STEPS IN PROGRAM DEVELO

Structured Programming	Object-Oriented Programming
1. State in one sentence what the program should do.	**1.** State in one sentence what the program should do.
2. Divide the main task into subtasks until each subtask is a clear logical step. Avoid language details.	**2.** Decide which objects should be used and what each object needs to know how to do. Avoid language details.
3. Decide broad details, such as global and local variables, data structures, and so forth. Hide as much as possible inside subroutines; create the program framework.	**3.** Decide broad details, such as global and local variables, data structures, and so forth. Hide everything possible inside object types; create the program framework.
4. Code and test each routine individually before plugging it into the main program framework. Make sure that any outside variables used by a routine are declared as parameters.	**4.** Code and test each object type individually before plugging it into the main program framework. Make sure that each object type has all the methods it needs to handle the data in its fields.
5. Plug all subroutines into the main program framework and test the program under a variety of conditions.	**5.** Plug all object types into the main program framework and test the program under a variety of conditions.

Computer users are not all alike.
Neither are SYBEX books.

We know our customers have a variety of needs. They've told us so. And because we've listened, we've developed several distinct types of books to meet the needs of each of our customers. What are you looking for in computer help?

If you're looking for the basics, try the **ABC's** series. You'll find short, unintimidating tutorials and helpful illustrations. For a more visual approach, select **Teach Yourself**, featuring screen-by-screen illustrations of how to use your latest software purchase.

Mastering and **Understanding** titles offer you a step-by-step introduction, plus an in-depth examination of intermediate-level features, to use as you progress.

Our **Up & Running** series is designed for computer-literate consumers who want a no-nonsense overview of new programs. Just 20 basic lessons, and you're on your way.

We also publish two types of reference books. Our **Instant References** provide quick access to each of a program's commands and functions. SYBEX **Encyclopedias** provide a *comprehensive reference* and explanation of all of the commands, features and functions of the subject software.

Sometimes a subject requires a special treatment that our standard series doesn't provide. So you'll find we have titles like **Advanced Techniques, Handbooks, Tips & Tricks**, and others that are specifically tailored to satisfy a unique need.

We carefully select our authors for their in-depth understanding of the software they're writing about, as well as their ability to write clearly and communicate effectively. Each manuscript is thoroughly reviewed by our technical staff to ensure its complete accuracy. Our production department makes sure it's easy to use. All of this adds up to the highest quality books available, consistently appearing on best seller charts worldwide.

You'll find SYBEX publishes a variety of books on every popular software package. Looking for computer help? Help Yourself to SYBEX.

For a complete catalog of our publications:

SYBEX Inc.
2021 Challenger Drive, Alameda, CA 94501
Tel: (415) 523-8233/(800) 227-2346 Telex: 336311
Fax: (415) 523-2373

SYBEX is committed to using natural resources wisely to preserve and improve our environment. As a leader in the computer book publishing industry, we are aware that over 40% of America's solid waste is paper. This is why we have been printing the text of books like this one on recycled paper since 1982.

This year our use of recycled paper will result in the saving of more than 15,300 trees. We will lower air pollution effluents by 54,000 pounds, save 6,300,000 gallons of water, and reduce landfill by 2,700 cubic yards.

In choosing a SYBEX book you are not only making a choice for the best in skills and information, you are also choosing to enhance the quality of life for all of us.

Mastering
Turbo Pascal 6

Mastering
Turbo Pascal® 6

Scott D. Palmer

SYBEX®

San Francisco • Paris • Düsseldorf • Soest

Acquisitions Editor: Dianne King
Developmental Editor: James A. Compton
Copy Editor: Kayla Sussell
Technical Editor: Charles Russel
Word Processors: Scott Campbell, Ann Dunn, Lisa Mitchell
Series Design: Eleanor Ramos
Chapter Art: Lucie Živny
Technical Art: Delia Brown
Screen Graphics: Cuong Le
Desktop Publishing Production: M.D. Barrera
Proofreaders: Sylvia Townsend and Rhonda Holmes
Indexer: Nancy Guenther
Cover Designer: Thomas Ingalls + Associates
Cover Photographer: Mark Johann
Screen reproductions produced by XenoFont.
XenoFont is a trademark of XenoSoft.

Dedicated to Karen Hanson, who's a diamond in a coal bin;

to Dennis Hamilton, whose literary talent is almost as big as his heart;

to Roberta Yerkes Blanshard, who was always there for us;

und an Wolfgang Petersen, in unendlicher Dankbarkeit für die Anregung.

ACKNOWLEDGMENTS

A good book is a team effort, and there were many people "on the team" in the production of this book.

First among those who helped was Charlie Russel, Sybex technical reviewer, whose astute comments and suggestions made this a much better book. In addition, Sybex editor Kayla Sussell spent many long hours working on the manuscript, and deserves considerable credit for her dedication in the face of tight deadlines.

Sybex developmental editor Jim Compton helped us launch the project, while managing editor Barbara Gordon and Editor-in-Chief Rudolph Langer stepped in occasionally when we needed their advice. Dianne King, acquisitions editor for Sybex, also helped launch the project and guide it in its early stages.

Nan Borreson at Borland International was a great help in obtaining timely copies of the Beta software and getting answers to difficult questions about Turbo Pascal 6 internal features.

I owe a special debt to Jeff Duntemann, who is always generous with his advice, and whose magazine, *PC Techniques*, is essential reading for serious PC programmers. Professor Mike Richey of George Mason University also provided many helpful ideas and suggestions.

Last but not least, of course, I owe thanks to the members of my family, especially my kids, for their support during the months of writing this book.

CONTENTS AT A GLANCE

TABLE OF CONTENTS

2. Programming and Program Design 25

3. An Overview of Pascal Programming 47

4. The Turbo Pascal Development Environment   83

PART II: Programming in Turbo Pascal 129

5. Simple Data Types 131

6. Simple Pascal Statements 169

7. More Advanced Pascal Statements   195

8. Structured and User-Defined Data Types   231

9. Procedures and Functions   273

10. Using Turbo Pascal Units   307

11. Pointers and Dynamic Allocation   333

12. Handling Text Files   371

13. Typed and Untyped Files   393

Part III: Advanced Programming Techniques 413

14. Debugging Your Programs 415

15. Graphics in Turbo Pascal 455

16. Accessing DOS Services   489

17. Elementary Data Structures   511

18. Elementary Algorithms   545

19. Sound and Music Programming   569

PART IV: Object-Oriented Programming 609

22. Introducing Turbo Vision   643

APP. A Turbo Pascal Reserved Words   667

APP. B The Ten Most Common Programming Mistakes   669

APP. C Solutions to Selected Exercises   671

Index   693

INTRODUCTION

THIS BOOK IS FOR YOU

This book is designed as a fast-track way for you to learn practical programming skills in Turbo Pascal 6, as well as in other versions of the Pascal language on computers from PCs to mainframes. If you want to catch up on the latest techniques, it also helps you to develop fundamental skills in object-oriented programming. Whether you are

- a beginner who's never written a program before,

- an experienced programmer who needs a quick, authoritative introduction to Turbo Pascal, or

- a student in a college or university programming course,

this book will help you acquire the knowledge, skills, and insight required to write the programs you need. It is structured so that you can read as much or as little as you want. If you are adventurous, you can simply work through Part I, "The Basics," and then jump straight into writing your own programs—dipping into the rest of the book only when needed. Or, if you are more comfortable with a conventional approach, you can start at the beginning and work straight through to the end.

In addition to standard topics such as graphics, data structures, and file handling, we will look at how to design and debug your programs. A special chapter shows how to add sound and music to your programs, and we will also develop a toolkit of general-purpose routines that you can use any time you need them. You will even learn how to use Turbo Pascal to write programs for other versions of Pascal on mainframes and minicomputers.

Furthermore, there is another side to this book—in some ways, an even more significant aspect than the practical skills you will learn. This is an adventure book, with thrills, narrow escapes, and triumphant discoveries. It is a book about the excitement of solving puzzles and the fun of teaching a computer to do things for you. If you merely learn to write programs, you will have missed the most important point of all: because, in the final analysis, programming is not about skill, getting a good grade, or even getting a high-paying job. Programming is about joy. Leave out the joy, and you might as well be flipping burgers at a fast-food place.

In short, this book will teach you not only how to program in Pascal and Turbo Pascal, but how to *have fun* doing it. And *fun*—no matter how much people talk about "productivity" or lucrative salaries—is one of the most important reasons for learning how to program.

You will receive the greatest benefit from this book if you actually type in the example programs, run them, and then study them to see how they work. Programming, like driving a car, involves both knowledge and skill. You can acquire knowledge by reading; skill, however, can be acquired only by *doing*. Just as you cannot learn to drive a car by reading a driver's ed book, so you cannot learn to program merely by reading a programming book.

Although writing program code is important, this book also spotlights the most important programming skill of all: the ability to *think through* a programming project; to organize and design it for error-free and efficient performance, for easy modification, and for the shortest possible development time. The truth is that with a little practice, almost anyone can write program code; the real trick is in knowing what code to write. Once you know that, you can write your program in almost any programming language.

A RESOURCE FOR YOUR COLLEGE COURSEWORK

One further note is in order here. Many people use Turbo Pascal in their college computer science courses. In addition to this book's in-depth coverage of Turbo Pascal's special features, it generally follows the guidelines developed by the Association for Computing Machinery (ACM) for a one-semester programming course (CS1), and includes some material that ACM recommends for a second-semester programming course (CS2)—as well as examples and exercises suitable for undergraduate courses. The ACM guidelines are currently being updated, so this book omits some material called for by the older (1983) document (*ACM Curricula Recommendations for Computer Science*, volume 1) when it is less relevant to the programming challenges of the 1990s.

In addition, most of the material in this book applies to *any* version of the Pascal language. When *Turbo Pascal* is discussed, that means features specific to Turbo Pascal. On the other hand, when Pascal is discussed, that means the discussion applies to all versions of Pascal.

How much of the material you use is entirely up to you; but you have in your hands a resource not only for self-teaching, but also a resource to help you with formal class work.

TURBO PASCAL AND OBJECT-ORIENTED PROGRAMMING

"Turbo Vision," one of the most exciting features of Turbo Pascal 6, is a built-in library of object-oriented program routines that allow you to add pull-down menus, mouse support, and a snazzy screen interface to all of your own programs. Since its previous version (5.5), Turbo Pascal has led the way in providing support for object-oriented programming in Pascal.

Some astute readers may ask this question: If Turbo Vision is so great (it is), and object-oriented programming is the wave of the future (well, somewhat), then why spend the first three parts of the book on traditional structured programming techniques? Why not jump right into object-oriented programming with Turbo Vision?

The answer is that object-oriented programming is a logical extension of structured programming. You can no more understand object-oriented programming without understanding structured programming than you can understand geometry without knowing how to add and subtract.

The heart of object-oriented programming, for example, is the idea of an "object," which is similar to a Pascal record but contains its own procedures and functions. The ideas concerning Pascal records, procedures, and functions are all part of structured programming. The basic ideas of object-oriented programming, such as information hiding and encapsulation, have evolved directly from the *structured* programming concepts that Niklaus Wirth originally designed Pascal to teach.

Further, as we'll discover, object-oriented programming stands beside structured programming (and even unstructured programming!) as just one more arrow in the programmer's quiver. In spite of its power, object orientation is not the single best solution for every programming problem.

HOW THIS BOOK IS STRUCTURED

This book is designed so that you can read as much or as little of it as you need. If you are a beginner and want a full introduction to Turbo Pascal, you can start on page 1 and work straight through. Chapters 1–4 give you all the basic information you need to get started writing simple programs. Chapters 5–13 discuss specific aspects of Turbo Pascal programming in detail. Chapters 14–20 introduce you to advanced programming techniques, and in Chapters 21–22, you will learn object-oriented programming.

On the other hand, once you have finished Chapters 1–4 and understand what Pascal and programming are all about, you can dip into a chapter here and a chapter there, picking up information as you need it when writing your programs.

If you are an "old pro" with Turbo Pascal, you may want to go straight to Chapter 4, which gives you a step-by-step guide to the new Turbo Pascal development environment. Then, you can go directly to the topics that interest you at the moment—whether it is object-oriented programming, graphics, debugging, or Turbo Pascal's DOS functions.

Part I, "The Basics," consists of Chapters 1–4. It provides an overview of Turbo Pascal in Chapter 1, an extensive discussion of program design in Chapter 2, and an overview of Pascal programming in Chapters 2 and 3. There is also a detailed tutorial on the Turbo Pascal Integrated Development Environment (IDE) in Chapter 4.

Part II, "Programming in Turbo Pascal," provides a step-by-step tutorial on Pascal programming, from simple data types and program statements to pointers and file handling. Most of the material in this section applies to any version of Pascal, whether it is Turbo Pascal, Microsoft

Pascal, or a mainframe version such as Digital Equipment Corporation's Vax Pascal.

Part III, "Advanced Programming Techniques," includes an in-depth look at debugging your programs, from general techniques that you can apply in any programming language to the specific debugging tools provided by Turbo Pascal. Chapters 17 and 18 show you how to implement some elementary data structures and algorithms, emphasizing the idea of data abstraction. (Don't worry: we'll explain what that all means and why it's important.) You will also learn how to use Turbo Pascal's graphics capabilities, how to call MS-DOS services, and how to add sound effects or music to your programs.

Part IV, "Object-Oriented Programming," introduces you to the basic concepts and amazing possibilities of this new approach. It also shows you how to use Turbo Vision, Turbo Pascal 6's built-in library of object-oriented routines, to jazz up your own programs.

PREPARE FOR TAKEOFF...!

Turbo Pascal 6 is an outstanding tool for learning programming skills and putting them to work. This book will be your guide for an unforgettable learning adventure.

So fasten your seat belts, extinguish all cigarettes, and prepare for takeoff. There won't be an in-flight movie: this is going to be better than a movie. You don't believe it now, but you will. Trust me on this one.

P A R T

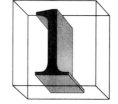

The Basics

In this part, Chapters 1–4, we look at the concepts and techniques of programming in Pascal and Turbo Pascal. We cover the basic features of the Pascal language, the nature of computer programming and computer operations, some methods for program design, and the special features provided by the Turbo Pascal Integrated Development Environment (IDE).

These four chapters will provide ample information to get you started in programming. If you are in a hurry, you can work through this part and refer to the other chapters in the book whenever you need more complete explanations or reference information.

C H A P T E R

A First Look at Turbo Pascal

All sides of our nature press for
satisfaction, and if left unsatisfied, will
manifest themselves so in idea.

— F.H. Bradley, *Essays on Truth and Reality*

AMAZING TURBO PASCAL!

If you are a son or daughter of the microcomputer revolution, you may
not realize what an amazing tool Turbo Pascal is. The first programs I ever
wrote were in the programming language called Fortran on an old IBM
teletype terminal: no video screen, no text editing, no help feature, no in-
teractive debugging, nothing. You typed in your program, sent it off to the
mainframe, and 15–30 minutes later (depending on how many people
were using the system at the time), got back a cryptic printout listing all
the reasons why your program wouldn't work.

Even today, most programming tools on large computers are far less
helpful than Turbo Pascal. On a mainframe computer, you use a clunky,
hard-to-use text editor to enter your program; then you compile it; then
you try to figure out the error messages; and then you recompile it. If
you're lucky and it compiles the second time, you have to do a separate
step to link it (to turn it into a functional program), and run it. Maybe.
Good luck. Don't hold your breath.

Contrast this with Turbo Pascal 6. You get an integrated text editor
with pull-down menus, on-screen help, easy debugging, automatic linking, and a wealth of other features including Turbo Vision, a library of
pre-written routines to use in your own programs. You also get a programming language (Pascal) designed to teach you how to do it right, along
with special Turbo Pascal features for graphics, object-oriented programming, and for working with other languages such as C and assembler. And
though Pascal is ideal for learning how to program, it has all the power
you'll ever need for the majority of real-world programming projects.

Twenty years ago, we would have killed to get something like this—at any price. Now, it's at the neighborhood computer store for about two hundred dollars, and you can save all your aggression for debugging.

INSTALLING AND STARTING TURBO PASCAL

Installing Turbo Pascal is very easy. You simply put disk No. 1 (the installation disk) into your A: drive or whatever floppy drive you have. Then switch to that drive; if your floppy drive is **A:**, key in **A:** and press Enter. Key in **install**, press Enter, and simply follow the on-screen prompts of Turbo Pascal's installation program. It is a good idea to make a backup copy of each Turbo Pascal disk before you do anything else. Keep the backup copies in a safe place, preferably away from your computer.

You will need at least 3.2Mb of free hard disk space to install the whole thing. If you need to free some disk space, you can tell the installation program not to unpack the example files; this will save about 700K of disk space. After installation, you can also delete the files in the \TURBO3 directory and remove the directory if you are not going to work with Turbo Pascal version 3. These files are included only to maintain compatibility with that early version.

To start Turbo Pascal, key in **turbo** at the DOS prompt and press Enter.

A QUICK TOUR OF THE IDE

When you start Turbo Pascal, you are taken directly into the Integrated Development Environment (IDE). See Figure 1.1. We'll look at this in detail in Chapter 4, but for now, let's just take a quick tour to get our bearings.

If Turbo Pascal starts up with a program file on the screen, as shown in Figure 1.2, then press Alt-F3 to close that file window.

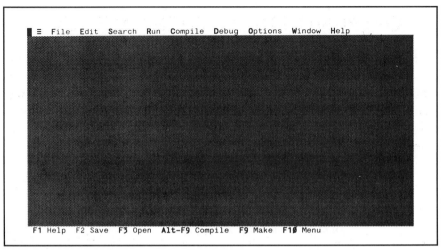

Figure 1.1: The Turbo Pascal Integrated Development Environment (IDE).

```
 ≡  File  Edit  Search  Run  Compile  Debug  Options  Window  Help
[■]                      DOC\DEMOS\HELLO.PAS                        1=[‡]
(**************************************************)
(                                                  )
(    Turbo Pascal 6.Ø                              )
(    Demo program from the Turbo Vision Guide      )
(                                                  )
(    Copyright (c) 199Ø by Borland International   )
(                                                  )
(**************************************************)

program Hello;

uses Objects, Drivers, Views, Menus, Dialogs, App;

const
  GreetThemCmd = 1ØØ;

type
  PHelloApp = ^THelloApp;
  THelloApp = object(TApplication)
    procedure GreetingBox;
    procedure HandleEvent(var Event: TEvent); virtual;
  1:1
 F1 Help  F2 Save  F3 Open  Alt-F9 Compile  F9 Make  F1Ø Menu
```

Figure 1.2: IDE with a file window open.

Turbo Pascal's IDE is a centralized control center from which you can do three main jobs: keying in your program, debugging it, and compiling it. To support you in these jobs, it provides pull-down menus, on-screen help, a variety of shortcuts, and some fairly sophisticated debugging facilities.

OPENING THE TOP-LINE MENUS

The menu bar, from which Turbo Pascal's menus pull down, is located across the top line of the screen. The bottom line of the screen shows some brief help information telling you how to do things like opening or saving a file, compiling a program, or calling Turbo Pascal's on-screen help system. Right now, let's take a quick look at the menus. There are three ways to open a menu:

- If you're using a mouse, you can click on the appropriate word in the menu bar. For example, you click on File to open the File menu.

- You can hold down the Alt key and press the highlighted letter in the name of the menu, for example, F for the File menu, E for the Edit menu, and W for the Window menu.

- You can press the F10 key, use the cursor keys to highlight the menu name you want, and then press Enter.

Many of Turbo Pascal's menu options have associated speed keys to save time. For example, to close a window, you can just press Alt-F3, or you can use your mouse to click on the button at the top left corner of the window frame. To save a file, you can press F2 instead of opening the File menu and selecting Save. Speed keys are shown in the menus, located to the right of the menu option they activate.

To get the feel of Turbo Pascal's menus, open the File menu now as shown in Figure 1.3. Press the right arrow key several times to look at some of the other menus, then return to the File menu.

QUITTING TURBO PASCAL

When you want to leave Turbo Pascal, you have two options. The easiest way is simply to press Alt-X (hold down the Alt key and press X), or, if you prefer, press Alt-F to open the File menu, and then select the Exit option.

If you are writing a program and try to quit without first saving the file to disk, Turbo Pascal will prompt you to save the file, as shown in Figure 1.4.

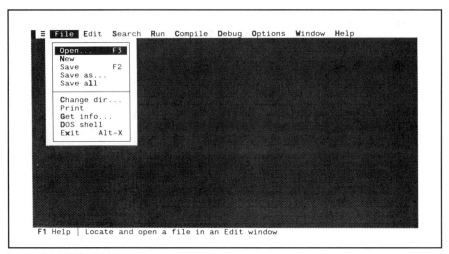

Figure 1.3: The File menu.

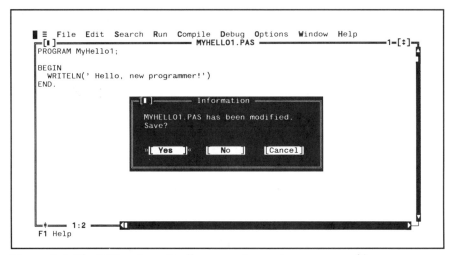

Figure 1.4: The IDE automatically prompts you to save your file.

When you restart Turbo Pascal, it can automatically remember which file(s) you were working with earlier, and, depending on the option settings, it will automatically reload those files for you.

CREATING AND USING A DATA DIRECTORY

It will make your life a lot easier if, before creating your first program, you set up a data directory to hold the programs you write. That way, your own Pascal programs won't be in the same directory as Turbo Pascal itself, making them a lot easier to find when you need them.

To create and use a data directory, take the following steps. If you don't understand any of the concepts used, you should consult your DOS manual.

1. If you're in the Turbo Pascal IDE, exit to DOS by pressing Alt-X.

2. At the DOS prompt, make sure that you are at the root directory by keying in **cd** and pressing Enter.

3. To make DOS show the directory that you are in, key in **prompt pg** and press Enter.

4. From the root directory, key in **md\tp\files** and press Enter. (Here, we are assuming that Turbo Pascal itself is in the *c:\tp* directory.) This step creates your data directory.

5. With Edlin or some other text editor (you can use Turbo Pascal's editor), find the AUTOEXEC.BAT file in your root directory and load it into the text editor. Do *not* use a word processor.

6. If your AUTOEXEC.BAT file does not have a PATH statement, then add this statement on a separate line: **PATH=C:\TP**. (Don't include the period.)

7. If your AUTOEXEC.BAT file *does* have a PATH statement, then add the *\tp* directory to the end. For example, if your PATH statement says **PATH=C:\;C:\DOS** then change it to read **PATH=C:\;C:\DOS;C:\TP**. Don't include the period at the end, and make sure that you proofread the changes you've made.

8. Save the new version of your AUTOEXEC.BAT file.

Now, after you've rebooted your PC, you can start Turbo Pascal from the *c:\tp\files* directory instead of from the *c:\tp* directory. Any files that you create will be put into the *c:\tp\files* directory.

CREATING YOUR FIRST PROGRAM

The first program we'll create is called the HELLO program, which is the program that almost every computer book ever written starts with. With the File menu open, select the New menu option by pressing N or by clicking on New with your mouse. An empty window, labeled NO-NAME00.PAS, will appear on the screen. Now, you can use the Turbo Pascal program editor, which creates plain text (ASCII) files that can be converted into usable programs.

Key in the program shown in Listing 1.1, making sure you type it exactly as it appears here. Note that single quote marks (or apostrophes) are used to enclose our "Hello" message. This differs from some other programming languages, such as BASIC, which use standard quote marks to enclose text material.

```
PROGRAM MyHello1;

BEGIN
  WRITELN(' Hello, new programmer!')
END.
```

Listing 1.1: The HELLO program.

SAVING YOUR PROGRAM

After you've finished keying in the program, reopen the File menu and select Save. A dialog box will appear on the screen; in the blank at the top, under Save file as, key in **myhello1** as shown in Figure 1.5, then press

Enter to save the file. Unless you specify otherwise, Turbo Pascal automatically adds a .PAS extension to any filename, so that your file is named MYHELLO1.PAS. (If you don't understand extensions of filenames, check your DOS manual.)

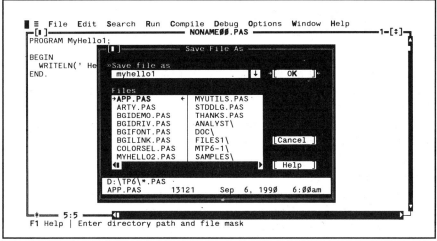

Figure 1.5: The Save File dialog box.

Upper and Lowercase Letters

You may have noticed that certain words in the program appear only in capital letters, others in lowercase, while still others include both upper and lowercase letters. Most of the time, Pascal does not distinguish between upper and lowercase; our use of capital letters is simply to make the program easier for you to read. If you prefer, you can use all upper or all lowercase. Some programming languages, such as C, do distinguish between upper and lowercase, but Pascal does not.

The HELLO program is so popular because it illustrates some of the most basic elements for writing a Pascal program. The Pascal word PROGRAM appears at the top, followed by the name of the program, and then by a semicolon. The main body of the program starts with BEGIN and ends with END, followed by a period. In between, a WRITELN command displays the text enclosed in parentheses and single quotes on-screen.

Notice that in the WRITELN statement, there's a space after the first quote mark. The space is not required, but when it is there, the message will appear one space over from the left edge of the screen. This is a minor trick used to make your screen displays easier to read.

COMPILING AND RUNNING YOUR PROGRAM

Your PC can't understand ordinary words, either in English or Pascal. Before you can run your program, you have to compile it—that is, translate it into a form that your PC can understand and execute. Because this is just a quick exercise, we'll take a compiling shortcut. After you've saved your file, press Alt-F9. This will convert your program from words (source code) into object code, which your PC will understand.

This is a test of whether you keyed in the program correctly. Turbo Pascal won't accept even a single typing mistake, so if you made any errors in the program commands, they will be caught here. However, neither Pascal nor any other programming language will check the words that you enclose in quotes, such as 'Hello, new programmer!', so you're on your own in that regard. The errors that are caught when you compile the program are called *compile-time errors.*

If there are any typing errors, the cursor will stop on the line where the mistake occurs, and an error message will display. Once you have corrected all the errors (if there were any), you can press Alt-F9 again to compile the program. After all these years, I still get a thrill when I see the next message (the good one): "Compile successful: press any key."

If you made any changes to correct your program, save it to disk again by pressing the F2 key. Then, to run your program, press Ctrl-F9.

Whoosh! That program went by so fast that you hardly got to see anything. However, it really did display the message "Hello, new programmer!" on your PC's screen. If you want to see it, press Alt-F5, which displays the output screen, and then press any key to return to the editing window.

In the following section, we will modify the MYHELLO1 program so that it will be a little more fun to watch.

ENTERING THE MYHELLO2 PROGRAM

Let's enter a new version of the HELLO program. This is a bit more complicated than the original, but it demonstrates some of the key ideas and features in Turbo Pascal programming. It also includes a **pause** at the end so that you can see what your program did.

To enter the new program, open the File menu and select New. A brand-new screen window opens up, superimposed just below and to the right of the first one that has your MYHELLO1 program in it. (See Figure 1.6.) Key in the program shown below in Listing 1.2, then save it under the filename MYHELLO2.PAS.

USING COMMENTS TO CLARIFY YOUR PROGRAM

MYHELLO2 is slightly more interesting than our original program. Note that under the program name, there is a comment that explains

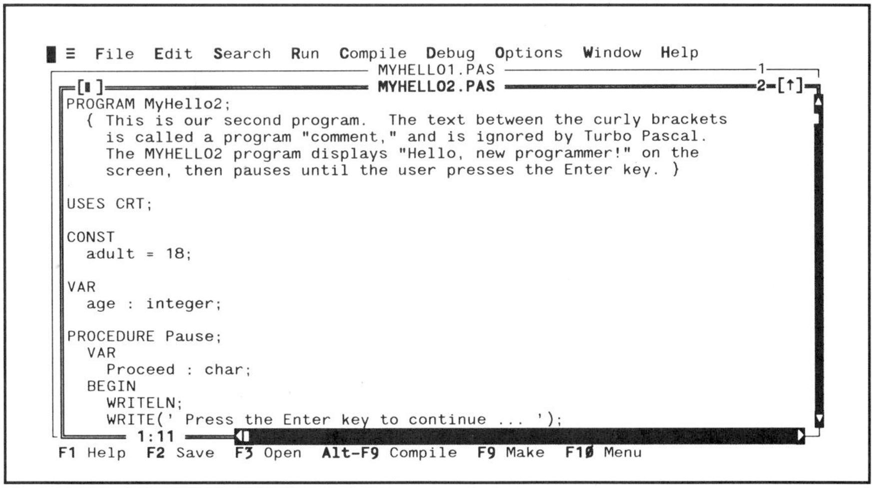

≡ File Edit Search Run Compile Debug Options Window Help
MYHELLO1.PAS 1
[▪] MYHELLO2.PAS 2 [↑]
PROGRAM MyHello2;
{ This is our second program. The text between the curly brackets
is called a program "comment," and is ignored by Turbo Pascal.
The MYHELLO2 program displays "Hello, new programmer!" on the
screen, then pauses until the user presses the Enter key. }
USES CRT;
CONST
adult = 18;
VAR
age : integer;
PROCEDURE Pause;
VAR
Proceed : char;
BEGIN
WRITELN;
WRITE(' Press the Enter key to continue ... ');
1:11
F1 Help F2 Save F3 Open Alt-F9 Compile F9 Make F10 Menu

Figure 1.6: Two file windows open.

what the program does. We will discuss how to use comments in Chapter 2. For the moment, simply observe that the comment begins with a left curly bracket { and ends with a right curly bracket }. Some Pascal compilers may not accept curly brackets as comment delimiters. If yours does not, then you should use the left parenthesis (and an asterisk * as the beginning delimiter, and an asterisk * and a right parenthesis) as an ending delimiter.

In addition to using explanatory comments at the beginning of a program, you can also insert a comment wherever something calls for an explanation; for example, the purpose of a particular line of code, what a variable represents, and so forth. Turbo Pascal ignores everything between the two brackets, so comments do not affect the size or the speed of your program.

```
PROGRAM Hello;
   { This is our second program.  The text between the curly brackets
     is called a program "comment," and is ignored by Turbo Pascal.
     The MYHELLO2 program displays "Hello, new programmer!" on the
     screen, then pauses until the user presses the Enter key. }

USES CRT;

CONST
  adult = 18;

VAR
  age : integer;

PROCEDURE Pause;
  VAR
    Proceed : char;
  BEGIN
    WRITELN;
    WRITE(' Press the Enter key to continue ... ');
    READ(proceed)
  END;


BEGIN
  CLRSCR;
  WRITELN;
  WRITELN(' Hello, new programmer!');
  WRITELN(' If you don''t mind my asking, how old are you? ');
  READLN(age)
  WRITELN;
  IF age < adult
    THEN WRITELN(' Why, you''re just a kid! You must be very smart!')
    ELSE WRITELN(' It''s nice to deal with a grown-up!');
  pause
END.
```

Listing 1.2: A beefed-up version of the HELLO program.

USING UNITS

Underneath the comment, there is a line that reads **USES CRT**. Turbo Pascal comes with several ready-to-use units that contain extra routines not found in the Pascal language itself. **USES CRT** means that if Turbo Pascal can't find a certain routine in the program being compiled (MYHELLO2), then it should look in the CRT unit.

In addition to the units that come with Turbo Pascal, you also can create your own units. This lets you break large programs down into smaller, more manageable parts. Furthermore, you can reuse a unit's routines in many different programs without ever having to rewrite them. Units are discussed in detail in Chapter 10.

DECLARING
CONSTANTS AND VARIABLES

The constants and variables that we intend to use in the program appear in the lines under **USES CRT**. Unlike BASIC (which is easier because it lets you make things up as you go along), Pascal insists that you declare everything that you are going to use at the beginning of the program. This means that names (identifiers) of variables, constants, procedures, and any other items that you create must be declared and defined before you can use them for anything.

But look at the bright side. Pascal is just like your old algebra teacher who insisted that you learn the quadratic formula so that you would be able to solve algebraic problems. Pascal demands that you learn to think through a program before you write it—which, more than anything else, is the secret of writing good programs to solve real problems.

DECLARING
PROCEDURES AND FUNCTIONS

After declaring the constants and variables in MYHELLO2, next we declare a procedure to create a pause in the program. There's nothing inherently difficult about a procedure. Essentially it's just a block of program code that gets its own name and performs a particular job. Wherever we want MYHELLO2 to pause, for example, we simply call the pause procedure instead of having to write the same code each time. The procedure is like a miniprogram itself, with its own BEGIN and END statements. It can even have its own constants, variables, and procedures.

Note, however, that simply defining this procedure does not make the program pause; the procedure goes to work only when we call it in the main body (the action part) of the program. To call the pause procedure in the action part of the program, we simply key in its name on a separate line of code; then the procedure carries out its own internal instructions, one line at a time.

THE ACTION PART OF THE PROGRAM

At last, we've arrived at the main body of MYHELLO2. This demonstrates a feature that may puzzle you at first, especially if you've written programs in an unstructured language like BASIC. Intuitively, you would expect a program to start running at the first statement you see (at the top) and go straight through to the bottom, except for the occasional LOOP or GOTO statement. Pascal and structured programming, however, are not like that.

The action part of a Pascal program typically comes at the end of the listing, and, usually, is only a few lines long. A structured Pascal program is something like a Chinese puzzle box: one box contains another, which in turn contains still more boxes. It's an odd way of thinking, but, in the long run, it makes your programs much easier to understand, debug, and modify.

At any rate, the main reason the action part of the program appears at the bottom is that in Pascal, everything has to be declared before it is used. This means that at the top of the program, you are not actually doing anything. You are simply defining all the actions and variables that you are going to use when you finally get around to the action part, at the bottom.

In the action part of the MYHELLO2 program, the first line is CLRSCR, which clears the screen. The CLRSCR routine comes from the CRT unit, which we declared in the USES statement. If we had neglected to tell Turbo Pascal that we intended to use the CRT unit, then we would have gotten an error message when we tried to compile MYHELLO2, because it wouldn't be able to find the CLRSCR routine.

The next item is WRITELN, which we've already seen. The first WRITELN is by itself; this causes the cursor to move down one line on the screen. The next WRITELN displays the text string "Hello, new programmer!", while the third WRITELN asks the user to enter his or her age.

Note that a piece of text that is input or displayed is called a *string*. (See Chapter 5 for more on strings.)

Getting User Input with READLN

Keying in data at the keyboard is something like passing a football: it doesn't do much good unless there's someone there to catch it. READLN, on the next line, "catches" the user's age and puts it into a variable called Age. A *variable* is a part of the PC's memory that your program sets aside to keep data that may change. It can be useful to think of variables simply as boxes that hold a particular kind of thing. Some variables hold numbers, others hold text, lists, and other kinds of data. Anytime that you are prompted to key in some data, you must include some sort of read statement to catch the data and put it into a variable. If you don't do this, your program won't work.

In this case, READLN pauses the program until the user keys in something on the keyboard and presses Enter. (This is the same trick as in the pause procedure.) Note that, at this stage, there's absolutely no error trapping, so you can enter anything at the age prompt. However, typing a nonnumeric entry such as "Fred" will cause a run-time error and stop the program. More subtle errors, such as entering an age of 749, will be accepted and, in a "real-life" program, can cause havoc.

After you enter your age, the IF..THEN..ELSE statement tells the program how to respond. If you are under 18, one message is shown; if you are 18 or older, a different message is displayed.

COMPILING AND RUNNING MYHELLO2

Now that you've had a chance to peruse the code a bit, let's open the Compile menu, noting that the menu choice for Destination is Memory. Select Compile to compile your program.

This time, it looks like there's a mistake: Turbo Pascal stops after the READLN statement and displays the message **Error 85: ";" expected** as shown in Figure 1.7. Although the cursor stops at the beginning of the next line, it is actually saying that the two lines should be separated by a semicolon. You must use a semicolon to separate statements in a Pascal program; in this case, it is needed to separate the READLN and the subsequent WRITELN statement.

```
  ▀ ≡  File  Edit  Search  Run  Compile  Debug  Options  Window  Help
 ┌─[■]─────────────────────── LIST1-2.PAS ──────────────────1=[↕]─┐
 ▐Error 85: ";" expected.                                          ▲
   END;


 BEGIN
   CLRSCR;
   WRITELN;
   WRITELN(' Hello, Turbo programmer!');
   WRITELN(' If you don''t mind my asking, how old are you? ');
   READLN(age)
   WRITELN;
   IF age < adult
     THEN WRITELN(' Why, you''re just a kid! You must be very smart!')
     ELSE WRITELN(' It''s nice to deal with a grown-up!');
   pause
 END.



 ├─ 31:3 ──┤◄▌                                                    ►│▼
  F1 Help  F2 Save  F3 Open  Alt-F9 Compile  F9 Make  F10 Menu
```

Figure 1.7: The IDE catches an error in MYHELLO2.

When to End Lines with Semicolons

There are many exceptions to the rule about semicolons, but only practice will familiarize you with them. It's like knowing when to sacrifice a pawn for a positional advantage in chess; eventually, you will just *know* when to do it. Generally, however, you put a semicolon at the end of a program line unless

- it is a label for part of the Pascal program (BEGIN, END, VAR, TYPE, and so forth), in which case it is technically not a statement;

- it is a clause in an IF..THEN..ELSE statement, all of which are considered to be part of the same statement; or

- it comes immediately before an END, in which case there's no subsequent statement from which it needs to be separated.

For the time being, just put a semicolon at the end of the READLN statement so that it now says **READLN(age);**. If you made any typing errors, you can correct them at this time. Then, open the Run menu and select Run to execute your program.

This time, the program clears the screen, displays the message "Hello, new programmer!", and then asks you how old you are. If you enter an integer under 18, the program congratulates you on being smart; if the integer is greater than or equal to 18, it congratulates you on being a grown-up. It then pauses and prompts you to press the Enter key; when you do so, the program finishes and you return to Turbo Pascal.

Getting Input from the User—Revisited

There's only one thing wrong with this program, apart from its rather facile assumption that anyone over 17 is a "grown-up." When it prompts you for your age, the cursor doesn't stay on the same line as the prompt; instead, it moves down to the next line on the screen.

The reason for this is that in coding the age prompt, we used WRITELN, which automatically moves the cursor to the next line on-screen without waiting for a response from the user. A better choice to code messages that require user input is WRITE, which is just like WRITELN except that it leaves the cursor on the same line as the message. If you're back in Turbo Pascal (as you should be at this point), change the age prompt so that the line reads

```
WRITE(' If you don''t mind my asking, how old are
you? ');
```

Apostrophes in Quoted Strings

There are two other notable aspects about this. First, observe that in the word "don't" the apostrophe is doubled. This is because Pascal uses the apostrophe as a quote mark, and it needs a way to determine whether or not the apostrophe in "don't" is intended to mark the end of the message that is displayed on-screen.

The way it does this is to ignore double-apostrophes. When Pascal encounters a double-apostrophe, it knows that it is a part of a word in the text, not the end of a message. (This is similar to the use of quote marks in BASIC.) Whenever you include a contraction in your text string, such as "don't," "you're," and so forth, you must double the apostrophe.

Second, at the end of the prompt message, you might have noticed that we left an extra space before the right quote mark. That's so the cursor will be one space to the right of the prompt message when you enter your age. It makes the on-screen prompt easier to read.

GETTING ON-SCREEN HELP

When you need information quickly and don't want to use the manuals, Turbo Pascal offers you on-screen help in a variety of ways. We'll discuss this in detail in Chapter 4, but here's how it works in outline:

- To get help for a specific Pascal feature in your program, position the cursor so that it is on the word for which you need help (e.g., PROCEDURE, IF, CONST). Then press Ctrl-F1.

- To open a general help window so that you can browse through the help information, just press F1.

- Note that whenever you are in a help window, the bottom line of the PC screen gives additional information about how to navigate through the help system.

CUSTOMIZING TURBO PASCAL

If you've used earlier versions of Turbo Pascal, then you are probably familiar with the TINST.EXE program, which lets you customize many aspects of Turbo Pascal. In version 6, however, TINST has been replaced by a more extensive ability to customize Turbo Pascal from the Options menu, as shown in Figure 1.8.

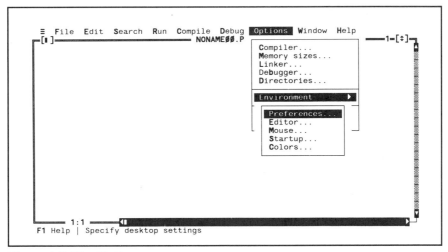

Figure 1.8: The Options menu.

We'll look at the Options menu in more detail in Chapter 4, but there are some things you should know about it now.

- The Directories menu choice lets you tell Turbo Pascal where to find important files such as units. If you use the File menu to change the default directory so that it isn't the Turbo Pascal program directory, then you need to use the Directories choice; otherwise, Turbo Pascal may not be able to find the files it needs.

- The Environment choice takes you to a submenu where you can set options for the editor (such as automatic file backup, tab size, and so forth), as well as screen colors and automatic loading of last-used files.

- The settings that you choose are stored in a file called TURBO.TP. This file is put in the current default directory when you save it. You can also create different sets of options and save them under other file names.

SUMMARY

Turbo Pascal 6 provides amazing facilities for programming and debugging—facilities that were unheard of even 10 years ago. You install Turbo Pascal 6 by running its installation program, which automatically sets up Turbo Pascal on your hard disk.

The central feature of Turbo Pascal is the Integrated Development Environment, or IDE, which provides pull-down menus that help you write and debug your programs. Pressing the F1 key also brings up an extensive on-screen help system.

A Pascal program begins with the word BEGIN and ends with the word END. Before you can run a program, you must compile it, which translates it from Pascal source code (what you see on the screen) into a form that the computer can understand. In any program, you should include comments to explain what is done by various parts of the program, as well as to explain the overall purpose of the program.

REVIEW EXERCISES

1. True or false: *ThisName* and *thisname* are considered different identifiers by Pascal.

2. Give three ways to open Turbo Pascal's drop-down menus.

3. How does Pascal enclose text that is to be displayed on the screen?

4. Give two ways to save a file in Turbo Pascal.

5. Explain the basic structure of a Pascal program as illustrated by the HELLO program in Listing 1.2.

6. Explain what it means to compile a program, and give two ways to compile a program in Turbo Pascal.

7. Explain how to mark the beginning and ending of a program comment in Pascal. Do comments help Pascal to compile the program more efficiently?

8. Explain Turbo Pascal units and why they are important.

9. True or false: Like BASIC, Pascal lets you make up new variables whenever you need them in a program. Explain why Pascal does (or doesn't) do this.

10. Explain what WRITELN does in Listings 1.1 and 1.2. How does it differ from WRITE? Create your own short program using WRITELN.

11. Explain how READLN works. Write your own short program using READLN.

12. True or false: In Pascal, you should end every program line with a semicolon. If the statement is false, explain Pascal's rules for using semicolons.

13. Explain how to include an apostrophe in a quoted string.

14. Give three ways to get on-screen help in Turbo Pascal.

15. True or false: A structured Pascal program starts running at the first line of the program code and runs line-by-line to the end. If false, explain how a Pascal program actually does run.

C H A P T E R

Programming and Program Design

The limits of my language mean the limits of my world.

— Ludwig Wittgenstein, *Tractatus Logico-Philosophicus*

WHAT IS A COMPUTER PROGRAM?

Essentially a computer program is very simple. It takes data (input), manipulates it in some way (processing), and then returns the processed data back to you (output). Apart from the fact that it *does* something, the main difference between a computer program and a few paragraphs of ordinary English prose is that the program must be far more precise than the prose.

For example, if you ask a human being "Do you know what time it is?," he or she is likely to respond by telling you the current time. However, that *wasn't* what you asked for: humans, who are much smarter than the most powerful computers, normally look beyond what is *said* and try to infer what is *meant*. Computers, on the other hand, understand only what is *said*. They can't "fill in the blanks" the way a person can. If (using a programming language) you ask a computer "Do you know what time it is?," it most likely will answer with a simple "Yes." Because human beings communicate in so many nonverbal ways (gestures, expressions, intonations, and the contexts in which we speak), English and other human languages are ill-equipped for talking with a computer.

Basically, a computer program is a sequence of instructions that tells the computer *precisely* what to do and when to do it. To achieve this level of precision, we use specially-designed computer languages such as Pascal.

HOW COMPUTERS OPERATE

Before you can understand how computer languages work, you need to understand something about how computers themselves work. Any computer—whether it's your PC or a 20-million dollar IBM mainframe—works on the principle of on/off switches. The computer stores and processes information (both data and instructions) as sequences of ons and offs, which programmers represent as sequences of zeroes and ones.

That's a pretty neat trick, and there's nothing supernatural about it; Morse code does the same thing with sequences of short and long signals representing letters. In the earliest computers, the ons and offs were represented by mechanical switches that the programmer had to set by hand in the machine itself. The idea of program "bugs" originated with these machines. In the 1940s, computer pioneer Grace Murray Hopper (then a Naval officer) found that one of her programs malfunctioned because a moth had flown into the back of the machine and jammed one of the switches. It isn't known if this incident motivated her to help create Fortran, the first high-level programming language, but it might have. Ever since, though, all programmers have hated bugs.

Any computer, including your PC, has four main components:

1. A central processing unit (CPU), which does the "thinking" for the computer;

2. A primary storage or random-access memory unit (RAM), which serves as an electronic desktop where the computer keeps its current work;

3. A secondary storage unit (disk drives or tapes), where the computer keeps things that it is not working on currently, but which may be needed later; and

4. An I/O (input-output) device(s), which the computer uses to communicate with the outside world (human users, printers, etc.).

So you can see that although the details are complex, a computer is fundamentally a simple device. Just as Morse Code uses combinations of short and long signals to represent letters, the computer uses ons and offs to represent letters, numbers, and special characters. The capital letter "A", for example, is on-off-off-off-off-off-on, and the period (.) is off-on-off-on-on-on-off.

The computer's CPU has certain built-in operations that it can perform. These operations are called its *instruction set*. The operations must be very simple, for example, comparing two numbers, moving a tiny piece of information from one part of the computer to another, or checking whether a switch is on or off. Each type of processor has its own unique instruction set. The IBM PC and compatible computers, for which Turbo Pascal is designed, are based on the Intel 80x86 family (8086, 80286, 80386, and 80486) of processors, which has a rich instruction set.

Although computers work very well with sequences of ons and offs, represented in machine language (the computer's internal lingo) as sequences of zeroes and ones, people find it difficult to work at this level. It's not that easy for a person to see the difference between 00111010 and 00110010 at a glance, particularly when dealing with page after page of zeros and ones. For this reason, *high-level languages* were invented.

PROGRAMMING LANGUAGES

A high-level language consists of words that are easier for a human being to recognize and remember than sequences of zeroes and ones. It consists of words (source code) like those we've already seen in Chapter 1, such as WRITE, PROGRAM, BEGIN, and END. When a program is compiled, each high-level word is translated into many strings of zeroes and ones, which represent both instructions and data. In fact, that's basically all a compiler really does. Today, the ons and offs are electronic switches that the computer sets by itself in response to the statements in your program.

High-level languages vary greatly in just how "high" they are—that is, in how much they insulate you from the details of your PC's operations. At the lowest level is assembly language, each word of which corresponds to just one instruction in the PC's processor. Assembly language is useful when you need to manipulate the computer directly and when you know *exactly, precisely* what you want to do. If you don't, you can get into real trouble.

A bit higher up are languages such as C, which are sometimes used (to the outrage of assembly-language programmers) for writing compilers and operating systems. C provides more shorthand than assembly language, but it gives a significant amount of access to the PC's low-level functions. And, like assembly language, C has few "guard rails" to keep you from getting into trouble if you don't know what you are doing.

Still higher are languages like Pascal, which combine easy-to-remember shorthand, some low-level access, and at least a few safety features for the novice programmer. Turbo Pascal provides the best of both worlds by letting you include assembly-language routines in your Pascal programs whenever you need sophisticated low-level access, and by extending the Pascal language to support graphics and object orientation. The Pascal language itself was designed by Niklaus Wirth in the early 1970s as a way to teach structured programming ideas to students of computer science, and to this day, it still exhibits that tutorial heritage.

At the highest level are languages such as Paradox and dBase, which provide little if any low-level access but offer powerful shorthand for specialized functions such as data management and graphics.

The vocabulary of a particular high-level language is referred to as its set of "reserved words." Because these words have a very precisely defined meaning in the language itself, they cannot be used for anything else in your program. A list of Turbo Pascal's reserved words is included here as Appendix A.

COMPILERS AND INTERPRETERS

As already noted, a compiler translates the words of a high-level programming language into the binary machine language of zeros and ones that the computer understands. Normally, the compiler creates an object file in machine language with the extension .OBJ in its filename. The final step in making a functional program is to link the file, which converts it into a file with an .EXE or .COM extension in its filename. In Turbo Pascal, compiling and linking are combined in a single step.

Similar to a compiler is an interpreter, such as the GW-BASIC interpreter included with the MS-DOS operating system. Database managers
such as Paradox and dBase are also interpreters, although they are not
usually thought of that way. Instead of creating a stand-alone program, an
interpreter runs your program's source code one line at a time, which is
good for testing program code. On the down side, however, interpreted
programs run very slowly compared to compiled programs, and you need
a copy of the particular language interpreter (such as GW-BASIC) to run
your program at all.

Turbo Pascal goes beyond being just a compiler; it provides a complete
development environment that gives you the benefits of both an interpreter and a compiler. You can run your program one line at a time to test
it, and, when you're sure it works right, you can compile it to a stand-alone
program. Moreover, in addition to the development environment, you
also get two other versions of the Turbo Pascal compiler (TPC.EXE and
TPCX.EXE in Turbo Pascal Professional) which you can use to get special
features not available in the Turbo Pascal IDE itself.

THE RIGHT TOOL FOR THE JOB

In programming, there is a simply stated but often overlooked truth.
You should choose a tool to fit the job that you are doing. Just as when you
build a house, the same tool will not serve every purpose and need. Some
programs call for low-level access that only assembly language can provide; others are very simple programs for which structured or object-
oriented programming is a waste of time; still others virtually demand
that you use object-oriented programming, for example, creating graphic
interface windowing systems on the PC's screen.

To illustrate this simple point, take a look at Listings 2.1 through 2.4,
which show four different approaches to the MYHELLO1 program. The
first, in Microsoft QuickBASIC, requires only a single line of program
code. In Turbo Pascal, the same program requires four lines. In assembly
language, it requires 15 lines; and to code the same program in object-
oriented Pascal with Turbo Vision requires 78 lines of code, *not counting*
the code in Turbo Vision itself—a clear case of programming overkill for
such a simple program.

```
'The HELLO1 program in Microsoft QuickBASIC

PRINT "Hello, new programmer!"
```

Listing 2.1: The HELLO program in MicroSoft QuickBASIC.

```
PROGRAM MyHello1;

BEGIN
  WRITELN(' Hello, new programmer!')
END.
```

Listing 2.2: The HELLO program (normal version) in Turbo Pascal.

```
;The HELLO1 program in Turbo Assembler

    dosseg
    .model small
    .stack 100h
    .data
Greeting db 'Hello, new programmer!',13,10,'$'
    .code
    mov  ax,@data
    mov  ds,ax
    mov  ah,9
    mov  dx,offset Greeting
    int  21h
    mov  ah,4ch
    int  21h
    end
```

Listing 2.3: The HELLO program in Turbo Assembler (assembly language).

```
{ The object-oriented version of HELLO1 in Turbo Pascal with
  Turbo Vision, included as an example file with Turbo Pascal
  6; Copyright 1990 by Borland International. This is a good
  example of object-oriented programming, and a great example
  of programming "overkill." }

program Hello;

uses Objects, Drivers, Views, Menus, Dialogs, App;

const
  GreetThemCmd = 100;

type
  PHelloApp = ^THelloApp;
  THelloApp = object(TApplication)
    procedure GreetingBox;
    procedure HandleEvent(var Event: TEvent); virtual;
    procedure InitMenuBar; virtual;
    procedure InitStatusLine; virtual;
  end;

{ THelloApp }
procedure THelloApp.GreetingBox;
var
  R: TRect;
  D: PDialog;
  C: Word;
begin
  { Create a dialog }
  R.Assign(21, 5, 56, 16);
  D := New(PDialog, Init(R, 'Hello, new programmer!'));

  { Create and insert controls into the dialog}
  R.Assign(3, 5, 15, 6);
  D^.Insert(New(PStaticText, Init(R, 'How are you?')));

  R.Assign(16, 2, 28, 4);
  D^.Insert(New(PButton, Init(R, 'Terrific', cmCancel, bfNormal)));

  R.Assign(16, 4, 28, 6);
  D^.Insert(New(PButton, Init(R, 'Ok', cmCancel, bfNormal)));

  R.Assign(16, 6, 28, 8);
  D^.Insert(New(PButton, Init(R, 'Lousy', cmCancel, bfNormal)));

  R.Assign(16, 8, 28, 10);
  D^.Insert( New(PButton, Init(R, 'Cancel', cmCancel, bfNormal)));

  { Execute the modal dialog }

    C := DeskTop^.ExecView(D);
  end;

  procedure THelloApp.HandleEvent(var Event: TEvent);
  begin
    TApplication.HandleEvent(Event);
    if Event.What = evCommand then
    begin
      case Event.Command of
        GreetThemCmd: GreetingBox;
```

Listing 2.4: The HELLO program in object-oriented Pascal with Turbo Vision.

```
    else
      Exit;
    end;
    ClearEvent(Event);
  end;
end;

procedure THelloApp.InitMenuBar;
var
  R: TRect;
begin
  GetExtent(R);
  R.B.Y := R.A.Y + 1;
  MenuBar := New(PMenuBar, Init(R, NewMenu(
    NewSubMenu('~H~ello', hcNoContext, NewMenu(
      NewItem('~G~reeting...','', 0, GreetThemCmd, hcNoContext,
      NewLine(
      NewItem('E~x~it', 'Alt-X', kbAltX, cmQuit, hcNoContext,
      nil)))), nil))));
  end;

procedure THelloApp.InitStatusLine;
var
  R: TRect;
begin
  GetExtent(R);
  R.A.Y := R.B.Y-1;
  StatusLine := New(PStatusLine, Init(R,
    NewStatusDef(0, $FFFF,
      NewStatusKey('', kbF10, cmMenu,
      NewStatusKey('~Alt-X~ Exit', kbAltX, cmQuit, nil)),
      nil)));
  end;

var
  HelloWorld: THelloApp;

begin
  HelloWorld.Init;
  HelloWorld.Run;
  HelloWorld.Done;
end.
```

Listing 2.4: The HELLO program in object-oriented Pascal with Turbo Vision. (cont.)

BASIC, PASCAL, AND STRUCTURED PROGRAMMING

Because it is included with the PC's operating system, many more people know how to write programs in BASIC than in any other language. BASIC and Pascal share a common purpose—to teach people how to program. The crucial difference between them is that BASIC (Beginners'

All-Purpose Symbolic Instruction Code) is designed simply to teach programming, while Pascal is designed to teach *structured* programming. BASIC allows you "to get away with" some bad programming practices that you'll need to unlearn as a Pascal programmer.

In particular, Pascal requires you to declare all identifiers before using them, while BASIC allows you to make up new variables anywhere, without ever having to explicitly define them. In some versions of BASIC, such as GW-BASIC, there is very limited support for separate subroutines to which you can pass variables. These subroutines are a key feature of Pascal. And while BASIC encourages you to sit down and start coding, Pascal almost *requires* a separate step to design your program before you ever write a line of code.

STRUCTURED VS. UNSTRUCTURED PROGRAMMING

The vast difference between structured and unstructured ("spaghetti") programming is shown clearly in Listings 2.5 and 2.6. Listing 2.5

```
10 REM Program MakeChange, coded in GW-BASIC.
20 CLS
30 PRINT "This is a program to make change. You will be prompted"
40 PRINT "to enter two integers: the first represents the amount due,"
50 PRINT "while the second represents the amount paid."
60 PRINT
70 PRINT "Press any key to continue ..."
80 WHILE INKEY$ = ""
90 WEND
100 PRINT
110 INPUT "Please enter the amount due in cents (an integer): ",AMOUNTDU
120 PRINT
130 INPUT "Please enter the amount paid in cents (an integer): ",PAYMENT
140 PRINT
150 CHANGE = PAYMENT - AMOUNTDUE
160 PRINT "Your change is "; CHANGE; " cents."
170 PRINT "Have a nice day."
180 INPUT "Do you want to go again (Y/N)? ", DOANOTHER$
190 CLS
200 IF DOANOTHER$ = "Y" OR DOANOTHER$ = "y" THEN GOTO 100
210 PRINT "Press any key to continue ..."
220 WHILE INKEY$ = ""
230 WEND
240 CLS
250 END
```

Listing 2.5: A spaghetti-code program in GW-BASIC.

```
PROGRAM MakeChange;
   ( This program illustrates how structured programming makes
     a program easier to understand than a "spaghetti" approach. )

USES CRT;  ( for CLRSCR )

VAR
   Payment,
   Change  : integer;

PROCEDURE Pause;
  VAR
    proceed : char;
  BEGIN
    WRITELN;
    WRITE(' Press the Enter key to continue ...');
    READ(proceed)
  END;

PROCEDURE ExplainProgram;
  BEGIN
    CLRSCR;
    WRITELN(' This is a program to make change.  You will be prompted');
    WRITELN(' to enter two integers: the first represents the amount');
    WRITELN(' due, while the second represents the amount paid.');
    pause;
    WRITELN
  END;

PROCEDURE CountMoney(var Payment, Change : integer);
  VAR
    AmountDue : integer; ( declare private variables for )
    DoAnother : char;( the CountMoney routine       )
  BEGIN
    DoAnother := 'Y';  ( put the letter 'Y' into DoAnother )
    WHILE UPCASE(DoAnother) = 'Y' DO( set up a loop )
      BEGIN
      WRITELN;
      WRITE(' Please enter the amount due in cents (an integer): ');
      READLN(AmountDue);
      WRITELN;
      WRITE(' Please enter the amount paid in cents (an integer): ');
      READLN(Payment);
      Change := Payment - AmountDue;( calculate change )
      WRITELN;
      WRITELN(' Your change is ', Change, ' cent(s).');
      WRITELN(' Have a nice day.');
      WRITE(' Do you want to go again (Y/N)? ');( exit from loop? )
      READLN(DoAnother);
      CLRSCR
      END          ( of the WHILE .. DO loop )
   END;            ( of the CountMoney procedure )


BEGIN
  ExplainProgram;
  CountMoney(payment, change);
  pause
END.
```

Listing 2.6: A structured Pascal version of Listing 2.5.

shows an unstructured GW-BASIC program that makes change for a purchase, somewhat like a cash register. When the user first starts the program, a screen is displayed that explains how the program works; then the
program pauses. After the pause, it asks the user to enter the amount owed
and the amount paid. By subtracting the amount owed from the amount
paid, it computes the change, and then asks the user if he or she wants to
go again. It then pauses and either goes again or terminates, depending on
the user's answer.

There are two things to note about Listing 2.5. First, it's confusing;
lines of code are jumbled together, making it harder to understand what
the program does. Second, each time we wanted to pause the program, we
ended up writing the same code all over again. (This case is slightly artificial, but if we wanted to pass some variables to the pause routine, we really *would* be forced to repeat the code.)

The program in Listing 2.5 is a very short and simple one; but if you
can imagine trying to understand a 100-page program written in the same
unstructured way, it's clear that the "spaghetti" approach can cause some
real problems.

Compare this to Listing 2.6, which illustrates a structured Pascal program that does the same thing. The program in Listing 2.6 is harder to
write in the first place than the unstructured version, which starts at the
beginning and runs straight through to the end. The Pascal program uses
the quirky kind of Chinese puzzle-box thinking that is the hallmark of
structured programming, and you simply *must* plan the program before
you write it.

The benefits of this extra initial effort are considerable. The program
in Listing 2.6 is far easier to *understand, debug,* and *modify* than the unstructured program in Listing 2.5. It is even easier to fine tune a structured program to make it run faster. Let's examine each of these points in turn.

UNDERSTANDING THE PROGRAM

It is true that for a 25-line program such as the one shown in Listing 2.5,
understanding the program is a fairly trivial matter. However, note that
even in this short program, all the different tasks that the program performs are jumbled together. You have to look carefully to be sure where the
pause lines end and the prompt the user lines begin. If the program were

even a few pages long, this could become a significant problem. With a real-world program, which could run to 100 or more pages, you'd be in deep trouble—as, indeed, some old COBOL programmers are today.

In Listing 2.6, however, each specific job is handled by a separate subroutine, and each subroutine has a name that describes what it does. To achieve this separation of program tasks you must carefully think through your program before you start to code, and you must decide beforehand what the basic subparts of the program should be. The end result, however, is that you will easily understand what each part of the program does, even if it is 100 pages long. Note that although parts of the structured program are indented, Pascal itself pays no attention to indenting. The indentation is there simply to make the program easier for humans to read.

There is a trick to understanding structured programs. Instead of starting at the beginning and reading to the end, you start at the end and work your way back to the beginning. At the end of the code listing, the action part of the program shows you the main outline of how the program works—a sort of bird's-eye view. The first line of the action part is almost always a call to a subroutine (a procedure or function) defined earlier in the program, so you go back and examine how that subroutine works. That routine itself may call earlier routines (such as pause), and you look at them, too. Finally, when you have a good understanding of what is done by the first line of the program's action part, then you can go on to the second line.

In the case of Listing 2.6, there are only three lines in the action part. The first line calls the ExplainProgram procedure, which in turn calls the Pause procedure. The second line calls the CountMoney procedure, passing two variables to that procedure (see Chapter 9 for passing variables to procedures). The third line calls the Pause routine directly. And that's all there is to the program. The overall structure of the program in Listing 2.6 is shown in Figure 2.1.

DEBUGGING THE PROGRAM

Structured design is a tremendous help in debugging any program of more than trivial complexity. In Listing 2.5, a bug could occur anywhere

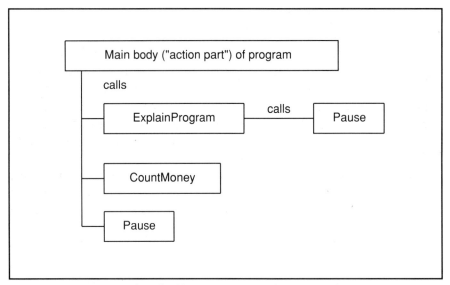

Figure 2.1: Structure of MakeChange Program (Listing 2.6).

in the program. A minor change in a variable, a change in an arithmetic statement, and kaboom! The program crashes and you don't know why. In a long unstructured program, the crash could occur at a place in the code listing some distance away from the actual source of the trouble. When the program crashes on line 2550, but the cause of the problem is on line 830, you can have an extraordinarily difficult time trying to find out what's wrong.

In Listing 2.6, however, you can localize bugs by treating each different routine as a "black box" whose content is hidden from the rest of the program. The conceptual notion of a black box is like a compartment in a submarine: each compartment is sealed off from all the others. If one compartment springs a leak and floods with water, all the other compartments stay dry. That way, the damage is contained and it's easier to find which compartment is leaking.

Structured programming works the same way to localize bugs and to limit the mischief they can create. Listing 2.7 shows how you might write the first code for the MakeChange program in Listing 2.6.

Top-Down and Bottom-Up Debugging

Listing 2.7 illustrates two features of developing structured programs that are tremendously helpful in debugging: top-down and bottom-up development. You start with the main part of the program as a framework on which to place your (as yet empty) subroutines. Each subroutine performs an essentially vacuous task, displaying a message that it has run. You then develop the subroutines one at a time, debugging them separately before adding them to the main program.

Because each subroutine is a black box as far as the main program is concerned, nothing that happens inside a subroutine should have any direct effect on either the main program or the other subroutines. The only

```
PROGRAM MakeChange;
   ( Listing 2.7. This illustrates top-down design and debugging,
     using "stubs" for the program's subroutines. )

USES CRT;   ( for CLRSCR )

VAR
   Payment,
   Change  : integer;

PROCEDURE Pause;
  VAR
    proceed : char;
  BEGIN
    WRITELN;
    WRITE(' Press the Enter key to continue ...');
    READ(proceed)
  END;

PROCEDURE ExplainProgram;
  BEGIN
    WRITELN(' The ExplainProgram procedure has run.');
    pause
  END;

PROCEDURE CountMoney(var Payment, Change : integer);
  BEGIN
    WRITELN(' The CountMoney procedure has run.');
    pause
  END;


BEGIN          ( main body of program )
  ExplainProgram;
  CountMoney(payment, change);
END.
```

Listing 2.7: Top-down development of a Pascal program.

things that are visible to the main program and the other subroutines are
(a) what *goes into* a given subroutine, and (b) what *comes out of* a given subroutine. And the items that go in and out of a subroutine should always
go through the "front door" as "parameters." See Chapter 9 for a discussion of parameters.

This means that if a bug does occur in a subroutine, it is easy to isolate.
You know exactly what is going in and what is coming out. To develop a subroutine separately from the main program, you need to write a *driver* to assign input values to the subroutine. When you think the subroutine has been
coded correctly, you run the test program (like that shown in Listing 2.8) and

```
PROGRAM TestCount;
  ( This program illustrates how to use subroutine drivers
    to develop a subroutine separately from the main program. )

USES CRT;   ( for CLRSCR )

VAR
  AmountDue,
  Payment,
  Change  : integer;
  Proceed : char;

PROCEDURE Driver(var Payment, AmountDue : integer);
  BEGIN
    CLRSCR;
    WRITE(' Initial value for payment? ');
    READLN(payment);
    WRITE(' Initial value for amount due? ');
    READLN(AmountDue)
  END;

PROCEDURE CountMoney(var Payment, AmountDue, Change : integer);
  BEGIN
      Change := Payment - AmountDue;    ( calculate change )
      WRITELN;
      WRITELN(' Your change is ', Change, ' cent(s).');
      WRITELN(' Have a nice day.')
  END;          ( of the CountMoney procedure )

BEGIN
  proceed := 'Y';
  WHILE UPCASE(proceed) = 'Y' DO
    BEGIN
    Driver(payment, amountdue);
    CountMoney(payment, amountdue, change);
    WRITE(' Do another (Y/N)? ');
    READLN(proceed)
    END
END.
```

Listing 2.8: Testing a subroutine with a driver program.

try one set of values after another to see if the subroutine works correctly.

In addition to ordinary values (such as 25 or 100 in the case of Count-Money), you should try very large and very small values (e.g., 1,000,000 and 0); values that don't make sense (e.g., a payment of 75 when the amount due is 100); and values that are the wrong type (e.g., "F" or "&" instead of integers). The goal is to ensure the following:

1. The subroutine runs correctly when it receives the sort of input it expects (in this case, integers where the payment is greater than the amount due).

2. The subroutine has ways to handle input that it doesn't expect (such as receiving letters instead of numbers for the amount due, or receiving an amount due of zero). This is called bullet-proofing the routine.

MODIFYING THE PROGRAM

Structured design is also very helpful when you need to modify a program. You may need a new feature, or need a change in an existing feature, or you may find, long after the program is in use, a subtle bug that you'd like to fix.

With an unstructured program, making changes can be a nightmare, because any part of the program can have unexpected effects on any other part of the program. You can make a change on page 19 and then, suddenly, the code on page five won't work right anymore—and you won't have the faintest idea why.

With structured programming, each part of the program is a black box whose internal features are hidden from the rest of the program, and whose interactions with other parts of the program are tightly controlled *by you*. Changes in the internal structure of a routine should have no effect on its work with other parts of the program. As long as it takes the expected input values and returns the correct output values, that's all the rest of the program is concerned with.

Moreover, to add a new feature, you need to make only minor changes either in the main program or in one of the main subroutines, so that the subroutine for the new feature will be called when needed.

Today there is an entire discipline called software maintenance that is devoted to rescuing people from unstructured code written in the 1960s and 1970s. Fortunately, you'll never have to worry about this. With Pascal, you'll learn how to do it right the first time.

USING PROGRAM COMMENTS

In Chapter 1 we briefly discussed how comments can clarify a program. You can create a comment in one of the following two ways:

- By enclosing the comment material in left and right curly brackets, { and }.

- By enclosing the comment material in a left comment bracket, (* and a right comment bracket, *).

Either combination of symbols will cause Pascal to ignore anything that's between the two brackets. You must be careful, however, not to combine the two types of brackets into a single comment. When Pascal sees a {, it will ignore everything until it comes to the next }. Likewise, when Pascal sees a (*, it ignores everything until it comes to a *). Thus, the following piece of code will cause an error:

```
BEGIN

  WRITELN(' Comments are beautiful.') { Our opinion.
*)

END;
```

In the case above, the first comment bracket does not match the second. In any single comment, both comment brackets must be of the same type.

WHAT COMMENTS ARE GOOD FOR

In addition to explaining particular parts of your code, comments are used in two other ways. The first is to "comment out" the parts of your program that are still under development. Once you have part of your program working, you can tell Turbo Pascal to ignore any new, untested code by enclosing it in comment brackets until you're sure that it works right. Generally, it's a good idea to use one type of comment bracket for explanations and the other for "commenting out" sections of code. If you use the same type for both jobs, you run the risk that a stray unmatched comment bracket will cause your program to go haywire.

The other use of comment brackets is to insert *compiler directives* into your program. These tell the Pascal compiler to do things it would not ordinarily do, such as to add some extra error checking to your program. See Chapter 7 for details on compiler directives.

OBJECT-ORIENTED PROGRAMMING

The most exciting developments in recent Pascal history have been Turbo Pascal's development of support for object-oriented programming, and the "Turbo Vision" object library that is included with Turbo Pascal 6.

We'll discuss the details of object-oriented programming in Chapters 22–24. Here, we only want to take a quick look at how it naturally evolved from—and differs from—structured programming.

Object-oriented programming, like structured programming, uses the idea that the internal features of each program part should be hidden from all the other parts. Where object-oriented programming differs from structured programming is in the notion that program parts are not subroutines, but intelligent data that have their own subroutines; data that know how to do things for themselves.

Most programming languages (such as BASIC) still do not provide direct support for object-oriented programming. However, for languages that have procedure and function data types (such as standard Pascal), object orientation can be simulated.

SUMMARY

A computer program is a very specific, unambiguous sequence of instructions that takes data (input), manipulates it in some way (processing), and returns data (output). The instructions must be specific because a computer (which consists of a central processing unit or CPU, data storage devices, and input-output devices) understands instructions as sequences of on-off switches that permit no ambiguity.

Turbo Pascal is a general-purpose programming language that is suitable for a wide range of applications. It provides both high-level capabilities such as graphics commands, and low-level access to the operating system and CPU. Pascal is also designed to teach structured programming methods that make programs easier to debug and modify. Turbo Pascal, as distinguished from standard Pascal, also supports object-oriented programming, which further extends the capabilities provided by structured programming.

REVIEW EXERCISES

1. What are the basic operations of any computer program?

2. How does a computer store and process information? Explain how this method works.

3. What are the four main components of any computer?

4. The instruction set of a computer is which of the following?

   (a) The set of instructions in Pascal.

(b) The built-in operations of its central processing unit.

(c) The instructions MOV, CALL, JMP, and CMP.

(d) The instructions for safe use of a computer by students.

5. Explain what a compiler does and how it differs from an interpreter.

6. Explain the characteristics of a high-level programming language.

7. True or false: The best way to write a Pascal program is simply to start writing code. Explain your answer.

8. Explain the three main advantages of structured programming. Does unstructured programming have any advantages? If so, what?

9. True or false: In a structured program, each specific task should be handled by a separate line of code. Explain your answer.

10. Explain how one should read a structured program to understand how it works.

11. How and why do subroutines make debugging easier? Is it simply the *use* of subroutines that is important, or is there a specific method for implementing subroutines that makes the difference?

12. Explain the basic ideas of top-down and bottom-up program development.

13. Explain the basic methods involved in debugging a subroutine. What values should you try? Why?

14. Give three uses for program comments, and devise an example that shows each type of use.

15. Explain the basic way in which object-oriented programming differs from structured programming.

An Overview of Pascal Programming

Prior planning prevents poor performance.

—The five P's, traditional Army adage

DESIGNING YOUR PROGRAM

Regardless of the programming language you use, you must spend some time at the beginning to plan and design your program. This requires more than just knowing that you should split the program into subroutines. The question is, *which* subroutines? How should different tasks be divided so that the chief goals of the program are achieved efficiently, with clear, easy-to-understand code?

I don't want to give you the idea that this is a simple problem. Many books have been written about program design, but people are still arguing about the best ways to do it. Nevertheless, there are a few simple rules that you can follow to create a good design without having to become a master theoretician. These rules are similar to remembering "control the center" and "castle early" in the game of chess, in that they are basic principles you should observe to create efficient, easy-to-understand programs.

STATE WHAT
THE PROGRAM SHOULD DO

The first step for planning a program design is to summarize in one sentence what the program is supposed to do. For the Turbo Tunemaker program, which we will develop later in Chapter 20, this sentence would be something like the following:

```
Allow the user to play music on his or her PC.
```

That is, of course, very general. It does not tell us anything about where the music comes from, how it is to be selected by the user, or if it can be edited by the user, but it does state the main task that the program must accomplish.

DIVIDE
THE MAIN TASK INTO SUBTASKS

As a second step, we will make our problem definition somewhat more specific by dividing the main task into several subtasks.

```
Allow the user to play music on his or her PC, mean-
ing that the program should
```

- Explain itself to the user
- Let the user enter tunes from the keyboard
- Let the user save tunes to a disk file
- Let the user load tunes from a disk file
- Let the user play tunes
- Let the user edit existing tunes

Notice that I have not said anything about Pascal in this design; I've simply identified the major tasks that the program has to perform. In this case, the major tasks divide rather neatly, and each receives its own subroutine. At this stage, there are three main principles to follow:

1. Subdivide the program's tasks in outline form until each subroutine performs a clear logical step, such as playing a tune or saving a tune to a disk file.

2. Avoid becoming involved in language details. Keep your focus on what the program is supposed to accomplish.

3. Attend to housekeeping details such as setting up the program to run and explaining the program to the user. Each of these may need its own subroutine.

DECIDE ON BROAD IMPLEMENTATION

Once you have created a usable outline of the tasks that the program must perform and how they are to be divided into subroutines, you need to consider some of the specifics of how to implement the program. If you ask yourself the following three questions, the answers should provide some of these specifics.

1. *What must be global and what can be local?* Remember that the code inside each subroutine is hidden both from the main program and from the other subroutines. Parts of the program that are hidden inside a subroutine are local to that subroutine, because they are not accessible to other parts of the program. Parts that are not in a subroutine, on the other hand, are called global. One programming principle is so important it deserves special emphasis as a rule of thumb:

   •Within reason, hide everything you can.

   This means that the main structure of the program should not be cluttered up with a lot of details about how various parts of the program work. Those details should be hidden inside subroutines, which can contain their own variables, data structures, and local subroutines.

   Some parts, however, do need to be global. If a variable is shared by several subroutines, such as the variable for a tune in Turbo Tunemaker, then it must be global so that it is accessible to all those subroutines. Hiding it inside one of the subroutines would not make sense. Similarly, a subroutine to pause the program, which will be called by many other subroutines, must be global. Anything that doesn't really need to be global, however, should be hidden inside a subroutine.

2. *Which data structures will work best?* The parts of your program that hold data are called *data structures,* and you design many of these structures yourself. At this stage, you simply need to decide what the data structures must do—never mind how they will coded in a particular language. In Turbo Tunemaker, we will need some kind of list to hold the notes of the tune being

played. Because some tunes are longer than others, ideally it should be the type of list whose length can vary while the program is being run.

3. *Which language is best suited for the program at hand?* In some ways, it would be easier to code Turbo Tunemaker in Microsoft QuickBASIC than Turbo Pascal, because QuickBASIC has a built-in music Play command. QuickBASIC, however, lacks support for object-oriented programming and other Turbo Pascal features that we'll be using.

STARTING TO WRITE CODE

At this stage of program development, you have two options. First, you can do as many people advise and write the program in *pseudocode*, which means, essentially, that you code it in English. For example:

```
start program

clear the screen

display on screen "Welcome to Turbo Tunemaker!"

pause


subroutine to set up a tune list

    initialize the list

    end of subroutine

~... etc.
```

There's no question that this extra step will give you a more detailed understanding of your program, but what you end up with is in English, not in Pascal. If you do your design work properly, then you don't need pseudocode. If you haven't done your design work properly, then the additional pseudocode is not that helpful. For small programs particularly, pseudocode is redundant; however, for larger programs, it may help you gain a better understanding of your program. To me, however, it makes

more sense to go directly to your second option, which is to start coding your program in the language you've chosen. We will design and code the Tunemaker program in Chapter 20.

SPECIFIC FEATURES OF PASCAL

If you are like me, you've probably been chomping at the bit, wondering when we are going to start talking about Pascal. Well, chomp no more: we have arrived.

PASCAL IDENTIFIERS

The fundamental building blocks of a Pascal program are called *identifiers* which are essentially just names for different parts of the program. Each part of the program must have its own identifier, and, with a few key exceptions, no two parts of a program can have the same identifier. Thus, the following code will cause an error if you try to compile it:

```
PROGRAM ClientNames; { same name as variable, below }
USES CRT,              { for CLRSCR }
CONST
  NumberOfClients = 5;
VAR
  ClientNames : ARRAY[1..NumberOfClients] of STRING[15];
  Counter : integer;
PROCEDURE Pause;
  VAR
    ch : CHAR;
  BEGIN
   WRITE ('Press any key...');
```

```
      REPEAT UNTIL Keypressed;
       Ch:= READKEY
     END;
 BEGIN
    CLRSCR;
    FOR Counter := 1 to NumberOfClients DO
       BEGIN
       WRITE(' Enter a client name: ');
       READLN(Clients[Counter])
       END;
     pause
 END.
```

The reason, as shown in Figure 3.1, is that two parts of the program have the same name—that is, both the program name and one of the variables are called **ClientNames**. Remember that it would not make any difference if one were called **ClientNames** and the other were called **CLIENTNAMES** or

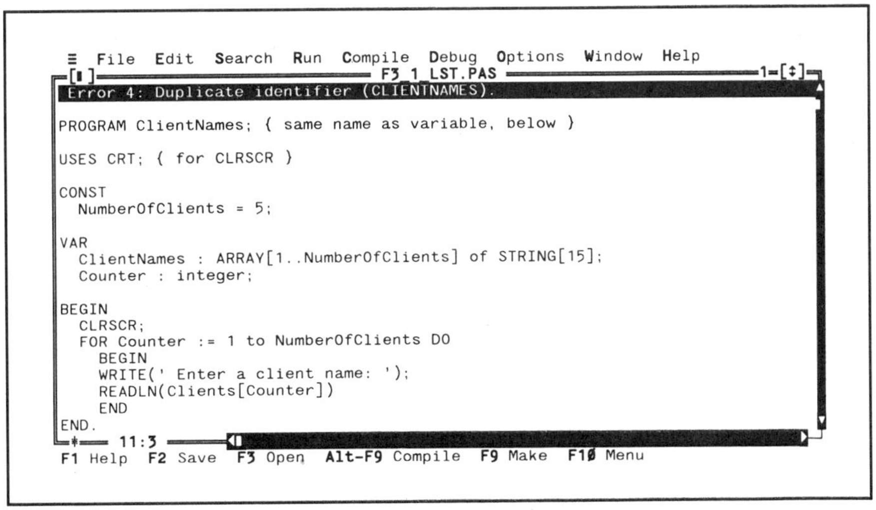

Figure 3.1: Compile-time error because of duplicate identifiers.

clientnames, because Pascal does not distinguish between upper and lowercase letters.

I know I have introduced some things in this short program that you have not seen before. Don't worry: you will get to them very soon. In the meantime, you can learn a lot by trying to figure them out on your own. If you want to enter and run the program, just change one of the **Client-Names** identifiers to another legal identifier, such as **Clients**.

Reserved Words

Turbo Pascal's vocabulary constitutes its own built-in set of identifiers called *reserved words*. These are words such as BEGIN, PROCEDURE, TYPE, UNIT, and VAR. In addition to reserved words, there are also *standard identifiers* such as WRITELN and READLN. You should not use either reserved words or standard identifiers to name parts of the program that you create. If you do try to use reserved words, your program won't compile. If you use standard identifiers, your program probably will compile, but most likely it won't run correctly because you've redefined one or more of Pascal's key words.

A list of Turbo Pascal's reserved words and standard identifiers is included as Appendix A at the back of the book.

Rules for Identifiers

You cannot use just any old word or string of characters as an identifier. You have to follow certain rules. A Pascal identifier must observe the following conventions:

1. It must begin with a letter or an underline character ("_").

2. It cannot contain any spaces or other special characters such as ., !, ?, #, or -.

3. It can have any combination of letters, digits, and underline characters after the first character.

4. It can be as long as you like, but Turbo Pascal pays attention only to the first 63 characters.

Thus, the following are legal, user-defined identifiers:

ClientRecord	COUNTER
_AnyOldThing	file2read
Number_Of_Loops	NumberOfLoops
mrspeel	general_george_s_patton

The following list contains some *il*legal identifiers that will cause an error when you try to compile the program:

Identifier	Mistake
Client Record	contains a space
2motleycrue	doesn't start with a letter or underline
Number-Of-Loops	contains illegal characters ("-")
Begin	same as a Pascal reserved word
data.txt	contains illegal character (".")

OVERALL PROGRAM STRUCTURE

Unlike spaghetti code, Pascal programs have a very definite structure that has to be followed. Each program is broken up into sections. The main sections of a Pascal program (demonstrated in Listing 3.1) are as follows:

- **The PROGRAM statement.** This gives the name of the program and marks the official beginning of the program for your Pascal compiler. In standard Pascal (though this is not required in Turbo Pascal), the program statement also has to identify any files that the program will be using, such as a data file containing a list of names and addresses.

- **The USES clause.** This tells Turbo Pascal what units the program uses. *Units* are separately-compiled libraries of routines and/or object types. By naming a unit in your USES clause, you can use material from the unit without having to include it in

```
PROGRAM Listing3_1;

  ( This listing demonstrates how to use an array to
   hold multiple variables in a list structure- -in
   this case, a client list. The maximum number of
   clients in the list is declared as a constant in
   the constant section; the advantage of doing this
   is that you can change every occurrence of this
   number in the program simply by changing the value
   declared for NumberOfClients in the CONST section.
   Notice also how we set up a FOR loop to load the
   client names into the array. )

USES CRT;        ( for CLRSCR )

CONST
  NumberOfClients = 5;

VAR
  Clients : ARRAY[1..NumberOfClients] of STRING[15];
  Counter : integer;

PROCEDURE Pause;
  VAR
    Proceed : CHAR;
  BEGIN
    WRITE(' Press any key to continue ...');
    Proceed := READKEY;
    WRITELN; WRITELN
  END;

BEGIN
  CLRSCR;
  FOR Counter := 1 to NumberOfClients DO
    BEGIN
    WRITE(' Enter a client name: ');
    READLN(Clients[Counter])
    END;
  pause
END.
```

Listing 3.1: The main sections of a Pascal program.

your program. If Turbo Pascal cannot find a given subroutine (or object type) in the current program, it looks in the units named by the USES clause to find them. This feature is not supported by standard Pascal, but many versions (such as Microsoft QuickPascal and DEC Vax Pascal) have similar features.

- **The LABEL section.** This is a section that your computer science professor might not tell you about, because it involves the hated GOTO statement. With a GOTO statement, you jump from one place in your program to another, and structured-programming purists maintain that you should never, ever use GOTOs.

In the LABEL section, you list labels for program lines that are GOTO destinations. In standard Pascal, labels must be integers that range from 0..9999, and leading zeroes don't count (e.g., 000125 and 125 are considered the same label). Turbo Pascal also lets you use ordinary identifiers for labels, such as Destination-Line, though of course they must be unique within your program (or at least within a subroutine).

- **The CONST (constant) section.** In this section, you declare any constants used by your program. Constants can be either simple or complex expressions, such as the following:

  10
  'stockfile'
  CHR(13)
  1000 div 5

  Each constant receives its own identifier. The number 10, for example, could be NumberOfClients. In this section, you also can declare typed constants, which are not really constants, but are variables whose initial value is preset in the constant section.

  You declare constants as follows:

  Name = 'stockfile';

  MaximumNumberofRecords = 100;

  Company : STRING[20] = "; {a typed constant}

  Except for typed constants, which are really variables, the values you set in the CONST section cannot be changed during the program run.

- **The TYPE section.** In this section, you can create and declare your own data types beyond those supported by Pascal. While Turbo Pascal supports data types of numbers, text, and so forth, you can use the TYPE section to create data types that are tailored to your own needs, such as the following:

```
TYPE
   String10 = STRING[10];        { needed for passing  }
   String15 = STRING[15];        { string variables to }
   String20 = STRING[20];        { subroutines         }
   DaysOfWeek = (Sunday, Monday, Tuesday, Wednesday,
                    Thursday, Friday, Saturday);
   Digits = 0..9;
   FirstSixLetters = 'A'..'F';
   Weekdays = Monday..Friday; {uses "DaysOfWeek" type}
   WorkDays = ARRAY[Monday..Friday] of String20;
   Client = RECORD
              Firstname,
              Lastname  : string[15];
              Address   : string[30];
              City      : string[15];
              State     : string[2];
              Zipcode   : string[5];
              Balance   : real;
              PaidUp    : Boolean  { True or False }
   END;
```

It is important to understand that merely defining a data type in the TYPE section does not automatically put that type to use in your program. The above section does not, for example, give you a variable named Client into which you can start loading clients' names, addresses, and other information. In order to do that, you have to declare a variable of the Client data type—a job you can do in the VAR section, which follows next.

Remember that you do not have to declare any simple Pascal types in this section—only types that you create.

- **The VAR (variable) section.** In this section, you declare the names and data types of variables that you use in the program. A variable name can be any legal identifier, and the data type can be a standard Turbo Pascal data type or a data type you defined in the TYPE section. The only variables not declared in this section are a special type called dynamic variables, which are created while the program is actually running. (See Chapter 11 for a discussion of dynamic variables.)

- **The procedures and functions section.** This is the section for your program's subroutines, and it is the only section of the program that does not begin with an explicit section label. As soon as you declare a procedure or a function, Turbo Pascal knows that you've started this section. If you are writing a medium-sized program with many subroutines, you should use comments to break up this section into subsections such as utility routines, input routines, help routines, and so forth. (In a very large program, you should create some units and put as many subroutines as possible into them.)

- **The main body of the program.** In a well-designed program, this part is usually only a few lines long. The main body of the program should show only the overall structure of what happens in the program, leaving all the details to the subroutines.

SPECIFIC FEATURES OF PASCAL

Now that you have seen the overall structure of a Pascal program, we are ready to delve deeper into how that structure is implemented. In the following sections, I will present an overview of the specifics of writing Pascal code. If and when you need complete details, you should look ahead to the appropriate chapters in Parts II and III.

BEGIN AND END

In order to understand the functions of BEGIN and END in a Pascal program, you must grasp an odd idea: *a Pascal program is just a single big statement*. Think of it in terms of the English language for a moment. The following is a legal sentence in English:

```
Go to the grocery store.
```

So is this:

```
Go to the grocery store and

pick up the kids after school.
```

The second example is not *two* sentences, but one sentence with two subsentences as its component parts. It is, of course, called a compound sentence.

In the same way, a Pascal program is a big compound statement composed of simpler statements. By using BEGIN and END, you signal to Pascal where a compound program statement is supposed to begin and end. Semicolons are used in the same way that the word "and" is used in English: to tie two simpler statements together into a compound statement. Thus, you must use BEGIN and END to show the start and finish of a compound statement. Here are some legal Pascal statements:

```
WRITELN(' This is a simple statement.');  { simple }
IF a = 1 THEN DoOneThing ELSE DoAnotherThing; { simple }


IF a = 1  { simple IF..}
    THEN BEGIN  { THEN which }
        WRITELN(' a = 1');  {contains a }
        pause { compound   }
        END  {THEN clause }
    ELSE WRITELN(' a doesn''t equal 1');
```

```
BEGIN  { compound   }
  WRITELN(' Block is a compound statement.');
  WRITELN(' Substatements linked by semicolons.');
  WRITELN(' No semicolon right before the END');
  WRITELN(' There's no next statement from');
  WRITELN(' the last line must be separated.') END;
```

The bottom line is that any time you are constructing a compound statement from simpler statements, you should start with BEGIN, separate the simpler statements with semicolons, and finish with END. Moreover, because each BEGIN..END sequence is itself a statement, it must be separated from other statements by a semicolon after the word END. The only exception occurs at the very end of the entire program, when you must put a period after END (see Listing 3.2).

SIMPLE DATA TYPES

The idea behind data types is a fairly commonsensical one. In the real world, there are, of course, many different types of things, such as gases, solids, colors, people, minerals, and diskettes. Because computer programs are ultimately about the real world, a programming language uses different data types so that it can manipulate information about the many different types of things in the real world more efficiently.

Pascal supports both simple and complex data types. You can use the simple data types as building blocks to define your own complex data types. Essentially, Pascal's simple data types break down into numbers, text, truth values, and pointers.

Numeric Data Types

Numeric data types are divided into integers (whole numbers) and real numbers (numbers with a decimal point). Turbo Pascal's integer type ranges from –32,768 to 32,767, so some examples of Pascal integers would

```
PROGRAM Listing3_2;

        { This program illustrates how BEGIN, END, and semicolons
        are used to define and separate program statements. }

USES CRT;

PROCEDURE Pause;
  VAR
    Proceed : CHAR;
  BEGIN
    WRITELN(' Press any key to continue ...');
    Proceed := READKEY;
    WRITELN; WRITELN
  END;

PROCEDURE ExplainProgram;
        BEGIN
        WRITELN;
    WRITELN(' This program shows how compound statements');
    WRITELN(' are formed with BEGIN, END, and semicolons.');
    pause
  END;

PROCEDURE ExplainPunctuation;
        BEGIN
    WRITELN;
    WRITELN(' Note that each simple statement within a');
    WRITELN(' compound statement is separated from the');
    WRITELN(' others by a semicolon, except for the very');
    WRITELN(' last one before the END.');
    pause
  END;

PROCEDURE ExplainENDs;
        BEGIN
        WRITELN;
    WRITELN(' Furthermore, each END in the program has a');
    WRITELN(' semicolon after it to separate it from the rest');
    WRITELN(' of the program unless (a) it comes just before');
    WRITELN(' another END, or (b) it comes at the end of the');
    WRITELN(' program, in which case it has a period after it.');
    pause
  END;

{ ---------------------------------------------------------------- }
{                      MAIN BODY OF PROGRAM                         }
{ ---------------------------------------------------------------- }
BEGIN

        CLRSCR;
  ExplainProgram;
  ExplainPunctuation;
  ExplainENDs;
END.
```

Listing 3.2: Put a period after the last END in the program.

be 123, 5, 30000, and –555. Real numbers in Turbo Pascal range from 2.9 times 10^{-39} to 1.7 times 10^{38}, which is an astronomical range.

Each type has several subtypes (see Chapter 5). For the time being, you need to be aware only of the following:

- If you do an arithmetic calculation with integers and real numbers, the result will be a real number—a fact which can occasionally get you into trouble. In Listing 3.3, we multiplied an integer (3) by a real number (2.00) and tried to put the result in an integer-type variable (c). The result is a compile-time error, as shown in Figure 3.2.

- Your real numbers will look extremely odd unless you format them. Turbo Pascal displays real numbers in scientific notation, which means that they are displayed in terms of powers of 10. Thus,

$$12.5 = 1.25 \times 10^1 \text{ is displayed as } 1.2500000000E+01$$

```
PROGRAM Listing3_3;

    ( This program demonstrates how mixing numeric types in an
      arithmetic operation can lead to trouble. Multiplying an
      integer by a real number gives a real number. )

USES CRT;

var
  a, c : integer;
  b : real;

PROCEDURE Pause;
  VAR
    Proceed : CHAR;
  BEGIN
    WRITELN(' Press any key to continue ...');
    Proceed := READKEY;
    WRITELN; WRITELN
  END;

BEGIN
  a := 3;                    ( assign integer value to a )
  b := 2.00;                 ( assign real value to b     )
  c := a*b;                  ( assign a times b to c      )
  WRITELN(' The value of c is ', c, '.');
  pause
END.
```

Listing 3.3: A compile-time error from incompatible data types.

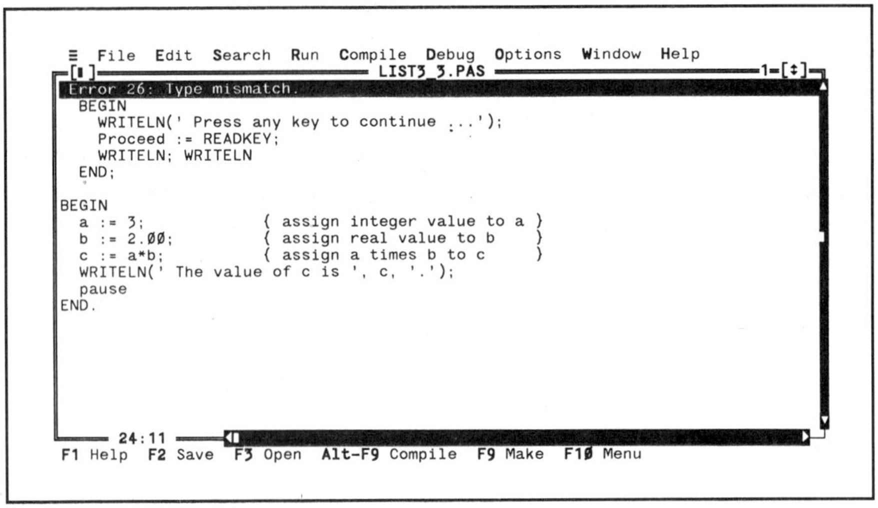

```
 ≡  File  Edit  Search  Run  Compile  Debug  Options  Window  Help
[■]══════════════════════ LIST3_3.PAS ═══════════════════1═[‡]
 Error 26: Type mismatch.
  BEGIN
    WRITELN(' Press any key to continue ...');
    Proceed := READKEY;
    WRITELN; WRITELN
  END;

BEGIN
  a := 3;              ( assign integer value to a )
  b := 2.00;           ( assign real value to b     )
  c := a*b;            ( assign a times b to c      )
  WRITELN(' The value of c is ', c, '.');
  pause
END.



    ── 24:11 ──
 F1 Help  F2 Save  F3 Open  Alt-F9 Compile  F9 Make  F10 Menu
```

Figure 3.2: Compile-time error because of incompatible data types.

You can put a stop to this by telling Turbo Pascal how many digits you want in your real number. For instance, if the real-number variable

a

has a value of 12.5, then you can make it show up as 12.5 (and in other formats) like this:

```
WRITELN(' The value of a is ', a:0:1, '.');
WRITELN(' The value of a is ', a:0:5, '.');
{with five decimal places}
WRITELN(' The value of a is ', a:10:1, '.');
{in a 10-character-wide column}
```

Putting the **:0:1** after the name of the variable does the trick. The number after the first colon denotes the total number of digits you want in the number; if you make this 0 (zero), then the length stretches to fit the actual number. The number after the second colon is the number of digits that you want to the right of the decimal point.

Text Data Types

There are two text data types in Turbo Pascal—characters (called CHAR) and strings. A character is any single letter, digit, or special symbol, such as 'g', 'P', '5', '&', or '+'; and it must be enclosed in single-quote marks. A string is an ordered sequence of characters, such as 'U.S.S. Enterprise' or 'Pascal', and must also be enclosed in single-quote marks.

You will use characters often to get user's answers to on-screen prompts, such as "Proceed (Y/N)?" You will use strings most often to display text and to give text input, such as

```
WRITE(' Enter your name: ');   { displays a string }

READLN(Name);                  { gets input string }
```

Standard Pascal does not have a string data type. It treats strings as packed arrays of characters. (See "Arrays" below.) If you have to do a program in standard Pascal, use packed arrays instead of strings. Turbo Pascal will ignore the packed part, which it does not support, and will handle arrays of characters in much the same way that it handles strings. The only problem is that it is much harder to read strings into and out of arrays, but don't worry—we will develop some routines for that later.

There is also a data type called *text* that is used to represent unstructured disk files. See Chapter 12 for a discussion of this data type.

Truth-Value Data Types

In standard logic, there are two truth values, true and false, and a factual statement is either one or the other. The same conditions apply in programming languages. In Pascal, truth values are denoted by the words true and false; the true/false data type is called Boolean, named after the English mathematician George Boole (1815-1864). The reason for calling truth value statements "factual" (Boolean) statements is that most program statements are not factual; instead, they are imperatives, such as "shut the door" or "put this value in variable x," which are neither true nor false.

You can use Boolean variables and expressions to control the flow of your program. For example, if PaidUp is a Boolean variable, then you could write

```
IF PaidUp = TRUE

    THEN SendThankYou

    ELSE BugForMoney;
```

Because factual statements are true or false, you can use them to set the truth values of Boolean variables, as follows:

```
PaidUp := (CustomerBalance = 0.00)
```

Because the statement **CustomerBalance = 0.00** makes an assertion, it is either true or false. Its value therefore can be assigned to a Boolean variable. You can combine factual statements or Boolean variables with logical operators such as AND, OR, and XOR to form more complex expressions. See Chapter 5 for a discussion of the Boolean type.

Pointer Data Type

The pointer data type differs markedly from the types that I have discussed so far. Instead of holding something ordinary, like a number or a text string, a pointer holds the memory address of a variable. Pointers are used to keep track of dynamic variables. (See Chapter 11.) For the time being, do not try to do anything with pointers unless you are sure that you understand them.

STRUCTURED DATA TYPES

There are three structured data types to be discussed here: arrays, records, and objects. Arrays are used to hold static lists of data, while records and objects can be used to create your own customized data types.

Arrays

You can think of an array as a row of slots into which you can fit data items of a single type. Thus, an array can hold numbers, text items, truth values, pointers, and even user-defined types such as records and objects.

To declare an array, you must specify three main things: the name of the array, the number of slots it will have, and the type of data item that the slots will need to hold. Note, however, that because ARRAY is a built-in data type, you do not strictly have to declare it in the type section. Either of the following will do fine:

```
TYPE

        Enrollment = ARRAY[1..100] of Student; { Where
Student is a previously defined data type }

VAR

        StudentList : Enrollment; { Declares variable
to be of enrollment data type }
```

or, more economically,

```
VAR

        StudentList : ARRAY[1..100] of Student;
```

You do need to declare an array type in the TYPE section if you intend to pass variables of that array type into subroutines. Therefore, even though the second method is easier, it's usually better to declare array types in the TYPE section.

You refer to the individual items in an array by using the name of the array variable combined with its array index. To refer to the fifth element in an array named **TextList**, which holds text strings, for example, we would write **TextList[5]**. With the **StudentList** array, which holds records, it is more complicated: to refer to the name part of the student record in position 5, we would write **StudentList[5].Name**.

Records

Records are used in Pascal to hold together different pieces of information that can be of different types. For example, a student record would hold name and address (strings), grade-point average (a real number), and whether or not the student was on academic probation (a Boolean value). A record is defined in the TYPE section by naming the record type, defining its data slots, called fields, and ending the definition with END:

```
TYPE

   Student = RECORD

            Name      : STRING[20];

            Address   : STRING[30];

            City      : STRING[10];

            State     : STRING[2];

            Zipcode   : STRING[5];

            GPA       : real;

            Probation : Boolean

            END;
```

You then can create variables of this type and use them as follows:

```
VAR

   Pupil : Student; { declares individual variable}
                    { of Student record type }

   StudentList : ARRAY[1.100] of Student;

                 { declares an array of student }

                 { records                      }


BEGIN

   Pupil.Name := 'Gerald Ford';
```

```
    Pupil.Address := '30 Rockefeller Center'

    StudentList[1].Name := 'Jimmy Carter';

    StudentList[1].Address := '10 Maple Street';

    StudentList[1].City := 'Plains'

    StudentList[1].State := 'California'

    StudentList[1].Zipcode := '90069'

    StudentList[1].GPA := 4.00;

    StudentList[1].Probation := false
END;
```

There are also some special tricks that you can do with records, such as using them to hold arrays of records (see Chapter 9).

Objects

Objects are the central data type used by Turbo Vision. They look similar to records, but they have very special properties:

- Object types include their own subroutines (procedures and functions).

- They can be derived from previously defined object types (ancestor types) and inherit the features of those types.

- They can override the features of their ancestor types and add their own new features, including new data fields and subroutines.

CONSTANTS AND VARIABLES

Constants and variables are pretty much self-explanatory. A constant is a data item that never changes its value during a program run, while a variable can have new values assigned to it at any time. Both can be any legal Pascal data type. It is best to think of a variable as a kind of "box" that can hold data of a certain type.

Declaring Constants

You declare constants in your program as we've already seen, by assigning values to them in the CONST section of your program. Some typical constant declarations might be the following:

```
CONST
    MaxCount = 100;
    Interest = 0.18;
    Space    = ' ';
```

One question that frequently arises is: Why do we need to declare constants in the first place? What's the point of declaring

```
NumberOfCustomers = 100;
```

when we could simply insert 100 at any place where we use the constant **NumberOfCustomers**?

The answer is that by declaring constants, we make a program easier to understand and modify than it would be otherwise. For example, after declaring **NumberOfCustomers** as a constant at the start of your program, you might in a later procedure define a variable as the following:

```
CustomerList = ARRAY[1..NumberOfCustomers]
               of Customer
```

The use of a named constant has two benefits. First, it makes the code easier to understand than **ARRAY[1..100]**. Calling the upper limit of the list **NumberOfCustomers** makes it clear what's going on. Second, if you later want to *change* the number of customers in your program, you need to change only the constant declaration at the very beginning, instead of having to search through the program for every instance where you referred to the number of customers.

Declaring Variables

Before a normal variable can be used in a program, it has to be named and its type has to be declared. A variable can be any data type, whether a built-in type or a user-defined type that's been declared in the TYPE section. To declare a variable, you simply give its name, a colon, and then its type:

```
VAR
      Counter          : INTEGER;
      StudentList      : ARRAY[1..100] of Student;
      String20         : STRING[20];
      YesNo            : CHAR;
```

PASCAL STATEMENTS

There are several different types of statements in Pascal. The most important are *assignment* statements, *input/output* (I/O) statements, and *control* statements. We've already seen examples of all three types in the program listings, but let's take an "official" look at them now.

Assignment Statements

Assignment statements assign a value to a variable. If a variable is a kind of box that can hold data of a certain type, then an assignment statement essentially takes an item of that type and puts it into the box. There is one thing to be careful about, however, especially if you've done programming in BASIC. Pascal uses a combination of the colon and the equal sign to make its assignment operator :=, while BASIC uses the equal sign by itself, =. If you use an equal sign by itself in Pascal, the program interprets it as a Boolean operator to compare two values; at best, your program won't compile.

Some examples of assignment statements are the following:

```
counter := 15;
```

```
Name := 'Zardoz';

PaidUp := TRUE;

StudentList[5].Name := 'Frank Borland';
```

Input/Output Statements

Input/output (I/O) statements are used to transfer data from one place to another: for example, to get it from the keyboard, display it on the screen, write it to a disk file, or print it on a printer. We've already seen several of these. Examples are:

```
WRITELN(' This displays text on the screen.');

READLN(Name);    { Gets a string from the keyboard }

WRITELN(myfile, 'This writes text to a disk file.');
```

There are two things to notice in these examples. First, you can use I/O statements to assign values to variables. In line 2 of the example, the READLN statement not only gets a string from the keyboard, but puts that string into the variable *Name.*

Second, the WRITELN statement at the bottom writes a line of text to a disk file that's denoted by the file variable *myfile*. WRITELN and READLN can take the name of a file as either the destination (with WRITELN) or the source (with READLN) of the information they use. Note that if you don't specify a file name, Pascal assumes that you want to *read* from the keyboard and *write* to the screen. If you want to read from or write to a disk file, you must first associate it with a file variable and then open the file (see Chapter 12).

Control Statements

Control statements are used to direct the flow of your program in one direction or another based on the value of some variable. We've already seen examples of IF..THEN..ELSE, which is one of the most common control statements. Others set up loops or test for a variety of values. We'll just summarize them below.

IF..THEN..ELSE   You use IF..THEN..ELSE (or just IF..THEN when you don't need an ELSE) when you want the program to go in one of two directions based on an either/or situation. For example:

```
IF PaidUp

   THEN SendThankYou

   ELSE BugForMoney;


IF GPA < 2.00

   THEN SendProbationLetter

   ELSE BugForMoney;
```

In this case, **PaidUp** is either true or it isn't; there is no third alternative. (Well, it could be undefined, but in that case, your program won't compile in the first place.) You don't strictly need an ELSE clause; you might not want the program to do anything about late bill-payers, so you would write simply:

```
IF PaidUp = true

   THEN SendThankYou;
```

FOR Loops   Sometimes, you simply want to repeat an operation a certain number of times. In that case, you would use a FOR loop. A good example of using a FOR loop would be to assign initial values to the slots in an array:

```
VAR

   Letters = ARRAY[1..50] of char;

   Counter : integer;

BEGIN

   FOR counter := 1 to 50 DO

      Letters[counter] := ' '

END;
```

This assigns initial values to the Letters array so that each slot has a space in it. Notice that we used an integer-type counter variable. In the FOR statement itself, we used the assignment operator and not the equal sign. The DO part of the statement can be any legal Pascal statement, whether simple (as in the example) or compound (a BEGIN..END statement).

Other Control Statements   There are several other types of control statements (CASE, WHILE..DO, REPEAT..UNTIL), but we'll defer our discussion of these until Chapter 7.

PROCEDURES AND FUNCTIONS

You have already seen several examples of procedures. Functions are similar to procedures except that they actually have a data type. A good analogy is to think of procedures as being like complete sentences, while functions are like nouns. A function is simply an operator that takes a value of a certain type and gives back another value—a value that is normally, but does not need to be, different from the original value. That is why functions are usually written with parentheses after them; the parentheses indicate that the function "has a hole" in it that must be filled by a value of a certain type. An example of a function might be the following:

```
FUNCTION PaidUp (balance: real) : Boolean;
  BEGIN
    IF balance <= 0.00
      THEN PaidUp := TRUE
      ELSE PaidUp := FALSE
  END;


  BEGIN             { main body of program }
    IF PaidUp(215.00)
      THEN SendThankYou(Customer)
```

```
        ELSE BugForMoney(Customer)

END;
```

When you pass the value *215.00* to the function **PaidUp**, it returns a value of false, which you can then use in an IF..THEN statement.

Parameters and Scope

The above example also shows another new idea: the idea of passing values to a subroutine. Because each subroutine (whether it is a procedure or a function) is a "black box," you want to maintain complete control over what goes into it and what comes out of it. Therefore, if the subroutine will handle any values from outside, they should be declared as "parameters" when you define the subroutine in the procedures and functions section of the program. Listing 3.4 is an example.

Notice that in Listing 3.4, you declare each type of value that goes into and comes out of the procedure when you first define the procedure.

```
PROGRAM Listing3_4;

   ( Illustrates a subroutine to add two integers. )

USES CRT;

VAR
  a,b,c : integer;

PROCEDURE AddTwoNumbers(a,b : integer; var c: integer);
  BEGIN
    c := a + b
  END;


BEGIN             ( main body of program )
  a := 1;
  b := 2;
  AddTwoNumbers(a,b,c)
END.
```

Listing 3.4: Passing parameters to a subroutine.

You then pass the values (integers) to the procedure as parameters by calling the procedure and listing the appropriate variables in parentheses after the procedure name.

Three variables are passed to the procedure. The first two, *a* and *b*, already have values and won't be changed by the procedure. Therefore, we simply make a copy of their values (**1** and **2**) and pass those values to the procedure. Variable *c*, however, will be changed by the procedure; that's why there is a **var** before it in the parameter list when we defined the **AddTwoNumbers** procedure.

There's one other interesting thing to note—perhaps you've caught it already. The parameter names are the same as the names of the variables we passed to the procedure, but this did not cause a "duplicate identifier" error when you compiled Listing 3.4. This is an exception to the rule that identifiers must be unique. An even more important exception is shown in Listing 3.5.

At the global level of Listing 3.5, outside the **AddTwoNumbers** procedure, we defined *MyName* as a string variable and assigned it the value 'Scott'. Inside the **AddTwoNumbers** procedure, however, we created an integer variable with the same name and assigned it the value **10**. Not only do we *not* get a "duplicate identifier" error message when we compile Listing 3.5, but the value of *MyName* is one thing outside the procedure and something else inside the procedure!

The reason for this strange situation is that, as you'll remember, each subroutine is a black box whose content is hidden from the outside world. When we declare a new variable inside the **AddTwoNumbers** procedure, it is not visible to anything outside the procedure. Inside the procedure, it simply replaces the global variable, so there's no conflict between the two variable names. We really have two different variables: one that exists at the global level, and another that exists only inside the **AddTwoNumbers** procedure.

It is important to realize, however, that it is just the inside of each subroutine that is hidden from the global level and from other subroutines. The global level of the program is visible everywhere else in the program, including from inside the subroutines. If we had not declared a new, local variable inside the **AddTwoNumbers** procedure, we would have had a completely different result, as in Listing 3.6.

In Listing 3.6, we did not declare a local variable inside the procedure, so when we tried to assign the integer value 10 to the *MyName* variable, the program thought we were talking about the global *MyName* variable. Because this is a string variable instead of an integer variable, Listing 3.6 won't compile. To correct the error, simply take out the line that says **MyName := 10;** and run the program. This time, *MyName* remains 'Scott' all through the program.

```pascal
PROGRAM Listing3_5;

  { Illustrates the meaning of "scope." The global variable
    MyName is a string variable outside of the AddTwoNumbers
    subroutine. However, a new, local variable called MyName
    is declared inside the AddTwoNumbers subroutine. Inside
    the subroutine, this integer variable overrides the global
    MyName variable, but is invisible everywhere outside the
    subroutine. }


USES CRT;

VAR
  a,b,c : integer;
  MyName : string[5];

PROCEDURE Pause;
  VAR
    Proceed : CHAR;
  BEGIN
    WRITELN(' Press any key to continue ...');
    Proceed := READKEY;
    WRITELN; WRITELN
  END;

PROCEDURE AddTwoNumbers(a,b : integer; var c: integer);
  VAR
    MyName : integer;
  BEGIN
    c := a + b;
    MyName := 10;
    WRITELN(' Inside the procedure, MyName is ', MyName, '.');
  END;


BEGIN           { main body of program }
  a := 1;
  b := 2;
  MyName := 'Scott';
  WRITELN(' Outside the procedure, MyName is ', MyName, '.');
  pause;
  AddTwoNumbers(a,b,c);
  pause;
  WRITELN(' Outside again, Myname is ', MyName, '.');
  pause
END.
```

Listing 3.5: Inside a subroutine, local names override global names.

There is an important lesson in Listing 3.6. The lesson is that even though you should "never say 'never'," you should *never, ever directly change global variables from within a subroutine.* If a subroutine is going to deal with a global variable, the variable should be passed to the subroutine as a parameter—never sneaked "through the back door" as in Listing 3.6. There are exceptions to this rule, but they are few and you should stick to the rule until you get some more programming experience.

```
PROGRAM Listing3_6;

    ( Unlike the AddTwoNumbers routine in Listing 3.5, the
      routine in this listing does NOT declare a local integer
      variable to override the global string variable MyName.
      Therefore, the program won't compile because the global
      variable MyName is visible inside the AddTwoNumbers
      routine, and the routine tries to assign an integer to
      it -- in spite of the fact that MyName is a string
      variable. )


USES CRT;

VAR
   a,b,c : integer;
   MyName : string[5];

PROCEDURE Pause;
   VAR
      Proceed : CHAR;
   BEGIN
      WRITELN(' Press any key to continue ...');
      Proceed := READKEY;
      WRITELN; WRITELN
   END;

PROCEDURE AddTwoNumbers(a,b : integer; var c: integer);
   BEGIN
      c := a + b;
      MyName := 10;
      WRITELN(' Inside the procedure, MyName is ', MyName, '.');
   END;


BEGIN           ( main body of program )
   a := 1;
   b := 2;
   MyName := 'Scott';
   WRITELN(' Outside the procedure, MyName is ', MyName, '.');
   pause;
   AddTwoNumbers(a,b,c);
   pause;
   WRITELN(' Outside again, Myname is ', MyName, '.');
   pause
END.
```

Listing 3.6: Global variables are accessible inside subroutines.

SUMMARY

Good programming begins not with writing code, but with a carefully thought-out program design. The main task of the program should be divided into subtasks, each of which performs a clear logical step in the program. Each subtask will be coded in a separate procedure or function.

Words that stand for data, programs, and subroutines in a Pascal program are called *identifiers*, and must be constructed according to certain very specific rules. A program has a structure that begins with its name, then a list of *units* used by the program, then sections for labels, constants, user-defined data types, variables, subroutines, and the main body of the program.

Pascal's built-in vocabulary is called its set of *reserved words*, and should not be used to stand for user-defined parts of the program. Pascal also has a wide variety of predefined data types that can be used in programs.

REVIEW EXERCISES

1. Explain (don't merely list) the three main steps in program design.

2. What are the rules for creating Pascal identifiers?

3. Which of the following are legal as user-defined Pascal identifiers? For those that are not legal identifiers, explain why they are not.

    (a) BEGIN

    (b) ThisRoutine

    (c) that_routine

    (d) 3rd_routine

    (e) an-amount

CHAPTER THREE

(f) an-amount3

(g) payroll total

(h) _3majorroutines

(i) checknumber2345_paid

(j) record

(k) studentfile.dat

(l) No#_of_records

(m) number_of_integers

4. List the eight main parts of a Pascal program and explain what each part does.

5. True or false: all data types used in a program must be declared in the TYPE section of the program. If the statement is false, explain why it is false.

6. Consider the following code fragment:

```
TYPE
       MyNumber = INTEGER;
```

Is **MyNumber := 15** a legitimate program statement? If not, why not?

7. Which of the following are legal Pascal program statements? In each case, explain your answer.

(a) IF TRUE THEN WRITELN(' The statement is true.');

(b) WRITELN(' "I am now lying," said Epimenides the Cretan.);

(c) BEGIN WRITELN END;

(d) BEGIN

```
IF a = 1
    THEN BEGIN
            a := a + 1
            WRITELN(' Variable has increased by 1.')
            END;
    ELSE WRITELN(' Variable was not equal to 1.')
            END;
```

(e) WRITELN(' The variable doesn't equal 1.');

(f) READLN(item1, item2, item3);

(g) { in CONST section } MaxCount := 15;

(h) { in VAR section } Counter : INTEGER;

8. What are the main numeric types in Pascal, and what is the range of values in each type?

9. Write a simple program that uses numeric formatting to display a 10-digit-wide column of real numbers on the screen. Include the following numbers: 1.00, 345.786, 20.15, 10.1, 1234.0, and 6.023.

10. Write a simple program that prompts the user to enter his or her first and last names, address, city, state, and zip code. The program should then display this information on the screen with explanatory text such as "Name: ", "Address: ", and so forth.

11. True or false: Most program statements in Pascal are true or false. Explain your answer.

12. Explain the basic idea of an array. Give at least two possible applications for arrays.

13. Explain the three main types of statements in Pascal as they are given in this chapter.

14. Explain what procedures and functions are, as well as how they differ.

15. Explain the idea and importance of "hiding" the inside of a subroutine from the rest of the program. Also, explain the ideas of global and local variables, and how these are related to hiding the internal features of a subroutine.

The Turbo Pascal
Development Environment

What stands fast does so, not
because it is intrinsically obvious or
convincing; it is rather held fast by
what lies around it.

—Ludwig Wittgenstein, *On Certainty,* No. 144.

In Chapter 1, we took a brief tour of the Turbo Pascal integrated development environment, called the IDE. Now, we return for a more detailed look at the different parts of the IDE and will discuss how to put them to work. If you are already comfortable using the IDE, you might want to browse through this chapter and come back to it for reference as needed, or, if you wish, you can work through it. Either way, you will see that there are some neat new features in Turbo Pascal 6.

MAIN PARTS OF THE IDE

When you first start Turbo Pascal, you see the Turbo Pascal desktop on the screen, as in Figure 4.1. Across the top line of the screen is the menu bar, from which Turbo Pascal's menus pull down. Across the bottom line is help information about operations you can perform with various key combinations. No matter what you are doing in the IDE, the bottom line always displays some relevant help information for the current window.

You can activate the menu bar and open menus in any of the following three ways:

- Press F10 to activate the menu bar, use the arrow keys to high-light the menu you want, and then press Enter to open the menu.

- Hold down the Alt key and press the highlighted letter in the menu name, e.g., Alt-F to open the File menu. To open the

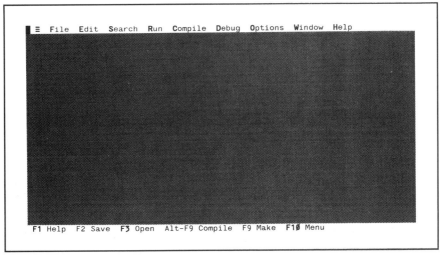

Figure 4.1: The Turbo Pascal desktop.

System menu, which is shown in the menu bar by three stacked horizontal lines, press Alt-spacebar.

- If you are using a mouse, click on the name of the menu that you want to open.

Once you've opened a menu, you can choose menu options in much the same way: by highlighting the option you want and pressing Enter, by pressing the highlighted letter (if any) in the menu choice, or by clicking on the menu choice with the mouse. Table 4.1 shows how to activate the different pull-down menus. Table 4.2 summarizes the jobs performed by the different function keys and function key combinations. Note that some of these jobs, such as using F8 to "step current subroutine" (used in debugging), won't become clear until you have more programming experience.

USING THE IDE WINDOWS

Opening an IDE window lets you enter a program or view information about that program. When you are in a particular window, it's called

Table 4.1: Menu Activation Keys

KEY	RESULT
F10	Activate menu bar (use arrow keys to highlight menu name, then press Enter)
Alt-spacebar	Open System menu
Alt-F	Open File menu
Alt-E	Open Edit menu
Alt-S	Open Search menu
Alt-R	Open Run menu
Alt-C	Open Compile menu
Alt-D	Open Debugging menu
Alt-O	Open Options menu
Alt-W	Open Window menu
Alt-H	Open Help menu

the *active* window, and any commands or text that you enter will be directed to that window. In previous versions of Turbo Pascal, you could have only one file window open at a time, but Turbo Pascal 6 lets you have as many open windows as can fit into your PC's available memory.

The active window has several features that provide information and let you manipulate the window with a mouse. If you do not have a mouse, you can do the same things using the menus or speed keys. Here, we're going to look at file windows containing Turbo Pascal program listings. However, most of the features we will discuss apply to all on-screen windows, including other types of windows. Table 4.3 shows the most important windowing commands and speed keys.

OPENING A WINDOW

Let's open a window that will contain Listing 3.1 from the previous chapter. You can open a file window in two ways: first, by choosing Open

Table 4.2: Tasks Performed by Function Keys

FUNCTION KEY:	ALONE	ALT	SHIFT	CONTROL
F1	Activate help	Prev. help	Help index	Find help
F2	Save File	-	-	Reset program
F3	Open File	Close File	-	Call stack
F4	Run to Cursor	-	-	Evaluate expr.
F5	Zoom /Unzoom	User screen	-	Size/move window
F6	Next window	-	Previous window	-
F7	Trace into subroutine	-	-	Add watch
F8	Step over current subroutine	-	-	Toggle breakpoint
F9	Make	Compile	-	Run program
F10	Open menu bar	-	-	-

or New from the File menu, or second, by pressing the F3 key. Either method opens up the Open File dialog box, as shown in Figure 4.2.

There are a few other things to notice about the Open File dialog box. At the top, it has a blank that shows the name of the currently highlighted file or directory in the file list. The file list, below, is in a miniwindow and shows all the files and subdirectories that are in the current directory. Across the bottom of the file list window is a scroll bar.

Table 4.3: Windowing Commands and Keys

KEY	RESULT
Alt-W	Opens Window menu. Can also be done by clicking on Window with the mouse.
Alt-0	Opens dialog box with window list. You then use the arrow keys to highlight the window you want and press Enter to move to that window.
Alt-N	Jumps directly to window number N. The window number (N) is displayed at the top right of the window frame. Can also be done by clicking on the window frame of the desired window with the mouse.
Alt-F3	Closes current window or file. This applies to all windows, not just file windows. Can also be done by clicking on the Close button with the mouse.
F5	Zoom a window to take up the entire screen, or unzoom a window that's already been zoomed. Can also be done by clicking on the Zoom button with the mouse.
Control-F5	Move/resize current window (arrow keys to move, Shift-arrow keys to resize). To resize with the mouse, grab onto the lower right corner of the window and drag. To move with the mouse, grab onto the top edge of the frame and drag.
F6	Jump to next window (e.g., from No. 3 to No. 4).
Shift-F6	Jump to previous window (e.g., from No. 4 to No. 3).

At the bottom of the Open File dialog box is detailed information about the currently highlighted file or directory, including file size and the date it was created. Finally, on the right side of the box, there are four push-buttons that you use to tell Turbo Pascal to perform different actions.

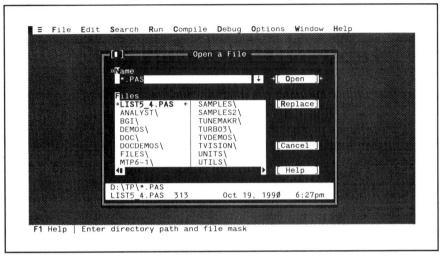

Figure 4.2: The Open File dialog box.

- Open: This opens a new file window and loads the highlighted file into that window.

- Replace: If you already have a file open in a file window, this loads the highlighted file into the current window—replacing the file that was already there. If you have changed the already opened file, you will be prompted to save your changes before the new file is loaded.

- Cancel: This button, which appears in all dialog boxes, lets you cancel the current operation if you change your mind. Pressing Escape will also cancel the current operation.

- Help: This button, which also appears in all dialog boxes, opens up a screen of help information and provides information about the various operations you can perform with it.

If you have been saving your program files in the TP\FILES subdirectory, then press the Tab key once to move to the file list, highlight FILES\, and press Enter to open that directory. Move the highlight to LIST3_1.PAS and press Enter to open the file. (If you have a mouse, you can do the same sequence by double-clicking on FILES\ to open the directory and double-clicking on LIST3_1.PAS to open the file.)

PARTS OF A SCREEN WINDOW

Because there is only one file open, the window we opened is automatically the active window. At the top left of the frame is the close button. You click on this button with the mouse cursor to close the active window. Or, if you are not using a mouse, you press Alt-F3 to close the window. Either way, if you've made changes in the current file, you will be prompted to save the file before closing the window.

In the middle of the top line is the name of the file that is in the current window. In Figure 4.3, this file is LIST3_1.PAS. At the top right is the number of the current window (useful if you have more than one window open) and the zoom arrow, which lets you zoom and unzoom a window with your mouse to occupy the entire screen, or only a part of the screen. You can also zoom and unzoom the current window by pressing the F5 key.

At the lower left of the frame are two numbers separated by a colon; here, they are 1:1. These numbers give the current location of the regular

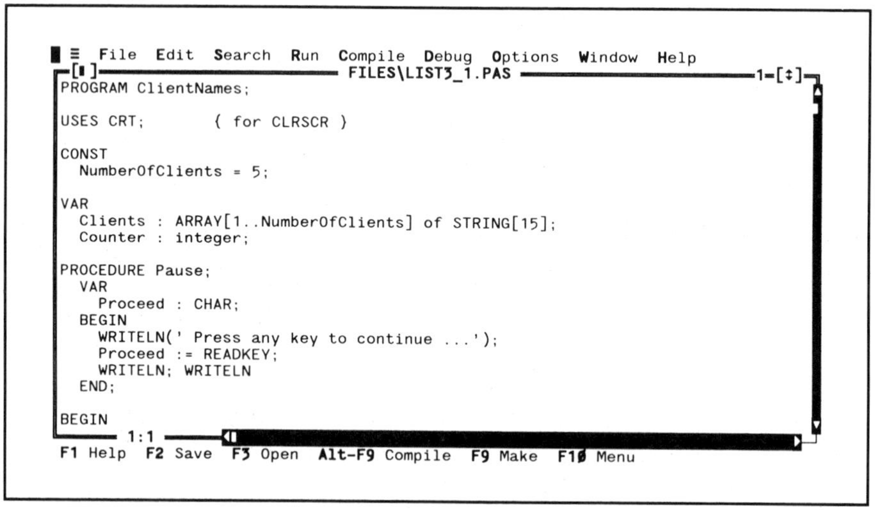

```
 ▪ ≡  File  Edit  Search  Run  Compile  Debug  Options  Window  Help
┌[▪]━━━━━━━━━━━━━━━ FILES\LIST3_1.PAS ━━━━━━━━━━━━1=[‡]┐
│PROGRAM ClientNames;                                              █
│                                                                  
│USES CRT;        ( for CLRSCR )                                   
│                                                                  
│CONST                                                             
│  NumberOfClients = 5;                                            
│                                                                  
│VAR                                                               
│  Clients : ARRAY[1..NumberOfClients] of STRING[15];             
│  Counter : integer;                                              
│                                                                  
│PROCEDURE Pause;                                                  
│  VAR                                                             
│    Proceed : CHAR;                                               
│  BEGIN                                                           
│    WRITELN(' Press any key to continue ...');                   
│    Proceed := READKEY;                                           
│    WRITELN; WRITELN                                              █
│  END;                                                            ▓
│                                                                  ▓
│BEGIN                                                             ▓
└━━━━ 1:1 ━━━━◀▌━━━━━━━━━━━━━━━━━━━━━━━━━━━━━━━━━━▶┘
 F1 Help  F2 Save  F3 Open  Alt-F9 Compile  F9 Make  F10 Menu
```

Figure 4.3: Parts of file window.

cursor (not the mouse cursor): the first number shows the current line and the second number shows the current column. Thus, if the cursor were on line 25 and in column 15, the frame would show 25:15.

Scroll Bars

On the right edge of the frame and the right part of the bottom edge are two shaded areas called scroll bars. If you have a mouse, you can use these bars to move instantly around your file. Looking closely at the vertical scroll bar, you can see that it has an up arrow and a down arrow. To move up in your file, you move the mouse cursor to the up arrow and either click on it with the left mouse button (to move one line at a time) or hold down the left mouse button (to move continuously). The little square inside the scroll bar shows your current position in the file: when it is at the top of the scroll bar, you are at the top of the file; when it is in the middle, you are in the middle of your file, and so forth. The scroll bar in the bottom edge of the frame works the same way, except that it moves you left and right instead of up and down.

If you are not using a mouse, you can use the PgUp, PgDn, Home, End, and arrow keys to move around your file. In this particular case, it is often easier than using a mouse.

Resizing and Moving Windows

At the bottom right-hand corner of the window is the resize button. You grab this button by highlighting it with the mouse cursor and holding down the left mouse button. You then can resize the current window by dragging the bottom right corner. You also can move the window by grabbing and dragging the top edge of the frame around the screen.

You also can resize or move a window by using menus and speed keys. To resize a window, select Size/Move from the Window menu or press Ctrl-F5, the corresponding speed key for that menu choice. Then, you can resize the window by holding down the Shift key and pressing the arrow keys, or you can move it by pressing the arrow keys alone, as shown in Figure 4.4.

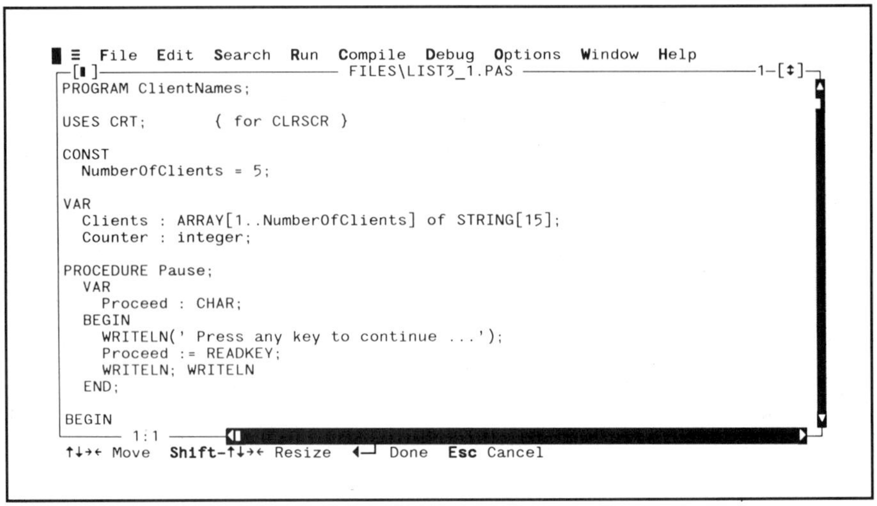

```
 ■ ≡  File  Edit  Search  Run  Compile  Debug  Options  Window  Help
 ─[■]──────────────────── FILES\LIST3_1.PAS ──────────────1─[↕]─┐
 PROGRAM ClientNames;                                          █
                                                               ░
 USES CRT;        ( for CLRSCR )                               ░
                                                               ░
 CONST                                                         ░
   NumberOfClients = 5;                                        ░
                                                               ░
 VAR                                                           ░
   Clients : ARRAY[1..NumberOfClients] of STRING[15];          ░
   Counter : integer;                                          ░
                                                               ░
 PROCEDURE Pause;                                              ░
   VAR                                                         ░
     Proceed : CHAR;                                           ░
   BEGIN                                                       ░
     WRITELN(' Press any key to continue ...');                ░
     Proceed := READKEY;                                       ░
     WRITELN; WRITELN                                          ░
   END;                                                        ░
                                                               ░
 BEGIN                                                         ▒
 ──── 1:1 ──────────◀█──────────────────────────────────────▶
 ↑↓→←  Move   Shift-↑↓→←  Resize   ◀┘ Done   Esc  Cancel
```

Figure 4.4: Moving and resizing a window.

After moving and resizing the windows, restore them to their original full-screen condition.

Note two other things about Figure 4.4. First, you can tell if the window is in Size/Move mode because the frame looks different. When you press Enter to tell Turbo Pascal that you are finished, it goes back to looking normal. Second, the bottom line of the screen—as usual—displays help information for whatever you are doing at the moment.

WORKING WITH MULTIPLE WINDOWS

Now that you are familiar with the parts of a screen window, let's see how Turbo Pascal allows you to work with several windows open at once. We've already got a window open with Listing 3.1 in it; now, use the Open File dialog box as before to open new windows with Listings 3.2 and 3.3 in them. Your screen should look like the screen shown in Figure 4.5.

What we have here is called *cascading* windows. Each new window is below and to the right of the previous window, so that the top edge of each window is visible, showing the filename and window number.

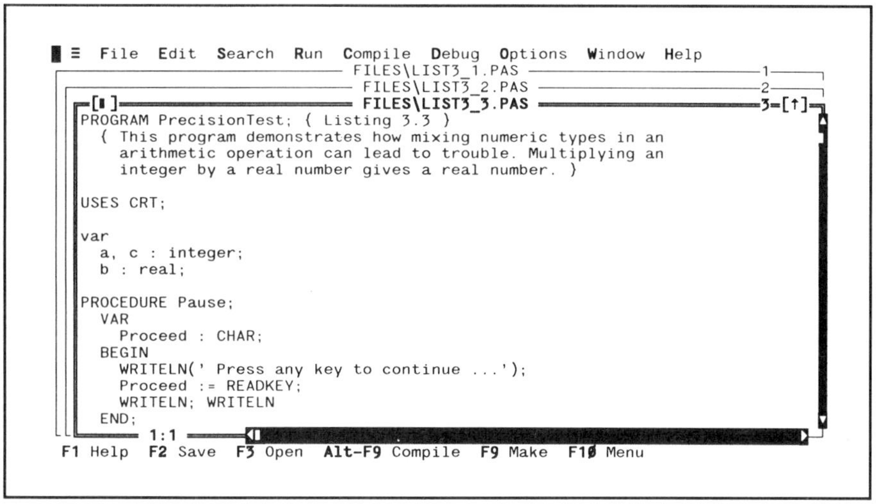

```
 █ ≡  File  Edit  Search  Run  Compile  Debug  Options  Window  Help
                 ┌──────────── FILES\LIST3_1.PAS ────────────────────1──────┐
                 │         ┌────── FILES\LIST3_2.PAS ─────────────────2─────┐│
         ┌─[■]───┴─────────┴────── FILES\LIST3_3.PAS ═════════════════3─[↑]─┐│
         │PROGRAM PrecisionTest; ( Listing 3.3 )                            ▲│
         │   ( This program demonstrates how mixing numeric types in an     ░│
         │     arithmetic operation can lead to trouble. Multiplying an     ░│
         │     integer by a real number gives a real number. )             ░│
         │                                                                 ░│
         │USES CRT;                                                        ░│
         │                                                                 ░│
         │var                                                              ░│
         │  a, c : integer;                                                ░│
         │  b : real;                                                      ░│
         │                                                                 ░│
         │PROCEDURE Pause;                                                 ░│
         │  VAR                                                            ░│
         │    Proceed : CHAR;                                              ░│
         │  BEGIN                                                          ░│
         │    WRITELN(' Press any key to continue ...');                   ░│
         │    Proceed := READKEY;                                          ░│
         │    WRITELN; WRITELN                                             ░│
         │  END;                                                           ▼│
         └───── 1:1 ═══◄▌───────────────────────────────────────────────►─┘
 F1 Help  F2 Save  F3 Open  Alt-F9 Compile  F9 Make  F10 Menu
```

Figure 4.5: Cascading file windows.

Jumping Between Windows

Currently, the active window is window number 3. You can switch to a different window in one of the four following ways:

1. Press F6 to go to the "next" window and Shift-F6 to go to the "previous" window. In this case, pressing F6 would take you to window number 1, then to number 2, and finally back to number 3. Shift-F6 would take you back to window number 2, then 1, then back to 3 again.

2. Choose List from the Window menu or press Alt-0 (Alt-zero, not Alt-O) to open up a list of open windows, as shown in Figure 4.6. In the list, move the highlight to the window you want and press Enter.

3. Use the mouse to click on the frame of the window you want (or click inside the window, if it is visible). This will move you directly to that window.

4. Press Alt-*n* to move to window number *n*.

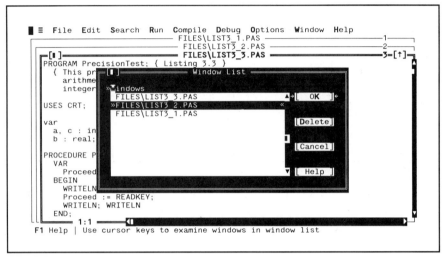

Figure 4.6: The List Windows dialog box.

Unless you are a hardcore mouse user, or you have a lot of windows open, methods 1 and 2 are generally the most efficient.

Tiled Windows

At the moment, only one window is really visible, with the others peeking out from behind it. There are many situations, however, where you will want to see two or more windows simultaneously. That's when tiled windows are used. To display your three windows in tiled format, open the Window menu and select Tile. Your windows should now be displayed as shown in Figure 4.7.

With the windows tiled, you now have the opportunity to try out some of the windowing commands discussed earlier. To see how these commands work, do the following:

- Press F6 a few times to jump forward between windows; then press Shift-F6 a few times to jump backward.

- Press F5 to zoom one of the windows to full screen size; then press F5 again to return it to its previous size.

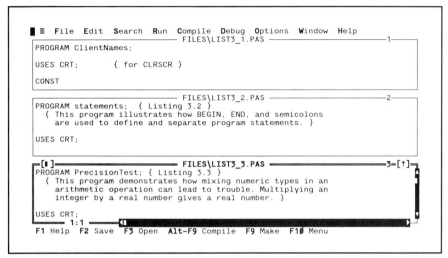

Figure 4.7: Tiled file windows.

- With window 3 as the current window, press Ctrl-F5 and move the window around some; then change its size. Finally, return it to its original size and position on the screen.

- If you have a mouse, try these same operations with the mouse. Click in a window to jump to that window; zoom a window by clicking on the zoom arrow at the top right of the frame; resize and move the window by grabbing the appropriate part of the frame with the mouse cursor. Remember to return the window to its original size and position when you're finished.

CLOSING A WINDOW

To prepare to close a window, choose Cascade from the Window menu and return the windows to cascading format.

Closing a window is even easier than opening it. Make sure that window 3 (with Listing 3.3) is the current window. Then either press Alt-F3 or click on the close button at the top left of the frame. Window 3 and the file with Listing 3.3 will close, leaving the other two windows still on-screen. You can use these methods to close any on-screen window, not just file windows. If you have changed your file since the last time you saved it, Turbo Pascal will prompt you to save your changes.

USING DIALOG BOXES

Dialog boxes are very similar to windows. The difference is that although windows allow you to write programs or see information about your programs, dialog boxes are designed specifically to let you give commands to Turbo Pascal itself. Let's look at a typical dialog box. From the Options menu, select Environment, then choose Preferences from the submenu that opens up. Your screen should look like the one in Figure 4.8.

Along the top edge of the dialog box you will see the close button and the name of the dialog box, just as with a regular window. However, the zoom button, scroll bars, cursor position, and move/resize buttons are missing. This is because you must work with a dialog box in a more structured way than an ordinary window. To move from one section of the box

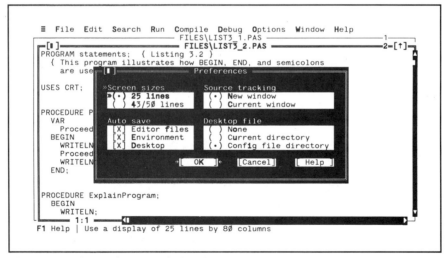

Figure 4.8: The Preferences dialog box.

to another, or from one button to another, you must do the following:

- To move from one section of the box to another, for example, from the Screen sizes to the Source tracking section, press the Tab key, or press the highlighted key letter for the option you want. For example, while the cursor is in Screen sizes, press "f" to toggle the AutoSave option for Editor files, and move to that box. To move backward, press Shift-Tab. You can move directly to a section by clicking in it with the mouse.

- To move from one radio button or checkbox to another, use the arrow keys or the mouse.

- To move from one push-button to another, use Tab/Shift-Tab. Clicking on a push-button with the mouse will cause its command to be executed instantly.

TYPES OF BUTTONS IN A DIALOG BOX

There are three types of buttons in a dialog box, though not all three types are in every dialog box. In Figure 4.8, the buttons are divided into five groups; you move from one group to another by using Tab (forward) and Shift-Tab (backward), or by using the mouse. The different types of buttons are as follows:

- **Radio buttons**. These let you select only one option out of several. In Figure 4.8, the Screen sizes, Source tracking, and Desktop file options have radio buttons. Screen size, for example, must be either 25 lines or 43/50 lines; it cannot be both. You select one of the radio buttons by moving the highlight with the arrow keys. (Do not do this right now.)

- **Checkboxes**. These let you select as many of the options as you want. In Figure 4.8 under Auto save, for example, you can tell Turbo Pascal to automatically save just the Editor files, or the Environment files, or the Desktop files, or any combination of the three options. In Figure 4.8, all three options are chosen. You select (or deselect) a checkbox by moving the cursor to the box and pressing the spacebar; alternatively, you can click inside the box's brackets with the mouse.

- **Push-buttons**. These buttons, along the bottom of the dialog box in Figure 4.8, tell Turbo Pascal what to do with the options you've selected via radio buttons and checkboxes. The OK button means go ahead, the Cancel button means cancel the operation, and the Help button calls up an explanation of how to use this particular dialog box.

We will not do anything with the Preferences dialog box right now, so close it by pressing Alt-F3. You can also close dialog boxes by pressing Escape, although this will not close a regular window.

Reopening a File

We closed the window with Listing 3.3 to show you how to use the buttons in dialog boxes. Reopen the Open File dialog box by pressing F3. Now, instead of tabbing to the file list to select LIST3_3.PAS, just press the down arrow key. A list of the files you've recently opened, with the highlight on LIST3_3.PAS, will pop up, as shown in in Figure 4.9. To reload this

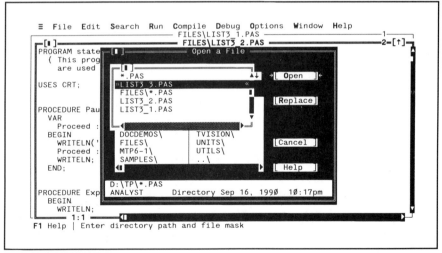

Figure 4.9: A pick list in the Open File dialog box.

file, press Enter twice; to load any other recently used file, highlight the file name and press Enter twice.

The list of recently used files is called a *pick list*. If you look at Figure 4.2 again, you can see that the blank (called an input box) above the file list has a down arrow on its right end. This means it has a pick list and that you can open the pick list by pressing the down arrow. Pick lists are used in several different dialog boxes, not just the Open File box.

One thing can go wrong here: the file you pick *must* be in the current directory. If you saved LIST3_3.PAS to the \TP\FILES directory, and you are currently in the \TP directory, then all you will get on your screen is an empty file window. To reload the file, you must select Change Dir from the File menu to switch to the directory where the file is located.

USING THE
TURBO PASCAL EDITOR

The new Turbo Pascal editor in version 6 is a vast improvement over the editor in earlier versions of Turbo Pascal. Until now, you couldn't have more than one file open at a time; you couldn't use box-drawing characters; and you couldn't use a mouse. That's just my personal list of gripes; other users could add to it. The editor in Turbo Pascal 6, however, does pretty much anything you need. It is still not as powerful as some stand-alone editors, such as Brief and Sage, but these editors owe their enormous power to the expense of great complexity. The Turbo Pascal editor, on the other hand, is relatively easy to learn and use. Tables 4.4–4.6 list some miscellaneous editor commands that you may find helpful.

USING COPY AND PASTE

From the File menu, select New. In the empty file window, enter the program shown in Listing 4.1. Don't try to compile or run it just yet. If and when it works, Listing 4.1 will ask "What is programming?" and will keep displaying the answer, "It's a GAS!!!!" until the user presses Escape.

Table 4.4: Opening and Closing File Commands

COMMAND	METHOD
Open file	Press F3 or select Open from File menu. Then highlight file in dialog box and press Enter; with mouse, double-click on filename in list.
Close file window and file	Press Alt-F3 or, with mouse, click on Close button at top left of window frame.
Close file but keep file window open	Press F3 or select Open from File menu. Then type new file name or highlight file in list; select Replace push-button instead of Open.
Save file and continue editing	Press F2 or select Save from File menu.
Save file under a different name	Select Save as from File menu. Then type in the new file name in the dialog box and press Enter.
Abandon changes to file	Press Alt-F3 or click on Close button; then answer no when prompted to save changes.

Table 4.5: Insert/Delete Commands

RESULT	KEY COMMAND
Toggle between insert and overstrike	Press Ctrl-V or Insert key
Insert new line at cursor position	Press Ctrl-N or Enter
Delete line at cursor position	Ctrl-Y
Restore line just deleted	Select Restore Line from Edit menu
Delete from cursor position to end of line	Ctrl-Q-Y
Delete character to left of cursor	Backspace or Ctrl-H
Delete character at cursor position	Del or Ctrl-G
Delete word at cursor position	Ctrl-T
Delete selected block	Ctrl-K-Y

Table 4.6: Cursor Movement Commands

RESULT	KEY COMMAND
Go to top of file	Ctrl-PgUp
Go to bottom of file	Ctrl-PgDn
Go to top of current screen	Ctrl-Home
Go to bottom of current screen	Ctrl-End
Go up one screen	PgUp
Go down one screen	PgDn
Go to beginning of line	Home
Go to end of line	End
Go right one word	Ctrl-Right Arrow
Go left one word	Ctrl-Left Arrow
Go right one column	Right Arrow
Go left one column	Left Arrow
Go up one line	Up Arrow
Go down one line	Down Arrow
Create bookmark (mark cursor position for instant return)	Ctrl-K-n, where n is an integer from 0 to 9
Jump back to bookmark	Ctrl-Q-n, where n is the number of the bookmark

If you looked carefully at Listing 4.1 after you entered it, you saw that there's a key element missing. We used the Pause routine at the end of the program, but we didn't declare it anywhere!

The reason was that there is absolutely no necessity to retype the pause routine into every program. There are two ways to make retyping unnecessary. One is to create a separate unit to hold utility routines such as the pause routine. (For a discussion about this method see Chapter 10.) The other, simpler way is to use Turbo Pascal's copy-and-paste feature to copy the routine from one window into another. And that's what we will do here.

```
PROGRAM Listing4_1;

USES CRT;


CONST
  Escape = CHR(27);               ( 'Escape' = the Escape key, ASCII 27 )

VAR
  YesNo,
  Proceed : char;


BEGIN
  CLRSCR;

  gotoXY(20,5);
  WRITELN('What is programming?');

  WRITELN; WRITELN;
  delay(1000);
  Proceed := ' '; YesNo := 'Y';
  window(8, 8, 80, 21);
  WHILE Proceed <> Escape DO
        BEGIN
        WRITELN('It''s a GAS!!!!!');
        WRITELN;
        DELAY(1000);
        IF KEYPRESSED then Proceed := READKEY;
        END;
  window(1,1,80,24);
  gotoXY(1,24);
  pause
END.
```

Listing 4.1: A loop that repeats until the user presses Escape.

At the moment, you should have Listings 3.1–3.3 and Listing 4.1 in separate windows on-screen. Press F6 to move from Listing 4.1 to one of the other windows; it doesn't really matter which one, since the pause routine is in all of them. Using the arrow keys or the mouse, move the cursor down to the first **P** in **PROCEDURE Pause;**. Then, do one of the following:

- Hold down one of the Shift keys and tap the down arrow key until the entire pause routine is highlighted.

- Hold down the left mouse button and drag the cursor down until the entire pause routine is highlighted.

Your screen should now look like Figure 4.10. The pause routine is ready to copy to the clipboard, from which we can then paste it into Listing 4.1.

```
  ≡  File  Edit  Search  Run  Compile  Debug  Options  Window  Help
┌─[■]─────────────────────── LIST3_1.PAS ───────────────────────1═[‡]─┐
PROGRAM ClientNames;

USES CRT;        ( for CLRSCR )

CONST
  NumberOfClients = 5;

VAR
  Clients : ARRAY[1..NumberOfClients] of STRING[15];
  Counter : integer;

PROCEDURE Pause;
  VAR
    Proceed : CHAR;
  BEGIN
    WRITELN(' Press any key to continue ...');
    Proceed := READKEY;
    WRITELN; WRITELN
  END;

BEGIN
── 20:1 ──────
F1 Help  F2 Save  F3 Open  Alt-F9 Compile  F9 Make  F10 Menu
```

Figure 4.10: Copying a selected block.

Open the Edit menu and select Copy; or you could use the Ctrl-Insert speed key to do the same thing. This copies the highlighted text to the clipboard. Now, press Shift-F6 to jump back to the window with Listing 4.1. Move the cursor down so that it is one line above the **BEGIN** that starts the main body of the program; press the Enter key a few times to open up some space. Then, with the cursor two lines above **BEGIN**, reopen the Edit menu and select Paste. Presto! The pause routine is now pasted into Listing 4.1. To remove the highlight, press Ctrl-K-H, then save your file. (Instead of opening the Edit menu and selecting Paste, you can also use the Paste speed key, Shift-Insert.)

There are some other interesting things in Listing 4.1. In fact, it demonstrates some pretty special Turbo Pascal features. Here is a quick summary of some of these features:

- It shows how to define a constant as a certain key being pressed, in this case the Escape key.

- It shows how to use **gotoXY** to move the cursor directly to a given screen location. The two numbers in **gotoXY**(x,y) are the x and y coordinates on the screen.

- It shows how to use the Window command to create a screen window (without visible borders) in a program. The numbers in Window(x1, y1, x2, y2) are the coordinates of the top right and lower left corners of the window on the screen.

- It shows how to use **Delay(n)** to pause the program momentarily; the number in the parentheses is in milliseconds (thousandths of a second), so DELAY(1000) causes the program to pause for one second.

- It shows how to set up a WHILE loop, which is discussed in detail in Chapter 7.

- Finally, it shows how to use KEYPRESSED and READKEY to get input from the user without requiring the user to press the Enter key.

BLOCK OPERATIONS

Copy and paste is one of the most useful examples of a block operation, in which you select a block of text and do some operation on it. There are different ways to select a block in Turbo Pascal 6. The easiest way is to position the cursor at the beginning of the block, hold down the Shift key, and press the down-arrow key until the entire block is highlighted. You can do the same thing with the mouse by positioning the mouse cursor at the beginning of the block, holding down the left mouse button, and dragging the cursor downward until the whole block is selected.

Finally, there's the traditional method: you mark the beginning of the block with Ctrl-K-B and the end of the block with Ctrl-K-K. If you're using an earlier version of Turbo Pascal, this is the method you'll have to use. Table 4.7 summarizes the different block operations that you can perform.

CREATING AND JUMPING TO BOOKMARKS

One of the most useful features of Turbo Pascal's editor is its ability to create up to 10 bookmarks which let you instantly return to a particular

Table 4.7: Block Commands

RESULT	KEY COMMANDS
Mark beginning of selected block*	Ctrl-K B
Mark ending of selected block	Ctrl-K K
Select a single word	Ctrl-K T
Copy selected block to current cursor position	Ctrl-K C
Move selected block to current cursor position	Ctrl-K V
Delete selected block	Ctrl-K Y
Read file from disk into current file	Ctrl-K R
Write selected block to disk as a text file	Ctrl-K W
Highlight/dehighlight selected block	Ctrl-K H
Print selected block	Ctrl-K P
Indent selected block	Ctrl-K I
Unindent selected block	Ctrl-K U

* Blocks also can be selected by one of the following two methods: You can position the cursor at the beginning of the block. Hold down the Shift key and tap the appropriate arrow key (down, right, etc.) until the entire block is highlighted. Or you can use a mouse and position the mouse cursor at the beginning of the block. Hold down the left mouse button and drag the cursor to the end of the block so that the entire block is highlighted.

place in your program. In the listings we've developed up to this point, this feature may not seem very valuable. Real-life programs, however, can be over 1,000 lines long. The main program of a fairly small PC game I once wrote is 1,677 lines long, and that *doesn't* count the other parts of the program that were in separate units. When you have a very long program, bookmarks can make it a lot easier to find your way around.

To create a bookmark, you move the cursor to the place you want to mark, then press Ctrl-K-*n*, where *n* is an integer from 0 to 9. To return to a bookmark from anywhere else in the program, press Ctrl-Q-*n*, where *n* is the number of the bookmark to which you want to return. At any one time, as the numbering indicates, you can have up to 10 different bookmarks in a program. About the only thing Turbo Pascal does not do for you is keep track of which bookmark is which; you have to remember that on your own.

The Turbo Pascal 6 IDE supports the following <Ctrl>Q keys:

A -Search and Replace

B -Moves the cursor to the beginning of the selected block

C -Move to the end of the file

D -Move to the end of the line (<End> key)

E -Move to the top of the screen

F -Forward search

K -Moves the cursor to the end of the selected block

L -Restore Line

R -Move to the start of the file

S -Move to the beginning of the line

X -Move to the bottom of the screen

Y -Deletes to the end of the line, from the cursor

[-Find matching delimiter

] -Find matching delimiter (backward search)

USING SEARCH AND REPLACE

If you have used a word processor, then you have a good idea of how search and search and replace features work. In Turbo Pascal, you can use

Search to find the first (or every) occurrence of a particular subroutine or other identifier. Search and Replace is most useful when you must make a global change in a piece of text; for example, you might change a variable name at the top of your program, and need to hunt down and change every occurrence of the old name to change it to the new one.

Both operations have been considerably improved in Turbo Pascal 6. In any version of Turbo Pascal, you can search for a given text string by pressing Ctrl-Q-F. You will then be prompted in the Find dialog box to enter the text you want to find, along with options such as whether to search the whole file, to ignore uppercase/lowercase differences, or to search only for whole words. To use Search and Replace in any version of Turbo Pascal, you press Ctrl-Q-A; then you choose similar options in the Replace dialog box, including whether you should be queried before each replacement is made.

This all works the same in Turbo Pascal 6 as in earlier versions. Where Turbo Pascal 6 differs is that it has a Search menu that takes care of everything for you. Also, instead of having to remember what the search options are (g for global, u for ignore uppercase/lowercase, etc.), you can specify them in a dialog box. Figure 4.11 shows the dialog box for search, while Figure 4.12 shows the dialog box for Search and Replace.

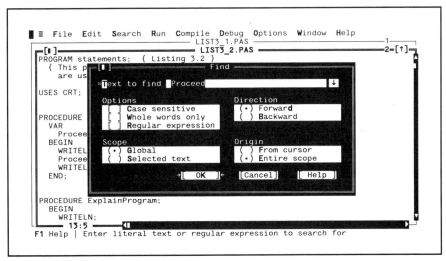

Figure 4.11: The Search dialog box.

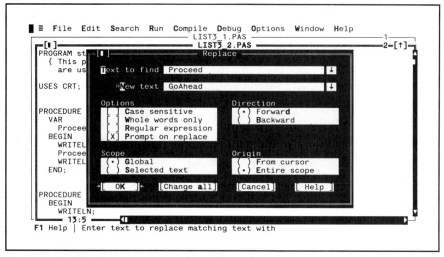

Figure 4.12: The Search and Replace dialog box.

USING BOX-DRAWING AND SPECIAL CHARACTERS

Now, we come to one of the most interesting new features in the Turbo Pascal 6 Editor. In previous versions of Turbo Pascal, the editor did not allow you to type in box-drawing and other special characters. As you undoubtedly know, your PC supports 256 different characters, far more than just letters, numbers, and punctuation. Each character has an ASCII number by which it's identified. Normally, to type in a special ASCII character, you hold down the Alt key and type the ASCII number on the numeric keypad. Then you release the Alt key, and the special character appears on the screen.

The old Turbo Pascal editor, however, did not allow you to do this. As a result, you had two options: to write your programs in an external editor, which many people didn't have, or to use loops and Pascal CHR statements to do your box-drawing. Using either was a pain in the neck. Just to show you what you are missing (or how to do it, if you have an earlier version of Turbo Pascal), enter and run Listing 4.2.

```
PROGRAM Listing4_2;

  ( Demonstrates the "bad old way" of drawing boxes in Turbo Pascal. )

USES CRT;

VAR Counter : INTEGER;

PROCEDURE Pause;
  VAR
    Proceed : CHAR;
  BEGIN
    WRITELN(' Press any key to continue ...');
    Proceed := READKEY;
    WRITELN; WRITELN
  END;


BEGIN
    CLRSCR;
    WRITELN;
    WRITE('                    ');
    WRITE(CHR(201));
    FOR Counter := 1 to 39 DO WRITE(CHR(205));
    WRITELN(CHR(187));
    WRITE('                    ');
    WRITE(CHR(186));
    WRITE(' This is the old way of drawing boxes. ');
    WRITELN(CHR(186));
    WRITE('                    ');
    WRITE(CHR(200));
    FOR Counter := 1 to 39 DO WRITE(CHR(205));
    WRITELN(CHR(188));
    WRITELN;
    pause
END.
```

Listing 4.2: Drawing a box using FOR loops and CHR functions.

Note that we used the **CHR()** function to get the box-drawing characters (putting the ASCII number of the character between the parentheses). We then set up a FOR loop to write the same character on the screen the appropriate number of times.

You can do it that way if you want to, but now since Turbo Pascal 6 lets you type in ASCII characters directly, Listing 4.3 is a lot easier to write.

Even when you can type them in, of course, holding down the Alt key and typing **205** over and over can become tiresome very quickly. Use the copy block feature as a shortcut. Once you've typed a character a few times, select it as a block and keep recopying it until you've got enough.

```
PROGRAM Listing4_3;

  { Demonstrates how to draw boxes in Turbo Pascal 6. }

USES CRT;

PROCEDURE Pause;
  VAR
    Proceed : CHAR;
  BEGIN
    WRITELN(' Press any key to continue ...');
    Proceed := READKEY;
    WRITELN; WRITELN
  END;


BEGIN
    CLRSCR;
    WRITELN;
    WRITELN('                                              ');
    WRITELN('         This is the new way to draw boxes.   ');
    WRITELN('                                              ');
    WRITELN;
    pause
END.
```

Listing 4.3: Drawing a box in the new Turbo Pascal editor.

PAIR MATCHING

No, this has nothing to do with computer dating services. The editor's pair matching feature helps you to prevent one of the most common causes of program bugs: unterminated delimiters.

Certain things in Pascal come in pairs: for example, comment brackets, quote marks, and parentheses. If you put in the first member of a pair but forget to put in the second, your program probably won't compile; and it certainly won't run the way it is supposed to. Turbo Pascal can do pair matching with:

- square brackets ("[" and "]")
- parentheses ("(" and ")")
- curly brackets ("{" and "}")
- double quote marks (")
- single quote marks (')

These brackets and marks are called delimiters because they mark the beginning and ending of a certain piece of the program. In the simplified examples we've been using, this may seem trivial. After all, how hard is to remember the second parenthesis mark in **CHR(186)**? When we get into complex code structures, however, Turbo Pascal's pair-matching feature will prove to be very valuable indeed.

To find the mate of a given delimiter, position the cursor on the first member of the pair; then press Ctrl-Q-[(that's Ctrl-Q-left square bracket). The cursor will immediately jump to the second member of the pair, if there is one. You can do the same thing with the second member of a pair; in that case, Turbo Pascal searches backward to find the first member of the pair. If you want to search backward with quote marks, you must enter a special command, Ctrl-Q-] (Ctrl-Q-right square bracket).

The one type of pair that Turbo Pascal still doesn't pair-match is the BEGIN..END pair. Mismatched ENDs and unterminated BEGINs are probably the greatest single cause of bugs in novices' programs, particularly when they involve compound IF statements, CASE statements, and RECORD data types, each of which needs its own END. To see the pairing of your BEGINs and ENDs, as well as the overall structure of your program, you need a tool such as TurboPower Software's *Turbo Analyst,* which can be an enormous help in debugging and fine-tuning real-life programs. Otherwise, you simply have to print out a program listing and trace the pairings by hand.

TURBO PASCAL MENUS

Turbo Pascal 6 provides full menu support for almost everything you need in program development. Here, we will take a step-by-step tour of each menu in the IDE. Some of the menu choices will not be completely explained until later chapters, because they deal with issues that haven't been covered yet. In this chapter, I will indicate what each menu choice does; if further explanation is needed, I will provide it in the appropriate chapter.

THE SYSTEM MENU (ALT-SPACEBAR)

The System menu has one major and two minor functions. The major function is Clear Desktop, which closes all open windows and clears all pick lists (such as the list of recently used files in the Open File dialog box). The two minor functions are About, which displays information about Turbo Pascal, and Refresh Display, which redraws the IDE screen if it is accidentally overwritten.

THE FILE MENU (ALT-F)

The following options are available in the File menu:

- Open: This opens a new file and file window by going through the Open File dialog box. The speed key for this menu choice is F3.

- New: This opens an empty file window into which you can enter a new program file. There is no speed key.

- Save: This saves the file in the active file window to disk in the current default directory, though you are given the option of saving it in a different directory. If you haven't yet named your file, you will be prompted for a filename. The speed key is F2.

- Save As: This lets you save the file under a different filename, which you are prompted to enter. This is most useful when you are developing a medium-to-large program and need to keep copies of the program at different stages of development and debugging.

- Save All: This saves all files in all open file windows, not just the file in the active window.

- Change Dir: This lets you change the default directory where files will be saved. The Change Directory dialog box is shown in Figure 4.13. The current directory is shown in the input box at the top. You can change to a different directory by pressing Tab once to get to the directory tree, using the arrow keys to highlight

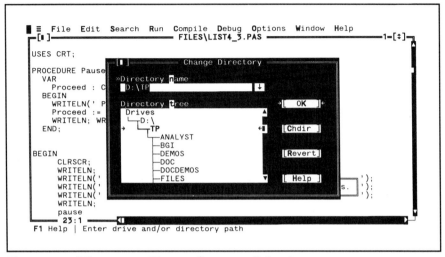

Figure 4.13: File menu—Change directory dialog box.

the directory you want, and pressing Enter. When the tree changes to show that the directory you want is selected, then Tab to the OK button and press Enter again. Or, if you're using a mouse, you can skip all the tabbing and just double-click on the directory you want, then single-click on the OK button. There are two other things to note about the Change Directory dialog box. First, observe that there's a down arrow at the right end of the input box; this means that there's a pick list of recently used directories.

Second, be careful: all files are saved to the current directory, not just program files. If you change your Turbo Pascal options and save them while the directory is changed to something other than the Turbo Pascal program directory, then Turbo Pascal will not be able to find your changed options the next time you start the program. If you need to use the Options menu during a session, be sure to switch back to the \TP directory first.

The following options are available with the Change directory dialog box.

- Print: This prints the file in the active file window. The speed key, Ctrl-K-P, also can be used to print a selected block of text.

- Get Info: This shows information about the current program file and about Turbo Pascal's use of your PC memory. Most of this information is of interest only for advanced programming tasks.

- DOS Shell: This lets you suspend Turbo Pascal and temporarily exit to MS-DOS, where you can run DOS commands such as dir and rename, as well as other programs. When you are ready to go back to Turbo Pascal, simply type **exit** at the DOS prompt. You'll return to Turbo Pascal at the exact place where you were when you suspended work, for example, on line 10 of Listing 4.2.

- Exit: This quits Turbo Pascal completely. If you've set the Options menu to save your file and desktop configuration, Turbo Pascal will remember what files were open when you quit and reopen them when you start it up again. The speed key is Alt-X.

THE EDIT MENU (ALT-E)

Most of the options on this menu have to do with manipulating selected blocks of text.

- Restore Line: This lets you undo the last change you made to a program line, even if you deleted the entire line. This works only on the *last* line that you changed before invoking Restore Line.

- Cut: This deletes a highlighted block of text from your file and copies it to the clipboard, from where it can be copied elsewhere in the same file or to a different file. The speed key is Shift-Delete.

- Copy: This copies a highlighted block of text to the clipboard without deleting the original highlighted block. You can then copy the text from the clipboard in the same way as with the Cut menu choice. The speed key is Ctrl-Insert.

- Paste: This copies text from the clipboard to the current cursor position (the text cursor, *not* the mouse cursor). The speed key is Shift-Insert.

- Copy Example: This lets you copy text from an on-screen help window into your program without first having to highlight the text that you want. The entire help example will be copied into your program. (You also can use standard copy-and-paste techniques if you want to copy only part of a help example.)

- Show Clipboard: This opens a window that displays the current text contained in the clipboard.

- Clear: This deletes highlighted text from your file *without* copying it to the clipboard, so that it can't be copied elsewhere. You also can use this to clear the clipboard itself by selecting the text in the clipboard window from Show Clipboard. The speed key is Ctrl-Delete.

THE SEARCH MENU (ALT-S)

The following options are available in the Search menu.

- Find: This searches your file for a text string which you specify in the Find dialog box, mentioned earlier in this chapter. The speed key is Ctrl-Q-F.

- Replace: This searches your file for a text string and replaces it with another text string; you specify both strings in the Replace dialog box mentioned earlier in this chapter. The speed key is Ctrl-Q-A.

- Search again: Repeats the last Find or Replace that you did. This is useful for finding multiple occurrences of a text string in a file.

- Go to Line Number: This is a quick way of jumping around in a large program file without having to do a lot of paging up and down.

- Find Procedure: This lets you search for a procedure or function during a debugging session. This menu choice is not available at other times, but when it is not, you can use the standard Find menu choice.

- Find Error: For most programs, you won't need to worry about this menu choice. It gives you the memory address where a run-time error occurred, and is useful for advanced programming and debugging only. Normally, when you run your program from the IDE and an error occurs, the cursor automatically stops on the line where the error occurred and displays an error message to tell you what the problem is (*e.g.,* it cannot find a file).

THE RUN MENU (ALT-R)

The Run menu lets you run your programs from within the IDE so that you can test and fine-tune them before you compile them to stand-alone program files.

- Run: This menu choice compiles, links, and runs the program in the active file window. Whether it compiles the program to memory or to a disk file depends on how the Destination menu choice is set in the Compile menu. The speed key is Ctrl-F9.

- Program Reset: When you are debugging a program, you will frequently step through it a line at a time, or have it run to a specified point in the program (called a *breakpoint*). When you do this, the program is ready to start running again at the *next line* after the place that it is currently stopped. Using this menu choice lets you reset the program run, so that when you restart the program, it will run from the beginning. The speed key is Ctrl-F2.

- Go to Cursor: This runs the program but makes it stop at the line where the cursor is located. For example, if the cursor were on line 556, the program would stop on line 556. Remember, however, that a structured program typically does *not* start on line 1 of the code and run to the end, so there will be a few twists and turns along the way. The speed key is F4.

- Trace Into: This lets you run your program one line at a time, which is called *stepping through* the program. It differs from Step Over, the next menu choice, in that it *always* goes one line at a time. For example, if you are tracing and come to the Pause routine, you will go through the pause routine line-by-line. Step Over, on the other hand, will execute the pause routine as a single line in your program, because that's all that the sub-routine call, **pause;**, takes. The speed key is F7.

- Step Over: This steps through your program line-by-line, but jumps over any subroutines without stepping through them. (Normally, you'll use *both* tracing into and stepping over.) The speed key is F8.

- Parameters: This lets you give your programs command-line parameters while running them in the IDE. A command-line parameter is something that comes after the name of a program when you start the program. When you select this menu choice, you enter command-line parameters in a dialog box for your IDE program.

THE COMPILE MENU (ALT-C)

The Compile menu gives you various options for compiling your program in the IDE.

- Compile: This compiles and links your program to the currently selected destination (memory or disk) that you chose with the Destination menu choice in the Compile menu. The speed key is Alt-F9.

- Make: This compiles and links not only the primary file (the file in the current editor window if you haven't specified a different file), but all other files that are used by the primary file. This includes units and object files; units are recompiled only if they have been changed since the previous compilation. The speed key is F9.

- Build: This is similar to Make except that *all* files are recompiled, whether they've changed or not since the previous compilation.

- Destination: This tells Turbo Pascal whether the result of a compile, make, or build operation should be sent to memory or to a disk file. If it is sent to a disk file, then the filename is the same as the primary file, except that it has an .EXE extension instead of a .PAS extension.

- Primary File: This tells Turbo Pascal which file should be the master program file. If you do not use this option, the file is automatically the file in the current file window.

THE DEBUG MENU (ALT-D)

The Debug menu provides various features to help you find any problems in your programs and correct them.

- Evaluate/Modify: This lets you see the current value of a variable at any point in your program. In addition to merely seeing the value, you also can assign a new value to the variable to find out how it would change the actions and results of your program. For example, you could change the value of an integer variable from 15 to 25. The Evaluate/Modify dialog box is shown in Figure 14.4. To use it, you enter the name of the identifier (normally a variable) in the Expression input box; the current value will be displayed in the Result box. To change the

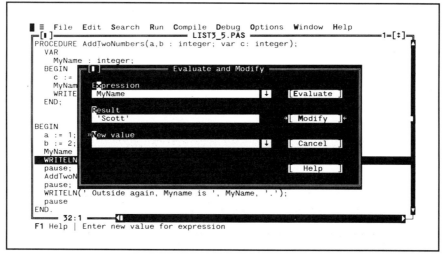

Figure 4.14: Debug menu—Evaluate/Modify dialog box.

value, you simply enter a new value in the New Value box at the bottom and then select the Modify push-button at the right. The speed key is Ctrl-F4.

- Watches: Unlike the Evaluate/Modify choice, which basically gives you a snapshot of a variable's value at a certain point, this menu choice lets you continuously monitor the value of one or more variables as you step through the program. Putting a watch on a variable allows you to observe the value of the variable in the watch window at the bottom of the screen. With this menu choice, you can also remove and edit watch instructions. If the watch window is not visible, you can use the Tile option in the Window menu to make it visible.

  To put a watch on a variable, you select Add Watch and then, in the dialog box, key in the name of the variable. As a shortcut, you can position the cursor on the name of the variable you want to watch; then, when you open the Add Watch dialog box, the name is already keyed in for you. Figure 14.15 shows a program with a watch on the *Counter* variable. The speed key is Ctrl-F7.

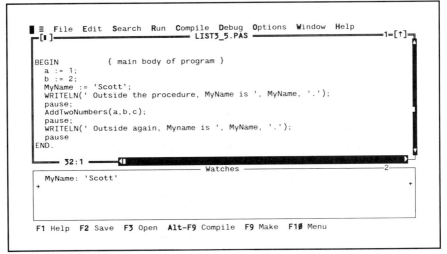

Figure 4.15: Debug menu—program with watch window open, on MyName variable.

- Toggle Breakpoint: This lets you put breakpoints into your program. A breakpoint is like a stop sign. To insert a breakpoint, you move the cursor to the line where you want the program to stop, then select this menu choice. When you run the program, it will run until it reaches the breakpoint and then stop. This allows you to inspect the current values of variables and other items manipulated by the program. The speed key is Ctrl-F8.

- Breakpoints: This takes you to a dialog box that allows you to delete and change the location of breakpoints.

THE OPTIONS MENU (ALT-O)

This menu lets you set various options for the Turbo Pascal IDE, including how much error checking it does on your programs, how the editor acts, and what colors the IDE uses (if any) on your PC's screen.

- Compiler: This lets you set compilation options in the IDE, as shown in Figure 14.6. Most of these are for advanced programming and debugging, but for now, let's note that while you're

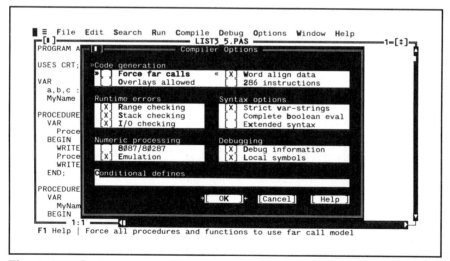

Figure 4.16: Options menu—Compile Options dialog box.

developing your program, it's a good idea to have the IDE trap all the run-time errors it can, so that Range Checking, Stack Checking, and I/O Checking should all be turned on. When you are sure that your program works right, you should turn these options off before your final compilation; this will reduce the size of your compiled program file.

- Memory Sizes: This lets you manipulate the amount of memory reserved for the stack and the heap. (See Chapter 11.)

- Linker: This lets you change options for linking your programs. Because Turbo Pascal automatically takes care of linking your program, you will seldom have to worry about this option.

- Debugger: This lets you tell Turbo Pascal whether you will be using the integrated IDE debugging capabilities alone, or if you will also be using Turbo Debugger, a stand-alone program that works with Turbo Pascal.

- Directories: This opens a dialog box that lets you specify where Turbo Pascal should look for programs, units, and other files if it can't find them in the current directory (see Figure 4.17).

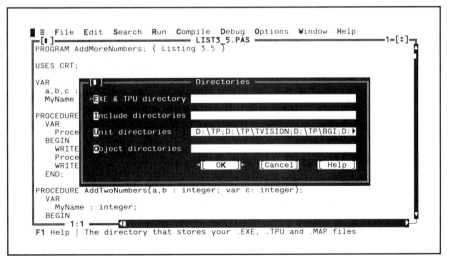

Figure 4.17: Options menu—Directories.

- Environment: This takes you to a submenu from which you can set options for global preferences (shown in Figure 4.18), and for the editor, the mouse (if you have one), startup options, and screen colors. The two most important options are these: (1) in the Preferences dialog box, where you can tell Turbo Pascal to remember the files and IDE configuration whenever you quit the program, so it can reload them when you start Turbo Pascal again; and (2) in the Startup dialog box, where you can tell Turbo Pascal to use expanded (EMS) memory, if you have it, for faster performance.

- Save Options: This lets you save the current Turbo Pascal options. If you want the options used as the default, then you can save them in a file called TURBO.TP; otherwise, you can save them in a different file.

- Retrieve Options: This lets you reload a set of options different from those stored in the default options file TURBO.TP.

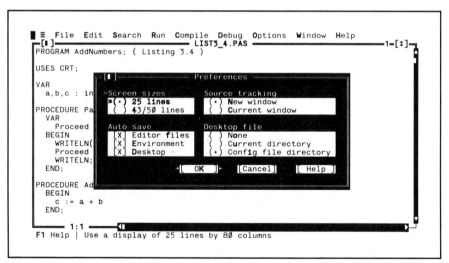

Figure 4.18: Options menu—Environment/Preferences.

THE WINDOW MENU (ALT-W)

We've already seen several uses of the Window menu, such as to zoom, tile, and resize windows. Here are the menu choices:

- Size/Move: This lets you resize or move windows, as we've already seen. The speed key is Ctrl-F5.

- Zoom: This zooms a window to take up the whole screen, or unzooms a window that was previously zoomed. The speed key is F5.

- Tile: This arranges multiple screen windows so that they do not overlap and at least part of each window is visible.

- Cascade: This arranges multiple screen windows so that they overlap, with each window slightly below and to the right of the previous window. Only the active window is fully visible.

- Next: This jumps from one window to the next, making the next window the active window. The speed key is F6.

- Previous: This jumps from one window to the previous window, making the previous window the active window. The speed key is Shift-F6.

- Close: This closes the active window. The speed key is Alt-F3.

- Watch: This opens the watch window, used in debugging.

- Register: This opens a window which displays the contents of the PC's processor registers. It is for advanced and assembly-language programming only.

- Output: This displays a small output window, which contains anything that your program displays on the PC screen during its run.

- Call Stack: This shows a list of the subroutines that your program called during its run, in the reverse order from the order in which they were called.

- User Screen: This is a full-screen version of the output window. The speed key is Alt-F5.

- List: This displays a list of the currently open file windows. By highlighting a file window in the dialog box, as we saw earlier, you can switch directly to that window. The speed key is Alt-0.

THE HELP MENU (ALT-H)

The following options are available in the Help menu.

- Contents: This displays a table of contents for the IDE's on-screen help system, as shown in Figure 4.19. You move from one help topic to another by using the Tab key or the mouse.

- Index: This displays an alphabetical index of Turbo Pascal commands, procedures, functions, operators, and compiler directives. By moving the cursor to the word you want and pressing Enter, you can see a help screen on that topic. You can move instantly to words beginning with a certain letter by pressing the key for that letter. The speed key for calling up the Help index is Shift-F1.

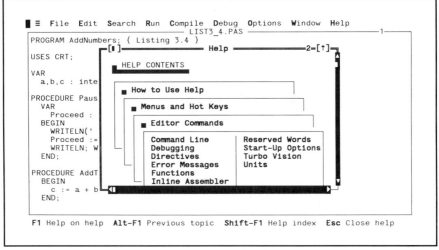

Figure 4.19: Help menu—Help system table of contents.

- Topic Search: This displays a help screen about the word at the current cursor position in your file. The speed key is Ctrl-F1.

- Previous Topic: This takes you back to the help screen you looked at before the current help screen. The speed key for calling up the Previous topic is Alt-F1.

- Help on Help: This gives you some basic information about how to use the Help system.

SUMMARY

Turbo Pascal's Integrated Development Environment (IDE) provides a powerful but easy-to-learn program editor, as well as pull-down menus for programming tasks. Menus are provided to open and manipulate on-screen windows, to open and close files, to perform editing tasks such as search-and-replace, to debug programs, and to compile and run programs.

Dialog boxes allow the user to interact directly with Turbo Pascal, using on-screen buttons and checkboxes to set various options in the IDE.

REVIEW EXERCISES

1. List the different pull-down menus in the Turbo Pascal Integrated Development Environment, and explain the primary purpose of each.

2. Which pull-down menu (and menu choice) would you use to do each of the following?

    (a) Create a new program file.

    (b) In a program listing, replace every occurrence of the word "ThisVariable" with the word "ThatVariable".

    (c) Close all open file windows.

(d) Put a watch on a variable during a debugging session. What's a watch?

(e) Change the tab size in the editor.

(f) Compile a program to disk.

(g) Arrange file windows so that they are all visible on the screen, with each window slightly below and to the right of the preceding one.

(h) Run a program one line at a time (*i.e.,* "step through" a program).

(i) Move the cursor to a specific line number in a program.

(j) Copy a block of text to the clipboard so that it can be "pasted" into a different location.

(k) Print a program file.

(l) Switch from one file window to another.

(m) Activate the on-screen help system.

3. Name the different parts of a screen window and explain how each part works. If it helps, draw a picture and label it.

4. Name the different parts of a dialog box and explain how each part works. If it helps, draw a picture and label it.

5. Give the menu and speed key methods for doing each of the following:

   (a) Open a file.

   (b) Close a file.

   (c) Save a file.

   (d) Switch from one file window to the next.

   (e) Zoom a file window to occupy the entire screen.

   (f) Open the Compile menu.

   (g) Compile a program.

   (h) Run a program.

   (i) Do pair matching.

   (j) Quit Turbo Pascal.

(k) Suspend Turbo Pascal and exit to DOS.

(l) Look up a program word in the Help index.

(m) Copy a selected block of text to the clipboard.

6. Explain how to use the Open Files dialog box to load a file that is not in the current directory.

7. What is a "pick list"? Explain how to determine if one is available, as well as how to open and use it.

8. When multiple file windows are displayed on-screen, how can you determine which one is currently the active window?

9. Explain how to create box-drawing and other extended ASCII characters in the Turbo Pascal 6 editor. (What does ASCII stand for?)

10. List three ways to select a block of text, two ways to copy it to the clipboard, and two ways to paste it to another location. (Challenging: speculate on what the clipboard really is and how it works.)

11. Suppose you wanted to use easy-to-remember names in your program for certain keys on your keyboard, such as the Escape key and the space bar. How would you do it?

12. Explain how to create a bookmark and how to jump back to it from elsewhere in a file. How many bookmarks can you have in a single program file?

13. Explain how to open the Search and Search/Replace dialog boxes, and explain the options available in each.

14. Explain how to save a program file under a different name.

15. Explain how to copy a program example from the on-screen help system into your own program file.

P A R T

Programming in Turbo Pascal

Part II provides detailed explanations of the most important features of programming in Pascal and Turbo Pascal. Chapters 5–13 explore data types, different kinds of program statements, subroutines, units, pointers, and file handling.

These chapters include material that will help you to use Turbo Pascal to develop programs for large computers and other Pascal compilers, such as Vax/VMS Pascal on Digital Equipment Corporation mainframes and minicomputers.

Simple Data Types

Whatever is deep is also simple, and can be reproduced as such, if only its relation to the whole of reality is preserved.

—Albert Schweitzer, *The Decay and the Restoration of Civilization*

In Chapter 3, I introduced the idea of a data type and showed you some simple examples. Now, we're ready to go into the subject in greater depth. In this chapter, I will discuss simple data types. Normally, when programmers use one of these types, we are talking about a single thing—such as a number, a letter, or a piece of text—and not a collection of things. This is in contrast to structured data types. As a rule, structured data items are complex, made up of collections of other items. An array of integers, for example, is a structured data item that can hold more than one integer. (See Chapter 7.)

From our previous discussion, recall that a variable is like a box that can hold a certain kind of thing: an integer, a piece of text, or a truth value (true or false). Just as you cannot put a square peg into a round hole, so you cannot put a truth value into a box designed to hold a number, any more than you can put a text string into a box designed to hold a truth value. With very few exceptions, a Pascal variable will accept and hold only items of the correct type.

This kind of restriction on what-can-go-into-what is called *strong typing*. Essentially, strong typing is a safeguard to prevent the programmer from accidentally doing things that would make the program blow up, and Pascal is a strongly typed language.

Some languages, such as C, are weakly typed, which means that often you can mix different data types and have them automatically converted into a compatible type. Turbo Pascal stands somewhere in between, letting you do some type mixing but stopping anything that looks too dangerous. We'll see some examples of both in this chapter.

ORDERED (ORDINAL) DATA TYPES

Although the common sense division of data types is into numbers, text, and "other," there is a more useful way to classify simple data types in Pascal: as ordinal and nonordinal types.

An *ordinal type* is a type whose members come in a certain order, such as 1,2,3,4,5 or a,b,c,d,e. Moreover, the members of the type must be discrete and not continuous. Integers, for example, are an ordinal type because

- They come in a definite order, i.e., 1,2,3,4,5,....

- Between any two adjacent members of the type, there are no other members of the type. For example, between the integers 1 and 2, there are no other integers; this is what is meant by calling the type discrete and not continuous.

Real numbers, on the other hand, are *not* an ordinal type because even though they are in order, they are continuous. Between any two real numbers, there is always an infinite number of other real numbers. For example, between the real numbers 2.141 and 2.142, there's 2.1411, 2.1412, 2.1413, and so forth. Similarly, pebbles on the seashore are not an ordinal type, because they're discrete but not in any kind of order.

The point of all this is that ordinal types let us do some fairly interesting operations, which depend on being able to pick out the *next* or *previous* member of the type. For any integer, no matter how large or how small, we can pick out the next or previous integer. With real numbers, on the other hand, there is *no* definable "next" or "previous" number to choose. For example, no matter how precisely we pick out the next real number after 2.1413, we can always find a slightly smaller next number between 2.1413 and the number we picked.

Because members of ordinal types have definite successors and predecessors, they are often used as loop counters. Listing 5.1 illustrates the use of a subrange of the CHAR type as a loop counter.

```
PROGRAM Listing5_1;

        { Shows how any ordinal type can be used as a counter, as
        long as the inherent limitations of the type are not
      exceeded. Here, we use a subset of the ASCII characters
      as values for a loop counter. }

uses crt;

const
        space = ' ';

var
  counter : char;

procedure pause;
  var
    ch : char;
  begin
  writeln;
  writeln('Press any key to continue ...');
  repeat until keypressed;
  ch := readkey;
  writeln
  end;


begin
  clrscr;
  writeln(' List of letters from "a" to "z":');
  writeln(' ------------------------------');
  for counter := 'a' to 'z' do
        write(space, counter);
  pause
end.
```

Listing 5.1: Using ordinal-type items to control a FOR loop.

INTEGER TYPES

Turbo Pascal has two basic numeric types: integers (whole numbers) and real numbers (those with decimal points). Each basic type is subdivided into several subtypes used for different purposes. Here, I'll discuss integer types.

One of the most important features of all of Turbo Pascal's numeric types is that they take up different amounts of space in your PC's memory. Remember the on/off switches discussed in Chapter 2? Well, each on/off switch can hold a single binary digit (*bit*) of information, which means it holds either a zero or a one. Put eight of those bits together and you have a byte, which is the smallest meaningful piece of information (e.g., a letter, digit, or other symbol) in the computer.

With an ordered sequence of eight zeroes and ones, you can represent 256 different symbols: enough for all 26 letters of the alphabet (upper and lowercase), 10 digits (zero through nine), and special characters such as carriage returns and linefeeds.

At any rate, sometimes you may write programs where the amount of memory needed is critical, and this is precisely when you can reap benefits from some of the more unusual number types in Turbo Pascal. In most situations, however, it's probably better to stick with the ordinary integer type: it uses more PC memory, but it is less likely to cause problems than some of the other types. This illustrates the general principle that you should keep your code as simple as possible. Doing so makes your programs more reliable and easier to understand.

Integers

Integers are whole numbers (for example, 1, -15, 207, and 60) and can range from a low value of -32,768 to a high value of 32,767, for a total range of 65,536. Integers cannot have a decimal point, and each integer requires 16 bits (two bytes or one "word") of memory to hold it. (See Table 5.1.) This two-byte memory requirement is much less than that required by real numbers, which need three times as much memory (six bytes per real number), so whenever you can get by with integers instead of real numbers, do it.

Note that although I am using commas to make it easier for you to read numbers in the text, you should *never* use commas when typing

Table 5.1: Integer Data Types

TYPE	RANGE	MEMORY REQUIRED (BYTES)
Shortint	−128..+127	1
Integer	−32,768..+32,767	2
Longint	−2,147,483,648 .. +2,147,483,647	4
Byte	0..255	1
Word	0..65,535	2

numbers into a Pascal program. Thus, if you want to declare a constant **A** whose value is 1,500, you would write it in the program as **A = 1500**.

You declare a variable to be of type integer in the following way:

```
VAR

    Counter : INTEGER;{Counter is an integer variable}
```

It is worth noting that when you declare constants in a Pascal program, generally, you do not need to declare the data type. The constant declaration itself, e.g., **Maximum = 100** makes it clear what the type of the constant is, and Turbo Pascal will automatically select the most appropriate data type.

Bytes

The Turbo Pascal byte data type is different from the generally understood meaning of byte as the smallest meaningful piece of information in your PC. In Turbo Pascal, bytes simply are a more economical version of integers, taking up only eight bits of your PC's memory—that is, one byte's worth.

Bytes pay for this reduced memory requirement, however, with a more limited range than integers. A byte can be any integer from 0 to 255, which is a range of only 256 numbers, instead of the integer type's range of 65,536 numbers. The reason for the range limitation is that there are only 256 different ordered combinations of eight bits (zeroes and ones), so that is the largest number of symbols that is possible to represent with eight bits. (Similarly, integers have a range of 65,536 numbers because there are 65,536 ordered combinations of 16 bits.) Also, unlike integers, bytes can represent only positive numbers. To see some of the difficulties that can occur with bytes, enter and run Listing 5.2.

If you look at the code for Listing 5.2, it is fairly obvious that my point is to generate an error by assigning a value of −5 to **c**, which is a byte-type variable. When you compile the program, however, you might think that everything is fine, because it compiles with no error messages.

```
PROGRAM Listing5_2;

USES CRT;

VAR
  a, b, c : BYTE;

PROCEDURE Pause;
  VAR
    Proceed : char;
  BEGIN
    WRITELN;
    WRITE(' Press any key to continue ...');
    REPEAT UNTIL KeyPressed;
      Proceed := Readkey;
    WRITELN; WRITELN;
  END;

BEGIN
  CLRSCR;

  a := 10;
  WRITELN(' The value of a is ', a, '.');
  pause;

  b := 15;
  WRITELN(' The value of b is ', b, '.');
  pause;

  c := (a-b);
  WRITELN(' C = a - b, so ', a, ' - ', b, ' equals ', c, '.');
  pause
END.
```

Listing 5.2: A potential problem with the BYTE data type.

However, this is the most dangerous type of error, because it sneaks up on you after the program is running. When you actually run Listing 5.2, you'll be amazed to learn that 10 minus 15 is 251! Of course, that's actually a run-time error caused by trying to assign a negative value to a byte-type variable.

A More Sophisticated Pause Routine

Listing 5.2 also introduces a more sophisticated version of the Pause procedure. Instead of requiring you to press the Enter key, now you can simply press any key as in commercially developed programs such as Turbo Pascal itself. This requires just a few tricks, which will become clearer as we go along. This routine has definite advantages over the previous Pause routine, which can require the user to to press the Enter key more than once, if used more than once in a program.

Short Integers

Like bytes, short integers are more economical with your PC's memory than ordinary integers, but they pay for it with a more limited range. Because short integers use only eight bits of memory, we know at the outset that the overall range is going to be 256 different numbers; the only question is, which 256 numbers? Although characters (discussed later in this chapter) and short integers both take up eight bits, short integers are *numbers* and can be used in arithmetic calculations, while characters cannot be used for arithmetic.

Short integers differ from bytes in that they are *signed* numbers, i.e., they can be either positive or negative. This means that one bit out of the eight has to show whether the number is positive or negative—leaving seven bits, with 128 possible combinations, left for the numbers themselves. Therefore, short integers have a range of −128 to +127. You declare a short integer variable as follows:

```
VAR

    MinutesLeft : SHORTINT;
```

Just as with bytes, you should only use short integers when you really need to economize on memory. Otherwise, you can get into the sort of trouble illustrated by Listing 5.3, which generates an error because the loop counter must go up to 150 while a short integer's maximum value is 127.

Words

Words are unsigned, like bytes, and take up 16 bits of memory, like standard integers. Their 16-bit status means that they have a range of 65,536; in this case, the range is 0..65,535. This type does not save any memory over integers; its only advantage is when you need to deal with positive numbers greater than 32,767. As with the other special integer types, you should use the word type only when you're very sure that it is

```
PROGRAM Listing5_3;

   { Illustrates potential problems with "shortint" and other
     fancy integer types. In this case, the loop counter variable
     NumberOfLoops needs to go up to 150, but the maximum value
     of a shortint variable is 127. }

VAR
   NumberOfLoops : shortint;  { Make loop counter a short integer }

PROCEDURE Pause;
   VAR
      Proceed : CHAR;
   BEGIN
      WRITE(' Press any key to continue ...');
      Proceed := READKEY;
      WRITELN; WRITELN
   END;


BEGIN      { main body of program }
   FOR NumberOfLoops := 1 TO 150 DO
   WRITELN(' Don''t promiscuously use short integers!');
   pause
END.
```

Listing 5.3: A potential problem with the SHORTINT data type.

appropriate. You declare a word as follows:

VAR

    RecordCounter : WORD;

Long Integers

Long integers are the "big gun" of whole numbers: big not only in the huge range of integers they can handle, but also in the amount of PC memory required—a whopping 32 bits, twice as much as standard integers. Because they use 32 bits, long integers can represent a total range of 4,294,967,296 different numbers; and because longint is a signed type, including both positive and negative numbers, the range is from -2,147,483,648 to +2,147,483,647: over four billion integers.

You declare a long integer variable as follows:

VAR

    ReallyBigCounter : LONGINT;

CHARACTERS

"Characters" in Pascal refers not merely to the letters A to Z, but to all the characters of the extended ASCII character set. ASCII, which stands for American Standard Code for Information Interchange, defines the set of characters that your PC can handle. It includes letters (upper and lower-case), digits (0..9), punctuation, and special characters such as the Enter key. In all, there are 256 ASCII characters. A character variable takes up eight bits of memory.

The ASCII Character Set

The order of ASCII characters is determined by the ASCII number of the character. For example, the first 32 ASCII characters (that is, 0 to 31) are nonprinting control characters, such as the Enter character (ASCII 13) and the Escape key (27). The rest of the ASCII characters are as follows:

- ASCII 32-47, 58-64, 91-96, and 123-127: Various punctuation and other special characters, such as the spacebar, parentheses, brackets, at sign (@), and question mark.

- ASCII 48-57: The ten digits 0 to 9, treated as characters instead of being treated as numbers. I'll come back to what this means in the section "Treating Digits as Characters" below.

- ASCII 65-90: The uppercase letters A through Z.

- ASCII 97-122: The lowercase letters a through z. Notice that the number of each lowercase letter is 32 more than its corresponding uppercase letter: for example, the number of "A" is 65 and the number of "a" is 97.

- ASCII 128-255: Various foreign-language and box-drawing characters.

For many ordinary operations, you can ignore all the ASCII numbers and simply work with the characters themselves. For example, the next character after A is B, the next character after 5 is 6, and so on. The ASCII numbers become important when you want to do something with a non-printing character, such as the Enter key, the Escape key, or one of the arrow keys.

Treating Digits as Characters

It may seem puzzling that we include the digits 0 through 9 in the set of characters. The fact is that there are two ways of looking at these digits. Viewed as numbers, they can be used in arithmetic operations. Viewed as characters, they cannot be used for arithmetic: in this case, they're simply more letters displayed on the screen. Note, however, that you can't put a character digit such as 5 into an integer variable, because the character 5 is not an integer.

There are times when it is advantageous to treat digits as characters: for instance, when you're setting up a list of numbered menu choices. There is a slight decrease in memory requirements and code size because integers take 16 bits and characters only 8. There is also a slight increase in safety because you cannot accidentally do an arithmetic calculation with characters. Listing 5.4 shows how to use digits as characters.

```
PROGRAM Listing5_4;

USES CRT;


CONST
  a = '5';                              { 'a' = the character '5'  }
  Escape = CHR(27);          { 'Escape' = the Escape key, ASCII 27 }

VAR
        Proceed : char;

BEGIN
  CLRSCR;
        Proceed := ' ';
  WHILE Proceed <> Escape DO
                BEGIN
        WRITELN(' There''s no place like home.');
                WRITELN;
    DELAY(1000);
                IF KEYPRESSED THEN Proceed := READKEY
                END
END.
```

Listing 5.4: Using digits as characters.

THE BOOLEAN DATA TYPE (TRUTH VALUES)

Remember that every factual statement has a Boolean value (a truth value) of either true or false. The two values of true and false are an ordinal type. In the ordering, false comes first and is represented by 00. True comes next and is represented by 01, so the order is *False, True*.

Normally, you'll use Boolean values to control the flow of your program. Any time you see an IF..THEN, CASE, WHILE..DO, or other statement that makes your program go in one direction or another, you're using Boolean values. Consider, for example:

```
IF Name = 'Sledge Hammer'

  THEN WRITELN(' What a nice name.')

  ELSE WRITELN(' Well, that''s a nice name, too!');
```

The IF clause of this statement is not really about anybody's name: it's about a truth value. What it says is that IF this statement is true (i.e., has the Boolean value of true), THEN do one thing; otherwise, do something else.

Boolean Ordering

Listing 5.5 illustrates the ordering of the two Boolean values, and also gives us our first look at two of the functions we can use with ordinal types: the Predecessor function **PRED()** and the Successor function **SUCC()**. These two functions work pretty much as you'd expect: whatever ordinal value you put between the parentheses, **PRED()** returns the previous value, while **SUCC()** returns the next value. For example, if you ever got tired of the day being Monday, you could apply the **PRED()** function to it and get

```
PRED(Monday) = Sunday
```

or the **SUCC()** function and get

```
SUCC(Monday) = Tuesday
```

```
PROGRAM Listing5_5;

   { Illustrates the use of Booleans to control the flow of the
program, and introduces PRED and SUCC functions.}


USES CRT;

VAR
   Statement1,
   Statement2,
   Statement3,
   Statement4     : BOOLEAN;
   FirstNumber,
   SecondNumber   : INTEGER;

PROCEDURE Pause;
   VAR
      Proceed : char;
   BEGIN
      WRITELN;
      WRITELN(' Press any key to continue ...');
      Proceed := READKEY;
      WRITELN
   END;


{ Main body of program }
BEGIN
   CLRSCR;
   FirstNumber := 100;
   SecondNumber := 200;

   IF FirstNumber = 100
      THEN Statement1 := (FirstNumber > SecondNumber)
      ELSE Statement1 := (FirstNumber <= SecondNumber);
   WRITELN(' The truth-value of Statement1 is ', Statement1, '.');
   pause;

   { ------------------------------------------ }
   { Use the Predecessor function to assign     }
   { the "previous" boolean value to Statement2 }
   { ------------------------------------------ }
   Statement2 := PRED(Statement1);
   WRITELN(' The truth-value of Statement2 is ', Statement2, '.');
   pause;

   { ------------------------------------- }
   { Use the Successor function to assign   }
   { the "next" boolean value to Statement3 }
   { ------------------------------------- }
   Statement3 := SUCC(Statement1);
   WRITELN(' The truth-value of Statement3 is ', Statement3, '.');
   pause;

   Statement4 := SUCC(statement3);
   WRITELN(' The truth-value of Statement4 is ', Statement4, '.');
   pause

END.
```

Listing 5.5: The ordering of the two Boolean values.

There is another neat trick in Listing 5.5. Notice that I never specifically assigned a truth value to **Statement1**. Instead, it looks as though I assigned a statement to it. What happened is that because **FirstNumber > SecondNumber** makes a factual assertion, it has a truth value of true or false. As it happens, this value is false, so that is the truth value that was assigned to Statement1. I also covered myself by putting in an ELSE clause to take care of all the other possibilities.

Finally, Listing 5.5 illustrates a problem you can run into frequently with certain ordinal types. Sometimes, when you get to the end of an ordinal type, you want the **SUCC()** function to cycle back to the beginning; in this case, you want **SUCC(True)** to be False. Similarly, at the beginning, you want **PRED()** to cycle to the end, which would make **PRED(False)** = True. In Listing 5.5, **PRED(False)** is true, as it should be, but **SUCC(True)** is incorrectly evaluated as true. You will learn how to solve this problem in the following section, where enumerated types are discussed.

ENUMERATED-DATA TYPES

An enumerated-data type is a type you define by enumerating its members; the order in which you list the members becomes their order in the type. Thus, for example,

```
TYPE

    Stooges = (Larry, Moe, Curly);
```

defines a perfectly good enumerated-data type in Pascal. You can apply the **SUCC()** and **PRED()** functions to get things like **SUCC(Moe) = Curly**. A more useful enumerated type would be something like:

```
TYPE

    DaysOfWeek = (Mon, Tue, Wed, Thu, Fri);
```

Usually, enumerated types are used for indexing arrays. Arrays are a structured type that we discussed briefly in Chapter 3 and to which we'll return in Chapter 8 to explore fully. For the time being, note that enumerated types can make the structure and purpose of arrays a little clearer:

```
TYPE
      DaysOfWeek = (Sun, Mon, Tue, Wed, Thu, Fri, Sat);
VAR
      ThingsToDo : ARRAY[Mon..Fri] of STRING[20];
```

By using the enumerated type **DaysOfWeek** to index the array **ThingsToDo**, you can refer to individual slots in the array by the name of a particular day, such as **ThingsToDo[Wed]**. It makes no difference to Pascal whether you use **Mon..Fri** or **1..5**; this is just somewhat easier to read and understand. Also, note that you don't have to use everything in your enumerated type to index the array; if you wish, you can use only part of it, in this case, Monday to Friday.

Another use for enumerated types is as loop counters, for example:

```
TYPE
   DaysOfWeek = (Sun, Mon, Tue, Wed, Thu, Fri, Sat);
VAR
   Day = DaysOfWeek;  { loop counter }


BEGIN

   . .

   FOR Counter := Mon TO Fri DO     { loop five times }
WRITELN(' Another workday!');  { do this each time }

   . .

END;
```

Displaying Enumerated-Data Type

It is important to understand that the members of an enumerated type are not text strings. You cannot, for example, use a line of code like the following:

```
WRITELN(' The next stooge after Moe was ', SUCC(Moe), '.');
```

If you do, you'll get an error message that says "Cannot read or write variables of this type," meaning that you cannot print an enumerated data item to the screen. To display or print the words in an enumerated type, you have to set up some text items (strings) that contain the names of the type's members. The best way to do this is to use an array, as follows:

```
TYPE
   Stooges = (Larry, Moe, Curly);
VAR
   StoogeNames : ARRAY[Larry..Curly] of STRING[5];
   BEGIN
   StoogeNames[Larry] := 'Larry';
   StoogeNames[Moe]   := 'Moe';
   StoogeNames[Curly] := 'Curly';


   { And then print the strings in the array }
   WRITELN('The first stooge was ',StoogeNames[Larry],'.');


   { .. and so on }
END;
```

Cycling Back in Enumerated Types

Sometimes, you have an ordinal type in which applying **SUCC()** to the last member of the type should take you back to the first member of the type, and applying **PRED()** to the first member should take you to the last member. Usually, this happens with enumerated types, but it can be applied generally to other ordinal types.

A typical example of this situation would be the days of the week. Sunday is the first day of the week, and **PRED(Sunday)** should give a value of Saturday; likewise, Saturday is the last day, and **SUCC(Saturday)** should give a value of Sunday. However, if you simply code it like this, you'll get an error, because **SUCC(Saturday)** is undefined.

```
TYPE

    DaysOfWeek =

    (Sunday,Monday,Tuesday,Wednesday,Thursday,Friday);

VAR

    Day1,

    Day2 : DaysOfWeek;

BEGIN

    Day1 := Saturday;

    Day2 := SUCC(Day1)

END;
```

The solution to this problem is to anticipate the possibility of calls to **SUCC(Saturday)** or **PRED(Sunday)** and write your assignment statements to account for those situations. An example of how to do this is shown in Listing 5.6.

SUBRANGE TYPES

With any ordinal type, it is also possible to create a *subrange type*. To create a subrange type, you simply take part of the original ordinal type (the *base type*) and declare it as its own type. For example, with the character type as the base type, you could declare subrange types as follows:

```
TYPE

    UpperCaseLetters = 'A'..'Z';
```

```
PROGRAM Listing5_6;

TYPE
  DaysOfWeek = (Sunday, Monday, Tuesday, Wednesday, Thursday,
                Friday, Saturday);
VAR
  Day1,
  Day2,
  Day3 : DaysOfWeek;

BEGIN
  Day1 := Sunday;
  IF Day1 = Sunday
    THEN Day2 := Saturday
    ELSE Day2 := PRED(Day1);
  IF Day1 = Saturday
    THEN Day3 := Sunday
    ELSE Day3 := SUCC(Day1)
END.
```

Listing 5.6: Cycling back with enumerated-data types.

With integers as the base type, you could declare

TYPE

   OneToAHundred = 1..100;

Note that if the base type is a built-in Turbo Pascal type (such as characters or integers), you don't have to declare it. On the other hand, if it is an enumerated type, you must declare it:

TYPE

   DaysOfWeek =
   (Sunday, Monday, Tuesday, Wednesday, Thursday, Friday, Saturday);

   WorkDays = Monday..Friday;

Because the **WorkDays** type is a subrange of the **DaysOfWeek** type, the **DaysOfWeek** type has to be declared first. Otherwise, Turbo Pascal will not recognize *Monday..Friday* as a legitimate type. And because subrange data types are derived from ordinal data types, the subrange types themselves are *also* ordinal data types.

FUNCTIONS THAT WORK WITH ORDINAL DATA

We have already seen a few examples of applying the successor and predecessor functions to members of ordinal data types. Now, I'll explain ordinal functions a little more completely.

- The value that a function takes is called its *argument*. Thus, in **SUCC(Saturday)** and **PRED(15)**, the arguments are Saturday and 15, respectively.

- Normally, a function can take only arguments of a certain type or group of types. Thus, for example, **SUCC()** can take only arguments of an ordinal type.

- The value returned by the function does not have to be of the same data type as the argument. For example, as we'll see in a moment, the **ORD()** function takes a base ordinal type and returns a number, as in **ORD(Saturday) = 7**.

SUCC(), PRED(), and Other Ordinal Routines

Now that we've seen some examples of how **SUCC()** and **PRED()** work, here is a summary of the functions and procedures you can apply to ordinal data types:

- **ORD()**: This function returns the position of an ordinal data item in the ordinal type. In the **DaysOfWeek** type, **ORD(Sunday) = 1**, **ORD(Tuesday) = 3**, and **ORD(Saturday) = 7**. Likewise, in the set of ASCII characters, **ORD('A') = 65**, **ORD('B') = 66**, which are the numbers of **'A'** and **'B'** in the order of ASCII characters. (For the character data type, the opposite of **ORD()** is **CHR()**, which takes an ASCII number and returns a character, e.g., **CHR(65) = 'A'**.)

- **SUCC()**: This function returns the next member of an ordinal data type, for example, **SUCC('B') = 'C'**.

- **PRED()**: This function returns the previous member of an ordinal data type, for example, **PRED('C') = 'B'**.

- **DEC()**: This decreases an ordinal value by one position, and is a procedure rather than a function. For example, if the variable *letter* has a value of **'C'**, then **DEC**(letter) changes its value to **'B'**.

  Notice that we didn't say *DEC(letter) = 'B'*: this is because **DEC()** and **INC()** are procedures, not functions. You can think of **DEC()** as the "complete sentence" counterpart of **"PRED()"**. Although you can use **PRED()** and **SUCC()** as words in a sentence, as shown in Listing 5.7 and Figure 5.1, you can use procedures such as **DEC()** and **INC()** only as whole statements that stand on their own. When you try to compile Listing 5.7, you get an error message because you're trying to use **INC()** as a function. If you delete the last two lines of the program (not **END**), the program will compile and run properly.

- **INC()**: This increases an ordinal value by one position, and works in the same way as **DEC()**.

```
 ≡  File  Edit  Search  Run  Compile  Debug  Options  Window  Help
[■]                        FILES1\LIST5_6.PAS                      1─[↕]
  Error 42: Error in expression.
BEGIN
  CLRSCR;
  WRITELN;
  WRITELN(' The third capital letter is ', SUCC('B'), '.');
  pause;

  RegLtr := 'B';
  WRITELN(' The RegLtr variable now holds ', RegLtr, '.');
  pause;

  INC(RegLtr);
  WRITELN(' The RegLtr variable now holds ', RegLtr, '.');
  pause;

  WRITELN(' The fourth letter is ', Inc('C'), '.');
  pause;

END.
  31:37
 F1 Help  F2 Save  F3 Open  Alt-F9 Compile  F9 Make  F10 Menu
```

Figure 5.1: PRED() and SUCC() are functions, similar to words in English.

```
PROGRAM Listing5_7;

USES CRT;

VAR
  RegLtr : char;

PROCEDURE Pause;
  VAR
    Proceed : char;
  BEGIN
    WRITE(' Press any key to continue ...');
    Proceed := Readkey;
    WRITELN; WRITELN
  END;

BEGIN
  CLRSCR;
  WRITELN;
  WRITELN(' The third capital letter is ', SUCC('B'), '.');
  pause;

  RegLtr := 'B';
  WRITELN(' The RegLtr variable now holds ', RegLtr, '.');
  pause;

  INC(RegLtr);
  WRITELN(' The RegLtr variable now holds ', RegLtr, '.');
  pause;

  WRITELN(' The fourth letter is ', Inc('C'), '.'); { Error! }
  pause;

END.
```

Listing 5.7: Error from trying to use INC() as a function.

NONORDINAL TYPES

As we have seen, members of ordinal data types are simple data items that come in a specific order, and each ordinal data item has an identifiable successor and predecessor. Members of nonordinal data types have little in common except that they fail to satisfy at least one of the requirements for being an ordinal type. Either they lack a specific order (e.g., text strings), or they fail to have identifiable successors and predecessors (e.g., real numbers).

The two nonordinal types are real numbers and strings. The real number type is further subdivided into types REAL, SINGLE, DOUBLE, EXTENDED, and COMP.

REAL NUMBERS

Real numbers differ from the other numeric types we've been discussing because, as noted earlier, real numbers are not an ordinal type. No matter which real number we pick, it is impossible to pick out the next or previous real number; neither is it possible to figure out where our chosen real number stands in the order of all real numbers. Examples of real numbers are 2.0, 3.15, 1.414, and 6.023.

In Turbo Pascal, real numbers are expressed in scientific notation, i.e., as powers of 10. This means, for example, that the real numbers:

$$2.2 = 2.2 \times 10^0 = 2.2000000000E+0$$

$$3{,}456.75 = 3.45675 \times 10^3 = 3.4567500000E+3$$

$$100 = 1.00 \times 10^2 = 1.0000000000E+2$$

Because most PC screens cannot display exponents (at least not when they are running in character mode), Turbo Pascal uses a modified scientific notation to handle the exponents, with E and a plus or minus sign showing which power of 10 the number should be raised to. To bypass this, you must specify the total number of digits and decimal places in your number. You do it by adding a format after the Pascal identifier which represents the number, as shown in Listing 5.8.

The first digit after the identifier indicates the total number of spaces that you want your number to take up; the second tells how many decimal places you want in your number, that is, how many digits should be to the right of the decimal point.

If you specify **0** for the total number of digits, then Turbo Pascal automatically expands the format to fit the number. You can specify other total numbers of digits when you want to line up columns of numbers as shown in Listing 5.8.

Listing 5.8 also provides several examples of passing variables as parameters to subroutines. When you define a subroutine, you must include in the definition the number, type, and order of any variables that the subroutine will need to get from outside itself. Then, when you call the subroutine, you can simply include the names of the appropriate variables in parentheses after the name of the subroutine. Any variables to be

```
PROGRAM Listing5_8;

  { This program shows how to format real numbers. }

USES CRT;

VAR
  a,b,c : REAL;

PROCEDURE Pause;
  VAR
    Proceed : CHAR;
  BEGIN
    WRITE(' Press any key to continue ... ');
    Proceed := READKEY;
    WRITELN; WRITELN
  END;

PROCEDURE SetValues(VAR a,b,c : REAL);
  BEGIN
    a := 1.1;
    b := 21.59;
    c := 350.1167
  END;

PROCEDURE DisplayWithNoFormat(a,b,c : REAL);
  BEGIN
    WRITELN;
    WRITELN(' List of real number variables "a" to "c" with no format');
    WRITELN(' ----------------------------------------------------');
    WRITELN(' ',a);
    WRITELN(' ',b);
    WRITELN(' ',c);
    WRITELN;
    pause
  END;



PROCEDURE DisplayFirstFormat(a,b,c : REAL);
  BEGIN
    WRITELN;
    WRITELN(' List of real number variables "a" to "c" with formatting');
    WRITELN(' ---------------------------------------------');
    WRITELN(' ',a:0:1);
    WRITELN(' ',b:0:2);
    WRITELN(' ',c:0:4);
    WRITELN;
    pause
  END;

PROCEDURE DisplayColumnFormat(a,b,c : REAL);
  BEGIN
    WRITELN;
    WRITELN(' List of real number variables in column format');
    WRITELN(' ---------------------------------------------');
    WRITELN(' ',a:8:4);
    WRITELN(' ',b:8:4);
    WRITELN(' ',c:8:4);
    WRITELN;
    pause
  END;
```

Listing 5.8: Formatting real numbers for display on the screen.

```
{ -------------------------------------------------------------- }
{                       MAIN BODY OF PROGRAM                      }
{ -------------------------------------------------------------- }
BEGIN
  CLRSCR;
  SetValues(a,b,c);
  DisplayWithNoFormat(a,b,c);
  DisplayFirstFormat(a,b,c);
  DisplayColumnFormat(a,b,c)
END.
```

Listing 5.8: Formatting real numbers for display on the screen. (cont.)

changed by the subroutine *must* be declared as VAR parameters when you first define the subroutine. We will examine subroutines and parameters more thoroughly in Chapter 9.

Types of Real Numbers

Just as with integers, real number types differ primarily in their range and in the amount of PC memory that they require. The different types are shown in Table 5.2. As with integers, it's better to use the plain "real" data type unless you have a special reason for needing one of the others. Even with the plain "real" data type, you get an almost unimaginably large range of numbers, quite large enough to count all the stars in our galaxy and several other galaxies, as well.

USING FANCY REAL TYPES

If you ever need to use Turbo Pascal's specialized real-number types (single, double, extended, and comp), there are two ways to do it. Technically, these data types require an 80x87 (8087, 80287, or 80387) math coprocessor in your PC in order to work, and if you have some extra money, that is the best solution.

On the other hand, for a cheaper solution that's almost as good, use Turbo Pascal's built-in library of routines for handling real numbers and turn on 80x87 software emulation, which tells Turbo Pascal to use 80x87 instructions to handle the fancy real-number types. This is slower and slightly less powerful than using an 80x87 math coprocessor, but you can use this method on all PCs—most of which are not 80x87-equipped.

Table 5.2: Real Number Data Types

TYPE	RANGE	SIGNIFICANT DIGITS	MEMORY REQUIRED (BYTES)
Real	2.9×10^{-39} .. 1.7×10^{38}	11-12	6
Single	1.5×10^{-45} .. 3.4×10^{38}	7-8	4
Double	5.0×10^{-324} .. 1.7×10^{308}	15-16	8
Extended	3.4×10^{-4932} .. 1.1×10^{4932}	19-20	10
Comp*	$-2^{63} + 1$ .. $2^{63} - 1$	19-20	8

The Comp type holds integers between -9.2×10^{18} and $+9.2 \times 10^{18}$

There are two ways to do this. The first is to use the Compiler Options dialog box (opened from the Options menu) to turn on 80x87 emulation as the default. (If you choose this method, then 80x87 emulation will be used in all of your programs.)

Numeric Processing Compiler Directives

The second way is to put two "compiler directives" at the beginning of your program that tell Turbo Pascal to turn on 80x87 emulation. A compiler directive is a special kind of program comment that tells Turbo Pascal (or any other Pascal compiler) how to handle certain situations when it compiles your program. We'll discuss compiler directives in detail in Chapter 7, but for the time being, here are instructions on how to use them to handle precise real numbers.

Usually, a compiler directive is a *toggle*, which means that it works like a light switch. Flip it up, and the light is turned on; flip it down, and the light is turned off. The equivalent of up for most compiler directives is the plus sign, while the equivalent of down is the minus sign.

There are two numeric processing compiler directives that you can use for floating-point arithmetic, that is, with real numbers:

- {$N+} and {$N-}, which turn 80x87 code generation on and off, respectively. When 80x87 code generation is on, Turbo Pascal generates floating-point instructions that take advantage of your math coprocessor's arithmetic capabilities. If you don't have a math coprocessor, you also must have *80x87 emulation* turned on; otherwise, you will get a compilation error message that says you need a math coprocessor.

- {$E+} and {$E-}, which turn 80x87 emulation on and off, respectively. When emulation is turned on, Turbo Pascal links your program with a run-time library of routines that handle floating-point arithmetic in approximately the same way as the 80x87 does. It is slower than having an extra processor in your PC, but it works.

You should use both of these compiler directives if your program must handle precise floating-point arithmetic but you do not know if your PC has a math coprocessor. This program will use a math coprocessor if one is present; and will use 80x87 emulation routines if one is not present.

```
PROGRAM VeryPreciseNumbers;

{$N+}            { turns on 80x87 code generation }

{$E+}            { links 80x87 emulation routines
                   in case 80x87 not present      }

{...details of program }
```

Of course, there's no point in using either of these compiler directives if you are only using integers and real numbers without many digits. They will make your compiled program slightly bigger.

Notice one unusual thing about compiler directives. I said earlier that Pascal ignores anything between two comment brackets. Compiler directives are the single exception to this rule. When Turbo Pascal encounters a left comment bracket that is immediately followed by a dollar sign, as in the example above, it knows it is dealing with a compiler directive instead of an ordinary comment. As a result, it carries out the directive's instructions on how the program is to be compiled.

Cautions about Real Numbers

One point that needs to be made is that although integers are handled by Turbo Pascal as exact values, *real numbers* are handled only as approximate values. This results more from the limitations of the PC's processor (8086, 80286, 80386, or 80486) than it does from Turbo Pascal itself, but it must be reckoned with if you are using real numbers with many digits.

In most situations, this won't cause you any trouble. Turbo Pascal has no problem distinguishing between 1.00 and 0.99, or between 1000.151 and 1000.152. The real-number data type has 11 to 12 significant digits, depending on the circumstances, and so as long as you are within that limit, you are fairly safe.

When you are doing calculations that require a high degree of precision, however, you should bear in mind that real numbers (and other real types) have a limited number of "significant digits." This means that only the significant digits (from left to right) count as part of the number. If you need greater precision than is provided by standard real numbers, you can use a double-precision or an extended-data type, which provides 15-16 and 19-20 significant digits, respectively. Remember that to use these types, you must have 80x87 code generation turned on and either 80x87 emulation or a math coprocessor.

ARITHMETIC OPERATIONS WITH INTEGERS AND REAL NUMBERS

Most of Turbo Pascal's arithmetic operations are quite ordinary: addition, subtraction, and multiplication work just as you would expect. There are, however, a few special points of which you need to be aware.

Integer and Real Division

First, there are two kinds of division in Pascal: integer division and real-number division. Integer division is denoted by the word *div*, while real-number division is denoted by the forward slash ("/"). When you use integer division, both of the numbers involved must be integers, and the result is also an integer, as in:

6 div 3 = 2

20 div 4 = 5

15600 div 15 = 1040

11 div 3 = 3

That last result might have surprised you. Eleven divided by three is *three*? However, we are using *integer division*, which is a special kind of division that only handles whole numbers—and the number of times that three will *evenly* divide eleven is indeed three. It is wise to remember this potential pitfall whenever you use integer division: the result is always an integer, and any fractions are discarded.

Real division, on the other hand, is exactly what you would expect. It takes two real numbers or integers, divides one into the other, and gives back a third real number as the result. For example,

7.50 / 3.0 = 2.50

12.25 / 2 = 6.125

6 / 3 = 2.0

The result of real division is a real number even if the operands are both integers and there is no remainder: for example, *6 / 3 = 2*, but the '2' that is the solution is a real number. If you try to assign it to an integer variable, you will get a compile-time error because the data types do not match. Thus, the following code will not compile:

```
PROGRAM MisMatch;
```

```
VAR

  WholeNum : integer;


BEGIN

  WholeNum := 6 / 3        { type mismatch }

END.
```

The MOD Operator

The other arithmetic operator that might be unfamiliar is the *mod* (modulus) operator, which returns the *remainder* of an integer division. Thus,

15 mod 2 = 1; { two divides 15 7 times, remainder = 1 }

12 mod 12 = 0; { 12 divides 12 once, remainder = 0 }

The *mod* operator is often used to set up loops in which a variable cycles from a low value to a high value and then starts again at the low value. The North American clock, for example, gives the hour of day as *mod 12*:

7th hour of the day = 7 mod 12 = 7 o'clock

15th hour of the day = 15 mod 12 = 3 o'clock

24th hour of the day = 24 mod 12 = 0 o'clock

As the third time indicates, normally, you need to set up a separate statement to handle the maximum value in the range that you are using: the 24th hour of the day is not zero o'clock, but 12 o'clock.

Turbo Pascal's arithmetic operators are summarized in Table 5.3.

Table 5.3: Arithmetic Operations with Integers and Real Numbers

OPERATOR	OPERATION	DATA TYPE OF OPERANDS	DATA TYPE OF RESULTS
+	Addition	Integer or real	Integer or real
−	Subtraction	Integer or real	Integer or real
* (asterisk)	Multiplication	Integer or real	Integer or real
div	Integer division	Integer	Integer
/ (slash)	Real division	Real or integer	Real
mod	modulus	Integer	Integer

Evaluating Arithmetic Expressions

Sometimes, the exact meaning of an arithmetic expression is ambiguous. For example, does *120 div 3 + 5* mean that you should

divide 3 into 120 and then add 5 to the result, or

add 5 to 3 and then divide the sum into 120?

Parentheses are the main tool for eliminating this kind of ambiguity. By grouping parts of an expression in parentheses, you indicate which operations are to be performed first. Operations inside parentheses are done first, then at the next level out of the parentheses, and so forth. Thus,

(120 div 3) + 5 = 40 + 5 = 45

120 div (3 + 5) = 120 div 8 = 15

120 div (3 + (5 * 3)) = 120 div (3 + 15) = 120 div 18 = 6

If parentheses do not resolve the issue, then operations are done in the following order: multiplication, division, modulus, addition, and subtraction. And, if there is still an ambiguity, any operations equal in priority are done from left to right.

THE STRING DATA TYPE

Strings, as pieces of text, are the most familiar type to human beings. Unfortunately, Standard Pascal (as defined by the International Organization for Standardization) provides no string data type; instead, you have to treat strings as packed arrays of characters, which can be quite tedious.

Fortunately, Turbo Pascal does provide a string data type. Turbo Pascal does see strings as arrays of characters but for most purposes we can ignore this and allow Turbo Pascal to handle it for us. When we need to think of a string as an array, we can do it (as, for example, when we want to pick out the nth character in a string by using the array index).

It is worth noting that in most of the cases where we have had to deal with strings, we have not had to worry about declaring a string data type. The program statement

```
WRITELN(' This is a string.');
```

automatically displays a string on the screen for us. It is only when we want to create string variables and/or constants that we have to worry about string types.

Even so, there is little to worry about except for how much memory the string will require. You declare a string variable as follows:

```
VAR

   Firstname : STRING[10];
```

You can also, of course, declare string constants if you want. The number between the square brackets in **STRING[10]** indicates how long the string

is supposed to be; the length can be anything from 1 to 255. If you do not
include a length, as in

```
VAR

    Firstname : STRING;
```

Turbo Pascal assigns a default length of 255 characters.

Now, there is a puzzle here: what happens if you assign a length of 10
to a string, but use only five characters, as in **Firstname := 'Steve'**? The
answer is that Turbo Pascal keeps track of the actual length (called the *logical length*) of the string as well as its physical length, which is the amount
of PC memory it requires, determined by the number you put between the
brackets. A string, remember, is really an array of characters; Turbo Pascal
keeps the logical length of the string in a special 0 slot at the very beginning of the array.

Thus, while a program is running, the logical length of a string can
vary from zero (the minimum) to its physical length (the maximum) as it
receives new pieces of text assigned to it.

```
VAR

    Firstname : STRING[10];      { physical length 10 }


BEGIN

    Firstname := 'Joe' { logical length 3, physical
                          length 10 }


    Firstname := 'Philippe' { logical length 8,
                                physical length 10 }

    { ... etc. }

END;
```

PASSING STRINGS TO SUBROUTINES

Ordinarily, you do not have to declare string types in the TYPE section of your program, because STRING is a built-in data type in Turbo Pascal. You will need to declare strings in the TYPE section whenever you need to pass string variables as parameters to subroutines (procedures and functions). Turbo Pascal will not allow you to declare a subroutine with a standard string type, such as in

```
PROCEDURE DisplayYourName(Name : STRING[20]);
```

This program line will not compile because Turbo Pascal won't accept **STRING[20]** or any similar expression (**STRING[5]**, **STRING[255]**) in a subroutine definition. To pass a string as a parameter to a subroutine, you have to declare a string type in the TYPE section and use that type in defining your subroutine:

```
TYPE
  String20 = STRING[20];


{ ... etc. }


PROCEDURE DisplayYourName(Name : String20);


{ ... etc. }
```

TYPED CONSTANTS

Typed constants suffer from a seriously misleading name. First, all constants have a data type. Second, typed constants are not constants: they are variables that you declare in the TYPE section of your program. A typed constant declaration includes the name, data type, and *the initial value* of the variable you are declaring.

Thus, in spite of their name, typed constants do have a role of sorts. You can use typed constants to declare variables and set their initial values at the same time. For example, the following two code fragments are equivalent:

```
TYPE
   Distance : integer = 600;
```

does the same job as

```
VAR
   Distance : integer;
BEGIN
   Distance := 600;
{ ... etc. }
END;
```

SUMMARY

Pascal has both simple and complex data types that are predefined in the language. Simple data types divide neatly into two categories: ordinal and nonordinal types. The characteristics of an ordinal data type are that its members (a) come in a definite order and (b) are discrete. These characteristics allow ordinal functions such as the successor and predecessor functions to work with these data types, which include integers, characters, and Boolean values (truth values). Ordinal data types can also include enumerated and subrange types which are defined by the programmer.

Nonordinal types are real numbers (which are in a definite order but are not discrete) and string types.

Pascal supports a variety of arithmetic operations with both integers and real numbers, including addition, subtraction, multiplication, division, and modulus (which returns the remainder from integer division).

Typed constants are actually not constants at all, but are instead pre-initialized variables that are declared in the CONST section of the program.

REVIEW EXERCISES

1. Explain what a variable is and how the nature of a variable is related to the idea of a data type in Pascal.

2. Explain the characteristics of an ordinal data type. List (a) the predefined ordinal types in Turbo Pascal, and (b) two predefined Pascal functions that are used with ordinal data items.

3. Which of the following are ordinal data types? For the ones that are not ordinal types, explain why they are not.

   (a) short integers

   (b) the range of lowercase letters 'a' through 'f'

   (c) integers

   (d) In TYPE section: Weekdays = (Mon, Tue, Wed, Thu, Fri)

   (e) the real numbers between 1.0 and 2.0

   (f) the Boolean values True and False

   (g) the integers 1..200

4. List the different integer data types in Turbo Pascal, along with the range and amount of memory required by each. Should you normally use special integer types, such as byte and shortint, to save memory?

5. List the different real number types in Turbo Pascal, along with the range and amount of memory required by each. When should you use special real number types, such as single and extended? (Challenging: How many real numbers are there

between 1.0 and 2.0? Are there twice as many between 1.0 and 3.0? Justify your answer.)

6. Explain what compiler directives are and how "toggle" compiler directives work. List the compiler directives to turn on 80x87 code generation and emulation; to turn off 80x87 code generation and emulation. What is the odd feature of compiler directives?

7. List the different arithmetic operations that you can perform with integers and real numbers in Turbo Pascal.

8. Explain the three factors that Turbo Pascal uses to determine the order in which arithmetic operations should be performed.

9. Give the solution and data type of each of the following:

    (a) 6 + 10

    (b) 10 / 2

    (c) 10 mod 2

    (d) (10 mod 3) * 2.0

    (e) 2.0 mod 1.0

    (f) 5 * 4

    (g) 5 * (4 div 2)

    (h) 5.0 + 1.23456 (Challenging: Is there a special problem here? If so, explain the problem.)

    (i) 5 mod 10

    (j) (10 * ((42 mod 5) + 17) / 6

    (k) 20 div 6

10. Why are there only 256 ASCII characters?

11. Explain the contents of the different sections of the ASCII character set.

12. Create an enumerated type with at least five members.

13. Given the enumerated type Week = (Sun, Mon, Tue, Wed, Thu, Fri, Sat), what is the value of each of the following?

    (a) SUCC(Sun)

    (b) PRED(Mon)

(c) SUCC(SUCC(Mon))

(d) SUCC(PRED(Mon))

(e) SUCC(Sat)

(f) PRED(Sun)

(g) ORD(Wed)

14. Given the enumerated type in exercise 12, what is wrong with the following Pascal statements?

(a) PRED(Wed);

(b) WRITELN(' The day before Wednesday is ', DEC(Wed), '.');

(c) WRITELN(INC(Sun));

15. What is wrong with this code fragment and why is it wrong? How would you correct it?

```
VAR
        Name : STRING[10];
PROCEDURE GetName(VAR Name : STRING[10]);
        BEGIN
          CLRSCR;
          WRITE(' Please enter your first name: ');
          READLN(Name)
        END;
```

Simple Pascal Statements

*[**A**n important distinction] is be-*
tween the language of statements and
prescriptive language...Telling someone
to do something, or that something is
the case, is answering the question
"What shall I do?" or "What are the
facts?"

—R. M. Hare, *The Language of Morals*

FUNDAMENTAL TYPES OF STATEMENTS

At the highest level there are only two fundamental kinds of statement in any Pascal program: first, statements that move *data* to one place or another, and second, statements that move *the program* in one direction or another.

Examples of statements that move data to one place or another are *assignment statements,* which move a value into a variable; *I/O (input/output) statements,* which move data from your PC's memory to the screen, disk drive, printer, or some other device; and *definitional statements,* which set the values of constants. Thus, the following are *data moving* statements:

- **Counter := 1;** { assignment statement; moves a value into a variable }

- **WRITELN(' This is displayed on the screen.');** { I/O statement; moves a text string from memory to the PC's screen }

- **Pi = 3.1415927;** { definitional statement; defines Pi as the real number specified }

- **Name : STRING[10];** { definitional statement; defines the Name variable as being of type STRING with physical length 10 }

Examples of statements that move the program in one direction or another (officially called *control statements*) are *looping statements*, which make the program repeat a sequence of operations until a certain condition is fulfilled; and *branching statements*, which, based on the value of some control variable, make the program take one path instead of another. Thus, the following are *program moving* statements:

- **FOR counter := 1 TO 10 DO WRITELN(' This is loop number ', counter, '.');** { looping statement; causes the program to execute an I/O statement (display a text string) 10 times }

- **IF PaidUp THEN SendThankYou ELSE BugForMoney;** { branching statement; causes the program to go in one direction or another based on the truth value of the Boolean variable "PaidUp" }

Serving in support of these two official kinds of statements is a third kind of statement, which *asserts* some fact or another. Examples of this kind of statement are *Boolean statements,* such as those involving NOT, and OR; and *arithmetic comparisons,* such as those involving the relational operators >, <, and =. Thus, the following are assertion statements:

- **Counter = 10 OR Name = 'Smith'** { asserts that either the counter variable equals 10 or the name variable = 'Smith' }

- **Balance >= 100.00** { asserts that the balance variable is greater than or equal to the real number 100.00 }

Observe that neither of these examples would qualify by itself as a legal statement in Pascal. Assertion statements in Pascal are used exclusively to help program-moving statements direct the program into one path or another. Ironically, this is exactly the opposite of how humans talk. As a rule, most of our statements assert something, like "There's a camel in the kitchen." The type of statement that Pascal uses, called an *imperative,* is used less frequently in English; for example, "Call the zoo!" The reason for this is that human communication is fact-oriented, and program statements are almost exclusively action-oriented.

SIMPLE AND COMPOUND STATEMENTS

Pascal statements can be either simple or compound. A simple statement performs a single Pascal action, while a compound statement does several actions in sequence. Some examples of simple statements are the following:

- **WRITELN(' This is a simple statement.');**

- **Counter := Counter + 1;**

- **IF Counter = 10 THEN Finish ELSE KeepOnTruckin;**

A compound statement is composed of simple statements. You might have looked at the third example, above, and wondered why it is not a compound statement. To see why it is a simple statement, remember the definition: a simple statement performs a single Pascal action. Depending on the value of **Counter**, the IF..THEN..ELSE statement performs a single program action. That is why it is a simple statement.

Compound statements use BEGIN, END, and the semicolon (;) to show Pascal where they begin and end. The following are examples of compound statements:

```
BEGIN

   WRITE(' Enter your name: ');

   READLN(Name)

END;


BEGIN

   IF Name = 'Albert Einstein'

      THEN BEGIN

            WRITELN(' E = mc²');
```

```
          END
      ELSE WRITELN(' That's a nice name!');
    Counter := Counter + 1
  END;
```

Notice that I enclosed a compound statement within one of the simple statements of the second example. You can do this to as many levels as you like, enclosing statements within statements, within other statements, although it is generally a good idea to keep things as simple as you can.

INDENTATION AND LINES DO NOT MATTER

You should realize that the indentation and separate lines of a Pascal program are there entirely for the benefit of the programmer. Pascal is a statement-oriented language, not a line-oriented one. How your program code indents and divides into different lines makes no difference to Pascal. A line-oriented language, such as BASIC, executes a program one *line* at a time, while a statement-oriented language, such as Pascal, executes a program one *statement* at a time. This is why, for example, a Pascal statement can be split into two or more program lines, while a BASIC statement (even in Microsoft QuickBASIC) cannot. Thus, the following two code fragments are equivalent:

```
BEGIN
  IF Counter = 10
    THEN BEGIN
        WRITELN(' End of list.');
        WRITE(' Do another (Y/N): '):
        READLN(YesNo);
        IF UPCASE(YesNo) = 'Y'
```

```
    THEN DoAnother

    ELSE Quit

END;

  pause

END;
```

is the same as

```
BEGIN IF Counter = 10 THEN BEGIN

WRITELN(' End of list.');

WRITE(' Do Another (Y/N): ');

READLN(YesNo); IF UPCASE(YesNo) = 'Y' THEN DoAnother

ELSE Quit END; pause END;
```

It is important to understand this, particularly because many beginning programmers think that structured programming means simply indenting your code. It is true that most structured programs are indented, but indenting and other devices that make code more readable have no necessary connection with structured programming.

To convince yourself, enter and run Listing 6.1, which is hard to read but runs just fine. Actually, Listing 6.1 includes some formatting, which makes it easier to read than some professionally written Pascal programs that have no formatting at all.

The idea that Pascal is statement-oriented is usually explained by saying that semicolons are statement *separators*, not statement *terminators*. If that idea seems unclear, just remember the following rules:

1. A simple program statement performs a single Pascal action.

2. All statements in a Pascal program must be separated by semicolons.

3. Compound statements are made up of one or more simple statements.

```
PROGRAM Listing6_1;

USES CRT; VAR Counter : integer; YesNo : char;

PROCEDURE Pause;
   VAR Proceed:char; BEGIN WRITE(' Press a key to continue ...');
   Proceed := READKEY; WRITELN; WRITELN END;

PROCEDURE DoAnother;
   BEGIN WRITELN(' The DoAnother routine has run.'); pause END;

PROCEDURE Quit;
   BEGIN WRITELN(' The Quit Routine has run.'); pause END;

BEGIN CLRSCR; Counter := 10; IF Counter = 10 THEN BEGIN
WRITELN(' End of list.'); WRITE(' Do Another (Y/N): ');
READLN(YesNo); IF UPCASE(YesNo) = 'Y' THEN DoAnother
ELSE Quit END END.
```

Listing 6.1: Indentation is ignored by Pascal.

4. Compound statements start with BEGIN and end with END.
    BEGIN and END are not themselves statements; rather, they
    mark the beginning and ending of a compound statement.

5. If a compound statement contains more than one component
    statement, you must use semicolons to separate its compo-
    nent statements.

6. You do not need to put a semicolon before an END or before a
    THEN or ELSE in an IF..THEN..ELSE statement.

The only situation when Pascal is somewhat line oriented occurs in
handling text strings: you cannot break a string across more than one line.
If we were to write

```
IF Counter = 10 THEN WRITELN(' End of
list.');
```

then the program would not compile and we would get the error message, "String constant exceeds line."

SPECIFIC TYPES OF SIMPLE STATEMENTS

Now that we've discussed the general ideas, let's move on to look at the general types of simple statements in Pascal. The basic types are assignment statements, definition statements, I/O statements, and control statements, such as IF..THEN..ELSE.

ASSIGNMENT STATEMENTS

We have seen several examples of assignment statements already. An assignment statement takes a value and puts it into a variable. To do this, Pascal uses the assign operator, which consists of a colon and an equal sign, as in the following:

```
Counter := 10;

Name := 'Smith';

Students[55].GPA := 3.21;

Area := Height * Width;

SuccessfulRead := IORESULT;
```

If you need a nickname for the assignment operator, it is best to think of it as "gets" so you don't accidentally confuse it with "equals." For example, think of it as "Counter gets 10" instead of "Counter equals 10." Another reason to think of the assignment operator as "gets" is to remind you that you're not in BASIC, which uses the equals sign as its assignment operator.

There are two things to watch out for when using assignment statements. First, the expressions on the left and right of the assignment operator must be compatible. This means that they must either be of the same type (e.g., character) or that they can be converted easily between the two types; e.g., integer and shortint, and so forth.

Second, the item on the right side of the assignment operator must *already be defined*. In other words, you can't assign the value of variable *b*, as in

```
b := a;
```

unless you have previously assigned a value to *a*.

DEFINITION STATEMENTS

Definition statements occur mainly in the TYPE, CONST, and VAR sections of your program and its subroutines (procedures and functions). These tell Pascal that, for the duration of your program, a certain identifier is either

- A name for a certain value declared in the CONST section, or
- Of a certain built-in or user-defined data type.

We've seen many examples of definition statements. Here are a few more:

```
CONST
  Pi = 3.14159;


TYPE
  StudentPtr = ^Student;
  Student = RECORD
            Firstname,
            Lastname : STRING[15];
            GPA      : REAL;
            Probation: BOOLEAN;
            Next     : StudentPtr
            END;
```

```
VAR
    StudentList : StudentPtr;
    Counter     : INTEGER;
    YesNo       : CHAR;
```

Just in case you're wondering what **StudentPtr** means, it is a pointer that points to variables of the "user-defined type Student." Of course, it is also a teaser, meant to spark your curiosity about pointers, which will be covered in Chapter 11.

I/O STATEMENTS

Input/output, or I/O, statements move data between your PC's memory and input/output devices, such as the PC's screen, the disk drives, the printer, or the modem. At the moment, we are going to look at two ways to exchange data with the PC screen and with the disk drives.

WRITELN and WRITE

The most familiar I/O statements are the WRITELN and WRITE statements. These take a sequence of printable values (strings, characters, numbers, etc.) and "write" them to an I/O device. You might think that WRITELN and WRITE are only for displaying things on screen; but as we will see, they do a lot more than that.

WRITELN and WRITE differ in that WRITELN displays whatever you want and then adds an end-of-line marker (a carriage return and line feed) at the end of the line. The result is that after displaying what it is supposed to display, WRITELN moves you down to the next line. WRITE, on the other hand, simply displays what it is supposed to display and then leaves the cursor wherever it is.

This makes WRITE ideal for on-screen prompts and for displaying sequences of values on the same line. Listing 6.2 shows how to use WRITE for both of these tasks.

Note that in Listing 6.2, the cursor pauses on the same line as the *Please enter the number of loops you want* prompt. Similarly, all the numbers are

```
PROGRAM Listing6_2;

USES CRT;

VAR
  Counter,
  NumberOfLoops : INTEGER;

PROCEDURE Pause;
  VAR
    Proceed : CHAR;
  BEGIN
    WRITE(' Press any key to continue ...');
    Proceed := READKEY;
    WRITELN; WRITELN
  END;

BEGIN
  CLRSCR;
  WRITE(' Please enter the number of loops you want: ');
  READLN(NumberOfLoops);
  WRITELN;
  FOR Counter := 1 TO NumberOfLoops DO
    BEGIN
    WRITE(' ',counter);
    DELAY(500)              { delay writing next for 1/2 second }
    END;
  WRITELN; WRITELN;
  pause
END.
```

Listing 6.2: Using WRITE for on-screen prompts.

displayed on the same line. The two WRITELN statements after the loop are there to move the cursor down two lines on the screen.

Files in WRITELN and WRITE: Although it is not obvious from what you have seen so far, both WRITELN and WRITE are designed to send output to disk files. If you do not specify a file name, then they assume that you want to use the standard output file—OUTPUT, which is just the PC's screen. Thus, a WRITELN statement such as **WRITELN('Display on screen')** will send its output to the screen. Turbo Pascal's printer unit also defines a standard output file called "LST" that allows you to send output to the printer.

You can, however, specify other file names with WRITELN and WRITE. To illustrate this, examine Listing 6.3. (See Chapters 12–13 for working with disk files.)

The program in Listing 6.3 prompts the user for information by writing text strings to the standard output file (the screen). It then gets

```
PROGRAM Listing6_3;

USES CRT;

TYPE
  String20 = STRING[20];

VAR
  Name     : String20;
  Namefile : TEXT;     { "text" is a type of file variable }
  YesNo    : CHAR;

PROCEDURE Pause;
  VAR
    Proceed : CHAR;
  BEGIN
    WRITE(' Press any key ... ');
    Proceed := READKEY;
    WRITELN; WRITELN
  END;

PROCEDURE Init(VAR YesNo : CHAR; VAR Namefile : text);
  BEGIN
    YesNo := 'Y';
    ASSIGN(Namefile, 'Names.txt');
    REWRITE(Namefile)
  END;

PROCEDURE Shutdown(VAR Namefile : text);
  BEGIN
    CLOSE(Namefile)
  END;

PROCEDURE ReadInNames(VAR Name : string20;
                      VAR YesNo : CHAR;
                      VAR Namefile : text);
  BEGIN
    WHILE UPCASE(YesNo) = 'Y' DO
      BEGIN
      WRITELN;
      WRITE(' Enter a name for the file: ');
      READLN(Name);
      WRITELN(Namefile, Name);
      WRITE(' Add another name (Y/N)? ');
      READLN(YesNo)
      END
  END;


BEGIN

  CLRSCR;
  Init(YesNo, Namefile);
  ReadInNames(Name, YesNo, Namefile);
  Shutdown(Namefile);
  pause
END.
```

Listing 6.3: Writing information to a text file.

the information the user enters by reading it from the standard input file (the keyboard). Finally, it writes the information to a text file, NAMES.TXT, on disk.

Notice that the key difference from what we have seen before occurs in the *ReadInNames* procedure, where the second WRITELN statement includes the name of a file variable as well as the text string that is supposed to be written. Before you can use this file variable, you must associate it with a DOS filename through the ASSIGN statement, then open the file with REWRITE (if you want to write to the file) or RESET, if you want to read from the file. Finally, at the end of the program, you must CLOSE the file.

By using Turbo Pascal's built-in Printer unit, you also could have sent the names to your printer. To send text to the printer using the Printer unit, you use the unit's predefined file variable LST, which automatically sends output to the printer, as in

```
USES CRT, Printer;

  CONST

    FormFeed = #12;    { to make printer eject page }

  BEGIN

    WRITELN(LST,' This goes to the printer.');

    WRITELN(LST, formfeed)

  END.
```

READLN and READ

READLN and READ work in exactly the same way as WRITELN and WRITE, except that they get input from some file (normally the keyboard) and put it into a variable. Listing 6.2 shows an example of READLN, and we've seen many others. Listing 6.4 shows how READLN can be used to display the names that we entered in the disk file from Listing 6.3.

```
PROGRAM Listing6_4;

USES CRT;

TYPE
  String20 = STRING[20];

VAR
   Name : String20;
   NameFile : text;

PROCEDURE Pause;
  VAR
    Proceed : CHAR;
  BEGIN
    WRITE(' Press any key ... ');
    Proceed := READKEY;
    WRITELN; WRITELN
  END;


PROCEDURE Init(VAR Namefile: text);
  BEGIN
    ASSIGN(Namefile, 'names.txt');
    RESET(Namefile)
  END;

PROCEDURE Shutdown(VAR Namefile : text);
  BEGIN
    CLOSE(Namefile)
  END;

PROCEDURE DisplayNames(VAR Namefile : text;
                       VAR Name : string20);
  BEGIN
    CLRSCR;
    WHILE NOT EOF(Namefile) DO  ( has end of file been reached ?
)
      BEGIN
        READLN(Namefile, Name);
        WRITELN(Name);
        WRITELN;
        pause
      END
  END;

BEGIN
  Init(Namefile);
  DisplayNames(Namefile, Name);
  Shutdown(Namefile)
END.
```

Listing 6.4: Using READLN to get information from a text file.

EVALUATING ASSERTION STATEMENTS

As I noted earlier, statements that assert something is true or false are
"second class citizens" in Pascal, because the only official program statements
are commands. However, assertive statements do have an important role to

play in directing the flow of a Pascal program. Based on whether an assertion statement is true or false, Pascal control statements move the program in one direction or another. Statements like **IF Balance = 0.0 THEN SendThanks** depend on the evaluation of the truth value of an assertion statement.

Boolean Operators

Sometimes, you will encounter statements that are not quite as simple as **Balance = 0.0**. For example, suppose that you had a statement like the following:

```
IF (WaterLevel > 25 AND NoLifeJacket) OR Temperature < 30

    THEN YellForHelp

    ELSE TakeASwim;
```

It is not quite as obvious how to evaluate whether the IF statement is true or false. AND and OR are Boolean operators, meaning that they take truth values and, based on what the truth values are, determine whether the entire statement is true or false. If there is any ambiguity about what goes with what, you should use parentheses to make things clear. In the example above, I used parentheses to make it clear that the statement breaks up into

```
(WaterLevel > 25 AND NoLifeJacket) OR Temperature < 30,
```

instead of using

```
WaterLevel > 25 AND (NoLifeJacket OR Temperature < 30)
```

Beyond that, there are some simple rules for figuring out this type of statement. These rules are shown in Tables 6.1 through 6.4.

Tables 6.1 through 6.4 are known as truth tables. They show how you can determine the truth values of statements that use Boolean operators. The statements **P** and **Q** are components of the statements constructed with the Boolean operators. On each line of the truth table, you see the truth value of the compound statement if P and Q have the values shown.

Table 6.1: Truth Table for a Statement P Used with NOT

P	NOT P
TRUE	FALSE
FALSE	TRUE

Table 6.2: Truth Table for Two Statements P and Q Connected by AND

P	Q	P AND Q
TRUE	TRUE	TRUE
TRUE	FALSE	FALSE
FALSE	TRUE	FALSE
FALSE	FALSE	FALSE

Table 6.3: Truth Table for Two Statements P and Q Connected by OR

P	Q	P OR Q
TRUE	TRUE	TRUE
TRUE	FALSE	TRUE
FALSE	TRUE	TRUE
FALSE	FALSE	FALSE

Table 6.4: Truth Table for Two Statements P and Q Connected by XOR

P	Q	P XOR Q
TRUE	TRUE	FALSE
TRUE	FALSE	TRUE
FALSE	TRUE	TRUE
FALSE	FALSE	FALSE

For example,

```
P       Q        P OR Q

-----   ------   -------

TRUE    FALSE    TRUE
```

means that if **P** is true and **Q** is false, then **P** OR **Q** will be true. Likewise, Table 6.2 shows that whenever **P** is true, **NOT P** is false, and whenever **P** is false, then **NOT P** is true; **NOT** simply reverses whatever truth value it is applied to.

Other Relational Operators

In addition to the Boolean operators, Turbo Pascal has a large number of other operators that are used in assertion statements. These operators are shown in Table 6.5.

Order of Evaluation

Turbo Pascal uses precedence rules to decide which expressions are evaluated first. For example, expressions containing NOT are evaluated before expressions containing OR. If you forget to include parentheses in your assertion statement, Turbo Pascal will figure out its truth value by (1) applying precedence rules, and (2) reading and evaluating the statement from left to right.

However, it is easy to make a mistake in remembering or applying the precedence rules, so I strongly recommend that you rely on parentheses instead.

Even if you do use parentheses, it's essential that you understand the precedence rules for Boolean expressions. The precedence levels of Boolean operators, which are referred to informally above, are summarized in Table 6.6.

Let's look at a few examples of how these rules apply. Where p, q, and r are Boolean statements, the following expressions are equivalent:

- **NOT p OR q** is equivalent to **(NOT p) OR q**, because NOT has a higher precedence level than OR.

Table 6.5: Relational Operators for Assertion Statements

OPERATORS	MEANING	TAKES WHAT TYPES AS ARGUMENTS?	RESULT
=	Equals	Compatible simple, pointer, set, string, and array types	Boolean
<>	Does not equal	Same	Boolean
<	Less than	Same	Boolean
>	Greater than	Same	Boolean
>=	Greater than or equal to	Same	Boolean
<=	Less than or equal to	Same	Boolean
SET OPERATOR			
>=	Superset of	Compatible set types	Boolean
<=	Subset of	Same	Boolean
in	Member of	Same	Boolean

Table 6.6: Precedence of Operators in Turbo Pascal

OPERATORS	PRECEDENCE
@, NOT	first
*, /, div, mod, AND, shl, shr	second
+, −, OR, XOR	third
=, <>, <, >, <=, >=, IN	fourth

- **p AND NOT q OR r** is equivalent to **(p AND (NOT q) OR r)**. NOT q is evaluated first because NOT has a higher precedence level than both AND and OR. Moreover, AND has a higher precedence level than OR, so NOT q goes with the AND p instead of with the OR r.

- **p AND q AND r** is equivalent to **(p AND q) AND r**, because when operators are equivalent in precedence level, Turbo Pascal evaluates the expression from left to right. (In fact, because AND is commutative, you can group this expression any way you like and it will come out the same.)

Table 6.6 also shows some other operators that you may find in Boolean expressions, including arithmetic operators. Just like Boolean operators, these are evaluated according to their level of precedence.

SHORT-CIRCUIT BOOLEAN EVALUATION

Sometimes, it is not necessary for Turbo Pascal to read an entire Boolean expression to know if it is true or false. For example, in

```
(6 < 5) AND (Name = 'Sam');
```

Turbo Pascal could conclude that the entire expression is false as soon as it reads the first statement, which says that six is less than five. Because AND statements evaluate to true if and only if both of the statements connected by AND are true, and six is *not* less than five, the overall expression is obviously false as soon as you read the first statement.

Normally, however, some versions of Pascal read Boolean expressions in their entirety before evaluating them as true or false—even if, as in our example, they do not need to do so. Usually, this will simply slow down your program and result in a slightly larger compiled program file, but there are a few cases in which it will actually cause a run-time error. The most common situation for an actual error is in searching a *linked* list (a topic covered in detail in Chapters 11 and 18). For example, you might have a search statement that says the following:

```
WHILE currptr <> nil

AND currptr^.keyfield <> searchkey

{...continue the search }
```

This tells Pascal that if you haven't reached the end of the list (i.e., **currptr** doesn't equal **nil**) and the current item's key field does not contain what you are searching for, then it should continue the search. However, if you *have* reached the end of the list and Pascal tries to look at the key field of the current item, the program will crash because there *is* no current item. It is trying to look for something that is not there.

To avoid this problem, Turbo Pascal's default setting uses what is called *short-circuit* Boolean evaluation, which stops evaluating a Boolean expression as soon as the truth value of the expression is clear. The second part of the AND statement above—the part that causes the run-time error—would never be evaluated if the first part turned out to be false.

Because it is the default setting, you need not do anything to make Turbo Pascal use short-circuit evaluation. In rare cases, you may want to turn off this option so that Turbo Pascal does a full evaluation of Boolean expressions. In such cases, you can use the complete evaluation compiler directive, {**$B+**}, to turn on full Boolean evaluation. When full evaluation is no longer needed in your program, you can turn complete evaluation off with the {**$B-**} compiler directive so that Turbo Pascal will resume doing short-circuit evaluations.

SIMPLE CONTROL STATEMENTS

In this chapter, we will look at two kinds of simple control statements: IF..THEN..ELSE statements and FOR statements. Both of these statements direct the flow of your program: IF..THEN..ELSE statements into one branch or another, and FOR statements into a loop that will execute a predetermined number of times.

In Chapter 7, we will look at more complex and powerful control statements that build on the basic concepts introduced in this section.

IF..THEN..ELSE STATEMENTS

We've already seen many IF..THEN..ELSE statements in our program examples. Normally, this type of statement is most useful when you want the program to go in one direction or another based on a single value that either *is* or *is not* a certain value. This means that IF statements are good to test single conditions, such as whether or not a statement is true.

Where IF statements are not quite as good is in making the program branch in one of several directions based on one of several possible values. For example, in an on-screen menu that has six choices, you cannot simply say

```
IF Menuchoice = 1

   THEN OpenFile

   ELSE Quit;
```

That gives you only two possibilities. In such situations, you would use a CASE statement, which will be discussed in Chapter 7.

FOR.. STATEMENTS

There are really only two varieties of FOR statements: FOR..TO and FOR..DOWNTO. As is probably obvious, FOR..TO counts upward and FOR..DOWNTO counts downward.

The counter variable in a FOR statement can be any ordinal type, including integers, characters, or enumerated types. Thus, a perfectly good FOR statement would be

```
FOR Counter := 10 DOWNTO 1 DO

   WRITELN(' Counting down, count ', Counter, '.');
```

Note two key differences between Pascal's FOR statement and FOR statements in BASIC. First, you use the assignment operator, not the equal sign, in setting up your counter loop. Second, the counter variable is automatically increased or decreased with each pass through the loop; there is no need for a NEXT statement.

You must be careful about how you set up FOR statements (and most others, for that matter). FOR takes a single statement and repeats it in the loop. Thus, if you wrote the code in Listing 6.5, the first line after the FOR statement would repeat five times, but the second line would display only once. That's because the FOR statement repeats only the first statement after it; to include multiple statements in the loop, you must use BEGIN and END to combine them into a single statement, as shown in Listing 6.6.

SUMMARY

There are two fundamental kinds of statement in a Pascal program: statements that move *data* from one place to another, and statements that move

```
PROGRAM Listing6_5;

USES CRT;

VAR
  Counter : INTEGER;

PROCEDURE Pause;
  VAR
    Proceed : CHAR;
  BEGIN
    WRITE(' Press any key ... ');
    Proceed := READKEY;
    WRITELN; WRITELN
  END;


BEGIN
  CLRSCR;
  FOR Counter := 1 TO 5 DO
      WRITELN(' Ho, ho, ho!');
      WRITELN(' This one doesn''t repeat!');
  pause
END.
```

Listing 6.5: A FOR statement repeats only the next statement after it.

the *program* in one direction or another. A third kind of statement, called a *Boolean expression*, is true or false and is used primarily to assist program-moving statements in deciding which way the program should go.

Statements in a Pascal program can be either simple or compound. A statement that performs only a single program action is a simple statement, regardless of how long or complicated it is. A compound statement, which performs multiple program actions, starts with the word BEGIN and ends with the word END. Statements are separated from each other by the use of semicolons.

Indentation of program lines is ignored by Pascal and is used solely to make the program easier for people to read.

The four types of simple statement are assignment statements, definition statements, I/O statements, and control statements. Boolean expressions are determined to be true or false based on definite rules for Boolean operators.

IF..THEN..ELSE statements are useful for making the program branch in one direction or another based on either/or situations. FOR statements cause a program statement to repeat for a predetermined number of times.

```
PROGRAM Listing6_6;

USES CRT;

VAR
  Counter : INTEGER;

PROCEDURE Pause;
  VAR
    Proceed : CHAR;
  BEGIN
    WRITE(' Press any key ... ');
    Proceed := READKEY;
    WRITELN; WRITELN
  END;


BEGIN
  CLRSCR;
  FOR Counter := 1 TO 5 DO
      BEGIN
      WRITELN(' Ho, ho, ho!');
      WRITELN(' This one does repeat!')
      END;
  pause
END.
```

Listing 6.6: Using BEGIN and END to repeat multiple statements with FOR.

REVIEW EXERCISES

---

1. What are the three kinds of data-moving statements in Pascal? Give an example (other than the ones already given in the chapter) of each kind of statement and explain how it works.

2. What are the two kinds of program-moving statements in Pascal? Give an example (other than the ones already given in the chapter) of each kind of statement and explain how it works.

3. What are the two kinds of assertive statements in Pascal, and what are they used for? Give an example (other than the ones already given in the chapter) of each kind of assertive statement and explain how it works.

4. Are assertive statements considered "official" statements in Pascal? If not, why not?

5. Explain the difference between simple and compound statements in Pascal, and give an example (other than the ones already given in the chapter) of each.

6. Which of the following are simple statements and which are compound statements?

    (a) WRITE(' Enter your name: ');

    (b) BEGIN WRITE(' Enter your name: ') END;

    (c) WRITE(' Enter your name: '); READLN(name);

    (d) BEGIN WRITE(' Enter your name: '); READLN(name) END;

    (e) IF name = 'Smith' THEN WRITELN(' Hello, Smith.');

    (f) IF (name = 'Smith') AND (age >= 18)

       THEN WRITELN(' Hello, Smith.')

       ELSE IF (name = 'Jones') and (age >= 18)

         THEN WRITELN(' Where"s Smith?')

         ELSE WRITELN(' Where are Smith and Jones?');

7. Explain why indentation is important in structured programming. Can you give an example in which Pascal interprets two pieces of code differently because of their indentation? If so, explain how the indentation makes a difference. If not, explain why not.

8. Explain the difference between a statement-oriented programming language (such as Pascal) and a line-oriented programming language (such as BASIC).

9. Explain what is done by an assignment statement. What are the two requirements for an assignment statement to work?

10. What does an I/O statement do? Give four examples of I/O statements and explain what each statement does.

11. Challenging: Based on the example in Listing 6.3, write a short program to create and open a file, write your name in it, and close the file. Don't forget to include all four steps.

12. Evaluate each of the following Boolean expressions: that is, say if it is true or false. Assume that you are using short-circuit Boolean evaluation, and mark the place in each statement where you could stop evaluating because the truth value of the statement has been determined.

    (a) 6 > 4
    (b) (6 > 4) AND (5 > 3)
    (c) (6 > 4) OR (5 > 3)
    (d) (6 > 7) OR (5 > 3)
    (e) (6 > 7) OR (5 > 3) XOR FALSE
    (f) ((6 > 7) AND (5 > 3)) XOR (17 div 3 = 5)

13. Explain when you should use an IF..THEN..ELSE statement. Write a simple program that uses an IF..THEN..ELSE statement.

14. Explain when you should use a FOR statement and give the two types of FOR statements. What, if anything, is incorrect about

this code fragment?

```
FOR counter = 'a' TO 'f' DO
    WRITELN(counter);
```

15. Write a simple program that uses an IF..THEN..ELSE statement inside a FOR loop.

C H A P T E R

More Advanced Pascal
Statements

In the previous chapter, we looked at some fairly simple Pascal statements—from WRITELN to the slightly more complex IF..THEN and FOR statements. Here, we'll continue that discussion by examining some more complex statements, as well as when—and when not—to use them.

CASE STATEMENTS

In the examples we have seen of IF..THEN..ELSE statements, there were only two alternatives in the IF clause: either true or false. Thus, in the following, we are dealing with only two possible branches in the program.

```
IF Name = 'Smith' THEN WRITELN(' Another Smith!');

IF Balance = 0.00

    THEN SendThankYou

    ELSE BugForMoney;
```

In the first case, the program executes an extra statement if the **Name** is **'Smith'**, while if the name is not **'Smith'**, it does not execute the statement. In the second case, if the balance is zero, then the program branches one way and sends a thank you note; otherwise, it branches in a different direction and sends a bill.

Sometimes, however, there are more than two alternatives. In that situation, things can get fairly messy with IF statements, as in Listing 7.1. (Actually, as nested IF statements go, the one in Listing 7.1 is hardly messy at all.) This is a common programming situation in which you are setting up a user menu. Depending on the number that the user enters, you want the program to do one of several different things.

The nested IF statement, of course, is in the **DoChoice** procedure. In passing, note several other things about Listing 7.1:

- Each subroutine that deals with variables from outside itself declares those variables as parameters.

- A separate subroutine initializes the variables. Strictly speaking, you do not have to initialize the *Choice* variable, because its value is set in the **GetMenuChoice** subroutine before any action is taken that depends on its value. However, it certainly doesn't hurt to initialize global variables, and it is somewhat safer.

- We set up a WHILE..DO loop to run the main body of the program until you press Escape. This is a fairly common approach. WHILE..DO loops are discussed below.

The program in Listing 7.1 does the job, but that series of nested IF..THEN..ELSE statements is messy: and messy code is always more prone to hidden bugs than clear, easy-to-understand code. Situations like this call for using a CASE statement, as shown in Listing 7.2.

The general form of a Pascal CASE statement is as follows:

```
CASE variable OF
     constantvalue1 : statement1;
     constantvalue2 : statement2;
     constantvalue3 : statement3;
     { ... etc. }
     END;
```

The values in the list must be constants of an ordinal data type, such as CHAR, INTEGER, or an enumerated type. They can also be lists or

```
PROGRAM Listing7_1;

   { Demonstrates the relative inefficiency of nested
     IF..THEN..ELSE statements compared to CASE statements in
     handling several alternatives. }

USES CRT;

CONST
   Escape = CHR(27);

VAR
   Choice : INTEGER;
   Continue : CHAR;

PROCEDURE Pause;
   VAR
     Proceed : CHAR;
   BEGIN
     WRITE(' Press any key to continue ...');
     Proceed := READKEY;
     WRITELN; WRITELN
   END;


PROCEDURE Init(VAR Choice : INTEGER; VAR Continue : CHAR);
   BEGIN
     Choice := 0;
     Continue := ' '
   END;

PROCEDURE AddRecords;
   BEGIN
     WRITELN('The AddRecords procedure has run.')
   END;

PROCEDURE EditRecords;
   BEGIN
     WRITELN('The EditRecords procedure has run.')
   END;

PROCEDURE DisplayRecords;
   BEGIN
     WRITELN('The DisplayRecords procedure has run.')
   END;

PROCEDURE DeleteRecords;
   BEGIN
     WRITELN('The DeleteRecords procedure has run.')
   END;
PROCEDURE GetMenuChoice(VAR Choice : INTEGER);
   BEGIN
     WINDOW(26,5,75,24);
     WRITELN('   MASTER MENU');
     WRITELN('------------------');
     WRITELN('1. Add Records');
     WRITELN('2. Edit Records');
     WRITELN('3. Display Records');
     WRITELN('4. Delete Records');
     WRITELN('5. Quit');
     WRITELN;
```

Listing 7.1: Using nested IF statements.

```
      WRITE('Enter your choice (1-5): ');
      READLN(Choice)
   END;

PROCEDURE DoChoice(VAR Choice : INTEGER);
   BEGIN
      WRITELN;
      IF Choice = 1 THEN AddRecords
         ELSE IF Choice = 2 THEN EditRecords
            ELSE IF Choice = 3 THEN DisplayRecords
               ELSE IF Choice = 4 THEN DeleteRecords
                  ELSE IF Choice = 5 THEN Continue := Escape;
      WRITELN
   END;


{ ------------------------------------------------------------ }
{                   MAIN BODY OF PROGRAM                        }
{ ------------------------------------------------------------ }
BEGIN
   Init(Choice,continue);
   WHILE Continue <> Escape DO
      BEGIN
         CLRSCR;
         GetMenuChoice(Choice);
         DoChoice(Choice);
         window(1,1,80,24);
         GoToXY(1,22);
         pause
      END
END.
```

Listing 7.1: Using nested IF statements. (cont.)

ranges of ordinal values, such as 1,2, 'A'..'Z', or 50..100, so that if **constantvalue1** in the above example were 50..100 and the variable's value were 75, then statement 1 would be carried out. The maximum range of the constant values in the CASE statement is 0..255, so you can use characters, integers, and enumerated types as long as you do not exceed that range. Also, of course, the type of the constant values has to be compatible with the type of the control variable.

Turbo Pascal goes beyond standard Pascal and lets you add an ELSE clause. This is useful in cases where the control variable might not have *any* of the values you listed in the CASE statement:

```
CASE variable OF
      constantvalue1 : statement1;

      constantvalue2 : statement2;

      constantvalue3 : statement3;
```

```
PROGRAM Listing7_2;

   { Demonstrates how to use a CASE statement to handle multiple
     alternatives. }

USES CRT;

CONST
   Escape = CHR(27);

VAR
   Choice : INTEGER;
   Continue : CHAR;

PROCEDURE Pause;
   VAR
      Proceed : CHAR;
   BEGIN
      WRITE(' Press any key to continue ...');
      Proceed := READKEY;
      WRITELN; WRITELN
   END;
   BEGIN
      Choice := 0;
      Continue := ' '
   END;

PROCEDURE AddRecords;
   BEGIN
      WRITELN('The AddRecords procedure has run.')
   END;

PROCEDURE EditRecords;
   BEGIN
      WRITELN('The EditRecords procedure has run.')
   END;

PROCEDURE DisplayRecords;
   BEGIN
      WRITELN('The DisplayRecords procedure has run.')
   END;

PROCEDURE DeleteRecords;
   BEGIN
      WRITELN('The DeleteRecords procedure has run.')
   END;

PROCEDURE GetMenuChoice(VAR Choice : INTEGER);
   BEGIN
      WINDOW(26,5,75,24);
      WRITELN('   MASTER MENU');
      WRITELN('-------------------');
      WRITELN('1. Add Records');
      WRITELN('2. Edit Records');
      WRITELN('3. Display Records');
      WRITELN('4. Delete Records');
      WRITELN('5. Quit');
      WRITELN;
      WRITE('Enter your choice (1-5): ');
      READLN(Choice)
   END;
```

Listing 7.2: Using a CASE statement in place of nested IF statements.

```
PROCEDURE DoChoice(VAR Choice : INTEGER);
  BEGIN
    WRITELN;
    CASE Choice OF
         1 : AddRecords;
         2 : EditRecords;
         3 : DisplayRecords;
         4 : DeleteRecords;
         5 : Continue := Escape
         END;
    WRITELN
  END;


{ -------------------------------------------------------------- }
{                      MAIN BODY OF PROGRAM                       }
{ -------------------------------------------------------------- }
BEGIN
  Init(Choice,continue);
  WHILE Continue <> Escape DO
    BEGIN
      CLRSCR;
      GetMenuChoice(Choice);
      DoChoice(Choice);
      window(1,1,80,24);
      GoToXY(1,22);
      pause
    END
END.
```

Listing 7.2: Using a CASE statement in place of nested IF statements. (cont.)

```
{ ... etc. }

ELSE statement4

END;
```

This tells Turbo Pascal that if the variable has value 1, it should do statement 1; if it has value 2, do statement 2; and on to the end of the value list. If the variable doesn't have *any* of the values listed, the ELSE clause tells it to do statement 4. The ability to include an ELSE clause is fairly important, because if a control variable did not match any of the values in your CASE statement, your program could crash or, even worse, malfunction in a subtle way that you would not notice.

Listing 7.3 shows how to build some error-checking into your CASE statements, first with an IF..THEN..ELSE clause in standard Pascal, then with a CASE..ELSE clause in Turbo Pascal. When we arrive at the section on sets in Chapter 8, we will show how to create more sophisticated error-checking for *all* values entered by the user.

```
PROGRAM Listing7_3;

   { Demonstrates how to use an ELSE clause in a CASE statement. Also
     shows how to use an IF clause in standard Pascal to substitute
     for an ELSE clause. }

USES CRT;

VAR
   Choice1 : INTEGER;
   Choice2 : CHAR;

PROCEDURE Pause;
   VAR
      Proceed : CHAR;
   BEGIN
      WRITE(' Press any key to continue ...');
      Proceed := READKEY;
      WRITELN; WRITELN
   END;

PROCEDURE NumberChoice(VAR Choice1 : INTEGER);
   BEGIN
      CLRSCR;
      WRITE(' Enter your choice (1-10): ');
      READLN(Choice1);
      IF (Choice1 < 1) OR (Choice1 > 10)
         THEN WRITELN(' You dolt! You didn''t enter a valid choice.')
         ELSE CASE Choice1 OF
            1,2 : WRITELN(' Your choice was 1 or 2.');
            3..9: WRITELN(' Your choice was in the range 3..9.');
            10  : WRITELN(' Your choice was 10.')
            END;
      pause
   END;

PROCEDURE CharacterChoice(VAR Choice2 : CHAR);
   BEGIN
      CLRSCR;
      WRITE(' Enter your choice (A..Z, 0..9): ');
      READLN(Choice2);
      CASE Choice2 OF
         'A'     : WRITELN(' Your choice was the letter A.');
         'B','C' : WRITELN(' Your choice was B or C.');
         'D'..'Z' : WRITELN(' Your choice was in the range D..Z.');
         '0'..'9' : WRITELN(' You chose a digit from 0 to 9.')
         ELSE WRITELN(' You dolt! You didn''t enter a valid choice.')
      END;
      pause
   END;

   { ---------------------------------------------------------------- }
   (                        MAIN BODY OF PROGRAM                       )
   { ---------------------------------------------------------------- }
BEGIN
   NumberChoice(Choice1);
   CharacterChoice(Choice2)
END.
```

Listing 7.3: Building some error-checking into a CASE statement.

WHEN NOT TO USE CASE STATEMENTS

There is an important fact that you should remember about CASE statements: they are merely a convenient (and somewhat limited) shorthand for a series of nested IF statements. IF statements can do everything CASE statements can do. In fact, IF statements can do things that CASE statements *cannot* do.

For example, the following statements are perfectly legal with IF:

```
IF Name = 'Smith'

  THEN SendSmithLetter

  ELSE IF Name = 'Jones'

    THEN SendJonesLetter

    ELSE IF Name = 'Quayle'

      THEN SendQuayleLetter;


IF (Reading > 100) AND (Reading <= 200)

  THEN SoundAlarm

  ELSE IF (Reading > 200) AND (Reading <= 300)

    THEN Evacuate

    ELSE IF Reading > 300

      THEN Goodbye;


IF number1 = number2          { number1, 2, 3, and 4  }

  THEN DoRoutine1             { are integer variables }

  ELSE IF number1 = number3

    THEN DoRoutine2

    ELSE IF number1 = number4

      THEN DoRoutine3;
```

However, if you tried to code these statements with CASE, your program wouldn't compile. The first statement uses text strings to tell the program which way to go—and text strings *are not* an ordinal data type. The second statement tries to use greater than and less than operators; but **> 100** is neither a constant, a finite list of constants, nor a range of constants. The third statement tries to use variables as CASE selectors: however, the CASE selectors (as distinguished from the control variables) have to be constants.

So, in a nutshell, all of the following should be coded with IF..THEN..ELSE instead of CASE. *Do not* use a CASE statement in the following situations:

- When you need to use a nonordinal data type as the CASE selector, such as a text string.

- When you need to make a greater than or less than comparison with the CASE selector.

- When you need to use a variable as a CASE selector.

- When you might need to deal with a range of CASE selectors that is greater than 0..255.

WHILE..DO STATEMENTS

Like FOR statements, which were discussed in Chapter 6, WHILE..DO statements set up a loop that carries out a series of statements over and over. The key differences between WHILE and FOR statements are as follows:

- A FOR statement sets up a loop to run for a specified number of times. A WHILE statement, on the other hand, sets up a loop to run only while a certain condition is true. If the loop condition is never true, then the statements in the loop *never* execute at all.

- A FOR statement requires a counter variable. This counter variable has its value set by the FOR statement, so you do not need a separate step to set an initial value for the counter variable. A

WHILE statement does not require a counter variable, although it can use one to set the truth value of its loop condition.

- Although a WHILE statement does not require a counter variable, it does depend on the loop condition being true. If the WHILE statement is meant to run at least once, then the condition must be initialized so that it is true when the program arrives at the WHILE statement. In such circumstances, however, it may be better to use a REPEAT..UNTIL statement, which is discussed below.

- If the loop condition in a WHILE statement is initially true and never becomes false inside the loop, the WHILE statement will continue to execute forever unless you break out of the loop (by pressing Ctrl-Break or by rebooting your PC).

Thus, you should use a WHILE statement when you want a certain sequence of actions to be performed as long as a certain condition is true, but you are not sure exactly how long that condition will continue to be true. The general form of a WHILE statement is as follows:

```
WHILE (Boolean value of true) DO (loop statement);
```

The Boolean value of true that controls the WHILE loop can be anything that evaluates to a Boolean value of TRUE. This includes equals statements, comparisons, and, of course, the Boolean value of TRUE itself (though you probably would not use a naked Boolean value). Thus, the following are legal WHILE statements:

```
WHILE TRUE DO Readfile;


WHILE NOT EOF(MyFile) DO Readfile;


WHILE Name = 'Smith' DO
  BEGIN
  SmithCounter := SmithCounter + 1;
```

```
READLN(MyFile, Name)

END;


WHILE (1+5 > 17) DO

    WRITELN(' The laws of arithmetic are suspended.');


WHILE Continue <> Escape DO

DisplayMenu;
```

It is very important to make sure that the Boolean expression (loop condition) used by the WHILE statement is defined and meaningful *before* the program arrives at the WHILE statement. Note that this does not mean it has to be *true*—only that its variables and constants must have values, and that the Boolean expression must have a truth value.

Thus, for instance, if you hadn't assigned any value to **Continue** in the final example above, anything might happen. The memory address reserved for the value of **Continue** would probably contain garbage instead of meaningful information; and with a million-to-one shot, it could even have the exact configuration of garbage to look like **Escape**. In any event, you'd be in trouble. Therefore it is essential to observe the following procedures:

- Make sure that your program assigns appropriate values to variables used in WHILE statements before the WHILE statements are invoked in the program.

- Make sure that any constants used in the WHILE statement's Boolean expression are defined and of the correct type.

It is perfectly possible, of course, to use a WHILE statement as a substitute for a FOR loop, as shown in Listing 7.4. However, a FOR loop is both more economical (requiring fewer lines of code) and *safer* than a WHILE loop. It is better to reserve WHILE loops (and REPEAT..UNTIL loops) for times when you *are not* sure how long the loop will go on. Listing 7.5 shows how, if you know how many loops to make, a FOR loop needs fewer lines of code than a WHILE loop.

```
PROGRAM Listing7_4;

   ( Demonstrates use of a WHILE loop as a substitute for a FOR
     loop. In this case, a FOR loop is better. )

USES CRT;

VAR
   Counter : INTEGER;

PROCEDURE Pause;
   VAR
      Proceed : CHAR;
   BEGIN
      WRITE(' Press any key to continue ...');
      Proceed := READKEY;
      WRITELN; WRITELN
   END;

BEGIN
   Counter := 0;
   CLRSCR;
   WHILE Counter <= 15 DO
      BEGIN
      WRITELN(' The counter now equals ', Counter, '.');
      WRITELN;
      Counter := Counter + 1
      END;
      pause
END.
```

Listing 7.4: Building a WHILE loop where a FOR loop would be better.

AVOIDING ENDLESS LOOPS

I mentioned that FOR loops are safer than WHILE loops. That is because a FOR loop will always terminate eventually; but a WHILE loop can continue forever if you are not careful. Not only will this cause you to miss lunch—and dinner, and breakfast, until you die of starvation at your PC—but it tends to upset your friends, who think you should be out working for a living.

Listing 7.6 shows an unterminating WHILE loop. Look at it, study it, enjoy it, but *do not run it*. It sets up an endless loop because the WHILE condition never becomes false.

```
PROGRAM Listing7_5;

  ( Demonstrates how a FOR loop requires fewer lines of code than
    a WHILE loop when you know in advance how many loops to make. )

USES CRT;

VAR
  Counter : INTEGER;

PROCEDURE Pause;
  VAR
    Proceed : CHAR;
  BEGIN
    WRITE(' Press any key to continue ...');
    Proceed := READKEY;
    WRITELN; WRITELN
  END;

BEGIN
  CLRSCR;
  FOR Counter := 1 TO 15 DO
    BEGIN
    WRITELN(' The counter now equals ', Counter, '.');
    WRITELN;
    END;
    pause
END.
```

Listing 7.5: Listing 7.4 recorded with a FOR loop.

```
PROGRAM Listing7_6;

  ( DO NOT RUN THIS PROGRAM. SIMPLY STUDY IT TO SEE WHY
    THE LOOP NEVER TERMINATES. )

USES CRT;

VAR
  Counter : INTEGER;

BEGIN
  CLRSCR;
  Counter := 0;
  WHILE Counter <= 10 DO
    BEGIN
    WRITELN(' Going through the loop again!');
    WRITELN(' That''s ', Counter, ' times so far!');
    WRITELN;
    WRITELN(' Press Control-Break to exit.');
    DELAY(1000)
    END
END.
```

Listing 7.6: An unterminating WHILE loop.

Getting Out of Endless Loops

Normally, you should be able to exit from an endless loop, particularly if it is running in the Turbo Pascal IDE, by pressing Ctrl-Break. However, if you are using certain memory-resident programs on your PC (such as a disk cache), then getting stuck in the loop and trying to Ctrl-Break out of it can scramble your hard disk—as Listing 7.6 did to my hard disk when I tested it.

If you ever do get stuck in an endless loop, however, there are three different remedies you can apply, in this order:

- Press Ctrl-Break; if nothing happens, try it again.

- Try to warm boot your PC by pressing Ctrl-Alt-Delete. (If your PC has a warm boot button, press it.)

- Turn your PC off. Wait 30 seconds (allow the hard disk time to stop completely), then turn your PC back on again. At the DOS prompt, key in **chkdsk** to check your disk for problems.

WHEN AND WHEN NOT TO USE WHILE

You *should* use a WHILE statement when:

- You want a (simple or compound) statement to execute as long as a certain condition is true, but you are not sure how long that will be.

- You want to allow for the possibility that the loop condition will never be true and, therefore, the DO part of the WHILE statement will never execute.

You should *not* use a WHILE statement when:

- You know in advance (or the program can determine in advance) how many loops are needed. In that case, use a FOR statement.

- You need to make sure that the loop executes at least once. If the loop condition of a WHILE statement is false when the program

arrives at the WHILE statement, then the WHILE loop will
never execute.

REPEAT..UNTIL STATEMENTS

REPEAT..UNTIL statements are very similar to WHILE statements. In
both cases, you set up a loop that will run (or not run) depending on
whether a loop condition is true or false. The key differences are:

- In a WHILE statement, the loop continues to execute as long as
  a certain condition (the loop condition) is true. In a REPEAT
  statement, on the other hand, the loop executes as long as the
  loop condition is false—e.g., *until* it becomes true.

- In a WHILE statement, the loop condition is evaluated *before*
  you go through the loop, in order to determine whether or not
  you should go through the loop. On the other hand, in a
  REPEAT statement, the loop condition is not tested until *after*
  you go through the loop. As a result,

- In a REPEAT statement, your program will always go through
  the loop at least once.

The general form of a REPEAT statement is as follows:

```
REPEAT {loop statements} UNTIL

(Boolean value of true);
```

Unlike a WHILE loop, you can have multiple statements in a REPEAT
loop without having to make them into a single compound statement
with BEGIN and END. This is because Pascal needs some way to tell
where the statements in the WHILE loop are supposed to end, but in a
REPEAT statement, the keyword UNTIL marks the end of the loop:

```
WHILE counter <= 10 DO    { incorrect WHILE loop }

    statement;
```

```
statement;

statement;

{ ... Where does this WHILE statement end? You must
   use BEGIN and END so that WHILE is followed by a
   single statement. }


REPEAT

   statement;

   statement;

   statement

UNTIL Counter > 10;      { marks end of REPEAT loop }
```

The Boolean value that controls the loop can be anything that has a truth value. Thus, the following are legal REPEAT statements:

```
REPEAT UNTIL True;


REPEAT ReadName(MyFile) UNTIL EOF(MyFile);
{ read names until end of file }


REPEAT
NameCounter := NameCounter + 1;
READLN(MyFile, Name)
UNTIL Name = CHR(13);


REPEAT
   WRITELN(' The laws of arithmetic are suspended.')
   UNTIL (1+5 < 17);
```

```
REPEAT DisplayMenu UNTIL Continue = Escape;
```

WHEN AND WHEN NOT TO USE REPEAT

You *should* use a REPEAT statement when:

- You want a (simple or compound) statement to execute until a certain condition becomes true, but you are not sure how long it will take.

- You want to make sure that your program goes through the loop at least once no matter what.

You should *not* use a REPEAT statement when:

- You know in advance (or the program can determine in advance) how many loops are needed. In that case, use a FOR statement.

- There are circumstances under which the program should *not* go through the loop even one time. In that situation, use a WHILE statement instead of REPEAT.

GOTO STATEMENTS

Among structured programming purists, the GOTO statement is the black sheep of Pascal statements. It lets you jump directly from one line of your program to another without using structured programming methods. If you are taking a course in Pascal, you would be well-advised to avoid GOTO statements—they could hurt your grade!

In practical programming situations, however, there are some cases in which GOTO offers a reasonable way to solve a problem. These are usually exit-if-error types of situations. For example, in the middle of its run, your program might find that a necessary file is nowhere to be found! Then, you could (but would not have to) use a GOTO statement to jump to the end and terminate the program or subroutine, as shown in Listing 7.7. Listing 7.8

shows how you would prompt the user for a different filename.

The general form of a GOTO statement, as you can see, is

```
GOTO <label>;
```

where **<label>** is a line identifier that you declared in the LABEL section of the program (see Chapter 3).

There are very definite limitations on GOTO in Turbo Pascal to prevent it from being used indiscriminately. In particular, you cannot use GOTO to jump out of the current code block. This means that if you are inside a subroutine, you can jump only to another place inside that subroutine; you cannot jump out of it to another subroutine, nor can you jump to the main body of the program.

```
PROGRAM Listing7_7;

USES CRT;

LABEL GetOut;              ( Line label to GOTO in case of error. )

VAR
  Name   : STRING[10];
  MyFile : TEXT;           ( Declares a file variable to use in
                             opening a text file. )

PROCEDURE Pause;
  VAR
    Proceed : CHAR;
  BEGIN
    WRITE(' Press any key to continue ...');
    Proceed := READKEY;
    WRITELN; WRITELN
  END;


BEGIN
  ASSIGN(MyFile, 'students.txt');
  ($I-)                    ( Turn off input checking. )
  RESET(MyFile);
  ($I+)                    ( Turn input checking back on. )
  IF IORESULT <> 0
    THEN GOTO GetOut
    ELSE BEGIN
         WRITELN(' The file is there!');
         READLN(MyFile, Name)
         END;
  pause;

GetOut: END.
```

Listing 7.7: Using GOTO to jump out of an error situation.

```
PROGRAM Listing7_8;

   ( Shows how to prompt the user for a different filename if
     the initial attempt to open a file doesn't work. )

USES CRT;

TYPE
   String10 = STRING[10];
   String12 = STRING[12];

VAR
   Name     : String10;
   NewFileName : String12;
   MyFile : TEXT;          ( Declares a file variable to use in
                             opening a text file. )

( ------------------------------ )
( MAIN-LEVEL PROCEDURE DECLARATION )
( ------------------------------ )
PROCEDURE Pause;
   VAR
      Proceed : CHAR;
   BEGIN
      WRITE(' Press any key to continue ...');
      Proceed := READKEY;
      WRITELN; WRITELN
   END;


( ------------------------------ )
( MAIN-LEVEL PROCEDURE DECLARATION )
( ------------------------------ )
PROCEDURE EnterNewFile(VAR NewFileName : string12;
                       VAR MyFile : text);
   BEGIN
      WRITELN;
      WRITELN(' That file can''t be opened!');
      WRITE(' Please enter a new filename or press <Enter> to exit: ');
      READLN(NewFileName);
      IF NewFileName = ''   ( If the user only pressed Enter )
         THEN Halt          ( then halt the program.        )
         ELSE BEGIN
              ASSIGN(MyFile, NewFileName);  ( assign new filename )
              {$I-}
              RESET(Myfile);                ( try to open file )
              {$I+}
              IF IORESULT = 0      ( was file opened okay? )
                 THEN BEGIN
                      WRITELN(' File opened successfully!');
                      CLOSE(MyFile)  ( Must close all open files  )
                      END            ( before the program ends.   ) .
                 ELSE Halt
              END
   END;

( ---------------------------------------------------------------- )
(                       MAIN BODY OF PROGRAM                        )
( ---------------------------------------------------------------- )
BEGIN
   CLRSCR;
```

Listing 7.8: Allowing the user to try again in an error situation.

```
    ASSIGN(MyFile, 'students.txt');
    ($I-)                 ( Turn off input checking. )
    RESET(MyFile);
    ($I+)                 ( Turn input checking back on. )
    IF IORESULT <> 0      ( If file-open wasn't a success )
      THEN EnterNewFile(NewFileName, MyFile)
      ELSE BEGIN
           WRITELN(' The file is there!');
           READLN(MyFile, Name);
           CLOSE(MyFile);   ( must close file before program ends. )
           END;
    pause;

END.
```

Listing 7.8: Allowing the user to try again in an error situation. (cont.)

GOTO is pretty much your only option in standard Pascal, but Turbo Pascal provides two other commands that permit you to make jumps: EXIT and HALT. EXIT jumps you out of the current subroutine and returns you to the next line in the calling program or subroutine. HALT, on the other hand, stops the program completely and returns you to DOS. Listing 7.9 shows how you could use HALT instead of GOTO in a situation where you want to password-protect your program.

COMPILER DIRECTIVES

As the name suggests, *compiler directives* are statements in your program that tell the compiler to do things in a certain way. You have already seen one compiler directive in Listing 7.7: there, we used {$I-} to turn off input/output (I/O) checking before we tried to open a nonexistent file, and then we used {$I+} to turn I/O checking back on again before proceeding with the program.

If we had not turned off I/O checking, then the program would have stopped with a run-time error when it tried to open the file. Turning off I/O checking, however, allowed us to handle the situation in a more controlled way. By checking the built-in variable *IORESULT*, which equals zero if the previous I/O operation was a success, we were able to tell if the file had been opened properly. Then, we either could shut down

```
PROGRAM Listing7_9;

  { Shows how to use HALT in place of GOTO. }

USES CRT;

TYPE
  String10 = STRING[10];

CONST
   ThePassword = 'frankcapra';

VAR
  Password: String10;

PROCEDURE Pause;
  VAR
    Proceed : CHAR;
  BEGIN
    WRITE(' Press any key to continue ...');
    Proceed := READKEY;
    WRITELN; WRITELN
  END;


PROCEDURE GetPassword(VAR Password : string10);
  BEGIN
    CLRSCR;
    WRITE(' Please enter the password: ');
    READLN(Password);
    IF Password <> ThePassword
       THEN HALT                     ( unauthorized access! )
  END;


BEGIN
  GetPassword(Password);
  WRITELN(' Congratulations! You know the password!');
  pause
END.
```

Listing 7.9: Using HALT instead of GOTO.

the program or give the user an opportunity to specify another file.

The compiler directives that you can use, and how you must set them up, are determined by the Pascal compiler you are using. Turbo Pascal, for instance, has different compiler directives than Vax Pascal.

Normally, Turbo Pascal compiles your program with certain default settings: I/O and stack checking are ON, range checking is OFF, Debug Information is ON, and complete Boolean evaluation is OFF. Some of these default settings are shown in Figure 7.1, which shows the compiler options dialog box from the Options menu. If you change the settings in this dialog box (and save your changes with the Save Options choice in the Options menu), then the new settings will apply to all of your Turbo Pascal programs until you change the settings again.

Compiler directives, however, allow you to change the default settings and have your changes apply only to a particular program—even just to one part of a particular program, as shown in Listing 7.7. A compiler directive is a special kind of comment that *is not* ignored by Turbo Pascal. It begins with a left curly bracket, then a dollar sign, then the name of the directive, and finally it closes with a right curly bracket, as we saw in the {$I-} and {$I+} compiler directives discussed above.

There are three kinds of compiler directives: *switch directives*, which turn a particular compiler option ON or OFF (as with I/O checking); *parameter directives*, which specify values that affect how the program is compiled (such as the size of the heap; see Chapter 11); and *conditional directives*, which tell Turbo Pascal how to handle "conditional compilation" of parts of your program.

There are quite a few compiler directives; here are the ones you are most likely to need often:

- {$I-} and {$I+}: The first turns input checking off, the second turns it back on again. Input checking will stop your program if

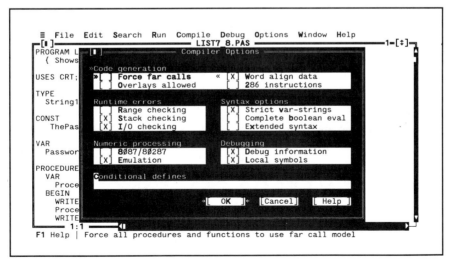

Figure 7.1: The Compiler Options dialog box.

it attempts to open a file that is not there, or if it expects a certain kind of input (for example, an integer) but receives something else (such as a letter). Turning off input checking allows you to anticipate these situations and to build some sophisticated error-trapping into your program.

- {$R-} and {$R+}: The first turns range checking off, the second turns it back on again. When you compile your program, Turbo Pascal normally will not check to see if (for example) you tried to assign a negative number to a BYTE-type variable (legal range 0..255), or if you have referred somewhere to the 101st slot in a 100-slot array variable. This type of error can come out and clobber you (with unpredictable results) when you try to run the program. It is a good idea to turn range checking ON at least while you are developing and debugging your program. You do this by putting the compiler directive {$R+} at the beginning of your program. Then, when you are certain that everything is working properly, you can turn it back OFF by deleting the {$R+} before your final compilation; this will make your .EXE file slightly smaller.

- {$S+} and {$S-}: The first turns stack-overflow checking ON, the second turns it OFF. Normally, Turbo Pascal operates with stack-overflow checking ON. The *stack* is an area of your PC's memory that Turbo Pascal uses to store variables and the addresses of subroutines. If you have a lot of subroutine calls and local variables, the amount of memory required can exceed the available stack space—particularly if you have made an error somewhere and your program is spinning out of control. With stack-overflow checking ON, the program will halt with a run-time error if it exceeds the available stack space; with stack-overflow checking OFF, the program will crash, with unpredictable results.

AN ERROR-CHECKING
SUBSTITUTE FOR READLN

We've seen in Listing 7.7 that the compiler directive to turn off I/O checking (and turn it on again) can be used to trap errors when opening files. Let's use it to create a generally more useful error-trapping routine: **GetGoodInt**.

It is sad but true that we all make errors at the keyboard. We mean to press one key but press another: a letter instead of a number, for example. Computer programs are extremely unforgiving of even the slightest mistake. Any of the following can cause a run-time error that will halt our program:

- Entering a letter when the program expects a number. For example, we might have an integer variable *Choice* and get input from the keyboard by READLN(*Choice*). If you enter a number, the program will halt because it expected an integer and it got a letter. I/O checking will not allow this, but at the same time, we cannot simply allow a letter get through to the program—that could result in consequences that would be even worse!

- Entering a number that is outside the range the program expects. We may have set up a CASE statement that expects to get a number from 1 to 4. We've seen how to build error-checking into a CASE statement with ELSE and IF..THEN..ELSE, but it would be even better if we could trap the errors before they ever get to the CASE statement.

Listing 7.10 shows what can happen when we use a naked READLN statement to get input from the keyboard. Enter and run this program, but instead of keying in a number from 1 to 4 at the menu prompt, type a letter instead. The result is shown in Figure 7.2.

Even if you protect your CASE statement with an ELSE (or IF clause), the program will still stop if you enter something that is the wrong data type for the variable in the READLN statement. To protect against these kinds of errors, we need something more sophisticated—and we need to use the I/O checking compiler directive to let us get the input and to handle it without errors.

Before we start coding, we need to have a clear idea of what we are trying to accomplish. We want to create an input routine that will do the following:

- Get integer input from the keyboard, just like a READLN statement with an integer variable.

```
PROGRAM Listing7_10;

  { Demonstrates potential problems that can arise if we don't
    have an error-trapping input routine. }

USES CRT;

CONST
   Escape = CHR(27);

VAR
  Choice : INTEGER;
  Continue : CHAR;


{ ============= UTILITY ROUTINES FOR THE PROGRAM =============== }

{ ------------------------------- }
{ MAIN-LEVEL PROCEDURE DECLARATION }
{ ------------------------------- }
PROCEDURE Pause;
  VAR
    Proceed : CHAR;
  BEGIN
    WRITE(' Press any key to continue ...');
    Proceed := READKEY;
    WRITELN; WRITELN
  END;


{ ------------------------------- }
{ MAIN-LEVEL PROCEDURE DECLARATION }
{ ------------------------------- }
PROCEDURE Init(VAR Choice: INTEGER; VAR Continue : CHAR);
  BEGIN
  CLRSCR;
  Choice := 0;
  Continue := ' '
  END;


{ ------------------------------- }
{ MAIN-LEVEL PROCEDURE DECLARATION }
{ ------------------------------- }
PROCEDURE AddRecords;
  BEGIN
  WRITELN;
  WRITELN(' The AddRecords routine has run.');
  WRITELN;
  pause
  END;


{ ------------------------------- }
{ MAIN-LEVEL PROCEDURE DECLARATION }
{ ------------------------------- }
PROCEDURE EditRecords;
  BEGIN
  WRITELN;
  WRITELN(' The EditRecords routine has run.');
  WRITELN;
  pause
  END;
```

Listing 7.10: READLN gives no protection against run-time errors.

```
( ------------------------------- )
( MAIN-LEVEL PROCEDURE DECLARATION )
( ------------------------------- )
PROCEDURE DisplayRecords;
  BEGIN
  WRITELN;
  WRITELN(' The DisplayRecords routine has run.');
  WRITELN;
  pause
  END;


( ------------------------------- )
( MAIN-LEVEL PROCEDURE DECLARATION )
( ------------------------------- )
PROCEDURE Displaymenu(VAR Choice : INTEGER);
  BEGIN
    CLRSCR;
    WRITELN; WRITELN;
    WRITELN('       MAIN MENU');
    WRITELN('       ---------');
    WRITELN('       1. Add Records');
    WRITELN('       2. Edit Records');
    WRITELN('       3. Display Records');
    WRITELN('       4. Quit');
    WRITELN;
    WRITE('        Enter your choice (1-4): ');
    READLN(Choice)
  END;


( ------------------------------- )
( MAIN-LEVEL PROCEDURE DECLARATION )
( ------------------------------- )
PROCEDURE DoChoice(VAR Choice : INTEGER);
  BEGIN
    CASE Choice OF
        1 : AddRecords;
        2 : EditRecords;
        3 : DisplayRecords;
        4 : Continue := Escape
        END
  END;


( --------------------------------------------------------------- )
(                        MAIN BODY OF PROGRAM                      )
( --------------------------------------------------------------- )
BEGIN
  Init(choice, continue);
  REPEAT
    DisplayMenu(choice);
    DoChoice(choice)
  UNTIL Continue = Escape;
  CLRSCR
END.
```

Listing 7.10: READLN gives no protection against run-time errors. (cont.)

```
 ≡  File  Edit  Search  Run  Compile  Debug  Options  Window  Help
┌[▪]─────────────── LIST7_9.PAS ─────────────────1─[‡]─┐
│Error 106: Invalid numeric format.                     │
│    WRITELN; WRITELN;                                   █
│    WRITELN('          MAIN MENU');                     █
│    WRITELN('          ---------');                     █
│    WRITELN('          1. Add Records');                █
│    WRITELN('          2. Edit Records');               █
│    WRITELN('          3. Display Records');            █
│    WRITELN('          4. Quit');                       █
│    WRITELN;                                            █
│    WRITE('          Enter your choice (1-4): ');       █
│    READLN(Choice)                                      █
│  END;                                                  █
│                                                        █
│                                                        █
│( ------------------------------- )                     █
│( MAIN-LEVEL PROCEDURE DECLARATION )                    █
│( ------------------------------- )                     █
│PROCEDURE DoChoice(VAR Choice : INTEGER);               █
│  BEGIN                                                 █
│    CASE Choice OF                                      █
│         1 : AddRecords;                                █
└──── 90:1 ────◄▯──────────────────────────────────────►┘
 F1 Help  F2 Save  F5 Open  Alt-F9 Compile  F9 Make  F10 Menu
```

Figure 7.2: Run-time error caused by entering an unexpected data type.

- Take *any* input character from the user and inspect it before passing it to the integer variable.

- Check to make sure that the input character is the correct data type; i.e., that it is an integer.

- Check to make sure that the input integer is in the acceptable range—in this case, that it is an integer from 1 to 4.

- If the input character *is not* the correct data type or *is not* in the acceptable range, then blank the screen where the user typed the character and continue to display the prompt.

This is what the **GetGoodInt** procedure in Listing 7.11 does. It uses a few Turbo Pascal features that we have not covered yet, but here is how it works. After we've used WRITE to prompt the user for a number between 1 and 4, we call **GetGoodInt** just as we would normally call READLN. The difference is that with READLN, we specify only the variable that gets the input value.

With **GetGoodInt**, on the other hand, we specify the minimum acceptable value, the maximum acceptable value, and the variable, in that order. If the user tries to enter something that is not an integer, or is not between

```
PROGRAM Listing7_11;

USES CRT;

CONST
   Escape = CHR(27);

VAR
  Choice : INTEGER;
  Continue : CHAR;


( ============== UTILITY ROUTINES FOR THE PROGRAM ============== )

( ------------------------------- )
( MAIN-LEVEL PROCEDURE DECLARATION )
( ------------------------------- )
PROCEDURE Pause;
  VAR
    Proceed : CHAR;
  BEGIN
    WRITE(' Press any key to continue ...');
    Proceed := READKEY;
    WRITELN; WRITELN
  END;


( ------------------------------- )
( MAIN-LEVEL PROCEDURE DECLARATION )
( ------------------------------- )
PROCEDURE GetGoodInt(MinNum, MaxNum: INTEGER;  VAR InNum: INTEGER);

 ( An error-trapping substitute for "readln" to get integer
   input from the keyboard. This procedure takes two parameters:
   a set of "acceptable" integers for input, and a variable
   parameter that is the actual integer input.  If the input
   integer is not in the set of acceptable integers, this
   procedure returns to the original screen position and waits
   for the user to enter an acceptable integer. )

  VAR
    markX, markY  : BYTE;
    LoopControl   : INTEGER;
  BEGIN
    REPEAT
      markX := whereX;     ( mark cursor location )
      markY := whereY;

      {$I-}                ( I/O checking off )
      Readln(InNum);       ( Get character from keyboard )
      {$I+}                ( I/O checking back on )

    LoopControl := ioresult; ( Was input a "Good Integer"? )

    IF (LoopControl <> 0) THEN  ( if not integer type )
      BEGIN
      gotoXY(markX, markY);      ( return to orig. cursor pos. )
      ClrEOL                     ( clear to end of line        )
      END;

    IF (inNum < MinNum) or (inNum > MaxNum) THEN ( not in range )
      BEGIN
      gotoXY(markX, markY); ( returns to original cursor pos. )
      ClrEOL                ( clears to end of line           )
      END
```

Listing 7.11: Creating the GetGoodInt procedure as an error-trapping substitute for READLN.

```
      until (LoopControl = 0) { correct data type entered }
            and (InNum >= MinNum) and (InNum <= MaxNum)
                              { number entered in acceptable range }
   END;


   { ------------------------------ }
   { MAIN-LEVEL PROCEDURE DECLARATION }
   { ------------------------------ }
   PROCEDURE Init(VAR Choice: INTEGER; VAR Continue : CHAR);
     BEGIN
     CLRSCR;
     Choice := 0;
     Continue := ' '
     END;


   { ------------------------------ }
   { MAIN-LEVEL PROCEDURE DECLARATION }
   { ------------------------------ }
   PROCEDURE AddRecords;
     BEGIN
     WRITELN;
     WRITELN(' The AddRecords routine has run.');
     WRITELN;
     pause
     END;

   { ------------------------------ }
   { MAIN-LEVEL PROCEDURE DECLARATION }
   { ------------------------------ }
   PROCEDURE EditRecords;
     BEGIN
     WRITELN;
     WRITELN(' The EditRecords routine has run.');
     WRITELN;
     pause
     END;

   { ------------------------------ }
   { MAIN-LEVEL PROCEDURE DECLARATION }
   { ------------------------------ }
   PROCEDURE DisplayRecords;
     BEGIN
     WRITELN;
     WRITELN(' The DisplayRecords routine has run.');
     WRITELN;
     pause
     END;


   { ------------------------------ }
   { MAIN-LEVEL PROCEDURE DECLARATION }
   { ------------------------------ }
   PROCEDURE Displaymenu(VAR Choice : INTEGER);
     BEGIN
       CLRSCR;
       WRITELN; WRITELN;
       WRITELN('        MAIN MENU');
       WRITELN('        ---------');
       WRITELN('        1. Add Records');
       WRITELN('        2. Edit Records');
       WRITELN('        3. Display Records');
```

Listing 7.11: Creating the GetGoodInt procedure as an error-trapping substitute for READLN. (cont.)

```
      WRITELN('          4. Quit');
      WRITELN;
      WRITE('          Enter your choice (1-4): ');
      GetGoodInt(1,4,Choice)
    END;


( ------------------------------ )
( MAIN-LEVEL PROCEDURE DECLARATION )
( ------------------------------ )
PROCEDURE DoChoice(VAR Choice : INTEGER);
  BEGIN
    CASE Choice OF
         1 : AddRecords;
         2 : EditRecords;
         3 : DisplayRecords;
         4 : Continue := Escape
         END
  END;


( ---------------------------------------------------------- )
(                     MAIN BODY OF PROGRAM                    )
( ---------------------------------------------------------- )
BEGIN
  Init(choice, continue);
  REPEAT
    DisplayMenu(choice);
    DoChoice(choice)
  UNTIL Continue = Escape;
  CLRSCR
END.
```

Listing 7.11: Creating the GetGoodInt procedure as an error-trapping
substitute for READLN. (cont.)

the minimum and maximum values (inclusive), then **GetGoodInt** will
erase what the user typed and sit there, waiting patiently for valid input.

Notice one other important thing about Listing 7.1. As soon as we
checked the data type of the input item with IORESULT, we assigned the
value of IORESULT to the *LoopControl* variable and used *LoopControl*
for all other tests. The reason for doing this is that the value of IORESULT
changes as soon as your program does another operation, such as comparing it to zero. Thus, the only way to use the value of IORESULT in succes-
sive program statements is to assign it to another variable *immediately* after
the I/O operation you are using IORESULT to test.

We will use **GetGoodInt** often in later chapters. In the next chapter, we
will create an error-trapping routine for getting character input. It is not
easy, but you now possess the knowledge and skills to do it.

SUMMARY

Pascal provides more flexible program control statements to handle more complex situations. CASE statements allow the program to branch in one of several directions depending on the value of a variable. Strictly speaking, IF statements can do anything that CASE statements can do, but CASE statements are often much easier to code and understand. CASE statements, however, are limited in some ways that IF statements are not.

WHILE statements cause a series of program actions (embodied in a single compound statement) to repeat until the condition in the WHILE statement becomes false. If the condition is false when the WHILE statement is reached in the program, then the WHILE loop will never execute.

REPEAT statements are similar to WHILE statements, but they cause a series of program actions to repeat until a certain condition becomes true. A REPEAT loop will always execute at least once. WHILE and REPEAT loops should be used instead of FOR when the number of loops that will be needed is not known in advance.

GOTO statements allow the program to jump from one place to another within a given block of code. They should be used sparingly and only when no other solution makes sense.

Compiler directives are a special type of program comment that allow you to give direct instructions to Pascal on how the program should be compiled.

REVIEW EXERCISES

1. What are the main advantages of CASE statements? The main disadvantages? How do they differ from IF..THEN..ELSE statements?

2. What is wrong with the following code fragment?

```
VAR
     choice, QuitNum : integer;
```

```
BEGIN
      WRITE(' Enter a "quit" value for the menu: ');
      READLN(QuitNum);
      { ... Display a menu on the screen }
      WRITE(' Enter your choice (1/2/3): ');
      READLN(choice);
      CASE choice OF
            1 : DoFirstThing;
            2 : DoSecondThing;
            3 : DoThirdThing;
            QuitNum : Halt;
      ELSE WRITELN(' Error: nonmatching choice.')
            END;
      { ... etc. }
```

3. Explain when and when not to use a CASE statement.

4. Explain the key differences between FOR and WHILE statements.

5. Write a simple program to perform each of the following tasks:

   (a) Prompt the user to enter five numbers in a five-slot array.

   (b) Run a loop that will display a menu and get the user's choice as long as the user does not enter 'Q' for 'Quit'.

6. Explain three potential pitfalls of WHILE loops, as well as how to avoid them.

7. Is there anything wrong with the following code fragment? If so, what is it? What would happen if you ran it? How could you fix it?

```
Continue := 'Y';
WHILE UPCASE(Continue) = 'Y' DO
     BEGIN
       WRITELN(' This is a WHILE loop.');
       WRITELN(' It executes while a certain');
       WRITELN(' condition remains true.')
     END;
     WRITE(' Run the loop again (Y/N)? ');
     READLN(Continue);
```

8. Explain when you should and should not use WHILE loops.

9. Explain the key differences between WHILE and REPEAT statements.

10. Will the following code compile and run? If there is an error, what is it? (Some errors will compile and run.)

```
Continue := ' ';
REPEAT
    BEGIN
    WRITELN(' This is a REPEAT loop.');
    WRITELN(' It runs until a certain
condition');
    WRITELN(' becomes false.');
    WRITE(' Run the loop again (Y/N)? ');
    READLN(Continue);
    END
UNTIL UPCASE(Continue) <> 'Y';
```

11. Explain when you should and should not use REPEAT statements.

12. Is there anything wrong with the following code fragment? If so, what would happen and how would you fix the problem?

```
LABEL 100;
PROCEDURE DoingSomething;
  VAR age : INTEGER;
  BEGIN
    WRITE(' Enter your age: ');
    READLN(age);
    IF age >= 18
      THEN WRITELN(' You''re officially an
adult!');
        ELSE GOTO 100
      END;
  100: WRITELN(' You''re officially still a kid!');
```

13. Explain the three different kinds of compiler directives in Turbo Pascal.

14. Explain what happens when range and stack checking are on; when they are off.

15. What is IORESULT, how does it work, and what can you use it for?

Structured and User-Defined Data Types

*Information that is to be processed,
in some sense, represents an* abstraction
of the real world.

—Niklaus Wirth, *Algorithms + Data Structures = Programs*

In Chapter 6, we looked at simple data types, such as text strings and numbers. These data types are not only simple, they are also predefined in Turbo Pascal, so you do not need to set them up in each program yourself.

In this chapter, we will discuss some more complex data types. These, in addition to being complex, are data types that you define for yourself. Far from being an extra burden, this gives you a great deal of flexibility to make your Pascal program work the way *you* want it to—whether or not your ideas agree with the ideas that are built into the language.

ABSTRACT DATA TYPES

Before I begin our discussion about particular data types, I need to make a very important point. Pascal lets you create complex data types—often called data structures—in some fairly specific ways. For example, it has a built-in data type called ARRAY that allows you to set up lists and tables (as well as other structures) to hold a fixed number of items of a given type. The items can be integers, characters, strings, records, pointers, objects, or even other arrays.

The important point is that you must keep two concepts separate. There is a clear distinction between an *idea* and its *implementation* as in:

1. The idea of a fixed-length list that holds items of a particular type, and

2. The specific way that fixed-length lists are implemented in Pascal and the specific words used to describe them.

The idea of a fixed-length list is called an *abstract data type*. Fixed-length lists can be implemented in many different ways, not all of them having anything to do with the word ARRAY, which is the data type normally used to create them in Pascal. In Pascal, you can set up a fixed-length list by creating the list type in the TYPE section and then declaring a variable of that type in the VAR section, as in the following:

```
TYPE
    Student = RECORD
                Name : STRING[10];
                GPA  : REAL;
                Probation : BOOLEAN
                END;
        { creates a data type for student records }


    StudentList = ARRAY[1..100] of Student;
        { creates a data type for listing student records }


    NumberList = ARRAY[1..50] of INTEGER;
        { creates a data type for listing integers }


VAR
    Enrollment    : StudentList;
        { creates a list to hold 100 student records }


    Top50         : NumberList;
        { creates a list to hold 50 integers }
    UnitedStates : ARRAY[1..50] OF STRING[15];
        { creates a list to hold 50 15-character strings }
```

(Note that you don't absolutely have to declare an ARRAY data type in the TYPE section. As with the *UnitedStates* variable above, you can simply declare an ARRAY variable in the VAR section.)

In BASIC, however, you create an array with a DIM (dimension) statement, as in the following:

```
TYPE Student

    Name AS STRING * 10

    GPA AS SINGLE

    Probation AS INTEGER

END TYPE

; Creates a data type for student records


DIM StudentList(1 TO 100) AS STUDENT

; Creates a list variable to hold 100 student
records
```

Although these BASIC data structures are usually referred to as arrays, the word ARRAY is not part of the BASIC language. In addition, BASIC allows you to create what are called dynamic arrays that are, in fact, *variable*-length arrays—an idea that is almost a self-contradiction in Pascal.

The bottom line is this: *Do not be misled* into thinking that the way a programming language implements an idea is the only way to do it—or that the *idea* has some necessary connection with the *words* used to describe it in a particular language. By keeping these distinctions in mind, you will gain two important benefits:

1. You will understand what you are *actually doing* when you set up data types, instead of doing everything just by rote. This is more fun, makes you a better programmer, and (in class work) gets you a better grade.

2. You will see that there are different ways to accomplish the same thing. For example, in Chapter 11, we will create variable-length

lists by using pointers. However, you also can create a variable-length list by using several arrays. If you think you can only create a variable-length list by using pointers, then you will be helpless if you ever need to create variable-length lists in a language that does not have pointers, such as BASIC or FORTRAN. But if you keep the clear distinction in your mind between an idea and its implementation, then you will be able to handle such situations with the confidence that comes when you know what you are really doing.

ARRAYS

With that rather philosophical introduction, let's begin with Pascal's ARRAY data type, which is ideally suited to handling fixed-length lists.

The best way to think of an array is as a sort of "rack" having a predetermined number of slots that can hold items of a certain type (see Figure 8.1). It is similar to a compact disc or cassette tape rack. You create an array data type by using the Pascal word ARRAY, indicating the number of slots in the array, and indicating the type of items that will go into the slots of the array. You refer to the individual slots of the array by combining the name of the array variable with the slot index (usually a number).

You can declare an array type in the TYPE section of your program as follows:

```
TYPE
     MyList = ARRAY[m..n] OF <slot type>
```

where:

- **MyList** is the name of the new data type you are declaring.

- **M** and **n** are members of an ordinal type (called the *index type* for the array), with **m** lower than **n**. They can be any ordinal data type, including characters, integers, and Boolean values. Normally, you will use a subrange of the full data type, e.g.,

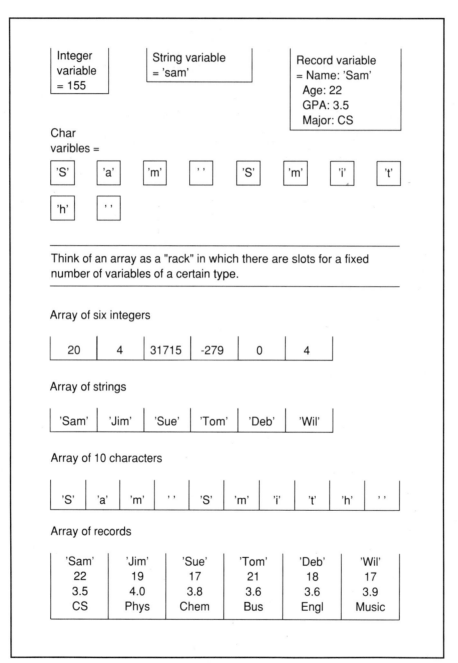

Figure 8.1: Individual variables vs. arrays.

instead of using all integers (which is too many), you will use [1..10], [0..999], or [50..59]. Note that [1..10] and [50..59] both define a 10-slot array; the only difference is in the indexes by which you refer to the slots. You also can use enumerated types that you have defined yourself (e.g., **ARRAY[Sun..Sat]**).

- **M** and **n** must be constants; they cannot be variables. The size of the array is determined when the program is compiled, and if you try to use a variable as the upper or lower bound of the array indexes, Pascal cannot determine the size of the array.

- The **<slot type>** is the type of item that you intend to hold in the array. This can be any legal data type except a file or a stream (the object-oriented counterpart of a file).

Thus, the following are all valid array types:

```
TYPE
     MyList = ARRAY[1..100] OF STRING[10];


     ToDoItems = ARRAY[1..10] OF STRING[15];

     Days = (Sun, Mon, Tue, Wed, Thu, Fri, Sat);

     Week = ARRAY[Sun..Sat] OF ToDoItems;


     CapLetters = ARRAY['A'..'Z'] OF CHAR;
```

DECLARING ARRAY VARIABLES

It is important to remember—and easy to forget—that simply *declaring* an array data type does not create any arrays. Thus, if you attempted to put something into **MyList** (above), such as

```
MyList[55] := 'Sam';
```

your program would not compile, because the **MyList** declaration in the TYPE section only defines a data type: it does not create any members of that type. We can define the *concepts* of unicorns and gryphons, but it doesn't automatically mean that there *are* any of them. In the same way, before you can use an array type, you have to represent the idea as a concrete instance of the variable in the VAR section.

Strictly speaking, with most array variables, you do not have to declare the array type in the TYPE section of your program. This is because ARRAY is a predefined type in Pascal, and you are just specifying how big it is and what it will hold. Thus, the following two code fragments are equivalent:

```
TYPE

   MyList : ARRAY[1..10] of STRING[10];

VAR

   NameList : MyList;
```

and

```
VAR

   NameList : ARRAY[1..10] OF STRING[10];
```

However, if you ever want to pass an array variable to a subroutine (as you will very often need to do), then you *do* have to declare the type in your TYPE section. A parameter that you pass to a subroutine has to be of a predefined type, so you could not write something like

```
PROCEDURE AddName(VAR NameList : ARRAY[1..10] OF
STRING[10]);
```

Instead, you have to use a type that is either predefined in Pascal or declared in the TYPE section of your program, as in

```
TYPE

   MyList = ARRAY[1..10] OF STRING[10];

{ ... etc. }
```

```
PROCEDURE AddName(VAR NameList : MyList);

{ ... etc. }
```

You refer to individual elements of an array by combining the name of the array with the index of the particular slot, such as

```
VAR

  NameList : ARRAY[1..10] OF STRING[10];

BEGIN

  NameList[1] := 'Bill';  { assigns 'Bill' to slot 1 }

  WRITELN(' Name in slot 1 is ', NameList[1], '.');

END;
```

Arrays make our programs neater, faster, and easier to understand. For example, we could keep the names of students in a programming class in separate string variables as in Listing 8.1; however, arrays permit us to keep the names all together in a single list, as in Listing 8.2.

There are several things to notice about Listing 8.2. First, the array should be initialized. Second, because the array will hold only a predetermined number of items, we need to test it to make sure that it is not already full.

INITIALIZING ARRAYS

When Pascal sets up an array variable, it reserves an area of your PC's memory to hold the variable, i.e., the array and the values in its slots. This memory area could contain almost anything, so it is important to initialize an array before you use it. This means putting an *empty* value into all the slots so that you can tell which slots are empty and which are occupied. It doesn't really matter what value you use for empty, as long as (1) it is something that cannot be mistaken for any of the values that eventually will be put into the slots, and (2) it is the right data type to fit into the array's slots.

Thus, in Listing 8.2, the array holds 10-character strings. To initialize the array, we used a FOR loop to assign an empty value of a space character to

```
PROGRAM Listing8_1;

  ( Using separate string variables for the items in a list.)

USES CRT;

TYPE
  String10 = STRING[10];

VAR
  Student1,
  Student2,
  Student3,
  Student4,
  Student5      : String10;

PROCEDURE Pause;
  VAR
    Proceed : CHAR;
  BEGIN
    WRITE(' Press any key to continue ...');
    Proceed := READKEY;
    WRITELN; WRITELN
  END;


BEGIN
  Student1 := 'Jim';
  Student2 := 'Tammy';
  Student3 := 'Oral';
  Student4 := 'Billy';
  Student5 := 'Elmer';

  CLRSCR;
  WRITELN(' The name of student # 1 is ', Student1, '.');
  WRITELN(' The name of student # 2 is ', Student2, '.');
  WRITELN(' The name of student # 3 is ', Student3, '.');
  WRITELN(' The name of student # 4 is ', Student4, '.');
  WRITELN(' The name of student # 5 is ', Student5, '.');
  pause
END.
```

Listing 8.1: Student names in string variables.

each slot. This enabled us, in the **EnterStudentName** subroutine, to find the first empty slot for a new student name, or to determine that the array was full. If the array had been set up to hold integers instead of strings, we might have used '0' to fill all the slots—as long as we knew that a zero value would never be assigned as an *actual* value for a slot in the array.

```
    PROGRAM Listing8_2;

  ( Demonstrates use of array type to hold students names. This
    makes the program much more flexible, because if the class
    size changes, all that is required to change the progam is to
    modify the constant "NumberOfStudents." )

USES CRT;

CONST
  NumberOfStudents = 5;

TYPE
  String10 = STRING[10];
  StudentList = ARRAY[1..NumberOfStudents] OF String10;

VAR
  Class : StudentList;
  Continue : CHAR;

PROCEDURE Pause;
  VAR
    Proceed : CHAR;
  BEGIN
    WRITE(' Press any key to continue ...');
    Proceed := READKEY;
    WRITELN; WRITELN
  END;

PROCEDURE Initialize(VAR Class : StudentList;
                     VAR Continue : CHAR);
  VAR
    Counter : INTEGER;
  BEGIN
    Continue := 'Y';
    FOR Counter := 1 TO NumberOfStudents DO
      Class[Counter] := '          '
  END;

PROCEDURE EnterStudentName(VAR Class : StudentList);
  VAR
    Counter : INTEGER;
  BEGIN
    Counter := 1;                   ( initialize counter variable )

    WHILE (Class[Counter] <> '          ')    ( find first empty slot )
      AND (Counter < NumberOfStudents) DO
        Counter := counter + 1;

    IF (Counter = NumberOfStudents)            ( test to see if )
    AND (Class[Counter] <> '          ')       ( array is full. )
      THEN WRITELN(' Sorry. The array is full.')

      ELSE BEGIN
           WRITELN;
           WRITE(' Enter the student name: ');
           READLN(Class[Counter]);
           WRITELN;
           WRITELN(' The name you entered was ', Class[Counter], '.');
           pause
           END
  END;                    ( of EnterStudentName subroutine )
```

Listing 8.2: Student names in array of strings.

```
BEGIN
  CLRSCR;
  Initialize(class, continue);
  REPEAT
    EnterStudentName(class);
    WRITE(' Enter another (Y/N)? ');
    READLN(Continue)
    UNTIL UPCASE(Continue) = 'N'
END.
```

Listing 8.2: Student names in array of strings. (cont.)

TESTING FOR A FULL ARRAY

The other task you have to do, before trying to put data into the array, is to see if it is already full (as in Listing 8.2). If you try to put additional values into an array that is already full, you will either get a run-time error in your program or you will corrupt your data.

In the section of this chapter called "Records," you will learn an easier way to handle this problem.

TRAVERSING AN ARRAY

Now that you know how to set up an array, we should discuss a few basic ideas about how to use the data in an array. In Listing 8.3, we will look at how to *traverse* an array, which means starting at the first slot and moving through the array slot-by-slot until we reach the end. After that, we will consider how to search an array for a particular target value, such as a name in a record.

In Listing 8.3, we set up a simple record type called *Student* which contains the first name and grade-point average of each student. Then, using an array, we set up a list type to hold the student records and, in the VAR section, create a variable of that list type. Then, we create procedures to do the following:

- **InitializeList** enters "blank" values in the fields of every record in the array. When we are traversing the list, this enables us to determine if the end of the list has been reached even when the list does not occupy the entire array.

```
PROGRAM Listing8_3;

  ( Demonstrates how to traverse an array-based list. )

USES CRT;

CONST
  NumberOfStudents = 3;


TYPE
  string10 = STRING[10];

  Student = RECORD
              Fname  : string10;
              GPA    : REAL
              END;

  Roster = ARRAY[1..10] OF Student;

VAR
  SList : Roster;

PROCEDURE Pause;
  VAR
    Proceed : CHAR;
  BEGIN
    WRITE(' Press any key to continue ...');
    Proceed := READKEY;
    WRITELN; WRITELN
  END;

PROCEDURE InitializeList(VAR SList : Roster);
      ( Note that because SList is an array of records (explained
        in the next section), each item in SList is itself a
        record. Therefore, we can use the WITH notation (explained
        in the next section) to refer to the fields in the record. )
  VAR
    LoopCounter : INTEGER;
  BEGIN
    FOR LoopCounter := 1 TO 10 DO
      BEGIN
      SList[LoopCounter].Fname := ' ';
      SList[LoopCounter].GPA := 0.00
      END
  END;

PROCEDURE LoadUpList(VAR SList : Roster);
  VAR
    LoopCounter : INTEGER;
  BEGIN
    CLRSCR;
    FOR LoopCounter := 1 TO NumberOfStudents DO
      WITH SList[LoopCounter] DO
        BEGIN
        WRITE(' Enter the name of student number ', LoopCounter, ': ');
        READLN(SList[LoopCounter].Fname);
        WRITELN;
        WRITE(' Enter his/her GPA, from 0.00 TO 4.00: ');
        READLN(GPA);
        WRITELN
        END
  END;
```

Listing 8.3: Traversing an array-based list.

```
PROCEDURE TraverseList(SList : Roster);
  VAR
    Slot : INTEGER;
  BEGIN
    Slot := 1;
    CLRSCR;
    REPEAT
      WRITE(' The name in node ', slot, ' of the list ');
      WRITELN('is ', SList[Slot].fname, ',');
      WRITELN(' with a GPA of ', SList[Slot].GPA:0:2, '.');
      Slot := Slot + 1;
      WRITELN;
      pause
    UNTIL (SList[Slot].Fname = ' ') OR (Slot = 10);
    WRITELN;
    WRITELN(' That''s the end of the list!');
    WRITELN(' There were ', (slot - 1), ' student records counted.');
    WRITELN
  END;


{ ----------------------------------------------------------------- }
{                      MAIN BODY OF PROGRAM                          }
{ ----------------------------------------------------------------- }
BEGIN
  CLRSCR;
  InitializeList(SList);
  LoadUpList(SList);
  TraverseList(SList);
  pause
END.
```

Listing 8.3: Traversing an array-based list. (cont.)

- **LoadUpList** enables us to load some student names and grade-point averages into the list. When we traverse the list, these names and grade-point averages will be displayed on the screen.

- **TraverseList** visits each record in the array, displays its contents on the screen, and then moves on to the next record. This process continues until the end of the list is reached: the REPEAT statement tells the program to continue moving forward in the list until it reaches either a blank record or the end of the array. Note how, in the program line that begins with UNTIL, we use the "blank" contents of empty records (put there by the **InitializeList** routine) to determine if the end of the list has been reached.

Note that in the **TraverseList** routine, we could have declared **SList** as a VAR parameter even though **TraverseList** is not supposed to make any changes in it. For reasons to be discussed in Chapter 9, "Procedures and Functions," this would reduce the memory requirements of the program, but would introduce the risk of an accidental change to the **SList** array. Here, for both simplicity and safety, we've chosen not to declare it as a VAR parameter.

The main body of the program, as usual, is only a few lines long and shows the overall structure of the program.

SEQUENTIAL SEARCH OF AN ARRAY

Traversing the array in Listing 8.3 is useful if you want to see all the records in the list, but it is an inefficient method to find a specific record. For that task, you need a more specialized routine to search the list until it finds the record you want.

The search routine we will use here is called *sequential search*. It is slower and less sophisticated than some other search routines we will see in Chapter 18, "Elementary Algorithms," but it does an adequate job. It also works with unsorted lists, while the more sophisticated search routines often require that lists be sorted before they can be searched. Sequential search is illustrated in Listing 8.4.

Listing 8.4 is identical to Listing 8.3 except for the fact that we have replaced the **TraverseList** routine with a **SearchList** routine. As expected, **SearchList** takes **SList** as a parameter and has three local variables:

- **Slot**, an integer variable which is used to hold the number of the array slot we are currently inspecting;

- **SearchKey**, a string variable which holds the name for which we are searching; and

- **Found**, a Boolean variable which indicates whether or not the string in **SearchKey** has been found in the **SList** array.

First, the **SearchList** sets the *Slot* and *Found* variables to their initial values. Then, it prompts the user to enter a search string, which is

```
PROGRAM Listing8_4;

  { Demonstrates how to search an array-based list. }

USES CRT;

CONST
  NumberOfStudents = 3;


TYPE
  string10 = STRING[10];

  Student = RECORD
            Fname  : string10;
            GPA    : REAL
            END;

  Roster = ARRAY[1..10] OF Student;

VAR
  SList : Roster;

PROCEDURE Pause;
  VAR
    Proceed : CHAR;
  BEGIN
    WRITE(' Press any key to continue ...');
    Proceed := READKEY;
    WRITELN; WRITELN
  END;

PROCEDURE InitializeList(VAR SList : Roster);
      { Note that because SList is an array of records (explained
        in the next section), each item in SList is itself a
        record. Therefore, we can use the WITH notation (explained
        in the next section) to refer to the fields in the record. }
  VAR
    LoopCounter : INTEGER;
  BEGIN
    FOR LoopCounter := 1 TO 10 DO
      BEGIN
      SList[LoopCounter].Fname := ' ';
      SList[LoopCounter].GPA := 0.00
      END
  END;

PROCEDURE LoadUpList(VAR SList : Roster);
  VAR
    LoopCounter : INTEGER;
  BEGIN
    CLRSCR;
    FOR LoopCounter := 1 TO NumberOfStudents DO
      WITH SList[LoopCounter] DO
        BEGIN
        WRITE(' Enter the name of student number ', LoopCounter, ': ');
        READLN(SList[LoopCounter].Fname);
        WRITELN;
        WRITE(' Enter his/her GPA, from 0.00 TO 4.00: ');
        READLN(GPA);
        WRITELN
        END
  END;
```

Listing 8.4: Sequential search of an array.

```
PROCEDURE SearchList(SList : Roster);
  VAR
    Slot      : INTEGER;
    SearchKey : string10;
    Found     : BOOLEAN;
  BEGIN
    Slot := 1;
    Found := FALSE;
    CLRSCR;
    WRITE(' Enter the student name for which to search: ');
    READLN(SearchKey);
    WHILE (Found = FALSE) AND (Slot <= 10) DO
      BEGIN
        IF SList[slot].fname = SearchKey
        THEN BEGIN
            WRITELN(' Search target found at slot #', slot, '!');
            Found := TRUE
            END
        ELSE slot := slot + 1
      END;
    IF Found = FALSE THEN WRITELN(' Search string not found.');
    pause
  END;


{ ---------------------------------------------------------------- }
{                       MAIN BODY OF PROGRAM                        }
{ ---------------------------------------------------------------- }
BEGIN
  CLRSCR;
  InitializeList(SList);
  LoadUpList(SList);
  SearchList(SList);
  pause
END.
```

Listing 8.4: Sequential search of an array. (cont.)

stored in the *SearchKey* variable. Then, a WHILE loop begins stepping through the array, one slot at a time. At each slot, it compares the **Fname** field of the student record to the *SearchKey* variable.

If the two match, the program displays a message on-screen that the search string has been found. It then sets the *Found* variable to true and drops out of the WHILE loop. If there is not a match, it increases the slot number by one and goes through the loop again, repeating the process until either the *Found* variable becomes true or the end of the array is reached. If the search string is never found, then the program displays a "not found" message on the screen.

The main body of the program matches Listing 8.3 exactly, except for calling **SearchList** instead of **TraverseList**.

MULTIDIMENSIONAL ARRAYS

Although we have used an array to create a list, you also can use arrays to create more complex two- and three-dimensional table structures, as shown in Figure 8.2. You create a multidimensional array by declaring

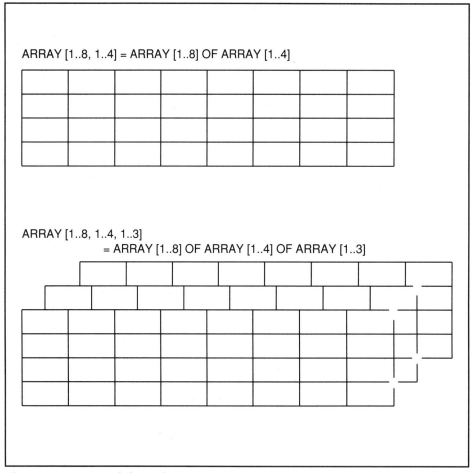

Figure 8.2: Two- and three-dimensional arrays.

multiple coordinates in your array definition, as in the following:

```
TYPE
  TwoDTable = ARRAY[1..8, 1..4] OF STRING[15];

  ThreeDTable = ARRAY[1..8, 1..4, 1..3] OF STRING[15];
```

You then can refer to slots in variables of these array types by multiple coordinates, as in:

```
MyTwoDTable[3,4]

MyThreeDTable[3,4,2]
```

Internally, Pascal treats all arrays as one-dimensional lists. In your PC's memory, Pascal stores everything in the first slot of the first array (including other array slots), then everything in the second slot, and so forth. But, fortunately, you don't often have to worry about this.

ADVANTAGES AND DISADVANTAGES OF ARRAYS

The biggest advantage of arrays, in terms of what we have looked at so far, is that they allow us to create a unified list or table of values that we can traverse from one end to the other, as we did in the **EnterStudent-Name** procedure of Listing 8.2. In a list, there are usually next and previous members of the list, which you reach by moving forward or backward in the list. With stand-alone variables, however, there is no easy way to create such a unified list. When you need to search for a given value or put a group of values in a certain order, it helps tremendously to have them in a list.

The biggest disadvantage of arrays, in terms of what we have looked at so far, is that they tend to waste memory. When you set up a list or a table with an array, you need to give it the maximum number of slots that you will ever possibly need. This means that most of the time, some—or even a majority—of the slots in the array will be empty. One way is to set up a special index function (called an *access function*) to create triangular, diagonal, or other odd-shaped tables that provide multidimensional arrays but require less memory.

Compared to other ways of setting up lists (for example, with pointers, which will be discussed in Chapter 11), array operations are much faster because all the elements of the array are stored side-by-side in your PC's memory. To find the next element in a list by using a pointer, you first have to look at the pointer, and then you have to go to the memory address to which it points. This two-step process is slower than going directly to the *n*th slot of an array, but it usually requires less memory.

STANDARD PASCAL: HANDLING STRINGS AS ARRAYS

Even though Turbo Pascal provides a string data type for us, there are two major benefits of learning how to handle strings as arrays of characters. The first benefit, of course, is a deeper understanding of exactly how Turbo Pascal manipulates strings for us—what goes on "behind the scenes" when we create and use a data item of type STRING. Thus, if we ever need to work with text strings in a language that does not support the string data type, we will know how to solve the problem.

The second, related benefit is that it enables us to develop more "portable" programs that will run under any Pascal compiler. As noted above, most popular Pascal compilers do support a string data type, but some do not. If you must "port" a Turbo Pascal program to another type of computer, such as a mainframe or a minicomputer, you may run into a version of Pascal that does not support strings. A program that uses the string type, therefore, will need more extensive modification than one that uses arrays.

Of course, portability isn't always a concern. If the program needs to run only on PCs, then you should compile it under Turbo Pascal and use strings to your heart's content. Likewise, if you are porting your program to another Pascal compiler and the target compiler supports strings, it is a waste of effort to implement the strings as arrays. But to develop maximally portable programs and to understand how strings really work, there is no better exercise than implementing strings as arrays—which is probably the reason many computer science courses do not allow the use of the string type.

Here, we will develop two routines for handling strings as arrays. These two routines, called *ReadString* and *WriteString*, correspond to Pascal's built-in READ and WRITE procedures. Note that they do *not* correspond to READLN and WRITELN: the reason is that any place you need an end-of-line character, you can always insert an actual READLN or WRITELN statement. Omitting the end-of-line character from *ReadString* and *WriteString* makes them more generalized and flexible in their application. Both of these routines are shown in Listing 8.5.

Note that we declared our string type, **astring**, as a **PACKED ARRAY** of characters. The word **PACKED** has no significance for Turbo Pascal (which ignores it). However, it instructs some other Pascal compilers, principally on mainframes and minicomputers, to cram as many of the characters as possible into a single memory location, thereby reducing the memory requirements of your program. Another benefit is that some Pascal compilers allow you to use READLN and WRITELN with packed arrays, thereby avoiding the need for special array-handling routines as we are demonstrating here.

Packed arrays do slow down the program, so if memory usage is not a problem, and your target compiler does not let you use READLN and WRITELN with packed arrays, then standard arrays of characters will work equally well—and your program will be slightly faster.

The size of the array that you use for your strings should be large enough to accommodate the biggest string you expect to use. Thus, if your program will handle 20-character names, 30-character addresses, 10-character city names, and 2-character state names, then you must use a 30-character array as your base type. Anything smaller would not be able to hold the addresses; anything larger would waste memory.

The ReadString Procedure

The ReadString procedure takes three parameters:

1. The name of the file variable from which characters will be read;

```
PROGRAM Listing8_5;

  ( Demonstrates how strings can be created and manipulated
    in ISO standard Pascal by using packed arrays. }

USES CRT;

TYPE
  astring  = PACKED ARRAY[1..20] of char;
              ( Turbo Pascal ignores the word PACKED, which is needed
                in some other Pascal compilers to create a string. The
                size of the array should be the size of the largest
                string you will use in the program. }

VAR
  UserName : astring;

( ---------------------------------------------------------------- )
(                 UTILITY ROUTINES FOR THE PROGRAM                  )
( ---------------------------------------------------------------- )
PROCEDURE Pause;
  VAR
    Proceed : CHAR;
  BEGIN
    WRITE(' Press any key to continue ...');
    Proceed := READKEY;
    WRITELN; WRITELN
  END;

PROCEDURE ReadString(var myfile:text;          ( input device )
                     var FakeString:astring;   ( string array )
                     length:integer);          ( length of string )
  VAR
    a  : char;
    i  : integer;
  BEGIN
    i := 0; a := 'x';
    while (ord(a) <> 13) and (i <= length) do
      begin
      i := i + 1;
      read(myfile,a); if ord(a) = 10 then read(myfile,a);
      if ord(a) <> 13 then FakeString[i] := a;
      if ord(a) = 13 then
                        begin
                        repeat
                          begin
                          FakeString[i] := ' ';
                          i := i + 1
                          end
                        until i = length + 1;
                          i := 0
                          end
        end
    END;

PROCEDURE WriteString(var myfile:text;          ( output device )
                      var FakeString:astring;   ( string array )
                      length:integer);          ( length of string )
    VAR
      i  : integer;
```

Listing 8.5: Standard Pascal using arrays for strings.

```
      BEGIN
        i := 1;
        repeat
          begin
          write(myfile,FakeString[i]);
          i := i + 1
          end
        until (FakeString[i] = ' ') or (i >= length);
        i := i + 1;
        if FakeString[i] <> ' '
          then begin
              write(myfile, ' ');
              repeat
                begin
                write(myfile, FakeString[i]);
                i := i + 1;
                end
              until (i >= length) or (FakeString[i] = ' ')
            end
      END;

 { ---------------------------------------------------------------- }
 (                        MAIN BODY OF PROGRAM                       )
 { ---------------------------------------------------------------- }
 BEGIN
   CLRSCR;
   WRITE(' What''s your name? ');
   ReadString(input,UserName,20);
   WRITELN;
   WRITE(' ');
   WriteString(output,UserName,20);
   WRITELN('.  That''s a nice name.');
   pause
 END.
```

Listing 8.5: Standard Pascal using arrays for strings. (cont.)

2. The name of the array variable into which the characters will be placed; and

3. The length of the array type being used as a base type (in this case, 20).

Normally, with READLN, you do not need to specify the name of the file variable from which characters are being read. If you do not specify anything, Turbo Pascal assumes that characters will be read in from the keyboard. The only time you need to specify the file variable is when you're reading from a disk file. **ReadString**, however, is not quite that sophisticated, so you must specify the file variable involved. To get keyboard input, it is the built-in Turbo Pascal file variable named *input*.

The name of the array variable is needed for the same reason that you include the name of a string variable with READLN: Pascal has to know where to send the characters it is reading in from the keyboard. Finally, the length of the array type is needed so that, after characters are read in, **ReadString** can pad out the rest of the array with space characters—a feature that becomes important when we use **WriteString**.

The WHILE statement that is the main part of the **ReadString** procedure says that Turbo Pascal should keep on reading characters from the input device until a character (variable *a*) is a carriage return, or a loop counter (variable *i*) reaches the maximum size of the array. If input is from the keyboard, a carriage return would mean that the user pressed the Enter key. If input is from a disk file, it would mean that the end of the line has been encountered.

The ASCII number of a carriage return is 13, and the ASCII number of a linefeed is 10. The **ReadString** routine uses Pascal's **ORD()** function to find the ASCII number of the input character and then compares this number to 13 and 10 to determine what to do.

It then adds one to the loop counter, indicating the first character read into the array, and reads a character. The routine tests the character to determine if it is a linefeed (a special kind of character we do not want in the string). If the character is a linefeed, another read statement is executed to read in the actual first character in the string.

If the character is not a carriage return, then it is added to the current slot in the array. Because the loop counter starts at 1 and increases by 1 each time we go through the loop, we use the loop counter to determine which slot in the array should receive the input character. On the first pass through the loop, the character goes into the first slot; on pass 2, into the second; and so forth.

If a carriage return is encountered before the array is completely full (that is, if *ord(a) = 13*), then the routine pads out the rest of the array with space characters.

The WriteString Procedure

The **WriteString** routine is very similar to **ReadString**. It takes a variable representing the output device, a variable for the array string, and the length of the array type as parameters. If you want to display output on the PC's screen, you simply use the built-in Pascal file variable *output*; otherwise, you use a file variable that represents a disk file.

WriteString moves through the array one slot at a time, sending each character in the array to the output device, until it encounters a space character. This space character could mean that the end of the string has been reached; but what if the string has a space in the middle, such as in the string 'Richard Kimble'?

To handle this possibility, **WriteString** looks ahead one more slot in the array to see if the space character is repeated. If it is, WriteString assumes that it has reached the end of the string; if not, it continues to write characters from the array until it reaches another space character or the limit of the array.

RECORDS

In Pascal, a *record* is simply a way to combine several different data items in the same wrapper. The data items can be of the same or different data types; there can be only one, or there can be many. In a record definition, each slot for a data item is called a *field*.

Therefore, you must be clear at the outset that although you can use Pascal records for what are ordinarily called records (such as student records), there is no necessary connection between the two concepts. Records in Pascal are used for many other things.

To define a record type in your program, you use the reserved word RECORD and then list the field names of the record along with the data type of each field. You finish the record type definition with the word END. Thus, the following are all legal record types:

```
CONST

  NumberStudents = 5;


TYPE

  String2  = STRING[2];
```

```
String5  = STRING[5];

String10 = STRING[10];

String20 = STRING[20];



Students = RECORD

      List : ARRAY[1..NumberStudents] of String10;

      Current : INTEGER

      END;



StudentRec  = RECORD

          Fname,

          Lname  : String10;

          Address: String20;

          City   : String10;

          State  : String2;

          Zip    : String5;

          GPA    : SINGLE;

          Class  : INTEGER

          END;



Enrollment = ARRAY[1..NumberStudents] of StudentRec;
```

Just as with arrays, it is important to remember that simply declaring a record type in the TYPE section of your program does *not* create any records. To do that, you have to declare a variable in the VAR section of your program and specify that it is of the record type you want, as in:

```
VAR

   Class : Students;
```

```
Joe    : StudentRec;
```

You refer to the fields of a record by using the name of the record variable, a period, and the field name. Thus, for example, if we created (as above) a variable called *Class* that is of type **Students**, we could refer to the individual elements of the array in the list field by **Class.list[*n*]**, where *n* is the index of the array slot we want to refer to. Listing 8.6 shows how to use a record in this way to simplify the **EnterStudentName** procedure in Listing 8.2.

Notice that in Listing 8.6, we no longer had to start at the beginning of the list and look for the first open slot. By using a record, we added a slot counter (**Class.Current**) to keep track of which slot we should use next. Each time we added a new item to the array, we added 1 to **Class.Current**. When **Class.Current** finally exceeded the upper limit of the list, we automatically knew that the array was full.

USING A WITH CLAUSE

Of course, if you have many statements with the same record variable, the dot-notation can become pretty tedious. With a student record, for example, we might write the following:

```
Joe.Fname := 'Joe';

Joe.Lname := 'Smith';

Joe.Address := '123 Maple Drive';

Joe.City := 'Delafield';

Joe.State := 'WI';

Joe.Zip := '53018';

Joe.GPA := 3.50;

Joe.Class := 4;
```

Using a WITH clause makes it unnecessary to repeat the name of the record variable each time you want to access its fields. You need to remember, however, that a WITH clause applies only to the very next

```
PROGRAM Listing8_6;

  { Shows how to embed an array inside of a record to make
    list operations easier. }

USES CRT;

CONST
   NumberStudents = 3;

TYPE
  String10 = STRING[10];
  Students = RECORD
               List: ARRAY[1..NumberStudents] OF String10;
               Current : INTEGER
               END;

VAR
  Class : Students;
  Continue : CHAR;

PROCEDURE Pause;
  VAR
    Proceed : CHAR;
  BEGIN
    WRITE(' Press any key to continue ...');
    Proceed := READKEY;
    WRITELN; WRITELN
  END;

PROCEDURE Initialize(VAR Class : Students;
                     VAR Continue : CHAR);
  VAR
    Counter : INTEGER;
  BEGIN
    Continue := 'Y';
    FOR Counter := 1 TO NumberStudents DO
      Class.List[Counter] := ' ';
    Class.Current := 1
  END;

PROCEDURE EnterStudentName(VAR Class : Students);
  VAR
    Counter : INTEGER;
  BEGIN
    Counter := 1;                  { initialize counter variable }

    IF Class.Current <= NumberStudents
      THEN BEGIN
           WRITELN;
           WRITE(' Enter the student name: ');
           READLN(Class.list[Class.current]);
           WRITE(' The name you entered was ');
           WRITELN(Class.list[Class.current]);
           Class.current := Class.current + 1;
           END
      ELSE BEGIN
           WRITELN(' Sorry. The array is full.');
           pause;
           halt
           END;
  END;                     { of EnterStudentName subroutine }
```

Listing 8.6: Embedding array in a record with counter field.

```
BEGIN
  CLRSCR;
  Initialize(class, continue);
  REPEAT
    EnterStudentName(Class);
    WRITE(' Enter another (Y/N)? ');
    READLN(Continue)
    UNTIL (UPCASE(Continue) = 'N')
END.
```

Listing 8.6: Embedding array in a record with counter field. (cont.)

statement that comes after it. To do the same thing as above by using a
WITH clause, you would write

```
WITH Joe DO

BEGIN

        Fname := 'Joe';

        Lname := 'Smith';

        Address := '123 Maple Drive';

        City := 'Delafield';

        State := 'WI';

        Zip := '53018';

        GPA := 3.50;

        Class := 4

END;
```

If you had an array of records, such as a list of student records, you would
use the WITH clause as follows:

```
WITH List[n] DO { List[n] is the record in array slot n }

    BEGIN

            Fname := 'Sue';

            Lname := 'Storm';

            { ... etc. }

    END;
```

Of course, you could set up a loop to increase *n* to keep adding new records to the array as long as you wanted to (at least until the array was full).

VARIANT RECORDS

Sometimes, you will need a record type that can use different fields depending on the values of other fields. For example, a university might have some students who live in dormitories on campus, while others live in apartments off-campus. In that case, you can set up your record type to have a "dorm rent" field if the student lives on campus. To do this, you embed a CASE statement in the record definition, as follows:

```
TYPE

  StudentRec  = RECORD
                Fname,
                Lname  : String10;
                Address: String20;
                City   : String10;
                State  : String2;
                Zip    : String5;
                GPA    : SINGLE;
                Class  : INTEGER;
                CASE OnCampus : BOOLEAN of
                    TRUE : (DormRent : SINGLE;
                            RentPaid : BOOLEAN);
                    FALSE: (Age : INTEGER;
                            ParentPermission : BOOLEAN)
                END;
```

In student records where the **OnCampus** field is true, then the record will also have the **DormRent** and **RentPaid** fields. If the **OnCampus** field is false, then the record will have the **Age** and **ParentPermission** fields.

SETS

A set is just a collection of things. In Pascal, a set is a collection of simple-data-type items. To create a set variable, you declare it in the **VAR** section of your program, as follows:

```
VAR

   GoodChars : SET OF CHAR;    { declares set variable }

BEGIN

GoodChars := ['Y','y','N','n']; {assigns value to set}
```

The specific syntax of a set declaration is as follows, where *BaseType* is the simple data type of the items included in the set:

```
VAR

        MySet : SET OF BaseType;
```

Note that this declaration simply creates *MySet* as a set variable which can hold members of the base type; it does not actually load any members into the set. To do that, you must use an assignment statement, as in the following:

```
MySet := [ element1, element2, ... elementN];
```

where the elements are members of the base type and *N*, of course, is less than or equal to 256, because a Turbo Pascal set cannot have more than 256 elements. Observe also that the members assigned to *MySet* are enclosed in square brackets, not parentheses or curly brackets, and that they are separated by commas.

Sets are obviously quite similar to lists, but there are some very important differences. The main difference is that lists are intrinsically *ordered* data structures, but sets are intrinsically *unordered.* Thus:

- 'A', 'B', 'C' is a different list from 'C', 'B', 'A', but
- ['A', 'B', 'C'] is the same set as ['C', 'B', 'A'].

For the same reason, items can appear more than once in a list, but can appear only once in a set:

- 'A', 'B', 'C', 'A' is different from 'A', 'B', 'C', but
- ['A', 'B', 'C', 'A'] is the *same set* as ['A', 'B', 'C'].

The elements of a set can be of any simple type, as long as the type does not have more than 256 members. Thus, CHAR is a perfectly good base type for a set, because it has 256 members; likewise, the user-defined type **CLASS = 1..4** is a good base type. However, the INTEGER type is not a legal base type for a set, because it has more than 256 members. To use integers, as in the CLASS type example, you have to define a type as a subrange of the integers and use that subrange type. Moreover, only integers from 0 to 255 are allowed.

LIMITS AND ADVANTAGES
OF TURBO PASCAL SETS

The reason why Turbo Pascal (unlike some other Pascal compilers) allows only 256 elements in a set, and elements can have ordinal values only from 0 to 255, is that Turbo Pascal uses a special scheme for storing sets in memory. This scheme minimizes the amount of memory that sets require, and maximizes the speed of set operations, but it also imposes the 256-element limit.

Internally, Turbo Pascal handles a set as an array of bits, the maximum size of which is 32 bytes (32 bytes multiplied by 8 bits per byte = 256). Each bit in the array indicates if the corresponding member of the base type is an element of the set or not. Thus, a set of CHAR would be stored as a 32-byte (256-bit) array: In each slot of the array there is a bit (1 or 0) which tells if the corresponding ASCII character is in the set (bit = 1) or not in the set (bit = 0). For example, if Set ARRAY is a set variable of TYPE Char, then:

- If SetArray[65] = 1, then the upper case letter 'A' is in the set, because the ASCII number (ordinality) of 'A' is 65.

- If SetArray[97] = 0, then the lower case letter 'a' is *not* in the set, because the ASCII number (ordinality) of 'a' is 97.

- If SetArray[13] = 1, then the carriage return character (Enter key) is in the set, because its ASCII number (ordinality) is 13.

COMPATIBLE SET TYPES

Normally, set operations can be performed only between two or more sets that are "compatible." For instance, you cannot use the union operator to unite two sets with a different base type. Similarly, you cannot use IN to see if an integer is a member of a set whose base type is CHAR, as in Listing 8.7; this causes a compile-time error.

The base type of a set determines if the set is type-compatible with another set or with a potential set member. Two sets that have the same base type are compatible; a data item is compatible with a set if it is a member of the set's base type.

One of the most obvious uses of sets is to create lists of acceptable values. In Listing 8.8, we create a **GetGoodChar** subroutine that serves as an error-trapping substitute for READLN. It allows us to specify a set of acceptable characters. If the user keys in an unacceptable value (whether it is a letter that is not on the list, or something that is not a letter), then **GetGoodChar** just sits there waiting for valid input—just like the **GetGoodInt** routine we developed in the previous chapter.

For any set, it has to be completely clear whether something is in the set or not. You can test for something being in a set, as in Listing 8.4, by using IN:

```
IF InChar IN GoodOnes

    THEN Congratulations;
```

```
PROGRAM Listing8_7;

  { Demonstrates the use of "IN" to test for set membership. }

USES CRT;

VAR
  Letters : SET OF CHAR;

PROCEDURE Pause;
  VAR
    Proceed : CHAR;
  BEGIN
    WRITE(' Press any key to continue ...');
    Proceed := READKEY;
    WRITELN; WRITELN
  END;

BEGIN
  CLRSCR;
  Letters := ['A', 'B', 'C'];

  IF 'A' IN Letters
     THEN WRITELN(' The letter "A" is in!');

  IF NOT ('a' IN Letters)
     THEN WRITELN(' The letter "a" is out!');

  IF 5 IN Letters
     THEN WRITELN(' The number 5 is in!');

  pause
END.
```

Listing 8.7: Incompatible set types.

However, to test if something is not in a set, you must use a slightly odd way of phrasing it (see Table 8.1). If you write **IF InChar NOT IN Good-Ones**, then your program won't compile. You have to write

```
IF NOT(InChar IN GoodOnes)

   THEN ToughLuck;
```

SET OPERATIONS

The most common use of sets is to determine if a certain value is acceptable or not by checking to see if it is in the set. In **GetGoodChar**, for example, we specify a set of "good characters" for user input. When the user keys in a value, the routine checks the value against the set of good

```
PROGRAM Listing8_8;

   ( Demonstrates the use of a set to create a list of
     acceptable values. )

USES CRT;

TYPE
   GoodChars = set of char;   ( used with the GetGoodChar procedure )

CONST
   YNchars : GoodChars = ['Y', 'y', 'N', 'n'];
             ( set of acceptable characters )

VAR
   YesNo : CHAR;

PROCEDURE Pause;
   VAR
      Proceed : CHAR;
   BEGIN
      WRITE(' Press any key to continue ...');
      Proceed := READKEY;
      WRITELN; WRITELN
   END;

PROCEDURE GetGoodChar(GoodOnes:GoodChars; var InChar:char);
   ( An error-trapping substitute for "readln" to get character
   input from the keyboard. This procedure takes two parameters:
   a set of "acceptable" characters for input, and a variable
   parameter that is the actual character input.  If the input
   character is not in the set of acceptable characters, this
   procedure returns to the original screen position and waits
   for the user to enter an acceptable character.)

   VAR
      markX, markY  : byte;

   BEGIN
      REPEAT
         markX := whereX;
         markY := whereY;
         READLN(InChar);
         IF NOT (InChar IN GoodOnes)
            THEN BEGIN
                   gotoXY(markX, markY);
                   ClrEOL
                   END
      UNTIL InChar IN GoodOnes
   END;

BEGIN
   CLRSCR;
   WRITE(' Have you stopped beating your flagellum (Y/N)? ');
   GetGoodChar(YNchars, YesNo);
   WRITELN;
   IF UPCASE(YesNo) = 'Y'
      THEN WRITELN(' Congratulations! You''re promoted to eucaryote!')
      ELSE WRITELN(' I''ve never seen a cilia fellow!');
   pause
END.
```

Listing 8.8: Demonstration of the GetGoodChar routine.

Table 8.1: Set Operators

OPERATORS	OPERATION	OPERAND TYPES
IN	Set membership: determines if the item on the left of IN is a member of the set on the right. Returns a Boolean value (true or false).	Simple type, set (must be compatible)
+	Union: adds the members of two sets together to produce a new, consolidated set. For two sets A and B, an item is in the union if it is a member of *either* set. If any item is in both original sets, it appears only once in the union set.	Compatible sets
−	Difference: With two sets A and B, $A - B$ subtracts from A any members that are also in B. The result is a set containing all those items that were in A but were not also in B.	Compatible sets

characters to determine if it is acceptable. If it is, then the value is passed to the program; if not, then the on-screen character is erased and the prompt is redisplayed.

Table 8.1: Set Operators (cont.)

OPERATORS	OPERATION	OPERAND TYPES
*	Intersection: The opposite of union (above). For sets A and B, the intersection $A * B$ includes those items that are members of *both* A and B. If any item is in only one of the sets, it is not in the intersection.	Compatible sets

There are, however, several other useful set operations. You may even be familiar with some of them already. They are:

Set union, denoted in Pascal by **+**. This combines the elements in two sets. For example:

- If set1 = ['a', 'b'] and set2 = ['b', 'c'], then set1 + set2 = ['a', 'b', 'c']. (Remember that ['a', 'b', 'b', 'c'] is the same set as ['a', 'b', 'c'].)

- If set1 = ['a', 'b'] and set2 = ['c', 'd'], then set1 + set2 = ['a', 'b', 'c', 'd'].

- If set1 = 'a', 'b'], set2 = ['c', 'd'], and set3 = ['e', 'f'], then set1 + set2 + set3 = ['a', 'b', 'c', 'd', 'e', 'f'].

Set intersection, denoted in Pascal by ***. This produces a set containing only the elements that are in both sets. Stated another way, an item is in the intersection of two or more sets if and only if it is a member of *every* set that is being intersected. For example:

- If set1 = ['a', 'b'] and set2 = ['b', 'c'], then set1 * set2 = ['b'];

- If set1 = ['a', 'b'] and set2 = ['c', 'd'], then set1 * set2 = [] (the empty set).

- If set1 = ['a', 'b'], set2 = ['a', 'c'], and set3 = ['a', 'd'], then set1 * set2 * set3 = ['a'].

Set difference, denoted in Pascal by the minus sign, −. This produces a set containing only the elements which are in the set on the left of the difference sign but not in the set on the right. For example:

- If set1 = ['a', 'b', 'c'] and set2 = ['b', c'], then set1 − set2 = ['a'].

- If set1 = ['a', 'b'] and set2 = ['c', 'd'], then set1 − set2 = ['a', 'b'].

- If set1 = ['a', 'b'] and set2 = ['a', 'b', 'c'], then set1 − set2 = [] (the empty set).

Several other set operators produce Boolean expressions that are true or false. These operators are:

Set equality, denoted in Pascal by the equal sign, =. This produces an expression which is true if and only if the sets being compared have exactly the same elements. For example:

- If set1 = ['a', 'b'] and set2 = ['a', 'b'], then set1 = set2 is true.

- If set1 = ['a', 'b'] and set2 = ['a', 'b', 'c'], then set1 = set2 is false.

Set inequality, denoted in Pascal by the left and right angle brackets, <>. This produces an expression which is true if and only if the sets being compared do *not* have exactly the same elements. For example:

- If set1 = ['a', 'b'] and set2 = ['a', 'b'], then set1 <> set2 is false.

- If set1 = ['a', 'b'] and set2 = ['a', 'b', 'c'], then set1 <> set2 is true.

Subset, denoted in Pascal by the left angle bracket and the equal sign, <=. This produces an expression which is true if and only if every element in the set on the left of the subset sign is also a member of the set on the right of the subset sign. For example:

- If set1 = ['a', 'b'] and set2 = ['a', 'b', 'c'], then set1 <= set2 is true.

- If set1 = ['a', 'b', 'c'] and set2 = ['a', 'b', 'c'], then set1 <= set2 is true (every set is a subset of itself).

- If set1 = ['a', 'b', 'c'] and set2 = ['a', 'b'], then set1 <= set2 is false ('c' is in set1 but not in set2).

- If set1 = [] (the empty set) and set2 = ['a', 'b'], then set1 <= set2 is true. Note that the empty set is a subset of all other sets, so this expression is true no matter what elements are in set2.

Superset, denoted in Pascal by the right angle bracket and the equal sign, >=. This produces an expression which is true if and only if every element in the set on the right of the superset sign is also a member of the set on the left of the superset sign. For example:

- If set1 = ['a', 'b'] and set2 = ['a', 'b', 'c'], then set1 >= set2 is false.

- If set1 = ['a', 'b', 'c'] and set2 = ['a', 'b', 'c'], then set1 >= set2 is true (every set is a superset of itself).

- If set1 = ['a', 'b', 'c'] and set2 = ['a', 'b'], then set1 >= set2 is true (everything in set2 is also in set1).

- If set1 = [] (the empty set) and set2 = ['a', 'b'], then set1 >= set2 is false. Note that the empty set is only a superset of itself, so this expression is almost always false.

SUMMARY

In addition to simple data types, Pascal lets the programmer create custom-defined data types for specific needs. In designing a program, these custom-defined data types should be thought of without regard for how they are handled in a specific programming language.

Arrays permit the creation of fixed-length lists of items, all of which must be the same type. The main disadvantage of arrays is that they tend to waste memory; the main advantage is that individual items in the array can be found very fast. To pass a variable of an array type to a subroutine, the array type must be declared in the TYPE section of the program. Standard

Pascal does not support a string data type, which means that arrays can be used for handling text strings if a program must be moved from one Pascal compiler to another.

Records allow multiple data elements of different types to be combined in a single data structure. The individual data elements in a record are called its *fields*. Variant records can have different fields depending on the value of a key field.

Sets are collections of items like lists. Unlike lists, however, the items in a set are not in any particular order. Turbo Pascal sets can contain only members of ordinal data types and can have no more than 256 members.

REVIEW EXERCISES

1. Explain what an array is and how it differs from simple data types.

2. Explain the idea of an "abstract data type." Is a fixed-length list basically the same thing as an array? Explain.

3. Is there anything wrong with this code fragment? If so, what is wrong and how would you correct it? Will it compile in its current form?

```
TYPE
    String15 = STRING[15];
    NameList = ARRAY[1..10] OF String15;
VAR
    MyList   : NameList;
    Continue : CHAR;
    Counter  : integer;
BEGIN
  Continue := 'Y'; { initialize loop control variable }
  Counter  := 1; { initialize counter variable }
  REPEAT
        WRITE(' Enter a name for the list: ');
```

```
         READLN(MyList[counter]);
         counter := counter + 1;
         WRITE(' Do another (Y/N)? ');
         READLN(Continue)
      UNTIL UPCASE(Continue) <> 'Y'
   END;
```

4. Is there anything wrong with this code fragment? If so, what is wrong and how would you correct it? Will it compile in its current form?

```
VAR MyList : ARRAY[1..10] OF CHAR;
PROCEDURE Init(VAR MyList : ARRAY[1..10] OF
CHAR);
   VAR counter : INTEGER;
   BEGIN
      FOR counter := 1 to 10 DO MyList[counter] := ' '
   END;
```

5. Write a simple program to use an array-based list of names. Load several names into the list.

6. What does it mean to initialize an array? When is this step particularly important and why? How should you decide what value to use?

7. To the program that you created in Exercise 5, add a routine to prompt the user for a name and then search for that name in the list. Don't forget to deal with the case in which the searched-for name is not in the list.

8. What are the advantages and disadvantages of arrays for keeping lists? For handling text strings?

9. Explain the RECORD data type in Pascal. Could you have a list that was contained in a single record? If you could, can you think of any reason why you might want to do it that way?

10. Write a simple program that uses the RECORD data type and a WITH clause.

11. Write a simple program that uses variant records to keep sales data. Using an array field inside a different record type, create a list of sales records and load some data into it.

12. Explain the following:

    (a) the idea of a set

    (b) the idea of compatible set types

    (c) the idea of membership in a set

    (d) the limitations of sets in Turbo Pascal

13. Give all the different lists can you form with the items 'a', 'b', 'c', 'd', and 'e'. Give all the different sets. If the number of sets is different from the number of lists, explain the difference.

14. Challenging: Write a simple program that uses sets to create a group of "acceptable values" for a variable. Don't forget to handle the situation in which the item entered by the user is not in the set.

15. Challenging: Can you think of a way to implement a variable-length list with Pascal arrays?

16. Challenging: Define set G as the set of all sets which are not members of themselves. For example, the set of integers is not itself an integer, hence, it is not a member of itself. Because of this fact, it is a member of the set containing all sets which are not members of themselves. Here is the problem: is set G a member of itself or not? Justify your solution.

Procedures and Functions

Now someone tells me that he knows what pain is only from [introspection]. Suppose everyone had a box with something in it; we call it a "beetle." No one can look into anyone else's box, and everyone says that he knows what a beetle is only by looking at his beetle. Here, it would be quite possible for everyone to have something different in his box.

— Ludwig Wittgenstein, *Philosophical Investigations, #293*

In the previous chapters, we've seen many examples of procedures and functions. In this chapter, we'll go into full details of how to use them. And like Wittgenstein's "beetle in the box," we will find that one of the most important things about them is the part that remains hidden.

WHAT PROCEDURES AND FUNCTIONS ARE

Procedures and functions are two different kinds of subroutines—that is, they are named blocks of program code to which you can pass values. Where they differ is that procedures are meant primarily to *do something*, to perform a sequence of actions. On the other hand, functions also may perform actions, but their *main* job is to take one value (or group of values) and return another value. A procedure is like a complete sentence, while a function is like an individual word. Both are like miniprograms in that they can contain their own constants, variables, data types, procedures, and functions.

Of course, if that's *all* they were, then procedures and functions would be a useful but essentially trivial programming tool. But that is not all they are. The most important thing about subroutines is that they embody the very *essence* of structured programming: to separate different tasks into different, "air-tight" compartments of the program; to hide the internal details of each compartment; and to keep total control over how the different compartments interact with each other and with the main body of the program. All this has, of course, several benefits:

- It reduces the number of things you have to worry about. Instead of a disorganized and very large number of interactions between different parts of a mixed-up program, you have to deal only with a small number of interactions between different air-tight compartments—interactions that you define and control.

- Given an overall program design, it allows you to develop and test a program "one piece at a time"—coding and debugging each compartment by itself without requiring you to worry about any of the others. Just like the adage about how to eat an elephant (one bite at a time), this lets you develop large, complex programs without having to think about anything but the part you are doing at that moment.

- It makes your program easier to understand and modify. Because each subroutine is concerned only with what comes into it and what goes out of it, you can add new subroutines or change the inner workings of existing subroutines with minimal and easy-to-see impact on the rest of the program.

Sometimes, the best way to explain an idea is to point to a simple example. So far, we have seen many examples of procedures and quite a few examples of functions. To spotlight the most basic features, though, let's look at two that are built into the Pascal language: the WRITELN procedure and the **SUCC()** function. (WRITELN is sometimes referred to loosely as a "command," but it actually is a built-in procedure.)

HOW PROCEDURES WORK

WRITELN has the classic features of a procedure. It takes a value (or group of values) that you pass to it, and then it does something with those values: in this case, it sends them to an output device. Usually, the WRITELN output device is the PC's screen, but it also can be a disk file, a printer, or some other device. Thus, for example,

```
WRITELN(' Frank Borland and his burro, Lotus');
```

displays a constant text string on the PC's screen. Similarly,

```
WRITELN(studentlist[n].fname, studentlist[n].lname);
```

displays the first and last names of student number **n** on the screen, where **studentlist** is an array of student records. In this case, however, it uses string *variables* to determine what it should display on the screen. Notice that the WRITELN statement stands by itself; in Pascal, a WRITELN statement, as a procedure, is a "complete sentence."

HOW FUNCTIONS WORK

Just like procedures, functions start by taking in a value or group of values. What happens then, however, is quite different. Based on the values it has received, the function assigns to *itself* a new value which it then passes back to the program. The **SUCC()** function, for example, takes an ordinal value and returns the next value in order after it, as in:

```
SUCC(5) = 6;

SUCC('a') = 'b';

SUCC(false) = true;
```

Most people have some trouble getting a grip on this idea. Perhaps the plot of the movie *Invasion of the Body Snatchers* offers a good analogy. There, pods from outer space turned themselves into look-alikes of individual Earth people—and then *took the places* of those Earth people in human society. Just like a pod from outer space, a function takes values, does something with them, and then replaces them with itself. Thus, both

```
WRITELN(' The successor of 5 is ', 6, '.');
```

and

```
WRITELN(' The successor of 5 is ', SUCC(5), '.');
```

will display the sentence, "The successor of 5 is 6" on your PC's screen. Listing 9.1 illustrates how a user-defined function can make this sort of transformation take place.

INFORMATION HIDING

Here's a trick question: what happens inside the WRITELN procedure and the **SUCC()** function to the values that have been passed to them? If you don't know, don't feel bad—you don't *need* to know, nor should you ever *have* to know. All that matters is that something goes into them (values), and something comes out the way you want it (either text on the screen or an ordinal value).

As far as the rest of the program is concerned, all of its procedures and functions—whether they are built into Pascal or created by you—should be like this. Particular data goes into them, and particular data comes out in the desired way. That's all the rest of the program should ever have to know.

This is a very important structured programming concept: it is called *information hiding*. What that means is, as I've said, the inside of each subroutine is hidden from everything outside itself, both from other subroutines and from the main part of the program. Because of this, you do not have to worry that anything inside a subroutine might have an unexpected effect on anything outside. Information hiding puts *you* in complete control of how your program works.

THE IDEA OF "SCOPE"

Until this point, we have been using the terms "global" and "local" variables fairly loosely, without discussing what they mean. The central idea that makes it all make sense is the idea of *scope*. And although this is a fairly simple idea, it is easier to understand than it is to explain.

The best way to understand the idea of scope is to consider how a Pascal program is structured. Figure 9.1 shows the overall structure of the

```
PROGRAM Listing9_1;

  { Illustrates a simple procedure and a simple function. }

USES CRT;

CONST
   Tax = 0.05;

VAR
   Amount : REAL;


( ------------------------------ )
( MAIN-LEVEL PROCEDURE DECLARATION )
( ------------------------------ )
PROCEDURE Pause;
   VAR
      Proceed : CHAR;
   BEGIN
      WRITE(' Press any key to continue ...');
      Proceed := READKEY;
      WRITELN; WRITELN
   END;


( ------------------------------ )
( MAIN-LEVEL FUNCTION DECLARATION )
( ------------------------------ )
FUNCTION WithSalesTax (VAR Amount : REAL; TaxRate : REAL) : REAL;
   BEGIN
   WithSalesTax := Amount + (Amount * TaxRate)
   END;


( ------------------------------ )
( MAIN-LEVEL PROCEDURE DECLARATION )
( ------------------------------ )
PROCEDURE GetAmount(VAR Amount : REAL);
   VAR
      Continue : CHAR;

   ( ------------------------- )
   ( Local procedure           )
   ( ------------------------- )
   ( Under GetAmount           )
   ( ------------------------- )
   PROCEDURE PromptForAmount;
      BEGIN
      CLRSCR;
   WRITELN;
   WRITE(' Enter amount of purchase: ');
   READLN(Amount);
   WRITELN;
   WRITELN(' With sales tax, that comes to ',
                     WithSalesTax(Amount,Tax):0:2, '.');
   WRITELN;
   WRITE(' Do Another (Y/N)? ');
   READLN(Continue)
   END;
```

Listing 9.1: A simple user-defined function shows how functions work.

```
( --------------------------------- )
( Main body of higher-level procedure )
( --------------------------------- )
( Procedure name: GetAmount          )
( --------------------------------- )
BEGIN
    Continue := ' ';
    REPEAT PromptForAmount
    UNTIL UPCASE(Continue) <> 'Y'
END;


( ----------------------------------------------------------- )
(                         MAIN BODY OF PROGRAM                 )
( ----------------------------------------------------------- )
BEGIN
    GetAmount(Amount);
    pause
END.
```

Listing 9.1: A simple user-defined function shows how functions work.
(cont.)

program in Listing 9.1. Notice that the main body of the program is at the top, which is only appropriate, since it has the highest level of control over what happens and when. Just below it, on the same level, are the **Pause**, **WithSalesTax**, and **GetAmount** subroutines. On the lowest level is the **PromptForAmount** procedure, which connects directly only to the **GetAmount** routine.

In a way, the hierarchy of a program resembles a company's organization chart. Global identifiers, which are declared at the very top of the hierarchy, are visible from everywhere in the program, just as everyone in a company is likely to know the name of the company president. In Listing 9.1, the constant **Tax** and the variable *Amount* are global in scope; which means that they are visible everywhere in the program, even from inside subroutines.

On the other hand, identifiers declared inside a subroutine are "local" to that subroutine. They are visible everywhere inside the subroutine, but *not* visible outside of the subroutine—just as people who work in one department of a company know everyone in their own department; but people in other departments and in the company's top management might not know *anyone* in that department.

In Figure 9.1 note that if one subroutine is declared inside another (as **PromptForAmount** is declared inside the **GetAmount** procedure), then it,

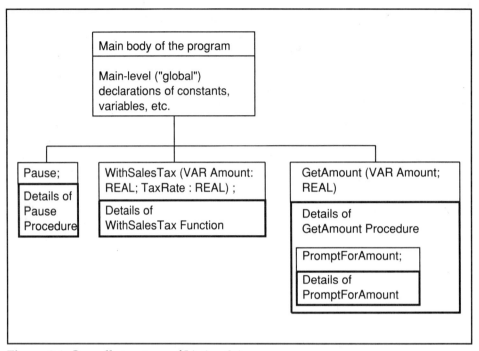

Figure 9.1: Overall structure of Listing 9.1.

too, is local to the higher-level subroutine. This means two things:

- Because it is inside the higher-level subroutine, it can see everything that is above it in the hierarchy, including local variables (and other identifiers) that are inside the higher-level subroutine.

- Because it is local to the higher-level subroutine, it is hidden from everything outside the higher-level subroutine, just as any other internal detail.

In Figure 9.1, parts of program blocks that are surrounded by single lines are visible to everything underneath them in the tree diagram, as well as to everything on the same level and to the main body of the program.

Parts that are surrounded by double lines are hidden from all other program blocks, as well as from the main program.

At the bottom right, the **PromptForAmount** procedure is a special case. It is declared *inside* the **GetAmount** procedure, so it is visible inside **GetAmount** but hidden from everything outside. Even inside the **GetAmount** routine, however, the details of **PromptForAmount** are still hidden.

It all boils down to this: the *scope* of any identifier includes (1) the program block in which it is named and (2) any program block below it in the program's hierarchy tree unless the lower block has a local identifier with the same name. One block is "below" another block if and only if you can follow the tree downward from the upper to the lower block without ever having to move up or move to a different branch of the tree.

Declaring and Using Identifiers

Pascal enforces a rule that is very similar to the idea of scope: *identifiers must be declared before they can be used.* This is why we must declare all our global constants, variables, and data types at the very beginning of the program code: that way, they can be used anywhere else in the program, whether in a subroutine or way down at the bottom in the main body of the program.

Similarly, subroutines must be declared before they are used. If subroutine A is used by subroutine B, then it must be declared *before* subroutine B. Otherwise, when Pascal compiles the program and arrives at the line where subroutine B calls subroutine A, it will stop with an "unknown identifier" error message because subroutine A has not been declared yet.

There are two minor exceptions to this rule. As we'll see in Chapter 11, you can declare a pointer data type before you declare the data type it points to. And, later in this chapter, we'll see how to use "forward declarations" to circumvent the declare-before-use rule with subroutines.

The rule that identifiers must be declared before they are used is a simple one, but it goes to the very heart of structured programming: the idea that you should plan and design your program before you start to write code. The rule is just another way that Pascal teaches you how to create efficient, bug-free programs.

HOW TO DECLARE
PROCEDURES AND FUNCTIONS

Normally, you declare subroutines after the VAR section of your program and before the main body of the program. Remember: the section where you declare subroutines is different from the main body of the program, where the subroutines actually do something. Here, you are just spelling out the details of what they are, what values they use from outside themselves, and how they work. Thus, each procedure or function declaration must contain the following information (see Figures 9.2 and 9.3):

- *The name of the procedure or function.* This follows the standard rules for Pascal identifiers. It must begin with a letter and can be as long as you like. It can have digits and underlines, but no dashes or other special characters. No distinction is made between upper

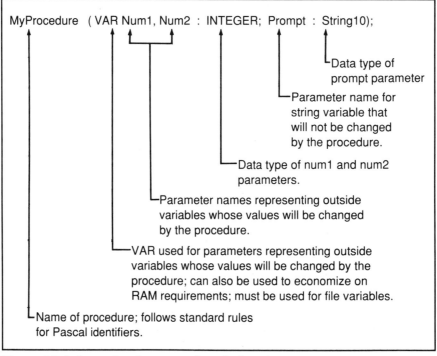

Figure 9.2: Information in a procedure declaration.

and lowercase letters, so you can use them to make the purpose of the routine clearer, such as **GetNumberFromUser**. However, the name shouldn't be the same as a Pascal reserved word (such as "case") or standard identifier (such as "writeln").

- *The names and data types of parameters.* The parentheses that come after the name of the subroutine make up the "front door" through which values can be passed to the subroutine. Just like a real-life security checkpoint, each item you intend to go in or out the door must be properly identified by name and data type. Any item that tries to enter the subroutine without proper identification papers will be detained by the security guard, i.e., Turbo Pascal will stop the program with either a compilation or a run-time error.

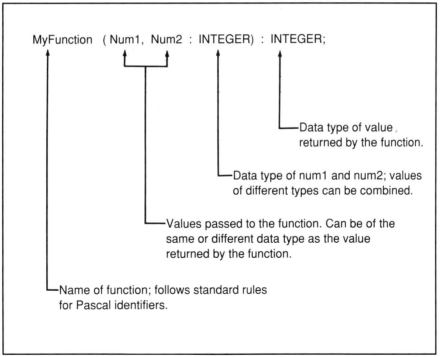

Figure 9.3: Information in a function declaration.

- *In a procedure, whether the parameters are value or VAR parameters.* In Figure 9.2, the first two parameters (*num1* and *num2*) are VAR parameters, while the third (*prompt*) is not. Note that you can have any combination of data types and parameter types. Some parameters may be VAR parameters, while others are not; some parameters can be of type INTEGER, while others are CHAR, BOOLEAN, REAL, or structured types such as ARRAY and STRING. For reasons that I'll explain in the next section of this chapter, only VAR parameters can be changed by a subroutine. One of the most common programming mistakes is to forget to use VAR in front of parameters that need to be changed by a subroutine.

- *In a function, the data type of the value returned by the function.* This is the data type of the value that the function itself will assume. Although the **SUCC()** function returns a value that is the same data type as the value it gets, things don't have to be this way. A function can get integer values and return a string, get a character value and return a Boolean, or any other combination. For example, the Turbo Pascal **STR()** function takes an integer and returns the string-type version of the same integer, e.g., replacing the integer 1555 with the string '1555'.

PASSING PARAMETERS TO SUBROUTINES

I've referred several times to the "parameters" used by a subroutine. Here, I'll discuss the meaning of this concept and how it works.

When we're using subroutines, we often need to pass values to the subroutines from outside. Sometimes, these are constant values that won't be changed by the subroutine, such as the text strings (e.g., **'This is a string constant'**) that we pass to the WRITELN procedure or the ordinal constants (e.g., **15**, **'a'**) we might pass to the **SUCC()** function. At other times, these values will actually be changed by the subroutine, such as when we pass an integer variable to a procedure that adds up numbers and gives us a total.

As we saw in our discussion of scope, two kinds of identifiers are visible from within a subroutine: identifiers that are local to that subroutine, and identifiers that are above that subroutine in the program hierarchy. Thus, in Listing 9.2, both the global variable *TotalStock* and the local variables *InStock*, *NewNum*, and *Continue* are accessible from inside the **GetNumberInStock** subroutine.

However, in Listing 9.2, we've got an obvious problem. The subroutine lets us add up numbers and get a total, but it gives us no way to

```
PROGRAM Listing9_2;

USES CRT;

VAR
  TotalStock: INTEGER;

PROCEDURE Pause;
  VAR
    Proceed : CHAR;
  BEGIN
    WRITE(' Press any key to continue ...');
    Proceed := READKEY;
    WRITELN; WRITELN
  END;

PROCEDURE GetNumberInStock;
  VAR
    InStock,
    NewNum   : INTEGER;
    Continue : CHAR;
  BEGIN
    CLRSCR;
    Continue := 'Y';
    InStock := 0;
    WHILE UPCASE(Continue) = 'Y' DO
      BEGIN
      WRITELN;
      WRITE(' Enter number to add to total: ');
      READLN(NewNum);
      InStock := InStock + NewNum;
      WRITE(' Add another (Y/N)? ');
      READLN(Continue)
      END;
    WRITELN;
    WRITELN(' The total number in stock is ', InStock, '.');
    pause
  END;


BEGIN
  TotalStock := 0;
  GetNumberInStock;
  WRITELN(' The total number in stock is ', TotalStock, '.');
  pause
END.
```

Listing 9.2: The inside of the procedure needs a way to connect with the outside.

hook up to the global variable (*TotalStock*) that we want to change. Thus, we are able to get the result we want inside the **GetNumberInStock** routine, but we are cut off from the outside.

For this obvious problem, most people seize upon the obvious solution: just put an extra line into the **GetNumberInStock** procedure to copy the value of the local variable *InStock* to the global variable *TotalStock*, as shown in Listing 9.3. This solution will work, and Turbo Pascal won't stop

```
PROGRAM Listing9_3;

  { Shows the WRONG way to change the value of a global variable. }

USES CRT;

VAR
  TotalStock: INTEGER;

PROCEDURE Pause;
  VAR
    Proceed : CHAR;
  BEGIN
    WRITE(' Press any key to continue ...');
    Proceed := READKEY;
    WRITELN; WRITELN
  END;

PROCEDURE GetNumberInStock;
  VAR
    InStock,
    NewNum   : INTEGER;
    Continue : CHAR;
  BEGIN
    CLRSCR;
    Continue := 'Y';
    InStock := 0;
    WHILE UPCASE(Continue) = 'Y' DO
      BEGIN
      WRITELN;
      WRITE(' Enter number to add to total: ');
      READLN(NewNum);
      InStock := InStock + NewNum;
      WRITE(' Add another (Y/N)? ');
      READLN(Continue)
      END;
    WRITELN;
    WRITELN(' The total number in stock is ', InStock, '.');
    TotalStock := InStock;
    pause
  END;


BEGIN
  TotalStock := 0;
  GetNumberInStock;
  WRITELN(' The total number in stock is ', TotalStock, '.');
  pause
END.
```

Listing 9.3: Directly changing a global variable: this is a very bad move.

you from doing it. From a structured programming viewpoint, however, it's just about the worst thing you could do.

The reason that it is a bad move is that the inside of each subroutine is supposed to be hidden from the rest of the program. In Listing 9.3, you allow part of the outside program to "break into" the inside of the subroutine, thus violating the principle of information hiding. *TotalStock*, in effect, sneaks into the **GetNumberInStock** routine through a back window. And whether it is a subroutine or your own house, you don't want anybody sneaking in through the windows. Figure 9.4 illustrates the situation.

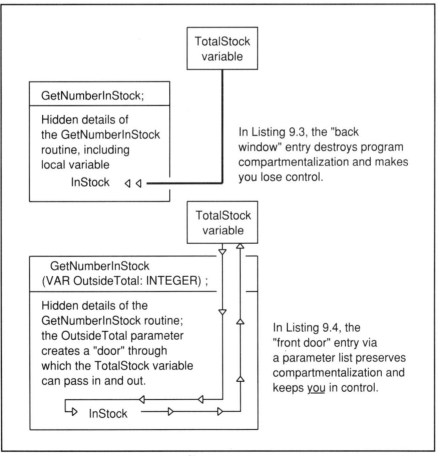

Figure 9.4: Keeping control of outside access to the details of a subroutine.

The whole point of structured programming is that it puts you *in control* of your program. You can develop your program one piece at a time and isolate different parts of the program in air-tight compartments. When you allow back-window access to subroutines, you give up control of your program and break the air-tight seals on the compartments. In a simple program like Listing 9.3, this is not a major problem. If you're developing a medium or large-sized program with dozens of subroutines, however, you'll find that this sort of back-window access makes it almost impossible to keep track of what is interacting with what—which variables are being changed by which subroutines, where your program bugs are coming from, and so on.

The solution is found in the idea of *passing parameters* to your subroutines. Passing parameters is a way of controlling what goes into your subroutines and what comes out of them. It also makes it easier for you to see, at a glance, with which outside variables and values a subroutine is dealing.

To pass parameters to a subroutine, you add a *parameter list* to your original declaration of the subroutine. This list gives the parameter names and data types of each item that needs to go into the subroutine. When you call the subroutine in the main body of the program, you include the names of the items that you want to pass to the subroutine. Thus, in Listing 9.4, we created an **OutsideTotal** parameter through which the *Total-Stock* variable is able to enter the **GetNumberInStock** procedure. In this case, the *TotalStock* variable is changed by the procedure, so it has to be a VAR parameter—a concept that I'll explain below.

When it enters a subroutine via a parameter list, an outside item temporarily takes on the name of the parameter with which it is associated. Thus, in Listing 9.4, the *TotalStock* variable gets into the subroutine via the **OutsideTotal** parameter, and travels under that name while it is inside the subroutine. When it leaves the subroutine, it takes back its original name of *TotalStock*.

In Listing 9.4, we used a parameter name that was different from Total-Stock because we wanted to make it clear that what was happening inside the procedure was being done *to the parameter*, not directly to the global variable. Whenever possible, however, it is simpler (and easier to remember) if you use the same name for the parameter as for the item it is replacing. Normally, therefore, we would have

```
PROGRAM Listing9_4;

   ( Shows the RIGHT way to change the value of a global variable,
     by declaring it as a parameter in a subroutine. )

USES CRT;

VAR
   TotalStock: INTEGER;


PROCEDURE Pause;
   VAR
     Proceed : CHAR;
   BEGIN
     WRITE(' Press any key to continue ...');
     Proceed := READKEY;
     WRITELN; WRITELN
   END;

PROCEDURE GetNumberInStock(VAR OutsideTotal : INTEGER);
   VAR
     InStock,
     NewNum   : INTEGER;
     Continue : CHAR;
   BEGIN
     CLRSCR;
     Continue := 'Y';
     InStock := 0;
     WHILE UPCASE(Continue) = 'Y' DO
       BEGIN
       WRITELN;
       WRITE(' Enter number to add to total: ');
       READLN(NewNum);
       InStock := InStock + NewNum;
       WRITE(' Add another (Y/N)? ');
       READLN(Continue)
       END;
     WRITELN;
     WRITELN(' The total number in stock is ', InStock, '.');
     OutsideTotal := InStock;
     pause
   END;


BEGIN
   TotalStock := 0;
   GetNumberInStock(TotalStock);
   WRITELN(' The total number in stock is ', TotalStock, '.');
   pause
END.
```

Listing 9.4: Using a parameter to bring a global variable into a subroutine.

declared the **GetNumberInStock** procedure as

```
PROCEDURE GetNumberInStock(VAR TotalStock : INTEGER);
```

Because the **TotalStock** parameter is temporarily replacing the global *TotalStock* variable, there is no conflict between the two identifiers.

CREATING PARAMETER LISTS

To create a parameter list, you first have to decide which items from outside need to be passed to the subroutine. These can include both constants and variables. Then you should decide:

- What parameter names to use.

- Which outside values need to be changed by the subroutine. These will need to be declared as VAR (variable) parameters. Other parameters can be declared as "value" parameters.

- In what order you will list the parameters. Generally, it saves extra work to list all parameters of the same type together.

Thus, the following are acceptable parameter lists:

```
PROCEDURE MyRoutine1(VAR num1 : INTEGER);

        { one variable parameter of type INTEGER }
PROCEDURE MyRoutine2(num1, num2 : INTEGER;
                VAR total : INTEGER);

        { two value parameters of type INTEGER and

          one variable parameter of type INTEGER }
PROCEDURE MyRoutine3(Name : String10;
VAR PaidUp : BOOLEAN);

        { a value parameter of type String10 and a

          variable parameter of type BOOLEAN }
FUNCTION MyRoutine4(num1, num2 : INTEGER;
                Operation : String10) : INTEGER;

        { two value parameters of type INTEGER and

          one value parameter of type String10. }
```

Rules for Parameter Lists

There aren't many rules for creating parameter lists, but there are a few. First, when you actually call the routine in the action part of your program, the items you pass to it must be of *exactly the same type* as the parameters that you declared, as well as being in the correct order. Thus, for example, if you declared a parameter list as

```
PROCEDURE MyRoutine(num1 : INTEGER; YesNo : CHAR);
```

and tried to call the procedure in your program by writing **My-Routine('Y', 5)**, then your program wouldn't compile. The first value you passed to the procedure, **'Y'**, is a different data type from the **num1** parameter that stands in for it inside the procedure. The second value, **5**, is also a different data type from the **YesNo** parameter. If you reversed the order of the values in your procedure call, though, and made it **My-Routine(5, 'Y')**, then everything would work fine.

Identical and Compatible Types   When I said that parameters and the items they receive must be exactly the same type, I meant it in a stronger sense than in most situations. For example, if you have two string variables that are both of type **STRING[10]**, then you can assign the value of one string variable to the other string variable, as shown in Listing 9.5.

Listing 9.5 *looks* a little odd, since there's really no reason to declare **name1** and **name2** in separate statements, but it is perfectly legal. However, because **name1** and **name2** were defined as the **STRING[10]** data type in separate statements, they are only of *compatible*, not *identical*, data types. To be of an *identical* data type, two identifiers must refer to the same type definition statement. If we were to substitute

```
VAR
    Name1, Name2 : STRING[10];
```

in Listing 9.5, then **Name1** and **Name2** would be identical in their data type, not merely compatible. Notice that this is not a problem with built-in Pascal types such as integers and characters.

```
PROGRAM Listing9_5;

  { Illustrates compatible data types. }

USES CRT;

VAR
  name1 : STRING[10];
  name2 : STRING[10];

PROCEDURE Pause;
  VAR
    Proceed : CHAR;
  BEGIN
    WRITE(' Press any key to continue ...');
    Proceed := READKEY;
    WRITELN; WRITELN
  END;

BEGIN
  CLRSCR;
  WINDOW(5,3,75,22);
  name1 := 'Jonas Salk';
  name2 := name1;
  WRITELN(' The name in variable name1 is ', name1, '.');
  WRITELN;
  WRITELN(' The name in variable name2 is ', name2, '.');
  WRITELN;
  pause
END.
```

Listing 9.5: Compatible string types are usually all right.

The reason it is sometimes a problem in declaring parameters is that data types such as strings and arrays are partly defined by you. It is true that both are built-in data types in Turbo Pascal (strings being just a special kind of array), but *you* specify how many slots each string or array type is supposed to have.

This means that when you pass a string to a subroutine, you can end up with two type-declaration statements, as in

```
VAR

  name1 : STRING[10];

PROCEDURE MyRoutine(ParameterName : STRING[10]);

  { ... etc. }
```

Because you declared **name1** to be of **STRING[10]** type in one place and the parameter name to be of **STRING[10]** type in another place, the variable and parameter are merely *compatible,* not identical, in their data type. And a parameter will accept only an item whose data type is identical to its own. Therefore, Listing 9.6 won't compile.

The solution to this predicament, when you need to pass a structured type such as a string or an array, is to put a special definition in the TYPE section of your program, as shown in Listing 9.7. Then, the variable or other item you pass to the parameter will have a data type identical to that of the parameter itself, since both will refer to the same type definition statement. This is a small but significant change—which works fine.

VALUE AND VARIABLE PARAMETERS

Now we have come to a very important distinction: that between value and variable parameters. When you put VAR in front of a parameter name in a subroutine declaration, it means that the item that gets passed

```
PROGRAM Listing9_6;

  { Shows how you can't pass an item to a parameter when their
    data types are merely compatible; the types must be identical. }

USES CRT;

VAR
  Name1 : STRING[10];

PROCEDURE Pause;
  VAR
    Proceed : CHAR;
  BEGIN
    WRITE(' Press any key to continue ...');
    Proceed := READKEY;
    WRITELN; WRITELN
  END;

PROCEDURE SetName(VAR ParameterName : STRING[10]);
  BEGIN
    ParameterName := 'Sam'
  END;

BEGIN
  CLRSCR;
  SetName(Name1);
  WRITELN(' The name in variable Name1 is ', name1, '.');
  pause
END.
```

Listing 9.6: Compatibility is not enough; the value and the parameter must be identical data types.

```
PROGRAM Listing9_7;

  { Shows how to pass an item to a parameter by including a
    special TYPE statement in the program. }

USES CRT;

TYPE
  String10 = STRING[10];

VAR
  Name1 : String10;

PROCEDURE Pause;
  VAR
    Proceed : CHAR;
  BEGIN
    WRITE(' Press any key to continue ...');
    Proceed := READKEY;
    WRITELN; WRITELN
  END;

PROCEDURE SetName(VAR ParameterName : String10);
  BEGIN
    ParameterName := 'Sam'
  END;

BEGIN
  CLRSCR;
  SetName(Name1);
  WRITELN(' The name in variable Name1 is ', name1, '.');
  pause
END.
```

Listing 9.7: Putting a special TYPE statement in the program solves the problem.

to this parameter is passed "by reference." If you do not put VAR in front of the parameter, then the item is passed "by value."

As usual, the technical jargon tends to obscure rather than to clarify what's really happening. Let's take things one at a time. When you first declare a variable in your program, Pascal sets aside a location in your PC's memory to hold that variable. When you pass a variable to a parameter "by reference," it means that you are making that parameter refer to *the same memory address* as the original variable.

Thus, any value that you assign to that parameter will be sent to the memory location for the outside variable that was passed (by reference) to the parameter. This means that anything you do to the parameter is done simultaneously to the outside variable. And this is why VAR parameters are called "variable" parameters: they can actually change the values of the outside variables that they receive.

Contrast this with a parameter that was not declared as a VAR parameter. In this case, the outside item is passed "by value." Instead of making the parameter refer to the same memory location as the item itself, Pascal makes a *copy* of the item's value and passes *that* to the parameter. The parameter does not refer to anything outside the subroutine, and changes made in the parameter can affect only the copied value—*not* the outside variable.

In a nutshell, when you use a VAR parameter, you are passing the *actual outside variable* into the subroutine. When you do not use a VAR parameter, you are passing only a *copy* of the outside variable into the subroutine, and the outside variable itself will not and cannot be changed.

You should use VAR parameters when:

- The item passed to the subroutine needs to have its value changed by the subroutine.

- The item passed to the subroutine is a variable that represents a disk file. In this case, Turbo Pascal requires that you use a VAR parameter because it is impractical to make a copy of the original file.

- You need to economize on the memory used by your program. Because value parameters make copies of the original variables, they require more memory than VAR parameters. When you are passing some very large data items (such as large arrays) to a subroutine, the memory required for making copies can be considerable, so VAR parameters may be a better choice.

You should use value parameters when:

- The item passed to the subroutine does not need to be changed by the subroutine.

- You want a little extra safety against accidental changes to an outside variable.

FORWARD DECLARATIONS

There are many situations in which one subroutine in a program calls another. Because nothing can be used in a Pascal program before it is declared, this means that you have to declare the subroutine that gets called *before* you declare the subroutine that calls it, as in

```
PROCEDURE MyRoutine1(SomeParameter : INTEGER);

  { code for the procedure }

PROCEDURE MyRoutine2(AnotherParameter : CHAR);

  BEGIN

     MyRoutine1(15);

     { ... etc.}

  END;
```

But what happens if sometimes **MyRoutine2** calls **MyRoutine1**, but at other times **MyRoutine1** calls **MyRoutine2**—as in the following:

```
PROCEDURE MyRoutine1(SomeParameter : INTEGER);

  BEGIN

     IF SomeParameter < 10 THEN MyRoutine2('Y');

     { ... etc.}

PROCEDURE MyRoutine2(AnotherParameter : CHAR);

  BEGIN

     MyRoutine1(15);

     { ... etc.}

  END;
```

We seem to be in an impossible situation. If **MyRoutine2** is to be able to call **MyRoutine1**, then **MyRoutine1** has to be declared first. But if

MyRoutine1 has to call **MyRoutine2**, then **MyRoutine2** has to be declared first. But we cannot declare both of them first.

Or can we? The solution to our problem is called a *forward declaration*. Pascal does not care if we spell out all the details of a subroutine before we call it, just so long as we've declared it. A forward declaration tells Pascal that a routine needs to be declared at a certain place, but that the details will be given later. To make a forward declaration, we simply give the first line of the subroutine declaration and, at the end, we add the word **FOR-WARD**, as in

```
PROCEDURE MyRoutine2(AnotherParameter : CHAR);

FORWARD;

PROCEDURE MyRoutine1(SomeParameter : INTEGER);

   BEGIN

      IF SomeParameter < 10 THEN MyRoutine2('Y');

      { ... etc.}

PROCEDURE MyRoutine2(AnotherParameter : CHAR);

   BEGIN

      MyRoutine1(15);

      { ... etc.}

   END;
```

Because we've declared **MyRoutine2** before **MyRoutine1** (even though we have not given the details), we can now have **MyRoutine1** call **MyRoutine2** and **MyRoutine2** call **MyRoutine1**.

COMMON MISTAKES WITH PROCEDURES AND FUNCTIONS

There are three mistakes that beginning programmers make again and again with procedures and functions. These errors are common enough to warrant some discussion. In order of priority, the mistakes are as follows:

FAILURE TO USE VAR WHEN NEEDED

By far, the most common mistake is failing to put VAR in front of a parameter for an outside variable that needs to be changed by the subroutine. This means that only a *copy* of the outside variable actually will be passed into the subroutine, and the outside variable won't be changed at all. This mistake is illustrated in Listing 9.8.

```
PROGRAM Listing9_8;

  ( Shows how failure to use VAR when needed to indicate a
    variable parameter will cause a program to malfunction.
    Here, the error is in the AddSalesTax procedure, where
    "OutsideAmount" should be declared as a VAR parameter. )

USES CRT;

VAR
  Amount : REAL;

PROCEDURE Pause;
  VAR
    Proceed : CHAR;
  BEGIN
    WRITE(' Press any key to continue ...');
    Proceed := READKEY;
    WRITELN; WRITELN
  END;

PROCEDURE AddSalesTax(OutsideAmount : REAL);
  CONST
    SalesTax = 0.05;
  BEGIN
    OutsideAmount := OutsideAmount + (OutsideAmount * SalesTax)
  END;

BEGIN
  CLRSCR;
  WRITE(' Enter the amount of purchase: ');
  READLN(Amount);
  WRITELN(' The amount without tax is ', Amount:0:2, '.');
  pause;
  AddSalesTax(Amount);
  WRITELN(' The amount with tax is ', Amount:0:2, '.');
  pause
END.
```

Listing 9.8: Failure to use VAR with a parameter that must change.

DIRECTLY CHANGING GLOBAL VARIABLES

The second most common mistake is directly changing the values of global variables. Beginning programmers often think that they can get away with this practice because, in the simple example programs they are most likely to see, it does no special harm. If you are writing any program of reasonable complexity, however, it will certainly land you in deep trouble. It's better to get into the habit of doing things right from the very beginning.

PARAMETERS IN THE WRONG ORDER

The third most common error is passing parameters in the wrong order. Just as parameters are *declared* in a specific order, the items that will be passed to the parameters must be listed in the *same* order when the subroutine is actually used in the program. Otherwise, the program either will not compile at all (if there is a data-type mismatch) or the subroutine will malfunction, as in Listing 9.9.

Although you might think that the error in Listing 9.9 is a harmless one because the program does compile all right, it is, in fact, the *worst* kind of program bug: one that compiles without any error messages but gives you the wrong answers when you run the program. Though anyone can see that 10 + 25 isn't equal to 0, the errors in a complex program are not nearly as obvious—and therefore can be catastrophic.

ABOUT BREAKING THE RULES

Much of this chapter has been an extended sermon on the evils of failing to compartmentalize subroutines properly. In an ideal world, all outside variables used in subroutines would be passed to the subroutines as parameters, and the internal details of each subroutine would be completely sealed off from the rest of the program in which it occurs.

```
PROGRAM Listing9_9;

   ( Demonstrates problems that can arise from incorrectly-ordered
     values passed to a subroutine. The values must be in the same
     order as the parameter list. )

USES CRT;

VAR
  num1, num2, num3  : INTEGER;

PROCEDURE Pause;
  VAR
    Proceed : CHAR;
  BEGIN
    WRITE(' Press any key to continue ...');
    Proceed := READKEY;
    WRITELN; WRITELN
  END;

PROCEDURE Initialize(VAR a,b,c : INTEGER);
  BEGIN
    CLRSCR;
    a := 0;
    b := 0;
    c := 0
  END;


PROCEDURE AddTwoNumbers(a,b : INTEGER; VAR c : INTEGER);
  BEGIN
    c := a + b
  END;

BEGIN
  Initialize(num1, num2, num3);
  num1 := 10;
  num2 := 25;
  AddTwoNumbers(num3, num1, num2);
  WRITELN(' The sum of ', num1, ' and ', num2, ' is ', num3, '.');
  pause
END.
```

Listing 9.9: Values passed to a subroutine must be listed in the correct order.

In the real world, however, there is no denying the truth: sometimes, highly skilled programmers fail to declare outside variables as parameters. Instead, they violate the principle of information hiding and pull some global variables directly into their subroutines. And their programs work fine.

In part, they can do this precisely *because* they are highly skilled. Nobody tells Jimmy Connors how to play tennis, Gata Kamsky how to play chess, or Mike Tyson how to throw a punch. (Nobody would dare!) If an expert decides to break the rules, the presumption must be that the expert knows the "correct" method but, based on experience, thinks that a different approach will work better in solving the current problem.

The novice programmer is in a different situation. Lacking the expert's years of experience, he or she should follow the rules whenever possible. Later, after acquiring more experience, he or she will be better equipped to decide if a particular rule can be ignored in a specific case.

At the same time, there are some situations in which it is safer to break the rules than in others. Although I am not saying it is "all right" to use outside variables in a subroutine without declaring them as parameters, here are four situations in which it is less dangerous to do so:

1. *When the program is very simple.* In this case, it's foolish to be a stickler about information hiding. The main purpose of structured programming is to make complex programs easier to code, debug, understand, and modify. If the program is very simple, then structured programming becomes less important.

2. *When you are the one and only programmer.* Another benefit of structured programming is that it allows you to divide a large programming project between the members of a project team. Each subroutine can be coded and tested separately, and because of information hiding, the individual programmer does not need to worry about how other programmers are coding their subroutines. If you are the only programmer working on the project, however, then strict information hiding becomes less important. Note that it does *not* become *un*important. To the extent that your code fails to follow structured methods, it will be more difficult to understand and modify in the future. If you forget how you coded a part of the program, or someone else needs to modify your program in the future, unstructured code will make things more difficult.

3. *When a subroutine is local within another subroutine.* When one subroutine is declared inside another, often it is unnecessary to pass variables as parameters to the local subroutine. Global variables will already have been passed as parameters to the main subroutine, and the level of complexity *within* a subroutine is normally (and should be) quite manageable. Thus, you should pass global variables as parameters to the main subroutine, but if you declare a local subroutine inside the main subroutine, it can get away with not declaring everything it uses as a parameter.

4. *When a subroutine simply abbreviates code.* Sometimes, you will find that the main body of your program has too many lines in it and would be clearer if you moved some of those lines off into a separate subroutine. These lines of code, as part of the main body of the program, may already have been using global variables. If you create a subroutine simply to abbreviate the main program, particularly if the main program is fairly simple, then it does no great harm to adjust global variables directly, so long as it is very obvious what you did. Nevertheless, it is still a better practice to bring the global variables into the subroutine as parameters.

SUMMARY

Procedures and functions are named blocks of code that embody the very essence of structured programming. A procedure is used mainly to perform a sequence of actions and can return multiple values, while a function is used mainly to return a single value: a procedure is similar to an English sentence, while a function is similar to an individual word.

The most important advantage provided by procedures and functions is that they allow a program to be subdivided into smaller blocks. These smaller blocks can be designed, coded, and debugged separately, thereby reducing the complexity of the programmer's task and decreasing the probability of bugs.

The internal details of a procedure or function should be hidden from the rest of the program, in the sense that making a change in their internal details should have no effect on the operation of the rest of the program. One important way to achieve this goal is to make sure that all outside variables are passed to procedures and functions as parameters.

Parameters can be either value parameters or variable parameters, but only variable parameters can actually be changed by a procedure or function. A parameter's data type must be identical to the variable it stands for, which means that string and array types must be given special identifiers in the TYPE section of the program.

REVIEW EXERCISES

1. Explain the concept of a procedure and the concept of a function. How are they alike and different?

2. Explain the idea of information hiding and how it is related to procedures and functions.

3. Is there anything wrong with this code fragment? If so, what is the problem and how would you correct it? Will it compile in its present form?

```
VAR
  Name : string15;
PROCEDURE GetName;
  VAR
    Name : string15;
  BEGIN
    WRITE(' Enter a name: ');
    READLN(Name)
  END;
```

4. Is there anything wrong with this code fragment? If so, what is the problem and how would you correct it? Will it compile in its present form?

```
PROCEDURE GetName;
  VAR
    Name : string15;
  BEGIN
    WRITE(' Enter a name: ');
    READLN(name)
  END;
  BEGIN { main body of program }
    GetName;
    WRITELN('Name entered in GetName: ', name, '.')
  END.
```

5. Explain the idea of scope. State and explain a rule for determining the scope of any identifier.

6. Is there anything wrong with this code fragment? If so, what is the problem and how would you correct it? Will it compile in its present form?

```
TYPE
     Student = RECORD
                    name : string15;
                    GPA  : REAL
                    END;
     string15 = STRING[15];
     StudentList = ARRAY[1..100] OF Student;
VAR
     Class : StudentList;
```

7. What is a forward declaration? Under what circumstances would a forward declaration be needed?

8. What information must be included in a procedure declaration? In a function declaration? If there is any difference in the information that must be included, explain why there is a difference.

9. Explain the two different ways in which a parameter can be passed to a subroutine. How does each method work? When should you use each?

10. List three major blunders that you can make in setting up a parameter list.

11. Explain the meaning of identical and compatible data types. How are they different?

12. True or false: You can change the internal details of any properly designed subroutine without having to change anything in the program outside the subroutine. If the statement is false, explain why it is false.

13. Explain the significance of the Pascal rule that identifiers must be declared before they are used.

14. Is there anything wrong with this code fragment? If so, what is the problem and how would you correct it? Will it compile in its present form?

```
VAR Name : string15;
PROCEDURE GetName(Name : string15);
  BEGIN
    WRITE(' Enter a name: ');
    READLN(name)
  END;
  BEGIN { main body of program }
    GetName(name);
    WRITELN(' The name entered is ', name, '.')
  END.
```

15. Is there any reason you might decide to pass a variable to a subroutine as a VAR parameter even when it will not be changed by the subroutine? Explain your answer.

C H A P T E R

Using Turbo Pascal Units

One has to approach the radical novelty with a blank mind, consciously refusing to try to link history with what is already familiar, because the familiar is hopelessly inadequate.

– Edsger Dijkstra, *"On the Cruelty of Really Teaching Computing Science," Communications of the ACM, December 1989.*

If units are not a radical novelty, then at the very least they are a useful one. In previous chapters, we have often used the Pause routine to stop the execution of our programs so that we could look at the output. We have also used **GetGoodInt** and **GetGood-Char** to provide error-trapping input routines. But there is one major problem: we have always had to include the routines we wanted in each new program that used them. This task is made easier by Turbo Pascal 6's ability to cut and paste between different file windows, but it is still a minor irritation.

In this chapter, we will look at a cure for that irritant: Turbo Pascal units. A *unit* is a separately compiled Pascal file in which you can put frequently used routines. When you need to use one of the routines, you simply name the unit in the USES clause of your program. If Turbo Pascal cannot find the definition of a particular routine in your program itself, it looks for it in the units you have named.

Turbo Pascal comes with several predefined and precompiled units that you can use with your programs. We have used the CRT unit in almost every listing so far to provide routines for clearing the screen and detecting keypresses (in the Pause procedure). Later in this chapter, we will discuss Turbo Pascal's predefined units

In addition to its predefined units, Turbo Pascal allows you to create your own units with routines that you develop yourself. These are used in exactly the same way as the predefined units, by including their names in a USES statement after the name of your program:

```
PROGRAM MyProgram;

USES CRT, MyUtils;
```

A NOTE FOR USERS
OF TURBO PASCAL 3.0

Units were first introduced in version 4.0 of Turbo Pascal, so if you are using an earlier version—such as version 3.0, which is a very popular educational version of Turbo Pascal—then you will have to use "include" files instead of units.

The main practical differences between units and include files are that (1) include files must be recompiled each time you compile your program, and (2) include files are inserted in your program with the {**$I** filename} compiler directive instead of a USES clause. Include files are discussed in detail at the end of this chapter.

The other key difference of Turbo Pascal 3.0 is that it contains some routines that, in later versions, were tucked into their own units. The CLRSCR routine from the CRT unit is a good example. In Turbo Pascal 3.0, you simply call this routine as a built-in part of the language, but in later versions, it is tucked into the CRT unit. To use CLRSCR in Turbo Pascal 4.0 or later, you must name the CRT unit in a USES clause.

PARTS OF A UNIT

A unit is divided into two main parts, as shown in Figure 10.1. In Figure 10.1, the publicly accessible part of the unit is surrounded by a single line; the hidden part of the unit is surrounded by a double line.

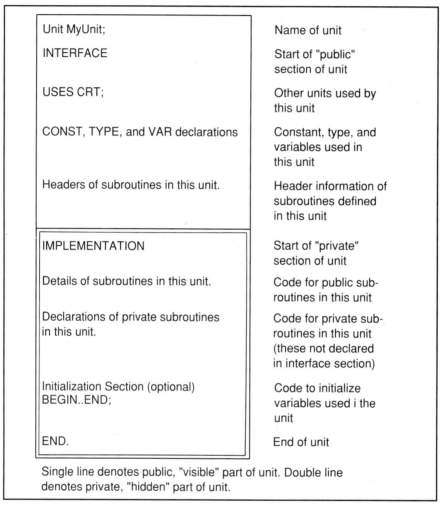

Unit MyUnit;	Name of unit
INTERFACE	Start of "public" section of unit
USES CRT;	Other units used by this unit
CONST, TYPE, and VAR declarations	Constant, type, and variables used in this unit
Headers of subroutines in this unit.	Header information of subroutines defined in this unit
IMPLEMENTATION	Start of "private" section of unit
Details of subroutines in this unit.	Code for public sub-routines in this unit
Declarations of private subroutines in this unit.	Code for private sub-routines in this unit (these not declared in interface section)
Initialization Section (optional) BEGIN..END;	Code to initialize variables used i the unit
END.	End of unit

Single line denotes public, "visible" part of unit. Double line denotes private, "hidden" part of unit.

Figure 10.1: Structure of a Unit.

INTERFACE

The public part of a unit, which is visible to other program modules that use the unit, consists of (1) the name of the unit and (2) the INTERFACE section of the unit. Other program modules that use the unit can use any subroutines, constants, variables, data types, or other program elements that are declared in this section of the program. It begins with the word INTERFACE and ends with the word IMPLEMENTATION, which marks the beginning of the next section of the unit.

It is important to note that this public section contains everything that a user or program needs to know in order to use the routines in the unit. For example, a unit could be declared as shown in Listing 10.1. In the INTERFACE section of the unit, you provide the name of each subroutine, what goes into it, and what comes out of it. And, remember, whether a subroutine is in a unit or not, in structured programming, that information is *all* that the rest of the program should need to be able to use the subroutine.

Units do have one peculiar aspect. In program listings, it did not matter if the program name declaration matched the filename of the program. If a program was named Register, you could save it just as easily under the name LIST5_X.PAS as you could under the name REGISTER.PAS. With units, however, Turbo Pascal must (1) locate the file on your hard disk and (2) use it by the unit name you have specified in your USES statement. Thus, the name of a unit must match its filename on disk. A unit called MyUtils, for example, must be saved under the name MYUTILS.PAS, not under another name such as LIST10_3.PAS. This limits the names of units to eight characters, but you can always clarify the unit's purpose by inserting a comment under the unit name.

IMPLEMENTATION

The IMPLEMENTATION section of the unit is "private" and is hidden from any other program modules that use the unit. It contains, as shown in Listing 10.1, the details of how subroutines named in the INTERFACE section actually work. It can also contain private declarations of subroutines, variables, constants, data types, and any other identifiers that you want to use in the unit but which should not be visible to anything outside the unit.

This ability to include such private declarations is very important. It lets you avoid some rather tricky bugs that can occur when another program module accidentally uses a variable, constant, or other identifier in a unit when it is not supposed to. Then, when you try to find the bug, you think you are looking at one variable when, in fact, you're looking at a completely different one. When it is appropriate, creating some private

```
Listing 10_1;

Unit MyUtils;  { Listing 10.1: miscellaneous utility routines. }

INTERFACE
{ =================== PUBLIC section of unit ====================
}

USES CRT, GRAPH;

TYPE
  GoodChars = set of char;    { used with the GetGoodChar
procedure }

CONST
  YNchars : GoodChars = ['Y', 'y', 'N', 'n'];


PROCEDURE Pause;    { accepts any key }

PROCEDURE GetGoodChar(GoodOnes:GoodChars; var InChar:char);

PROCEDURE GetGoodInt(MinNum, MaxNum: integer; var InNum:integer);


IMPLEMENTATION
{ =================== PRIVATE section of unit ===================
}


PROCEDURE Pause; { Pauses the program until user presses a key. }
  VAR
    Proceed : char;
  BEGIN
    Writeln;
    Write(' Press any key to continue ... ');
    Proceed := readkey;
    Writeln; Writeln
  END;


PROCEDURE GetGoodChar(GoodOnes:GoodChars; var InChar:char);

  {An error-trapping substitute for "readln" to get character
  input from the keyboard. This procedure takes two parameters:
  a set of "acceptable" characters for input, and a variable
  parameter that is the actual character input.  If the input
  character is not in the set of acceptable characters, this
  procedure returns to the original screen position and waits
  for the user to enter an acceptable character.}

  VAR
    markX, markY  : byte;
  BEGIN
    repeat
      BEGIN
        markX := whereX;
        markY := whereY;
        Readln(InChar);
        if not (InChar in GoodOnes) then
```

Listing 10.1: Structure of a Turbo Pascal unit.

```
              BEGIN
                gotoXY(markX, markY);
                ClrEOL
              END
          END
        until InChar in GoodOnes
    END;


PROCEDURE GetGoodInt(MinNum, MaxNum: integer;  var InNum:
integer);

    {An error-trapping substitute for "readln" to get integer
    input from the keyboard. This procedure takes two parameters:
    a set of "acceptable" integers for input, and a variable
    parameter that is the actual integer input.  If the input
    integer is not in the set of acceptable integers, this
    procedure returns to the original screen position and waits
    for the user to enter an acceptable integer.}

    VAR
      markX, markY  : byte;
      LoopControl   : integer;

    BEGIN
      repeat
          BEGIN
            markX := whereX;
            markY := whereY;

            {$I-}
            Readln(InNum);
            {$I+}
            LoopControl := ioresult;

            if (LoopControl <> 0) then
              BEGIN
                gotoXY(markX, markY);
                ClrEOL
              END;

            if (inNum < MinNum) or (inNum > MaxNum) then
              BEGIN
                gotoXY(markX, markY);
                ClrEOL
              END
          END
        until (LoopControl = 0) and (InNum >= MinNum) and (InNum <=
    MaxNum)
      END;




    END.     { of the "MyUtils" unit }
```

Listing 10.1: Structure of a Turbo Pascal unit. (cont.)

declarations in the IMPLEMENTATION section of the unit means that this problem cannot happen—at least not with the private identifiers. Remember the programming maxim: *Hide everything you can.*

The IMPLEMENTATION section begins with the word IMPLEMENTATION and ends with the word END, which marks the end of the unit.

INITIALIZATION

The initialization section of the unit allows you to assign values to variables and do other setup work that needs to be done before the subroutines in the unit are actually used. The initialization section, which is just like the main body of a regular program file, carries out its instructions when the unit is called. If you are using multiple units, then their initialization sections (if any) run in the order that they are named in your USES statement. As you can see in Listing 10.1, the initialization section is hidden inside the IMPLEMENTATION section:

```
Unit MyStuff;

INTERFACE

   { public declarations }

IMPLEMENTATION

   { private declarations }

   BEGIN { initialization section }

   { initialization statements }

   END;

END. { of MyStuff unit }
```

Depending on the situation, you also can use the initialization section of a unit to make sure that it is possible for the unit to work. For example, if certain files or memory-resident drivers are needed to run the unit, then the initialization section can determine if these are present. If they are not, then it can take the appropriate action, from warning the user to shutting down the entire program.

If your initialization needs are simple and the variables you are initializing are public, then you can use typed constants in the INTERFACE
part of the unit as a simpler alternative to having an initialization section.
For example, in Listing 10.1, we used the initialization section only to assign the string **'James'** to the public variable *Name*. In this case, it would
have been better to declare **Name** as a typed constant (a preinitialized
variable) as follows:

```
Unit List10_1;

INTERFACE

TYPE

   String10 = STRING[10];

CONST

   Name : string10 = 'James'

{ ... etc. }
```

This would create *Name* as a public variable and initialize it with the
value **'James'**. (If you need to review typed constants, they are discussed
in Chapter 5.)

Listing 10.2 demonstrates how to name a unit in a USES statement.
Note that the CRT unit is named first. In Turbo Pascal 4.0, if you used multiple units, and unit No.1 used unit No.2 (as Listing10.1 uses the CRT unit),
then you had to list unit No.2 first in the USES statement, in accordance
with Pascal's general rule that everything must be declared before it is
used. Turbo Pascal 5.0 relaxed this rule so for that and later versions, you
can list units in any order you desire.

In the main body of Listing 10.2, we first assign the **NumberOfNames**
constant from the unit to a *NewNumber* variable in our program,
demonstrating that constants in the INTERFACE section are indeed
visible to the calling program. Then, we called the **GetName** routine from
the unit and let it load a value into the *Name* variable, also from the unit.
Finally, we used **GetName** with a variable from the calling program—
which is much more common than using it with a variable from the unit.
In both cases, it loaded the name you entered into the correct variable.

```
PROGRAM Listing10_2;

USES CRT, List10_1;

VAR
  NewName : string10;
  NewNumber : INTEGER;

PROCEDURE Pause;
  VAR
    Proceed : CHAR;
  BEGIN
    WRITELN;
    WRITE(' Press any key to continue ...');
    Proceed := READKEY;
    WRITELN; WRITELN
  END;

BEGIN
  CLRSCR;
  NewNumber := NumberOfNames;
  WRITE(' The current value of "Name" in the List10_1 unit is ');
  WRITELN(Name, '.');
  pause;

  GetName(Name);     { uses Name variable from unit }
  WRITE(' The new value of "Name" in the List10_1 unit is ');
  WRITELN(Name);
  pause;

  GetName(NewName);  { uses NewName variable from this program }
  WRITELN(' The current value of "NewName" is ', NewName, '.');
  pause
END.
```

Listing 10.2: How to name a unit in a USES statement.

WHY USE UNITS?

There are three main reasons to use units. The first, as I have already mentioned, is to store frequently used subroutines in a separate file from which they can be called *without* having to include them in the main program each time. The second, which was celebrated as "shattering the 64K barrier" when units were first introduced, provides a practical way to create programs larger than the 64K size limit of Turbo Pascal 3.0. The third, which makes programming easier in the long run, is "procedural abstraction" that allows you to hide details about how subroutines in a unit actually work.

PACKAGING
FREQUENTLY USED ROUTINES

Packaging frequently used subroutines is more than just a matter of saving effort. By keeping subroutines in a separate unit, you can reduce the amount of time needed to compile a large program, because the units do not have to be recompiled each time you recompile your main program. This means that you can make as many changes as you want to in your main program, and not have to worry about those changes having any effect on the units.

If you are developing software for other Turbo Pascal programmers, you can distribute your work in precompiled units, which they can incorporate into their own programs. The people at TurboPower Software and Blaise Computing, two vendors of programming tools for Turbo Pascal, make a very nice living at this. Even if you are developing routines only for use in your own organization, this lets you distribute standardized units without the fear that they will be modified by anyone but you.

DEVELOPING LARGE PROGRAMS

One of the greatest benefits of using units is that they provide a practical way to develop programs larger than 64K. The 64K limit on program size is not an arbitrary feature of Turbo Pascal, but results from the limitations of the Intel 8086 processor, which with its descendants (the Intel 80286, 80386, and 80486) power virtually all PCs. The 8086, as a 16-bit microprocessor, handles data in 16-bit chunks. This means that it can directly handle 2^{16} (64K) different numbers to stand for memory locations; 64K is the number of different 16-digit combinations of zeroes and ones.

In order to deal with more memory, however—a full one megabyte, or 1,024K—the 8086 divides your PC's memory into 64K *segments*, each of which begins at a paragraph address. To calculate a given memory location, the 8086 combines two 16-bit pieces of information: the paragraph address where the 64K segment starts, and the offset, which gives a specific address within that segment. Thus, through some complex maneuvering, your PC can handle a full megabyte of RAM.

Even with this segmented-addressing scheme, however, the 8086 is still only a 16-bit processor and cannot easily handle information in chunks larger than 64K—the size of a single memory segment. This means that Turbo Pascal cannot compile a program file larger than 64K because all the code has to fit into a single segment. And, although the 80386 and 80486 processors are 32-bit chips that can address 2^{32} memory locations, we still have the 64K limit to keep compatibility with less powerful 8086 and 80286-based PCs.

Units provide a way around this problem. By splitting off groups of subroutines into their own units and then naming them in a USES clause at the beginning of your program, you can evade the 64K size limitation on your programs because no single program file is larger than 64K. You can even do the same trick with units themselves, which can USE other units.

PROCEDURAL ABSTRACTION

Procedural abstraction is a less obvious, but in the long run, no less important reason for using units. An important feature of subroutines, as you should recall from Chapter 9, is that their details remain hidden from the main part of the program. If you include a subroutine in the main program, then you are able to violate this information-hiding principle—even though it is not a good idea to do so. Units, however, enforce information hiding very strictly: the details of a unit's subroutines are completely invisible to the main program.

As we saw in Figure 10.1, the only public parts of a unit are its name and its INTERFACE section, which gives "headers" of the unit's subroutines without any of their details, for example,

```
PROCEDURE Pause;
```

Everything except the unit's name and its Interface section is hidden from the main program. You can even include private subroutines that are accessible only within the unit by defining them in the Implementation (hidden) section and omitting their headers from the Interface section. Like units themselves, these can make your main program easier to read and provide subroutines that are local to a group of procedures but do not have to be included in each procedure.

Suppose, for example, that you want to use a local subroutine **DoBalance** inside two other subroutines **OnTimePayment** and **LatePayment**, but you do not want it accessible to other parts of the program. If you declared it as follows,

```
{ ... other declarations }

PROCEDURE DoBalance(VAR balance : REAL);

{ details of DoBalance routine}

PROCEDURE OnTimePayment(VAR balance : REAL);

{ details of OnTimePayment routine }

PROCEDURE LatePayment(VAR balance : REAL);

{ details of LatePayment routine }

{ ... the rest of the program }
```

then **DoBalance** would be accessible to both **OnTimePayment** and **LatePayment**, but it would *not* be hidden from the rest of the program as you wish. However, making it local to the two subroutines involves some redundancy, as in

```
{ ... other declarations }

PROCEDURE OnTimePayment(VAR balance : REAL);

    { ... }

    PROCEDURE DoBalance;

    { details of DoBalance }

PROCEDURE LatePayment(VAR balance : REAL);

    { ... }

    PROCEDURE DoBalance;

    { details of DoBalance }

{ ... the rest of the program }
```

Of course, there are other ways around this problem, but using **DoBalance** as a private subroutine in a unit with **OnTimePayment** and

LatePayment gives you a fairly neat solution. Assuming that **DoBalance** is declared before **OnTimePayment** and **LatePayment** in the implementation section of the unit, it would then be accessible to both subroutines, and would be hidden from the main program.

SETTING UP THE MYUTILS UNIT

Now that we have a good idea of what units are and how they work, let's create a new unit called MyUtils to hold frequently-used utility routines. In this chapter, we'll add the **Pause**, **GetGoodInt**, and **GetGood-Char** routines to MyUtils. As we develop new utility routines in later chapters, we will add them as well.

To create the MyUtils unit, enter Listing 10.3 and save it under the filename MYUTILS.PAS. If you want to avoid rekeying, you can use Turbo Pascal's paste feature (discussed in Chapter 4) to paste the three routines into the implementation section of the unit. **Pause** can be found in Listing 10.2, **GetGoodInt** in Listing 7.11, and **GetGoodChar** is in Listing 8.4.

There are several things to note about the MyUtils unit. First, like all units, it begins with the reserved word UNIT and the name of the unit. An explanatory comment tells what the unit is to be used for.

Then, in the Interface part of the unit, we include the following:

- A USES statement that names other units used by the MyUtils unit. You already know that we use the CRT unit for the CLRSCR routine and several other routines. The GRAPH unit will be used in Chapter 15 for both text and graphics-oriented routines, such as determining the type of video adapter in the user's PC and setting screen colors.

- A TYPE declaration that defines a data type for use with the **Get-GoodChar** routine.

- A CONST declaration that sets up a typed constant (a pre-initialized variable) of the data type we just defined. In this case, the type is the set of characters; the typed constant is a set that can include any characters we assign to it. In the typed constant

```
Unit MyUtils;  { Listing 10.3: miscellaneous utility routines. }


INTERFACE
{ ================== PUBLIC section of unit ====================
}

USES CRT, GRAPH;

TYPE
  GoodChars = set of char;    { used with the GetGoodChar
procedure }

CONST
  YNchars : GoodChars = ['Y', 'y', 'N', 'n'];



PROCEDURE Pause;    { accepts any key }

PROCEDURE GetGoodChar(GoodOnes:GoodChars; var InChar:char);

PROCEDURE GetGoodInt(MinNum, MaxNum: integer; var InNum:integer);


IMPLEMENTATION
{ ================== PRIVATE section of unit ==================
}

PROCEDURE Pause; { Pauses the program until user presses a key. }
  VAR
    Proceed : char;
  BEGIN
    Writeln;
    Write(' Press any key to continue ... ');
    Proceed := readkey;
    Writeln; Writeln
  END;


PROCEDURE GetGoodChar(GoodOnes:GoodChars; var InChar:char);

  {An error-trapping substitute for "readln" to get character
  input from the keyboard. This procedure takes two parameters:
  a set of "acceptable" characters for input, and a variable
  parameter that is the actual character input.  If the input
  character is not in the set of acceptable characters, this
  procedure returns to the original screen position and waits
  for the user to enter an acceptable character.}

  VAR
    markX, markY  : byte;
  BEGIN
    repeat
      BEGIN
        markX := whereX;
        markY := whereY;
        Readln(InChar);
        if not (InChar in GoodOnes) then
```

Listing 10.3: The MyUtils unit.

```
          BEGIN
            gotoXY(markX, markY);
            ClrEOL
          END
      END
    until InChar in GoodOnes
  END;


PROCEDURE GetGoodInt(MinNum, MaxNum: integer;  var InNum:
integer);

  {An error-trapping substitute for "readln" to get integer
  input from the keyboard. This procedure takes two parameters:
  a set of "acceptable" integers for input, and a variable
  parameter that is the actual integer input.  If the input
  integer is not in the set of acceptable integers, this
  procedure returns to the original screen position and waits
  for the user to enter an acceptable integer.}

  VAR
    markX, markY  : byte;
    LoopControl   : integer;

  BEGIN
    repeat
        BEGIN
          markX := whereX;
          markY := whereY;

          {$I-}
          Readln(InNum);
          {$I+}
          LoopControl := ioresult;

          if (LoopControl <> 0) then
            BEGIN
              gotoXY(markX, markY);
              ClrEOL
            END;

          if (inNum < MinNum) or (inNum > MaxNum) then
            BEGIN
              gotoXY(markX, markY);
              ClrEOL
            END
        END
    until (LoopControl = 0) and (InNum >= MinNum) and (InNum <=
MaxNum)
  END;



END.    { of the "MyUtils" unit }
```

Listing 10.3: The MyUtils unit. (cont.)

declaration, we load 'Y', 'y', 'N', and 'n' into the set and refer to them by the variable name **YNchars** (for Yes-No characters).

- Headers for the subroutines that are currently defined in this unit. Each header lists the name of the subroutine and the parameters it takes, as well as the data type of each parameter and whether or not it is a VAR parameter.

In the implementation part of the unit, we repeat the header of each subroutine, but this time, we include the full details of how the subroutine works. Note that the header in the interface section must exactly match the header in the implementation section; otherwise, Turbo Pascal will not be able to compile the unit and will give you an "undefined forward" error message. (The headers in the interface section are, in a certain sense, forward declarations of subroutines to come. The only difference is that in the interface part of a unit, you do not have to specify that they are forward declarations, because it is assumed.)

The MyUtils unit ends with the reserved word END and a period. If we had wanted to, we could have declared **YNchars** in the interface section as a variable instead of a typed constant. In that case, we could have included an initialization section to load it with the characters we wanted.

STANDARD TURBO PASCAL UNITS

Turbo Pascal comes with several predefined and precompiled units that add new features to the Pascal language. We will be using each of these units later, so at this point, let's just take a quick look at what each unit is and what it contains.

SYSTEM

The System unit provides a wide variety of low-level features, and is automatically linked with every program; therefore, you do not have to specify the System unit in a USES clause. Because of this, you can consider the routines in the System unit to be a built-in part of the Turbo Pascal language.

DOS

The DOS unit, which will be discussed in Chapter 16, has routines that let you call a variety of MS-DOS functions, from reading directories of files on disk to executing outside programs from your Turbo Pascal program.

CRT

The CRT unit contains several useful routines that we have seen already: CLRSCR, WINDOW, GotoXY, KeyPressed, ReadKey, and ClrEOL. Other important routines in the CRT unit are the following:

- TextMode, which allows you to set the screen mode (color or monochrome) with either a 40- or an 80-column screen width and 25, 43, or 50-line screen height.

- TextColor and TextBackground, which allow you to set the color of text and the background over which it is displayed.

- AssignCRT, which associates a text file with the screen.

- Sound and NoSound, which we will use in creating Turbo Tunemaker in Chapters 20.

PRINTER

The printer unit has only one task to carry out, and that is to let your program direct output to a printer. The printer unit automatically assigns the filename LST to your PC's LPT1 printer port, and any output you direct to LST will be sent to the printer, as in

```
WRITELN(LST, 'This will print on your printer.');
```

If your printer is connected to a different port than LPT1, do not despair. You can create your own printer-file variable and assign a different port to it, just as you would assign a DOS name to any other file variable. If your printer is connected to the LPT2 port (or the COM1 or COM2 port), you can direct output to the printer by including the following lines in your program:

```
PROGRAM PrintDemo;

USES PRINTER;

VAR MyPrinter : text;

BEGIN

  ASSIGN(MyPrinter, 'LPT2');

  REWRITE(MyPrinter);

  { ... etc. }

  CLOSE(MyPrinter)

END.
```

GRAPH

The graph unit allows you to create a wide range of graphics displays, from bar charts and fractals to fancy type styles and sizes. We'll discuss the graph unit in detail in Chapter 15.

OVERLAY

The overlay unit allows you to develop very large programs whose size exceeds your PC's available DOS memory. Normally, when you start a program, the entire program is loaded into your PC's RAM. With very large programs, however, this is not possible. The overlay unit lets your program swap pieces of itself in and out of memory as they are needed. Pieces that are not currently being used can be held on disk or in expanded memory.

Because of its specialized application for very large programs, we will not discuss the overlay unit any further in this book.

TURBO VISION UNITS

Turbo Pascal 6 comes with nine predefined units of objects that you can use to create programs with Turbo Vision. These units include objects that let you add pull-down menus, mouse support, dialog boxes, multiple windows, and memory management to your programs without having to write the extra code yourself. Turbo Vision will be discussed in Chapter 22.

SPECIAL UNIT FILES

There are four special unit files that you need to know about. The first, TURBO.TPL, contains all the standard Turbo Pascal units except for the graph unit; hence, you won't find separate unit files on disk for the CRT, graph, overlay, or other built-in units: they are all included in the TURBO.TPL file.

Second, if you wish, you can also include your own units in TURBO.TPL by using the TPUMOVER program, which should be in your Turbo Pascal main program directory. However, there isn't much to be gained by this, because you can still use your units whether or not they are in the TURBO.TPL file.

Third and fourth are the Graph3 and Turbo3 units, which you can use to produce programs that are backward-compatible with Turbo Pascal 3.0.

USING INCLUDE FILES

Even though Turbo Pascal now supports units, there may be times when you want to use the include files instead. In particular, if you are using Turbo Pascal 3.0, this is the only way that you can create libraries of standard routines for re-use.

Using include files is a three-step process. First, you must create the include file itself. Second, you must mark the place in your program where the file is to be included. This cannot be in any statement part of your program, i.e., it cannot be between any BEGIN and END. This means that, normally, you'll place an include file near the top of your program, possibly just after the variable declarations and before the procedure and function declarations.

The third step is to compile your program, at which time Turbo Pascal automatically "includes" the named file in your program.

You place an include file in your program with the include compiler directive {$I filename}, where filename is the DOS name of your include file. The include file itself is neither a program file nor a unit; hence, it cannot have a PROGRAM heading or any of the usual trappings of ordinary program and unit files. All the include file can contain is the group of routines that you want to include in your programs. Listings 10.4 and 10.5 demonstrate the use of include files.

The main disadvantage of include files is that because they are not precompiled, they must be recompiled each time you recompile your main program. This slows down the compilation process. Also, because they are in source code form, you do not have much quality control if you are distributing them to others as libraries of Pascal routines.

```
PROGRAM Listing10_4;   { uses include file }

USES CRT;

VAR
  MyName : STRING[10];

{$I LIST10_4.PAS}        { "Includes" Listing 10.4 here. }

BEGIN
  CLRSCR;
  WRITE(' Enter your first name: ');
  READLN(MyName);
  pause
END.
```

Listing 10.4: A program that uses the include file in Listing 10.5.

```
PROCEDURE Pause;  { include file }
  VAR
    Proceed : CHAR;
  BEGIN
    WRITELN;
    WRITE(' Press any key to continue ...');
    Proceed := READKEY;
    WRITELN; WRITELN
  END;
```

Listing 10.5: An include file containing the Pause routine.

PORTABILITY CONSIDERATIONS

Although standard Pascal (as defined by the American National Standards Institute and the International Organization for Standardization) does not officially support units, most real-world Pascal compilers do support some way to break up a program into more manageable chunks.

Microsoft's QuickPascal, because it is almost totally compatible with Turbo Pascal (at least in its non-object-oriented features), supports units with exactly the same syntax as Turbo Pascal itself. Digital Equipment Corp.'s Vax Pascal, which runs on Vax minicomputers under the VMS operating system, supports unit-like files called *modules* that are very similar to Turbo Pascal units except that they cannot have any executable sections, which means that they cannot have an initialization section.

Other versions of Pascal offer similar features, so you can use units in your programs with at least some confidence that you won't need to throw everything out if you move your program to a different Pascal compiler. You should, however, be alert to the fact that different compilers have both different terminology and different methods for handling units.

Note that if portability is an important concern, you should avoid using units whenever possible. You should also keep all unit-using routines together in your program and clearly indicate (by program comments) which routines depend on which units.

SUMMARY

Units are a feature of Turbo Pascal (versions 4.0 and later) that allow you to compile some parts of a program separately from the main program. This has two chief benefits. First, it allows you to save often-needed routines (such as the Pause routine) in a precompiled unit. You can then use the routines whenever you need them without having to type them into your program. Second, units allow you to create programs larger than 64K by putting most routines into units that are compiled separately from the main program. Many versions of Pascal other than Turbo Pascal have features similar to units: the generic term for this feature is separate compilation.

In versions of Turbo Pascal prior to version 4.0, units were not supported. Users of these versions can still reap some of the benefits of units by using include files, which are similar to units but are not precompiled.

A unit consists of two mandatory and one optional section. The mandatory sections are (a) the Interface section, which contains the names and parameter lists of subroutines defined in the unit, as well as publicly accessible declarations; and (b) the Implementation section, which contains the details of the subroutines defined in the unit as well as private declarations. The optional section of a unit is called the Initialization section, and it sets up the values of variables used by the unit.

Turbo Pascal comes with several predefined units that add features to the Pascal language. These include the System unit (which is automatically linked to Turbo Pascal programs), the CRT unit, the DOS unit, the Graph unit, and various Turbo Vision units for object-oriented programming.

REVIEW EXERCISES

1. Explain what units are, how they are used, and why they are important.

2. How are subroutines and units similar? How are they different?

3. What are the main differences between units and include files? Are there any advantages in using units instead of include files?

4. How do you tell your program to use a particular unit? To use a particular include file?

5. What are the two main parts of a unit? What is contained in each part?

6. True or false: You need a solid understanding of the Implementation section of a unit in order to use the routines in the unit. If the statement is false, explain why it is false.

7. True or false: The initialization section of a unit allows you to initialize variables in the program that uses the unit.

8. What is the initialization section of a unit and where is it located? Will a unit compile properly without an initialization section?

9. Explain a strategy for designing, coding, and compiling a program that takes up 128K of disc space.

10. Name five routines that we have used from the CRT unit and explain what each routine does.

11. Is there anything wrong with the following code fragment? If so, explain the problem and how you would correct it.

```
PROGRAM Including;
{$I+ Utils }
PROCEDURE DoSomething;
  BEGIN
    { ... details }
  END;
BEGIN { main body of program }
END.
```

12. List the standard Turbo Pascal units and explain what general kinds of routines are provided by each one.

13. True or false: If you distribute compiled units for other people to use in their programs, you must include the source code for the units so that they can understand how the routines work. If

false, explain why it is false, and explain what you do need to include with the compiled units.

14. True or false: If you use a unit in your program, then all the routines contained in the unit can be used in your program.

15. True or false: The Interface section of a unit cannot contain private declarations that are hidden from programs using the unit. If the statement is false, explain why it is false and how to correct it.

11

Pointers and Dynamic
Allocation

Take anything which can stand for anything else, and you have a sign ... its content carries us direct to the object of which it is used.

— F.H. Bradley, *Principles of Logic*

In Chapter 8, we saw how to create fixed-length lists of items by using arrays. This allowed us to put student records, for example, into a single array instead of having to create a separate variable for each record.

This approach has many advantages. Because the elements of an array are stored next to each other in the computer's memory, it takes very little time to go from one record in an array to the next. It is also simple: declare an array variable with a certain number of slots of the appropriate type, and you can then simply "load it up" by putting values into each slot.

DISADVANTAGES OF ARRAYS

There is also a large disadvantage in this approach: Pascal arrays are inflexible and sometimes tend to waste space in your computer's memory. To be certain of having enough space for all the data items you need, you must make the array large enough to contain all the data items that you might ever possibly need. If there are many large items in the array, you could easily run out of available memory. If you try to cut down the size of the array to save memory, however, you run the risk of "overflow"—i.e., of having more data items than can fit into the array.

For that reason, arrays (and fixed-length lists in general) can be a bad choice when you are not sure of how many data items you will need. In some obvious cases, this is not a problem: for example, you could create a 50-slot array to hold data about the states in the United States. Or, if the data items are small and there will never be too many of them, you can "overbook" your array with many extra slots and never have any problems.

In some other cases, however, fixed-length lists like those you create with an array just will not do the job. The Turbo Tunemaker program that we will develop in Chapter 20 is such an example. It must be able to play tunes of widely different lengths, but we do not want an array large enough to hold Beethoven's Fifth Symphony when all we want to play is "Row, Row, Row Your Boat."

There are other problems. Suppose that you have a sorted list in an array and you have to insert a new item into the middle of the list. Even if the array is not full, this can be a major undertaking. First, you must identify the correct place to insert the new item. Then, you must open up that array slot by moving all the items that come after it (each of these items must be moved up one position in the array). Finally, you can insert the new item into the list. Although this is *possible* (unlike the case of trying to insert an item into a full array, which is not possible), it involves a great deal of extra work both for the program and the programmer.

To handle situations like this, we need a way to create variable-length lists and other more flexible data structures. These data structures will use only as much memory as they need on a particular run of the program.

DYNAMIC ALLOCATION

Dynamic memory allocation is the solution to the problem. Although the name is intimidating, the idea is fairly simple. Consider, first, the case of ordinary, static variables such as array variables. When a program is compiled, Turbo Pascal sets aside (allocates) a certain amount of memory for all the variables and other data items declared in the program. Later, when the program is run by the user, these decisions about memory allocation have already been made and cannot be changed. For that reason, this kind of memory allocation is called *static*.

Dynamic memory allocation, however, takes place after the program is actually running; memory allocation decisions can be made and new variables can be created "on the fly." The feature (in Pascal and many other languages) that makes this possible is the *pointer*. When used in a few clever ways, which we will discuss presently, pointers give us tremendous flexibility for creating new variables whenever we need them, and also for getting rid of old variables when they are no longer needed.

THE IDEA OF POINTERS

It is important to understand the problems we meet with in any attempt to create new variables after the program is running. The main problems are (1) keeping track of which variables are being used and (2) locating where each variable is situated in the computer's memory. With static variables, these are not problems at all; these decisions are made at compile time and each variable is declared explicitly and named in the Pascal source code. But to create new variables *after* the program is running, we must determine the following:

- How to refer to each new variable. Although static variables are named in the source code, e.g., "Counter," dynamic variables do not have names. If we need to talk about one of them or assign a value to it, how do we accomplish this task?

- How to locate each new variable. Because the memory addresses of dynamic variables are not pre-assigned at compile time, we must have some way to find the dynamic variables when we need them.

A pointer is a special kind of variable that solves these problems for us. Instead of holding an integer, a string, an array, a record, or some other *substantive* item, a pointer holds the *memory address* of another variable—a variable that may or may not exist at the time the program is compiled. After the program is running, we can take a pointer, point it at a memory location (in an area called the *heap*), and create a new dynamic variable in that location.

Normally, a pointer variable, like any other variable, is set up so that it will work only with items of a given type. Just as an integer variable can hold only integers, a string variable can hold only strings, and so forth, each pointer variable is designed to *point to* only one specific type of dynamic variable. As a result, when you use that pointer to create a new dynamic variable, Turbo Pascal knows how much space to reserve in the heap for the new variable: for instance, it must allocate more space for an array variable than for a character variable.

A pointer can point to any data type *except* file types. You declare a pointer data type as follows:

```
TYPE

    MyFirstPointer = ^INTEGER;

    MySecondPointer = ^MyPointerDataItem;

    MyPointerDataItem = RECORD

                        Name : string10;

                        Age  : INTEGER;

                        Paid : BOOLEAN

                        END;
```

The caret (^) in the type declaration indicates that the type being defined is a pointer type. The key to produce the caret is located on the top row of most PC keyboards, and is produced by holding down the shift key and pressing the 6 key. In some mainframe computer versions of Pascal (and many books about Pascal), the up-arrow symbol (↑) is used instead of the caret, but the caret will work fine with the vast majority of Pascal compilers.

The first pointer type we declared will point only to dynamic variables of type INTEGER. The second pointer type, **MySecondPointer**, is designed to point only to items of type **MyPointerDataItem**. If you try to point it at anything else, your program either will not compile or will crash while running. Turbo Pascal does permit the use of untyped pointers (see discussion below), but these require special procedures and extra caution.

If you look carefully at the type declaration above, you will see an apparent paradox. Pascal requires all identifiers to be declared before they are used; however, we used the data type **MyPointerDataItem** in setting up the **MySecondPointer** type one line *before* we declared it in the program code.

This is one of the few exceptions to the rule that all identifiers must be declared before they are used. When we declare a pointer type that points to a user-defined data type, Pascal assumes that we are going to declare the second type before the end of the TYPE section. If we fail to do so, the program will not compile. This exception to the declare-before-use rule becomes very important when we use pointers to create linked data structures, some of which we will see later in this chapter.

One issue has come up previously but is worth repeating. What we have done so far *does not create any dynamic variables;* indeed, it does not even create any pointer variables. All that the TYPE section does is to set up user-defined data types that we can then use for specific data items, i.e., variables and constants.

CREATING DYNAMIC VARIABLES

Once we have declared pointer types in the TYPE section of the program, we can proceed to create variables of those types in the VAR section. You declare a pointer variable just as any other:

```
TYPE

    MyFirstPointer = ^INTEGER;

    MySecondPointer = ^MyPointerDataItem;

    MyPointerDataItem = RECORD

                        Name : string10;

                        Age  : INTEGER;

                        Paid : BOOLEAN

                        END;

VAR

    NumPtr : MyFirstPointer;

    RecPtr : MySecondPointer;
```

Note that both of these pointer variables are *static,* not dynamic, variables: they are embedded in the program code and are fixed at compile-time. They cannot be changed by the user.

This is the normal situation. *Some* variables must always be static so that dynamic variables have a known memory location to which they can be connected. Moreover, although it can point to an integer variable, **NumPtr** itself is not an integer, but a pointer. In the same way, **RecPtr** is not a record but a pointer *to* a record. In both cases, the pointers point to dynamic variables, but are themselves static variables.

To create dynamic variables, we use Pascal's built-in **New** procedure with a pointer variable. This procedure allocates a portion of memory for a variable of the appropriate type; then points the pointer at that memory location (i.e., it loads that memory address into the pointer variable). The process is shown in Listing 11.1. (Turbo Pascal also extends the **New**

```
PROGRAM Listing11_1;

   { Demonstrates how to set up pointer types and create
     dynamic variables. }

TYPE
  String10 = STRING[10];

  MyFirstPointer = ^INTEGER;

  MySecondPointer = ^MyPointerDataItem;
  MyPointerDataItem = RECORD
                        Name : string10;
                        Age  : INTEGER;
                        Paid : BOOLEAN
                        END;

VAR
  NumPtr : MyFirstPointer;
  RecPtr : MySecondPointer;

BEGIN
  NumPtr := NIL;          { Initializes the variable to NIL. }
  RecPtr := NIL;

  New(NumPtr);
  NumPtr^ := 5;           { Refers to the variable that NumPtr points
                            to by "dereferencing" NumPtr. }

  New(RecPtr);
  WITH RecPtr^ DO         { Refers to the variable that RecPtr points
                            to by "dereferencing" RecPtr. }
    BEGIN
      Name := 'Sam';      { Assigns values to the fields in RecPtr^, }
      Age  := 25;         { the dynamic record variable pointed to   }
      Paid := TRUE        { by the pointer RecPtr.                    }
    END

END.
```

Listing 11.1: Setting up pointer types and creating dynamic variables.

procedure with object-oriented features that go beyond standard Pascal, but we will defer our discussion of those features until Chapter 21.)

Of course, it is very convenient that we have a pointer that tells us where a dynamic variable is located—but how do we refer to the variable itself? **NumPtr** and **RecPtr** refer to pointers, not to the dynamic variables to which they point. Suppose we create a dynamic variable by calling the **New** routine with **NumPtr**, as in Listing 11.1. How do we assign a value to the new variable?

We do it by *dereferencing* the pointer. In the TYPE section, we put a caret *before* the name of a data type. To talk about what a pointer points to, we put a caret *after* the name of the pointer variable, as in *NumPtr^* and *Rec-Ptr^*. By dereferencing a pointer, we tell Pascal that we are talking about what the pointer points to, just as we do in Listing 11.1. In summary:

- **NumPtr** is a pointer that points to a dynamic integer variable; *NumPtr^* is a dynamic integer variable.

- **RecPtr** is a pointer that points to a dynamic record variable of type **MyPointerDataItem;** *RecPtr^* is a dynamic record variable of type **MyPointerDataItem.**

Avoid Dangling Pointers

Note that in Listing 11.1, the **NumPtr** and **RecPtr** variables are declared in the VAR section, just like any other static variables.

In the first two lines of the program body, we set both of these pointers to **NIL**. **NIL** is a predefined value that tells Pascal that a pointer does not point to anything. If we leave a pointer undefined—that is, if we do not assign a value to it—then it might contain anything, even a memory address used by the operating system or some other vital piece of software. Such a pointer is called a *dangling pointer.* If it is accidentally used, the results are unpredictable and can be potentially disastrous.

For this reason, it is wise to be very careful with pointers. Any time a pointer does not have a dynamic variable assigned to it, it should be set to the value **NIL.** You may get away with not doing this, but considering the risks, it is wiser to play it safe.

Linked Data Structures

What we have seen of dynamic variables so far is interesting but not very impressive. In Listing 11.1, we had two static pointer variables and used them to create two dynamic variables: one an integer and one a record. Where is the great flexibility that dynamic allocation was supposed to deliver?

The flexibility appears when we realize that pointers can point to almost any user-defined data element, *including* one that contains more pointers. This means that we can use pointers to create daisy-chained data structures. To create the first item in the daisy chain, we use **New** with the initial, static pointer. The dynamic record variable we create *also* contains a pointer, which we use with **New** again to create a second item in the chain, which has its own pointer we can use with **New** to create a third item, and so forth. A simple example of how this works is given in Listing 11.2.

Listing 11.2 performs an essentially trivial task, but it demonstrates the basic idea on which all linked data structures are built: a daisy-chain of records, each of which contains one or more pointers that point to other

```
PROGRAM Listing11_2;

  { Gives a simple example of a linked data structure
    using pointers. }

TYPE
  String10 = STRING[10];

  NodePtr = ^ListItem;
  ListItem = RECORD
             Number : INTEGER;
             next   : NodePtr
             END;


VAR
  ListHead : nodeptr;

BEGIN
  New(ListHead);                  { creates a new list node }
  ListHead^.Number := 1;          { assigns 1 to the number field }

  New(ListHead^.next);            { creates another new list node }
  ListHead^.next^.Number := 2;    { assigns 2 to the number field }

  New(ListHead^.next^.next);            { creates a third list node }
  ListHead^.next^.next^.Number := 3;    { assigns 3 to the number field }
  ListHead^.next^.next^.next := NIL     { sets the "next" pointer to NIL }
END.
```

Listing 11.2: A linked data structure using pointers.

records or to **NIL**. Using this concept, we start with a single static pointer, **ListHead**, and create a linked list that contains three integers. *None* of the list's three record variables exist before the program runs: all are created with the **New** procedure at run-time.

Here is how Listing 11.2 works. The **ListItem** record type contains two fields: an integer field and a pointer field that can point to another record of type **ListItem**. When the program first begins to run, there are no variables of this type. There is, however, a static pointer variable **ListHead** that can point to **ListItem**-type records. The details become somewhat complicated, so let's take it line by line:

- Line 1: We call the **New** procedure with the **ListHead** variable. This creates a dynamic record variable of type **ListItem** and points **ListHead** at that variable's memory location.

- Line 2: We dereference the **ListHead** pointer. Remember, what **List-Head** points to is a record, so we can manipulate the dereferenced pointer just as we would any other record variable. Using the dot notation (see the discussion of records in Chapter 8 if you are hazy on this point), we assign the integer **1** to the Number field of the record variable.

- Line 3: The Next field of the *ListHead^* record variable is itself a pointer variable. Therefore, we can use the **New** routine to create another new node in the list and point the Next field of *List-Head^* at the new node.

- Line 4: Because *ListHead^.next* points to a dynamic variable, we can dereference it (*ListHead^.next^*) and put the integer value **2** into the Number field of the dynamic variable.

- Line 5: Because *ListHead^.next^.next* is a pointer, we can use the **New** routine to create another list node and point the pointer at it.

- Line 6: Because *ListHead^.next^.next^* is a dynamic record variable, we can assign the integer value **3** to its Number field.

- Line 7: Because *ListHead^.next^.next^.next* is a pointer that is not going to point to anything, we set it to **NIL**.

In a certain sense, this is not a fair example, because we will see techniques later in this chapter that make it much easier to refer to items in a list. However, this example presents the basic idea of linked data structures without any extra features to complicate the picture. In fact, a picture makes it much easier to understand linked data structures, as shown in Figure 11.1.

DISPOSING OF DYNAMIC VARIABLES

So far, we have seen how to use pointers to create new variables while a program is running. Some of these variables, however, may be used in a

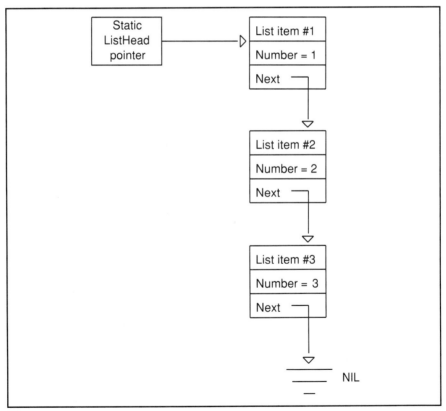

Figure 11.1: Linked data structures in Listing 11.1.

certain part of the program and then never be needed again. If there were no way to free up the memory used by dynamic variables, then—at least in terms of saving memory—they would be only a slight improvement over static variables.

Fortunately, there is a way to free up the memory used by dynamic variables that are no longer needed: Pascal's **Dispose** procedure. Using the **Dispose** procedure with a pointer variable frees the memory reserved for the variable that the pointer points to, and then disconnects the pointer from that memory address. The memory location that was used for the "disposed" dynamic variable can be used for other dynamic variables, and the pointer's value itself becomes undefined. Listing 11.3 shows how to use the **Dispose** procedure.

It is *very important,* when a pointer's value becomes undefined, that it is assigned either a new memory location or a **NIL** value. As I noted earlier, a "dangling" pointer is like a time bomb waiting to explode. Unless a

```
PROGRAM Listing11_3;

   { Shows how to use the Dispose procedure to free up
     memory used by dynamic variables when they are no
     longer needed. }

TYPE
  String10 = STRING[10];

  NodePtr = ^ListItem;
  ListItem = RECORD
             Number : INTEGER;
             next   : NodePtr
             END;


VAR
  ListHead : nodeptr;

BEGIN
  New(ListHead);                { creates a new list node }
  ListHead^.Number := 1;        { assigns 1 to the number field }

  New(ListHead^.next);          { creates another new list node }
  ListHead^.next^.Number := 2;  { assigns 2 to the number field }
  ListHead^.next^.next := NIL;  { end of the list              }

  Dispose(ListHead^.next);      { de-allocates memory }
  ListHead^.next := NIL         { sets undefined pointer to NIL }
END.
```

Listing 11.3: Using Dispose to free up memory.

pointer is going to receive a new value immediately after you use it with **Dispose**, then it should be set to **NIL** with the program line (for example)

```
ThisPtr := NIL;
```

THE STACK AND THE HEAP

We've referred earlier in this chapter to the *heap*, where Turbo Pascal reserves memory for dynamic variables. Another term you will hear frequently is the *stack*, and this is a good place to explain both terms.

The stack is an area of memory that Turbo Pascal reserves for local variables used by subroutines. When a procedure or function is called in your program, Turbo Pascal sets aside space in the stack for the local variables hidden inside that procedure or function. Immediately after that in the stack, Pascal places the "return address" of the line that called the subroutine, so that when the subroutine finishes its work, the program can continue from the exact point at which it called the subroutine.

The default size of the stack is 16,384 bytes (16K). You can use the {$M} compiler directive or the *Memory Sizes* choice on the Options menu to change the amount of memory reserved for the stack. Normally, however, you should not have to increase the amount of stack memory unless you are using many large local variables or running a recursive procedure (see Chapter 18). *Stack overflow*—running out of stack space—is a common problem for novice programmers, and usually means that some routine is incorrectly designed. If you have this problem, take a careful look at your code before you rush to increase the stack size.

Although the stack has nothing much to do with dynamic allocation, it provides a useful contrast to the heap. The heap is an area of memory that Turbo Pascal uses to store dynamic variables, *i.e.*, variables created by your program while it is running. When we say that Turbo Pascal allocates memory on the heap, this simply means that it reserves a certain location where you can store the values of dynamic variables. Because a variable is fundamentally a memory location that can take values of a certain type, allocating the memory is the same thing as creating the variables.

Normally, Turbo Pascal uses all the free memory in your PC for the heap. Suppose that you have 640K in your PC. If your program takes up 200K (including the stack), DOS 50K, and memory-resident programs

100K, then the heap size will be 640K minus (200K + 50K + 100K), or 290K. This is a lot of memory, but if you make extensive use of linked data structures, you will be surprised at how easy it is to fill. Figure 11.2 shows how PC memory is allocated between your program, the stack, and the heap.

Note that Figure 11.2 omits some details that are not relevant to our immediate purpose of understanding the heap, but it is accurate in its essentials.

MemAvail and MaxAvail

Two important functions for using the heap, particularly if you are making extensive use of dynamic variables or are using large dynamic variables, are **MemAvail** and **MaxAvail**. **MemAvail** informs you of the total amount of memory (in bytes) available on the heap, while **MaxAvail** informs you of the largest single (contiguous) piece of memory available on the heap.

These two functions are different because the heap allocates memory for dynamic variables wherever it can find some free space, and de-allocates

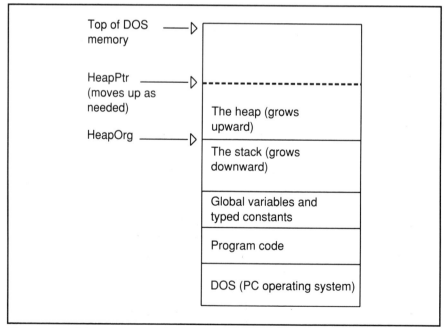

Figure 11.2: Memory map of the stack and the heap.

memory in no particular order. This means that you can have the bottom of the heap area, as shown in Figure 11.2, occupied by dynamic variables, have free space above it, and then have still more dynamic variables above the free space. Thus, the available memory on the heap is split into smaller pieces.

When it comes to creating a dynamic variable on the heap, however, the only thing that matters is the size of the pieces—not the total heap memory available. If there is 100K of heap space available but the largest contiguous piece is 25K, then your program will have a run-time error (heap overflow) if you try to create a dynamic variable that requires 30K.

You can use **MemAvail** to determine the total amount of free space on the heap, and **MaxAvail** as a safety mechanism to prevent heap overflow. Where **SizeOf** is a function that returns the amount of memory needed by a particular variable type, you can use **MemAvail** and **MaxAvail** as follows:

```
TYPE

      RecPtr = ^StudentRecord;

      StudentRecord = RECORD

                      Name : STRING[10];

                      GPA  : REAL

                      END;

VAR

      Student : RecPtr;

BEGIN

      { ... program statements }

      WRITELN('Total heap memory available: ', MemAvail);

      IF MaxAvail < SizeOf(StudentRecord)

          THEN WRITELN(' Inadequate heap space.')

          ELSE NEW(Student);

      { ... more program statements }

END.
```

The IF clause checks to make sure that an adequate-sized piece of memory is available on the heap before trying to create a dynamic variable, and thus prevents your program from suffering a heap overflow error.

The best solution, of course, is to prevent the problem from occurring in the first place. Shortages of heap space often can be avoided if you scrupulously dispose of dynamic variables as soon as they are no longer needed. As noted earlier, if you fail to do this, you have lost one of the major advantages that dynamic variables have over static variables. There is an old saying that someone who *does not* read is no better off than someone who *cannot* read. To this, we might add that a programmer who does not use the advantages of dynamic variables is no better off than someone who only knows how to use arrays.

USING UNTYPED POINTERS

Normally, a pointer variable can point only to dynamic variables of a specific type: the type that you declared when you set up the pointer type. Thus, in our previous example,

```
TYPE

    MyFirstPointer = ^INTEGER;

    MySecondPointer = ^MyPointerDataItem;

    MyPointerDataItem = RECORD

                            Name : string10;

                            Age  : INTEGER;

                            Paid : BOOLEAN

                        END;

VAR

    NumPtr : MyFirstPointer;

    RecPtr : MySecondPointer;
```

the pointer variable **NumPtr** can point only to integer variables, and the pointer variable **RecPtr** can point only to variables of the type **MyPointerDataItem**. In these cases, we may not know how many dynamic variables we will need, but we know, at least, what size they will be when we create them.

There are rare occasions, however, when we know that we will need to create dynamic variables, but we do not know at compile time how big they will be during a particular run of the program. For these situations, Turbo Pascal provides an *untyped pointer* type that can point at these un-known-at-compile-time data objects. It is declared as follows:

```
VAR

    MysteryPtr : Pointer;
```

This untyped pointer type is not supported by standard Pascal and is used mainly for low-level system programming, such as to save the contents of video memory to an array for later restoration. Untyped pointers cannot be dereferenced like normal pointers. Because they are not set up to point to variables of a specific type, they cannot be used with the **New** and **Dispose** procedures, which need to know how much heap memory to allocate or release.

GetMem and FreeMem

To allocate and de-allocate memory for untyped pointers, you must use Turbo Pascal's **GetMem** and **FreeMem** procedures. These work exactly like the **New** and **Dispose** procedures, except that in addition to the untyped pointer variable, you must also specify the amount of heap memory to allocate or de-allocate:

```
GetMem(MysteryPtr, 4000);

FreeMem(MysteryPtr, 4000);
```

where *MysteryPtr* is an untyped pointer variable and, in our example, 4000 is the number of bytes of memory that *MysteryPtr*'s referent uses on the heap.

DYNAMIC DATA STRUCTURES

Now, we arrive at a practical application of dynamic allocation: creating and manipulating a linked list. We will look at other dynamic data structures in Chapter 17, but this should be adequate to demonstrate their power.

It is always important to keep a clear idea of what one is doing, but nowhere is this more important than when handling linked data structures. If you think exclusively in terms of pointers and dereferencing and heap memory, you can become hopelessly confused. On the other hand, if you step back from the technical details and focus on what you are really trying to accomplish, the task of manipulating linked data structures begins to seem almost trivial.

The operations we are going to perform, and the results we will achieve, are illustrated in Figure 11.3.

CREATING A SINGLY LINKED LIST

Given that background, let's "think through" what we need to do to create a linked list. Suppose we have the following:

```
TYPE

    RecPtr = ^StudentRec;

    StudentRec = RECORD

                Name  : STRING[10];

                GPA   : REAL;

                Next  : RecPtr

                END;

VAR

    ListHead,

    ListTail  : RecPtr;
```

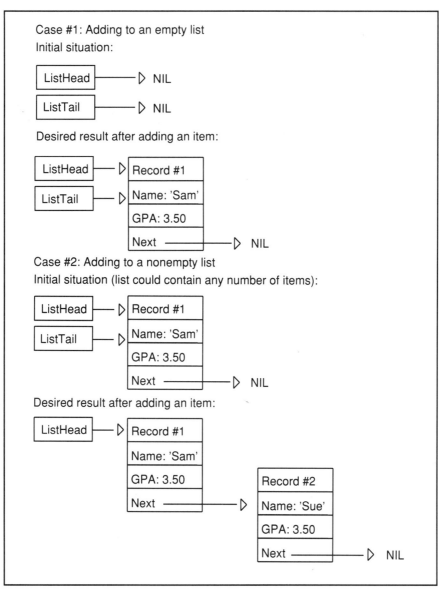

Figure 11.3: Adding items to a singly linked list.

This type of list is called *singly linked* because there is only one pointer link between each record and the next. Another kind of list, called *doubly linked,* offers some advantages but it is slightly more complicated to manipulate. Instead of having only a *next* pointer in each record, it also has a *previous* pointer that points to the previous record in the list. In this chapter, we will demonstrate only singly linked lists.

To add an item to the list, we must first determine where to add it. If the list is empty, we simply use the **New** procedure with the **Listhead** pointer; this creates a dynamic variable of the type **StudentRec** and points the **ListHead** pointer at its memory location in the heap. We then assign values to the record and set its Next field to **NIL** because, in a one-record list, there is no "next" record.

If the list is not empty, then our task is slightly more complicated. First, assuming that we are simply adding records as they come along (not in any sorted order), we have to find the end of the list. We could do this by starting at the **Listhead** record and moving down the list until we arrived at a record whose Next field was **NIL**, but there is an easier way. We can declare an extra pointer of the same type as **ListHead** to keep track of the end of the list. This means that in a list with only one item, both the **List-Head** and the **ListTail** pointers will point at the same record.

To add a new item to the end of the list, we call the **New** procedure with the Next pointer of the **ListTail** record. This creates a new dynamic record and points the Next pointer of the **ListTail** record at that record. We then assign values to the new record, set its Next field to **NIL**, and repoint the **ListTail** pointer so that it now points at the new end of the list.

This process of adding a node to a list is demonstrated in Listing 11.4.

TRAVERSING A LINKED LIST

Compared to creating a singly linked list, traversing the list is a fairly simple exercise. We create a new *current item pointer* to keep track of where we are in the list, along with a counter to keep track of the item number. Then we simply tell Pascal that until the current pointer is **NIL**—that is, until the end of the list has been reached—to visit each list item, report its contents, and then move on to the next item in the list. The process of traversing a linked list is demonstrated in Listing 11.5.

```
PROGRAM Listing11_4;

  { Shows how to create a linked list of student names and GPAs.
    Uses the MyUtils unit created in Chapter 10. }

USES CRT, MyUtils;

TYPE
  string10 = STRING[10];

  RecPtr = ^StudentRec;
  StudentRec = RECORD
               Name : string10;
               GPA : real;
               Next : RecPtr
             END;
VAR
   ListHead,
   ListTail : RecPtr;
   proceed  : CHAR;

PROCEDURE init(VAR ListHead, ListTail : RecPtr; VAR proceed : CHAR);
  BEGIN
    ListHead := NIL;
    ListTail := NIL;
    proceed := 'Y'
END;

PROCEDURE addname(VAR ListHead, ListTail : RecPtr);
  BEGIN
  CLRSCR;
  IF ListHead = NIL
     THEN BEGIN
          NEW(ListHead);
          WRITE(' Enter name: '); READLN(ListHead^.name); WRITELN;
          WRITE(' Enter GPA: '); READLN(ListHead^.GPA);
          ListHead^.next := NIL;
          ListTail := ListHead;
          pause
          END
     ELSE BEGIN
          NEW(ListTail^.next);
          IF ListHead = ListTail
             THEN ListHead^.next := ListTail^.next;
          ListTail := ListTail^.next;
          WRITE(' Enter name: '); READLN(ListTail^.name); WRITELN;
          WRITE(' Enter GPA: '); READLN(ListTail^.GPA); WRITELN;
          ListTail^.next := NIL;
          pause
          END
  END;

  BEGIN
       init(ListHead, ListTail, proceed);
       REPEAT
          addname(ListHead, ListTail);
          WRITE(' Do another (Y/N)? ');
          READLN(proceed)
       UNTIL UPCASE(proceed) <> 'Y';
       pause
  END.
```

Listing 11.4: Creating a linked list of student names and GPAs.

```
PROGRAM Listing11_5;

   { Shows how to traverse a linked list of student names and
     GPAs. Uses the MyUtils unit created in Chapter 10. }

USES CRT, MyUtils;

TYPE
  string10 = STRING[10];

  RecPtr = ^StudentRec;
  StudentRec = RECORD
                 Name : string10;
                 GPA : real;
                 Next : RecPtr
               END;
VAR
   ListHead,
   ListTail : RecPtr;
   proceed  : CHAR;

PROCEDURE init(VAR ListHead, ListTail : RecPtr; VAR proceed : CHAR);
   BEGIN
     ListHead := NIL;
     ListTail := NIL;
     proceed := 'Y'
   END;

PROCEDURE addname(VAR ListHead, ListTail : RecPtr);
   BEGIN
   CLRSCR;
   IF ListHead = NIL
      THEN BEGIN
           NEW(ListHead);
           WRITE(' Enter name: '); READLN(ListHead^.name); WRITELN;
           WRITE(' Enter GPA: '); READLN(ListHead^.GPA);
           ListHead^.next := NIL;
           ListTail := ListHead;
           pause
           END
      ELSE BEGIN
           NEW(ListTail^.next);
           IF ListHead = ListTail
              THEN ListHead^.next := ListTail^.next;
           ListTail := ListTail^.next;
           WRITE(' Enter name: '); READLN(ListTail^.name); WRITELN;
           WRITE(' Enter GPA: '); READLN(ListTail^.GPA); WRITELN;
           ListTail^.next := NIL;
           pause
           END
   END;

   procedure TraverseList(ListHead : RecPtr);
      VAR
        currptr : RecPtr;
        counter : integer;
      BEGIN
        currptr := ListHead;
        counter := 0;
        if currptr = NIL then WRITELN(' The list is empty.');
        while currptr <> NIL do
              BEGIN
              counter := counter + 1;
```

Listing 11.5: Traversing a linked list.

```
            WRITELN;
            WRITE(' The name in StudentRec number ', counter);
            WRITELN(' is ', currptr^.name, '.');
            WRITE(' The GPA of ', currptr^.name, ' is ');
            WRITELN(currptr^.GPA:0:2, '.');
            WRITELN;
            WRITELN(' So far, ', counter, ' records have been visited.');
            currptr := currptr^.next;
            pause
            END;
       currptr := NIL;      { not strictly needed }
    END;

BEGIN
     init(ListHead, ListTail, proceed);
     REPEAT
          addname(ListHead, ListTail);
          WRITE(' Do another (Y/N)? ');
          READLN(proceed)
     UNTIL UPCASE(proceed) <> 'Y';
     pause;
     TraverseList(ListHead);
END.
```

Listing 11.5: Traversing a linked list (cont.).

SEQUENTIAL
SEARCHING OF A LINKED LIST

Doing a sequential search of a linked list is quite similar to the search of an array-based list that we saw in Chapter 8. The main difference is that, instead of combining an *empty value* with a slot counter to tell us when we have reached the end of the list, we simply search the list until we find the searched-for value or run into the value **NIL**.

We traverse the list in the same way as shown in Listing 11.5, and at each list item, we compare the name field with the search target. If the name field equals the search target, then we set the Boolean *found* variable to true and drop out of the WHILE loop that does the search. If the name field does not match the search target, we then move ahead one item until we find the search target or reach the end of the list, either of which will cause us to drop out of the loop. This process is demonstrated in Listing 11.6.

```
PROGRAM Listing11_6;

    { Demonstrates a simple sequential search of a list containing
      student names and GPAs. Uses the MyUtils unit created in
      Chapter 10. }

USES CRT, MyUtils;

TYPE
   string10 = STRING[10];

   RecPtr = ^StudentRec;
   StudentRec = RECORD
                   Name : string10;
                   GPA : real;
                   Next : RecPtr
                END;
VAR
   ListHead,
   ListTail : RecPtr;
   proceed  : CHAR;

PROCEDURE init(VAR ListHead, ListTail : RecPtr; VAR proceed : CHAR);
   BEGIN
      ListHead := NIL;
      ListTail := NIL;
      proceed := 'Y'
   END;

PROCEDURE addname(VAR ListHead, ListTail : RecPtr);
   BEGIN
   CLRSCR;
   IF ListHead = NIL
      THEN BEGIN
           NEW(ListHead);
           WRITE(' Enter name: '); READLN(ListHead^.name); WRITELN;
           WRITE(' Enter GPA: '); READLN(ListHead^.GPA);
           ListHead^.next := NIL;
           ListTail := ListHead;
           pause
           END
      ELSE BEGIN
           NEW(ListTail^.next);
           IF ListHead = ListTail
              THEN ListHead^.next := ListTail^.next;
           ListTail := ListTail^.next;
           WRITE(' Enter name: '); READLN(ListTail^.name); WRITELN;
           WRITE(' Enter GPA: '); READLN(ListTail^.GPA); WRITELN;
           ListTail^.next := NIL;
           pause
           END
   END;

procedure SearchList(ListHead : RecPtr);
   VAR
      currptr : RecPtr;
      target  : string10;
      found   : BOOLEAN;
      counter : INTEGER;

   BEGIN
      currptr := ListHead;
      counter := 0;
```

Listing 11.6: Sequential search of a linked list.

```
      found := FALSE;
      WRITE(' Enter a name for which to search: ');
      READLN(target);
      if currptr = NIL then WRITELN(' Sorry. The list is empty.');
      while (currptr <> NIL) AND (NOT Found) DO
              BEGIN
              counter := counter + 1;
              IF currptr^.name = target
                 THEN BEGIN
                         Found := TRUE;
                         WRITE(' Search target found at list item # ');
                         WRITELN(counter, '.')
                      END
                 ELSE currptr := currptr^.next;
              END;
      IF found = FALSE THEN WRITELN(' Sorry. Target not found.');
      pause
   END;

BEGIN
     init(ListHead, ListTail, proceed);
     REPEAT
        addname(ListHead, ListTail);
        WRITE(' Do another (Y/N)? ');
        READLN(proceed)
     UNTIL UPCASE(proceed) <> 'Y';
     pause;
     SearchList(ListHead);
   END.
```

Listing 11.6: Sequential search of a linked list (cont.).

FREEING UP HEAP MEMORY

In the program examples we have seen so far, we have assumed that we have unlimited memory available for our dynamic data structures. Often, this is assumption is justified, because all DOS memory not occupied by the program is used for the heap, which holds dynamic variables (see Figure 11.2).

However, it is also possible to run out of heap space; this occurs, for example, when you run a routine repeatedly that creates new dynamic variables on each run, or when you use large dynamic arrays. Recall that each time you create a new dynamic variable, Pascal reserves space for it on the heap. If you do not have a way to free up heap memory when you are finished with your dynamic variables, then eventually you can run out of heap memory.

There are two ways that this can happen. As noted earlier in this chapter, Pascal allocates space on the heap wherever it can find a block of free memory. This means that (a) the *total* amount of memory (as reported by **MemAvail**) can be inadequate for the dynamic variables you want to create, or (b) the *largest single (contiguous) block* of memory can be smaller than an individual dynamic variable that you want to create.

As an example of the first problem, you might need to create 1000 dynamic variables with each dynamic variable taking up 100 bytes. Even if you had blocks of heap memory that were larger than 100 bytes, you would still run out of space if there were less than 1000 such blocks. As an example of the second problem, you might want to create a dynamic array that requires 50K of heap memory. However, if you had blocks of only 45K, 30K, 40K, and 35K, it would not matter that the *total* is more than 50K; you need a single block (as reported by **MaxAvail**) that is 50K or larger.

Pascal's **Dispose** procedure provides only a partial solution to these problems. It is very good for freeing up heap space that is reserved for a single variable, but it cannot be applied directly to a linked data structure. Remember, when you call the **Dispose** procedure with a dynamic variable, as in

```
Dispose(ThisDynamicVariable)
```

it frees up (de-allocates) the heap memory occupied by the dynamic variable and points the corresponding pointer to **NIL**.

Suppose, however, that this dynamic variable is the first item in a linked list. Our call to the **Dispose** procedure does indeed free up the heap memory occupied by the first item, but the memory for the other items is still officially *occupied*, even if we can no longer do anything with it.

What we need is a way to free up the memory occupied by a variety of dynamic variables: some of which are easily accessible, others not so easily. Furthermore, there will be times when we simply want to clear the entire heap and start afresh. Turbo Pascal 6 has two built-in procedures, **Mark** and **Release**, that provide us with a way to free up heap memory. These procedures, however, are not supported by standard Pascal and other versions of Pascal, so we will also discuss a more generalized way to clear heap memory.

USING THE MARK
AND RELEASE PROCEDURES

With the **Mark** procedure, you put a "bookmark" at a certain point in the heap; then you simply go about your business creating dynamic variables. Later, when you call the **Release** procedure, all the dynamic variables that you created since inserting the bookmark are destroyed, and the memory they occupied becomes free for use by other dynamic variables.

As an analogy, suppose that you have a short stack of papers on your desk. You want to keep the papers that you already have, but any new papers that come in should be thrown away at the end of the day. To handle this situation, you might put a large, brightly colored piece of cardboard on top of the original stack. Then, when any new papers come in, they are put on top of the colored piece of cardboard. When you need to throw new papers out at the end of the day, you just pick up the piece of cardboard (with the new papers on top) and dump them into the wastebasket.

Calling the **Mark** procedure is like putting that piece of cardboard on top of the original stack of papers. Calling the **Release** procedure is like picking up the cardboard and dumping any new papers into the wastebasket.

Mark and **Release** provide one of the few occasions to use untyped pointers. You call **Mark** and **Release** with an untyped pointer as follows:

```
Mark(UntypedPointerVariable)

Release(UntypedPointerVariable)
```

The pointer variable is the bookmark that you insert into the heap; it is declared simply as a pointer type, as shown in Listing 11.7.

In Listing 11.7, we declare a **heapmark** pointer variable in the VAR section; because this is an untyped pointer, we do not have to declare it in the TYPE section.

As the action part of the program begins, it uses the untyped pointer to mark the top of the heap; then it displays a message about the current heap space available. After that, it creates and loads a 100-slot dynamic array. (Strictly speaking, we do not have to load it, but arrays usually have something in them.) After creating the array, the program again displays a message about the current heap space available. Finally, it calls **Release**

```
PROGRAM Listing11_7;

   { Demonstrates the use of Mark and Release to free up heap
     memory. In this case, we mark a place in the heap at the
     beginning of the program. We then create a dynamic array
     which takes up some heap memory. Finally, we use Release
     to free up the memory occupied by the array. In a case
     like this, of course (with only one dynamic variable),
     Dispose would work just as well as Release. See Listing
     11.8 for a case in which Release provides a much easier
     solution than Dispose. }

USES CRT, MyUtils;

TYPE
   MyArray = ARRAY[1..100] of CHAR;
   arrayptr = ^MyArray;


VAR
    i        : INTEGER;
   mainptr  : arrayptr;
   heapmark : POINTER;

PROCEDURE LoadUpArray(VAR thisarray : myarray);
   VAR i : INTEGER;
   BEGIN
   FOR i := 1 TO 100 DO thisarray[i] := 'a'
   END;

BEGIN
   CLRSCR;
   mainptr := NIL;
   MARK(heapmark);
   WRITELN(' There are now ', memavail, ' free bytes on the heap.');
   WRITELN;
   pause;

   NEW(mainptr);
   loaduparray(mainptr^);
   WRITELN(' There are now ', memavail, ' free bytes on the heap.');
   WRITELN;
   pause;

   RELEASE(heapmark);
   mainptr := NIL;      { being a stickler for safety }
   WRITE(' After using release, there are now ', memavail);
   WRITELN(' free bytes on the heap.');
   pause
END.
```

Listing 11.7: Using Mark and Release.

with the same untyped pointer. Presto! All the heap space occupied by the array has been freed.

You can use the same method to de-allocate memory that is being used by the items in a linked list, as shown in Listing 11.8. There are situations,

```
PROGRAM Listing11_8;

    { Works in the same way as Listing 11.7. The key difference
      is that in this listing, the heap memory freed by Release
      is occupied by a dynamically linked list instead of an
      array. }

USES CRT, MyUtils;

CONST
  maxitems = 100;

TYPE
    nodeptr = ^node;
    node    = RECORD
                 item : CHAR;
                 next : nodeptr
                 END;

VAR
    i           : INTEGER;
    listhead,
    listtail    : nodeptr;
    heapmark    : POINTER;
    free1,
    free2,
    difference : LONGINT;


PROCEDURE init(VAR listhead, listtail : nodeptr;
                VAR heapmark : POINTER;
                VAR free1 : LONGINT);
  BEGIN
    listhead := NIL;
    listtail := NIL;
    MARK(heapmark);
    CLRSCR;
    WRITE(' Before creating the list, there are ', memavail);
    WRITELN(' bytes available on the heap.');
    free1 := MEMAVAIL;
    pause
  END;


PROCEDURE LoadUpList(VAR listhead, listtail : nodeptr);
  VAR i : INTEGER;
  BEGIN
  FOR i := 1 TO MaxItems DO
    BEGIN
      IF listhead = NIL
        THEN BEGIN
               NEW(listhead);
               listhead^.item := 'a';
               listhead^.next := nil;
               listtail := listhead
               END
        ELSE BEGIN
               NEW(listtail^.next);
               listtail := listtail^.next;
               listtail^.item := 'a';
               listtail^.next := NIL
               END
```

Listing 11.8: Using Mark and Release with a linked list.

```
        END  { of FOR statement }
    END;  { of PROCEDURE }
BEGIN
    CLRSCR;
    init(listhead, listtail, heapmark, free1);
    WRITELN;

    loaduplist(listhead, listtail);

    WRITELN(' After creating a ', maxitems, '-node list, there are now');
    WRITELN(' ', memavail, ' free bytes on the heap.');
    free2 := (free1 - memavail);
    WRITELN;
    WRITELN(' This indicates the the list is taking up ', free2);
    WRITELN(' bytes of heap space.');
    pause;

    RELEASE(heapmark);
    WRITELN(' After executing the release procedure with the heapmark,');
    WRITELN(' available heap memory is now ', memavail, ' bytes.');
    WRITELN;
    difference := (MEMAVAIL - free1);
    WRITELN(' The difference between the original amount of heap memory');
    WRITELN(' available and the current amount is ', difference, ' bytes.')

    pause

END.
```

Listing 11.8: Using Mark and Release with a linked list (cont.).

however, in which **Mark** and **Release** are not appropriate: for instance, when you need to free up space used by a linked data structure but do not want to disturb other dynamic variables on the heap. Also, **Mark**, **Release**, and untyped pointers are not supported by most versions of Pascal, so it is essential to learn the normal method to free up memory. This method is discussed in the following section.

DE-ALLOCATING A LINKED LIST

The great virtue of the **Mark** and **Release** procedures is that they are fairly easy to apply. They cannot, however, remove a single dynamic data structure from the middle of the heap. For that, you have to know how to use the **Dispose** procedure with linked data structures. In this section, we will see how to do this with a singly linked list.

The method takes a little thought. The head item in a singly linked list contains the pointer to the next item. If we simply use **Dispose** on the head item in the list, we will have no way to find the next item in the list, because the pointer to it will have been destroyed when we disposed of the head item. What we need is a way to free up the memory used by a list, item by item, while at each point keeping track of the next item in the list. This is provided by the method shown in Listing 11.9.

In Listing 11.9, we declare a simple node type for the items in the linked list: each node will contain only a character and a pointer to the next item. Then, in the VAR section, we declare head and tail pointers for the list, along with an integer-type counter variable and three **longint**-type variables for reporting the free heap memory with the **MemAvail** function.

The **Init** procedure initializes all the variables and reports the starting amount of heap memory. We then create the linked list, using the **New** procedure to create new, dynamic nodes for the list. After the list has been created, we again use **MemAvail** to check the available heap space.

Now comes the interesting part. In the **DeallocateList** procedure, we declare two local pointer variables that can point to items in the list. We then point the first local pointer at the head of the list and set up a WHILE loop to traverse the list. In each pass through the loop, we point the second local pointer at the current node, repoint the first pointer at the next node, and then dispose of the current node, freeing up the heap memory that it occupies. Unlike using the **Mark** and **Release** procedures, this method applies to any version of Pascal.

STATIC VS. DYNAMIC DATA STRUCTURES

Many people, when they first encounter dynamic linked lists, think that using dynamic variables is always a better approach than using static variables such as arrays. It is true that dynamic allocation offers many advantages in some situations. When correctly implemented, however, each approach has both strong and weak points in particular cases.

The strong point of using arrays is that they are slightly faster than dynamically linked data structures. Because all the elements of an array are located next to each other in the PC's memory, you can go directly to

```pascal
PROGRAM Listing11_9;

    { This listing demonstrates a method for de-allocating
      the memory used by a singly linked list. At each
      step, a temporary pointer keeps track of the next
      item in the list while the current item is disposed
      of. This process continues until the end of the list
      is reached. }


USES CRT, MyUtils;

CONST
  maxitems = 5;

TYPE
    nodeptr = ^node;
    node    = RECORD
                item : CHAR;
                next : nodeptr
                END;

VAR
    i          : INTEGER;
  listhead,
  listtail   : nodeptr;
  free1,
  free2,
  difference : LONGINT;


PROCEDURE init(VAR listhead, listtail : nodeptr;
               VAR free1 : longint);
  BEGIN
    listhead := NIL;
    listtail := NIL;
    CLRSCR;
    WRITE(' Before creating the list, there are ', MEMAVAIL);
    WRITELN(' bytes available on the heap.');
    free1 := MEMAVAIL;
    pause
  END;


PROCEDURE LoadUpList(VAR listhead, listtail : nodeptr);
  VAR i : INTEGER;
  BEGIN
  FOR i := 1 to maxitems do
    BEGIN
      IF listhead = NIL
        THEN BEGIN
             new(listhead);
             listhead^.item := 'a';
             listhead^.next := NIL;
             listtail := listhead
             END
        ELSE BEGIN
             new(listtail^.next);
             listtail := listtail^.next;
             listtail^.item := 'a';
             listtail^.next := NIL
             END
    END   { of FOR statement }
  END;  { of PROCEDURE }
```

Listing 11.9: De-allocating heap memory used by a linked list.

```
PROCEDURE DeallocateList(VAR listhead : nodeptr);
  VAR
    tempptr1,
    tempptr2 : nodeptr;
  BEGIN
    tempptr1 := listhead;
    while tempptr1 <> NIL do
      BEGIN
      tempptr2 := tempptr1;
      tempptr1 := tempptr1^.next;
      DISPOSE(tempptr2)
      END
  END;

BEGIN
  CLRSCR;
  init(listhead, listtail, free1);
  WRITELN;

  loaduplist(listhead, listtail);

  WRITELN(' After creating a ', maxitems, '-node list, there are now');
  WRITELN(' ', MEMAVAIL, ' free bytes on the heap.');
  free2 := (free1 - MEMAVAIL);
  WRITELN;
  WRITELN(' This indicates the the list is taking up ', free2);
  WRITELN(' bytes of heap space.');
  pause;

  DeallocateList(listhead);
  WRITELN(' After using the DeallocateList routine to dispose of list');
  WRITELN(' nodes, available heap memory is now ', MEMAVAIL, ' bytes.');
  WRITELN;
  difference := (MEMAVAIL - free1);
  WRITELN(' The difference between the original amount of heap memory');
  WRITELN(' available and the current amount is ', difference, ' bytes.')

  pause;

END.
```

Listing 11.9: De-allocating heap memory used by a linked list (cont.).

any array element in a one-step process. With a dynamically linked list, you have a two-step process: first, you look at the pointer to find the memory address of the variable you need, and second, you go to that address. So, in situations where speed is more important than memory economy, arrays and other static data structures have an edge over dynamically linked data structures.

Another factor to take into consideration with static data structures is flexibility. If you are creating a list in which new items must often be inserted and deleted in the middle of the list, then an array-based list will be terribly inefficient. Remember, to insert an item in the middle of an array, you must move many items over to open up a slot for the new item; the process is similar when deleting an item. This is terribly inefficient compared to inserting or deleting an item from the middle of a linked data structure, which simply involves re-arranging a few pointers.

This leads us to the strong point of using dynamically linked structures: their immense flexibility and memory economy. If you need to maintain lists whose size is unpredictable, or whose size varies widely from one program run to another, then linked data structures are probably better; likewise if you must insert and delete many items in the middle of a list. You will have to make a small sacrifice in terms of speed, but it will be more than offset by the flexibility that dynamic structures provide.

It is true that in these days of faster and faster PCs, people tend to think that program efficiency does not matter—that sloppy program code can be compensated for by incredibly efficient hardware. Although this idea has a grain of truth to it, that is no reason to use an inferior solution for a particular problem when a superior solution is available. You should analyze the situation carefully before deciding to use one type of data structure or another.

SUMMARY

Static data structures, such as arrays, must be declared in the program and cannot be changed at run-time. Pointers allow you to create *dynamic* data structures whose size can be changed at run-time, allowing the user to create new data items and to destroy old ones as needed.

A pointer is a special kind of variable that holds the memory address of another variable. To create a variable at run-time, the program uses the **New** procedure with a pointer to set aside memory space for a dynamic variable on the heap, and then loads that memory address into the pointer. To get rid of a variable at run-time, the program uses the **Dispose** procedure with the pointer; this frees up the heap space occupied by the dynamic variable and disconnects the pointer from that location.

It is very important that pointers be set to **NIL** at any time that they do not have a specific memory address loaded into them. Failure to do so can result in disaster.

A linked data structure can be created with pointers by including a pointer in each item of the list, thereby permitting a daisy-chain of pointer links from each item to the next.

Pointers give tremendous flexibility to the programmer, but they are a powerful tool that must be used with care.

REVIEW EXERCISES

1. Explain the differences between static and dynamic variables.

2. Explain the advantages and disadvantages of using static variables.

3. Explain what a pointer is and how it differs from other variables.

4. True or false: a pointer is always a dynamic variable. Justify your answer. Are there ever circumstances in which a pointer *cannot* be a dynamic variable?

5. Is there anything wrong with the following code fragment? If so, explain the problem and how you would correct it.

```
TYPE
     RecPtr = ^Rec;
Rec     =  RECORD
            Name : string10;
            GPA  : real;
            next : recptr
            END;
BEGIN
     New(RecPtr);
WITH RecPtr^ DO
     BEGIN
     Name := 'Jones';
     GPA  := 3.50;
     next := NIL
     END;
```

```
New(RecPtr^.next);
WITH RecPtr^.next^ DO
      BEGIN
      Name := 'Smith';
      GPA  := 3.55;
      next := NIL
      END
END;
```

6. Is there anything wrong with the following code fragment? If so, explain the problem and how you would correct it.

```
TYPE
      RecPtr = ^INTEGER
VAR
      MyNumRec : RecPtr;
BEGIN
      RecPtr^ := 10;
      WRITELN(' The value is ', recptr^, '.');
      pause
END;
```

7. Write a simple program to create a linked list of colors. Use a loop to allow the user to enter color names and, when finished, to exit from the loop.

8. Add a new routine to the program you created in exercise 7. This routine should traverse the list and, at each item, display the name of the color on the computer screen.

9. Add another new routine to the program from exercise 7. This routine should search the list for a specified target value.

10. Explain what the heap is and how it differs from the stack.

11. Suppose that at a certain point in your program, you need to create a fairly large dynamic variable, such as a dynamic array. Give step-by-step instructions and explain each step.

12. Are there any circumstances in which a pointer-linked list would require more memory than an array-based list with the

same number and type of items? Explain your answer.

13. (Challenging) Write a program to create and use a doubly-linked list—i.e., a list in which each item has a pointer to both the next and the previous items in the list.

14. Explain what happens to a dynamic variable when you use Dispose with the pointer that points to it.

15. (Challenging) To the program from exercise 7, add two new routines:

    (a) To add and remove items from the head of the list

    (b) To add and remove items from somewhere in the middle of the list.

Handling Text Files

Curious learning not only makes unpleasant things less unpleasant, but also makes pleasant things more pleasant.

—Bertrand Russell, *In Praise of Idleness*

DIFFERENT FILE TYPES

In previous chapters, we have seen several ways to create variables and lists. However, all of these approaches suffered from one major shortcoming: our data was always lost as soon as we turned off the computer.

In this chapter, we will look at how to remedy that shortcoming by creating and using files. Although the usual idea of a file is that it is a collection of information (such as text, records, and the like), Pascal uses the idea in a somewhat broader sense. In Turbo Pascal, files fall into one of two main categories:

- **Device files**, which are I/O devices in the computer, such as the keyboard, the screen, the printer port, and the modem; and

- **Disk files**, which are collections of related data on the computer's disk drives. The category of disk files is further subdivided into *text files*, *typed files*, and *untyped files*. We will show how to use text files in this chapter; typed and untyped files will be discussed in Chapter 13.

Turbo Pascal (and other implementations of the Pascal language) can read data from or write data to files in any of these categories. However, there is an important problem in doing so. Each different kind of computer and operating system has its own rules for naming and accessing different types of devices and disk files. Under MS-DOS, for instance, PC file names can be up to 11 characters long (eight characters plus a three-character extension). On the other hand, under VMS, Vax minicomputer file names can be up to 39 characters long, not counting additional information that can be included on the version number of the file and where the file is located in a computer network.

In this chapter, of course, our primary focus will be on text files, even though we must first introduce some general methods for handling any kind of file. The greatest advantage of text files is that they are simple and involve familiar ideas—an advantage that should not be ignored even by experienced programmers. Writing data to a text file is just like typing text on a page: you start at the top of the page and enter text one line at a time. Reading data from a text file is similar: start at the top line and read line-by-line until you arrive at the end. If you wish, you can send a text file to the printer or, with the DOS Type command, you can display it on-screen.

It is important to understand that although text files are easier to understand and work with than typed files, they are fundamentally similar. Any type of file is a sequence of items of a particular kind. In text files, the items in question are lines of text, while in typed files, the items are records, arrays, integers, or some other nontext data items. Untyped files, which are often discussed as if they were a third type of file, represent less a distinct file type than a special way to handle text and typed files.

FILE NAMES AND FILE VARIABLES

If Pascal had to incorporate all the different file and I/O conventions into the Pascal language itself, there would have to be a radically different version of Pascal for each different computer and operating system. Instead, Pascal uses *file variables* to insulate the programmer from having to worry about such details. A file variable is a Pascal identifier that serves inside a program as an "alias" for a disk file or an I/O device in the underlying computer hardware and operating system.

Before a file or device can be used in a Pascal program, it must be associated with a file variable that will be its name inside the program. So, for example, 'students.txt' is a legal file name in DOS, but it is illegal as a Pascal identifier because it contains a period. To use this DOS disk file in a program, we must first associate it with a file variable that *is* a legal Pascal identifier. To do this, Turbo Pascal uses its built-in **Assign** procedure:

```
ASSIGN(numberfile, 'numbers.txt');
```

Notice that just as 'numbers.txt' is illegal in Pascal, 'numberfile' would not be a legal file name in DOS because it is too long. The name of the file variable is part of a Pascal program, and follows the rules for Pascal identifiers.

Anytime the program writes data to or reads data from the file variable **numberfile**, Pascal directs the operation through the appropriate operating system services in DOS, which passes data to and from the associated disk file or device. Listing 12.1 illustrates the use of the **Assign** procedure with a file variable.

The VAR section of Listing 12.1 declares two variables: *numberfile*, which is a text file variable, and *counter*, a variable that we will use to control a loop. In the main body of the program, **ASSIGN** links the file variable with a disk file named **'numbers.txt'**, and **REWRITE** opens the file so the program can write data to it. Notice that to write data to the file, the WRITELN statements have the name of the file variable, a comma, and the names of the items to be written to the file.

After you enter and run the program in this listing, you can look at the file **'numbers.txt'** in the same directory as the listing itself. Your program

```
PROGRAM Listing12_1;

   {  This listing shows how to use the ASSIGN command to
      associate a file variable with an external disk file
      or device. Note that ASSIGN takes two parameters: a
      file variable, which in this case is numberfile, and
      a text string that is the name of the disk file or
      device. REWRITE opens the file for writing, which
      means that you can send data to the file but, with
      text files, cannot at the same time read data from
      the file. Finally, CLOSE closes the file; this is a
      very important step that is sometimes forgotten by
      novice programmers. }

VAR
   numberfile : TEXT;
   counter : INTEGER;

BEGIN
   ASSIGN(numberfile, 'numbers.txt');
   REWRITE(numberfile);
   WRITELN(numberfile, 'List of integers from 1 to 50:');
   WRITELN(numberfile, '-----------------------------');
   FOR counter := 1 TO 50 DO
        WRITELN(numberfile, counter);
   CLOSE(numberfile)
END.
```

Listing 12.1: Using Assign to associate a disk file with a file variable.

created the file, opened it, wrote the integers from 1 to 50 in it, and then closed the file.

When you pass a file variable to a subroutine, you *must* pass it as a VAR parameter. The reason is simple. When you pass a variable to a subroutine without using VAR, the variable is passed "by value," meaning that Pascal makes a copy of the variable and passes the copy to the subroutine. When you pass a variable as a VAR parameter, however, the variable is passed "by reference": instead of a copy, the subroutine receives a pointer to the actual variable that the parameter represents. It is not practical to pass files by value, i.e., to make a copy of a file any time you pass it to a subroutine. For that reason, files (of any type) can be only passed to subroutines as VAR parameters.

It is worth noting that even with the use of file variables, file operations (and other I/O operations) tend to vary from one implementation of the Pascal language to another. Sometimes, the differences are merely terminological: Vax Pascal has a command called *Open*, which works the same as Assign, except that it offers a large number of options for opening a file in different ways. At other times, the differences are more substantive: most mainframe and minicomputer Pascals use GET and PUT commands that are not in Turbo Pascal (see "File Handling in Standard Pascal" below).

If you are writing a program that has to be moved to a different Pascal compiler, then you should try to group all I/O operations into a few separate compartments of your program. When you move your program to the other compiler, the areas most likely to need modification will be easier to find.

Prompting the User for a Filename

In Listing 12.1, the actual name of the disk file is embedded in the program code itself. Of course, if this were the only way to use files in Turbo Pascal, it would create terrible problems. Any time the user had to work with a different file, we would have to produce a different version of our program.

Turbo Pascal (and Pascal in general) offers a simple solution to this problem. Instead of embedding the filename in the code, as is done in Listing 12.1, the user is prompted for a filename. This filename is then stored in a string variable whose contents—the name of the disk file—is then loaded into the file variable by the **ASSIGN** command. Listing 12.2 illustrates how to do this.

Listing 12.2 is basically the same as Listing 12.1 except that it creates and uses a new string variable, *NameOfFile*, to hold the filename entered by the user. We prompt the user to enter a filename with a WRITE statement; notice that there is no filename included in this statement because the output is going to the PC's screen. (The screen is denoted by the default output file variable, *output*. If you do not specify a filename, Turbo Pascal assumes that you want output directed to the screen.)

After the user enters a filename, **ASSIGN** links the filename with the file variable, **REWRITE** opens the file for writing, and the user is in business. Everything else works exactly the same as in Listing 12.1.

```
PROGRAM Listing12_2;

    ( Shows how to prompt the user for a file name. The file name
      is then loaded into the file variable with the ASSIGN command. )

USES CRT;

VAR
   NameOfFile : STRING[12];
   numberfile : TEXT;
   counter    : INTEGER;

BEGIN
   CLRSCR;
   WRITE(' Please enter the name of the file you want to use: ');
   READLN(NameOfFile);
   ASSIGN(numberfile, NameOfFile);
   REWRITE(numberfile);
   WRITELN(numberfile, 'List of integers from 1 to 50:');
   WRITELN(numberfile, '-----------------------------');
   FOR counter := 1 TO 50 DO
        WRITELN(numberfile, counter);
   CLOSE(numberfile)
END.
```

Listing 12.2: Prompting the user for a filename.

DOS Device Files

As noted above, a file variable can denote either a disk file or a device in the computer. Turbo Pascal has standard names for the various devices in your PC. To use one of these devices, for example, to direct output to the printer, you simply use the **ASSIGN** command to link the standard device name with a file variable. Then, exactly the same as with a disk file, any action performed on the file variable will apply to the device. The standard device names are shown in Table 12.1.

You use the names in Table 12.1 just as you would the names of disk files, except that some of the devices (i.e., the printer ports) are write-only: you can send data to them, but you cannot read data from them.

Table 12.1: Standard DOS Device Names in Turbo Pascal

NAME	FUNCTION	INPUT	OUTPUT
CON	Screen, keyboard	Yes	Yes
LPT1	Printer port #1	No	Yes
LPT2	Printer port #2	No	Yes
LPT3	Printer port #3	No	Yes
LST	Printer port #1*	No	Yes
PRN	Printer port #1	No	Yes
COM1	Communications port #1	Yes	Yes
COM2	Communications port #2	Yes	Yes
NUL	Wastebasket	Yes	Yes
Note: Defined in the Printer unit.			

A typical application of these device names is to send output to the printer. This is shown in Listing 12.3.

You declare the printer device **PRN** just like any other file, by using **ASSIGN** with the file variable and putting the name of the device within single quotes. After that, any output sent to the *MyPrinter* text file variable is routed to your PC's printer port #1. (A printer port is a device by which your PC can be connected to a printer.) If your printer is connected to one of the other ports, such as printer port #2 (LPT2) or a serial port (COM1

```
PROGRAM Listing12_3;

  ( Demonstrates how to use a standard device name with a
    file variable. The device name is treated just as if it
    were the name of a disk file. In this case, the device
    name stands for printer port #1. Instead of being written
    to a disk file, as in Listings 12.1 and 12.2, this list
    of integers is sent to the printer. Notice that after the
    list is sent to the printer, we send a "form feed" character
    (ASCII number 12) to advance the paper in the printer. )

VAR
  MyPrinter : TEXT;
  counter   : INTEGER;

BEGIN
  ASSIGN(MyPrinter, 'PRN');    ( link printer with file variable )
  REWRITE(MyPrinter);          ( open file for output )

  WRITELN(MyPrinter, 'List of integers from 1 to 50:');
  WRITELN(MyPrinter, '----------------------------');

  FOR counter := 1 TO 50 DO         ( write integers 1..50 )
       WRITELN(MyPrinter, counter);

  WRITELN(MyPrinter, chr(12));  ( Send form feed to the printer. )

  CLOSE(MyPrinter)      ( close file )
END.
```

Listing 12.3: Using a device name with a file variable.

or COM2), you can send output to the printer by substituting the appropriate device name for **'PRN'** in the **ASSIGN** statement.

The devices in Table 12.1 are pretty much what you would expect them to be. CON takes input from the keyboard and directs output to the screen. LPT1, LPT2, LPT3, LST, and PRN are names for printer ports. COM1 and COM2 are the names of communication ports; generally, you will use these for communicating with a modem. In certain situations, printers can also be connected to these COM ports.

The only device that may seem a little puzzling is NUL, which the table describes as a "wastebasket." NUL ignores anything that is sent to it. If you attempt to read from the NUL device, it tells your program that the end of the file has been reached. You will not use this frequently, but it can be helpful when you need to include an input or output file name in your program but do not want to deal with an actual file or device.

FILE HANDLING IN STANDARD PASCAL

It is also important to know that many versions of Pascal require you to declare all file variables in the header of your program. Thus, for example, a program called **ThisProgram**, which used the file variable *studentfile*, would have the following as the first line in the source code:

```
PROGRAM ThisProgram (input, output, studentfile);
```

Input and *output* denote the computer's keyboard and display screen, respectively. *Studentfile* is a file variable associated by the Assign procedure with an actual disk file or device in the computer. Turbo Pascal simply ignores these file declarations in the program header, so if you are writing a program that will be moved to another Pascal compiler, you might as well include them.

One common mistake in writing these headings is to confuse the file variable with the actual name of a disk file. Thus, for example, if *studentfile* stood for a file named 'students.txt', a beginner might mistakenly write:

```
PROGRAM ThisProgram(input, output, students.txt);
```

A program with this heading will not compile, because **'students.txt'** is not a legal Pascal identifier. It is the name of the file variable, not the file name itself, that should be included in the program heading.

Standard Pascal, along with most mainframe and minicomputer Pascals, implements two procedures called *Get* and *Put,* which correspond roughly (*very* roughly) with READ and WRITE. Get and Put work with a "buffer variable" that stands between the program and the file itself. Where x is a character or string variable, Get(x) reads the next component of a file into x, and Put(x) writes the value of x as the next component in the file.

Turbo Pascal does not support either the Get or Put procedure. The main reason you should know about them is that you can replace Get with READ and Put with WRITE if you ever have to move a Pascal program from another compiler to Turbo Pascal. Moving a program from Turbo Pascal to other Pascal compilers, however, is less of a problem, because all Pascals support READ and WRITE.

OPENING FILES

Once you have associated a device or disk file with a file variable in your Pascal program, you are almost ready to use the file. First, however, the file must be opened. A text file can be opened for (1) reading data from the file or (2) writing data to the file, but not both at the same time.

The attempt to write data to a text file open for reading or to read data from a text file open for writing is a very common error. If you want to write data to a text file that is open for reading, you must first re-open it for writing by using **REWRITE** or **APPEND**. Likewise, if you want to read data from a file that is open for writing, you must first re-open it for reading by using **RESET**. You do not have to close the file before re-opening it in either case.

Typed and untyped files, which will be discussed in Chapter 13, do not suffer from this limitation. No matter how typed and untyped files are opened, they are available for both reading and writing.

Turbo Pascal offers the three commands just mentioned for opening files: *Rewrite*, *Append*, and *Reset*. It has one command for closing files: *Close*.

REWRITE

As we have already seen in the listings, **REWRITE** opens a file for writing, i.e., it opens a file in such a way that you can put data into it. It also positions the *file pointer*—the location where the next line of text will be entered—at the very beginning of the file. The first use of WRITE or WRITELN with the file variable will write text to this line in the file.

If you use **REWRITE** with a name of a disk file that does not yet exist, then **REWRITE** will create the file for you. However, if you use **REWRITE** with a file that *already* exists, it will wipe out the existing file and replace it with a new, empty file that is ready for you to enter data into it. The use of **REWRITE** is illustrated in Listings 12.1–12.3, so it won't be repeated here.

APPEND

To add new data to an existing text file, you must open the file with **APPEND**. Instead of creating a new file or wiping out the old file, as **REWRITE** does, **APPEND** opens an existing file for writing and positions the file pointer at the current end of the file. Any new uses of WRITE or WRITELN with the file variable will add new text to the end of the file. The use of **APPEND** is illustrated in Listing 12.4.

Listing 12.4 is identical to Listing 12.1 except that (a) it opens the file **'numbers.txt'** with **APPEND** instead of **REWRITE**, and (b) it appends the numbers **51** to **100** to the bottom of the file. If you look at the file **'numbers.txt'** after running this program, you will see that the new numbers have been added at the end.

```
PROGRAM Listing12_4;

   { Demonstrates how to add new material to an existing text
     file by opening the file with APPEND instead of REWRITE. }

VAR
   numberfile : TEXT;
   counter : INTEGER;

BEGIN
   ASSIGN(numberfile, 'numbers.txt');
   APPEND(numberfile);
   WRITELN(numberfile);
   WRITELN(numberfile, 'List of integers from 51 to 100:');
   WRITELN(numberfile, '--------------------------------');
   FOR counter := 51 TO 100 DO
        WRITELN(numberfile, counter);
   CLOSE(numberfile)
END.
```

Listing 12.4: Using Append to add new data to an existing text file.

RESET

So far, we have seen several examples of writing to text files, but no examples of reading from them. To read from a text file, you open it with **RESET**. This opens the file for reading and positions the file pointer at the very beginning of the file. The first use of READ or READLN will read text from the first line of the file. Additional READs and READLNs after that will read from succeeding lines of the file, depending on whether you use READ or READLN. (See "Reading from Text Files" below.) Listing 12.5 demonstrates the use of **RESET**.

In addition to the file and counter variables, Listing 12.5 creates a new *line* variable. This is a text string that holds the contents of each line as it is read in from the file. After opening the file for reading with **RESET**, we do a few things that are relatively complex, at least, compared to what we have seen so far.

- The line **WHILE NOT EOF(numberfile) DO** uses the end-of-file function (discussed in "The EOF and EOLN Functions" section below) to tell the program that it should continue executing the WHILE loop until the end of the file is reached.

- Embedded in the WHILE loop is a FOR loop. If we did not include this extra loop, then the program would simply read the file from start to finish without any pauses. By using the FOR loop, we tell the program to read 20 lines from the file, display each line on the screen, and then pause so that we can look at what has been displayed. After the user presses a key, the FOR

```
PROGRAM Listing12_5;

 { Demonstrates the use of RESET to open a file for reading. }

USES CRT, MyUtils;

VAR
  numberfile : TEXT;
  counter    : INTEGER;
  line       : STRING[80];

BEGIN
  CLRSCR;
  ASSIGN(numberfile, 'numbers.txt');
  RESET(numberfile);
  WHILE NOT EOF(numberfile) DO
    BEGIN
    FOR counter := 1 TO 20 DO
      BEGIN
      READLN(numberfile, line);
      WRITELN(line);
      END;
    pause
    END;
  CLOSE(numberfile)
END.
```

Listing 12.5: Using Reset to open a file for reading.

loop executes again, bringing in another 20 lines from the file, and pauses again. This process continues until the end of the file is reached, at which point we drop out of the WHILE loop.

- Finally, after all the lines in the file have been read and displayed on-screen, the file is closed and the program ends.

These embellishments aside, the main point is that we opened the file for reading with **RESET**, read from it, and closed it. If you look at the **'numbers.txt'** file itself, you will see that it was completely unchanged by this operation.

There are two other tricks you can do with **RESET**. First, there may be times when you want to add data to a text file, but you are not sure if the text file already exists and holds data or not. Using **REWRITE** in this situation won't work, because if the file currently exists, **REWRITE** will wipe out the data it already contains. But **APPEND** won't work either, because if the file does *not* exist, then your program will have a run-time error because **APPEND**, unlike **REWRITE**, will not create a new file.

By using **RESET**, however, we can devise a *safe* way to open text files for writing, as shown in Listing 12.6.

Listing 12.6 is not a full program; it is a routine procedure that you can use in any program that manipulates text files. It takes the text file itself as a parameter and declares a local integer variable *FileExists*. It then turns off input checking and tries to open the file with **RESET**. (We had to turn off input checking because if the file doesn't exist and input checking is on, then we'll get a run-time error.) After the call to **RESET**, we immediately turn input checking back on.

```
PROCEDURE OpenFileForWriting (VAR this file : text);

  { Provides a safe way to open text files for writing. }

  VAR
    FileExists : INTEGER;
  BEGIN
    {$I-}
    RESET(thisfile);       { try to open the file }
    {$I+}
    FileExists := IORESULT; { file opened successfully? }
    IF FileExists = 0
       THEN APPEND(thisfile)
       ELSE REWRITE(thisfile)
  END;
```

Listing 12.6: "Safe" routine to open text files for writing.

If the call to **RESET** was a success, then the file was opened and **IORESULT = 0**, indicating that the file already exists. If the call to **RESET** was not a success, then **IORESULT <> 0** and we have learned that the file does not yet exist. With that information, it is a simple matter to set up an IF statement that uses **APPEND** if the file already exists and **REWRITE** if it does not.

The second trick is also quite useful. There may be times when you need to read from a text file, return to the beginning of the file, and start reading all over again. The simplest way to achieve this is to re-open the file by calling **RESET** again. Remember, in addition to opening the file for reading, RESET positions the file pointer at the very beginning of the file.

WRITING TO TEXT FILES

We have already seen the basics of writing to text files. There are just a few other things that you should know to be able to write to text files. None is particularly mysterious, and they are worth pointing out to help achieve efficiency.

First, there is the difference between WRITE and WRITELN. You have already seen this as it applies to the computer screen, and it has the same effect when you WRITE or WRITELN to a file. The following code will write a single integer on each line:

```
FOR counter := 1 TO 5 DO

     WRITELN(thisfile, counter);
```

The result is a file that contains five lines:

```
1

2

3

4

5
```

WRITE, on the other hand, does not add an end-of-line character (ASCII 13) after each operation. Thus,

```
FOR counter := 1 TO 5 DO

    WRITE(thisfile, counter);
```

will produce a file with a single line:

```
12345
```

You should also realize that though there are many times when you need to use separate WRITE statements, it is not always necessary. WRITE and WRITELN can take multiple parameters, so

```
WRITE(thisfile, 1, 2, 3, 4, 5);
```

will produce a file with the same single line containing '**12345**'.

Just as you would use WRITELN when you are sending text to the screen, you can insert a blank line in a file with a plain WRITELN statement and no parameters.

READING FROM TEXT FILES

Most of the operations for reading from text files are similar to those for writing to text files. A READ statement reads one or more items without moving the file pointer down to the next line. READLN also reads one or more items, but it *does* move the file pointer down to the next line. If you want to move the file pointer without reading anything, you use a READLN statement with no parameters.

Thus, suppose that you had a text file called *NumFile* with the following contents:

```
11 2 20 43 5
225 2 67 4 7
```

If you had some integer variables *a* through *j*, you could read these two lines in two different ways. First, you could use READ and insert an empty READLN statement at the end, as in

```
READ(numfile, a, b, c, d, e);

READLN(numfile);

READ(numfile, f, g, h, i, j);

READLN;
```

Alternatively, you could simply use two READLN statements, as in

```
READLN(numfile, a, b, c, d, e);

READLN(numfile, f, g, h, i, j);
```

That seems easy enough, but it becomes a little trickier if you are reading in a line of characters. To see why, enter and run Listing 12.7.

```
PROGRAM Listing12_7;

  { Illustrates a potential problem reading characters
    from a text file. There are two different solutions. }

USES CRT, MyUtils;

VAR
  a, b, c, d, e : CHAR;
  CharFile      : TEXT;

begin
  CLRSCR;
  ASSIGN(charfile, 'chars.txt');
  REWRITE(charfile);
  WRITELN(charfile, 'a', ' ', 'b', ' ', 'c', ' ', 'd', ' ', 'e');
  pause;

  RESET(charfile);
  READLN(charfile, a, b, c, d, e);
  WRITELN(a, b, c, d, e);
  pause;

  CLOSE(charfile)
end.
```

Listing 12.7: A potential problem reading characters from a text file.

Instead of displaying the line's contents as 'a b c d e', as it should, this program displays the line's contents as 'a b c'. The problem with Listing 12.6 does not occur when you are reading in a line of numbers separated by spaces. The problem is that the space character is itself a character, so instead of reading 'abcde', as you want it to, the READLN statement reads in 'a', space, 'b', space, 'c'—for five characters.

What you need is a way to filter out the characters (called *delimiters*) that separate the characters you want, whether the delimiters are spaces, commas, or some other ASCII character.

One way to do this is by using *dummy* character variables. If you know (as, normally, you will) the exact format of the lines you will be reading from the file, you can include separate READ statements with dummy variables to advance the file pointer past the spaces. A somewhat more elegant solution is to set up an IF statement that executes an extra READ statement if the last character read from the file was a space (or any other delimiter character). This approach is shown in Listing 12.8.

THE EOF AND EOLN FUNCTIONS

There are two important Boolean-type functions that give you control over how long your program reads from or writes to a file. These are the EOF (end of file) and the EOLN (end of line) functions. When Pascal creates a text file, it ends each line with an end-of-line marker (ASCII 13), which corresponds to the Enter key on your PC keyboard. In addition, Pascal marks the end of the file with a Ctrl-Z character.

Listing 12.7 illustrates the use of the EOLN function. After the file is re-opened for reading with **RESET**, the statement **WHILE NOT EOLN(charfile)** ... tells Pascal to keep on performing the read operation until it arrives at the end of the line, where EOLN becomes true and, therefore, NOT EOLN becomes false.

Likewise, Listing 12.5 illustrates the use of the EOF function to read a file until the end. This is a very typical example of setting up a loop to execute WHILE the end of the file has not yet been reached.

```
PROGRAM Listing12_8;

   { Illustrates one solution to the problem of reading characters
     from a line in a text file. }

USES CRT, MyUtils;

CONST
     space = ' ';

TYPE
     SomeLetters = ARRAY['a'..'e'] OF CHAR;

VAR
   letters   : SomeLetters;
   CharFile  : TEXT;
   counter   : CHAR;

BEGIN
     CLRSCR;
     ASSIGN(charfile, 'chars2.txt');
     REWRITE(charfile);
     FOR counter := 'a' TO 'e' DO
       BEGIN
         WRITE(charfile, counter);
         WRITE(charfile, space)
       END;
     pause;

     RESET(charfile);
     FOR counter := 'a' TO 'e' DO
         IF NOT EOLN(charfile) THEN
             REPEAT
                READ(charfile, letters[counter])
             UNTIL letters[counter] <> space;

     FOR counter := 'a' TO 'e' DO
         BEGIN
         WRITE(letters[counter]);
         WRITE(space)
         END;
     pause;

     CLOSE(charfile)
END.
```

Listing 12.8: A solution to the problem of reading characters from a text file.

CLOSING FILES

We have already seen how to close a file by using the CLOSE procedure with the file variable. There are two aspects of this, however, that we
have not yet discussed.

The first is to understand that disk I/O operations (such as reading data from a file or writing data to a file) are usually the slowest processes that your program performs. This is because such operations depend on mechanical components in the disk drives that are much slower than the electronic components in your computer's processor and memory. If your program had to do a disk access every time you wrote data to a file, it would seriously degrade the program's performance.

Pascal solves this problem by trying to minimize the number of times your program must physically access the disk drive. When a file is opened with **RESET** or **REWRITE**, Pascal sets aside an area of memory to hold data that is read from or written to the file. This area of memory is called the *file buffer*, and when you write data to a file in your program, normally, it goes into the file buffer rather than to the disk file itself.

Turbo Pascal periodically *flushes* the file buffer to the disk file and actually writes its contents to the disk file. This is why, if you forget to close a file at the end of your program, at least some of the things you wrote to the file will actually be there—some, but *not* all. Using the **CLOSE** procedure executes a final flush and writes all remaining data to the file. If you forget to close the file, data that is still in the file buffer will be lost.

The second thing to understand is that if you ever need to force the file buffer to flush, but do not want to close the file, you can use Turbo Pascal's **FLUSH** procedure. Its syntax is identical to that of **CLOSE**:

```
FLUSH(file variable);
```

This will cause all data currently written to the file buffer to be written to the disk file itself.

SUMMARY

Turbo Pascal supports two major types of files: device files, which are devices in the computer, and disk files, which are collections of data saved in a file on the computer's disk drives. Disk files, in turn, are divided into

(1) text files, which contain plain-text information that can be read on the screen or used by other programs; and (2) typed files, which contain non-text data items, such as records and arrays.

To work with a file, a Pascal program must first associate its name with a file variable. This variable is then used in the program to refer to the file. A file variable, like any other variable, must be a legal Pascal identifier.

A text file can be opened *for writing* by using the Rewrite procedure with the file variable. It can be opened *for reading* by using the Reset procedure with the file variable. Because a call to Rewrite wipes out any data that is already in a file, data can be added to an existing text file by opening it for writing with Append instead of Rewrite.

To write data to a text file, you include the file variable as the first parameter in a WRITE or WRITELN statement. To read data from a text file, you do the same thing with a READ or READLN statement.

All files must be closed with the Turbo Pascal Close procedure at the end of the program. Failure to do so can result in loss of data.

REVIEW EXERCISES

1. Explain the two main types of files in Turbo Pascal, as well as any subcategories within those main types of files.

2. Explain (a) what file variables are, (b) why they are important, and (c) how to set up and use a file variable in a Turbo Pascal program.

3. Explain the different ways of opening a file and when you should use each. Are there circumstances under which using one of these methods could be disastrous? If so, explain why.

4. Explain how to design your program's file-handling operations for maximum portability between different Pascal compilers and different hardware platforms.

5. Are there any problems in the following code fragment? If so, what are they and how would you correct them?

```
VAR
      MyFile : TEXT;
PROCEDURE OpenFile(MyFile : TEXT);
      BEGIN
            Assign(MyFile, 'thisfile.dat');
            RESET(Myfile);
            WRITELN(MyFile, 'This is a text
file.');
      END;
BEGIN { main body of program }
  OpenFile(MyFile)
END.
```

6. Explain what is done by each of the following:

   (a) Assign

   (b) Reset

   (c) Rewrite

   (d) Append

   (e) Close

7. Explain what is done by each of the following:

   (a) Write(thisfile, 'This is a text file.');

   (b) Writeln(thisfile, 'This is a text file');

   (c) Writeln(thisfile);

   (d) Read(thisfile, num_var);

   (e) Readln(thisfile, num_var);

8. Write a simple program to open a text file, write the names of several colors into it (one color on each line), and close the file.

9. With the program from Exercise 8, add a routine to read color names from the file and display them on the screen. The routine should not assume that there is a specific number of color names in the file; instead, it should read color names until it reaches the end of the file.

10. Explain the file functions EOF() and EOLN() and how they are used.

11. Write a routine using both EOF() and EOLN() that will read numbers from a file. Assume that there are several numbers on each line, with the numbers separated by spaces, as in:

```
56 72 5 0 134
2
80 6 1 9 178 23 4 11
5 7 3 9 1
```

12. Write a routine using both EOF() and EOLN() that will read characters from a file. Assume that there are several characters on each line, with the characters separated by spaces, as in:

```
e v i
l a s i s
i v l e t u b
d a e d s i
l u a p
```

13. Write a short program to send text to the printer. Test it on your printer with the message "Pascal is more fun than surfing!"

14. Are there circumstances in which you might use Reset with a file that is already open? If so, explain what the circumstances might be.

15. (Challenging) Write a program that gets data from the user, puts the data in a linked list, and then writes the data to a text file. The same program should have another routine, which reads the data from the text file into a linked list and displays it on the screen.

CHAPTER

Typed and Untyped Files

It isn't possible to get to the moon.

—Ludwig Wittgenstein, September 1950 *(On Certainty, No. 286)*

It isn't possible to get to the moon
without a rocket.

—Ludwig Wittgenstein, July 1969 *(probably apocryphal)*

In the previous chapter, we looked at some ways to use text files. The principal advantage of text files is that they are the computer equivalent of printed pages and, hence, are very easy to understand and manipulate. Also, they are highly portable between different versions of Pascal, most of which handle text files in about the same way. Finally, of course, they can be used to send text-format data to other programs or to a printer for reports.

In this chapter, we will look at typed and untyped files. Unlike text files, which consist (obviously) of text, typed files consist of items of a particular data type. And though the name "untyped files" suggests a third kind of file, untyped files are, in fact, a fast and powerful way to use both text and typed files.

TYPED FILES

In text files, the fundamental unit is the line of text—or, depending on your preference, the text character. In typed files, the fundamental unit is not a line of text but items of a specific data type. The items can be integers, real numbers, strings, characters, arrays, and other built-in Pascal types, as well as user-defined types such as records and objects.

In fact, the units in a typed file are commonly referred to as *records,* but you must be careful to avoid confusion on this point. The "records" in a typed file can indeed be items of the record data type, but they can also be integers, strings, or any other legal Pascal type except a file type. Thus, a file "record" might or might not be a Pascal record-type data item.

Unlike the lines in text files, the units in a typed file must all be of the same size. (The only exception is the unusual case of a typed file that contains variant records.) You declare a typed file as follows:

```
VAR

    ThisFile : FILE OF <type>
```

where <type> can be any built-in or user-defined data type except another file type. Thus, you could have the following as a typed file:

```
TYPE

    string15 = STRING[15];

    studentrec = RECORD

                    fname,

                    lname : string15;

                    GPA   : REAL

                    END;

VAR

    numfile : FILE OF INTEGER;

    ltrfile : FILE OF CHAR;

    strfile : FILE OF string15;

    stdfile : FILE OF studentrec;
```

A typed file can contain only items of the appropriate type: e.g., if a file is declared as a FILE OF INTEGER, it cannot have real numbers, characters, or any other noninteger value. In a certain sense, this is no different from text files, which also can contain only text items. With text files, however, text is also the *only* type that they can contain, requiring Pascal (or the programmer) to convert text file items to other types as needed by the program. Listings 13.1 and 13.2 illustrate two programs for storing integers in a file; the only difference between them is that Listing 13.1 uses a text file and Listing 13.2 uses a typed file.

The first difference between Listing 13.1 and Listing 13.2 appears, as expected, in the VAR section when we declare the file variable *Numfile*. In 13.1, this is declared as a text file, while in 13.2, it is declared as a file of integers (a typed file).

Linking the file variable with a disk file and opening the file for writing also work the same way, using **Assign** and **Rewrite**. In fact, almost everything is the same until we arrive at the last part of the program, where we read a number from the file.

In Listing 13.1, the text file was opened for writing with the **Rewrite** procedure. Before we can read from it, we must re-open it with **Reset**. We

```
PROGRAM Listing13_1;

   { This program uses a text file to store integers, in contrast
     with Listing 13.2, which uses a typed file. The purpose of this
     listing is to illustrate some of the differences between text
     and typed files. }

USES CRT, MyUtils;

VAR
   Numfile : TEXT;
   counter,
   HowMany : INTEGER;
BEGIN
   ASSIGN(numfile, 'numfile.txt');
   REWRITE(numfile);
   CLRSCR;
   WRITE(' How many integers to store in file? ');
   READLN(HowMany);

   { Now we write some numbers to the text file. }
   FOR counter := 1 TO HowMany DO
      WRITELN(numfile, counter);

   { ------------------------------------------------ }
   { Now we use RESET to re-open the text file for reading. }
   { ------------------------------------------------ }
   RESET(numfile);
   FOR counter := 1 TO 4 DO READLN(numfile);

   READLN(numfile, HowMany);  { the HowMany variable is available }
   WRITELN;
   WRITELN(' The number on line 5 is ', HowMany, '.');
   pause;

   CLOSE(numfile)
END.
```

Listing 13.1: Using a text file to store integers.

then execute four empty READLN statements to move the file pointer down to the fifth line, where we read the number on the file's fifth line and display it on the screen.

In Listing 13.2, however, we did not need to re-open the file with **Reset**. This is because an open typed file is available for both reading and writing *regardless* of how it was opened.

The next difference in Listing 13.2 occurs when we move the file pointer down to the fifth record in the file. Because a typed file consists of records instead of lines, we use the **Seek** procedure with a record number to move the file pointer to that record in the file. The first record in the file is always record number 0; therefore, to see the fifth number in the file, we

```
PROGRAM Listing13_2;

    { Demonstrates a very simple typed file. This stores the same
      data as the text file in Listing 13.1, and shows some of the
      differences between text and typed files. }

USES CRT, MyUtils;

VAR
   Numfile : FILE OF INTEGER;
   counter,
   HowMany : INTEGER;

BEGIN
   ASSIGN(numfile, 'numfile.dat');
   REWRITE(numfile);
   CLRSCR;
   WRITE(' How many integers to store in file? ');
   READLN(HowMany);

   FOR counter := 1 TO HowMany DO
     WRITE(numfile, counter);


   ( --------------------------------------------------------- )
   ( Observe what we have NOT done: we have not re-opened the   )
   ( file for reading, as we had to do in Listing 13.1 with the )
   ( text file. When open, a typed file is available for both   )
   ( reading and writing, regardless of how it was opened.      )
   ( --------------------------------------------------------- )
   SEEK(numfile, 4);
   READ(numfile, HowMany);
   WRITELN(' The number in record #5 is ', HowMany, '.');
   pause;

   CLOSE(numfile)

END.
```

Listing 13.2: Using a typed file to store integers.

seek record number 4. There are no other differences between Listings 13.1 and 13.2: in both, the files are closed in the same way.

COMPARATIVE SIZE OF TYPED FILES

Listings 13.1 and 13.2 illustrate another important point: sometimes a typed file will be smaller than a text file with the same data, and sometimes it will not. If you run Listing 13.1 and tell it to produce a file containing 50 integers, the file will take up 191 bytes of disk space. The typed file with 50 integers produced by Listing 13.2, however, takes up only 100 bytes of disk space. (These values are approximate; the size of the files on your machine will depend on your DOS version and how your disk is configured.)

To determine if a typed file will take up less disk space than a text file, a rule of thumb is this: If the data items to be stored are all the same size or very nearly so, then a typed file probably will take up less disk space than a text file. On the other hand, if the data items to be stored vary widely in their actual size, then a text file probably will be smaller.

That rule is still fairly abstract, so let's look at a concrete example. Listings 13.1 and 13.2 produced two files of integers, all of which were about the same size. That is, when considered as two characters in a text file, '20' takes up eight bits (one byte) for each character, for a total of two bytes. In a typed file, the same number stored *as an integer* takes up two bytes because that's how much space integers take up. But when you add in the overhead (end-of-line markers, etc.) of the text file, the text file ends up being bigger.

Listings 13.3 and 13.4 create files that hold text strings. Both use a string variable 15 characters long, and both write the names to a file. In Listing 13.3, the names are written to a text file, in which each name occupies only the number of characters it actually needs. This amount of space, plus the end-of-line characters and so forth, adds up to the amount of space required by the text file.

Listing 13.4, however, creates a file of 15-character strings. In the typed file that this program creates, each data item takes up 15 characters of space—*whether or not* the actual name is 15-characters long. This means that, because most names are shorter than 15 characters, a text file probably will be smaller than a typed file for this kind of information.

```
PROGRAM Listing13_3;

USES CRT;

CONST
  continue : CHAR = 'Y';     ( a "typed constant" )

VAR
  namefile : TEXT;
  student  : STRING[15];

BEGIN
  ASSIGN(namefile, 'names.txt');
  REWRITE(namefile);
  CLRSCR;
  WHILE UPCASE(continue) = 'Y' DO
    BEGIN
    WRITELN;
    WRITE('Enter a student''s first name: ');
    READLN(student);
    WRITELN(namefile, student);
    WRITELN(namefile);
    WRITELN;
    WRITE(' Add another (Y/N)? ');
    READLN(continue)
    END;
  CLOSE(namefile)
END.
```

Listing 13.3: A text file of student names.

```
PROGRAM Listing13_4;

USES CRT;

CONST
  continue : CHAR = 'Y';     ( a "typed constant" )

TYPE
  string15 = STRING[15];

VAR
  namefile : FILE OF string15;
  student : string15;

BEGIN
  ASSIGN(namefile, 'names.dat');
  REWRITE(namefile);
  CLRSCR;
  WHILE UPCASE(continue) = 'Y' DO
    BEGIN
    WRITELN;
    WRITE('Enter a student''s first name: ');
    READLN(student);
    WRITE(namefile, student);
    WRITELN;
    WRITE(' Add another (Y/N)? ');
    READLN(continue)
    END;
  CLOSE(namefile)
END.
```

Listing 13.4: A typed file of student names.

To test this theory, run Listing 13.3 and Listing 13.4, entering the following names in each: Rebecca, Sam, Nick, Susan, and George. This will produce (subject to the conditions noted earlier) a text file that requires 45 bytes of disk space and a typed file that requires 80 bytes of disk space.

ADVANTAGES AND DISADVANTAGES

As the joke says, there is good and bad news about typed files. ("Take my file—please!") The good news is that typed files can help your program run faster than it would if it used text files. Depending on the situation, typed files also can make it easier for you to program file I/O operations.

The bad news is that you've just heard all the good news. Typed files are not necessarily smaller than text files, nor are they always easier to handle. Moreover, different Pascal compilers handle typed files in far more varied ways than the ways in which they handle text files; so typed files and programs that use them are far less portable from one Pascal to another.

Typed files are faster than text files because typed files store data in Turbo Pascal's native format for that data type. Consider a simple example: a file of integers, with one integer on each line. You can store the same group of integers in a text file or a typed file. In the text file, however, the integers are stored as ASCII character representations of integers—that is, Turbo Pascal sees the file as containing text items such as '1543', '5', and '21', instead of the integers 1543, 5, and 21. When a program reads the content of each text line into an integer variable, Pascal must convert each text item from the file into an integer type.

File I/O is already the slowest operation that your program performs, and this extensive type-conversion just adds one more operation for your program to do when it reads from or writes to a text file. The extra work becomes even more obvious when you store the contents of complex data items (such as records) in a text file. In this case, you have to write the type-conversion routines into your program, converting values as needed and loading them one-by-one into your program's data structures.

Handling complex data elements is, in fact, the main area where typed files excel—not only in terms of speed, but also in terms of programming simplicity. For ease of programming, there is no difference between a text file containing numbers (actually, of course, representations of numbers as ASCII characters) and a typed file containing the same numbers. But when you have a complex type, matters become quite a bit easier with typed files.

Suppose you had the following record type in your program (a type which we will actually use later in this chapter):

```
TYPE

        student = RECORD

                fname,

                lname : string15;

                GPA    : REAL

                END;
```

With a text file, you could store the information for each field of the record on a separate line, with a blank line between records. But reading the information from the file into a program's record variables is somewhat laborious, as shown by this code fragment:

```
READLN(class, studentvariable.fname);

READLN(class, studentvariable.lname);

READLN(class, studentvariable.GPA);

READLN(class); { skips blank line between records }
```

That is four lines of code to read a single record: three lines actually to read the record, and the fourth line to move the file pointer ahead to the start of the next record. A typed file, however, stores each student record in exactly the same format as a variable of the student data type, so your code is much simpler:

```
READ(class, studentvar);
```

Because the file record is the same data type as the student variable, you can skip the process of reading information line-by-line and field-by-field; instead, you just pop the file record into the student variable with a single operation. Also, there's no need to move the file pointer to the next record, because a typed file is designed to be easy for Turbo Pascal (not people) to read, and the records are packed together. In this case, you end up with less work for Turbo Pascal (no type-conversion) and less work for you, the programmer (fewer lines of code to write). The cost is that you lose the intuitive familiarity of text files and the portability that they provide.

WRITING AND READING DATA

You write data to typed files in almost exactly the same way that you write data to text files. Using the WRITE procedure with the file variable for the typed file, you can write variables to the file. Similarly, you use the READ procedure to read data from typed files. Because typed files do not have lines, however, you cannot use WRITELN or READLN with typed files. The formal syntax of WRITE and READ statements with typed files is as follows:

```
WRITE(typedfile, variable1, variable2, ... );
READ(typedfile, variable1, variable2, ... );
```

Here, *typedfile* is the file variable that stands for the typed file, while *variable1*, *variable2*, and so forth are variables of the data type that the file is set up to hold. This points up another difference between typed and text files: you can only write variables to a typed file, not constants. With a text file, it is perfectly legal to write

```
WRITE(filename, 5);
```

where *filename* stands for a text file and **5** is the number 5. If you try to use the same statement with a typed file, however, your program will not compile, because **5** is a constant, not a variable.

USING SEEK

After you have written data to a typed file, sometimes you need to pluck data from somewhere in the middle of the file. To do this, you can use Turbo Pascal's **Seek** procedure to find data if you have the record number. The **Seek** procedure is not implemented in many versions of Pascal, but it makes things a little easier for the Turbo Pascal programmer.

Seek and similar routines are the reason that typed files are sometimes referred to as *random-access* files. To see why this is so, consider what you would have to do to read a data item on line 25 of a text file. From the beginning of the file, you would have to execute 24 empty READLN statements to move the file pointer to the 25th line. This is called *sequential access* because you have to go through all the lines in sequence until you arrive at the one you want.

With the **Seek** procedure, however, you can go directly to any record in the file, and you do not have to cycle past the preceding records in order to get to it. This is called random access. A more familiar example of random access is provided by a compact disc, which allows you to go directly to any song at random without having to play through the preceding songs first. A cassette tape, on the other hand, is a sequential access device. If you want to listen to a song in the middle of the tape, you must fast-forward through the other songs first.

Thus, typed files are random-access files in that they *permit* random access of the records they contain. However, they have no necessary connection with random access; if you prefer, you can go through a typed file's records in sequence just as easily, from the first record to the last.

You use the **Seek** procedure with a typed-file variable and a record number, as in

```
SEEK(numfile, 5);
```

Seek, however, must be used with caution; if there are only 10 records in a file and you try to seek record number 11 (or any other record number beyond the last record in the file), your program will halt with a run-time error. To avoid this, it is a good idea to use Turbo Pascal's **FileSize** function before using **Seek**; this will tell the user how many records are in the file. **FileSize** takes a typed-file variable as an argument and returns an integer, which is the number of records in the file. You use **FileSize** as follows:

```
WRITELN(' File contains ', FileSize(numfile), 'records.');
```

EDITING AND ADDING RECORDS

With typed files, you can also change data in the middle of a file or add new data to the end of the file. It's not always completely straightforward, but it's not that difficult, either. To change a record in the middle of a file, you use the **Seek** procedure to find the record number you want and then write new data into it.

Adding data to an existing typed file is a little more difficult than adding data to an existing text file. You may recall that with text files, we can use the **Append** procedure to open the file for writing, and we position the file pointer at the end of the file—precisely where we want to add new data. Unfortunately, we cannot use **Append** with typed files. Instead, we must set up a three-step process: (1) determine the number of records with the **FileSize** function; (2) use **Seek** to move the file pointer to the last record in the file; and (3) execute an empty READ statement to move the file pointer past the last record to the very end of the file.

Methods for editing current records and adding new records are demonstrated in Listing 13.5.

Inside Listing 13.5

Listing 13.5 demonstrates several techniques and tricks that you can use when working with typed files. The listing does the following things:

- It creates a file of integers, referred to in the program by the file variable *numfile*.

- It asks the user how many integers should be entered into the file, and then writes the integers in sequence from 1 to the number the user chooses.

- After closing the file variable to make sure that all records (integers) have been written to the disk file, it re-opens the file and changes a record in the middle of the file.

```
PROGRAM Listing13_5;

   { This listing illustrates how to change a value in the middle
     of a typed file and how to add a new value to the end of a
     typed file. More sophisticated operations, such as sorting the
     elements of a file or inserting a new item between two current
     items, would normally be handled by reading the file into a
     data structure, such as an array or linked list, performing
     the desired operation, and then writing the new data back to
     the disk file. Note that a special procedure is needed to add
     data at the end of a typed file because APPEND will not work
     with typed files as it will with text files. }


USES CRT, MyUtils;

TYPE
  NumberFile = FILE OF INTEGER;

VAR
  Numfile : NumberFile;


{ ------------------------------ }
{ MAIN-LEVEL PROCEDURE DECLARATION }
{ ------------------------------ }
PROCEDURE CreateAndLoadFile(VAR numfile : numberfile);
  VAR
    counter,
    SizeNum : INTEGER;
  BEGIN
    CLRSCR;
    ASSIGN(numfile, 'numbers.dat');
    REWRITE(numfile);
    WRITE(' How many integers do you want in the file? ');
    READLN(SizeNum);
    WRITELN;
    FOR counter := 1 TO SizeNum DO
        WRITE(numfile, counter);
    CLOSE(numfile)
  END;

{ ------------------------------ }
{ MAIN-LEVEL PROCEDURE DECLARATION }
{ ------------------------------ }
PROCEDURE ChangeRecord(VAR numfile : NumberFile);
  VAR
    NumberOfRecords,
    RealRecNum,
    RecNum,
    RecVal1,
    RecVal2  : INTEGER;
  BEGIN
    RESET(numfile);
    CLRSCR;
    NumberOfRecords := filesize(numfile);
    WRITE(' The current size of the file is ');
    WRITELN(NumberOfRecords, ' records.');
    WRITELN;
    WRITE(' Which record do you want to change? ');
    READLN(recnum);
    RealRecNum := recnum - 1;
    WRITELN;
```

Listing 13.5: Editing and adding records in a typed file.

```
      WRITE(' What integer do you want to change it to? ');
      READLN(RecVal2); WRITELN;

      SEEK(numfile, RealRecNum);
      READ(numfile, recval1);
      WRITE(' The old value of record #',recnum);
      WRITELN(' is ', recval1, '.');
      delay(1500);

      SEEK(numfile, RealRecNum);
      WRITELN(' Now writing a new value to record #', recnum, '.');
      WRITE(numfile, recval2);

      SEEK(numfile, RealRecNum);
      READ(numfile, recval2);
      WRITE(' The new value of record #', recnum);
      WRITELN(' is ', recval2, '.');
      pause;
      CLOSE(numfile)
   END;


  { ------------------------------ }
  { MAIN-LEVEL PROCEDURE DECLARATION }
  { ------------------------------ }
  PROCEDURE AddNewRecord(VAR numfile : NumberFile);
    VAR
      NumberOfRecords,
      LastRecord,
      LastRecordValue,
      NewValue    : INTEGER;
    BEGIN
      RESET(numfile);
      NumberOfRecords := FileSize(numfile);
      LastRecord := NumberOfRecords - 1;
      WRITE(' There are now ', NumberOfRecords);
      WRITELN(' records in the file.'); WRITELN;
      WRITE(' Enter a new integer to add at end of file: ');
      READLN(newvalue);
      SEEK(numfile, lastrecord);
      READ(numfile, lastrecordvalue);
      WRITE(numfile, newvalue);
      NumberOfRecords := FileSize(numfile);
      WRITELN;
      WRITE(' There are now ', NumberOfRecords);
      WRITELN(' records in the file.');
      pause;
      CLOSE(numfile)
    END;

  BEGIN
    CreateAndLoadFile(numfile);
    ChangeRecord(numfile);
    AddNewRecord(numfile)
  END.
```

Listing 13.5: Editing and adding records in a typed file. (cont.)

- It also finds the end of the file and adds a new record at the end.

The **ChangeRecord** procedure takes the typed file as a VAR parameter (remember that files can be passed to subroutines only as VAR parameters). After re-opening the file, it uses the **FileSize** function to determine the number of records in the file, then prompts the user for the number of a record to be changed.

Here is where the routine may look a little odd: we use an additional variable, *RealRecNum*, which is assigned a value one less than the record number that the user specified. This is because in typed files, records are numbered not from 1 but from *zero*. Thus, the first record is record 0, the fifth record is record 4, and so forth. To insulate the user from this complication, we use the *RealRecNum* variable for all program references to record numbers. Thus, when the user asks for record number five, he or she expects it to contain the integer 5; we do some behind-the-scenes manipulation to satisfy this expectation and thereby avoid confusing the user.

After converting the user's requested record number to a "real" record number, we use **Seek** to position the file pointer at the correct record and inspect the value of that record. However, this READ operation causes the file pointer to move ahead to the *next* record, so before we can change the selected record, we must use **Seek** again to reposition the file pointer. This WRITE operation, just like the preceding READ operation, again causes the file pointer to move ahead, so we use **Seek** a third time to move the file pointer back to where we want it and inspect the new value of the chosen record. We then close the file to make sure that all the values are written to disk.

The **AddNewRecord** routine uses some similar tricks. It uses the **File-Size** function to determine the number of records, and a *Lastrecord* variable to hold the number of the last record. Recall that because the record numbering starts with zero, if there are 25 records in a file, then the last record is record number 24. The **AddnewRecord** routine uses **Seek** to go directly to the last record; executes a READ statement to move the file pointer past the last record, to the end of the file; and then writes a new record at the end of the file. It uses **FileSize** again to find the new number of records in the file; displays the number on the screen; and closes the file.

If you wanted to add a new record in the middle of the file, you could do that, although it would be a fairly slow and fairly complicated process. A better solution, and one that is normally used, is to read the contents of the file into a linked list or other data structure, do any manipulations in the computer's RAM, and then write the revised list back to the file. This is faster and more flexible than trying to manipulate the file directly.

UNTYPED FILES

In spite of its name, the *untyped file* is not a third type of file: instead, it is a way of handling any DOS file without regard for the structure of the data it contains—even without regard for its origin. You can treat any file as an untyped file (whether or not it is wise to do so) by associating it with an untyped file variable, as in:

```
VAR

    ThisFile,

    ThatFile : FILE;    { untyped file variable }

    Buffer   : ARRAY[0..1024] OF BYTE;

BEGIN

    ASSIGN(ThisFile, 'miscfile.dat');

    RESET(ThisFile, 1);

    REWRITE(ThatFile, 1);

    REPEAT

    BLOCKREAD(ThisFile, Buffer, SizeOf(Buffer), Num);

    BLOCKWRITE(ThatFile, Buffer, Num, NumToFile);

    UNTIL (Num = 0) OR (NumToFile <> Num);

    CLOSE(ThisFile);

    CLOSE(ThatFile)

END.
```

Applications for untyped files do exist, but they are fairly uncommon. Their great advantage is that because they treat files without any regard for their structure, they provide a very fast way of reading and writing files.

The example above illustrates the main operations which are done with untyped files. First, the file is associated with an untyped file variable—*i.e.*, a file variable that is neither declared as a text nor as a typed file, but simply as a "file." Then, you need to create some storage in the computer's memory for the data that is read from the file. Normally, this will be an array, because this is the fastest form of storage and, after all, speed is a major reason for using untyped files.

RESET and REWRITE have an added feature when used with untyped files. Because data is read from and written to untyped files in blocks, you should specify the size of the blocks to be used. One byte is ideal as a block size because it divides evenly into a file of any size, whether the file is 128 bytes or 17. If you do not specify a block size when you open the file with RESET or REWRITE, then Turbo Pascal uses the default block size of 128 bytes, which may cause problems with files whose size is not evenly divisible by 128.

As is evident from the example, you cannot use READ and WRITE with untyped files. Instead, you need to use **BlockRead** and **BlockWrite**, which are discussed below.

BLOCKREAD AND BLOCKWRITE

BlockRead reads data from the untyped file into the storage area you have set up in the computer's memory. Its basic use is as follows:

```
BLOCKREAD(VAR f:FILE; VAR Buffer:ARRAY; Count:WORD;
    VAR Result:WORD);
```

The first parameter in **BlockRead** is the untyped file variable. The second is the variable representing the storage area for the data from the file, which is usually but not necessarily an array; the third is the maximum number of blocks to be read from the file; and the fourth is a variable that returns the actual number of blocks read in the **BlockRead** operation.

BlockWrite is similar. Its first parameter, as in the example, is an untyped file variable for the file that will be *written to;* second is the variable for the storage area; third is the maximum number of blocks to be written; and fourth is the actual number of blocks that are written in the operation.

One potential pitfall, if you do use **BlockWrite**, is that it inserts an end-of-file character (Ctrl-Z) at the end of a block. This means that if a block ends in the middle of an existing file and you look for the end of the file by using the EOF function, your program will stop at the end of the block. **BlockWrite** and **BlockRead** should both be used with caution.

SUMMARY

Typed files allow you to write program data directly to a disk file without first converting it to text. The main advantage of typed files is that they are faster than text files; depending on the situation, they can also result in simpler program code.

Writing to and reading from typed files is done exclusively with WRITE and READ; WRITELN and READLN cannot be used because typed files have no lines of text. Individual data items in a typed file can be found by using the Turbo Pascal Seek procedure, which is the reason that typed files are sometimes called *random access* files.

Untyped files are not actually a file type; instead, any file can be treated as an untyped file for very rapid writing and reading operations. Applications for untyped files, however, are fairly uncommon.

REVIEW EXERCISES

1. Explain what typed files are and how they differ from text files.

2. True or false: One of the main advantages of typed files is that they are always smaller than text files containing the same data. If the statement is false, explain why it is false.

3. Are there any problems with the following code fragment? If so, what are they and how would you correct them?

```
VAR
     MyFile : FILE OF INTEGER;
BEGIN
     Assign(MyFile, 'thisfile.dat');
  RESET(MyFile);
  WRITE(MyFile, 15, 20, 1, 4, 75);
  CLOSE(MyFile)
END.
```

4. Explain the differences, if any, between how Pascal reads and writes noncharacter data (a) with a text file and (b) with a typed file.

5. What are the main advantages and disadvantages of typed files compared to text files?

6. What are the main advantages and disadvantages of text files compared to typed files?

7. Are there any problems in the following code fragment? If so, what are they and how would you correct them?

```
VAR
     MyFile : FILE OF INTEGER;
  num1, num2,
  num3, num4 : INTEGER:
BEGIN
     Assign(MyFile, 'thisfile.dat');
  REWRITE(MyFile);
  WRITE(MyFile, '15', '20', '1', '4');
  READLN(MyFile, num1, num2, num3, num4);
  CLOSE(MyFile)
END.
```

8. Suppose you are designing a program that will use files, and you must decide whether the files should be text files or typed

files. Explain at least three factors that should be considered in making your decision.

9. Explain why typed files are sometimes called "random-access files."

10. Write a program to create a typed file containing the names of several colors. The program should prompt the user to enter color names, and provide a way to stop entering names when desired.

11. To the program from exercise 10, add a routine to read the color names from the file into a linked list and display them on the screen.

12. To the program from exercise 10, add a routine (using Seek) that allows the user to enter a record number and then view the data in that record. Do not forget to handle the case in which the user enters a number that is not a valid record number.

13. To the program from exercise 10, add a routine to add data to the end of an existing typed file.

14. Explain the idea of untyped files and when untyped files can be used.

15. Explain the use of **BlockRead** and **BlockWrite**. Are there any potential problems that can result from using **BlockWrite**? If so, explain them.

P A R T

Advanced
Programming Techniques

Part III explains and demonstrates advanced programming techniques in Pascal and Turbo Pascal. Chapters 14–20 discuss debugging techniques (finding and correcting errors in your programs), graphics, data structures, algorithms (sorting, searching, and hashing), and creating sound effects and music.

Chapter 20 provides a practical programming example: a reasonably complex programming project that creates "Turbo Tunemaker," a music construction program for the PC.

C H A P T E R

Debugging Your Programs

Knowledge which serves for the guidance of action must anticipate the future, but a future to which the action itself will make a possible difference.

C.I. Lewis, *An Analysis of Knowledge and Valuation*

In this chapter, we will look at the bane of programmers everywhere: the omnipresent, impossible-to-exterminate program "bugs." A bug is anything in your code that prevents a program from compiling and running correctly, *whether or not* the cause is technically an "error." Some program bugs are catastrophic in their effects, while others are innocuous and still others are so obscure that no one will ever discover them.

First, we will look at general methods for avoiding bugs and for dealing with them when they occur. Though Turbo Pascal 6 has powerful integrated debugging capabilities, the methods discussed in this section of the chapter can be applied with any version of Pascal, including Turbo Pascal versions 4 and earlier, which did not have integrated debugging. Moreover, ideas not specifically tied to Pascal can be applied in any programming language.

Second, we will look at a rogues' gallery of common program bugs—what they are, how they occur, and what to do about them. Like the first section, this material applies to any version of Pascal and, to a large extent, to programming in any language.

Third, we will look at the specific integrated debugging capabilities provided by Turbo Pascal 6, and show how these can help you debug your programs faster and more easily.

GENERAL DEBUGGING ISSUES

Many people, especially novice programmers, have the wrong idea about debugging. They think that debugging is something you do at the end of the program development process: first you write the program, then you debug it, then it sells a million copies and you retire to Bora Bora.

Retire to Bora Bora you might, but a comfortable retirement will be a lot more likely if you realize that debugging is an on-going process that begins with correct program design and careful coding. Far from treating debugging as a separate step, you should design your program with ease of debugging in mind. You should also develop it one subroutine at a time and debug each subroutine as it is completed, before "hooking it up" to the main program.

The truth is that in any program of more than minimal complexity, it is probably impossible to eliminate all bugs. The most popular PC database manager of the 1980s, Ashton-Tate's dBase, had hundreds of documented bugs. *TechNotes*, the Ashton-Tate magazine, devoted an entire section each month to newly-discovered "anomalies," which is a euphemism for bugs. The latest version of Lotus 1-2-3, a popular spreadsheet program, was reported to have over 10,000 bugs before it went through testing and debugging.

Dbase, 1-2-3, and other commercial software packages (including Turbo Pascal itself) are developed by top-notch programmers who have many years of experience. If even *they* can't totally eliminate bugs from their programs, then you shouldn't feel too bad if you have trouble eliminating bugs from yours.

Experienced programmers are also familiar with another painful truth: whatever the user *perceives* as a bug *is* a bug. Eliminating bugs is not simply a matter of making your program run correctly. It is also a matter of making your program run the way the user *expects* it to run—a task that is sometimes much more difficult because it involves a certain amount of mind reading.

There are eight different levels of *program correctness* that we work to achieve through the design and debugging process. These levels are shown in Table 14.1.

Most beginners think that compile-time errors are the most serious—that going from level 1 to level 2 is the most important hurdle. However, all that it means when a program compiles is that the source code follows the rules of Pascal. It does not mean that the program is error-free, or that it will produce correct results, or even that it will produce any results at all. Compile-time errors are the least serious and easiest to correct of

Table 14.1: Levels of Program Correctness

LEVEL	CORRECTNESS
1	Does not compile.
2	Compiles without errors.
3	Starts to run but halts with a run-time error.
4	Runs but produces incorrect results.
5	Produces correct results for small set of "normal" input data.
6	Produces correct results for large set of "normal" input data under all normal or expected run-time conditions.
7	Produces correct results for extreme, abnormal, and incorrect input data under normal, expected, and unexpected run-time conditions.
8	Produces correct results for any possible data and run-time conditions.

program errors. Also, because you literally *cannot* run a program that won't compile, such errors pose no threat to your data.

Run-time errors are almost in the same class as compile-time errors. Most common run-time errors are easy to identify because the program halts when it encounters them (e.g., a missing file) or the program does something else fairly obvious (e.g., going into an endless loop). Uncommon run-time errors usually result from running the program under unusual or unexpected conditions, such as with inadequate memory or disk space; these can be identified, if at all, only through exhaustive testing.

Virtually all other errors are *logic errors*, which result from the programmer's mistaken analysis of the problem he or she is trying to solve. Sometimes, the code is so intricate that getting the solution *right* is almost a matter of luck, such as trying to run a loop inside an IF statement inside another loop. It's in these situations that careful thought prior to coding is even more important than usual, and extra efforts should be made to produce the simplest, clearest code possible.

THE CONNECTION
BETWEEN DESIGN AND DEBUGGING

Another thing that makes debugging easier is to be a fanatic about structured design and compartmentalization. In a 1,000-line unstructured program, each line could conceivably interact with 999 other lines, meaning that there are 999! (999 factorial, or $999 \times 998 \times 997 \times \ldots 1$) possible interactions between different parts of the program: a level of complexity beyond any human mind's ability to grasp. In reality, of course, you would never have this many interactions, but you can see the problem.

Even when you divide the program into 30-line subroutines, you are still faced (inside each subroutine) with 29! possible interactions, and although this is still a large number, it is far more manageable than before. When one considers that the actual number of interactions is much lower than this, and that 30 lines will fit easily on a single page, it seems *very* manageable.

Achieving this reduction in complexity, however, requires strict adherence to structured programming methods. Any outside data items manipulated by a subroutine must be passed to it as parameters; otherwise, the compartmentalization of the subroutine is breached and it can no longer be treated as a black box. Its internal features could then interact in an uncontrolled way with any other part of the program—in which case, we might as well be writing unstructured "spaghetti" code.

GENERAL DEBUGGING METHODS

The most important weapon in debugging your program is to understand both the broad outlines of how the program works and the details of how each subroutine processes the parameters that are passed to it. With this in mind, you will see how the parts of your program fit together and why each part behaves in the way that it does.

Creating the Main Program First

The first step is to create a framework that eventually will become the main program. On this framework you will hang the individual subroutines which, eventually, will work together to make a complete program. Notice that, strictly speaking, this is a design method; however, design and debugging are so intimately connected that it must be discussed here.

The overall framework (sometimes called the *main control program* because it determines when subroutines are called and what values are passed to them) should contain as little detail as possible. It is all right to include a loop here or an IF..THEN statement there, but as much detail as possible should be hidden inside the subroutines. Naturally, at the start of the process, you cannot be sure that this detail-hiding will always work: you might need to bring some details out of a subroutine and keep them in the main program. The presumption, however, should always be in favor of hiding details inside subroutines. Listing 14.1 shows a program at this stage of development; however, don't try to run this listing, because although the incomplete program will compile, it will go into an endless loop.

You can see that at this stage, we have simply decided on the main tasks that the program should perform. Each of those tasks has been delegated to a subroutine, leaving very little in the main program framework itself. This is as it should be: the less detail that is included in the main framework, the fewer things that can go wrong without being noticed by the programmer.

Testing Each Subroutine Separately

Once you have decided what the subroutines should be, you should develop and debug each one separately before you plug it into the main program. This involves two basic steps: first, to define the initial and ending conditions for the subroutine; and second, to use a *driver program* to test the subroutine with a wide range of input values.

Define Initial and Final Conditions Defining initial and final conditions for a subroutine involves specifying exactly what output values the subroutine should produce for each set of input values. For example, in the subroutine **AddTwoNumbers**, we would specify that the subroutine should accept integers and return an integer as a result. Note that it is possible for the sum of two integers to exceed the limits of the integer

```
PROGRAM Listing14_1;

  { Illustrates how to create an empty "main program framework"
    which is filled in as subroutines are completed. }

USES CRT;

VAR
  Continue : CHAR;
  a, b,
  Result   : INTEGER;

PROCEDURE AddTwoNumbers(a, b: INTEGER; VAR result: INTEGER);
  BEGIN
  END;

PROCEDURE MultiplyTwoNumbers(a, b: INTEGER; VAR result: INTEGER);
  BEGIN
  END;

PROCEDURE Quit;
  BEGIN
  END;

PROCEDURE DisplayMenu;
  BEGIN
  END;

PROCEDURE GetMenuChoice;
  BEGIN
  END;


{ main body of program }
BEGIN
  Continue := 'Y';
  WHILE UPCASE(Continue) = 'Y' DO
    DisplayMenu
END.
```

Listing 14.1: A framework for the main program; do NOT run.

data type, which ranges only from −32,768 to +32,767: for example, 25,000 + 25,000 would generate an error. Depending on the situation, we could design the subroutine either to handle such situations or to refuse to input numbers whose sum exceeds the integer data type, but, in any case, we need to be aware of this limitation and decide how to deal with it.

Create a Driver Program   The next step is to develop each subroutine inside a driver program that will let you test a wide range of different input values. A simple driver program (all driver programs should be as simple as possible) is shown in Listing 14.2. This driver program works with the **AddTwoNumbers** procedure from Listing 14.1.

```
PROGRAM Listing14_2;

  { Illustrates a simple driver program for developing and
testing
     the AddTwoNumbers subroutine in Listing 14.1. }

USES CRT, MyUtils;

VAR
  continue : CHAR;
  a, b,
  result   : INTEGER;

PROCEDURE AddTwoNumbers(a, b: INTEGER; VAR result: INTEGER);
  BEGIN
  result := a + b;
  WRITELN;
  WRITELN(' The sum of ', a, ' and ', b, ' is ', result, '.');
  pause
  END;

{ main body of driver program }
BEGIN
  CLRSCR;
  continue := 'Y';
  REPEAT
    WRITELN;
    WRITE(' Enter the first number to add: ');
    READLN(a);
    WRITE(' Enter the second number to add: ');
    READLN(b);
    AddTwoNumbers(a,b,result);
    WRITE(' Do another (Y/N)? ');
    READLN(continue);
  UNTIL UPCASE(continue) <> 'Y'
END.
```

Listing 14.2: A simple driver program.

Listing 14.2 sets up a REPEAT loop that allows you to feed one pair of integers after another into the **AddTwoNumbers** routine to make sure that it works properly. Remember that to test the routine fully, you should try not only expected input such as 15 and 100, 2 and 2, or 40 and 10, but zero, negative, and very large values such as 0 and 0, –1000 and 85, or 30,000 and 30,000.

This last pair of integers, in fact, will reveal that, as suspected, the routine has a weak spot: it is possible for two integers to add up to a number that exceeds the range of the integer data type. In this case, the program will not stop on a run-time error, but will give a wildly erroneous result (between the two, a run-time error is infinitely preferable). Depending on how ambitious you are, you can include code to handle situations like that one, as well as to trap incorrect data type input such as 'c' and 'x'.

A driver program will help you identify where these traps need to be placed.

Tracing Code Blocks

Tracing code blocks is also an important debugging method. When your code reaches a certain level of complexity, it is hard to determine what goes with what: which END goes with which BEGIN or CASE statement, which ELSE goes with which IF, and so forth. This is one of the most common sources of programming errors. When you have one too few (or one too many) ENDs, a left comment bracket that isn't matched by a right bracket, or a REPEAT loop that goes who-knows-where, your program probably won't compile. Moreover, the error message you receive in this case is likely to be unhelpful. "Error in statement" is the usual error message, and it tells you only that there is probably an unterminated BEGIN somewhere above the line where you got the error message.

Tracing code blocks can help you master this complexity. To use this method, simply print out a listing of your program code (in Turbo Pascal 6, use the Print option in the File menu). Then start at the deepest level of nested statement and use a pencil to connect each BEGIN with its corresponding END, each REPEAT with its corresponding UNTIL, and so forth. Ultimately, this can lead you to bugs that would, otherwise, be very difficult to find.

Let's look at an example of this process. Consider the following code block:

```
BEGIN
    CASE num of
        1: BEGIN
            { ... details }
        END;
        2: BEGIN
            { ... details }
        END;
```

```
3: BEGIN
       IF num > 5
       THEN BEGIN
              { ... details }
       ELSE BEGIN
              { ... details }
            END
   ELSE BEGIN
       { ... details }
       END
   END
```

Although this code may seem messy and confusing, it is far less so than much of the code you will see in actual programming. Situations where you have END, END, ENDs stacked on top of each other are prime targets for bug-hunting. Let's see how tracing can help us find the errors in this block. We start at the deepest level of nesting: in this situation, that means the different BEGIN..END pairs in the CASE statement.

The reason for starting at the deepest level is that is where Pascal starts putting together (parsing) the statements. Each BEGIN or CASE at the deepest level takes the first END that it encounters; then the next BEGIN or CASE takes the next END, and so forth. This process continues until Pascal works its way though to the outermost level.

In this case, tracing reveals what was not apparent at a glance. The very first BEGIN is never terminated; as a result, it will probably grab hold of another section of code's END further down in the program. At that point, the compiler will stop and give you an "Error in statement" error message, but the real error is here at the very beginning. In fact, the END taken by the CASE was probably the END that was meant to go with the first BEGIN; the programmer forgot to include an END for the CASE statement. To complicate matters further, two BEGINs nested inside the CASE statement are never terminated, and will probably cause a compilation error as well.

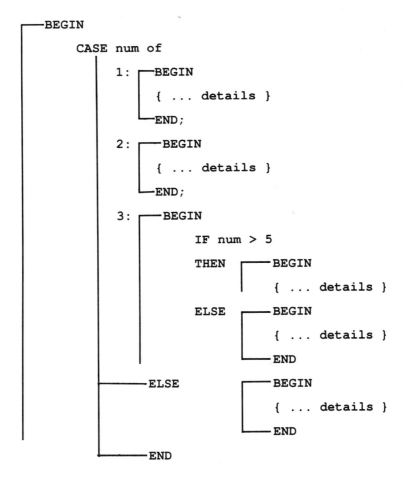

```
BEGIN

    CASE num of

        1:  BEGIN

               { ... details }

            END;

        2:  BEGIN

               { ... details }

            END;

        3:  BEGIN

               IF num > 5

                  THEN   BEGIN

                            { ... details }

                  ELSE   BEGIN

                            { ... details }

                         END

        ELSE            BEGIN

                            { ... details }

                        END

        END
```

You can do the same thing as we've done here with loops, comment brackets, and any other program structure that starts on one line and should terminate on another. If you have some extra money to spend, you might consider getting *Turbo Analyst* from TurboPower Software (1-800-333-4160), which can do the tracing (and several other types of program analysis) for you. A sample of Turbo Analyst's tracing work is shown in Figure 14.1.

```
                              EDIT
        Line 62   Col 1   Insert Indent      D:LIST13_6.LST
    40      ( ------------------------------ )
    41      ( MAIN-LEVEL PROCEDURE DECLARATION )
    42      ( ------------------------------ )
    43      PROCEDURE AddnameToList(VAR class : studentfile;
    44                              VAR ListHead, ListTail : RecPtr);
    45  ┌──── BEGIN
    46  │     CLRSCR;
    47  │     IF ListHead = NIL
    48  │  ┌── THEN BEGIN
    49  │  │       NEW(ListHead);
    50  │  │       READ(class, ListHead^.pupil);
    51  │  │       ListHead^.next := NIL;
    52  │  │       ListTail := ListHead;
    53  │  └─── END
    54  │  ┌── ELSE BEGIN
    55  │  │       NEW(ListTail^.next);
    56  │  │       IF ListHead = ListTail
    57  │  │          THEN ListHead^.next := ListTail^.next;
    58  │  │       ListTail := ListTail^.next;
    59  │  │       READ(class, ListTail^.pupil);
    60  │  │       ListTail^.next := NIL;

   F1-Help  F2-Save  F3-Load  F5-Zoom  F6-Switch  F9-Make  F10-Menu
```

Figure 14.1: Turbo Analyst's tracing of a subroutine.

Inserting Debug Code

Another general debugging technique is to insert *debug code* at various places in your program. Debug code allows you to monitor the values of variables as your program runs. It is not really needed in the Turbo Pascal IDE (for versions 5 and later), which lets you put *watches* on variables. However, if you are developing a Pascal program with version 3 or 4 of Turbo Pascal, with the Turbo Pascal command-line compiler, or with a different Pascal compiler, debug statements can be very helpful.

The most basic kind of debug statement simply displays the current value of a variable on the screen. If your program runs but gives incorrect results or behaves oddly, it may be that a variable is not getting the values you expected it to. Listing 14.3 shows a classic application of a debugging statement.

The error in Listing 14.3 may seem contrived (and remember that you should use FOR instead of WHILE when you have a loop counter variable), but it is a typical error made by beginning programmers. The program sets up a loop that is to execute 10 times, using a counter variable to

```
PROGRAM Listing14_3;

   { Illustrates the use of debug statements to track the
     values of variables. }

USES CRT, MyUtils;

VAR
  counter,
  a, b,
  result  : INTEGER;
  debugging: BOOLEAN;

PROCEDURE AddTwoNumbers(a, b: INTEGER; VAR result: INTEGER);
  BEGIN
  result := a + b;
  WRITELN;
  WRITELN(' The sum of ', a, ' and ', b, ' is ', result, '.');
  pause
  END;


BEGIN
  CLRSCR;
  counter := 0;
  debugging := TRUE;
  WHILE counter <= 10 DO
    BEGIN
    WRITE(' Enter the first number to add: ');
    READLN(a);
    WRITELN;
    WRITE(' Enter the second number to add: ');
    READLN(b);
    AddTwoNumbers(a,b,result);
    IF debugging THEN WRITELN(' Counter value is now ', counter,
'.')
    END;
  pause
END.
```

Listing 14.3: Using debugging statements in your program.

keep track of how many times it has gone through the loop so far. However, the programmer forgot to include a statement in the loop that will increase the value of the counter variable, so the counter stays at zero and the loop executes over and over unto eternity.

Without the debugging statement, it might take a while to identify the problem, even in a simple case like this one. With the debugging statement, however, the problem is immediately apparent because the value of the counter never changes.

Note that we used a Boolean variable to determine if the debugging statement executes or not. If there are many debugging statements scattered throughout a routine (or an entire program), then this provides an easy way to turn all of them on or off by adjusting the value of a single variable. Make "debugging" true and the debugging statements all go to work; make it false, and they become invisible. One caution: if you use this method, you should remove (or comment out) the debugging statements before you do the final compilation of your debugged program. Otherwise, the debugging statements (which no longer serve a purpose) will be included in the compiled version of your program, resulting in a larger .EXE file than necessary.

Test Under Different Conditions

The fact that a program runs properly on one computer under one set of conditions does not mean that it will run on another computer under a different set of conditions. A final step in debugging your program is to test it under a variety of different conditions. Try running it with less memory available, or with memory-resident utility packages such as Borland's Sidekick. If your program uses graphics or special effects such as reverse video, try it out on different types of monitors with different types of video adapters. A program that uses graphics may run fine with an EGA adapter and a color monitor, but it may behave oddly or not work at all with a Hercules adapter and a monochrome monitor.

Whether or not you do this level of testing, of course, will depend on the purpose of your program, who will be using it, and how ambitious you are. If you have a text-only program that will be run only on standard PCs, then it is a waste of effort to test it on a variety of machines. It's all up to you.

Give Your Program to a Kid

You might think that this is a frivolous suggestion, but it's quite serious. Kids (1) are imaginative, (2) have lots of free time, (3) love to "show up" adults, and (4) will conduct a bug hunt with the sort of fanatical devotion that you could never get even from the most conscientious adult programmer.

A DEMONOLOGY
OF COMMON BUGS

On the theory that "forewarned is forearmed" (or is it "forewarned is *four*-armed"?) in this section, we will look at some of the most common programming errors with Pascal and discuss what to do about them. Many of these errors also apply to programming in languages other than Pascal.

COMPILE-TIME ERRORS

Compile-time errors are the most innocuous of bugs, principally because they are caught by the compiler and therefore pose no threat to your data. However, they can be maddening for beginners, particularly when the error messages they generate are less helpful than they might be—even in Turbo Pascal, which is far better than many other compilers in this area.

Unknown Identifier

This bug means that Turbo Pascal cannot find a certain identifier that you have used in your program—whether it is a name for a variable, constant, subroutine, or some other program element. It is normally caused by one of three things:

1. A typing error when you keyed in the program. In this case, you simply misspelled the identifier when you attempted to call it in your program. This is a trivial mistake and is always easy to correct.

2. Forgetting to name a unit in the USES clause of your program; for example, forgetting to name the CRT unit in a program that uses the CLRSCR procedure. (This error cannot occur in versions of Turbo Pascal before version 4, which was the first to support units.) Like error No.1, this is easily corrected.

3. An error in structuring your program. This is the most difficult type of "unknown identifier" bug to correct. It means that for some reason, the identifier you used is inaccessible at the place in the code where you used it. In hunting for this kind of error, you should remember the following:

    (a) Identifiers must be declared before they are used. If subroutine X uses subroutine Y, then Y must be defined in the code *before* subroutine X. Make sure that general routines used by several other routines are either toward the beginning of the program code or are in their own unit; in either case, they will be accessible to routines that are declared later in the program code.

    (b) Identifiers inside subroutines are hidden from everything outside of the subroutine.

    (c) Even inside a subroutine, an identifier must be declared before it is used, so even local subroutines must be declared in the proper order.

";" Expected

This is a trivial but fairly common bug. As you will recall, semicolons are used to separate statements in a Pascal program from other statements. To correct this bug, just add a semicolon at the end of the line from which it is missing. Normally, the compilation error occurs on the line immediately after the line without the semicolon.

Missing END or Comment Bracket

The error message "Error in statement" is usually a dead giveaway for this kind of bug. When you get this error message, first check the highlighted statement to make sure that it is not the source of the trouble. If it isn't, then all you really know at the beginning is that *somewhere* in the code above that statement, another statement or a comment is not terminated properly: you may have too few ENDs, mixed-up comment brackets, or some variation on those errors.

The first and best weapon against this type of error is to have a firm knowledge of the rules for constructing statements and expressions in Pascal (the syntax of Pascal). Armed with this knowledge, you should trace through the code with a pencil, as we described above in the section on general debugging methods.

The best way to avoid this type of error in the first place is to stick with the proper methods for structured design, compartmentalization, and testing your code religiously. When such bugs do pop up, as inevitably they will from time to time, this will help localize them within a small block of code, making them much easier to find and correct.

Mixed-Up IFs and ELSEs

This bug is most likely to occur when you have two or more nested IF..THEN..ELSE and CASE statements. Remember that unless you tell it otherwise, an IF statement will try to grab the closest THEN and/or ELSE statement that it can find which isn't separated from it by a semicolon. Thus, the following code will cause a compile-time error:

```
CASE choice of
       1 : AddNewRecord;
       2 : EditCurrentRecord;
       3 : IF RecordsOpen
           THEN CloseRecords
  ELSE WRITELN(' You must enter a choice from 1 to 3.')
       END;
```

In this situation, the ELSE clause is intended to cover the situation in which the user enters a choice that does not match any of the items in the CASE statement. However, because the IF statement in case 3 is not terminated with a semicolon, it grabs onto the ELSE clause, which as a result will execute only if CASE 3 is chosen—*not* if the user's choice fails to match any of the choices in the CASE statement.

This kind of error may not stop the program, but may result in unexpected and incorrect program behavior. Like the missing END or comment bracket, the main remedy for this kind of error is to trace through your code with a pencil. It also helps to proofread your code.

RUN-TIME ERRORS

Run-time errors, as the name implies, get past the compiler and pop up only when someone tries to run your program. Some run-time errors will pop up immediately and on every program run; others will occur only under special conditions. Obviously, the first category of run-time errors is more important, but proper defensive programming should try to anticipate all but the most remote possibilities for run-time errors.

Failure to Initialize Variable Before Use

Some variables need to be initialized (set to initial values) at the beginning of a program or subroutine; other variables do not. The problem is that you often don't know which is which until you run into a bug. Variables that are used as counters in FOR loops do not have to be initialized, but variables used to control WHILE and REPEAT loops should be initialized. Likewise, expressions and variables that control IF and CASE statements may or may not need to be initialized.

The safest course is, at the beginning of a program or subroutine, to initialize all variables at that level with a separate subroutine, just as we have done in several of the program listings. You initialize a variable simply by assigning it a known initial value, as in **counter := 0**.

The only type of variable that absolutely *must* be initialized is the pointer. An uninitialized pointer variable conceivably could contain the memory address of part of the operating system, part of Turbo Pascal, or of some vital piece of data: the potential results are catastrophic. All pointer variables should be set to NIL at the beginning of a program or subroutine, and should be set to NIL again as soon as they are disposed of and are no longer needed.

Attempt to Assign Out-of-Range Value

This error can occur when you are using "fancy" numeric types such as bytes, which have a fairly limited range of values. It also can occur with integers, enumerated types, and subrange types. A typical example of this error would be an attempt to assign the integer 500 to a variable of type byte, which can take only values in the range 0 to 255.

It pays to anticipate and take steps to cope with the possibility that the user might enter some off-the-wall value. This is the purpose of using error-trapping input routines such as **GetGoodChar** and **GetGoodInt**.

Use Out-of-Range Array Index

This error is most likely to occur when you are using an array to hold a list. If the array is full and the user tries to enter another item into the list, then this error might pop up. The solution is to include code to keep track of how much space is left in the array and, if appropriate, to refuse the new input and inform the user of the array's full condition.

To trap this sort of error, it helps to test your program with range-checking turned on (use the Compiler options dialog box from the Options menu or insert a {$R+} compiler directive at the top of your program code).

Failure to Handle
Nonmatch in CASE Statement

In standard Pascal (and many real-world implementations of the standard), your program will stop with a run-time error if the user enters a choice for a CASE statement that doesn't match any of the choices included in the CASE statement. For example, consider the following code:

```
CASE choice of
    1 : DoThis;
    2 : DoThat;
    3 : DoSomethingElse
END;
```

As long as the user enters a value from 1 to 3, everything is fine. However, if the user enters 4, then the program will stop with a run-time error. In Chapter 7, we saw how to defend against this possibility in standard

Pascal by using an IF statement with the CASE statement.

Turbo Pascal provides two levels of protection against this kind of error. First, as we saw in Chapter 7, it allows you to use an ELSE clause with a CASE statement, thereby making an extra IF..THEN..ELSE statement unnecessary. Second, even if you don't use an ELSE clause, Turbo Pascal programs will not stop with a run-time error if the user's choice fails to match any of the CASE choices. On the one hand, this is good, because it prevents the program from stopping when it might not really need to stop. On the other hand, it's bad, because a nonmatching CASE could indicate a subtle error in the logic of the routine. The moral is, simply, that you should be careful in coding CASE statements.

Reading Incompatible Value into Variable

This is a fairly straightforward error. Your code contains a variable of one data type; the user is prompted to enter a value for the variable, but mistakenly enters a value of the wrong data type or a value that is not in the acceptable range of values. For example, you might ask the user how old he or she is; instead of entering an integer, the user might enter a letter; or instead of entering an integer that makes sense, he or she might enter a number such as 181 or 20,015.

The only defense against these errors is to replace Pascal's READ and READLN procedures with your own error-trapping input routines, such as **GetGoodInt** and **GetGoodChar**.

File Not Found

When this error occurs, usually you are trying to RESET or APPEND a file that isn't there. Of course, "isn't there" can mean two different things: either the file doesn't exist at all, or the file exists but is in a directory other than the one in which your program is looking for it. There is no simple solution for this problem; probably the most straightforward solution is to make sure that all the files needed to run the program are in the same directory on disk. Another solution is to include the directory path in the file name, as shown in the code fragment below:

```
VAR

  MyFile : TEXT;

BEGIN

  ASSIGN(MyFile, 'c:\tp6\oldfiles\data.txt');

  REWRITE(MyFile);

  WRITELN(MyFile, 'Uses a path in the file name.');

  close(MyFile)

END.
```

Turbo Pascal offers some more elegant ways to achieve the same result, but this solution is fairly portable across different Pascal compilers. When the "file not found" is a unit file, you need to make sure that Turbo Pascal's Directory Options dialog box includes the unit's home directory in its list of unit directories.

File Not Closed

Usually, this error pops up when you think you have written some data to a disk file. After your program runs, you check the file and discover that some (or all) of the data you entered is missing. This is a clue that your program did not close the file before finishing its run. Remember that any data written to a file is normally stored in a *file buffer* in your computer's memory before being physically written to the file. This speeds up your program, but it also means that if you fail to close the file at the end of the program, then some data may be left in the file buffer without having been written to the disk file.

Thus, when you find that data is missing from a disk file, the first thing to check is whether or not the file was closed properly in your program.

LOGIC ERRORS

Logic errors are the most difficult kind of errors to debug. They don't cause compilation errors; they don't cause run-time errors; they just cause programs to crash or produce incorrect results. It's important to understand that logic errors have nothing to do with Pascal. Logic errors occur when the programmer analyzes a problem incorrectly and comes up with the wrong solution, which is then written into Pascal program code. To debug a logic error requires not so much a knowledge of Pascal as a very careful analysis of what tasks need to be done and in what order.

By now, I probably sound like a broken record (a broken CD?) on this issue, but the best way to avoid or minimize logic errors is to keep your code as simple and as compartmentalized as possible.

Failure to Use VAR Parameter When Needed

This is probably the most common error involving subroutines. Remember, there are two ways to pass a variable to a subroutine: by value and by reference. Any variables that are to be changed by a subroutine must be passed to it as VAR parameters, that is, passed by reference. Otherwise, Pascal makes a copy of the variable and passes the copy to the subroutine. No changes made in the copy have any effect on the original variable itself. The following code, for example, does not use VAR parameters and has no effect on the variables a, b, and c.

```
VAR a, b, c : INTEGER;
PROCEDURE AddTwoNumbers(a,b,c : INTEGER);
    BEGIN
       c := a + b
    END;
BEGIN { main body of program }
    a := 1;
    b := 1;
    c := 0;
```

```
            AddTwoNumbers(a,b,c)

    END;
```

To correct this code, the word VAR has to be put in the procedure dec-laration before, at least, the c variable, which is the only one that is sup-posed to be changed by the subroutine. The new code would be as follows:

```
    VAR a,  b,  c  :  INTEGER;

    PROCEDURE AddTwoNumbers(a,b  :  INTEGER;

                                    VAR  c:  INTEGER);

        BEGIN

          c  :=  a  +  b

        END;

    BEGIN { main body of program }

        a  :=  1;

        b  :=  1;

        c  :=  0;

        AddTwoNumbers(a,b,c)

    END;
```

Loop Exit Condition Never Reached

This is the *endless loop* that we've already seen several times. What usually happens is one of two things: either (a) a counter variable is not increased on each pass through the loop, leading to a constant value for the counter and no exit from the loop; or (b) a *continue* variable controls the exit from the loop, and the programmer forgets to prompt the user for input into this variable, as in **WRITE(' Continue (Y/N)? ');**.

You may think that forgetting to prompt the user for input is a preposterous mistake for anyone to make, and it probably is. But wait until you've made this mistake yourself a few times; it won't seem quite so preposterous.

Loop Executes Wrong Number of Times

Unless this error involves a counter variable (see above), there are two main possibilities here: either the loop never executes when it should execute at least once, or it executes at least once when, under some conditions, it should never execute.

The solution is to remember the key difference between WHILE and REPEAT loops. A WHILE statement evaluates its loop control variable before going through the loop each time. If the control variable does not satisfy the loop condition when the program first reaches the loop, then the statements in the loop will never execute. A REPEAT statement, on the other hand, evaluates the control variable at the end of each loop, so no matter what the initial value of the control variable, a REPEAT loop will always execute at least once.

USING TURBO PASCAL'S INTEGRATED DEBUGGER

Now that you are familiar with the issues involved in debugging, as well as with some of the most common bugs, you are in for a treat. The integrated debugging capabilities in Turbo Pascal 6 (as well as in Turbo Pascal 5.0 and 5.5) make it much easier to find bugs and correct them than with most Pascal compilers.

Turbo Pascal's integrated debugger is what is called a "high level" debugger, in that it works with the statements of a high-level language, in this case, Pascal. Turbo Pascal also provides some facilities for low-level debugging, in which you go through a series of machine-language statements and directly inspect CPU registers and memory locations. Low-level debugging is, however, not relevant to most programming tasks, so we will not discuss it here. Full high-level and low-level debugging support is provided by Borland's Turbo Debugger, which works with Turbo

C and C++ as well as with Turbo Pascal. Borland's Turbo Assembler also provides low-level debugging for assembly language programs.

Turbo Pascal provides four main tools for debugging: the ability to step through a program one line at a time; the ability to watch the value of one or more variables as the program runs; the ability to change a variable's value in the middle of running a program to find out what effect the change will have; and the ability to set *breakpoints* at which the program will stop its run, so that you can inspect its results up to that point.

THE DEBUG MENU

Debugging operations are performed from the Debug menu and its submenus, as well as with speed keys. The four options on the Debug menu are (1) *Evaluate/Modify*, which lets you inspect and/or change the value of a variable at a certain point in the program; (2) *Watches*, which opens a submenu that lets you add, edit, and delete watches on variables; (3) *Toggle Breakpoint*, which lets you insert and remove breakpoints in your program code; and (4) *Breakpoints*, which opens a dialog box that lets you add, delete, and view breakpoints in your program code.

Normally, the values of variables that you see in the Evaluate/Modify dialog box and the Watch window are easy to understand. However, if you want the values displayed in a different format, you can add one of the *format specifiers* listed in Table 14.2. To add a format specifier, you key in the name of the variable, a comma, and then the format specifier, as in **My-Character,C** where **MyCharacter** is an ASCII character and **C** is the format specifier.

WATCHING A VARIABLE

Probably the most important thing you can do with Turbo Pascal's integrated debugger is to put a watch on one or more variables in your program. This allows you to monitor the values of the variables as your program progresses without the need to insert extra debugging statements into your

Table 14.2: Format Specifiers for Use in Debugging

FORMAT SPECIFIER	RESULTING FORMAT
C	Character. Displays nonprinting control characters (e.g., Enter) on the screen with special display characters.
D	Decimal. Displays all integer values in decimal (normal, base 10) form.
$, H, or X	Hexadecimal. Displays all integer values in hexadecimal (base 16) with the $ prefix.
Fn	Floating point. Displays real numbers with *n* significant digits.
P default	Pointer. Displays pointers (memory addresses) in segment:offset format instead of the default format, which is Ptr(segment, offset).
R names	Record. Displays record and object field names along with their values.

code. Before continuing, close any open windows in Turbo Pascal by selecting "Clear Desktop" from the System menu (the menu is opened by pressing Alt-spacebar). Then, open a new file window, enter and save the program shown in Listing 14.4. Be sure to include the bugs.

The menu-driven way to add a watch is to choose "Add Watch" from the Watches submenu, but the most efficient way is to position the cursor on the name of the variable you want to watch, then press Ctrl-F7. This opens up the "Add Watch" window as shown in Figure 14.2. Use this technique to put a watch on the "Continue" variable in Listing 14.4.

Listing 14.4 has two fairly common bugs. The first, a missing semicolon in the **AddTwoNumbers** subroutine, is caught when you compile the program. The second bug is more subtle. It will not generate either a compile-time or a run-time error, but will send your program into an endless loop because the value of the loop control variable *Continue* never changes. In the next section, we will see how to use the watch window while stepping through a program one line at a time.

```
PROGRAM Listing14_4;

  { Illustrates stepping and tracing through a program with
    the Turbo Pascal integrated debugger. }


USES CRT, MyUtils;

VAR
  continue : CHAR;
  a, b,
  result   : INTEGER;


PROCEDURE AddTwoNumbers(a, b: INTEGER; VAR result: INTEGER);
  BEGIN
  result := a + b   { missing semicolon }
  WRITELN;
  WRITELN(' The sum of ', a, ' and ', b, ' is ', result, '.');
  pause
  END;

PROCEDURE MultiplyTwoNumbers(a, b: INTEGER; VAR result: INTEGER);
  BEGIN
  result := a * b;
  WRITELN;
  WRITELN(' The product of ', a, ' and ', b, ' is ', result,
'.');
  pause
  END;


{ main body of program }
BEGIN
  CLRSCR;
  continue := 'Y';
  WRITELN(' This is a program that adds and then multiplies');
  WRITELN(' two numbers. You will first be prompted to enter');
  WRITELN(' the two numbers to add and multiply. Then, the');
  WRITELN(' AddTwoNumbers procedure will calculate the sum of');
  WRITELN(' the two numbers and pause so that you can see the');
  WRITELN(' result. Then, the MultiplyTwoNumbers procedure
will');
  WRITELN(' calculate the product of the two numbers and pause');
  WRITELN(' again so that you can see the result.');
  WRITELN;
  WRITELN(' After this process is complete, the program will
ask');
  WRITELN(' if you want to run the add and multiply routines
again.');
  WRITELN(' If you do, type Y at the prompt; otherwise, type
N.');
  pause;
  REPEAT
  CLRSCR;
  WRITELN;
  WRITE(' Enter the first number: ');
  READLN(a);
  WRITE(' Enter the second number: ');
  READLN(b);
  AddTwoNumbers(a,b,result);
  MultiplyTwoNumbers(a,b,result);
  WRITE(' Do another (Y/N)? ');
```

Listing 14.4: Stepping and tracing through a program.

```
      { The programmer forgot to include a Readln statement to get
 input, resulting in an endless loop. In addition, without a
 Readln statement to pause the program for input, the "Do
 Another?" prompt goes by so fast that it is virtually invisible.}

    UNTIL UPCASE(continue) <> 'Y'
 END.
```

Listing 14.4: Stepping and tracing through a program. (cont.)

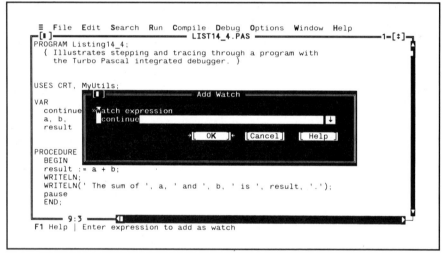

Figure 14.2: The Add Watch dialog box.

STEPPING THROUGH A PROGRAM

Turbo Pascal offers two ways to step through your program. The first method, called *stepping*, executes a single line of code at a time; if the line calls a subroutine, this method simply treats the subroutine as if it were a single statement. You step through a line of code by pressing the F8 function key; each time you press it, another line of your program is executed. The second method, *tracing*, is similar to stepping except that when a line has a subroutine call, the subroutine is executed a line at a time. Tracing is done by pressing the F7 function key. In Figure 14.3, we are stepping through Listing 14.4.

Note that the screen is now divided into two windows: the file window, which contains your program code, and the watch window, which contains the names of variables you are watching and their current values. Sometimes, when you have not yet run the program or a variable is hidden inside a subroutine, a variable will have the message "Cannot access this symbol" or "Unknown identifier" next to it. If you wish to make the screen a little neater, you can choose the Tile option from the Windows menu, although this won't affect how anything works.

The watch window shows that the current value of the **Continue** variable is **'Y'**, indicating that the loop should continue to execute. Keep pressing the F8 key, one press at a time, to step through the program until you get to the line that begins with **UNTIL**, as shown in Figure 14.4. At various points, you will be prompted to enter numbers or press a key.

Note that although we have completed the loop, the value of *Continue* is still **'Y'**, and we were given no opportunity to change it inside the loop. Thus, we have found the bug that caused the endless loop.

```
≡  File  Edit  Search  Run  Compile  Debug  Options  Window  Help
┌[■]══════════════════════ LIST14_4.PAS ════════════════════1=[↑]═┐
│ WRITELN(' The product of ', a, ' and ', b, ' is ', result, '.');    │
│ pause                                                               │
│ END;                                                                │
│                                                                     │
│                                                                     │
│ ( main body of program )                                            │
│ BEGIN                                                               │
│   CLRSCR;                                                           │
│   continue := 'Y';                                                  │
│   WRITELN(' This is a program that adds and then multiplies')       │
│   WRITELN(' two numbers. You will first be prompted to enter');     │
│   WRITELN(' the two numbers to add and multiply. Then, the');       │
│   WRITELN(' AddTwoNumbers procedure will calculate the sum of');    │
│   WRITELN(' the two numbers and pause so that you can see the');    │
└══ 35:1 ═══◄▮════════════════════════════════════════════════════►─┘
┌─────────────────────────── Watches ──────────────────────2────┐
│ continue: 'Y'                                                      │
│ →                                                               ← │
│                                                                   │
│                                                                   │
└───────────────────────────────────────────────────────────────┘
  F1 Help  F7 Trace  F8 Step  F9 Make  F1Ø Menu
```

Figure 14.3: Stepping through Listing 14.4.

DELETING A WATCH

Now that we have found the bug, we do not need the watch on the *Continue* variable any more. With the highlight bar in the watch window on the *Continue* variable, open the Debug menu and select the Watches option to open the Watches submenu. Select "Delete Watch" to delete the watch on the *Continue* variable, as shown in Figure 14.5. Then, enter the bug-fixed version of the program, as shown in Listing 14.5.

Notice one other interesting thing about Listing 14.5, apart from the fact that the bugs have been corrected. The lines that explain the program to the user have been bundled into their own subroutine. When you have multiple WRITELN statements as we do here, bundling them into a subroutine makes it easier to step through the program. Instead of having to step through each line one at a time, you simply press F8 and the **Explain-Program** routine executes all at once.

TRACING INTO SUBROUTINES

Sometimes, the bug you want to locate is in a subroutine. In this situation, tracing through a subroutine is helpful. In the previous example, when you

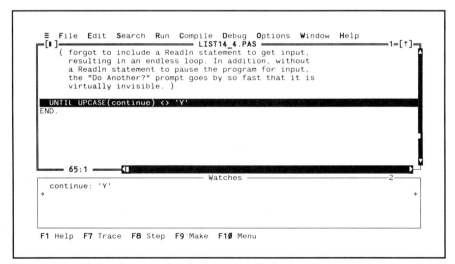

Figure 14.4: Using the watch window to find the loop error.

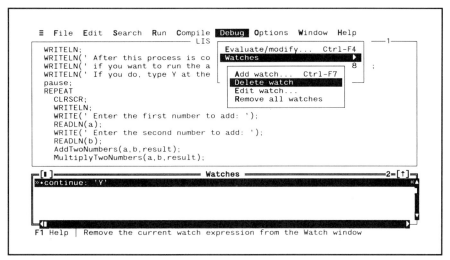

```
 ≡  File  Edit  Search  Run  Compile  Debug  Options  Window  Help
┌────────────────────── LIS ┌─────────────────────────────────┐─1─┐
│ WRITELN;                   │ Evaluate/modify...   Ctrl-F4    │   │
│ WRITELN(' After this process is co │ Watches               ▶ │   │
│ WRITELN(' if you want to run the a ├──────────────────────────┤8  │ ;
│ WRITELN(' If you do, type Y at the │ Add watch...   Ctrl-F7   │   │
│ pause;                     │▐ Delete watch             ▌ │   │
│ REPEAT                     │ Edit watch...            │   │
│   CLRSCR;                  │ Remove all watches       │   │
│   WRITELN;                 └──────────────────────────┘   │
│   WRITE(' Enter the first number to add: ');              │
│   READLN(a);                                              │
│   WRITE(' Enter the second number to add: ');             │
│   READLN(b);                                              │
│   AddTwoNumbers(a,b,result);                              │
│   MultiplyTwoNumbers(a,b,result);                         │
├─[■]───────────────────── Watches ─────────────────2=[↑]─┤
│»•continue: 'Y'                                           «▲│
│                                                          │ │
│                                                          │ │
├─[◄]──────────────────────────────────────────────────────┤
└──────────────────────────────────────────────────────────┘
  F1 Help │ Remove the current watch expression from the Watch window
```

Figure 14.5: Deleting a watch.

stepped through a program by pressing the F8 key, the internal details of
subroutines were skipped, or *stepped over*. When the highlight was on a line
with a call to a subroutine, pressing F8 executed the subroutine in a single
step, and then moved the highlight down to the next line.

Pressing F7 has the same effect as pressing F8 except when the line contains a subroutine call. Then, F7 takes you line-by-line through the subroutine
itself, just as F8 takes you line-by-line through the main program. This
process is shown in Figure 14.6, where we are tracing through Listing 14.5.

USING EVALUATE/MODIFY

The Evaluate/Modify option in the Debug menu allows you to inspect
and, if desired, to change the values of variables at any desired point in
your program. To see how this works, do the following:

1. Begin stepping through Listing 14.5 by pressing the F8 key.
   When you are prompted to enter numbers for the program,
   enter 20 for **a** and 25 for **b**.

```
PROGRAM Listing14_5;

   { Illustrates stepping and tracing through a program with
     the Turbo Pascal integrated debugger. }

USES CRT, MyUtils;

VAR
  continue : CHAR;
  a, b,
  result   : INTEGER;

PROCEDURE ExplainProgram;
  BEGIN
  CLRSCR;
  WRITELN(' This is a program that adds and then multiplies');
  WRITELN(' two numbers. You will first be prompted to enter');
  WRITELN(' the two numbers to add and multiply. Then, the');
  WRITELN(' AddTwoNumbers procedure will calculate the sum of');
  WRITELN(' the two numbers and pause so that you can see the');
  WRITELN(' result. Then, the MultiplyTwoNumbers procedure
will');
  WRITELN(' calculate the product of the two numbers and pause');
  WRITELN(' again so that you can see the result.');
  WRITELN;
  WRITELN(' After this process is complete, the program will
ask');
  WRITELN(' if you want to run the add and multiply routines
again.');
  WRITELN(' If you do, type Y at the prompt; otherwise, type
N.');
  pause
  END;


PROCEDURE AddTwoNumbers(a, b: INTEGER; VAR result: INTEGER);
  BEGIN
  result := a + b;
  WRITELN;
  WRITELN(' The sum of ', a, ' and ', b, ' is ', result, '.');
  pause
  END;

PROCEDURE MultiplyTwoNumbers(a, b: INTEGER; VAR result: INTEGER);
  BEGIN
  result := a * b;
  WRITELN;
  WRITELN(' The product of ', a, ' and ', b, ' is ', result,
.');
  pause
  END;


{ main body of program }
BEGIN
  continue := 'Y';
  ExplainProgram;
  REPEAT
    CLRSCR;
    WRITELN;
```

Listing 14.5: Stepping and tracing through a bug-fixed program.

```
        WRITE(' Enter the first number: ');
        READLN(a);
        WRITE(' Enter the second number: ');
        READLN(b);
        AddTwoNumbers(a,b,result);

        MultiplyTwoNumbers(a,b,result);

        WRITE(' Do another (Y/N)? ');
        READLN(continue);
    UNTIL UPCASE(continue) <> 'Y'
END.
```

Listing 14.5: Stepping and tracing through a bug-fixed program. (cont.)

```
  ≡ File  Edit  Search  Run  Compile  Debug  Options  Window  Help          1=[↑]
┌─[■]──────────────────────── LIST14_4.PAS ══════════════════════════════════┐
│  continue : CHAR;                                                          │
│  a, b,                                                                     │
│  result   : INTEGER;                                                       │
│                                          \                                 │
│                                                                            │
│ PROCEDURE AddTwoNumbers(a, b: INTEGER; VAR result: INTEGER);               │
│   BEGIN                                                                    │
│   result := a + b;                                                         │
│ ▐WRITELN;▌                                                                 │
│   WRITELN(' The sum of ', a, ' and ', b, ' is ', result, '.');             │
│   pause                                                                    │
│   END;                                                                     │
│                                                                            │
│ PROCEDURE MultiplyTwoNumbers(a, b: INTEGER; VAR result: INTEGER);          │
└──── 17:1 ─────────◄▌───────────────────────────────────────────────────►──┘
┌──────────────────────────── Watches ───────────────────────────2─┐
│  a: 1Ø                                                            │
│  b: 1Ø                                                            │
│  result: 2Ø                                                       │
│ →                                                               ← │
└───────────────────────────────────────────────────────────────────┘

 F1 Help  F7 Trace  F8 Step  F9 Make  F1Ø Menu
```

Figure 14.6: Tracing into a subroutine.

2. Stop when the highlight is on the line containing the **Multiply-TwoNumbers** subroutine.

3. With the highlight on the **MultiplyTwoNumbers** subroutine, open the Debug menu and pick Evaluate/Modify. The Evaluate/Modify dialog box opens up. (See Figure 14.7.)

4. In the "Expression" blank of the dialog box, enter **a**. The number 20 is displayed in the "Result" blank because that is the current value of the variable **a**.

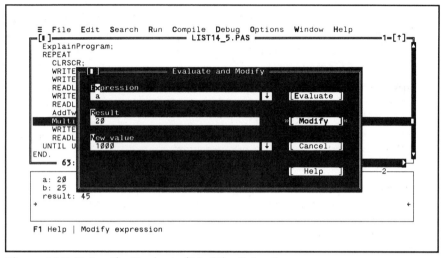

Figure 14.7: Using the Evaluate/Modify dialog box.

5. Tab to the "New value" blank and enter the number **1000**. Then press Enter to change **a** to the new value. Press Escape to exit from the dialog box.

6. Continue stepping through the program by pressing F8. With the value of **a** changed to **1000**, the **MultiplyTwoNumbers** procedure reports that the product of **a** and **b** is **25000**.

The primary use for Evaluate/Modify is to let you play "what if" with the values of variables: by changing the value of a variable in the middle of a program, you can see what the effect would be if it had that value.

SETTING BREAKPOINTS

Setting a breakpoint is like putting a stop sign in your code; in fact, "brakepoint" would be a more appropriate spelling. When you run the program, it will run up to the breakpoint and then stop. At that time, you can inspect the values of variables and anything else in the current state of the program. You insert a breakpoint in a program by moving the cursor to the line where you want to insert the breakpoint and then pressing

Ctrl-F8. To remove a breakpoint, you move the cursor to the line containing the breakpoint and then press Ctrl-F8 a second time.

The primary advantage of breakpoints over stepping through a program is that, in certain cases, breakpoints can be more efficient. If you want to inspect variables at a point toward the end of a long program, it would be time-consuming to step to that point one line at a time. Inserting a breakpoint allows you to go directly to the place you want to inspect.

You can use the Breakpoints option in the Debug menu to open the Breakpoints dialog box, from which you can view a list of the current breakpoints in your program, as shown in Figure 14.8. You can also add and delete breakpoints by using this dialog box, but it is more practical to do it with the Ctrl-F8 speed key method.

SUMMARY

A bug is anything that prevents a program from compiling and running correctly. Debugging should not be thought of as a step that begins only after the program is coded; instead, the program should be designed

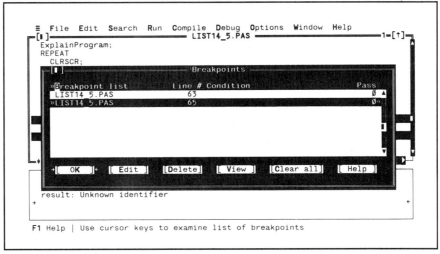

Figure 14.8: Using the breakpoint dialog box.

from the beginning for ease of debugging. Strict adherence to structured design methods and information hiding makes errors less likely and debugging easier.

In program development, a main program module should be developed first, with empty *stubs* for the subroutines that will be used by the program. These subroutines then can be developed and debugged separately.

Turbo Pascal provides powerful debugging tools that are adequate for most programmers' needs. It allows you to put a *watch* on a variable, which enables you to see how the value of the variable changes in the course of the program run. You can also step through a program one line at a time; you can either *step over* subroutines or *trace into* them line-by-line.

Breakpoints allow you to run your program up to a certain point and then permit you to inspect the values of variables and other items at that point. The Evaluate/Modify dialog box lets you view or change the values of variables in the middle of a program run.

REVIEW EXERCISES

1. Explain the idea of a program bug. Do bugs always result from programming error? Justify your answer.

2. Explain the three main types of bug. Which type is the most dangerous and why?

3. True or false: In a properly designed and coded program, there are no bugs. If the statement is false, explain why it is false.

4. Explain the connection between structured programming methods and ease of debugging, as well as the "why" of this connection.

5. Explain how to combine initial debugging with program design and coding. What are the three main stages of initial debugging?

6. Trace through the following code with a pencil. Are there any problems in the code? If so, what are they and how would you correct them?

```
BEGIN
  WRITELN;
  WRITE(' Enter DOS name of update file to use: ');
  READLN(input,updatename,18);
  ASSIGN(updatefile, updatename);
  RESET(updatefile);

  WHILE NOT EOF(updatefile) DO
    BEGIN
    IF updatehead = NIL
      THEN BEGIN
             NEW(updatehead);
             updatehead^.next := NIL;
             updatetail := updatehead;
             ReadInUpdateHead;
             Readln(updatefile)
           END
      ELSE BEGIN
             NEW(updatetail^.next);
             IF updatetail = updatehead
           THEN updatehead^.next:= updatetail^.next;
             updatetail := updatetail^.next;
             updatetail^.next := NIL;
             ReadInUpdateTail;
             Readln(updatefile)
           END;
    CLOSE(updatefile)
  END;
```

7. Design a routine to prompt the user for numbers to multiply; then create and run a driver program to test the routine.

8. Explain the idea of debug code and how it helps debug your programs. Write a simple program in which a variable is used to control a loop; then insert debug code to track the value of the variable during each pass through the loop.

9. Using any method you like, locate the bug in the following code fragment. Explain how the bug works and what needs to be done to correct it.

```
PROCEDURE GRead(VAR gtext: STRING);
    { This routine reads a string from the
      keyboard one character at a time. As
      each character is entered, the routine
      displays the character on the screen.
      It first initializes the string to be
      empty, then adds one character at a
      time until a character = Enter, which
      means that the user has pressed the
      Enter key. }
VAR
    ch : CHAR; { temporary character variable }
BEGIN
    REPEAT
    gtext := '';    { initialize gtext string }
    ch := READKEY;  { get character for string }
    IF ch <> Enter  { has user pressed Enter?  }
        THEN BEGIN
            WRITE(ch); { display character }
            gtext := gtext + ch { add to string }
        END
    UNTIL ch = Enter
END;
```

10. Explain how to step through a program in the Turbo Pascal IDE. Explain how to trace through a program. How do these two methods differ?

11. Explain how to put a watch on a variable—and why you might want to do so. How can you delete a watch?

12. Explain how to use Turbo Pascal's Evaluate/Modify feature to change the value of a variable in the middle of a program run. How can this feature help to debug your programs?

13. Explain how to set and remove breakpoints. When should you use breakpoints?

14. Are there any problems in the following code fragment? If so, what are they and how would you correct them?

```
VAR continue : char;
BEGIN
   WHILE UPCASE(continue) = 'Y' DO
      BEGIN
      GetNewRecord;
      WRITE(' Do another (Y/N)? ');
      READLN(continue)
      END
   END
END;
```

15. What does it mean to test a program under varying conditions? What kinds of conditions should be varied? Why is this important?

C H A P T E R

15

Graphics in Turbo Pascal

A picture is a model of reality. What a picture must have in common with reality, in order to be able to depict it, is its pictorial form. A picture cannot, however, depict its pictorial form: it displays it.

– Ludwig Wittgenstein, *Tractatus Logico-Philosophicus*

In this chapter, we turn to an area that can simultaneously be the most fun, the most frustrating, and the least portable in Turbo Pascal: graphics programming.

Although it is a general-purpose programming language, Turbo Pascal also provides extensive support for graphics programming on the IBM PC and compatible computers. The problem is that graphics programming relies so heavily on the specific hardware features provided by each computer that there is almost no portability in graphics code from one type of computer to another. Even worse, there is no official standard for graphics programming, so each Pascal compiler tends to handle graphics in its own unique way—if at all.

That's the bad news, but there is some good news: the basic ideas of graphics programming are pretty much the same in every programming language and on every computer platform. If you are working with another Pascal compiler or on a computer that is not a PC, you won't be able to use your Turbo Pascal graphics code, but you will have a good understanding of how to write graphics code in the other language.

GENERAL METHODS FOR GRAPHICS

In order to understand graphics programming in Turbo Pascal, you must first understand the basic elements of graphics in any language. So far, we have worked exclusively in *text mode*. This means that the PC's screen is normally set up to display 25 lines of text with 80 characters per line. If you have an EGA or VGA monitor and video adapter, your monitor may be able to display more than this.

By the way, a video adapter is a part of your computer (usually an add-in board) that controls how text and graphics are displayed on your computer's screen. The original video adapter in the IBM PC, the IBM Monochrome Adapter, supported only text. Soon thereafter, the Hercules Graphics Adapter was introduced and created a de facto standard for monochrome graphics on the PC. IBM itself introduced the Color Graphics Adapter (CGA), which provided color graphics on color (RGB) monitors, but text was fuzzy and somewhat hard to read. More recently, the Enhanced Graphics Adapter (EGA), Video Graphics Array (VGA), and IBM 8514 Graphics Card standards have brought even better support for color graphics while providing sharp, easy-to-read text displays.

LIMITATIONS OF TEXT MODE

ASCII characters displayed on the screen are predefined by your PC's hardware, in particular by its video adapter. When you include extended ASCII characters, such as box and line-drawing characters, you can do some fairly interesting things in text mode. There are, however, three significant limitations.

The first limitation is that you cannot vary the size of the characters displayed on-screen at the same time. Because the size and shape of the characters are controlled by your video adapter and monitor, they all will occupy the same amount of space on the screen so they can fit into the monitor's 25-line by 80-column grid. This does have an important advantage: it makes screen elements in text mode very easy to manipulate. Every line has the same height and every character has the same width. If we want to move up or down one line, we know exactly how far to go; ditto for moving left or right. However, if you want to make *some* text elements larger or smaller than others, you cannot do it.

The second limitation is that you cannot vary the shape of the characters displayed on the screen. Everything comes out in the same type font, which (theoretically) is easy to read but is not visually interesting. If you want to put some text in a plain font while others are in Gothic font, and still others are in Helvetica, you simply cannot do it.

The third limitation is that although you can draw boxes with extended ASCII characters, you cannot draw much else. You can only use the 256 pre-defined ASCII characters, and only in the 2,000 (25 times 80) text character positions on your screen.

ADVANTAGES AND DISADVANTAGES OF GRAPHICS

These limitations—as well as some of the advantages that go with them—are absent when you work in graphics mode. Instead of 25 lines, each 80 characters wide, you work with tiny dots on the screen, called *pixels* (picture elements). Even in character mode, pixels are present; they are used to form the characters that appear on the screen. Text characters themselves are predefined patterns of pixels. However, because the video adapter provides built-in support for ASCII characters, it constructs them out of pixels automatically, and neither the user nor the programmer has to deal with the problem of construction. Working in graphics mode, however, provides you with the ability to manipulate individual pixels that you do not have in text mode.

The tremendous advantage of this approach is that you can display literally anything you want to on the screen: fancy text fonts, bar charts, animation, and so forth. The main disadvantage is that creating a graphics screen requires you to provide far more information than a text screen does. Instead of 2,000 text positions, now you must deal with the total number of pixels on the screen.

The arrangement and number of pixels on the monitor's screen is called the *resolution* of the monitor and video adapter. With a Hercules Graphics Adapter, this is 720 pixels wide by 348 pixels high, or 250,560 pixels; the Hercules adapter is said to have a resolution of 720×348. Although other factors affect how characters and images appear on the screen, the general rule is that the higher the resolution (the more pixels), the sharper the images on the screen. What is usually called the resolution of a monitor and video adapter is, in fact, its maximum resolution; one or more lower resolutions usually are available as well.

With a color monitor and video adapter, pixels can be any of the colors in the available *palette*. With a monochrome monitor, pixels are either on (lit up) or off (dark). The combination of a particular resolution and a particular color palette is called a graphics mode. When your program first sets up the computer to run graphics, it must tell the video adapter and monitor which of the available graphics modes should be used.

GRAPHICS DRIVERS

Each different video adapter has different ways of handling graphics. Because of this, a program must be able to work with all or most of the currently used video adapters. However, to include support for all video adapters in every program would make the programs far bigger than necessary. Because of this, Turbo Pascal provides a separate *driver* file for each popular video adapter. When a Turbo Pascal program is run by the user, the program can detect which video adapter is installed in the computer and it uses the appropriate video driver.

This means, of course, that the required video drivers must be available to the program. Turbo Pascal provides six different video drivers, each of which will work with one or more of the currently popular video adapters. These driver files all have the extension *.BGI in their file names, and are normally found in the BGI directory created by the Turbo Pascal installation program. Other drivers for specific video cards are often available from the manufacturers of the video cards.

When you distribute a Turbo Pascal-compiled program that uses graphics, you must include copies of all these video drivers with the program. In addition, if you use special text fonts in graphics screens—as you almost certainly will—you must include copies of the font files. Turbo Pascal's video driver files are listed in Table 15.1; the font files are listed in Table 15.2.

One other point needs to be mentioned. As a conscientious computer user, you know that you cannot legally make copies of Turbo Pascal itself and distribute the copies to other people. However, this restriction does not apply to the video drivers and font files. You are free to copy these files and distribute them with your programs. Not only is this legal, of course, but it is the only solution that makes sense: if every user needed to have Turbo Pascal in order to run graphics programs written in Turbo Pascal, then it would be extremely impractical to write programs that included graphics.

Table 15.1: Video Driver Files Included with Turbo Pascal 6

DRIVER FILE NAME	VIDEO ADAPTERS SUPPORTED
ATT.BGI	AT&T 6300 (400 line)
CGA.BGI	IBM CGA, MCGA, and compatibles
EGAVGA.BGI	IBM EGA, VGA, and compatibles
HERC.BGI	Hercules Monochrome and compatibles
IBM8514.BGI	IBM 8514 and compatibles
PC3270.BGI	IBM 3270 PC

Table 15.2: Font Files Included with Turbo Pascal 6[*]

FONT FILE	FONT PROVIDED
GOTH.CHR	Stroked Gothic
LITT.CHR	Stroked small character
SANS.CHR	Stroked sans serif
TRIP.CHR	Stroked Triplex

[*]*Note: Unlike standard bit-mapped fonts, which are stored as patterns of pixels, stroked fonts are stored as a set of line segments. These segments are called strokes.*

SETTING UP THE SCREEN FOR GRAPHICS

Making your program set up the monitor and video adapter for graphics is quite similar to making it open and close files. In the beginning, you call the **InitGraph** procedure, which initializes your graphics hardware and puts your computer screen in graphics mode, normally with the maximum resolution available. When your work with graphics is finished, you call the **CloseGraph** procedure to return your computer screen to text mode.

InitGraph takes three parameters: the video driver to be used, the graphics mode (i.e., the screen resolution and color palette) to be used, and the path name of the directory where the program can find the video driver files. You will need to have two integer variables in your program to represent the video driver and the graphics mode.

Although you have the option of specifying which video adapter to use, normally, this does not make much sense. If you use **InitGraph** and specify the Hercules Monochrome video driver, then your program will not be able to work with any other video adapters. Fortunately, Turbo Pascal's Graph unit, which contains most of Turbo Pascal's graphics routines, has a predefined constant named *detect* that tells **InitGraph** to automatically detect which video adapter is being used and to load the appropriate driver. Table 15.3 lists the names and corresponding integers for Turbo Pascal's graphics drivers.

To use *detect*, you assign it to the graphic driver variable as shown in Listing 15.1. If you do not specify a value for the graphics mode, **InitGraph** uses the highest-resolution mode available for your video adapter and monitor.

Table 15.3: Graphic Driver Constants in Turbo Pascal 6

CONSTANT NAME	CORRESPONDING INTEGER VALUE
Detect	0
CGA	1
MCGA	2
EGA	3
EGA64	4
EGAMono	5
IBM8514	6
HercMono	7
ATT400	8
VGA	9
PC3270	10

```
    { Demonstrates fonts, text sizes, directions, and text
      justification modes that are pre-defined in the BGI. }

USES CRT, GRAPH;

CONST
  gd : INTEGER = detect;

VAR
  gm : INTEGER;

BEGIN
    INITGRAPH(gd, gm, 'c:\tp\bgi');
    OutText('A picture is a model of reality.');
    OutText('  Press any key ...');
    REPEAT UNTIL keypressed;
    CLOSEGRAPH
END.
```

Listing 15.1: Setting up graphics mode with InitGraph.

The first thing Listing 15.1 does is to name the CRT and Graph units in the program's USES statement. Then, the graphics driver variable, called **gd**, is created as a typed constant. You should recall from Chapter 5 that a typed constant is actually a variable with a preset initial value. In this case, we have set the value of *gd* to *detect*. The variable to represent graphics mode, *gm,* is declared as an integer variable in the VAR section.

In the action part of the program, the first line is a call to **InitGraph**. Because we set the value of the graphics driver variable to *detect*, **Init-Graph** automatically detects the type of graphics hardware in use and chooses the appropriate driver. The graphics mode variable *gm* is set to the highest-resolution mode available. Finally, the third parameter tells **Init-Graph** where to find the graphics driver files. This is most likely to be the \tp\bgi directory on your c: drive. If you have installed the files somewhere else, you should substitute the appropriate path name for 'c:\tp\bgi' in Listing 15.1.

After setting up the computer in graphics mode, the program uses the Graph unit's **OutText** routine to display text on the screen. The Pascal WRITE and WRITELN routines can be used only in text mode, so Turbo Pascal provides **OutText** as an approximate equivalent to the WRITE routine. Next comes a REPEAT loop to pause the program until the user presses a key. Finally, a call to **CloseGraph** shuts down graphics mode and returns the computer to text mode. The result of running Listing 15.1 is shown in Figure 15.1.

Note that this pattern of setting up graphics with **InitGraph** and shutting it down with **CloseGraph** is part of every program that uses graphics.

```
A picture is a model of reality.  Press any key ...
```

Figure 15.1: Displaying text in graphics mode.

HANDLING GRAPHICS ERRORS

The program in Listing 15.1 is fine as far as it goes. However, it is unable to cope with situations in which the necessary video driver cannot be found and where, as a result, the graphics hardware cannot be initialized. Listing 15.1 simply assumes that the video drivers will be found in the directory that the program specifies—an assumption which, in real-life situations, is sometimes not justified.

A solution to this problem is shown in Listing 15.2, which incorporates error-checking into its graphics initialization. A string variable **dpath** is set up with an initial empty value; in this case, the call to **Init-Graph** will succeed if the video driver is found in the same directory as the program itself. If not, a REPEAT loop keeps going until the call to **Init-Graph** succeeds.

Immediately after the call to **InitGraph**, we check a built-in variable called *GraphResult* and assign its value to an integer variable *gerror*. *GraphResult* works the same way for graphics as **IOResult** works for input-output operations. If the graphics operation is a success, then *GraphResult* returns a value of 0; otherwise, it returns an error code that indicates what problem was encountered. The *GraphResult* value 0 can also be referred to by the identifier **GrOK**, which is used to control the loop. The values and identifiers of various graphics errors are shown in Table 15.4.

Like the value of **IOResult**, the value of *GraphResult* is a slippery thing, liable to change without notice. Therefore, we need to store the

```
PROGRAM Listing15_2;

    { Demonstrates how to build error-checking into the graphics
      initialization. This is essential, because many PCs still do
      not have graphics capabilities. Note that the program uses
      GraphResult, a function from the Graph unit that tells if the
      InitGraph routine was successful in initializing the graphics
      hardware: GraphResult works just like IORESULT, which is used
      to determine if a file was opened successfully. GrOK and
      GrFileNotFound are constants defined in the Graph unit; if
      the call to InitGraph is successful, then GraphResult returns
      a value of GrOK; if the required graphics driver cannot be
      found, then it returns a value of GrFileNotFound. }


USES CRT, GRAPH;

CONST
  dpath  : STRING = '';

TYPE
  string80 = STRING[80];

VAR
  gd,
  gm,
  gerror : INTEGER;

BEGIN
  CLRSCR;
  REPEAT
    gd := detect;
    INITGRAPH(gd, gm, dpath);
    gerror := GRAPHRESULT;
    IF gerror <> grOK
      THEN BEGIN
           WRITELN(' Graphics error: ', GraphErrorMsg(gerror));
           IF gerror = GrFileNotFound
              THEN BEGIN
                   WRITELN(' Cannot find graphics driver. Please');
                   WRITE(' enter directory path for the driver: ');
                   READLN(dpath);
                   WRITELN
                   END
                ELSE HALT(1)
           END
  UNTIL gerror = grOK;

  OutText('A picture is a model of reality.');
  OutText(' Press any key ...');
  REPEAT UNTIL keypressed;
    CLOSEGRAPH
  END.
```

Listing 15.2: Building error-checking into graphics initialization.

value of *GraphResult* in the *gerror* variable immediately after the call to
InitGraph.

If an error is detected, an IF statement is activated. The first thing it
does is use Turbo Pascal's **GraphErrorMsg** function with the error code

Table 15.4: GraphResult Error Values

CONSTANT	VALUE	PROBLEM DETECTED
grOK	0	No problem
grNoInitGraph	−1	Graphics not yet initialized
grNotDetected	−2	Graphics hardware not found
grFileNotFound	−3	Cannot find video driver file
grInvalidDriver	−4	Invalid driver file
grNoLoadMem	−5	Not enough RAM for graphics
grNoScanMem	−6	Out of RAM in scan fill
grNoFloodMem	−7	Out of RAM in flood fill
grFontNotFound	−8	Font file not found
grNoFontMem	−9	Not enough RAM to load font
grInvalidMode	−10	Invalid graphics mode for driver selected
grError	−11	Generic graphics error
grIOError	−12	Graphics I/O error
grInvalidFont	−13	Invalid font file
grInvalidFontNum	−14	Invalid font number

returned by *GraphResult;* this displays an informative error message on the computer screen. If the problem is that the driver cannot be found in the current directory, it prompts the user to enter a new value for the *dpath* variable. If the driver is found in this directory, then the loop terminates. If the problem is something else, such as not enough memory, then the program simply halts.

Everything else in Listing 15.2 is the same as in Listing 15.1, with an important exception. In 15.2, the graphics driver is not initialized at the beginning of the program as a typed constant; instead, it is included in the REPEAT loop so that it is re-initialized by a call to DETECT before each call to **InitGraph**. This is because a call to **InitGraph**, if unsuccessful, clears the value of the graphics driver variable; if the variable is not reset to the correct value, then the next call to **InitGraph** will fail because it cannot find the graphics hardware that corresponds to the now-incorrect value of the graphics driver variable. This is a bug typical of many loop situations: a particular statement needs to be in (or out of) the loop, but it is currently somewhere else.

MANIPULATING ITEMS ON THE SCREEN

Working in graphics mode is different from working in text mode in some fundamental ways. Because text and art in a graphics screen can be any size and screen resolutions can vary, there is no straightforward way to position items on the screen.

In graphics, everything is calculated in terms of pixel coordinates. The topmost, leftmost pixel has coordinates of 0,0; the bottommost, rightmost pixel, at the lower-right corner of the screen, has coordinates that vary depending on the video adapter and graphics mode in use. In CGA graphics, for example, the resolution is 320 pixels horizontally and 200 pixels vertically (320×200); therefore, because the coordinate numbers start with 0,0, the bottom-right pixel has coordinates of 319,199. With Hercules graphics (resolution 720×348), the bottom-right pixel has coordinates of 719,347.

These differences in the number of pixels in different computer screens mean that it is extremely impractical to use *absolute* coordinates to position items in a graphics screen. For example, suppose that you are writing your program on a PC with a Hercules graphics card, which provides a screen resolution of 720×348. You find that a particular item looks very good when you place it at the pixel coordinates of 350,300—at the bottom center of the screen. If a user then runs your program on a PC with a CGA video adapter, the screen will not display properly because both pixel coordinates are beyond the limits of the CGA display's resolution (320×200).

This means that most of the time, you position items by using relative instead of absolute coordinates. This is probably the most difficult aspect of graphics programming; next to this, learning how to use graphics drawing routines is a piece of cake. Turbo Pascal's Graph unit provides two functions that enable you to use relative coordinates: **GetMaxX** and **GetMaxY**. A call to **GetMaxX** gives you the number of the maximum x-axis coordinate, while a call to **GetMaxY** gives the maximum y-axis coordinate. No matter what kind of adapter or graphics mode is in use, these functions enable your program to find out the pixel-dimensions of the screen and to position items accordingly, as in:

```
VAR
   gd, gm,
   maxX, maxY : integer;
BEGIN
   gd := detect;
   InitGraph(gd, gm, 'c:\tp\bgi');
   maxX := GetMaxX;
   maxY := GetMaxY;
   OutTextXY(maxX div 2, maxY div 2, 'Centered text.');
   { ... other details of program }
   CloseGraph
END.
```

When you need to position several items on the screen at the same time, sometimes you have to do some fairly tricky arithmetic with **maxX** and **maxY** to get your items positioned properly. The big advantage, however, is that once the items are positioned with this method, they will be in the same relative position on any PC screen with any video adapter and any graphics mode.

HANDLING TEXT

The most obvious thing to learn first, in a chapter on graphics, would be how to draw pictures on the computer screen. However, even in graphics mode, text is more fundamental, because some graphics screens will contain only text and most graphics screens will contain at least some text.

OUTTEXT AND OUTTEXTXY

The most basic text-manipulation routines in graphics mode are **OutText** and **OutTextXY**. Both of these routines work like the WRITE procedure instead of WRITELN; they do not move the cursor down to the next line of text because in graphics mode, there is no predefined "next line" on the screen. **OutText**, which we saw in Listings 15.1 and 15.2, displays a text string at the current (invisible) cursor position. In doing so, it uses the current values for text font, size, direction, and justification; these values can be changed by calls to **SetTextStyle** and **SetTextJust**, as we will see in the next section.

OutTextXY, as you might guess, allows you to display text at the pixel coordinates specified by x and y, whether or not this is the same as the current cursor position. **OutTextXY** is used in the **GWrite** and **GWriteln** routines in Listing 15.3. Enter and run this listing, which gives you a demonstration of the different fonts, text sizes, and text directions available.

OutTextXY, as you can see in Listing 15.3, takes three parameters: two integers representing the x (horizontal) and y (vertical) pixel coordinates at which you want text displayed, and a string that contains the text to be displayed. There is a lot of information in Listing 15.3, so let's take it one item at a time.

FONTS

The first result of running Listing 15.3 is shown in Figure 15.2, which shows different predefined text fonts and sizes in Turbo Pascal. When you

```
PROGRAM Listing15_3;


  { Demonstrates fonts, text sizes, directions, and text
    justification modes that are predefined in the BGI. }

USES CRT, GRAPH;

CONST
  x       : INTEGER = 10;
  y       : INTEGER = 10;
  lmargin = 10;

  BkSpc   = #8;
  enter   = #13;
  space   = #32;

TYPE
  string80 = STRING[80];

VAR
  gd,
  gm,
  maxX,
  maxY   : INTEGER;
  name   : STRING;
  FilePath : string80;

PROCEDURE FindFiles(VAR gd, gm: INTEGER;
                         VAR filepath:String80);

  VAR
    gerror: INTEGER;


  BEGIN (* Procedure FindFiles *)
   CLRSCR;
   REPEAT
    gd := detect;
    INITGRAPH(gd, gm, FilePath);
    gerror := GRAPHRESULT;
    IF gerror <> grOK
        THEN BEGIN (* Error Found *)
              WRITELN(' Graphics error: ', GraphErrorMsg(gerror));
              IF gerror = GrFileNotFound
                 THEN BEGIN  (* Prompt *)
                       WRITELN(' Cannot find graphics driver. Please');
                       WRITE(' enter directory path for the driver: ');
                       READLN(FilePath);
                       WRITELN
                       END     (* Prompt *)
                 ELSE HALT(1)
             END  (* Error Found *)
    UNTIL gerror = grOK;
  END;  (* Procedure FindFiles *)


PROCEDURE Init(VAR maxX, maxY : INTEGER);
  BEGIN
  maxX := GetMaxX;
  maxY := GetMaxY
  END;
```

Listing 15.3: Different fonts, sizes, and text directions.

```
PROCEDURE HomeCursor(VAR x, y: INTEGER);
  BEGIN
  x := 10;
  y := 10
  END;


PROCEDURE GWrite(VAR X, Y : INTEGER; gtext : STRING);
  { corresponds to WRITE }
  BEGIN
  OutTextXY(X,Y,gtext);
  x := x + textwidth(gtext)
  END;

PROCEDURE GWriteln(VAR X, Y : INTEGER; gtext : STRING);
  { corresponds to WRITELN }
  BEGIN
  OutTextXY(x, y, gtext);
  y := y + TextHeight('M');
  x := lmargin;
  END;


PROCEDURE Gpause;
  VAR
    ch : CHAR;
  BEGIN
    SetTextJustify(LeftText, TopText);
    GWriteln(x, y, '');
    Gwriteln(x,y, 'Press any key ...');
    REPEAT UNTIL keypressed;
    ch := READKEY;
    GWriteln(x,y, '');
  END;

PROCEDURE GpauseXY(VAR x, y : INTEGER);
  VAR
    ch : CHAR;
  BEGIN
    SetTextStyle(TriplexFont, HorizDir, 2);
    SetTextJustify(LeftText, TopText);
    GWriteln(x, y, '');
    Gwriteln(x,y, 'Press any key ...');
    REPEAT UNTIL keypressed;
    ch := READKEY;
    GWriteln(x,y, '');
  END;


PROCEDURE ShowFontsAndSizes(VAR x, y : INTEGER);
  BEGIN
    GWrite(x, y, 'This is the default font, size 1. ');
    Gpause;

    SetTextStyle(TriplexFont, HorizDir, 2);
    Gwrite(x, y, 'This is the triplex font, size 2. ');
    Gpause;

    SetTextStyle(SmallFont, HorizDir, 4);
    GWrite(x,y,'This is the "small" font, size 4. ');
    Gpause;

    SetTextStyle(SansSerifFont, HorizDir, 3);
    GWrite(x,y,'This is the Sans-serif font, size 3. ');
    Gpause;
```

Listing 15.3: Different fonts, sizes, and text directions. (cont.)

```
      SetTextStyle(GothicFont, HorizDir, 4);
      GWrite(x,y,'This is the Gothic font, size 4. ');
      Gpause;

      ClearDevice;
      HomeCursor(x,y)
   END;



PROCEDURE ShowJustAndDir(VAR x, y : INTEGER;
                             maxX, maxY : INTEGER);
   VAR
     xpos, ypos : INTEGER;
   BEGIN
      SetTextStyle(TriplexFont, HorizDir, 2);
      GWriteln(x, y, 'This is horizontal text, left-justified. ');
      Gpause;
      x := maxX div 3;
      y := y + TextHeight('M');

      SetTextJustify(LeftText, BottomText);
      OutTextXY(x, y, 'Left, bottom-justified');
      delay(1000);

      SetTextJustify(CenterText, CenterText);
      y := y + TextHeight('M');
      OutTextXY(x, y, 'Center, center-justified.');
      delay(1000);

      SetTextJustify(RightText, TopText);
      y := y + TextHeight('M');
      OutTextXY(x,y, 'Top, right-justified');
      delay(1000);

      x := maxX - maxX div 6;
      y := maxY;
      SetTextStyle(TriplexFont, VertDir, 7);
      SetTextJustify(LeftText,BottomText);
      OutTextXY(x,y, 'Vertical');
      delay(1000);

      SetTextStyle(TriplexFont, HorizDir, 2);
      y := maxY - maxY div 4;
      Gpause;
      ClearDevice;
      HomeCursor(x,y)
   END;


BEGIN
    gd := DETECT;
    FindFiles(gd, gm,FilePath);
    Init(maxX, MaxY);
    ShowFontsAndSizes(x,y);
    ShowJustAndDir(x,y, maxX, maxY);
    CLOSEGRAPH
END.
```

Listing 15.3: Different fonts, sizes, and text directions. (cont.)

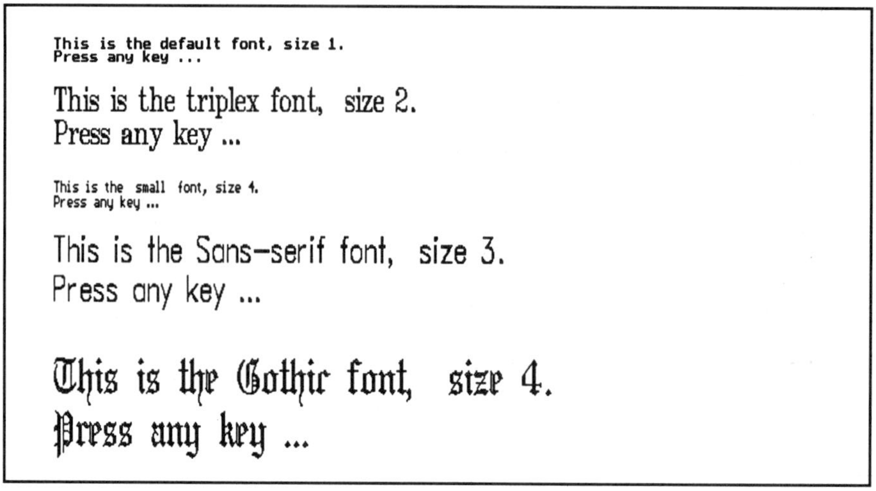

Figure 15.2: Different fonts and sizes of text in graphics mode.

use **OutText** or **OutTextXY**, the text is displayed with the current text font, direction, and size. In the first example we saw in Listing 15.1 and Figure 15.1, this was fairly unimpressive: small text at the top of the screen. In Listing 15.3, however, we use the **SetTextStyle** routine to change from the default settings to fonts and sizes that are a little more interesting.

The **SetTextStyle** routine takes three parameters: the font style to be used, the direction of the text (horizontal or vertical), and a magnification factor from 1 to 10. All three parameters are of type word, which is a special integer type. However, Turbo Pascal provides predefined names for the font styles and the directions, so you need not worry about remembering which number stands for a particular type font or text direction. These names are shown in Table 15.5.

The text font, direction, and size that you set with **SetTextStyle** remain in effect until you change them with another call to **SetTextStyle** or until graphics mode is shut down with a call to **CloseGraph**.

Notice that the **ShowFontsAndSizes** routine ends with a call to the **ClearDevice** routine. Because CLRSCR can be used only with text-mode screens, the Graph unit provides **ClearDevice** to blank the screen as a graphics counterpart of CLRSCR.

Table 15.5: Constants for Text Fonts and Directions

CONSTANT	VALUE
DefaultFont	0 (8x8 pixel bit-mapped font)
TriplexFont	1 (stroked fonts)
SmallFont	2
SansSerifFont	3
GothicFont	4
HorizDir	0 (left to right)
VertDir	1 (bottom to top)
UserCharSize	0 (user-defined character size)

TEXT JUSTIFICATION

Text justification is something that may have surprised you when you ran Listing 15.3. When we are working in text mode, the terms *left-justified, center-justified,* or *right-justified* have meanings that do not seem to apply in graphics mode. When we say that something is left-justified, we mean that it is against the left edge of the screen, while center-justified items are in the center of the screen and right-justified items are against the right edge of the screen.

In the **ShowJustAndDir** routine of Listing 15.3, however, things don't work that way. First, we call **SetTextJustify** to tell Turbo Pascal to left-justify text horizontally and bottom-justify it vertically. Then, we would normally expect the text to appear at the bottom-left corner of the screen. In graphics mode, however, text is justified not relative to the screen as a whole but relative to the current cursor position. A left-justified item will appear to the right of the current location, while a center-justified item will be centered on the current location and a right-justified item will be to the left of the current location. The results are shown in Figure 15.3.

The first text item, which says that "This is horizontal text, left-justified," seems fine: it is against the left edge of the screen. The next three items, however, are puzzling. "Left, bottom-justified" appears not on the left side of the screen, but in the center; "Center, center-justified" appears

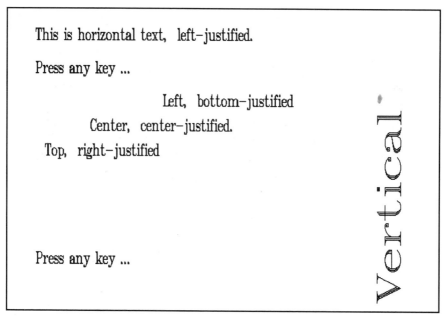

Figure 15.3: Different text directions and justifications.

a little below and to the left of the first item; and "Top, right-justified" appears below and to the left of "Center, center-justified."

The fact that each text item appears below the preceding one is no mystery. Before displaying the second and third items with **OutTextXY**, we move the current cursor location down by a distance equal to a "line" of text in the current font and size. This is done by changing the y (vertical) coordinate: to the original y coordinate, we add the height of a capital letter. Because the y axis increases as we go from the top to the bottom of the screen, this moves the cursor location down. This is the standard method for moving the cursor down a line in graphics mode.

However, the horizontal position of the text items is confusing until you notice that all three items are positioned in relation to the same horizontal location. The left-justified item is positioned to its right, the center-justified item is centered on it, and the right-justified item is to its left.

Vertical justification works in the same odd way, even though this fact is not quite as clear in Figure 15.3. A top-justified item appears below the current cursor position, a center-justified item appears at the same level, and a bottom-justified item appears above the current cursor position. The text justifications that you can use with **SetTextJustify** are shown in Table 15.6.

The **ShowJustAndDir** routine also provides several examples of the sort of travails you must go through to position items on the screen. Most of these positioning operations involve changing the value of the x or y coordinate by relating it to **maxX** or **maxY**, the maximum x and y coordinates of the screen. (Remember that **maxX** and **maxY** are variables that *we* defined, and they are not predefined variables in Turbo Pascal. They get their values from calls to **GetMaxX** and **GetMaxY**.) There really is no formula for this kind of positioning; it is partly a matter of experience, and partly a matter of trial and error.

GRAPHICS VERSIONS OF WRITE AND WRITELN

Another trick that we introduced in Listing 15.3 was to create **GWrite** and **GWriteln**, which are graphics-mode versions of WRITE and WRITELN. **OutText** and **OutTextXY** are fine as far as they go, but these

Table 15.6: Text Justification Constants

CONSTANT	VALUE
Horizontal justification	
LeftText CenterText RightText	0 (text appears to right of cursor) 1 (text centered on cursor location) 2 (text appears to left of cursor)
Vertical justification	
BottomText CenterText TopText	0 (text appears above cursor location) 1 (text centered on cursor location) 2 (text appears below cursor location)

routines give us a more familiar and flexible way to display text on the screen. Both routines take three parameters: two integers for the x and y coordinates at which the text is to be displayed, and the text string itself.

GWriteln displays text at the specified cursor location (using the current settings for font, size, and justification). It is designed to work only with horizontal text. After the text has been displayed, **GWriteln** moves the cursor down by a "line" and moves it back to the left margin, just the same as WRITELN does in text mode. **Lmargin** itself is a constant x-coordinate value of 10, which is just a little over from the far-left edge of the screen.

GWrite does the same thing as **OutText**, except that it allows you to specify the cursor location at which the text should be displayed. In fact, the main reason to create **GWrite** was to have a parallel graphics-mode routine for WRITE in the same way as we have one for WRITELN.

GETTING USER INPUT

Because we probably will use the routines from Listing 15.3 in the future, we should add them to the MyUtils unit that we created in Chapter 10. Add the new routines to the MyUtils unit so that the unit now contains everything shown in Listing 15.4. Then open the Compile menu, and change the Destination to "Disk." Compile the unit, change the Compile Destination back to "Memory," and make sure that the new MyUtils unit is in a directory where Turbo Pascal can find it (one of the directories listed for units in the Options/Directories dialog box).

Here are the new graphics routines in the MyUtils unit:

- GFilesLoc, which locates the graphics files needed for the other graphics routines.

- HomeCursor, which repositions the graphics cursor at the top left corner of the screen.

- GWrite, which displays text at a specified position on the screen.

- GWriteln, which displays text at a specified position on the screen, and then moves the cursor down one line and back to the left edge of the screen.

```
Listing 15.4:


Unit MyUtils;   { Listing 15.4: utility routines, including graphics. }


INTERFACE
{ =================== PUBLIC section of unit =================== }

USES CRT, GRAPH;

TYPE
  GoodChars = set of char;    { used with the GetGoodChar procedure }

CONST
  YNchars    : GoodChars = ['Y', 'y', 'N', 'n'];

  backspace  = #8;
  enter      = #13;
  space      = #32;

  x          : INTEGER = 10;
  y          : INTEGER = 10;
  lmargin    = 10;


TYPE
  string80 = STRING[80];


PROCEDURE Pause;    { accepts any key }

PROCEDURE GetGoodChar(GoodOnes:GoodChars; var InChar:char);

PROCEDURE GetGoodInt(MinNum, MaxNum: integer; var InNum:integer);

PROCEDURE GFilesLoc(VAR Gdriver,GMode:INTEGER;GPath:STRING);

PROCEDURE HomeCursor(VAR x, y: INTEGER);

PROCEDURE GWrite(VAR X, Y : INTEGER; gtext : STRING);
  { corresponds to WRITE }

PROCEDURE GWriteln(VAR X, Y : INTEGER; gtext : STRING);
  { corresponds to WRITELN }

PROCEDURE Gpause;

PROCEDURE GpauseXY(VAR x, y : INTEGER);

PROCEDURE GRead(VAR x, y : INTEGER; VAR gtext: STRING);

IMPLEMENTATION

{ =================== PRIVATE section of unit =================== }

VAR
  Gdriver,
  Gmode,
  maxX,
  maxY : INTEGER;

  Gtext: STRING;
```

Listing 15.4: Unit MyUtils; utility routines, including graphics.

```
PROCEDURE Pause; { Pauses the program until user presses a key. }
  VAR
    Proceed : char;
  BEGIN
    Writeln;
    Write(' Press any key to continue ... ');
    Proceed := readkey;
    Writeln; Writeln
  END;


PROCEDURE GetGoodChar(GoodOnes:GoodChars; var InChar:char);

  {An error-trapping substitute for "readln" to get character
  input from the keyboard. This procedure takes two parameters:
  a set of "acceptable" characters for input, and a variable
  parameter that is the actual character input.  If the input
  character is not in the set of acceptable characters, this
  procedure returns to the original screen position and waits
  for the user to enter an acceptable character.}

  VAR
    markX, markY  : byte;
  BEGIN
    repeat
      BEGIN
        markX := whereX;
        markY := whereY;
        Readln(InChar);
        if not (InChar in GoodOnes) then
          BEGIN
            gotoXY(markX, markY);
            ClrEOL
          END
      END
    until InChar in GoodOnes
  END;


PROCEDURE GetGoodInt(MinNum, MaxNum: integer;  var InNum: integer);

  {An error-trapping substitute for "readln" to get integer
  input from the keyboard. This procedure takes two parameters:
  a set of "acceptable" integers for input, and a variable
  parameter that is the actual integer input.  If the input
  integer is not in the set of acceptable integers, this
  procedure returns to the original screen position and waits
  for the user to enter an acceptable integer.}

  VAR
    markX, markY  : byte;
    LoopControl   : integer;

  BEGIN
    repeat
      BEGIN
        markX := whereX;
        markY := whereY;

        {$I-}
        Readln(InNum);
        {$I+}
        LoopControl := ioresult;
```

Listing 15.4: Unit MyUtils; utility routines, including graphics. (cont.)

```
           if (LoopControl <> 0) then
              BEGIN
                gotoXY(markX, markY);
                ClrEOL
              END;

           if (inNum < MinNum) or (inNum > MaxNum) then
              BEGIN
                gotoXY(markX, markY);
                ClrEOL
              END
        END
   until (LoopControl = 0) and (InNum >= MinNum) and (InNum <= MaxNum)
END;

PROCEDURE GFilesLoc(VAR Gdriver,Gmode:INTEGER;GPath:STRING);
                {Procedure to Locate the Path of BGI Files}

   VAR
     gerror: INTEGER;

   BEGIN (* Procedure GFilesLoc *)
    CLRSCR;
    REPEAT
     Gdriver := detect;
     INITGRAPH(Gdriver, Gmode, GPath);
     gerror := GRAPHRESULT;
     IF gerror <> grOK
         THEN BEGIN (* Error Found *)
                  WRITELN(' Graphics error: ', GraphErrorMsg(gerror));
                  IF gerror = GrFileNotFound
                     THEN BEGIN  (* Prompt *)
                              WRITELN(' Cannot find graphics driver. Please');
                              WRITE(' enter directory path for the driver: ');
                              READLN(GPath);
                              WRITELN
                              END     (* Prompt *)
                     ELSE HALT(1)
                  END  (* Error Found *)
     UNTIL gerror = grOK;
   END;  (* Procedure GFilesLoc *)

PROCEDURE HomeCursor(VAR x, y: INTEGER);
   BEGIN
   x := 10;
   y := 10
   END;


PROCEDURE GWrite(VAR X, Y : INTEGER; gtext : STRING);
   { corresponds to WRITE }
   BEGIN
   OutTextXY(X,Y,gtext);
   x := x + textwidth(gtext)
   END;

PROCEDURE GWriteln(VAR X, Y : INTEGER; gtext : STRING);
   { corresponds to WRITELN }
   BEGIN
   OutTextXY(x, y, gtext);
   y := y + TextHeight('M');
   x := lmargin;
   END;
```

Listing 15.4: Unit MyUtils; utility routines, including graphics. (cont.)

```
PROCEDURE Gpause;
  VAR
    ch : CHAR;
  BEGIN
    SetTextJustify(LeftText, TopText);
    GWriteln(x, y, '');
    Gwriteln(x,y, 'Press any key ...');
    REPEAT UNTIL keypressed;
    ch := READKEY;
    GWriteln(x,y, '');
  END;

PROCEDURE GpauseXY(VAR x, y : INTEGER);
  VAR
    ch : CHAR;
  BEGIN
    SetTextStyle(TriplexFont, HorizDir, 2);
    SetTextJustify(LeftText, TopText);
    GWriteln(x, y, '');
    Gwriteln(x,y, 'Press any key ...');
    REPEAT UNTIL keypressed;
    ch := READKEY;
    GWriteln(x,y, '');
  END;

PROCEDURE GRead(VAR x, y : INTEGER; VAR gtext: STRING);
  VAR
    ch : CHAR;
  BEGIN
    gtext := '';
    REPEAT
    ch := READKEY;
    IF ch <> enter
       THEN BEGIN
       GWrite(x, y, ch);
       gtext := gtext + ch
       end
    UNTIL ch = Enter
  END;


END.    { of the "MyUtils" unit }
```

Listing 15.4: Unit MyUtils; utility routines, including graphics. (cont.)

- Gpause, which pauses the program and displays a "Press any key" message at the current cursor position.

- GpauseXY, which pauses the program and displays a "Press any key" message at a cursor position that you specify.

- GRead, a graphics equivalent of the READ procedure, which gets keyboard input from the user, displays it on the screen, and loads it into a string variable.

The new version of MyUtils also adds some constant names for keys, as well as predefined x, y, and left-margin coordinates. But the routine we have not seen in action is **GRead**, which works in graphics mode almost the same as READ works in text mode.

GRead takes three parameters: two integers that represent the x and y coordinates where text input will be echoed to the screen, and a text string variable into which the input gets loaded. We first initialize the text variable to make sure that it is empty. Then we set up a REPEAT loop that continues until the user presses the Enter key.

Inside the REPEAT loop, each input character is loaded into a local variable *ch*. If the input character is not the Enter key, then it is echoed to the screen and added to the current contents of the text variable. Note, by the way, that we can use the plus sign ("+") with text strings in almost the same way that we can use it with numbers. We keep adding new input characters to the text string until an input character is the Enter key, at which point we drop out of the loop and the routine terminates. Listing 15.5 provides a demonstration of **GRead**, the on-screen results of which are shown in Figure 15.4.

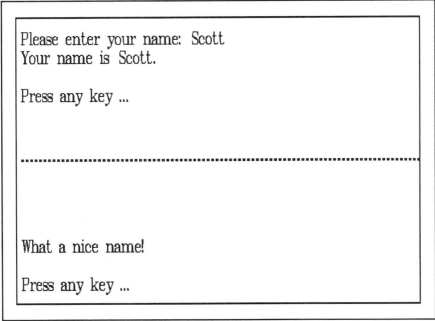

Figure 15.4: Screen result from a run of Listing 15.5.

```pascal
PROGRAM Listing15_5;


   { Demonstrates how to get keyboard input from the
     user. The fundamental routine used is GRead from
     the MyUtils unit; this new routine is defined in
     Listing 15.4. }

USES CRT, GRAPH, MyUtils;

VAR
  gd,
  gm,
  maxX,
  maxY : INTEGER;
  GPath,
  name : STRING;

PROCEDURE InitSettings(VAR maxX, maxY : INTEGER);
  VAR
    ViewPort : ViewPortType;
  BEGIN
    maxX := GetMaxX;
    maxY := GetMaxY;
    SetTextStyle(TriplexFont, HorizDir, 3);
    SetLineStyle(SolidLn, 0, ThickWidth);
    GetViewSettings(ViewPort);
    WITH ViewPort DO
      Rectangle(0,0, maxX, maxY)
  END;


PROCEDURE GetUserInput(VAR x, y : INTEGER);
  VAR
    username : STRING;
  BEGIN
    GWrite(x, y, 'Please enter your name: ');
    GRead(x,y, username);
    GWriteln(x,y, '');
    GWrite(x,y, 'Your name is ');
    GWrite(x, y, username);
    GWriteln(x, y, '.');
    Gpause
  END;

PROCEDURE Congrats(VAR x, y : INTEGER);
  BEGIN
    x := lmargin;
    y := maxY - maxY div 4;
    GWriteln(x,y, 'What a nice name!');
    gpause
  END;
  BEGIN
    gd := DETECT;
    GFilesLoc(gd,gm,GPath);
    InitSettings(maxX, maxY);
    Homecursor(x,y);
    GetUserInput(x,y);
    SetLineStyle(DashedLn, 0, ThickWidth);
    Line(lmargin, maxY div 2, maxX, maxY div 2);
    delay(1000);
    Congrats(x,y);
    CLOSEGRAPH
  END.
```

Listing 15.5: Using the GRead routine to get user input.

Listing 15.5 has another notable feature. It uses a variable called *View-Port* to hold the dimensions of the screen, and then calls Turbo Pascal's **Rectangle** graphics routine to draw a box around the screen window. **ViewPort** is defined as being of the data type **ViewPortType**, which is a predefined record type in the graph unit that holds the screen dimensions in its fields. A call to **GetViewSettings** loads the current screen dimensions into the *ViewPort* variable, which is then used to draw the rectangle.

DRAWING FIGURES

Creating images is where graphics programming really shows its power. Turbo Pascal has 19 different drawing routines, most of which we will not have the space to examine in this book. However, let's look at a few of the most important. Four are demonstrated in Listing 15.6, and the result of running Listing 15.6 is shown in Figure 15.5.

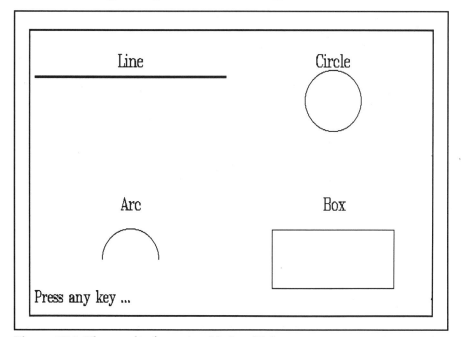

Figure 15.5: The result of running Listing 15.6.

```
PROGRAM Listing15_6;


    { Demonstrates four Turbo Pascal drawing routines. Also
      shows how to position multiple graphics items on the
      screen. }


USES CRT, GRAPH, MyUtils;

CONST
  gd : INTEGER = detect;

VAR
  gm,
  maxX,
  maxY : INTEGER;
  GFile: STRING;

PROCEDURE InitSettings(VAR maxX, maxY : INTEGER);
  VAR
    ViewPort : ViewPortType;
  BEGIN
    maxX := GetMaxX;
    maxY := GetMaxY;
    SetTextStyle(TriplexFont, HorizDir, 3);
    SetTextJustify(CenterText, CenterText);
    SetLineStyle(SolidLn, 0, ThickWidth);
    GetViewSettings(ViewPort);
    WITH ViewPort DO
      Rectangle(0,0, maxX, maxY)
  END;


PROCEDURE DrawLine(maxX, maxY : INTEGER);
  VAR
    rightborder,
    bottomborder : INTEGER;
  BEGIN
    rightborder := maxX div 2;
    bottomborder := maxY div 2;
    OutTextXY(rightborder div 2, bottomborder div 5, 'Line');
    Line(x, bottomborder div 3, rightborder - 10, bottomborder div 3);
  END;


PROCEDURE DrawCircle(maxX, maxY : INTEGER);
  VAR
    leftborder,
    bottomborder : INTEGER;
    radius       : WORD;
  BEGIN
    leftborder := maxX div 2;
    bottomborder := maxY div 2;
    SetLineStyle(SolidLn, 0, NormWidth);
    OutTextXY(leftborder + maxX div 4, bottomborder div 5, 'Circle');
    Circle(leftborder + maxX div 4, bottomborder div 2, 50)
  END;

PROCEDURE DrawArc(maxX, maxY : INTEGER);
  VAR
    topborder,
    rightborder,
    x, y         : INTEGER;
```

Listing 15.6: Some Turbo Pascal drawing routines.

```
          radius,
          startangle,
          endangle    : WORD;
      BEGIN
          topborder := maxY div 2;
          rightborder := maxX div 2;
          OutTextXY(maxX div 4, topborder + maxY div 10, 'Arc');
          Arc(maxX div 4, maxY - maxY div 5, 0, 180, 50)
      END;

    PROCEDURE DrawBox(maxX, maxY : INTEGER);
      VAR
        leftborder,
        topborder,
        x1, y1, x2, y2 : INTEGER;
      BEGIN
        leftborder := maxX div 2;
        topborder := maxY div 2;
        OutTextXY(maxX - maxX div 4, topborder + maxY div 10, 'Box');
        x1 := leftborder + maxX div 10;
        y1 := topborder + maxY div 5;
        x2 := maxX - maxX div 10;
        y2 := maxY - maxY div 10;
        Rectangle(x1, y1, x2, y2)
      END;


    BEGIN
      GFilesLoc(gd,gm,GFile);
      InitSettings(maxX, maxY);
      DrawLine(maxX,maxY);
      DrawCircle(maxX,maxY);
      DrawArc(maxX,maxY);
      DrawBox(maxX,maxY);
      x := lmargin;
      y := maxY - maxY div 6;
      GpauseXY(x, y);
      CLOSEGRAPH
    END.
```

Listing 15.6: Some Turbo Pascal drawing routines. (cont.)

In order, Listing 15.6 draws and labels a line, a circle, an arc, and a rectangle. Each is positioned in its own quadrant of the screen, an exercise which requires the programmer to do some more fiddling around with relative screen coordinates.

The **DrawLine** routine positions a line and its label in the top-left quadrant of the screen. To position it correctly, we use integer variables to represent the right and bottom borders of the quadrant. Turbo Pascal's **Line** routine itself takes four parameters: the x and y coordinates where the line begins, and the x and y coordinates where the line ends. The style and thickness of the line itself is set in the **InitSettings** routine with a call to Turbo Pascal's **SetLineStyle** routine.

The **DrawCircle** routine positions the circle and its label in the top-right quadrant of the screen, using the same scheme as in **DrawLine** for setting up borders and positioning the items. The Turbo Pascal **Circle** routine itself takes three parameters: the x and y coordinates of the center of the circle, and a word-type number which is the radius of the circle. As usual, x and y are relative coordinates, and the circle is drawn with the current line style and thickness.

In the **DrawArc** routine, Turbo Pascal's **Arc** routine takes five parameters: two integers for the x and y coordinates of the center of the arc, two word-type numbers for the starting and ending angles of the arc, and one word-type number for the radius of the arc. The starting angle of 0 indicates that the arc starts at the three o'clock position and then moves counter-clockwise around its center point for 180 degrees, ending up at the nine o'clock position. Arcs are always drawn in this fashion: counter-clockwise with 0 degrees at three o'clock, 90 degrees at 12 o'clock, 180 degrees at nine o'clock, and 270 degrees at six o'clock. (Of course, you can draw an arc with any starting and ending angle you choose, such as a starting angle of 77 and an ending angle of 121.)

In the **DrawBox** routine, we set up four relative coordinates as integer variables for the four corners of the box drawn by Turbo Pascal's **Rectangle** routine. The four statements assigning values to x1, y1, x2, and y2 are not actually necessary: they are included simply to make the **Rectangle** statement easier to read.

SUMMARY

Turbo Pascal provides tremendously versatile graphics capabilities for a general-purpose programming language. With graphics programming, you can create and use fancy type fonts, draw figures, and create business graphics. With graphics-oriented applications becoming increasingly important, graphics programming is a vital skill to have.

Unfortunately, graphics programming is the least portable of all Turbo Pascal features, but the skills and techniques used to write graphics programs are largely the same from one programming language to another.

REVIEW EXERCISES

1. Explain the differences between text mode and graphics mode.

2. Explain the most important advantages and disadvantages of programming in graphics mode.

3. Explain what a video driver is. List the video drivers provided by Turbo Pascal and explain which video driver is designed to work with which video adapter.

4. Explain what is done by **Initgraph** and show how to use it. Explain each of its three parameters.

5. Apart from the specific operations you might do in graphics mode, explain the two essential steps your program must take in order to work in graphics mode.

6. Write a simple program to display text on a graphics screen using **OutText** and **OutTextXY**.

7. Explain the purpose of the **GraphResult** function. List the values it can return and explain the meaning of each value.

8. Explain how to position items on a graphics screen so that your program will work correctly on any monitor and video adapter supported by Turbo Pascal.

9. With the program from Exercise 6, use the **SetTextStyle** routine to display all the different fonts provided with Turbo Pascal. Experiment with the text direction and magnification factors to see the result. Clear the screen after displaying each font.

10. With the program from Exercise 6, use the **SetTextJustify** routine to change the horizontal and vertical positioning of the text. Explain why "left justification," "top justification," etc. do not have their usual meanings when used in graphics mode.

11. Create a simple program that draws a circle inside of a square and then labels the drawing "Circle Inside Square."

12. With the program from Exercise 11, draw a border around the screen display by using the **Rectangle** routine.

13. Create a simple program that displays a line on the left side of the screen and an arc on the right side of the screen. Label each drawing.

14. (Challenging) The routine **GRead** will not recognize a backspace. Modify it to correct this deficiency.

16

Accessing DOS Services

Of two things one can hardly doubt.
One is that the rational temper—that
is, clearness of vision, justice in thought
and act, and the peace which is the har-
vest of the quiet eye—is an end that
men desire too waveringly. The other is
that to achieve it would transform life.

– Brand Blanshard, *Reason and Goodness*

Any program in any high-level programming language uses services that are provided by the computer's operating system. For example, when a program needs to open a file or display a text string on the screen, it normally sends a request to the operating system to perform the service. The operating system, in turn, sends the appropriate instructions through the computer's BIOS (Basic Input-Output System) to the disk drive or monitor, and the file is opened or the text is displayed on the screen.

When a program uses operating system services in this way, you as the programmer do not need to know any of the details of how the services are provided. This approach, however, does not allow you to work directly with the computer's operating system, BIOS, and hardware. If you want to perform an operation for which there is no predefined routine in the programming language, then you simply cannot do it.

Turbo Pascal 6 provides four main methods by which you can directly use services provided by the computer's operating system and BIOS. Because they are not part of standard Pascal, these methods are located in a separate unit called the DOS unit. Although they all provide access to DOS services, they vary considerably both in the amount of sophistication required to use them—and in the *danger* they present to the careless or inexperienced programmer. These four methods are:

1. Using the **MsDos** procedure to access DOS functions directly.

2. Using the **Intr** procedure to access BIOS services directly through software interrupts.

3. Using predefined DOS unit procedures and functions that access DOS and BIOS services.

4. Using the **Exec** procedure to suspend the current program and run an external program, including DOS itself.

We will look at three of these methods in this chapter. To understand how they work, however, you must first know something about the architecture of the PC's microprocessor, as well as how it works with the BIOS and operating system to provide services to application programs such as those you write in Turbo Pascal.

FUNDAMENTALS OF SYSTEM PROGRAMMING

Before you can understand how to use Turbo Pascal's DOS and BIOS routines (particularly the **MsDos** and **Intr** routines), you must have at least a minimum understanding of the architecture of the Intel 80x86 family of microprocessors, which are used in PCs. You must also understand hardware and software interrupts, know the functions provided by DOS and the PC's BIOS, and be able to figure out hexadecimal numbers when you see them.

PROCESSOR ARCHITECTURE

The central processing unit of a PC is normally a member of the Intel 80x86 family of microprocessors: an 8086, 8088, 80286, 80386, or 80486. The 8086, 8088, and 80286 chips are manufactured by many different chip makers, but the 80386 and 80486 are made only by Intel. PCs can also use 80x86-compatible chips such as the NEC V-20 (compatible with the Intel 8086) or chips that are compatible with the Intel 80386.

Although there are significant differences between these classes of microprocessors, they do have some characteristics in common. First, they all can perform the same basic operations performed by the 8086 chip, which was the first chip in the line. Second, each chip contains a variety of *registers* for on-chip storage of data that the processor needs to carry out its work. Each register can hold 16 bits of data, and each register has a different task to perform. The 8086 chip's registers are shown in Figure 16.1. Later members of the 80x86 family also have these registers.

General-Purpose Registers

The *general-purpose* registers AX, BX, CX, and DX are used for temporary storage of data that is being used in calculations. Most data, most of the time, is stored in the computer's random-access memory. For this data to be used in calculations, however, it must be transferred to the microprocessor over a communication channel called the *data bus*. While it is "at" the microprocessor being used in a calculation, each small piece of data is held in one of these registers.

The reason it is important for you to know about these registers is that Turbo Pascal's **MsDos** and **Intr** routines require you to load data into specific registers. If you know what the registers are, you will have a better understanding of what you are doing when you use these routines.

The AX, BX, CX, and DX registers have another important feature: each can be treated either as a single 16-bit (word) register or as two 8-bit (byte) registers. Thus, they can be used to store either a single 16-bit piece of data or two separate 8-bit pieces of data. For example, you can load a single 16-bit piece of data into the AX register, or you can load separate 8-bit pieces of data into the AL (AX-low) and AH (AX-high) registers.

You can store any kind of data in these registers, but in general, they are used in the following ways:

- *The AX register* is used to store operands and results in arithmetic operations, such as addition and subtraction. It also can be used to hold the number of a DOS routine from Turbo Pascal's **MsDos** procedure.

- *The BX (base) register* holds memory addresses and is used to find addresses in memory in relation to a *base* address. It also can be used in arithmetic operations.

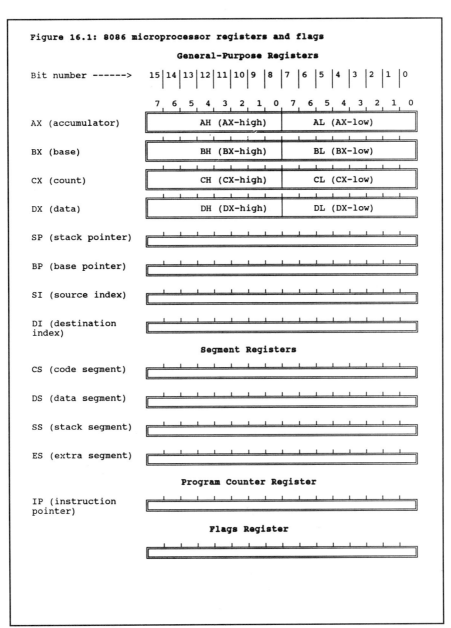

Figure 16.1: Registers in the 8086 microprocessor.

- *The CX (count) register* is used as a counter for loop control and other repeated program operations. It also can be used in arithmetic operations.

- *The DX (data) register* is used to store some of the results of multiplication and division operations. It also can be used for general data storage and to hold the addresses of I/O devices.

Segment Registers

In order to handle a full megabyte of random-access memory, the 8086 divides memory into 64K segments. To find a location in memory, it combines the starting address of the appropriate segment with an *offset* which indicates a location within that segment. This is very similar to dividing street addresses into "blocks": e.g., you can have an offset address of "22" in the 100 block of Maple Street (122 Maple Street), in the 200 block of Maple Street (222 Maple Street), and so forth.

In the same way, the 8086 combines a segment address (the "block") with an offset address (the house number) to identify a specific address in the PC's memory. The segment registers are used to hold the starting addresses of specific segments used by your program:

- *The CS (code segment) register* contains the starting address of the code segment, which contains the instructions from the program that is currently being run. This is used with the instruction pointer from the IP register to find the next program instruction that should be carried out.

- *The DS (data segment) register* contains the starting address of the data segment, which contains data being used by the current program.

- *The SS (stack segment) register* contains the starting address of the stack segment, which holds return addresses for subroutines, variables passed to subroutines, and other data that needs to be stored temporarily during a program run.

- *The ES (extra segment) register*, as its name implies, contains the starting address of an *extra segment*, which is used for miscellaneous data storage during a program run.

Offset Registers

Just as the segment registers contain starting addresses of specific segments in memory, the offset registers contain the "street addresses" of locations within those segments. The offset registers are as follows:

- *The SP (stack pointer) register* contains the address of the current top of the stack. When a subroutine is called, its return address and local variables are placed on the stack. If it calls another routine before terminating, then the return address and local variables of the second routine are placed on the stack *on top of* the corresponding information for the first routine. The top of the stack is the location in memory where the next stack data will be placed. As subroutines finish their work and terminate, their data is removed from the stack in reverse order—that is, the last routine called has its data removed first, then the second to last routine, and so forth.

- *The BP (base pointer) register* is also used for holding addresses of locations in the stack segment.

- *The SI (source index) and DI (destination index) registers* are used to hold miscellaneous addresses in memory. They also are used for string instructions (move and compare) that allow high-speed manipulation of the data in entire blocks of memory.

Instruction and Flags Registers

The other two registers are the *IP (instruction pointer) register* and the *Flags register*. The IP register contains the memory address of the next program instruction to be carried out; the instruction is, of course, somewhere in the code segment. The Flags register has 16 bits available to indicate the status of various processor operations and to handle control functions.

Turbo Pascal's **MsDos** and **Intr** routines allow you to send data to each of these registers through a predefined *registers* data type in the DOS unit. We will look at how to use this data type when we discuss the **MsDos** and **Intr** routines, below.

THE IDEA OF INTERRUPTS

The idea of an interrupt is a familiar one. Suppose that you are performing some task, such as shaving your cat, and the phone rings. As a result, you put the cat down and start talking on the telephone. The telephone ring was an *interrupt:* a signal that you should stop what you are doing temporarily and do something else for a while. When the second task—in this case, talking on the telephone—is finished, then you go back to what you were doing when you were interrupted.

A PC interrupt is almost exactly the same: it signals to the microprocessor that it should stop what it is doing temporarily and do something else that is more urgent. The 80x86 family of microprocessors allows both *hardware* and *software* interrupts. When it receives an interrupt, the processor saves the contents of its registers, handles the task requested by the interrupt, puts the saved information back in the registers, and returns to what it was doing when it received the interrupt.

The 8086 supports 256 different interrupts, numbered 0 to 255 (or 00H to FFH in hexadecimal numbering, which we'll discuss below). Each interrupt requests that the processor carry out a different routine, and the 32-bit (segment plus offset) memory addresses of these routines are located in the PC's *interrupt vector table,* which occupies the first 1K (1,024 bytes) of RAM. Turbo Pascal's DOS unit provides a procedure, **SetIntVec**, which allows you to tamper with the contents of the interrupt vector table, but it is extremely foolish to do so unless you are highly experienced and very careful.

The most common use of interrupts in Turbo Pascal is to call DOS functions, such as those to get disk information or to terminate a program. However, Turbo Pascal also provides high-level routines for many of these functions, so direct use of interrupts is often unnecessary. For a list of specific DOS interrupts see your DOS manual.

HEXADECIMAL NOTATION

If you look at your DOS manual, you will probably notice that the numbers of DOS interrupts are given in both "Hex" and standard decimal notation. That's because if you want to do low-level programming in Turbo Pascal (or any other language), you must have at least some familiarity with hexadecimal arithmetic.

If you went to school in the last 20 years, since the time when the "new math" substituted number theory for such arcane and useless skills as addition and subtraction, you already know the basic ideas behind hexadecimal (even if you can't add or subtract). Our everyday arithmetic uses base 10, but hexadecimal uses base 16. Thus, the first 16 numbers in each base are as shown in Table 16.1.

Table 16.1: Decimal, Hexadecimal, and Binary Numbers

DECIMAL	HEXADECIMAL	BINARY
0	0	0000
1	1	0001
2	2	0010
3	3	0011
4	4	0100
5	5	0101
6	6	0110
7	7	0111
8	8	1000
9	9	1001
10	A	1010
11	B	1011
12	C	1100
13	D	1101
14	E	1110
15	F	1111

Table 16.1 also shows the binary numbers that correspond to the first 16 decimal and hexadecimal numbers. This is the primary reason for the use of hexadecimal numbers. Recall that the main principle of the PC's operation is the on/off switch, and binary numbers can be used to represent sequences of on/off switches.

There are 16 possible combinations of four bits, and one hex digit can be used to stand for each of the combinations, thereby providing a convenient shorthand for the corresponding binary numbers. Thus, a 32-bit segment:offset address in memory can be written in hex in only eight digits, e.g., as 0CE8:0DBA instead of 0000110011101000:0000110110111010.

The most important aspect of this is simply to be *aware* of hex notation. The numbers of DOS functions and 8086 interrupts are often given in hex notation, and if you mistake it for decimal notation, you will probably call the wrong function or use the wrong interrupt. Hex numbers are *usually*, but not always, preceded by a dollar sign or followed by an uppercase "H". Thus, *$23* and *23H* both denote hex 23. Even if a number is not specially marked with a dollar sign or an "H", you should stay alert for the possibility that it is in hex instead of decimal notation.

To indicate that a number in a Turbo Pascal program is in hex rather than decimal, you use the dollar sign, e.g., $23.

HOW TO USE
THE MSDOS PROCEDURE

Turbo Pascal's **MsDos** procedure, defined in the DOS unit, provides one way to make a direct call to functions provided by the MS-DOS operating system. This is somewhat trickier than using those functions indirectly through ordinary Pascal commands, but it gives you more flexibility in using them.

To use the **MsDos** procedure, you need to know three things: first, about processor registers, which we looked at earlier in this chapter; second, about the various functions that DOS offers, which we will look at in the next section; and third, about the DOS unit's predefined *registers* data type.

The registers data type is a record type that mirrors the structure of the 8086 registers. It is defined as follows:

```
registers = RECORD
    CASE INTEGER OF
    0 :(AX,BX,CX,DX,BP,SI,DI,DS,ES, Flags: WORD);
    1 :(AL, AH, BL, BH, CL, CH, DL, DH: BYTE)
    END;
```

As you can see, the registers type is a variant record type that allows you to load data either 16 bits or eight bits at a time. Generally, you do not have to worry about this; when you load a value into a field, e.g., AH, Turbo Pascal picks the appropriate variant of the record type for you. If you are using a version of Turbo Pascal prior to version 4, of course, then you have no DOS unit and must declare the registers data type in your program.

To call a DOS function with the **MsDos** procedure, you must first create a registers-type variable in your program. Then, you load the number of the desired DOS function into field AH of your register variable and load any other data needed by the function into the appropriate fields. You then call the **MsDos** routine, which loads the information from the register variable into the actual processor registers and then executes DOS interrupt **$21**, which is the interrupt to carry out a DOS service. The service is carried out and, when appropriate, the results are loaded back into the fields of the register variable for use by your Turbo Pascal program. This process is illustrated in Listing 16.1.

The first thing done by Listing 16.1, of course, is to name the DOS unit in a USES statement. Then, it creates a typed string constant to be displayed on the screen and declares a variable of the registers data type. After clearing the screen, it loads DOS function number 9 (which, in this case, is the same number in hex or decimal) into field AH of the *regs* variable. DOS function 9 is the function to send a text string to the default output device—in this case, to the screen.

Before the processor can display the string, of course, it must know where to find it. Therefore, the next step is to load the string's segment address into field DS (corresponding to the data segment register) and its

```
PROGRAM Listing16_1;


  { Demonstrates the use of the Turbo Pascal MsDos procedure. In
    this program, we use the DOS "string output" function to display
    a text string on the screen. The function number is loaded into
    field AH (AX-high) of the "regs" variable, while the segment
    address of the text string is loaded into field DS of regs and
    the offset address is loaded into field DX of regs. The MsDos
    routine then calls the DOS function, loading the parameters from
    the "regs" variable into the actual processor registers. }

USES CRT, DOS, MyUtils;

CONST
  message : STRING = ' Hello, Pascal programmer!$';

VAR
  regs : Registers;

BEGIN
  CLRSCR;
  regs.ah := $9;      { Number for DOS string output function }
  regs.ds := Seg(message);
  regs.dx := Ofs(message[1]);
  MsDos(regs);
  pause
END.
```

Listing 16.1: Calling a DOS function with the MsDos procedure.

offset address into field DX (corresponding to the general purpose data
register). Calling the **MsDos** routine with the *regs* variable copies the data from
regs to the actual processor registers and carries out DOS function 9, displaying
the string on the screen. For information about specific DOS functions, you
should consult your DOS manual, or the *ABC's of DOS 4,* by Alan R. Miller
(1989 SYBEX).

THE TURBO PASCAL
INTR PROCEDURE

Turbo Pascal's **Intr** procedure gives you more flexibility than **MsDos**,
which is used simply to call DOS functions. **Intr** gives you the ability to
generate a software interrupt for a variety of purposes, *including* to call a

DOS function. Because of the Intr procedure's specialized nature, however, we will not discuss it any further in this book.

The program begins by loading the number of the DOS function (hex 30) into the AH field of the register-type variable *regs*. Then, the Turbo Pascal **Intr** procedure is called with **$21** (as the interrupt number) and the *regs* variable. This transfers the function number from the AH field of the *regs* variable to the AH register in the PC's processor, then executes interrupt **$21**. This is the pattern for calling DOS functions in any language, whether it is Turbo Pascal or assembly language: first load the function number into register AH, then call interrupt **$21**.

USING TURBO PASCAL DOS ROUTINES

Although it gives you the flexibility to call DOS functions when needed, Turbo Pascal also provides predefined DOS routines that often make it unnecessary to use **MsDos** or **Intr** to access DOS functions and software interrupts directly. These routines, which are described in your Turbo Pascal manuals, do the low-level work for you so that you can concentrate on what your program is trying to accomplish.

Listing 16.2 demonstrates the use of several of these predefined routines to display a file directory on the PC screen.

The first task performed by the program is to initialize the *dirsize* and *numfiles* variables: *dirsize* indicates the total number of bytes in the files displayed, while *numfiles* indicates the number of files displayed. Note, however, that **dirsize** will be smaller than the actual amount of disk space occupied by the files because each file, even a file with nothing in it, must take up a minimum amount of disk space.

The **GetFileSpec** routine then prompts the user to enter a specification for the file names to be listed in the directory; this follows the standard DOS rules for wildcards, e.g., "*.*" indicates that all files should be displayed, "*.pas" indicates that only files whose names end in ".pas" should be displayed, and so forth.

```
PROGRAM Listing16_2;


   { Demonstrates the use of Turbo Pascal's predefined
     DOS routines. In this program, we use the FindFirst
     and FindNext routines to display a file directory.
     We also use the GetFAttr procedure to prevent directory
     names from being included in our on-screen file list. }

USES CRT, DOS, MyUtils;

TYPE
  string5  = STRING[5];
  string12 = STRING[12];

VAR
  fileword  : string5;
  filespec,
  filename  : string12;
  dirsize   : LONGINT;
  numfiles  : INTEGER;

PROCEDURE init(VAR dirsize : LONGINT; VAR numfiles: INTEGER);
  BEGIN
  dirsize := 0;
  numfiles := 0
  END;

FUNCTION DrNo(filesfound : searchrec) : BOOLEAN;
  VAR
    f    : FILE;
    attr : WORD;
  BEGIN
    ASSIGN(f, filesfound.name);
    GetFAttr(f, attr);
    IF (attr AND Directory) = 0
       THEN DrNo := TRUE
       ELSE DrNo := FALSE
  END;

PROCEDURE GetFileSpec(VAR filespec : string12);
  BEGIN
    CLRSCR;
    WRITELN;
    WRITELN('   Please enter a file specification for');
    WRITELN('   file names to display. For example:');
    WRITELN('   ------------------------------------');
    WRITELN('   *.*  = display all files');
    WRITELN('   *.pas = display all pascal source code files');
    WRITELN('   *.doc = display all Microsoft Word documents');
    WRITELN;
    WRITE('   Enter a file specification: ');
    READLN(filespec);
    IF filespec = '' THEN filespec := '*.*';
  END;

PROCEDURE DisplayDir(filespec : string12);
  VAR
    filesfound : searchrec;
  BEGIN
    findfirst(filespec, anyfile, filesfound);
    CLRSCR;
    WRITELN;
    WRITELN(' Files found in the current directory: ');
```

Listing 16.2: Using predefined DOS routines to display a file directory.

```
        WRITELN(' -----------------------------------');
        WRITELN;
        WHILE DosError = 0 DO
           WITH filesfound DO
              BEGIN
              IF DrNo(filesfound)
                 THEN BEGIN
                      WRITELN(' ',name:12, ' .......... ', size, ' bytes');
                      dirsize := dirsize + size;
                      numfiles := numfiles + 1
                      END;
              findnext(filesfound)
              END;
        IF numfiles = 1
           THEN fileword := 'file' ELSE fileword := 'files';
        WRITELN;
        IF numfiles = 0
           THEN WRITELN(' No matching files were found.')
           ELSE BEGIN
                WRITE(' ',dirsize, ' bytes in ', numfiles);
                WRITELN(' ', fileword, '.');
                END
     END;


BEGIN
  init(dirsize, numfiles);
  getfilespec(filespec);
  DisplayDir(filespec);
  pause
END.
```

Listing 16.2: Using predefined DOS routines to display a file directory. (cont.)

The **DisplayDir** routine then uses Turbo Pascal's predefined **FindFirst** procedure to find the first file matching the user's specifications. Just in case the user has asked to see all of the files, it uses the predefined **GetFAttr** procedure in the **DrNo** routine to filter out names of directories; this is done to make the file list easier to read. **DisplayDir** then uses the predefined **FindNext** procedure to find the next matching file, and continues the process until all the matching files in the directory have been found and their names displayed on the screen.

FindFirst takes three parameters: the file specification that was entered by the user in **GetFileSpec**, an attribute that tells it which files to include in the search, and a variable of type **SearchRec**. **FindNext**, which is always used after **FindFirst**, takes the variable as its only parameter. In this case, we have specified **AnyFile** as the attribute, which means that all files matching the specification will be included in the search.

FindFirst and **FindNext** use a predefined data type from the DOS unit called **SearchRec**, which is set up as follows:

```
SearchRec = RECORD

          Fill : ARRAY[1..21] OF BYTE;

          Attr : BYTE;

          Time : LONGINT;

          Size : LONGINT;

          Name : STRING[12]

          END;
```

Listing 16.2 also illustrates a trick that you can use to display varying text on the screen depending on the situation. In this case, the word "file" is used in the directory display if only a single matching file is found; but the plural "files" is used if there is more than one file found.

HOW TO USE
THE EXEC PROCEDURE

Exec is at once the most powerful and the easiest tool provided by the DOS unit. It allows you to suspend the current program temporarily, exit to DOS and run other programs (memory permitting), and then to return to your original program. The **Exec** procedure takes two parameters: the name and directory path of DOS's command interpreter COM-MAND.COM, and the name of the external program to be executed.

There's only one hitch in using **Exec**: you must have some extra memory available to run the outside programs. Normally, a Turbo Pascal program reserves all extra DOS memory up to 640K for the heap—that is, the place where it stores dynamic variables. This means that *no* extra memory is left over for running outside programs with **Exec**. To change this, you must use the **$M** compiler directive to reduce the amount of memory reserved for the heap; if your program does not use dynamic variables at all, you can reduce this to zero. The **$M** compiler directive takes three parameters: the amount of memory reserved for the stack, the minimum amount of memory reserved for the heap, and the maximum amount of memory reserved for the heap. Thus, for a 16K stack and no memory reserved for the heap, you would write the directive at the top of your program as {**$M 16384, 0,0**}.

You should also call the **SwapVectors** routine before and after calling **Exec** to safeguard the integrity of your interrupt vector table.

RUNNING EXTERNAL PROGRAMS

Listing 16.3 illustrates how to use **Exec** to run an outside program—in this case, an internal DOS command. An internal DOS command is an operating system command that is kept resident in memory, as opposed to external DOS commands such as **format**, which must be read from disk each time they are used.

```
PROGRAM Listing16_3;

  { Demonstrates the use of EXEC to suspend the current program
    and run a DOS command. }

USES CRT, DOS, MyUtils;

{ Insert compiler directive to specify the amount of memory
  reserved for the heap, thereby leaving some memory for the
  external program to run. In this case, the stack is set at
  16384 bytes (the default setting), while the minimum and
  maximum sizes of the heap are both set at 0. }
{$M 16384, 0, 0}


BEGIN
  CLRSCR;
  swapvectors;
  EXEC('c:\command.com', '/c dir *.pas');
  swapvectors;
  pause
END.
```

Listing 16.3: Running an external program with Exec.

The program first uses the **$M** compiler directive to limit the amount of heap memory, in this case, to zero. It then calls **SwapVectors** to protect the interrupt vector table and executes **Exec**. **Exec** itself takes the name and path of COMMAND.COM; here, it is in the root directory of the C: drive. It also takes the name of the outside program to run. Here, this outside program is the internal DOS command **dir**, so—because it is an internal DOS command—it must be preceded by **"/c"**. After running the **dir** command, the program returns the user to the calling Pascal program. **SwapVectors** is called again and the program terminates.

This is, of course, only a very simple example of what you can do with **Exec**. Next, let's look at an even more powerful use of **Exec**: this time to exit to a DOS shell that lets you run any program or programs (memory permitting), and then return to the calling Pascal program.

RUNNING A DOS SHELL

Running a DOS shell with **Exec** is even simpler than running a specific external program. Instead of specifying the name of the outside program when you call **Exec**, you specify an empty string, as shown in Listing 16.4. This takes you directly to the DOS prompt, where, subject to memory limitations, you can execute any program you wish.

As you can see, the program in Listing 16.4 sets up a menu option to exit to DOS. Because running a DOS shell is the purpose of the program, this is the only menu choice that is implemented. When the user returns from DOS, the program redisplays the menu.

SUMMARY

Although it is a high-level language, Turbo Pascal's DOS unit provides sophisticated capabilities to access processor registers and send low-level instructions directly to the PC's microprocessor. The main low-level tools for doing this are the **MsDos** and **Intr** procedures, which give direct access

```
PROGRAM Listing16_4;

   { Demonstrates the use of EXEC to suspend the current program
     and run a DOS shell. }

USES CRT, DOS, MyUtils;

{ Insert compiler directive to specify the amount of memory
  reserved for the heap, thereby leaving some memory for the
  external program to run. In this case, the stack is set at
  16384 bytes (the default setting), while the minimum and
  maximum sizes of the heap are both set at 0 because this
  program does not use dynamic variables. }
{$M 16384, 0, 0}

VAR
  choice : INTEGER;


PROCEDURE Menu(VAR choice: INTEGER); FORWARD;
{ Forward declaration of menu routine; needed because it
  may be called by the GoToDOS routine. }

{ ------------------------------- }
{ MAIN-LEVEL PROCEDURE DECLARATION }
{ ------------------------------- }
PROCEDURE AddRecords;
  BEGIN
  WRITELN;
  WRITELN(' The AddRecords routine has run.');
  pause
  END;


{ ------------------------------- }
{ MAIN-LEVEL PROCEDURE DECLARATION }
{ ------------------------------- }
PROCEDURE EditRecords;
  BEGIN
  WRITELN;
  WRITELN(' The EditRecords routine has run.');
  pause
  END;


{ ------------------------------- }
{ MAIN-LEVEL PROCEDURE DECLARATION }
{ ------------------------------- }
PROCEDURE FormLetters;
  BEGIN
  WRITELN;
  WRITELN(' The FormLetters routine has run.');
  pause
  END;


{ ------------------------------- }
{ MAIN-LEVEL PROCEDURE DECLARATION }
{ ------------------------------- }
PROCEDURE GoToDOS;
  BEGIN
  WRITELN;
  WRITELN(' Suspending current program and going to DOS.');
  WRITELN(' Type EXIT at the DOS prompt to return to this program.');
  pause;
  CLRSCR;
```

Listing 16.4: Running a DOS shell with Exec.

```
  swapvectors;
  EXEC('c:\command.com', '');
  swapvectors;
  CLRSCR;
  GoToXY(27, 12);
  WRITE('***** Back from DOS! *****');
  delay(1500);
  Menu(choice);
  END;


{ ------------------------------- }
{ MAIN-LEVEL PROCEDURE DECLARATION }
{ ------------------------------- }
PROCEDURE Menu(VAR choice : INTEGER);

  { -------------------------- }
  { Local procedure           }
  { -------------------------- }
  { Under Menu                }
  { -------------------------- }
  PROCEDURE DisplayMenu;
    BEGIN
    CLRSCR;
    WRITELN;
    WRITELN('                        MAIN MENU');
    WRITELN('                        -------------------------');
    WRITELN('                        1. Add new records to file');
    WRITELN('                        2. Edit existing records');
    WRITELN('                        3. Create/print form letter');
    WRITELN('                        4. Exit to DOS');
    WRITELN('                        5. Quit this program');
    WRITELN;
    WRITE('            Enter your choice (1..5): ');
    READLN(choice);
    END;


  { -------------------------- }
  { Local procedure           }
  { -------------------------- }
  { Under Menu                }
  { -------------------------- }
  PROCEDURE DoChoice;
    BEGIN
      CASE choice OF
        1 : AddRecords;
        2 : EditRecords;
        3 : FormLetters;
        4 : GoToDOS;
        5 : EXIT
        ELSE HALT
        END { end of CASE statement }
    END;

  { ---------------------------------- }
  { Main body of higher-level procedure }
  { ---------------------------------- }
  { Procedure name: Menu              }
  { ---------------------------------- }
  BEGIN
  DisplayMenu;
  DoChoice
  END;
```

Listing 16.4: Running a DOS shell with Exec. (cont.)

```
{ ------------------------------------------------------------
-- }
{                         MAIN BODY OF PROGRAM
}
{ ------------------------------------------------------------
-- }
BEGIN
  choice := 0;
  REPEAT Menu(choice) UNTIL choice = 5;
  pause
END.
```

Listing 16.4: Running a DOS shell with Exec. (cont.)

to processor registers, DOS functions, and software interrupts, and therefore *require* the programmer to have a good understanding of how to use these features without causing a catastrophe.

At a higher level, predefined DOS routines provide safer and easier, but less flexible, access to many low-level DOS functions, and the **Exec** procedure allows the user of a program to suspend it temporarily and run external programs, including DOS itself. As is the case in most areas of programming skill, the more experience you get, the more powerful and creative ways you will find to use Turbo Pascal's DOS services.

REVIEW EXERCISES

1. List the four main methods which Turbo Pascal provides to access DOS services.

2. Explain what processor registers are and what task they perform.

3. List the 8086 processor registers and explain the purpose of each one.

4. Explain the idea of an interrupt. How do interrupts work in a PC?

5. Explain the difference between hexadecimal and decimal notation. How can you determine if a number is in hex or decimal notation? List the first 16 hex numbers.

6. How do you indicate a hex number in a Pascal program? Why are hex numbers used in programming?

7. Explain the 8086's segment:offset scheme for addressing PC memory.

8. Explain how to use the **MsDos** procedure. Write a simple program that uses the **MsDos** procedure but do *not* run it unless you have double-checked everything and are sure that it is correct.

9. Explain the purpose of the predefined registers data type. How is this type used in Turbo Pascal programs?

10. Which interrupt is used to call a DOS function, and how is this task accomplished? Write a short routine in pseudo-code to load a function number into the appropriate register and to call the appropriate software interrupt.

11. Which DOS functions correspond to the Turbo Pascal procedures **FindFirst** and **FindNext**?

12. Explain why heap memory is a problem for programs that use the **Exec** routine. What is the solution?

13. What should you always do before and after calling **Exec**? Why should you do it?

14. Explain how to use the **Exec** procedure. Write a simple program that uses the **Exec** procedure but do *not* run it unless you have double-checked everything and are sure that it is correct.

C H A P T E R

17

Elementary Data Structures

In earlier chapters, we have looked at some simple data structures, such as records, static lists, and dynamic lists with pointers. In this chapter, we will look at some more advanced data structures that put even more power at your fingertips. In the next chapter, we will look at some methods ("algorithms") for manipulating information in these and other data structures.

Once we go beyond simple data structures that are predefined in Pascal, such as arrays, the distinction between data structures and algorithms becomes somewhat artificial. A data structure is defined by (1) a specific way of arranging data, and (2) a set of operations performed on the data that make it behave in a certain way. Without the proper set of algorithms, the data structure is incomplete—just as an automobile without a person who knows how to drive it is only an inert pile of metal and glass.

ABSTRACT DATA STRUCTURES

The data structures we will look at in this chapter are stacks and queues, which are often used in real-life programming situations. Both are lists that can hold any type of data item except a file type.

ABSTRACT STACKS

A *stack* is a list in which all insertions and deletions are made at one end of the list, commonly called the "top" of the list. This is very much like a stack of trays in a cafeteria; the last tray put on top of the stack is the first one removed. For this reason, stacks are also referred to as *last-in-first-out* (or LIFO) lists. Adding an item to a stack is called *pushing* it onto the stack, while deleting an item from a stack is called *popping* it off the stack.

Thus, consider the example shown in Figure 17.1. The sequence of events is as follows:

1. At Step One, the stack is empty. We push the first item, A, onto the empty stack.

2. At Step Two, we push B and C onto the stack. B is added first, going on top of A, and C is added next, going on top of B.

3. At Step Three, we pop an item off the top of the stack. Because C was the last item added to the stack, it is on the top, and hence it is the item first in line to be popped (last in first out).

4. At Step Four, we pop another item from the top of the stack. Because B was added to the stack before C, it is now at the top of the stack and gets popped.

5. At Step Five, only item A is left in the stack. We now push two new items, D and E, onto the top of the stack in the same way that, before, we added B and C. If any more items are popped from the stack, they will be popped in the order opposite to that in which they were added—i.e., they will be popped in the order E, D, A.

Notice that at this stage, we are describing stacks as an abstract data type. Not a single word has been said about arrays, pointers, or any other detail of how stacks can be implemented in Pascal. The description we have given could be implemented in any language, using a variety of structured data types.

The most familiar application of stacks is one to which we referred in Chapter 11: *the* stack (which is an area in your PC's memory that Turbo Pascal reserves for local variables and return addresses of subroutines) is also *a* stack which pops off those variables and addresses in last-in-first-out order. Stacks also can be used for a variety of arithmetic operations.

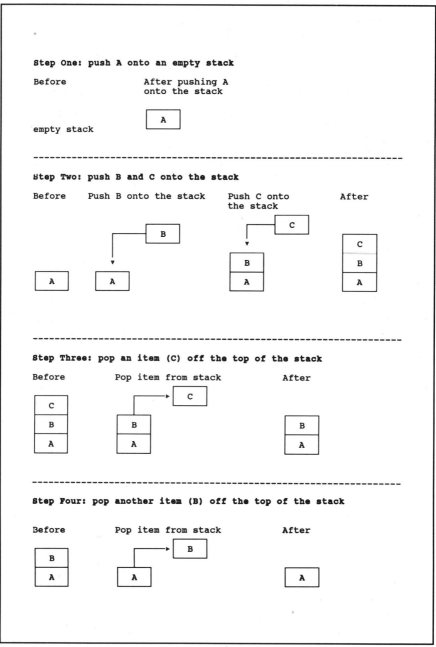

Figure 17.1: Adding and deleting items from a stack.

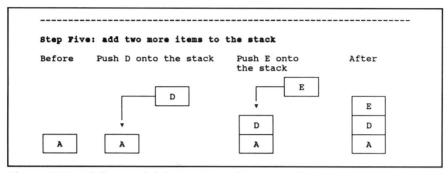

Figure 17.1: Adding and deleting items from a stack. (cont.)

ABSTRACT QUEUES

Unlike a stack, which is a last-in-first-out list, a *queue* is a first-in-first-out list. In a queue, all insertions are made at the back of the list and all deletions are made at the front. This works the same way as a line at an airline ticket counter. When new passengers arrive, they join the line at the end. People who arrived earlier, however, leave the line at the front as they get their tickets. Perhaps because queues are more familiar, there are no special terms to describe adding items to queues and deleting items from queues. The operation of a queue is shown in Figure 17.2. The sequence of events is as follows:

1. At Step One, the queue is empty. We add a single item, A, to the queue.

2. At Step Two, we add items B and C to the queue. However, because a queue is a first-in-first-out list, we picture the situation differently. Instead of being added to the "top," as with a stack, the new items are added to the end of the queue, just like new passengers lining up at an airline ticket counter.

3. At Step Three, we delete an item from the queue. Because A was the first item added to the queue, it is also the first item to be deleted.

4. At Step Four, we delete another item from the queue. Because B was the next item added after A, it is the next item to be deleted

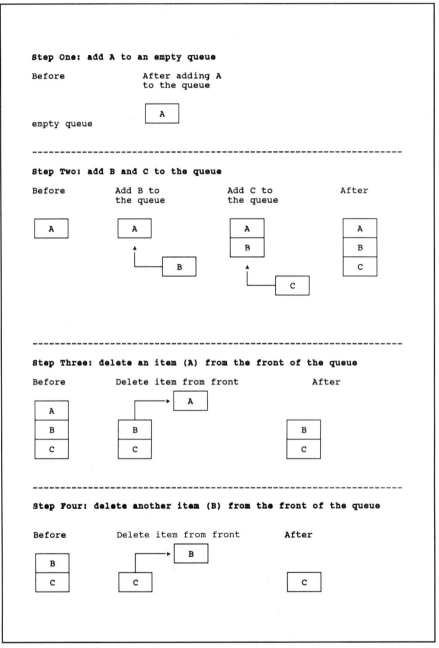

Figure 17.2: Adding and deleting from a queue.

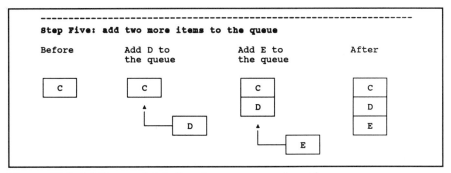

Figure 17.2: Adding and deleting from a queue. (cont.)

from the queue. Only item C, the last item added, is left in the queue—still "waiting in line."

5. At Step Five, we add two more items (D and E) to the back of the queue, one after the other. If the items currently in the queue were to be deleted, they would be deleted in the order C, D, E.

As was the case with stacks, we have said nothing about the specific way queues are to be implemented. We could use either static or dynamic data structures, depending on the situation and the programming language. In what follows, we will see how to implement stacks and queues using both static and dynamic data structures.

Because queues are so familiar in everyday life, they have many applications. A typical application would be to simulate the operation of a stoplight at a traffic intersection. (See Review Exercise 15.)

STATIC DATA STRUCTURES

Static stacks and queues are implemented in Pascal by using arrays. Because the size of arrays is fixed at compile time, it is necessary to make the arrays as large as the stacks and queues are ever going to be, and to include special routines to check for full stacks and queues.

ARRAY-BASED STACKS

Let's look at how to use arrays to implement a stack. The first thing to decide is precisely what data structure we will use to implement our stack. We know in advance that we are going to use an array, but we also need a way to keep track of the top of the stack so that we know where to add the next item. Consider Figure 17.3, which shows a stack implemented with a five-slot array. We know that we should add the first item in slot 1, but after that, the program must have some kind of counter so that it can determine which slot is next.

Suppose that we have three items A, B, and C in the stack. A counter variable attached to the stack would inform the program that the current top of the stack is at slot 3, meaning that a pop would delete an item from slot 3 and a push would add a new item to slot number 4. The same counter variable could also be used to indicate when the stack was full or empty.

As we discussed in Chapter 8, the record data type is the usual way to bring items of different data types together in the same data structure. We can thus define our stack data structure as follows:

```
CONST Max = 5;


TYPE

    Stack = RECORD

            stackitem : ARRAY[1..Max] OF item;

            stacktop  : 1..Max

            END;
```

Note that, just as we did in Chapter 8, we have included a counter field, *stacktop*, to keep track of a certain position in the array—in this case, the top of the stack. Given this stack data structure, we can now move on to identify the subroutines we will need to manipulate our stack. They are:

- **Init**, a procedure to initialize the stack
- **Push**, a procedure to push items onto the top of the stack

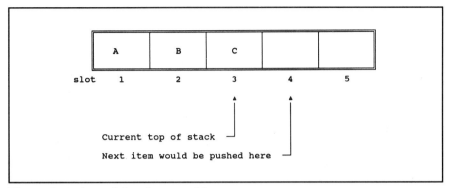

Figure 17.3: A stack implemented in an array.

- **Pop**, a procedure to pop items from the top of the stack
- **FullStack**, a function to indicate when the stack (i.e., the array in which the stack is implemented) is full
- **EmptyStack**, a function to indicate when the stack (i.e., the array in which the stack is implemented) is empty

FullStack and **EmptyStack** are not strictly necessary, because we can test for a full or empty stack merely by looking at the stack record's counter field. In fact, all of the routines we will create are quite simple, and could be written out wherever they are needed in the program. However, this spotlights two important benefits of structured programming.

First, suppose that instead of creating these procedures and functions, we simply inserted the relevant code wherever it was needed. If we later decided to make any change in our program—such as changing the stack from a static to a dynamic list—we would virtually have to rewrite the whole program. Every place where an item was pushed onto the stack or popped from the stack would have to be recoded. By packaging this code in subroutines, however, we need to change only the subroutines themselves. The changes will take effect automatically wherever the subroutines are called in the program.

Second, it's easier to see what is happening in the program when we use simple names such as push, pop, empty, and full for blocks of code. Instead of having to look at the code and figure out what it does each time, we can see at a glance that it does a "pop" or it checks to see if the stack is full. Listing 17.1 shows how to set up a stack using these ideas.

Inside Listing 17.1

The program begins by calling **Init**, which fills up the stack with space characters and sets the stacktop field to zero. It then calls the **PushItems-OnStack** routine, which prompts the user to enter characters for the stack and calls the **Push** routine to push each one onto the top of stack.

At this point, you might be wondering why the code for **Push** wasn't simply included in the **PushItemsOnStack** routine—as well as why the code for **Pop** wasn't included in the **PopItemsOffStack** routine. This is an example of separating different tasks into different subroutines. The main purpose of the **PushItemsOnStack** routine is to get input from the user, while the main purpose of the **PopItemsOffStack** routine is to display output for the user. Thus, these routines should be insulated from the details of how the push and pop operations actually take place. We can change our stack data structure, along with the **Push** and **Pop** routines, without having to make any changes in the **PushItemsOnStack** and **Pop-ItemsOffStack** routines.

Because the stack is a record type, the **Push** routine uses the WITH notation to simplify references to the stack's fields. The first thing it does is to determine if the stack is full by calling the **Full** function. If the stacktop field is equal to the maximum number of entries in the stack, then the **Full** function returns a value of true; otherwise, it returns a value of false.

Notice that although the **Full** and **Empty** functions perform the same basic operations, **Full** is coded with an IF statement, while **Empty** assigns the Boolean value of **(list.stacktop = 0)** to itself. This illustrates the equivalence of these two methods.

If the stack is not full, then the **Push** routine's next move is to add 1 to the stacktop field, thereby moving up one slot in the array. In this slot, it loads the value to be pushed onto the stack.

The **PopItemsOffStack** procedure calls **Pop** to get values from the stack. The **Pop** routine does essentially the same things as the **Push** routine, merely in reverse. It first checks to see if the stack is empty, because, obviously, it cannot pop anything from the stack if there's nothing

```
PROGRAM Listing17_1;


    { Demonstrates the use of a stack. In this case, the
      program prompts the user to enter enough characters
      to fill up the stack, then pops them off the stack
      in reverse order. }

USES CRT, MyUtils;

CONST
      Max = 5;
      space = ' ';
TYPE
     stack = record
                stackitem : ARRAY[1..Max] of CHAR;
                stacktop  : 0..Max
                END;
VAR
    list    : stack;
    item    : CHAR;

PROCEDURE init(VAR list : stack);
   VAR
     counter : INTEGER;
   BEGIN
     CLRSCR;
     FOR counter := 1 TO max DO
         list.stackitem[counter] := space;
     list.stacktop := 0
   END;

FUNCTION full(list : stack) : BOOLEAN;
   BEGIN
     IF list.stacktop = max
        THEN full := TRUE
        ELSE full := FALSE
   END;

FUNCTION empty(list : stack) : BOOLEAN;
   BEGIN
   Empty := (list.stacktop = 0)
   END;

PROCEDURE push(item : CHAR; VAR list : stack);
   BEGIN
     WITH list DO
     BEGIN
       IF full(list) { test FOR full stack }
       THEN BEGIN
            WRITELN(' Sorry, full stack!');
            exit
            END;
       stacktop := stacktop + 1;
       stackitem[stacktop] := item
     END
   END;

PROCEDURE pop(VAR item : CHAR; VAR list : stack);
   BEGIN
     WITH list DO
       BEGIN
         IF empty(list)
```

Listing 17.1: A stack implemented with an array.

```
                THEN BEGIN
                     WRITELN(' Sorry, stack is empty!');
                     exit
                     END;
              item := stackitem[stacktop];
              stackitem[stacktop] := space;
              stacktop := stacktop - 1
        END
     END;

PROCEDURE PushItemsOnStack(VAR list : stack);
   VAR
     newitem : CHAR;
     counter : INTEGER;
   BEGIN
     FOR counter := 1 TO max DO
        BEGIN
        WRITE(' Enter a character to push onto the stack: ');
        readln(newitem);
        push(newitem, list);
        WRITELN
        END
   END;

PROCEDURE PopItemsOffStack(VAR list : stack);
   VAR
     counter : INTEGER;
   BEGIN
     CLRSCR;
     WRITELN(' The stack items are popped off in reverse order');
     WRITELN(' because a stack is a last-in-first-out list.');
     WRITELN;
     WRITE(' Items popped from the stack: ');
     FOR counter := 1 TO max DO
        BEGIN
        delay(700);
        pop(item, list);
        WRITE(item, ' ')
        END
   END;


BEGIN
   init(list);
   PushItemsOnStack(list);
   PopItemsOffStack(list);
   pause
END.
```

Listing 17.1: A stack implemented with an array. (cont.)

to be popped. If the stack is not empty, then it assigns the value in the current top of the stack to the item parameter and then subtracts one from the stacktop field, moving the top of the stack down one slot in the array.

ARRAY-BASED QUEUES

Queues are a bit more complicated than stacks. In stacks, we need only keep track of one end of the list: the top. It is at this end that all insertions and deletions are made in the list. With queues, on the other hand, insertions are made at the rear of the list and deletions are made at the front. This means that, at minimum, our queue-handling routines must keep track of two ends of the list instead of just one.

Let's consider a "first draft" of a data structure for holding a queue. We know that we must keep track of both ends of the list, so the natural move is simply to upgrade our stack data type with an additional field:

```
CONST Max = 5;

TYPE

    queue = RECORD

            queueitem : ARRAY[1..Max] of CHAR;

            front,

            rear      : 0..Max

            END;
```

We would then use this data type for our queue, exactly as we used the stack type. The front would start out in slot 1 of the array, with the rear set to 0 (which isn't a slot in the array) to distinguish it from the front in the starting, empty position. Operations with this queue data structure are shown in Figure 17.4, which assumes a five-slot queue.

After adding four items to the queue, the front field of the queue record contains the value 1, indicating which array slot contains the next value that would be deleted from the queue. The rear field contains the value 4, indicating the current rear end of the queue. The next insertion would be made at slot number 5, filling the queue. Each time we make an insertion, we simply add 1 to the value of the rear field, until we arrive at the maximum size of the queue (i.e., the number of slots in the array).

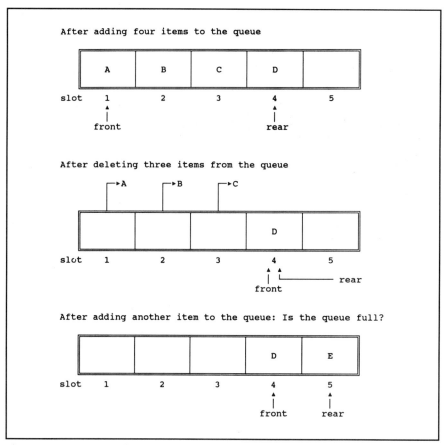

Figure 17.4: First draft of a queue implemented in an array.

So far, so good. The fact that the queue can be filled up was expected, because we are using arrays. However, the next step in Figure 17.4 begins to raise a problem. We deleted three items from the queue, in first-in-first-out order, just as we should. This leaves only one item in the queue at slot number 4, which is now both the front and the rear of the queue. Next, however, we add another item to the queue, and it goes into slot number 5. The queue is not full—there are three open slots earlier in the array—but it seems as if we have no place to go.

Obviously, something has to be done. We could simply make the array very large, allowing the queue to creep down toward the end of the array as insertions and deletions were made during a program run. This solution, however, would be terribly wasteful in terms of array space. A better approach would be somehow to allow the queue to "double back" to the beginning when it reaches the end of the array. That solution is shown in Figure 17.5.

This approach is conventionally referred to as using a "circular" array, even though there is really no such thing as a circular array. What we are actually doing is using the *mod* operator so that, when the rear of the queue arrives at the last slot in the array, it doubles back to the first slot.

We discussed the mod operator in Chapter 5, but this is a good place for a recap. Mod ("modulus") returns a value equal to the remainder left by integer division. For example, 3 goes into 10 three times, with a remainder of 1, so 10 mod 3 = 1. Likewise, 2 goes into 10 five times, with no remainder, so 10 mod 2 = 0.

In the case of our array-based queue, we will set up the routine to add a new item to the queue so that it does not simply add 1 to the rear, but instead, adds 1 to (rear mod max), where max is the highest slot in the array. Thus, here is where the next item would be placed in several situations, with max = 5:

- If rear = 0 (the situation at the start of the program), then (rear mod max) + 1 = (0 mod 5) + 1 = 1.
- If rear = 3, then (rear mod max) + 1 = (3 mod 5) + 1 = 4.
- If rear = 5, then (rear mod max) + 1 = (5 mod 5) + 1 = 1.

There's only one other problem that needs to be solved—a problem we conveniently glossed over in Figure 17.5. What happens if the queue *really is* full: that is, if rear = 5 so that (rear mod max) + 1 = 1, but slot 1 is still occupied by another item? We need some way to detect when the array really is full so that we will not accidentally "add" a new value to a full queue and thereby erase a previously entered value.

To solve this problem, we simply add a counter field to the record that defines the queue data structure. When this counter field contains a value

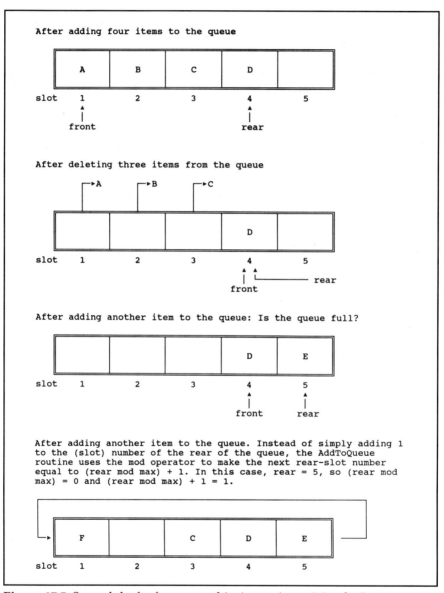

Figure 17.5: Second draft of a queue, this time using a "circular" array.

equal to max, then we know that the queue is full. This data structure is shown in Listing 17.2, which also contains the framework for a program to manipulate a queue.

Just as with our stack program in Listing 17.1, we need routines to initialize the queue, to add and delete items, and to determine if the queue is empty or full. The details of these routines are shown in Listing 17.3.

```
PROGRAM Listing17_2;


  { Framework for a program to create and manipulate an
    array-based queue. }

USES CRT, MyUtils;

CONST
     Max = 5;
TYPE
    queue = RECORD
              queueitem : ARRAY[1..Max] of CHAR;
              Qcount,
              front,
              rear      : 0..Max
              END;
VAR
   list    : queue;
   item    : CHAR;



PROCEDURE Init(VAR list : queue);
  BEGIN
  END;

FUNCTION Empty(VAR list : queue) : BOOLEAN;
  BEGIN
  END;

FUNCTION Full(VAR list : queue) : BOOLEAN;
  BEGIN
  END;

PROCEDURE AddToQueue(item : CHAR; VAR list : queue);
  BEGIN
  END;

PROCEDURE DeleteFromQueue(VAR item : CHAR; VAR list : queue);
  BEGIN
  END;
{ ----------------------------------------------------------- }
{                     MAIN BODY OF PROGRAM
}
{ ----------------------------------------------------------- }
BEGIN
END.
```

Listing 17.2: Framework for a program to manipulate a queue.

```pascal
PROGRAM Listing17_3;

    { Demonstrates a program to create and manipulate an
      array-based queue. }

USES CRT, MyUtils;

CONST
     Max = 5;
TYPE
    queue = RECORD
              queueitem : ARRAY[1..Max] of CHAR;
              Qcount,
              front,
              rear      : 0..Max
              END;
VAR
    list    : queue;
    item    : CHAR;

PROCEDURE Init(VAR list : queue);
   BEGIN
     WITH list DO
       BEGIN
       Qcount := 0;
       front := 1;
       rear := 0
       END
   END;

FUNCTION Empty(VAR list : queue) : BOOLEAN;
   BEGIN
     Empty := (list.Qcount = 0)
   END;

FUNCTION Full(VAR list : queue) : BOOLEAN;
   BEGIN
     Full := (list.Qcount = max)
   END;

PROCEDURE AddToQueue(item : CHAR; VAR list : queue);
   BEGIN
     WITH list DO
       IF full(list)
         THEN WRITELN(' Sorry, queue is full.')
         ELSE BEGIN
             Qcount := Qcount + 1;
             rear := (rear mod max) + 1;
             Queueitem[rear] := item;
             END
   END; { of AddToQueue routine }


PROCEDURE DeleteFromQueue(VAR item : CHAR; VAR list : queue);
   BEGIN
     WITH list DO
       IF empty(list)
         THEN WRITELN(' Sorry, queue is empty.')
         ELSE BEGIN
             Qcount := Qcount - 1;
             item := Queueitem[front];
```

Listing 17.3: A program to manipulate a queue.

```
                  front := (front mod max) + 1
                  END
        END;

PROCEDURE AddItems(VAR list : queue);
   VAR
      counter : CHAR;
      Qpos    : INTEGER;
   BEGIN
      Qpos := list.rear;
      WRITELN(' Now adding items to the queue ...');
      WRITELN(' -------------------------------');
      FOR counter :=  'a' TO 'e' DO
        BEGIN
        addtoqueue(counter, list);
        Qpos := (Qpos mod max) + 1;
        WRITELN(' Item ', counter, ' added at position ', Qpos, '.');
        delay(1000)
        END;
      WRITELN; WRITELN
   END;


PROCEDURE DeleteItems(VAR list : queue);
   VAR
      counter : CHAR;
      Qpos    : INTEGER;
   BEGIN
      Qpos := 0;
      WRITELN(' Now deleting items from the queue ...');
      WRITELN(' ----------------------------------');
      FOR counter := 'a' TO 'e' DO
        BEGIN
        deletefromqueue(item, list);
        Qpos := (Qpos mod max) + 1;
        WRITELN(' Item ', counter, ' deleted from position ', Qpos, ',');
        delay(1000)
        END
   END;


{ ---------------------------------------------------------------- }
{                      MAIN BODY OF PROGRAM                         }
}
{ ---------------------------------------------------------------- }
BEGIN
  CLRSCR;
  Init(list);
  AddItems(list);
  DeleteItems(list);
  pause
END.
```

Listing 17.3: A program to manipulate a queue. (cont.)

Inside Listing 17.3

The first task performed by Listing 17.3 is to initialize the queue. This means setting the **Qcount** and **rear** fields to 0 and setting the front field to 1.

The **AddItems** routine then fills up the queue by calling **AddToQueue** five times, each time adding a letter to the queue. The **AddToQueue** routine first checks to make sure that the queue is not full. If not, then it increases the **Qcount** by 1 each time an addition is made; the front of the queue remains the same unless a deletion is made, so **AddToQueue** needs to change only the **rear** field of the queue record; in doing so, it uses the *mod* scheme that was described above.

After the **AddItems** routine has filled up the queue, the **DeleteItems** routine removes items from the queue in first-in-first-out order, as it should. It calls the **DeleteFromQueue** routine. **DeleteFromQueue** first checks to make sure that the queue is not empty. If it is not, then **DeleteFromQueue** subtracts 1 from the **Qcount** field, copies the value from the front slot into a parameter, and increases the value in the **front** field by the mod approach, just as it did with the **rear** field. The letters are displayed on the computer screen as they are deleted from the queue.

DYNAMIC DATA STRUCTURES

As we have seen, static data structures can be used to create stacks and queues. However, because of the limitations of static variables, this approach tends to waste memory. It also imposes special requirements on the programmer to guard against *full list* conditions, and the array-based implementation of queues is slightly more complicated than we would probably like it to be.

These problems disappear when stacks and queues are implemented in dynamic linked lists. New nodes can be created as they are needed, and a counter field is no longer required. Linked data structures, of course, present their own problems, but are often a better choice than arrays for stacks and queues.

Because operations with pointers are sometimes a little complex, a brief recap is in order here. A pointer is a variable that contains the memory address of another variable and can be used to refer to that variable. If **MyPtr** is a pointer to a record variable with a field *item* that contains a character, then:

- **MyPtr** contains the memory address of a record variable.

- **MyPtr^** is the record variable itself.

- **MyPtr^**.item is the item field of the record variable; this item field is itself a character variable.

- If the record variable is in a linked list, then it has at least a **next** field containing a pointer to the next record. In that case, **MyPtr^.next** is itself a pointer, and points either to the **next** record or to **NIL**, which indicates that there is no next record.

If you need further review on pointer operations, you should refer back to Chapter 11.

LINKED STACKS

Before we discuss how to code linked stacks, it would be a good idea to have a clear picture of what we will be doing. In Figure 17.6, we can look at what actually happens in each step of pushing items onto a linked stack and popping them off.

Figure 17.6 assumes that we will create a stack of items (as yet unspecified) in a singly linked list. As was the case when we looked at stacks in arrays, all insertions and deletions are made at the head of the list, called the *top*. A pointer identifies the top of the stack.

In an empty stack, the stacktop pointer points to **NIL**. When we add a new item to the stack, we use the **New** procedure (see Chapter 11 if you're hazy on this) with a temporary pointer to set aside the appropriate amount of memory on the heap and point the temporary pointer at that memory location. We copy the values we want into the new item and point the stacktop pointer at it, setting the next field of the new item to **NIL**.

It's when we add another item to the stack that things get really interesting. We first call **New** again to create a dynamic variable of the appropriate type. Then we load values into the variable and set its next pointer to point to the current top of the stack. Finally, we repoint the stacktop pointer at the new item, which becomes the new top of the stack.

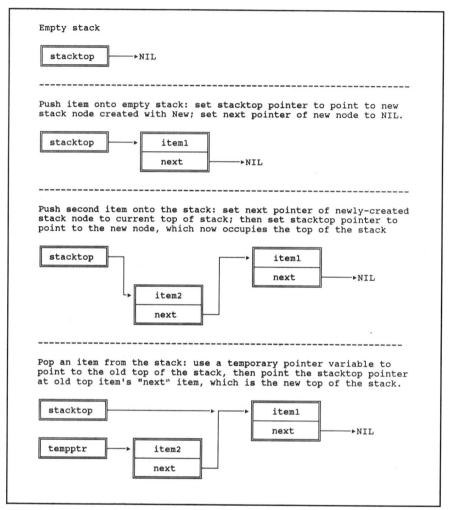

Figure 17.6: Operations with a linked stack.

To pop an item from the stack, we reverse this process. We use a temporary pointer to keep track of the item currently on top of the stack, then we repoint the stacktop pointer at the next item after the current top item. Note that it is important to do this in the correct order. If we first repointed the stacktop pointer, we would then have lost track of the item that had been at the top of the stack. By assigning its location to a temporary pointer as our first step, however, we keep track of the item at the original top of the stack. Finally, we copy the values out of this item and use Dispose with the temporary pointer to free up the heap space occupied by the item.

Listing 17.4 demonstrates the Pascal code version of these stack operations.

Inside Listing 17.4

Listing 17.4 first defines a data type for items in the stack, along with a pointer type for those items. Each item will contain a character as its *content* and a pointer to the next item in the list. Then, in the VAR section, we declare a global variable "item" for getting characters in and out of the stack, as well as a static pointer variable "stacktop" to point to the item at the top of the stack.

The **Init** routine's only purpose is to set the **stacktop** pointer to **NIL**. However, this is very important because the program uses the **stacktop** pointer's **NIL** value to determine if the stack is empty.

The **PromptUserForItem** routine is called next, and asks the user to enter characters to be pushed onto the top of the stack. It calls the **Push** routine, which uses Pascal's **New** procedure to create a dynamic stack node on the heap. Into this node, it then loads the character entered by the user. It points the new node's next pointer to the current top of the stack, then repoints the **stacktop** pointer toward the new node, so that the new node is now at the top of the stack. Back in the **PromptUserForItem** routine, we then cycle through a REPEAT loop until the user decides that enough items have been pushed onto the stack.

The **PopItemsOffStack** routine sets up a WHILE loop to pop items off of the stack until the end of the stack is reached. Note that we used a WHILE loop instead of a REPEAT loop to cover the possibility of there being *no* items in the stack, in which case nothing could be popped off. On each pass through the loop, the **Pop** routine is called.

The **Pop** routine creates a temporary (local) pointer to point to the top of the stack. It then checks to see if the stack is empty; if so, it exits back to the calling routine. If the stack is not empty, then it loads the value from the top node into the item parameter (which is standing in for the global variable *item*) and points the temporary pointer at the top

```
PROGRAM Listing17_4;


  { Demonstrates how to set up a linked stack by using pointers.
    Uses the MyUtils unit created in Chapter 10. }

USES CRT, MyUtils;

CONST
  space = ' ';

TYPE
  nodeptr   = ^stackitem;
  stackitem = RECORD
                item  : CHAR;
                next  : nodeptr
                END;
VAR
  item     : CHAR;
  stacktop : nodeptr;

PROCEDURE Init(VAR stacktop : nodeptr);
 .BEGIN
    stacktop := NIL
  END;

FUNCTION Empty(stacktop : nodeptr) : BOOLEAN;
  BEGIN
    Empty := (stacktop = NIL)
  END;

PROCEDURE Push(item : CHAR; VAR stacktop : nodeptr);
  VAR
    TempNode : nodeptr;
  BEGIN
    New(TempNode);
    TempNode^.item := item;
    TempNode^.next := stacktop;
    stacktop := TempNode
  END;

PROCEDURE Pop(VAR item : CHAR; VAR stacktop : nodeptr);
  VAR
    TempNode : nodeptr;
  BEGIN
    IF Empty(stacktop)
        THEN BEGIN
            WRITELN(' Sorry, stack is empty.');
            exit
            END
        ELSE BEGIN
            item := stacktop^.item;
            TempNode := stacktop;
            stacktop := stacktop^.next;
            Dispose(Tempnode)
            TempNode := NIL
            END
  END;

PROCEDURE PromptUserForItems(VAR stacktop : nodeptr);
  VAR
    item,
    continue : CHAR;
  BEGIN
```

Listing 17.4: Creating and using a linked stack.

```
      continue := 'Y';
      CLRSCR;
      WRITELN(' Pushing items onto the stack ...');
      WRITELN(' -----------------------------');
      REPEAT
        WRITELN;
        WRITE(' Enter a letter to push onto the stack: ');
        READLN(item);
        push(item, stacktop);
        WRITELN;
        WRITE(' Do another (Y/N)? ');
        READLN(continue);
      UNTIL UPCASE(continue) <> 'Y'
  END;

PROCEDURE PopItemsOffStack(VAR stacktop : nodeptr);
  VAR
    item : CHAR;
  BEGIN
    CLRSCR;
    WRITELN;
    WRITELN(' Popping items off the stack ...');
    WRITELN(' -----------------------------');
    WHILE stacktop <> NIL DO
      BEGIN
      pop(item, stacktop);
      WRITE(space, item);
      delay(1000)
      END;
    WRITELN
  END;
  { ---------------------------------------------------------------- }
  {                       MAIN BODY OF PROGRAM                        }
  }
  { ---------------------------------------------------------------- }
  BEGIN
    CLRSCR;
    init(stacktop);




    PromptUserForItems(stacktop);
    PopItemsOffStack(stacktop);
    pause
  END.
```

Listing 17.4: Creating and using a linked stack. (cont.)

node. It takes the value of the top node's next field and loads it into the **stacktop** pointer, thereby pointing the **stacktop** pointer at the next node and making it the new top of the stack. Finally, it calls **Dispose** to free up the heap memory occupied by the popped stack node and sets the temporary pointer to **NIL**.

The last step, which sets the temporary pointer to **NIL**, is probably not necessary because the pointer will cease to exist as soon as the **Pop** routine terminates. However, any time you are in doubt, play it safe and set unassigned pointers to **NIL**.

As each letter is popped off the stack, the **PopItemsOffStack** routine displays it on the screen. As you will see when you run the program, letters are popped off the stack in reverse order, because a stack—regardless of its implementation details—is a last-in-first-out list.

LINKED QUEUES

Just as we did with linked stacks, we will begin our discussion of linked queues by drawing a picture so that we can have a code-free idea of what we are doing. Figure 17.7 shows the operations we will be doing with linked queues.

Linked queues are slightly more complicated than linked stacks. Because insertions are made at one end (the rear) and deletions are made at the other end (the front), we need two pointers to keep track of the front and rear nodes of the queue. There are other ways to solve this problem, for example, with a circularly linked queue. (See Review Exercise 13.)

When the queue is empty, both the front and rear pointers are set to **NIL**. To add an item to the empty queue, we use the Pascal **New** procedure to create a new node variable on the heap. We load the appropriate values into the node variable's fields and set its next pointer to **NIL**. We then point both the front and rear pointers at the new node, which is the only node in the queue.

To add items to a *non*empty queue, we create a node variable on the heap. After loading its fields with the desired values, we set the next field of the current rear node to point to the new node, then repoint the rear pointer to point to the new node. As in other cases, the order of these operations is very important: if we had changed the rear pointer first, then we would have had no simple way to find the old rear node and could not have linked the new node into the list. Finally, we set the next field of the new rear node to **NIL**. Notice that because insertions are made at the rear, no changes had to be made in the front pointer.

To delete an item, we first use a temporary pointer to keep track of the old front node of the queue. Then we load the value from the next field of the old front node into the front pointer, thereby repointing it at the node

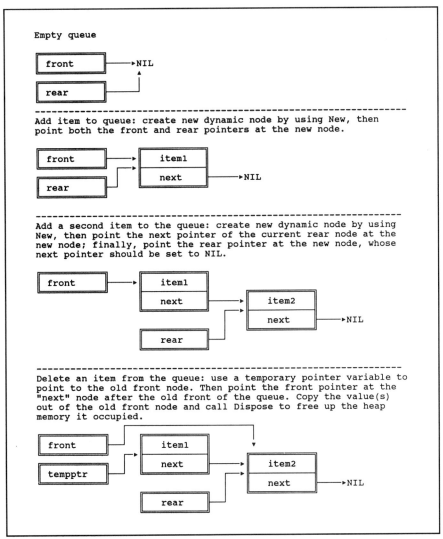

Figure 17.7: Operations with a linked queue.

after the old front node. We copy the values out of the old front node and then call **Dispose** to free up the heap memory that it occupied. Notice that because deletions are made at the front, no changes had to be made in the rear pointer.

Listing 17.5 demonstrates the Pascal code version of these queue operations.

Inside Listing 17.5

Listing 17.5 begins by initializing the queue. In this case, all that is required is to set the front and rear pointers to **NIL**. The **PromptUserForItems** routine is then called, setting up a REPEAT loop to prompt the user for one or more values to add to the queue.

Once the user has entered a letter to be added to the queue, the **AddNode** procedure is called. **AddNode** calls **New** to create a new node variable on the heap, loading the letter into the new node's item field and setting the new node's next field to **NIL** because this node will be the new rear of the queue. The routine then checks to see if the queue is empty; if so, it points both the front and rear pointers at the new node. If the queue is not empty, then the routine links the new node to the end of the list by pointing the current rear node's next field at it. It then repoints the rear pointer at the new node.

Back in the **PromptUserForItems** routine, the user is asked if he or she wishes to enter another item in the queue. Depending on the answer, the REPEAT loop either will run again or terminate.

Once the queue is loaded up, we are ready to delete its nodes one at a time and view the result. The **DisplayItemsOnScreen** routine sets up a WHILE loop (in case the queue is empty). The loop calls the **DeleteNode** procedure.

DeleteNode uses a temporary pointer to keep track of the current front node. It then loads the letter from the front node into the item parameter and loads the value from the current front node's next field into the front pointer, thereby repointing it at the next node in the queue. If the previous front node was the only node in the list, and the list is now empty, then the front pointer will now be **NIL**, and an IF statement sets the rear pointer to **NIL** as well. The routine then calls **Dispose** to free up the heap memory occupied by the old front node and, as an added safety measure, resets the temporary pointer to **NIL**.

Back in the **DisplayItemsOnScreen** procedure, the value from the deleted node is displayed on the screen. At the same time, a **Beep** procedure is called to sound a short tone each time a letter is displayed on-screen;

```
PROGRAM Listing17_5;


   { Demonstrates a linked-list implementation of a queue.
     Uses the MyUtils unit that was created in Chapter 10. }

USES CRT, MyUtils;

CONST
  space = ' ';

TYPE
  nodeptr = ^node;
  node    = RECORD
              item  : CHAR;
              next  : nodeptr
              END;

VAR
   item    : CHAR;
   front,
   rear    : nodeptr;

PROCEDURE Beep;
   { Causes the PC's speaker to emit a short beep. Intended
     as a preview of Chapter 19. }
   BEGIN
     sound(100);
     delay(150);
     nosound
   END;


PROCEDURE Init(VAR front, rear : nodeptr);
   BEGIN
   front := NIL;
   rear := NIL
   end;

PROCEDURE AddNode(item : CHAR; VAR front, rear : nodeptr);
   VAR
     TempNode : nodeptr;
   BEGIN
     New(TempNode);
     TempNode^.item := item;
     TempNode^.next := NIL;
     IF front = NIL
         THEN BEGIN
              front := TempNode;
              rear := TempNode
              END
         ELSE BEGIN
              rear^.next := TempNode;
              rear := TempNode
              END
   END;


PROCEDURE DeleteNode(VAR item : CHAR; VAR front, rear : nodeptr);
   VAR
     TempNode : nodeptr;
   BEGIN
     TempNode := NIL;
     IF front = NIL
```

Listing 17.5: Operations with a linked queue.

```
            THEN BEGIN
                 WRITE(' Sorry, queue is empty.');
                 exit
                 END
            ELSE BEGIN
                 TempNode := front;
                 item := front^.item;
                 front := front^.next;
                 IF front = NIL THEN rear := NIL;
                 Dispose(TempNode);
                 TempNode := NIL;
                 END
      END;

PROCEDURE PromptUserForItems(VAR front, rear : nodeptr);
   VAR
      item,
      continue : CHAR;
   BEGIN
      continue := 'Y';
      CLRSCR;
      WRITELN(' Now adding items to the queue ...');
      WRITELN(' ------------------------------');
      REPEAT
        WRITE(' Enter a letter to add to the queue: ');
        READLN(item);
        WRITELN;
        WRITELN(' Adding ', item, ' to the queue. ');
        delay(500);
        AddNode(item, front, rear);
        WRITE(' Add another item (Y/N)? ');
        READLN(continue);
        WRITELN;
      UNTIL UPCASE(continue) <> 'Y';
      WRITELN
   END;

PROCEDURE DisplayItemsOnScreen(VAR item : CHAR;
                               VAR front, rear : nodeptr);
   BEGIN
      CLRSCR;
      WRITELN(' Now deleting items from the queue ...');
      WRITELN(' ------------------------------------');
      WHILE front <> NIL DO
        BEGIN
        deletenode(item, front, rear);
        WRITE(space, item);
        beep;
        delay(1000)
        END;
      pause
   END;

{ ---------------------------------------------------------------- }
{                       MAIN BODY OF PROGRAM                        }
}
{ ---------------------------------------------------------------- }
BEGIN
  Init(front, rear);
  PromptUserForItems(front, rear);
  DisplayItemsOnScreen(item, front, rear)
END.
```

Listing 17.5: Operations with a linked queue. (cont.)

this is a "preview of coming attractions" for Chapter 19. **Beep** uses the Turbo Pascal **Sound** procedure, which takes the desired sound frequency as a parameter and causes the speaker to emit a tone until the **NoSound** procedure is called.

SUMMARY

When we go beyond simple data structures, the distinction between data structures and algorithms becomes somewhat artificial. Data structures such as stacks and queues consist of data structures, such as arrays or linked lists, and algorithms to manipulate the data in certain ways.

In a stack, all insertions and deletions are made at one end of the list, called the top of the stack. This makes stacks much simpler to manipulate than queues. In queues, insertions are made at one end, called the rear of the queue, and deletions are made at the other end, called the front of the queue. Both stacks and queues, however, are useful in a wide variety of applications.

REVIEW EXERCISES

1. Explain the idea of a stack, as well as the ideas of pushing and popping stack items.

2. Explain the idea of a queue, as well as how items are added to and deleted from a queue.

3. Draw a sequence of pictures that shows the state of a stack at each step in the following pseudocode:

   (a) Empty stack

   (b) Push('a', stack)

   (c) Push('b', stack)

   (d) Push('c', stack)

   (e) Pop(item, stack)

     (f) Push('d', stack)

     (g) Pop(item, stack)

     (h) Pop(item, stack)

     (i) Pop(item, stack)

4. Draw a sequence of pictures that shows the state of a queue at each step in the following pseudocode:

     (a) Empty queue

     (b) Add('a', queue)

     (c) Add('b', queue)

     (d) Delete(item, queue)

     (e) Add('c', queue)

     (f) Add('d', queue)

     (g) Delete(item, queue)

     (h) Add('e', queue)

     (i) Delete(item, queue)

5. Explain how to implement a stack in an array. Write a simple program to create a stack of student records. Each record should contain the student's last name and grade point average. Push and pop several student records from the stack, displaying each on the computer screen as it is deleted.

6. Explain the idea of a *circular* array and draw a series of pictures illustrating how to set up a queue in such an array.

7. Explain how to implement a queue in an array, and how it differs from implementing a stack in an array. Write a simple program to create a queue of cars at a stoplight. Each record should contain the car's number (with the first car as number 1) and the color of the car. Assume that the cars are all going in the same direction, so that there needs to be only a single queue. Add and delete several cars from the queue, displaying the results on the computer screen as the program runs.

8. Explain the mod operator and how it is used in setting up an array-based queue. If you can, devise an alternative method to cycle back without using the mod operator.

9. Draw a series of pictures showing how to set up and manipulate a linked stack.

10. Write a simple program to set up and manipulate a linked stack of student records, as in Exercise 5. Explain the differences between the array-based and the linked versions.

11. Write a simple program to set up and manipulate a linked queue of cars at a stoplight, as in Exercise 7. Explain the differences between the array-based and the linked version.

12. (Challenging) In a circularly linked list, the next node of the last item points not to NIL, but back to the first node in the list. If you set up a circularly linked queue, you need only a single pointer to the rear of the queue instead of needing two pointers, one for the front and one for the rear. Draw a series of pictures that show how a circularly linked queue would work.

13. (Challenging) Write a simple program to set up and manipulate a circularly linked queue of cars at a stoplight, as in exercise 7.

14. One method for setting up and manipulating a queue is to use a *doubly linked* list. In a doubly linked list, each node has two pointers instead of one: a pointer to the next node and a pointer to the previous node. Show how a doubly linked list might be used to create and manipulate a queue.

15. (Challenging) Consider a stoplight at a traffic intersection. Cars reach the stoplight going in four different directions; at the stoplight, cars can go straight ahead, turn left, or turn right. How many queues would you need to simulate this intersection? How would you simulate the operation of the traffic light, allowing cars to go through the intersection without collisions? Write the outline of a program to simulate such an intersection.

Elementary Algorithms

The decision as to the validity of an algorithm is not itself an algorithmic process! In order to decide whether or not an algorithm will actually work, one needs insights, *not just another algorithm.*

—Roger Penrose, *The Emperor's New Mind*

In this chapter, we will discuss *algorithms:* step-by-step recipes that tell a computer (or a person) what to do in certain situations. In the broadest sense of the term, algorithms have been an integral part of every chapter we have seen so far. In programming, however, the term is often used more narrowly, to refer to some fairly well-known recipes that have been thoroughly tested in practice. Here, we will look at several such recipes, with the understanding that there is much more to be learned than we can present in the short space we have here.

THE IDEA OF AN ALGORITHM

Before we discuss particular algorithms, however, we should get a better idea of what an algorithm is. The word is derived from the name of a Persian mathematician, Abu Ja'far Mohammed ibn Musa al Khowarizmi, who lived in the Middle Ages, around 800 C.E. An algorithm specifies a precise and totally unambiguous series of steps that will produce a certain result. Thus, an algorithm must have the following characteristics:

1. It must consist of a *finite* series of steps; that is, the conditions in which it will stop running must be clearly defined and must eventually be reached.

2. Each step must be *precise;* there can be no ambiguity about what is supposed to be done at any point in the running of the algorithm.

3. It must terminate in a reasonable amount of time, i.e., it must be *efficient*.

4. It must produce the desired results at least under any foreseeable or probable conditions of use, i.e., it must be *effective*.

The characteristics of an algorithm make it ideal for giving instructions to a computer, which takes everything literally and does exactly what it is told to do. Hence, the following is an example of an algorithm, in pseudocode rather than Pascal:

```
counter = 0
computer screen line = 5
repeat loop until counter = 10
   begin loop
         counter := counter + 1
         display counter value at screen column 0.
         screen line := screen line + 1
   end loop
```

EFFICIENCY OF ALGORITHMS

One of the important features of an algorithm is that it be as efficient as possible. This means that it should run as *fast* as possible and require as little computer *memory* as possible—two goals that are often in conflict.

Consider sequential search, which we looked at in Chapters 8 (for arrays) and 11 (for linked lists). To use this algorithm, you specify a *target* value that you want to look for in the list. The algorithm starts its search at the beginning of the list and compares each value to the target. If the value matches, then the search ends. Otherwise, the algorithm moves down to the next item in the list and does another comparison. It continues this process until it either finds the target value in the list or reaches the end of the list.

Observe that in the version of sequential search we have discussed so far, two operations are done at each position in the list—not just one. The first operation is to determine if the target value has been found. The second is to determine if the end of the list has been reached. Later in this chapter, we will see how to improve on this situation.

For small lists, sequential search is fast enough. It is faster in the array-based version than it is in the linked-list version, but the array-based version will normally require more memory. Thus, we face a trade-off: we can make the algorithm run faster by putting our list in an array, but this means a larger memory requirement. We can reduce the algorithm's memory needs by putting our list in a linked list, but this will cause somewhat slower performance.

BEST, WORST, AND AVERAGE PERFORMANCE

Another aspect of algorithm performance is how the speed of the algorithm varies with the number of items it has to process. In the case of sequential search, the amount of time it takes to find an arbitrary item in a list varies directly with the size of the list. There are three cases we need to consider:

- *Best-case performance,* which is the number of operations that the algorithm will have to perform under ideal conditions;

- *Worst-case performance,* which is the number of operations that the algorithm will have to perform under the most unfavorable set of conditions; and

- *Average-case performance,* which is the average number of operations that the algorithm will have to perform when all cases are considered.

Notice that these three points refer only to how many operations the algorithm must perform—*not* to how fast it will run. How fast it runs will depend on many factors that cannot be controlled by the programmer, such as the speed of the user's machine. However, the more operations an algorithm has to perform for an input of a certain size, the slower it will run. A more efficient algorithm, which has to do fewer operations for an input of the same size, will run faster on any computer.

As an example, let's look at sequential search to determine its approximate efficiency in searching a list of n items—ignoring, for the moment, the extra end-of-list test at each position. In the best case, the target item will be found at the first position in the list, so the algorithm will need to make only one comparison. In the worst case, the target item will not be found in the list, so the algorithm will make n comparisons and have nothing to show for it.

The average case is a little more complicated. Assume that values are distributed randomly throughout the list: i.e., that the target value has an equal chance of being at any position in the list. The target value might be at the first position, or the last, or any position in between. The algorithm might have to make one comparison, two, three, or any number of comparisons up to n. Therefore, using some math that we won't discuss here, the average number of comparisons is

$$\frac{1 + 2 + 3 + .. + n}{n} = \frac{n + 1}{2}$$

This is about half the number of comparisons for a worst-case, unsuccessful search. (If you are interested in learning how to do these calculations, see any book on discrete mathematics, such as *Discrete Mathematics* by Richard Johnsonbaugh or *Concrete Mathematics* by Graham, Knuth, and Patashnik.)

As you can see, the performance of sequential search varies directly with the number of items in the list to be searched. Not all algorithms are like this. A few algorithms take the same time regardless of how many items are in the list; for example,

```
VAR

    List : ARRAY[1..50000] OF CHAR;

BEGIN

    WRITELN(List[n])

END;
```

Of course, this is a trivial algorithm, but it is one that pops up occasionally in programs. On the other hand, some algorithms have much slower worst-case performance than sequential search. For example, **Quicksort**, which we will look at later in this chapter, has a worst-case performance of n^2. This means that if one list is 10 times the size of another, then in the worst case it will take 100 times as long to sort the bigger list. (What makes **Quicksort** valuable is that it gives excellent best-case and average-case performance.)

"BIG O" NOTATION

We've talked about how algorithm performance varies with the number of items to be processed, but it would make things easier if we had a simple way to refer to levels of efficiency. This is provided by "Big O" notation. Here, we will simply explain Big O notation enough so that you can understand it when you see it, but we will skip the mathematical details. If you want to develop a deeper understanding of Big O notation, see any of the books on discrete mathematics that were mentioned earlier.

The best way to proceed is with an example. Consider a list containing n items and some (unspecified) search algorithm that we will call F. Assume that $f(n)$ is the number of operations that have to be performed by F in dealing with n items, and $g(n)$ is some function of n, such as $5n$ or n^2. Then, using Big O notation, we say that the algorithm *F is O(g(n))* ("F is Big O of g(n)") if there is some constant c such that

$$| \mathbf{f}(n) | <= (c * | g(n) |)$$

This *sounds* a lot more complicated than it really is. Suppose that function $g(n)$ is "n squared," so that $g(n) = n^2$. Then if our algorithm is O of g(n), i.e., is O of n^2, it means simply that as n (the number of items in the list) increases, the number of operations that the algorithm must perform will grow *no faster* than n^2. Thus, the worst-case performance of **Quicksort**, which varies with the square of the number of items in the list, is O of n^2, meaning that with a list of n items the number of operations done by **Quicksort** grows proportionately to n^2 or slower than that. The worst-case performance of sequential search, which varies directly in proportion to the number of items in the list, is O of n, meaning it varies in proportion to n with a list of n items.

Table 18.1 shows the levels of algorithm efficiency that are commonly expressed in Big O notation, from most efficient (Big O of 1) to least efficient (Big O of n factorial).

Table 18.1: Common "Big O" Efficiency Ratings of Algorithms (from Most Efficient to Least Efficient)

BIG O NOTATION	HOW PERFORMANCE VARIES WITH n [*]
O(1)	Constant (the best: size of n doesn't matter)
O(lg n) [**]	Logarithmic
O(n)	Linear
O(n lg n)	N log n (common with "divide and conquer" algorithms)
O(n^2)	Quadratic
O(n^3)	Cubic
O(m^n) [***]	Exponential
O($n!$)	Factorial (the absolute worst!)

[*] *N is the number of items that must be handled by the algorithm.*

[**] *Logarithms normally use 10 as a base; Lg n means Log of n to the base 2, and is commonly used in computer science.*

[***] *M is a nonnegative constant integer greater than 1.*

TIPS FOR FINE-TUNING ALGORITHMS

Algorithm efficiency is important, but it is not equally important in every situation. If you have a simple program to display some text on the computer screen, then it is silly to spend too much time worrying about how efficiently you do it.

Likewise, a routine that is called only once in a program run can probably be as inefficient as you please: if it takes five seconds to run, then it's too bad but it's not a disaster. On the other hand, a routine that is called 1,000 or 1,000,000 times in a program run had better be as efficient as possible: if *it* wastes five seconds on a task that should take only a fraction of a second, then your program could still be running next week! (Turbo Profiler, which is included with Turbo Pascal Professional, can help you determine where you should concentrate your efforts.)

The point is that you should concentrate your optimization efforts where they will do the most good. There are two areas where efficiency is most important:

1. In routines that will be called very often during a run of the program. If one of these routines wastes time, then its inefficiency will be multiplied by the number of instances where it is called in the program.

2. In routines that handle user input and output. Users (PC users in particular) expect almost instant response when they do something on the computer. A routine that takes user input and displays a response on the screen should be as efficient as you can make it. If the user is forced to wait more than a second for a response, he or she will probably start pressing keys to see if your program is working properly—an action which could itself interfere with the operation of your program. (If some delay is unavoidable, then your program should display a message on-screen that says "Processing. Please wait ..." or something similar.)

If you focus on these areas, you do not need to spend too much time worrying about the efficiency of other parts of your program.

SEARCHING ALGORITHMS

Now we will examine two searching algorithms and do an analysis of each. First, we will look at an improved version of sequential search that does only half as many operations as the version we saw earlier. Second, we will look at an algorithm called *binary search* that is more difficult but is also much faster than sequential search.

SEQUENTIAL SEARCH WITH A SENTINEL NODE

As noted earlier, our current version of sequential search does two operations at each position in the list:

- First, it compares the item at that position to the search target.

- Second, if the item is not equal to the target, then the search determines if the end of the list has been reached.

If we were certain that the target value was in the list, then we could leave out the second operation (the end-of-list test) and our algorithm would run twice as fast because it would have to do only half the number of operations.

To pull off this trick, we use what is called a *sentinel node*. At the very beginning of our search, we take the target value and insert it at the end of the list. Then we can omit the end-of-list test because we know that the search will terminate when the target value is found. At the same time, we know that if it is found at the last position in the list, then the target value was not really in the list at all—but that our sentinel node was reached. This method is illustrated in Listing 18.1.

In Listing 18.1, we create a linked list of characters from 'a' to 'z'. The **Init** procedure simply sets the head and tail pointers of the list to **NIL**, then clears the screen. The **FillList** procedure actually creates the list, creating and linking nodes to hold the letters.

It is the **SearchList** procedure that is of greatest interest here. This procedure takes both the head and tail pointers of the list as parameters. Because the head pointer won't be changed by the procedure, it is passed by value. The tail pointer, on the other hand, will be changed when we add the new sentinel node at the end of the list, so it is passed as a VAR parameter.

The **SearchList** procedure first sets a temporary pointer to point at the head of the list and initializes a counter variable, just as in the version of sequential search we saw in Chapter 11. It then prompts the user to enter a letter as a search target. If the head pointer equals nil, then the procedure tells the user that the list is empty. Otherwise, it creates a new node, points

```
PROGRAM Listing18_1;

   { Demonstrates sequential search of a linked list with a
     sentinel node at the end. This is faster than "plain"
     sequential search because it does fewer operations. }

USES CRT, MyUtils;

TYPE
   CharPtr = ^CharRec;
   CharRec = RECORD
               Letter : CHAR;
               Next   : CharPtr
               END;
VAR
   ListHead,
   ListTail : CharPtr;

PROCEDURE init(VAR ListHead, ListTail : CharPtr);
   BEGIN
      ListHead := NIL;
      ListTail := NIL;
      CLRSCR;
   END;

PROCEDURE FillList(VAR ListHead, ListTail : CharPtr);
   VAR
      counter : CHAR;
   BEGIN
      FOR counter := 'a' TO 'z' DO
         BEGIN
            IF ListHead = NIL
               THEN BEGIN
                  NEW(ListHead);
                  ListHead^.letter := counter;
                  ListHead^.next := NIL;
                  ListTail := ListHead;
                  END
               ELSE BEGIN
                  NEW(ListTail^.next);
                  IF ListHead = ListTail
                     THEN ListHead^.next := ListTail^.next;
                  ListTail := ListTail^.next;
                  ListTail^.letter := counter;
                  ListTail^.next := NIL;
                  END
         END
   END;

PROCEDURE SearchList(ListHead: CharPtr; VAR ListTail: CharPtr);
   VAR
      currptr : CharPtr;
      target  : CHAR;
      counter : INTEGER;

BEGIN
   currptr := ListHead;
   counter := 1;
   WRITE(' Enter a letter for which to search: ');
   READLN(target);
   IF currptr = NIL
      THEN WRITELN(' Sorry. The list is empty.')
      ELSE BEGIN
         New(ListTail^.next);          { new node for sentinel }
```

Listing 18.1: Sequential search with a sentinel node.

```
              ListTail := ListTail^.next; { point tail at new node }
              ListTail^.letter := target; { load sentinel value }
              ListTail^.next := NIL;
              WHILE target <> currptr^.letter DO
                    BEGIN
                    counter := counter + 1;
                    IF currptr^.letter <> target
                       THEN currptr := currptr^.next
                    END;
              IF currptr = ListTail
                 THEN WRITELN(' Sorry, target not found in list.')
                 ELSE BEGIN
                      WRITE(' Target found at node #', counter);
                      WRITELN(' of list.')
                      END
              END;
        pause
  END;

{ main body of program }
BEGIN
  init(ListHead, ListTail);
  FillList(ListHead, ListTail);
  SearchList(ListHead, ListTail);
END.
```

Listing 18.1: Sequential search with a sentinel node. (cont.)

the tail pointer at the new node, and loads the target value into that node. This is our sentinel node.

Having completed this preparatory work, the **SearchList** procedure goes into the search loop. In the old version of the routine, the WHILE statement had to have two tests to make sure that the loop would eventually terminate: one to determine if the current list item matched the target value, and one to determine if the end of the list had been reached. However, we now know for sure that the target value will be found by the end of the list, so we don't need an end-of-list test to make sure that the loop terminates. Whenever the target value is found, the program drops out of the loop.

If the loop ends with the current pointer equal to the tail pointer, we know that the search routine has gone all the way to the sentinel node without previously finding the target value in the list. Hence, the target was not in the list. If the loop ends and the current pointer is *not* equal to the tail pointer, then we know that the target *was* found in the list because the loop ended before arriving at the sentinel node.

By reducing the number of operations that must be performed each time the search routine goes through the loop, we have made this search algorithm somewhat faster. Observe, however, that this version of sequential search is still $O(n)$, that is, its running time is directly proportional to the number of items in the list. If one list is 10 times larger than another, then its worst-case search time will still be 10 times longer, even though it will take *less* time in both cases than with the old sequential search routine.

Are there any ways to search a list more efficiently? Yes, indeed. In the next section we will look at binary search, which gives $O(lg\ n)$ performance.

BINARY SEARCH

The next search algorithm to examine is called *binary search*. Unlike sequential search, binary search requires that the list already be in order by the search field: e.g., if you are searching for a student record by last name, then the records must be in sorted order by last name. For lists that *are* already in order, binary search provides much faster performance than sequential search.

Binary search is what is called a "divide and conquer" algorithm. Instead of trying to search the whole list at once, you break it up into smaller pieces and determine which piece will contain the search target if it is in the list. Then you apply the same method to the new, smaller list (which is one-half of the original list) to get a list that is still smaller. You continue the process of narrowing the list until you either run out of list items or run into the target value.

Two versions of the binary search algorithm are shown in Listing 18.2. The first, **BSearch1**, continues to divide the list until it arrives at a single item, but does not check until then to find out if the target has been found. The second, **BSearch2**, checks at each loop to see if the target value has been found.

BSearch1 takes four parameters: a list to be searched, a target value, a variable representing the position in the list where the target is found, and a Boolean variable for whether or not the target value has been found. The

```
PROGRAM Listing18_2;

   { Demonstrates two versions of binary search. }

USES CRT, MyUtils;


CONST
  max = 8;

TYPE
  list = RECORD
           entry : ARRAY[1..max] of INTEGER;
           count : 0..max
           END;

VAR
  choice,
  target,
  position   : INTEGER;
  found      : BOOLEAN;
  SearchList : list;
  Again      : CHAR;


{ ------------------------------- }
{ MAIN-LEVEL PROCEDURE DECLARATION }
{ ------------------------------- }
PROCEDURE FillList(VAR searchlist: list; max: INTEGER);
  VAR
    counter : INTEGER;
  BEGIN
    for counter := 1 to Max do
    searchlist.entry[counter] := counter;
    searchlist.count := max
  END;

{ ------------------------------- }
{ MAIN-LEVEL PROCEDURE DECLARATION }
{ ------------------------------- }
PROCEDURE BSearch1(VAR SearchList: list; target: INTEGER;
                   VAR position: INTEGER; VAR found: BOOLEAN);
  { "Non-checking" binary search. This does not check at
        each loop to determine if the target has been found }
  VAR
    high,
    low,
    middle     : INTEGER;
  BEGIN
    high := SearchList.count;
    low := 1;
    while high > low do
    BEGIN
    middle := (high + low) div 2;
    IF target > SearchList.entry[middle]
      THEN low := middle + 1
      ELSE high := middle
    END;
  IF high = 0
    THEN found := FALSE
    ELSE found := (target = SearchList.entry[high]);
  position := high
END;
```

Listing 18.2: Two versions of binary search.

```
{ ------------------------------- }
{ MAIN-LEVEL PROCEDURE DECLARATION }
{ ------------------------------- }
PROCEDURE BSearch2(VAR SearchList:list; target:INTEGER;
                   VAR position:INTEGER; VAR found:BOOLEAN);
   { "Checking" version that determines at each loop whether
          or not the target has been found. }

   VAR
     high,
     low,
     middle      : INTEGER;
   BEGIN
     high := SearchList.count;
     low := 1;
     found := FALSE;
     while (not found) and (high >= low) do
       BEGIN
       middle := (high + low) div 2;
       IF target = SearchList.entry[middle]
         THEN found := TRUE
         ELSE IF target < SearchList.entry[middle]
                 THEN high := middle - 1
                 ELSE low := middle + 1
       END;
       position := middle
   END;


{ ------------------------------- }
{ MAIN-LEVEL PROCEDURE DECLARATION }
{ ------------------------------- }
PROCEDURE GetKey(VAR key:INTEGER);
   BEGIN
     CLRSCR; WRITELN; WRITELN;
     WRITE('Enter the number for which to search: ');
     READLN(key)
   END;


{ ------------------------------- }
{ MAIN-LEVEL PROCEDURE DECLARATION }
{ ------------------------------- }
Procedure InList(found:BOOLEAN; position:INTEGER; VAR Again:CHAR);
   BEGIN
     CLRSCR;
     IF found THEN
       BEGIN
       WRITE('The searched-for item was found at position ');
       WRITELN(position, '.');
       pause;
       CLRSCR
       END
     ELSE
       BEGIN
       WRITELN('The searched-for item was not found in this list.');
       pause
       END;
     WRITE(' Would you like to do another? (Y/N): ');
     READLN(Again);
     IF UPCASE(again) = 'Y'
        THEN BEGIN
             CLRSCR;
             WRITELN;
```

Listing 18.2: Two versions of binary search. (cont.)

```
                WRITELN
             END
   END;


PROCEDURE DisplayMenu(VAR choice:INTEGER);
  ( displays a menu on the screen )
    BEGIN
      CLRSCR; WRITELN; WRITELN;
      WRITELN('                    Search Operations Menu');
      WRITELN('            ===================================');
      WRITELN('                1. BSearch1 ("non-checking" search)');
      WRITELN('                2. Binary2 (checks if target found)');
      WRITELN('                3. Quit'); WRITELN;
      WRITE('             Enter your choice (1/2/3): ');
      READLN(choice)
    END;

PROCEDURE DoChoice(choice:INTEGER);
  BEGIN
    CASE choice OF
      1 : BSearch1(SearchList,target,position,found);
      2 : BSearch2(SearchList,target,position,found);
      3 : HALT
    END
  END;


{ ------------------------------------------------------------- }
{                    MAIN BODY OF PROGRAM                        }
{ ------------------------------------------------------------- }
BEGIN
  Again := 'Y';
  FillList(SearchList,Max);
  REPEAT
    GetKey(target);
    DisplayMenu(choice);
    DoChoice(choice);
    InList(found,position,again)
  UNTIL UPCASE(again) <> 'Y'
END.
```

Listing 18.2: Two versions of binary search. (cont.)

list, remember, must be in sorted order. The number of items in the list is assigned to the *high* variable, while the *low* variable is set to 1.

A WHILE loop begins the divide-and-conquer part of the routine. It divides the list into two parts, a high part and a low part, by picking a middle position. If the target value is higher in the order than the item in the middle position, then the low variable is set to be one above the middle position. If the target is lower than or equal to the item in the middle position, then the high variable is set to the middle position.

The same process is repeated with the high and low positions getting closer each time, until the two finally come together at some position in the list. If the target value is in the list, it will be in this position. Otherwise, the search is unsuccessful.

BSearch2 works the same way as **BSearch1**, except that at each pass through the loop, it tests the value at the middle position to determine if it matches the target value, in which case the target has been found.

The difference between **BSearch1** and **BSearch2** is that if the target value is found early in the search, then **BSearch2** will require fewer operations than **BSearch1**. However, **BSearch2** also makes twice as many comparisons as **BSearch1**, so in the average and worst cases, it is actually *less* efficient.

Both methods, however, are more efficient for sorted lists than sequential search. Binary search is $O(lg\ n)$, which Table 18.1 shows is faster than sequential search, which is $O(n)$.

SORTING ALGORITHMS

Now we will look at sorting algorithms. These algorithms are used to put list items in order. Some sorting algorithms, such as **Insertion Sort,** are very simple but have average-case performance that is $O(n^2)$. They are suitable for small lists of a few hundred items or less. Other sorting algorithms, such as **Quicksort**, are faster, with average-case performance that is $O(n\ lg\ n)$. These, however, are generally more difficult to code correctly and should be used only where a large number of items must be sorted. In certain circumstances, you can even do some *really* tricky things to get speed approaching $O(n)$, but we won't discuss those here.

Most sorting algorithms also excel in dealing with either array-based lists or linked lists—but not both. Insertion sort is a simple general-purpose sorting routine that can be used either with arrays or linked lists. **Quicksort** is a more powerful routine that does not do very well with linked lists, but is very fast in sorting arrays.

INSERTION SORT

Insertion sort is perhaps the most familiar of all sorting methods. It is the method that most people use to sort a hand of cards: keep each item in its proper position in a sorted sublist, adding new items one at a time to the sorted sublist. When a new item is inserted in the sorted part of the list, higher-ranking items are moved to the right. When all the items have been added to the sorted sublist, then the original list has been completely sorted. This method is illustrated in Listing 18.3.

The program in Listing 18.3 first creates a linked list of letters. In the list, the letters are in reverse alphabetical order, from 'z' to 'a'. It then traverses the list, displaying the order of the letters on the computer screen.

The **Insertion Sort** procedure, of course, is the star of the show. It first checks to make sure that the list is not empty, then sets up a WHILE loop to move node-by-node down to the end of the list. It moves to the next node, and if the letter in this node comes before the head node letter in the alphabet (as we know that it does), then it shuffles the link pointers to move the next node to the head of the list. If not, it creates two more temporary pointers and moves them down the list until they reach the location where the node should be inserted. This process is repeated until every item in the list is in its proper location and the list is completely sorted.

Even this simple sorting routine has its share of details, so you should study Listing 18.3 until you are sure you understand how **Insertion Sort** works.

QUICKSORT

Quicksort, which really is quick most of the time when it comes to sorting arrays, was invented by C. Antony Hoare, an Oxford University computer scientist who has won just about every award that his profession and the computer industry can bestow. **Quicksort** is a classic example of a divide-and-conquer sorting algorithm. Just as a large and complex program can be coded more efficiently when you divide it into smaller,

```
PROGRAM Listing18_3;

  { Demonstrates Insertion Sort with a linked list. }

USES CRT, MyUtils;

TYPE
  nodeptr = ^node;
  node    = RECORD
              item  : CHAR;
              next  : nodeptr
              END;
VAR
  head, tail: nodeptr;

PROCEDURE Init(VAR head, tail: nodeptr);
  BEGIN
    CLRSCR;
    head := NIL;
    tail := NIL
  END;


PROCEDURE TraverseList(VAR head: NodePtr);
  VAR
    TempPtr : nodeptr;
  BEGIN
    CLRSCR;
    WRITELN(' Now traversing the list from head to tail ...');
    tempptr := head;
    WHILE TempPtr <> NIL DO
      BEGIN
      WRITELN(' Current node contains: ', TempPtr^.item, '.');
      delay(500);
      TempPtr := TempPtr^.next
      END;
    pause
  END;


PROCEDURE addnode(VAR head, tail : nodeptr; newitem: CHAR);
  BEGIN
  IF head = NIL
      THEN BEGIN
            NEW(head);
            head^.item := newitem;
            head^.next := NIL;
            tail := head;
            END
      ELSE BEGIN
            NEW(tail^.next);
            IF head = tail
                THEN head^.next := tail^.next;
            tail := tail^.next;
            tail^.item := newitem;
            tail^.next := NIL;
            END
  END;


PROCEDURE CreateLinkedList(VAR head, tail: NodePtr);
  VAR
    counter : CHAR;
```

Listing 18.3: Demonstration of Insertion Sort.

```
   BEGIN
     CLRSCR;
     FOR counter := 'z' DOWNTO 'a' DO
       BEGIN
       WRITELN(' Now adding ', counter, ' to the list.');
       delay(500);
       AddNode(head, tail, counter)
       END
   END;


PROCEDURE InsertionSort(VAR head: NodePtr);
  VAR
    LocalTailPtr,
    TempPtr1,
    TempPtr2,
    TempPtr3 : nodeptr;
  BEGIN
    CLRSCR;
    WRITELN(' Now running Insertion Sort! ... ');
    IF head <> NIL
      THEN BEGIN
            LocalTailPtr := head;
            WHILE LocalTailPtr^.next <> NIL DO
              BEGIN
              TempPtr1 := LocalTailPtr^.next;
              IF TempPtr1^.item < head^.item
                  THEN BEGIN
                        LocalTailPtr^.next := TempPtr1^.next;
                        TempPtr1^.next := head;
                        head := TempPtr1
                        END
                  ELSE BEGIN
                        TempPtr3 := head;
                        TempPtr2 := TempPtr3^.next;
                        WHILE TempPtr1^.item > TempPtr2^.item DO
                          BEGIN
                          TempPtr3 := TempPtr2;
                          TempPtr2 := TempPtr3^.next
                          END;
                        IF TempPtr1 = TempPtr2
                          THEN LocalTailPtr := TempPtr1
                          ELSE BEGIN
                                LocalTailPtr^.next := TempPtr1^.next;
                                TempPtr1^.next := TempPtr2;
                                TempPtr3^.next := TempPtr1
                                END
                        END
              END;
            END;
    pause
  END;

{ ------------------------------------------------------------ }
{                     MAIN BODY OF PROGRAM                     }
{ ------------------------------------------------------------ }
BEGIN
  Init(head, tail);
  CreateLinkedList(head, tail);
  TraverseList(head);
  InsertionSort(head);
  TraverseList(head);
END.
```

Listing 18.3: Demonstration of Insertion Sort. (cont.)

simpler subroutines, so a large array-based list can be sorted more efficiently (most of the time) when you divide it into smaller lists.

Quicksort works by dividing (*partitioning*) a list into two parts. It does so by selecting a *pivot* location that is midway between the beginning and the end of the list; hopefully, the value in this location will be midway between the lowest and highest values in the list. It then scans through the whole list and puts all the items that are less than the pivot into one sublist and all the items that are greater than or equal to the pivot into another sublist.

Notice that the original list is now partly sorted: all the items less than the pivot are in one sublist, and all the items greater than or equal to the pivot are in the other sublist. If we were to put the two sublists back together at this point, the original list would be closer to being sorted than it was before.

This operation is repeated until each sublist contains only a single element. The sublists are then put back together, one step at a time, until the original list has been reconstituted—this time, in completely sorted order. Listing 18.4 illustrates the use of **Quicksort.**

In most respects, Listing 18.4 is just like Listing 18.3. The major differences are that it has an array-based list instead of a linked list, and, of course, it has **Quicksort** instead of **Insertion Sort**. The array-based list is loaded up with letters in reverse alphabetical order. Then, **Quicksort** is called to put them in normal alphabetical order.

Quicksort takes three parameters: the list itself, the array index for the beginning slot, and the array index for the ending slot. It calls a local routine called **Sort**, which does the actual work of sorting. **Sort** picks a location in the middle of the array and uses the value it contains (x) as the pivot.

Using two WHILE statements, it then scans forward through the array until it gets to a value that is greater than or equal to x, and scans backward until it finds another value that is less than or equal to x. If the array slot of the first value (the value which is greater than or equal to the pivot) is lower than the slot containing the second (which is less than or equal to the pivot), then the routine flip-flops the two items so that the one in the second slot gets moved into the first slot and the one in the first slot gets moved into the second.

```
PROGRAM Listing18_4;

  { Demonstrates the Quicksort algorithm for sorting arrays. }

USES CRT, MyUtils;

CONST
  ListSize = 26;

TYPE
  List = ARRAY[1..ListSize] OF CHAR;

VAR
  LetterList : list;
  i          : integer;


{ ------------------------------ }
{ MAIN-LEVEL PROCEDURE DECLARATION }
{ ------------------------------ }
PROCEDURE LoadUpList(VAR LetterList : list);
  VAR
    counter : CHAR;
    listpos : INTEGER;
  BEGIN
    CLRSCR;
    WRITELN(' Now loading the list in reverse alphabetical order,');
    WRITELN(' from "z" to "a" ...');
    listpos := 1;
    FOR counter := 'z' DOWNTO 'a' DO
      BEGIN
      LetterList[listpos] := counter;
      listpos := listpos + 1
      END;
    delay(1000);
    WRITELN;
    WRITELN(' List now loaded in reverse alphabetical order!');
    pause
  END;

{ ------------------------------ }
{ MAIN-LEVEL PROCEDURE DECLARATION }
{ ------------------------------ }
PROCEDURE TraverseList(VAR LetterList : list);
  VAR
    counter : INTEGER;
  BEGIN
    CLRSCR;
    WRITELN(' Now traversing the letter list ...');
    delay(1000);
    FOR counter := 1 TO ListSize DO
      BEGIN
      WRITELN(' Current node contains ', LetterList[counter], '.');
      delay(500)
      END;
    pause
  END;


{ ------------------------------ }
{ MAIN-LEVEL PROCEDURE DECLARATION }
{ ------------------------------ }
PROCEDURE Quicksort(VAR LetterList: list; Low,High: integer);
```

Listing 18.4: Sorting an array with Quicksort.

```
{ --------------------------- }
{ Local procedure            }
{ --------------------------- }
{ Under Quicksort }
{ --------------------------- }
PROCEDURE sort(l,r: INTEGER);
  VAR
    i,j : INTEGER;
    x,y : CHAR;
  BEGIN
  i:=l;
  j:=r;
  x:=LetterList[(l+r) DIV 2];    { pivot value in array }
  REPEAT
    WHILE LetterList[i] < x DO i := i+1;
    WHILE LetterList[j] > x DO j := j-1;
    IF i <= j
      THEN BEGIN
           y := LetterList[i];
           LetterList[i] := LetterList[j];
           LetterList[j] := y;
           i := i + 1;
           j := j - 1;
           END;
  UNTIL i > j;
  IF l < j THEN sort(l,j); { the sort routine calls itself:  }
  IF i < r THEN sort(i,r)  { a typical example of recursion. }
  END;

{ --------------------------------- }
{ Main body of higher-level procedure }
{ --------------------------------- }
{ Procedure name: Quicksort         }
{ --------------------------------- }
BEGIN
CLRSCR;
WRITELN(' Now sorting the list with Quicksort ...');
sort(Low,High);
WRITELN;
WRITELN(' WHOOSH !!!!');
WRITELN(' The list has been sorted! Pretty fast, eh? ');
pause
END;
{ --------------------------------------------------------------- }
{                       MAIN BODY OF PROGRAM                      }
{ --------------------------------------------------------------- }
BEGIN
  LoadUpList(LetterList);
  TraverseList(LetterList);
  quicksort(LetterList, 1, ListSize);
  TraverseList(LetterList)
END.
```

Listing 18.4: Sorting an array with Quicksort. (cont.)

This process continues until all the items less than the pivot are moved to one side of the array and all those greater than or equal to the pivot are moved to the other side of the array. The process then repeats within each sublist (i.e., each section of the array) until one-item lists are reached, at which point the array is in sorted order.

The **Quicksort** routine is complicated by the fact that, although we have been talking about sublists as if they were physically separate, all of the sorting goes on inside the array that is being sorted. Items are shuffled back and forth in the array until they finally end up in the correct order. This makes things more difficult to code, but it has the advantage of needing very little extra memory beyond the array itself.

As with **Insertion Sort**, you should examine Listing 18.4 carefully until you are sure that you understand how it works. Then, try to create your own implementation of **Quicksort**.

SUMMARY

An algorithm is a precise set of instructions that tells how to accomplish a certain result. It must be finite, precise, efficient, and effective. One aspect of efficiency is running as fast as possible, while another is requiring as little memory as possible: these two aspects are often in conflict.

There are three cases that have to be considered in evaluating an algorithm: best-case, worst-case, and average-case performance. Big O notation is a convenient way to talk about the efficiency of algorithms. Decision trees are one way to determine the approximate efficiency of a new algorithm.

There are well-known algorithms for searching and sorting lists. Sequential search is simple but relatively inefficient; binary search is more efficient, but harder to code.

Insertion sort, like sequential search, is simple but slow; **Quicksort**, which works with array-based lists, is complex but fast (in the best and average cases).

REVIEW EXERCISES

1. Explain the idea of an algorithm, as well as each of the four characteristics of an algorithm.

2. Explain the two aspects of algorithm efficiency, as well as why these aspects are often in conflict. What factors determine how efficiently an algorithm will process data?

3. Explain the idea of "Big O" notation and list the levels of algorithm efficiency, from most efficient to least efficient.

4. Explain where you should concentrate your efforts in making your program more efficient, and why this is so.

5. Explain how sequential search works in an array-based list and then in a linked list. What is the Big O rating of sequential search?

6. Explain the idea of a sentinel node. Write a simple program of your own that uses a sentinel node in sequential search.

7. Explain the idea of binary search and how the two versions of binary search are different. Compare the efficiency of the two versions in the best, worst, and average cases.

8. Explain the idea behind **Insertion Sort**, and write a simple program that uses **Insertion Sort**.

9. Explain how the **Quicksort** algorithm works.

10. (Challenging) Tracing through Listing 18.4, sort at least 10 items by using **Quicksort**, assuming that they are in an array. Divide each list into sublists and identify the pivot item in each sublist. You should divide the sorting process into two steps: dividing the list into sublists until one-item lists are reached, and recombining the sublists until a single sorted list is created.

C H A P T E R

Sound and Music
Programming

Without music, life would be a mistake.

– Friedrich Nietzsche, *The Twilight of the Idols*

Creating programs that work is one thing; creating programs that are *interesting to use* is something extra. One way to add zip to your programs is by using sound effects and music. A program can beep when the user makes an error, play an anthem when the user saves a file, or make an "exploding" noise when the user opens an on-screen window.

MS-DOS PCs are not designed with computer games and sound effects in mind, so an ordinary PC's sound and music capabilities are somewhat limited. However, Turbo Pascal has features that let you take advantage of what PCs *can* do. With a little imagination, experimentation, and practice, you can create some interesting sound effects. With some sheet music and a basic understanding of the notes, you can even make a PC play melodies.

In this chapter, we will show how to create some simple sound effects and explain the basics of PC music. This will lay the groundwork for Chapter 20, where—as a practical example of program design and development—we will create a basic music construction program for the PC.

MAKING SOUNDS IN TURBO PASCAL

Like so much else in computing, the PC's speaker works on the principle of an on/off switch. It is either on, in which case it is making a sound at a particular frequency, or it is off, in which case it is quiet.

The basic tools that Turbo Pascal provides to manipulate the PC's speaker are the **Sound**, **NoSound**, and **Delay** procedures. All are part of the CRT unit. **Sound** takes a single parameter for the frequency of the tone you want to make. Middle C, for example, is 512 Hertz (cycles per second), while the note (C) one octave lower has a frequency of 256 Hertz and the note (C) one octave higher has a frequency of 1024 Hertz.

The **Sound** routine works together with the **NoSound** routine. Once you have turned on the PC's speaker and made it emit a tone, it will continue to emit that tone until you either turn it off with the **NoSound** routine or call the **Sound** routine again with a different frequency. Normally, you will use Turbo Pascal's **Delay** procedure to make the tone continue for a specific amount of time before **NoSound** is called. **Delay** takes a single parameter, the number of milliseconds (thousandths of a second) that it is intended to work.

A typical use of these routines would be as follows:

```
SOUND(256);

DELAY(1000);

NOSOUND;
```

This causes the PC's speaker to emit a 256-Hertz tone (Low C) for 1,000 milliseconds, or one second. After one second has passed, the call to **NoSound** turns off the speaker and it is silent until it is activated again by another call to **Sound**.

These tools are fairly basic, but as we'll see in the next section, you can use them to create some surprisingly good sound effects. One word of caution: any time you use the **Sound** routine in your program, you *must* make a call to **NoSound** later on in the program to turn the speaker off again. If you forget to do this, you might end up in a situation in which the only way to make the speaker shut up would be to reboot your computer.

SOUND EFFECTS

Although the sound effects you can create on the PC are not very impressive compared to those on more game-oriented machines like the

Commodore Amiga, you can still make some interesting sounds if you use your imagination. Here, we will look at a few examples.

BEEP

The first sound effect we will look at is one that we have already seen—without much comment—in Chapter 17: a short "beep." This sound effect is demonstrated by Listing 19.1.

For the beep tone, we want a fairly low-pitched sound, so a frequency of 150 is just about right. Moreover, a beep should be short, so the **Delay** routine is told to run for 400 milliseconds, or four-tenths of a second. After the delay, a call to **NoSound** turns off the speaker.

Listing 19.1 shows a typical application of a beep: alerting the user to an error. It is simple but effective.

```
PROGRAM Listing19_1;

   { Demonstrates how to make the speaker emit a beep. }

USES CRT, MyUtils;

VAR mynum : integer;

PROCEDURE beep;
  BEGIN
     SOUND(150);
     DELAY(400);
     NOSOUND
  END;

BEGIN
  CLRSCR;
  WRITE(' Enter a number from 1 to 5: ');
  READLN(mynum);
  IF (mynum < 1) or (mynum > 5)
     THEN BEGIN
        beep;
        WRITELN(' You didn''t enter a number from 1 to 5!');
        pause
        END
     ELSE BEGIN
        WRITELN(' Congratulations! You followed
instructions!');
        pause
        END
END.
```

Listing 19.1: Creating a "beep" sound effect.

BUZZ

A buzzing sound is similar to a beep in that it is low-pitched, but it lasts longer and is more uneven. Listing 19.2 shows how to create a buzzing sound.

Because the buzz tone must be uneven, we want to alternate sound with silence. We set up a FOR loop to keep the buzz going while this process is taking place. The speaker emits a low tone (at 100 Hertz) for 30 milliseconds; then is silent for 30 milliseconds; and then repeats the same sequence of sound and silence, for a total of 30 times in the counter loop. This makes the buzz continue for 1.8 seconds.

BOUNCING BALL

For a bouncing ball sound effect, we want to alternate between low and high tones as the ball bounces, goes up, and then comes back down. Each time it bounces, it bounces a little lower, so the bouncing tones get closer together on each bounce. This is illustrated in Listing 19.3. The high and low tones are specified in integer parameters that are passed to the

```
PROGRAM Listing19_2;

    { Demonstrates how to create a buzzing sound. }

USES CRT;

PROCEDURE Buzz;
  VAR
    counter : integer;
  BEGIN
    FOR counter := 1 TO 30 DO
      BEGIN
        SOUND(100);
        DELAY(30);
        NOSOUND;
        DELAY(30)
      END
  END;

BEGIN
  Buzz
END.
```

Listing 19.2: Creating a buzzing sound.

Bouncing Ball routine. We used a WHILE loop instead of a FOR loop because we wanted to change the counter variable by more than 1 on each pass through the loop.

The bouncing ball loop is a little more complicated than the buzzing loop. Because the tones and their duration must change on each pass through the loop, we need some way to control these factors. The most obvious way is to make the tone frequency and duration depend in some way on the value of the counter variable, which itself changes automatically on each pass through the loop.

On the first pass through the loop, the first tone sounds at the "low" frequency minus two times the current counter variable. Because the counter variable decreases from its original value of 20 on each pass through the loop, the value of 2 * *counter* becomes smaller and smaller. Because it is subtracted from the low value to get the sound frequency of the first tone, this means that on each pass, the tone becomes higher, since a

```pascal
PROGRAM Listing19_3;

    { Demonstrates a bouncing ball sound effect. }

USES CRT;

VAR
  high, low : INTEGER;

PROCEDURE BouncingBall(high, low : INTEGER);
  VAR count : INTEGER;
  BEGIN
  count := 20;
  WHILE count > 1 do
    BEGIN
    SOUND(low - count * 2);
    DELAY((count *500) DIV 20);
    NOSOUND;
    DELAY(100);
    SOUND(high);
    DELAY((count * 500) div 15);
    NOSOUND;
    DELAY(150);
    count := count - 2
    END
  END;

BEGIN
  BouncingBall(350,200)
END.
```

Listing 19.3: Bouncing ball sound effect.

smaller number is subtracted from it. At the same time, the *duration* of the tone also becomes shorter as the value of *(count * 500) DIV20* decreases.

The high frequency itself stays the same, although the duration of the second, higher tone in the loop does become shorter on each pass through the loop. There is nothing very scientific about the mathematical formulas used to control the frequency and duration of tones in the loop: you just have to experiment until you discover a sound sequence you like.

BOMBS AWAY

This sound effect is similar to the one used in television war dramas when a plane drops its bombs. It takes three parameters: a high frequency, a low frequency, and an "altitude" integer variable that is used to control the duration of the tones. It is illustrated in Listing 19.4.

As the loop begins (again, a WHILE loop so that we have more flexibility in changing the counter variable), the counter is set at the low frequency value. The first tone is at this low frequency, lasting for a duration that is determined by dividing the altitude by the counter value, and multiplying the result by 75 to make the tone last longer. The counter variable is then increased by 10. On each pass through the loop, the counter value becomes bigger, so the pitch of the tone becomes higher and the length of the tone becomes shorter as *altitude DIV count* decreases. The loop finally ends when the counter is no longer less than or equal to the high value. A call to **Nosound** is made after the loop ends to shut down the PC's speaker.

RED ALERT

This sound effect simulates an alarm, such as the ones that always go off in space operas when a hostile ship is approaching. It simply alternates a high-pitched sound with a low-pitched sound until the user presses a key as shown in Listing 19.5.

A REPEAT loop is used because we want the tones to sound at least once. Outside the loop, we use a WRITE statement to put a message on the screen telling the user how to terminate the sound. This step is very easy to forget because it has nothing to do with generating the sound, but it is also very important: if a user starts the sound and does not know how to

```
PROGRAM Listing19_4;


   { Demonstrates a "bombs away" sound effect. }

USES CRT;

VAR
   high, low, altitude : INTEGER;

PROCEDURE BombsAway(high, low, altitude: INTEGER);
   VAR count : INTEGER;
   BEGIN
        count := low;
        WHILE count <= high DO
              BEGIN
              SOUND(count);
              DELAY((altitude DIV count) * 75);
              count := count + 10
              END;
        NOSOUND;

        SOUND(40);
        DELAY(500);
        NOSOUND;
        DELAY(100);

        SOUND(40);
        DELAY(500);
        NOSOUND;
        DELAY(100);

        SOUND(40);
        DELAY(500);
        NOSOUND;
        DELAY(100);

        SOUND(40);
        DELAY(3000);
        NOSOUND
   END;

BEGIN
   BombsAway(1200, 200, 500)
END.
```

Listing 19.4: "Bombs away" sound effect.

turn it off, extremely angry phone calls about the situation will result.

Note that we called **Readkey** to clear the keyboard buffer after the user presses a key. In normal programming situations, when the user presses a key that is not relayed into a variable, the character resulting from the keypress can still be in the keyboard buffer and can cause unpredictable malfunctions. Calling **Readkey** as we have done here clears the keyboard buffer.

```
PROGRAM Listing19_5;

   { Demonstrates "red alert" alarm sound effect. }

USES CRT;

PROCEDURE RedAlert(high, low: INTEGER);
   VAR ch : CHAR;
   BEGIN
      CLRSCR;
      WRITE(' Press any key to terminate red alert ... ');
      REPEAT
         SOUND(high);
         DELAY(400);
         SOUND(low);
         DELAY(400)
      UNTIL Keypressed;
      ch := Readkey;
      NOSOUND
   END;

BEGIN
   RedAlert(350,200)
END.
```

Listing 19.5: "Red alert" alarm sound.

MUSIC

The PC's speaker may not sound as good as your CD player, but at least it can carry a tune. By using the **Sound** procedure with the frequencies of musical notes, you can make your PC play any tune you like.

We will explore music programming in much more detail in the next chapter when we create Turbo Tunemaker. However, Listing 19.6 introduces many of the basic concepts involved in music programming with Turbo Pascal.

The first thing we have to do is to set up a group of constants to use in our program. Here are the constants used in Listing 19.6:

- **Sbrk** and **Lbrk** are amounts of time between notes.

- **Enote** is the amount of time for an eighth note.

- **Qnote** is the amount of time for a quarter note.

- **Hnote** is the amount of time for a half note.

```
PROGRAM Listing19_6;

    { Demonstrates how to play a simple tune. }

USES CRT;

CONST
  sbrk      = 30;
  lbrk      = 60;
  enote     = 150;
  qnote     = 300;
  hnote     = 600;
  dot_hnote = 900;
  wnote     = 1200;

  { octave below Middle C }
  c1 = 256; c1s = 271; d1 = 287; d1s = 304; e1 = 323; f1 = 342;
  f1s = 362; g1 = 384; g1s = 406; a1 = 431; a1s = 456; b1 = 483;

  { octave containing Middle C }
  c2 = 512; c2s = 542; d2 = 575; d2s = 609; e2 = 645; f2 = 683;
  f2s = 724; g2 = 767; g2s = 813; a2 = 861; a2s = 912; b2 = 967;

  { octave above Middle C }
  c3 = 1024; c3s = 1085; d3 = 1149; d3s = 1218; e3 = 1290; f3 =
1367;
  f3s = 1448; g3 = 1534; g3s = 1625; a3 = 1722; a3s = 1825; b3 =
1933;

PROCEDURE Off;
  BEGIN
  NOSOUND;
  DELAY(notebrk)
  END;


BEGIN
  SOUND(e1);
  DELAY(qnote);
  off;

  SOUND(e1);
  DELAY(qnote);
  off;

  SOUND(e1);
  DELAY(hnote);
  off;
{ ------------------- }
  SOUND(e1);
  DELAY(qnote);
  off;

  SOUND(e1);
  DELAY(qnote);
  off;

  SOUND(e1);
  DELAY(hnote);
  off;
{ ------------------- }
```

Listing 19.6: Playing a simple tune.

```
    SOUND(e1);
    DELAY(qnote);
    off;

    SOUND(g1);
    DELAY(qnote);
    off;

    SOUND(c1);
    DELAY(qnote);
    off;

    SOUND(d1);
    DELAY(qnote);
    off;
{ ------------------ }
    SOUND(e1);
    DELAY(dot_hnote);
    NOSOUND;
    DELAY(qnote);
END.
```

Listing 19.6: Playing a simple tune. (cont.)

- **Dot_hnote** is the amount of time for a dotted half note.

- **Wnote** is the amount of time for a whole note.

- Individual note names contain, first, the letter of the note; second, the octave number; and third, an "s" if the note is sharp. Only sharps are recognized in our table of note names, and this causes no problem because any flat note is the sharp note of the note below it—e.g., B-flat is A-sharp.

The listing also includes a short "off" procedure to insert breaks between notes. This is included simply to avoid writing **NoSound; Delay(notebrk)** over and over. The comment lines indicate the separate bars of the tune.

CREATING THE MUSIC UNIT

As helpful as our table of note names may be, it would be a terrible pain in the neck if we had to put it into every program that used music. The obvious solution is the correct one: we will put the musical notes into a unit that any program can use if it needs to play music. The music unit is shown in Listing 19.7.

```
UNIT Music; { Listing 19.7 }

INTERFACE

CONST

   sbrk      = 30;
   lbrk      = 60;
   enote     = 150;
   qnote     = 300;
   hnote     = 600;
   dot_hnote = 900;
   wnote     = 1200;

   { =============== TABLE OF MUSICAL NOTE FREQUENCIES
============== }
   { This table has mnemonic names for the frequencies of musical
     notes. It covers three octaves: the octave containing Middle
C,
     the octave below Middle C, and the octave above Middle C. The
     note frequencies are taken from the book Science & Music by
     Sir James Jeans.

     There is one thing to be careful about in using this table.
     Some programs use the text strings 'f1', 'f2', etc. to
     denote the function keys on the PC's keyboard. If you are
     adding music to a program that uses the function keys, you
     should make sure that the function keys are named in some
     other way, for example, f_1 for the F1 function key. This
     will prevent the program from becoming confused about which
     item (a function key or a musical note) a particular 'f1',
     etc. identifies. }

   { octave 1, below Middle C }
   c1 = 256; c1s = 271; d1 = 287; d1s = 304; e1 = 323; f1 = 342;
   f1s = 362; g1 = 384; g1s = 406; a1 = 431; a1s = 456; b1 = 483;

   { octave 2, containing Middle C }
   c2 = 512; c2s = 542; d2 = 575; d2s = 609; e2 = 645; f2 = 683;
   f2s = 724; g2 = 767; g2s = 813; a2 = 861; a2s = 912; b2 = 967;

   { octave 3, above Middle C }
   c3 = 1024; c3s = 1085; d3 = 1149; d3s = 1218; e3 = 1290; f3 =
1367;
   f3s = 1448; g3 = 1534; g3s = 1625; a3 = 1722; a3s = 1825; b3 =
1933;

TYPE
   string3 = STRING[3];

   noteptr = ^note;
   note    = RECORD
                freq,
                dur,
                brk  : integer;
                next : noteptr
                END;

IMPLEMENTATION

END.
```

Listing 19.7: The Music unit.

As you should recall from Chapter 10, a unit has three parts: an INTERFACE section, which contains material that is accessible to any programs that use the unit; an IMPLEMENTATION section, which contains material that is private to the unit and cannot be seen by calling programs; and an optional section to initialize the values of variables used by the unit.

Although a unit most often is used to hold subroutines, we can also use it to hold publicly accessible constants in its INTERFACE section. Therefore, we simply declare our note names (along with the note durations) as constants in the INTERFACE section of the unit. In anticipation of Chapter 20, where we will create Turbo Tunemaker, we also include a TYPE section with a note data type for a linked list of musical notes.

There is one thing to be careful about when using this unit. If you are creating constant names that will represent function keys, the natural name for the F1 key is 'f1'. However, this name is used by the table of musical notes to stand for the note F in octave 1; likewise for 'f2' and 'f3'. If your program uses music, you should use some other names for the function keys, such as 'f1key' for the F1 function key.

The music unit allows the programmer to embed musical notes in the source code of a program. One thing it does not do, however, is allow the user of a program to enter the names of musical notes into variables at the keyboard. You cannot simply prompt the user to enter the name of a musical note and then play that note. To get the note from the user, you would need to use a string variable, because the note names are text strings. If you try to play this note, however, you cannot use the **Sound** routine because it requires a parameter of the integer data type. Thus, a user cannot type 'c2' at the keyboard and expect the computer to sound Middle C.

In Chapter 20, we will see how to solve this problem. In the meantime, try some of your own ideas for a solution.

SUMMARY

The PC is not an outstanding music and sound effects machine—it was never intended to be—but with imagination, practice, and skill, you can create some respectable sound effects. The key routines for creating sound effects are **Sound**, **NoSound**, and **Delay**; all three are in the CRT unit.

REVIEW EXERCISES

1. List the three main routines used for sound effects and music in Turbo Pascal, and explain how each one works.

2. How long (in seconds) would each of these tones last?

    (a) Sound(500); Delay(1000);

    (b) Sound(700); Delay(1000);

    (c) Sound(500); Delay(200);

    (d) Sound(500); Delay(10500);

    (e) Sound(500); Delay(1);

3. Experiment on your own and try to write a short program to create an "exploding window" sound effect to run when the user opens a window on the computer screen.

4. Experiment on your own and try to write a short program to play "Yankee Doodle" or some other tune. (You will need sheet music.)

5. Challenging: Listing 19.6 uses only constants with the **Sound** procedure. Can you think of a way to let the user enter note names at run time, load those names into variables, and then play the corresponding notes with the **Sound** procedure? If so, explain how this might be accomplished.

Practical Example:
Creating Turbo Tunemaker

*The first thing to learn in [deal-
ings] with others is non-interference
with their own peculiar ways of being
happy, provided those ways do not assume to interfere by violence with ours
... The pretension to dogmatize about
them in each other is the root of most
human injustices and cruelties, and the
trait in human character most likely to
make the angels weep.*

– William James, *Pragmatism and Other Essays*

This chapter differs from earlier ones
in that it offers a practical exercise for the skills that we have built up in
the previous 19 chapters. In this exercise, we will design and code Turbo
Tunemaker, a music construction program for the PC. At each stage, we
will explain some of the reasoning involved in the most important design
and coding decisions. However, as a learning exercise, there is no substitute for examining the code yourself and making sure that you understand how it works.

PRACTICAL SKILLS
IN THIS CHAPTER

Most of the skills that we will demonstrate in creating Turbo
Tunemaker can be applied in any implementation of Pascal and, indeed,
in almost any programming language. These include:

- Define the main task and divide it into subtasks, each of which
  will be compartmentalized in its own subroutine.
- Set up appropriate looping structures to get input from the user.

- Create easy-to-understand screen displays that provide any information needed by the user.
- Build rudimentary error-checking into routines that call for user input or disk file I/O.
- Create functions to "translate" one type of data into another.
- Create, traverse, and edit linked lists.
- Read data from disk files into linked lists.
- Write data from linked lists into disk files.

In addition, Turbo Tunemaker will demonstrate some techniques that are specific to Turbo Pascal. These include:

- Create and manipulate on-screen windows.
- Create, edit, and play melodies on the PC.
- Create a simple routine to manage the heap.

Here and there, we will also demonstrate a few tricks that you have not seen yet.

Because the Turbo Tunemaker listing itself is about the size of an average chapter, we will not be able to explain everything in it, nor does everything *need* to be explained. Instead, we will focus on the most important points, as well as on points that are not entirely clear without additional explanation of the code.

OVERALL PROGRAM DESIGN

The overall design of the program is dictated to a large degree by the tasks it is intended to perform. As mentioned earlier in this book, Turbo Tunemaker should allow the user to do the following things:

- Create tunes at the computer keyboard.
- Edit tunes that have already been created.

- Play tunes through the PC's speaker.

- Save tunes to disk files.

- Retrieve tunes from disk files for playing or editing.

In addition to these specific tasks that the program should perform, the program should also be easy to use. There are two main areas where this ease-of-use requirement makes a difference. First, we will need to set up an on-screen menu from which the user can select different tasks, such as creating or playing a tune. This is a standard programming task that you will encounter many times in your programming career.

The second task is equally ordinary in general terms, but a little unusual in its specifics. You will recall from Chapter 19 that the Turbo Pascal **Sound** procedure takes as its parameter an integer that stands for a sound frequency. However, it is not reasonable to expect the user to remember (or even to know) all the frequencies of different musical notes. Therefore, we want to provide a way for the user to enter easy-to-remember "note names" at the keyboard: names that the program will then translate into the appropriate sound frequencies. Likewise, we want to provide names for the types of notes (eighth note, quarter note, and so forth) and the pauses between notes (no pause, short pause, and so forth).

It is not immediately obvious, but the reverse is also true. The musical notes, note types, and pause types are used by the program itself as integers. When the user edits a tune, however, the program should translate those integers back into the names of notes, note types, and pause types so that the user can see (in English) the characteristics of the note being edited.

All of these considerations together allow us to generate the overall program framework that is shown in Listing 20.1. Each major task to be performed by the program is assigned to its own subroutine, while a minimum of detail is included in the main program itself.

As you can see in Listing 20.1, there are functions to convert notes, note types, and pause types to and from integer form. There are also procedures for each of the main functions of the program: tune creation, editing, saving, retrieving, and playing. A sign-on routine will explain the

```
PROGRAM Listing20_1;

USES CRT, MyUtils, Music;

(* -------------------- DEVELOPMENT NOTES --------------------
    1. Be sure to substitute GetGoodInt and GetGoodChar for
       READLN whenever possible.
    2. Be sure that the appropriate calls to Mark and Release
       are made in routines that create linked lists.
   -------------------- END OF DEVELOPMENT NOTES --------------- *)

TYPE
  string12 = STRING[12];
  string20 = STRING[20];

VAR
  NewNote  : string3;
  tunehead,
  tunetail : noteptr;
  Heapmark : pointer;
  tunefile : TEXT;
  choice   : INTEGER;

PROCEDURE Init(VAR Tunehead, Tunetail: noteptr; VAR choice: INTEGER);
  BEGIN
  END;

PROCEDURE RestoreWindow;
  BEGIN
  END;

PROCEDURE FreeUpHeapSpace(tunehead : noteptr);
  BEGIN
  END;

PROCEDURE SignOnScreen;
  BEGIN
  END;

FUNCTION NoteName(notefreq: INTEGER) : string3;
  BEGIN
  END;

FUNCTION NoteType(NoteLength : INTEGER) : string20;
  BEGIN
  END;

FUNCTION NBrkType(nbreak : INTEGER) : string20;
  BEGIN
  END;

FUNCTION Frq(VAR NewNote :string3) : INTEGER;
  BEGIN
  END;

PROCEDURE DisplayNotes;
  BEGIN
  END;

PROCEDURE MakeBox;
  BEGIN
  END;

PROCEDURE AddNoteToTune(VAR tunehead, tunetail: noteptr;
                        nfreq, ndur, nbrk: INTEGER);
```

Listing 20.1: Main program framework for Turbo Tunemaker.

```
      BEGIN
      END;

PROCEDURE GetTuneFromUser(VAR tunehead, tunetail: noteptr;
                          VAR HeapMark: pointer);
      BEGIN
      END;

PROCEDURE GetTuneFromFile(VAR tunefile: text; VAR tunehead: noteptr;
                          VAR HeapMark: pointer);
      BEGIN
      END;

PROCEDURE PlayTune(tunehead: noteptr);
      BEGIN
      END;

PROCEDURE EditTune(tunehead: noteptr);
      BEGIN
      END;

PROCEDURE SaveTuneToFile(VAR tunefile : text; VAR tunehead : noteptr);
      BEGIN
      END;

PROCEDURE Menu(VAR choice: INTEGER);
      BEGIN
      END;

  { ---------------------------------------------------------------- }
  {                        MAIN BODY OF PROGRAM                       }
  { ---------------------------------------------------------------- }
  BEGIN
    Init(tunehead, tunetail, choice);
    SignOnScreen;
    REPEAT
      Menu(choice);
    UNTIL choice = { menu choice to quit Turbo Tunemaker };
    CLRSCR
  END.
```

Listing 20.1: Main program framework for Turbo Tunemaker. (cont.)

program to the user, while a menu routine will get the user's choice of the task to be performed.

There are also global routines to display the notes available in the program, to draw a box, to free up heap space, and to add notes to a tune. These routines do not work on their own, but are called by other parts of the program as needed. They must be global in scope because they are called by more than one other part of the program. If they were called only by a single routine, then they would be hidden inside it.

SPECIFIC SUBROUTINES

Now that we have had a brief look at the overall design of the program, we can proceed to examine some of the details of how the program is implemented in specific subroutines. Many of these details will already be familiar to you, so our discussion will focus on new techniques and on slightly more complex applications of old techniques. The completed Turbo Tunemaker program is shown in Listing 20.2.

SIGN-ON ROUTINES

The **SignOn** routines clear the screen, display a welcome message, and play an introductory tune ("Yankee Doodle"). Then, they explain the program to the user. The box in the sign-on screen is drawn in the Turbo Pascal IDE by using the ASCII numbers for box-drawing characters, as explained in Chapter 4. At the end of the sign-on, the **RestoreWindow** routine is called to restore the screen window to its original full-screen dimensions.

NOTE-CONVERSION FUNCTIONS

The note-conversion functions convert musical notes, note types, and pause types from text-string names to integers, and vice versa. **Frq** converts a three-character note name into an integer that represents its sound frequency; **NoteName** converts a sound frequency back into a note name; **NoteType** converts a note duration in milliseconds to a text string such as "quarter note" or "half note," and **NoteBrkType** converts a pause duration in milliseconds to a text string such as *short pause* or *long pause*.

Each of these routines consists of a series of nested CASE statements. Let's take the **Frq** function as an example. In this program, the user will enter three-character *names* for the various musical notes. In these names, the first character stands for the note itself, such as 'c' or 'g'. The second

```
PROGRAM Listing20_2; { Complete Turbo TuneMaker program }

USES CRT, MyUtils, Music;

TYPE
  string12 = STRING[12];
  string20 = STRING[20];

VAR
  NewNote  : string3;
  tunehead,
  tunetail : noteptr;
  Heapmark : pointer;
  tunefile : TEXT;
  choice   : INTEGER;


{ ------------------------------- }
{ MAIN-LEVEL PROCEDURE DECLARATION }
{ ------------------------------- }
PROCEDURE Init(VAR Tunehead, Tunetail: noteptr; VAR choice: INTEGER);
  BEGIN
    Tunehead := NIL;
    Tunetail := NIL;
    choice := 0;
    CLRSCR
  END;

{ ------------------------------- }
{ MAIN-LEVEL PROCEDURE DECLARATION }
{ ------------------------------- }
PROCEDURE RestoreWindow;
  BEGIN
  WINDOW(1,1,80,25);
  CLRSCR
  END;

{ ------------------------------- }
{ MAIN-LEVEL PROCEDURE DECLARATION }
{ ------------------------------- }
PROCEDURE FreeUpHeapSpace(tunehead : noteptr);
  { The procedures that create linked lists to hold tunes
    always BEGIN with a call to MARK. This marks the top of
    the heap before the linked list is created. If several
    tunes were created during a single run of Turbo Tunemaker,
    then the program might run out of heap space. Therefore,
    before a new linked list is created, any previous lists
    are disposed of by a call to RELEASE. This frees up heap
    space for the new linked list. }
  BEGIN
  IF tunehead <> NIL THEN RELEASE(heapmark)
  END;

{ ------------------------------- }
{ MAIN-LEVEL PROCEDURE DECLARATION }
{ ------------------------------- }
PROCEDURE SignOnScreen;
  VAR
    counter : INTEGER;

    { -------------------------- }
    { Local procedure            }
    { -------------------------- }
    { Under SignOnScreen         }
    { -------------------------- }
    PROCEDURE PlayIntro;
```

Listing 20.2: The completed Turbo Tunemaker program.

```
BEGIN
SOUND(f1); DELAY(enote); NOSOUND; DELAY(sbrk);
SOUND(f1); DELAY(enote); NOSOUND; DELAY(sbrk);
SOUND(g1); DELAY(enote); NOSOUND; DELAY(sbrk);
SOUND(a1); DELAY(enote); NOSOUND; DELAY(sbrk);

SOUND(f1); DELAY(enote); NOSOUND; DELAY(sbrk);
SOUND(a1); DELAY(enote); NOSOUND; DELAY(sbrk);
SOUND(g1); DELAY(enote); NOSOUND; DELAY(sbrk);
SOUND(c1); DELAY(enote); NOSOUND; DELAY(sbrk);

SOUND(f1); DELAY(enote); NOSOUND; DELAY(sbrk);
SOUND(f1); DELAY(enote); NOSOUND; DELAY(sbrk);
SOUND(g1); DELAY(enote); NOSOUND; DELAY(sbrk);
SOUND(a1); DELAY(enote); NOSOUND; DELAY(sbrk);

SOUND(f1); DELAY(qnote); NOSOUND; DELAY(sbrk);
SOUND(e1); DELAY(qnote); NOSOUND; DELAY(sbrk);

SOUND(f1); DELAY(enote); NOSOUND; DELAY(sbrk);
SOUND(f1); DELAY(enote); NOSOUND; DELAY(sbrk);
SOUND(g1); DELAY(enote); NOSOUND; DELAY(sbrk);
SOUND(a1); DELAY(enote); NOSOUND; DELAY(sbrk);

SOUND(a1s); DELAY(enote); NOSOUND; DELAY(sbrk);
SOUND(a1); DELAY(enote); NOSOUND; DELAY(sbrk);
SOUND(g1); DELAY(enote); NOSOUND; DELAY(sbrk);
SOUND(f1); DELAY(enote); NOSOUND; DELAY(sbrk);

SOUND(e1); DELAY(enote); NOSOUND; DELAY(sbrk);
SOUND(c1); DELAY(enote); NOSOUND; DELAY(sbrk);
SOUND(d1); DELAY(enote); NOSOUND; DELAY(sbrk);
SOUND(e1); DELAY(enote); NOSOUND; DELAY(sbrk);

SOUND(f1); DELAY(qnote); NOSOUND; DELAY(sbrk);
SOUND(f1); DELAY(qnote); NOSOUND; DELAY(sbrk);
END;   { of PlayIntro procedure }


{ --------------------------------- }
{ Main body of higher-level procedure }
{ --------------------------------- }
{ Procedure name: SignOnScreen        }
{ --------------------------------- }
BEGIN
WINDOW(10, 3, 80, 25);
WRITELN('/-----------------------------------------------------------\'
WRITELN('|                 WELCOME TO TURBO TUNEMAKER!               |'
WRITELN('|           Copyright 1991 by RGMS Computer Systems         |'
WRITELN('|-----------------------------------------------------------|'
WRITELN('|           * May be copied and exchanged freely *          |'
WRITELN('|        ** Not to be modified or sold for more than $5 **   |'
WRITELN('|-----------------------------------------------------------|'
WRITELN('|                                                           |'
WRITELN('|     This program allows you to create and play tunes on   |'
WRITELN('|     your PC. In addition, you can edit tunes that you     |'
WRITELN('|     have already created, save tunes to disk files, and   |'
WRITELN('|     read tunes from disk files for playing or editing.    |'
WRITELN('|     It presupposes only a very basic knowledge of music:  |'
WRITELN('|     if you know what Middle C is and can tell a quarter    |'
WRITELN('|     note from a half note, then you can compose and play   |'
WRITELN('|     tunes with Turbo Tunemaker.                           |'
WRITELN('|                                                           |'
WRITELN('\-----------------------------------------------------------/'
```

Listing 20.2: The completed Turbo Tunemaker program. (cont.)

```
    PlayIntro;
    NOSOUND;
    pause;
    RestoreWindow
  END;


{ ------------------------------ }
{ MAIN-LEVEL FUNCTION DECLARATION }
{ ------------------------------ }
FUNCTION NoteName(notefreq: INTEGER) : string3;
  { This function takes the frequency of a note
    and returns its mnemonic name (a three-character
    string. Its task, therefore, is essentially just
    the reverse of the Frq function. }
  BEGIN
    CASE notefreq OF
        { octave 1 }
        256: notename := 'c1';
        271: notename := 'c1s';
        287: notename := 'd1';
        304: notename := 'd1s';
        323: notename := 'e1';
        342: notename := 'f1';
        362: notename := 'f1s';
        384: notename := 'g1';
        406: notename := 'g1s';
        431: notename := 'a1';
        456: notename := 'a1s';
        483: notename := 'b1';
        { octave 2 }
        512: notename := 'c2';
        542: notename := 'c2s';
        575: notename := 'd2';
        609: notename := 'd2s';
        645: notename := 'e2';
        683: notename := 'f2';
        724: notename := 'f2s';
        767: notename := 'g2';
        813: notename := 'g2s';
        861: notename := 'a2';
        912: notename := 'a2s';
        967: notename := 'b2';

        { octave 3 }
        1024: notename := 'c3';
        1085: notename := 'c3s';
        1149: notename := 'd3';
        1218: notename := 'd3s';
        1290: notename := 'e3';
        1367: notename := 'f3';
        1448: notename := 'f3s';
        1534: notename := 'g3';
        1625: notename := 'g3s';
        1722: notename := 'a3';
        1825: notename := 'a3s';
        1933: notename := 'b3'
    ELSE BEGIN
        WRITELN(' The program has encountered a note that is not');
        WRITELN(' supported. Because there is no "normal" way for');
        WRITELN(' an unsupported note to be entered into a tune,');
        WRITELN(' this probably indicates an unknown software or');
```

Listing 20.2: The completed Turbo Tunemaker program. (cont.)

```
                  WRITELN(' hardware malfunction. The program will now shut');
                  WRITELN(' down.');
                  pause;
                  halt
                  END
     END       { of CASE statement }
     END;      { of NoteName function }


{ ----------------------------- }
{ MAIN-LEVEL FUNCTION DECLARATION }
{ ----------------------------- }
FUNCTION NoteType(NoteLength : INTEGER) : string20;
   BEGIN
      CASE NoteLength OF
           150  : NoteType.:= 'eighth note';
           300  : NoteType := 'quarter note';
           600  : NoteType := 'half note';
           900  : NoteType := 'dotted half note';
           1200 : NoteType := 'whole note'
      ELSE BEGIN
           WRITELN(' The program has encountered a note type that is');
           WRITELN(' not supported. There is no "normal" way for an');
           WRITELN(' unsupported note to be entered into a tune, so');
           WRITELN(' this probably indicates an unknown software or');
           WRITELN(' hardware malfunction. The program will now shut');
           WRITELN(' down.');
           pause;
           halt
           END
     END       { of CASE statement }
     END;      { of NoteType function }


{ ----------------------------- }
{ MAIN-LEVEL FUNCTION DECLARATION }
{ ----------------------------- }
FUNCTION NBrkType(nbreak : INTEGER) : string20;
   BEGIN
      CASE nbreak OF
           0  : NBrkType := 'no pause';
           30 : NBrkType := 'short pause';
           60 : NBrkType := 'long pause'
      ELSE BEGIN
           WRITELN(' The program has encountered a pause type that is');
           WRITELN(' not supported. There is no "normal" way for an');
           WRITELN(' unsupported pause type to be entered into a tune,');
           WRITELN(' so this probably indicates an unknown software or');
           WRITELN(' hardware malfunction. The program will now shut');
           WRITELN(' down.');
           pause;
           halt
           END
     END       { of CASE statement }
     END;      { of NBrkType function }


{ ----------------------------- }
{ MAIN-LEVEL FUNCTION DECLARATION }
{ ----------------------------- }
FUNCTION Frq(VAR NewNote :string3) : INTEGER;
```

Listing 20.2: The completed Turbo Tunemaker program. (cont.)

```
{ This function returns an integer corresponding to the
  frequency of the note name entered by the user. Only
  three octaves are supported: the octave containing
  Middle C, the octave above it, and the octave below it.
  If the user enters a note name that is not supported,
  then the function returns a value of 0.

  CAUTION: Some programs use the strings 'f1', 'f2', and
  'f3' to denote function keys, whereas in this function,
  they are used to denote musical notes. If you are adding
  music to a program, you must be sure to use some other
  names for the function keys to avoid possible conflicts
  between different 'f1', 'f2', and 'f3' identifiers. }


BEGIN
  CASE NewNote[2] OF
    '1' : CASE UPCASE(NewNote[1]) OF
          'C' : CASE UPCASE(NewNote[3]) OF
                space : Frq := c1;
                'S'   : Frq := c1s;
                END;
          'D' : CASE UPCASE(NewNote[3]) OF
                space : frq := d1;
                'S'   : frq := d1s
                END;
          'E' : frq := e1;
          'F' : CASE UPCASE(NewNote[3]) OF
                space : frq := f1;
                'S'   : frq := f1s
                END;
          'G' : CASE UPCASE(NewNote[3]) OF
                space : frq := g1;
                'S'   : frq := g1s
                END;
          'A' : CASE UPCASE(NewNote[3]) OF
                space : frq := a1;
                'S'   : frq := a1s
                END;
          'B' : frq := b1
          END;              { of CASE NewNote[2] = '1' statement }

    '2' : CASE UPCASE(NewNote[1]) OF
          'C' : CASE UPCASE(NewNote[3]) OF
                space : Frq := c2;
                'S'   : Frq := c2s;
                END;
          'D' : CASE UPCASE(NewNote[3]) OF
                space : frq := d2;
                'S'   : frq := d2s
                END;
          'E' : frq := e2;
          'F' : CASE UPCASE(NewNote[3]) OF
                space : frq := f2;
                'S'   : frq := f2s
                END;
          'G' : CASE UPCASE(NewNote[3]) OF
                space : frq := g2;
                'S'   : frq := g2s
                END;
          'A' : CASE UPCASE(NewNote[3]) OF
                space : frq := a2;
                'S'   : frq := a2s
                END;
```

Listing 20.2: The completed Turbo Tunemaker program. (cont.)

```
                 'B' : frq := b2
                 END;              { of CASE NewNote[2] = '2' statement }

        '3' : CASE UPCASE(NewNote[1]) OF
              'C' : CASE UPCASE(NewNote[3]) OF
                    space : Frq := c3;
                    'S'   : Frq := c3s;
                    END;
              'D' : CASE UPCASE(NewNote[3]) OF
                    space : frq := d3;
                    'S'   : frq := d3s
                    END;
              'E' : frq := e3;
              'F' : CASE UPCASE(NewNote[3]) OF
                    space : frq := f3;
                    'S'   : frq := f3s
                    END;
              'G' : CASE UPCASE(NewNote[3]) OF
                    space : frq := g3;
                    'S'   : frq := g3s
                    END;
              'A' : CASE UPCASE(NewNote[3]) OF
                    space : frq := a3;
                    'S'   : frq := a3s
                    END;
              'B' : frq := b3
              END               { of CASE NewNote[2] = '3' statement }
    ELSE frq := 0;
    END     { of big CASE statement }
  END;      { of function }


{ ------------------------------ }
{ MAIN-LEVEL PROCEDURE DECLARATION }
{ ------------------------------ }
PROCEDURE DisplayNotes;
  BEGIN
  CLRSCR;
  WRITE(space:15);
  WRITELN(' Notes available for tunes ("s" means "sharp")');
  WRITE(space:15);
  WRITELN(' -------------------------------------------');
  WRITE(space:24);
  WRITELN(' Octave1 (below Middle C):');
  WRITE(space:12);
  WRITELN(' ----------------------------------------------------');
  WRITE(space:12);
  WRITELN(' c1  c1s  d1  d1s  e1  f1  f1s  g1  g1s  a1  a1s  b1');
  WRITE(space:22);
  WRITELN(' Octave2 (containing Middle C):');
  WRITE(space:12);
  WRITELN(' ----------------------------------------------------');
  WRITE(space:12);
  WRITELN(' c2  c2s  d2  d2s  e2  f2  f2s  g2  g2s  a2  a2s  b2');
  WRITE(space:24);
  WRITELN(' Octave3 (above Middle C):');
  WRITE(space:12);
  WRITELN(' ----------------------------------------------------');
  WRITE(space:12);
  WRITELN(' c3  c3s  d3  d3s  e3  f3  f3s  g3  g3s  a3  a3s  b3');
  WRITELN;
  WRITELN(' Available Note Types and pauses between notes: ');
```

Listing 20.2: The completed Turbo Tunemaker program. (cont.)

```
   WRITE(' ---------------------------------------------------');
   WRITELN('-----------------------');
   WRITE(' 1. Eighth note   2. Quarter note    3. Half note');
   WRITELN('      4. Dotted half note');
   WRITE(' 5. Whole note    6. No pause        7. Short pause');
   WRITELN('      8. Long pause');
   WRITELN
   END;


{ ------------------------------ }
{ MAIN-LEVEL PROCEDURE DECLARATION }
{ ------------------------------ }
PROCEDURE MakeBox;
   { Note: each line of the box is broken into two statements,
     a WRITE and a WRITELN. This has nothing to do with the
     program, but is done so that we can print this program
     listing on a book page without having to use extremely
     small type. When you code this routine yourself, you can
     substitute a single WRITELN statement for each pair of
     WRITE and WRITELN statements. }
   BEGIN
   WRITE('/---------------------------------------------');
   WRITELN('--------------------------------\');

   WRITE('|                                              ');
   WRITELN('                            |');

   WRITE('|                                              ');
   WRITELN('                            |');

   WRITE('|                                              ');
   WRITELN('                            |');

   WRITE('|                                              ');
   WRITELN('                            |');

   WRITE('|                                              ');
   WRITELN('                            |');

   WRITE('\---------------------------------------------');
   WRITELN('--------------------------------/');
   WINDOW(5, 19, 78, 22)
   END;


{ ------------------------------ }
{ MAIN-LEVEL PROCEDURE DECLARATION }
{ ------------------------------ }
PROCEDURE AddNoteToTune(VAR tunehead, tunetail: noteptr;
                            nfreq, ndur, nbrk: INTEGER);
   BEGIN
   IF TuneHead = NIL
      THEN BEGIN
            NEW(TuneHead);
            TuneHead^.freq := nfreq;
            TuneHead^.dur := ndur;
            TuneHead^.brk := nbrk;
            TuneHead^.next := NIL;
            TuneTail := TuneHead;
            END
      ELSE BEGIN
            NEW(TuneTail^.next);
            IF TuneHead = TuneTail
```

Listing 20.2: The completed Turbo Tunemaker program. (cont.)

```
                 THEN TuneHead^.next := TuneTail^.next;
            TuneTail := TuneTail^.next;
            TuneTail^.freq := nfreq;
            TuneTail^.dur := ndur;
            TuneTail^.brk := nbrk;
            TuneTail^.next := NIL;
            END
     END;


{ ------------------------------- }
{ MAIN-LEVEL PROCEDURE DECLARATION }
{ ------------------------------- }
PROCEDURE GetTuneFromUser(VAR tunehead, tunetail: noteptr;
                          VAR HeapMark: pointer);

     { ------------------------- }
     { Local procedure           }
     { ------------------------- }
     { Under GetTuneFromUser     }
     { ------------------------- }
     PROCEDURE GetNotes;
     VAR
        MarkX, MarkY        : INTEGER;
        Another, noteOK     : CHAR;
        note, ndur, nbrk    : INTEGER;
        checknote           : string3;
        duration, notebrk   : INTEGER;

     BEGIN
        Another := 'N'; noteOK := 'N';
        Mark(HeapMark);
        MakeBox;

        { Set up REPEAT loop to add "OK" notes to the linked list that
          constitutes the tune. }
        REPEAT  { until the "another" variable gets set to "no" }

        { Set up another REPEAT loop (inside the first one) to prompt
          user for each note until the note is accepted as OK. }
        REPEAT { until user OKs the note entered }
        CLRSCR;
          WRITE(' Enter a note name such as "c1" (or X to exit): ');
          markX := WhereX; markY := WhereY;
          REPEAT
            READLN(checknote);
            IF UPCASE(checknote[1]) = 'X' THEN Exit;
            IF UPCASE(checknote[3]) <> 'S' THEN checknote[3] := space;
            note := Frq(checknote);
            IF note = 0
              THEN BEGIN
                   WRITE(' That note not supported. Try again.');
                   DELAY(1000);
                   gotoXY(1, WhereY);
                   clrEOL;
                   gotoXY(markX, markY);
                   clrEOL;
                   END
          UNTIL note <> 0;

          WRITE(' Enter the type of note (1 - 5, above): ');
          GetGoodInt(1,5,duration);
          CASE duration OF  { error trapping done by GetGoodInt }
```

Listing 20.2: The completed Turbo Tunemaker program. (cont.)

```
                1 : ndur := enote;
                2 : ndur := qnote;
                3 : ndur := hnote;
                4 : ndur := dot_hnote;
                5 : ndur := wnote
             END;

        WRITE(' Enter pause before next note (6 - 8, above): ');
        GetGoodInt(6,8,notebrk);
        CASE notebrk OF  { error trapping done by GetGoodInt }
             6 : nbrk := 0;
             7 : nbrk := sbrk;
             8 : nbrk := lbrk
             END;

     CLRSCR;
     WRITELN(' The current note is: ', checknote);
     WRITELN(' The note type corresponds to number: ', duration);
     WRITELN(' Pause corresponds to number: ', notebrk);
     WRITE(' Is this okay (Y/N)? ');
     GetGoodChar(YNchars,noteOK);

     { End of REPEAT loop that prompts user for note until note is
       accepted as OK. }
     UNTIL UPCASE(noteOK) = 'Y';

     AddNoteToTune(tunehead, tunetail, note, ndur, nbrk);
     CLRSCR;
     WRITELN;
     WRITE(' Add another note to the tune (Y/N)? ');
     GetGoodChar(YNchars,another);
     UNTIL UPCASE(Another) <> 'Y';
     { End of REPEAT loop that adds OK notes to the linked list. }

  END; { of GetNotes procedure }

{ -------------------------------- }
{ Main body of higher-level procedure }

  { -------------------------------- }
  { Procedure name: GetTuneFromUser    }
  { -------------------------------- }
  BEGIN
    FreeUpHeapSpace(tunehead);
    DisplayNotes;
    GetNotes;
    RestoreWindow
  END;


{ ------------------------------- }
{ MAIN-LEVEL PROCEDURE DECLARATION }
{ ------------------------------- }
PROCEDURE GetTuneFromFile(VAR tunefile: text; VAR tunehead: noteptr;
                          VAR HeapMark: pointer);
  VAR
    tunefilename : string12;
    FileExists   : INTEGER;
    Again        : CHAR;
```

Listing 20.2: The completed Turbo Tunemaker program. (cont.)

```
{ --------------------------- }
{ Local procedure            }
{ --------------------------- }
{ Under GetTuneFromFile       }
{ --------------------------- }
PROCEDURE GetTheFile;
  BEGIN
    REPEAT
      CLRSCR;
      WRITELN; WRITELN;
      WRITE(' Enter the name of the tune file to use: ');
      READLN(tunefilename);
      ASSIGN(tunefile, tunefilename);
      {$I-}
      RESET(tunefile);
      {$I-}
      FileExists := IORESULT;
      IF FileExists <> 0
         THEN BEGIN
              WRITE(' File does not exist. Try again (Y/N)? ');
              GetGoodChar(YNchars,again)
              END
    UNTIL (FileExists = 0) OR (UPCASE(again) <> 'Y')
  END;

{ --------------------------- }
{ Local procedure            }
{ --------------------------- }
{ Under GetTuneFromFile       }
{ --------------------------- }
PROCEDURE ReadTuneIntoList;
  VAR
    currnote,
    currdur,
    currbrk   : INTEGER;
  BEGIN
    MARK(heapmark);
    WHILE NOT EOF(tunefile) DO
      BEGIN
      READLN(tunefile, currnote);
      READLN(tunefile, currdur);
      READLN(tunefile, currbrk);
      READLN(tunefile);
      AddNoteToTune(tunehead,tunetail,currnote,currdur,currbrk)
      END
  END;

{ ------------------------------------ }
{ Main body of higher-level procedure }
{ ------------------------------------ }
{ Procedure name: GetTuneFromFile      }
{ ------------------------------------ }
BEGIN
  CLRSCR;
  FreeUpHeapSpace(tunehead);
  GetTheFile;
  IF FileExists = 0 THEN ReadTuneIntoList;
  pause;
  IF FileExists = 0 THEN CLOSE(tunefile)
END;
```

Listing 20.2: The completed Turbo Tunemaker program. (cont.)

```
{ -------------------------------- }
{ MAIN-LEVEL PROCEDURE DECLARATION }
{ -------------------------------- }
PROCEDURE PlayTune(tunehead: noteptr);
  { This routine simply traverses the linked list that holds
    the tune. At each list node, the routine sounds a note at
    the frequency specified in that node's "freq" field for the
    number of milliseconds specified in the "dur" field. }
  VAR
    CurrNote : noteptr;
  BEGIN
    CurrNote := tunehead;
    IF currnote = NIL
      THEN BEGIN
           WRITELN(' You must either compose a tune at the keyboard');
           WRITELN(' or load one from a disk file before it can be');
           WRITELN(' played with this routine.');
           pause;
           exit
           END;
    CLRSCR;
    WHILE CurrNote <> NIL DO
      BEGIN
      SOUND(currnote^.freq);
      DELAY(currnote^.dur);
      NOSOUND;
      DELAY(currnote^.brk);
      currnote := currnote^.next
      END;
    NOSOUND;
    pause
  END;


{ -------------------------------- }
{ MAIN-LEVEL PROCEDURE DECLARATION }
{ -------------------------------- }
PROCEDURE EditTune(tunehead: noteptr);
  VAR
    currnote : noteptr;
    another,
    changenote  : CHAR;
    notecounter : INTEGER;

  { --------------------------- }
  { Local procedure            }
  { --------------------------- }
  { Under EditTune             }
  { --------------------------- }
  PROCEDURE NoteChange;
    VAR
      ncnote : string3;
      ncdur,
      ncbrk  : INTEGER;
      noteOK : CHAR;
    BEGIN
      REPEAT
        CLRSCR;
        WRITE(' Enter a new note name such as "c1": ');
        READLN(ncnote);
        IF UPCASE(ncnote[3]) <> 'S' THEN ncnote[3] := space;
        currnote^.freq := Frq(ncnote);
```

Listing 20.2: The completed Turbo Tunemaker program. (cont.)

```
      WRITE(' Choose a new note type (1 - 5): ');
      GetGoodInt(1,5,ncdur);
      CASE ncdur OF   { error trapping done above }
           1 : currnote^.dur := enote;
           2 : currnote^.dur := qnote;
           3 : currnote^.dur := hnote;
           4 : currnote^.dur := dot_hnote;
           5 : currnote^.dur := wnote
           END;

      WRITE(' Choose a new pause type (6 - 8): ');
      GetGoodInt(6,8,ncbrk);
      CASE ncbrk OF
           6 : currnote^.brk := 0;
           7 : currnote^.brk := sbrk;
           8 : currnote^.brk := lbrk
           END;

      WRITE(' Is this okay (Y/N)? ');
      GetGoodChar(YNchars,noteOK);
      IF UPCASE(noteOK) = 'Y' THEN changenote := 'N'
    UNTIL UPCASE(noteOK) = 'Y'
  END;

{ --------------------------- }
{ Local procedure             }
{ --------------------------- }
{ Under EditTune              }
{ --------------------------- }
PROCEDURE DisplayCurrentNote;
  VAR
    thisnote : string3;
    ndur,
    nbrk : string20;
  BEGIN
    thisnote := NoteName(currnote^.freq);
    ndur := NoteType(currnote^.dur);
    nbrk := NBrkType(currnote^.brk);

    { Set up another REPEAT loop to ask the user if he wants
      to change the note settings in the current list node.
      The loop will continue until the user says that he does
      not wish to change the current settings. }
    REPEAT
      CLRSCR;
      WRITE(' The current note is: ', thisnote, '.');
      WRITELN(space:22,'This is note # ', notecounter, '.');
      WRITELN(' The current note type is: ', ndur, '.');
      WRITELN(' The current pause type is: ', nbrk, '.');
      WRITE(' Do you want to change these settings (Y/N)? ');
      GetGoodChar(YNchars,changenote);
      IF UPCASE(changenote) = 'Y' THEN NoteChange;
    UNTIL UPCASE(changenote) = 'N';
    CLRSCR
  END;

{ ---------------------------------- }
{ Main body of higher-level procedure }
{ ---------------------------------- }
{ Procedure name: EditTune           }
{ ---------------------------------- }
BEGIN
```

Listing 20.2: The completed Turbo Tunemaker program. (cont.)

```
      notecounter := 1;
      currnote := tunehead;
      DisplayNotes;
      MakeBox;
      REPEAT { traverse list until user quits or END reached }
        DisplayCurrentNote;
        IF currnote^.next = NIL
          THEN BEGIN
               WRITELN(' End of tune has been reached. That''s all.');
               another := 'N';
               pause
               END
          ELSE BEGIN
               WRITE(' Edit any more notes in this tune (Y/N)? ');
               GetGoodChar(YNchars,another);
               IF UPCASE(another) = 'Y'
                  THEN BEGIN
                       notecounter := notecounter + 1;
                       currnote := currnote^.next
                       END
               END
      UNTIL (UPCASE(another) = 'N') OR (currnote = NIL);
      pause;
      RestoreWindow;
      CLRSCR
   END;


{ ------------------------------ }
{ MAIN-LEVEL PROCEDURE DECLARATION }
{ ------------------------------ }
PROCEDURE SaveTuneToFile(VAR tunefile : text; VAR tunehead : noteptr);
  VAR
    tunefilename : string12;
    currnote     : noteptr;

  BEGIN
    CLRSCR;
    IF tunehead = NIL
      THEN BEGIN
           WRITELN(' Before you can save a tune to a disk file, you');
           WRITELN(' must first compose it at the keyboard or load it');
           WRITELN(' from a disk file.');
           pause;
           Exit
           END;
    currnote := tunehead;
    WRITELN; WRITELN;
    WRITE(' Enter a DOS file name under which to save the tune: ');
    READLN(tunefilename);
    ASSIGN(tunefile, tunefilename);
    REWRITE(tunefile);
    WHILE currnote <> NIL DO
      BEGIN
      WRITELN(tunefile, currnote^.freq);
      WRITELN(tunefile, currnote^.dur);
      WRITELN(tunefile, currnote^.brk);
      WRITELN(tunefile);
      currnote := currnote^.next
      END;
    Close(tunefile);
    WRITELN;
```

Listing 20.2: The completed Turbo Tunemaker program. (cont.)

```
      WRITELN(' Tune has been written to file ', tunefilename, '.');
      pause
   END;
{ ------------------------------ }
{ MAIN-LEVEL PROCEDURE DECLARATION }
{ ------------------------------ }
PROCEDURE Menu(VAR choice: INTEGER);
  VAR
    markX, markY : INTEGER;

    { -------------------------- }
    { Local procedure           }
    { -------------------------- }
    { Under Menu                }
    { -------------------------- }
    PROCEDURE DisplayMenu;
      BEGIN
      CLRSCR;
        window(17,5,80,25);
        WRITELN('/-----------------------------------------------\');
        WRITELN('|              TURBO TUNEMAKER MAIN MENU          |');
        WRITELN('|-----------------------------------------------|');
        WRITELN('|     1. Compose a tune at the keyboard          |');
        WRITELN('|     2. Read a tune from a disk file            |');
        WRITELN('|     3. Edit a tune (must be loaded)            |');
        WRITELN('|     4. Save a tune to a disk file              |');
        WRITELN('|     5. Play a tune                             |');
        WRITELN('|     6. Quit Turbo Tunemaker                    |');
        WRITELN('\-----------------------------------------------/');
        WRITELN;
        WRITE('        Enter your choice (1 - 6): ');
        GetGoodInt(1,6,choice);
        RestoreWindow
      END;

    { -------------------------- }
    { Local procedure           }
    { -------------------------- }
    { Under Menu                }
    { -------------------------- }
    PROCEDURE DoChoice;
      BEGIN
      CASE choice OF
          1 : GetTuneFromUser(tunehead, tunetail, heapmark);
          2 : GetTuneFromFile(tunefile, tunehead, heapmark);
          3 : EditTune(tunehead);
          4 : SaveTuneToFile(tunefile, tunehead);
          5 : PlayTune(tunehead);
          6 : Exit
          END
      END;

    { --------------------------------- }
    { Main body of higher-level procedure }
    { --------------------------------- }
    { Procedure name: Menu              }
    { --------------------------------- }
    BEGIN
      DisplayMenu;
      DoChoice
    END;
```

Listing 20.2: The completed Turbo Tunemaker program. (cont.)

```
{ ------------------------------------------------------------- }
{                    MAIN BODY OF PROGRAM                       }
{ ------------------------------------------------------------- }
BEGIN
  Init(tunehead, tunetail, choice);
  SignOnScreen;

  REPEAT
    Menu(choice);
  UNTIL choice = 6;

  CLRSCR
END.
```

Listing 20.2: The completed Turbo Tunemaker program. (cont.)

character is a digit that stands for the octave, such as '**2**' for the octave containing Middle C. The third character either contains an '**s**' if the note is sharp or a space if it is not sharp.

The CASE statement first determines the octave of the note by looking at the second position in the string. Remember, at this point, that strings can also be treated as arrays of characters. Thus, we can refer to the second character in the string as if it were the second slot in an array, i.e., as **NewNote[2]**. Based on the octave, the function then checks the first position in the string to find the note. Finally, it checks the third position to determine if the note is sharp.

One warning: if a note is not sharp, and the user enters only, for example, '**c2**', the third position of the string will not automatically be filled with a space character. You must (as we do in Listing 20.2) put in an extra line of code to fill that position with a space. If you forget to do this, your program will not work correctly.

The other note-conversion routines work very much like the **Frq** function. Each uses a CASE statement to convert either an integer to a string or a string to an integer.

THE GETTUNEFROMUSER PROCEDURE

The **GetTuneFromUser** procedure exercises your logical muscles as much as it does your Pascal skills. The first thing that the routine does is to mark the heap so that any tune it creates can be easily disposed of when you create or load another tune. Then, the routine creates two main loops to perform two tasks:

- Add notes to a linked list in the computer's memory until the user decides to quit adding notes.

- Run a loop each time the user adds a note that allows the user to change the note being entered until he or she says that it is "okay."

In the inner loop, we also use some error-trapping tricks that you saw in the **GetGoodInt** and **GetGoodChar** procedures. After each note is accepted, it is added to the linked list with the **AddNoteToTune** routine. The user is then asked if he or she wants to enter another note. If the answer is no, then the program drops out of the loop and the tune is considered finished.

The one "fancy" trick used by **GetTuneFromUser** is to display the note names on the screen, draw a box, and then use the Window command to restrict Turbo Pascal's screen window to the inside of the box. This means that any commands given after that (until the window is changed back to full-screen status) apply only to the inside of the box. A call to CLRSCR, for example, will only clear the screen inside of the box, leaving the box itself and the table of note names still on the screen.

You should analyze this routine on your own, paying special attention to how the REPEAT loops are set up.

THE EDITTUNE PROCEDURE

EditTune is very similar to **GetTuneFromUser**. It traverses the linked list that contains the tune and, at each note, asks the user if he or she wants to change the note. Instead of converting notes from string to integer format, however, it uses the **NoteName**, **NoteType**, and **NBrkType** functions to convert the integer values in the linked list to *names* that will make more sense to the user.

Like **GetTuneFromUser**, **EditTune** uses two REPEAT loops: one to keep traversing the linked list until the user decides to quit, and one to continue editing a specific note until the user says that the note is okay. It also uses the same windowing trick as **GetTuneFromUser** to create a box in which the user will edit the notes from the tune.

THE SAVETUNETOFILE PROCEDURE

The **SaveTuneToFile** routine is fairly simple. It prompts the user to enter a file name for a text file, opens the file for writing, and then traverses the linked list that contains the tune. At each note in the tune, it writes the contents of the note's fields to the file, with one field on each line and a blank line separating the notes. This process continues until the end of the linked list is reached.

THE GETTUNEFROMFILE PROCEDURE

The **GetTuneFromFile** procedure reverses the process performed by the **SaveTuneToFile** procedure. It opens the specified file for reading and then reads the notes into a linked list by calling the **AddNoteToTune** routine. This process continues until the end of the file is reached.

THE PLAYTUNE PROCEDURE

The **PlayTune** procedure is probably the simplest routine in the program. It merely traverses the linked list that contains a tune and, at each note in the list, uses the **Sound** and **Delay** procedures to sound a tone of the specified frequency and duration. It then moves to the next note in the list until the end of the list is reached.

THE MENU PROCEDURE

The **Menu** procedure is fairly standard stuff. It displays a list of choices on the screen, gets the user's choice, and executes a CASE statement that calls one of the other routines based on the user's choice. In the main body of the program, the menu is inside of a REPEAT loop that continues until the user chooses menu choice No. 6, which is to quit the program.

CONCLUSION

Because this chapter was itself a practical exercise in Turbo Pascal programming, the summary and exercises sections are omitted.

P A R T

Object-Oriented Programming

   Chapters 21–22 explain the basic concepts and techniques of object-oriented programming with Turbo Pascal. Chapter 22 provides an introduction to Turbo Vision, an exciting but intricate library of object types that is included with Turbo Pascal 6. Turbo Vision allows you to add pull-down menus, dialog boxes, mouse support, and many other features to your programs—*without* requiring you to write the program code for those features.

C H A P T E R

21

Concepts and Techniques

Creating a new theory is not like destroying an old barn and erecting a skyscraper in its place. It is rather like climbing a mountain, gaining new and wider views, discovering unexpected connections between our starting point and its rich environment ... The simpler our picture of the external world and the more facts it embraces, the stronger it reflects in our minds the harmony of the universe.

—Albert Einstein, *The Evolution of Physics*

Version 5.5 of Turbo Pascal introduced a new way of thinking about and structuring Pascal programs: *object-oriented programming.* Turbo Pascal 6 further extends the object-oriented capabilities of Turbo Pascal, as well as adding Turbo Vision, a library of object routines for use in your own programs. With the tools that Turbo Pascal offers for this powerful approach, you can—in complex programming projects—create better structured, more flexible, and easier to modify programs in less time. You do not have to use Turbo Pascal's object-oriented features if you do not want to (and for smaller programs, they are not always appropriate), but they are there when you need them.

Object-oriented programming is based on an idea that should be familiar by now. In Chapter 17, we saw that any sophisticated data structure, such as a stack, includes two things:

- A particular arrangement of data items, such as an array or a linked list.

- A set of operations that manipulates those data items, such as the **Push** and **Pop** routines used with a stack.

Without **Push** and **Pop** routines, an array is just an array. When you add those routines, you create a stack data structure. If, instead, you add the routines appropriate for a queue or a hash table, then you turn the array into a queue or a hash table. In standard Pascal, however, there is no way to *weld* the routines right into the data structure—no way to create a stack, queue, hash table, or other data structure that is smart enough to take care of itself and does not need outside routines to help it.

That kind of intelligent data structure is the essence of object-oriented programming. Instead of having a passive array on which external routines operate to create a stack or other data structure, object-oriented programming lets us create a "smart" data structure that contains *within itself* everything it needs to behave as it should. For example, instead of passing a stack to the **Push** routine to add an item, you send a message to the stack object to add an item to itself—an operation that it knows how to do. What makes this tricky is that it involves a totally new way of structuring and thinking about our programs.

Object-oriented programming originally came out of ideas in the Simula programming language of the 1960s. Most of the research work that developed the object-oriented approach, however, was done at Xerox Corporation's Palo Alto Research Center (PARC) in a 10-year project that developed Smalltalk, the first truly and completely object-oriented programming language. Xerox PARC is perhaps most famous for developing the "Xerox Star" microcomputer and its icon-based screen interface, which provided the inspiration for Microsoft Windows and the Apple Macintosh. The difficulty of creating such a screen interface was a key motivation in the development of object-oriented programming techniques, even though object-oriented programming has no necessary connection with icon-based screen displays.

Turbo Pascal traces its object-oriented heritage from Xerox PARC's original work on Smalltalk through Apple's Object Pascal and AT&T's C++ programming languages. It takes the best features of each, prunes what is redundant or of questionable value, and builds them into standard Pascal as added features that you can use or ignore as you wish.

Consider the following problems:

- You have a customer billing system and you want to create several different customer data types. They are all basically the same, but each differs from the others in some minor detail.

- You are creating a program with on-screen windows and menus. Although there are several different types of each, you want them all to perform certain operations in the same ways.

- You create a library of Turbo Pascal routines and distribute precompiled units containing those routines, but you want users to be able to modify your routines without having the Pascal source code.

Object-oriented programming has a clean, logical solution to all of those problems. In a customer billing system, for example, you can create a single *parent* customer data type that contains basic customer information such as name, address, and account number. Based on this parent type, you can then create as many specialized customer types as you need, *without* repeating any code from the parent type. Each specialized data type, called a *child* of the parent type, inherits all of the features of the parent type and can add its own new features. It can even cancel out parent features that do not apply to it. Extending the parent-child metaphor, a type that is derived from an earlier object type is called its *descendant*, while the earlier object type, likewise, is called the descendant type's *ancestor*.

Because these object data types inherit the characteristics of their ancestor types, you can extend the capabilities of already-compiled units of object routines even if you do not have the source code. You simply create new object types as descendants of already existing object types, and then add new features or cancel inherited features as needed. Procedures designed to work with ancestor object types will work with their descendant object types as well.

OBJECTS AND OBJECT-ORIENTED PROGRAMMING

That's the general idea of objects. Now let's take a look at the specifics. Object-oriented programming introduces several new concepts:

- *Objects*, which look similar to records but contain their own procedures and functions, called "methods."

- *Object types,* which define particular object data types and their capabilities.

- *Encapsulation,* which binds procedures and functions into a data structure with the data they process.

- *Messages,* which are instructions sent to objects that tell them to carry out their built-in methods.

- *Inheritance,* by which the characteristics of an object type are passed along to its descendant object types.

- *Polymorphism,* the ability of different objects to respond in their own unique ways to the same program command.

- *Extensibility of code,* by which already compiled units of object types can be used as a basis for creating and using new object types that were unknown at compile time.

Appropriately enough, the fundamental concept in object-oriented programming is that of an *object.* An object looks very much like a Pascal record, except that it has its own procedures and functions. Consider Listing 21.1, which shows a conventional structured programming approach to loading values into a student record. (Before running Listing 21.1 or any of the listings in this chapter, make sure that your printer is connected and ready to print.)

The student record itself uses the RECORD data type to bind together two string fields (for first name and last name) with a real-number field for grade point average. Routines are defined to initialize the record, load it with data, and then display the data on the computer screen. If the student's GPA is over 3.5, then a letter of congratulations is printed.

It is in the main body of the program that we will see the most dramatic change when we go from structured to object-oriented programming. In Listing 21.1, the program clears the screen and then passes the student record variable to the **Init** routine, which initializes its data fields with "blank" values. The variable is then passed to the **FillRecord** routine, which loads name and GPA information into its data fields. Finally, it is passed to the **DisplayInfo** routine, which takes the information in its data fields and displays it on the computer screen.

```
PROGRAM Listing21_1;

  { Shows standard structured programming techniques for
    entering data into a student record and displaying the
    data. }

USES CRT, MyUtils;

const
  formfeed = #12;

TYPE
  string15 = STRING[15];
  studentrec = RECORD
                 fname,
                 lname : string15;
                 GPA          : REAL;
                 END;
VAR
  student : studentrec;

PROCEDURE init(var student : studentrec);
  BEGIN
    WITH student DO
      BEGIN
        fname      := space;
        lname      := space;
        GPA        := 0.00
      END
  END;

PROCEDURE FillRecord(var student : studentrec);
  BEGIN
    WITH student DO
      BEGIN
        WRITE(' Enter the student''s first name: ');
        READLN(fname);
        WRITE(' Enter the student''s last name: ');
        READLN(lname);
        WRITE(' Enter the student''s current GPA: ');
        READLN(GPA);
      END
  END;

PROCEDURE SendHonorsLetter(student : studentrec);
  VAR
    letterfile: TEXT;
    counter   : INTEGER;
  BEGIN
    ASSIGN(letterfile, 'prn');
    REWRITE(letterfile);
    FOR counter := 1 TO 10 DO WRITELN(letterfile);
    WRITELN(letterfile, 'Dear Mr./Ms. ', student.lname, ':');
    WRITELN(letterfile);
    WRITELN(letterfile, 'Your grade point average is over 3.5. This');
    WRITELN(letterfile, 'means that you will graduate cum laude from');
    WRITELN(letterfile, 'this institution. Congratulations.');
    WRITELN(letterfile);
    WRITELN(letterfile, 'Sincerely,');
    WRITELN(letterfile);
    WRITELN(letterfile, 'V. Wormer');
    WRITELN(letterfile, 'Dean of Students');
```

Listing 21.1: Structured programming approach to a student record.

```
      WRITELN(letterfile, formfeed);
      CLOSE(letterfile)
   END;


 PROCEDURE DisplayInfo(student : studentrec);
   BEGIN
      CLRSCR;
      WITH student DO
        BEGIN
        WRITELN(' The student''s name is: ', fname, space, lname, '.');
        WRITELN(' The student''s GPA is: ', GPA:0:2, '.');
        IF GPA > 3.5 THEN SendHonorsLetter(student);
        pause
        END
   END;


 BEGIN
   CLRSCR;
   init(student);
   fillrecord(student);
   pause;
   displayinfo(student)
 END.
```

Listing 21.1: Structured programming approach to a student record. (cont.)

Through all this, the student record variable is a passive spectator that has things "done to it," like a hospital patient lying on a cart who gets wheeled from one examining room to the next. Poked, prodded, and (we imagine) slightly humiliated by all this, the student record variable nonetheless provides what we need. There is, however, a neater way to do the same thing.

METHODS AND ENCAPSULATION

The neater way is to declare the student record type as an *object type* instead of a record type. This allows us to include all the procedures and functions needed to manipulate the data in the object itself—an approach called *encapsulation* because it creates a hermetically sealed object "capsule" that includes all the data fields and methods it needs. To declare an object type, you simply use the Turbo Pascal reserved word *object* and then list the fields and methods of the object, in much the same way as you would do with a standard record-type declaration:

```
TYPE
studentrec = OBJECT
            fname,
            lname : string15;
            GPA   : REAL;
            PROCEDURE init;
            PROCEDURE fillrecord;
            PROCEDURE SendHonorsLetter;
            PROCEDURE DisplayNameAndGPA;
            END;
```

All the data fields must be listed in the type definition *before* any methods are listed, as in the example above. One quirk of object type declarations is that the last method or field declaration before the END must be followed by a semicolon; this is the only place in Pascal where a semicolon must be used right before an END.

Of course, this type declaration does not create an object, any more than declaring a record type creates any records. To create an object, you must declare a variable of the object type:

```
VAR
    student : studentrec
```

At some point, either before or after you declare the object variable, you must spell out the details of the object's methods, just as you would with any other subroutines. There are, however, two key differences:

- First, the name of each method must be preceded by the name of the object type. When we declare the details of our **Init** method for the **studentrec** object type above, for example, we would write the subroutine header as *studentrec.init* to make it clear that the subroutine is a method in the **studentrec** object type.

- Second, the header for a method does not have to take an object variable itself as a parameter. For example, in the **Init** declaration from Listing 21.1 (which uses standard structured programming), the record variable must be declared as a parameter because it is passed to the **Init** subroutine. With an object type, however, the **Init** routine is *part of* the object variable, so it automatically "knows" which variable it should initialize—i.e., itself. Therefore, instead of **Init(student: studentrec)** as in Listing 21.1, the declaration can be simply **studentrec.init,** with no parameters.

The best way to understand these concepts is to look at a simple example, as shown in Listing 21.2. This is exactly the same program as in Listing 21.1, but with a crucial difference: it is coded using object-oriented techniques.

In most of the program code, the differences seem fairly minor. Instead of declaring **studentrec** as a record type, we declare it as an object type. We include as methods in the object type all of the procedures that were formerly separate from the student record: this is an example of encapsulation. When we get to declaring the details of the methods, again, everything looks pretty much the same. The **Init** method initializes the object's data fields with a "blank" value, the **FillRecord** method loads data into the data fields, the **DisplayNameAndGPA** method shows the name and GPA on the screen, and if the GPA is over 3.5, then the **SendHonorsLetter** prints a congratulatory letter.

It is when we arrive at the main body of the program that the dramatic difference becomes clear. Instead of passing the student record variable to the **Init** routine, which would then initialize it (as in Listing 21.1), we send a message to the variable and tell it to initialize itself. It knows how to do this because it has a built-in **Init** method. We then tell the variable to get some data from the user and load the data into its fields. Finally, we tell it to display its data on the screen and, if appropriate, send a congratulatory letter to the student.

Note how we called the methods in the object: by using the name of the object variable (not the object type), a dot, and then the name of the method. The variable name tells the program which object *variable* is to get

```
PROGRAM Listing21_2;

   ( Shows object-oriented approach to entering data into a
     student record (an object) and displaying the data.
     Principal feature demonstrated: ENCAPSULATION. )

USES CRT, MyUtils;

const
  formfeed = #12;

type
  string15 = STRING[15];
  studentrec = OBJECT
               fname,
               lname : string15;
               GPA   : REAL;
               PROCEDURE init;
               PROCEDURE fillrecord;
               PROCEDURE SendHonorsLetter;
               PROCEDURE DisplayNameAndGPA;
               END;

PROCEDURE studentrec.init;
  BEGIN
  fname      := space;
  lname      := space;
  GPA        := 0.00
  END;

PROCEDURE studentrec.FillRecord;
  BEGIN
  CLRSCR;
  WRITE(' Enter the student''s first name: ');
  READLN(fname);
  WRITE(' Enter the student''s last name: ');
  READLN(lname);
  WRITE(' Enter the student''s current GPA: ');
  READLN(GPA);
  END;

PROCEDURE studentrec.SendHonorsLetter;
  VAR
    letterfile: TEXT;
    counter   : INTEGER;
  BEGIN
    ASSIGN(letterfile, 'prn');
    REWRITE(letterfile);
    FOR counter := 1 TO 10 DO WRITELN(letterfile);
    WRITELN(letterfile, 'Dear Mr./Ms. ', lname, ':');
    WRITELN(letterfile);
    WRITELN(letterfile, 'Your grade point average is over 3.5. This');
    WRITELN(letterfile, 'means that you will graduate cum laude from');
    WRITELN(letterfile, 'this institution. Congratulations.');
    WRITELN(letterfile);
    WRITELN(letterfile, 'Sincerely,');
    WRITELN(letterfile);
    WRITELN(letterfile, 'V. Wormer');
    WRITELN(letterfile, 'Dean of Students');
    WRITELN(letterfile, formfeed);
    CLOSE(letterfile)
  END;
```

Listing 21.2: Object-oriented approach to a student record.

```
PROCEDURE studentrec.DisplayNameAndGPA;
  BEGIN
  CLRSCR;
  WRITELN(' The student''s name is: ', fname, space, lname, '.');
  WRITELN(' The student''s GPA is:  ', GPA:0:2, '.');
  IF GPA > 3.5 THEN SendHonorsLetter;
  END;


VAR
  student : studentrec;


BEGIN
  student.init;
  student.fillrecord;
  student.displaynameandGPA
END.
```

Listing 21.2: Object-oriented approach to a student record. (cont.)

a message, and the method name tells the variable which of its *methods* it should use.

In this simple example, we can see that object-oriented programming gets rid of the traditional passive data structures that we saw in structured programming. In their place, it puts active, intelligent data structures that know how to do every task that they will be called on to perform.

WHICH METHODS TO INCLUDE

This leads to a key principle of object design: *make sure that your object type has all the methods it needs to manipulate the data in its fields.* It is possible in Turbo Pascal (but not in most other languages that support object-oriented programming) to access an object's fields directly. For example, instead of sending a message to the student variable to use its **Init** method, you could initialize its fields as follows:

```
student.fname := space;

student.lname := space;

student.GPA := 0.00;
```

As you might suspect, you can also use the WITH notation, just as you can with a record variable:

```
WITH student DO

    BEGIN

    fname     := space;

    lname     := space;

    GPA       := 0.00

    END;
```

Now, if *student* were a record variable, there would be nothing wrong with this: indeed, it would be the only way to initialize the record's data fields. But student is *not* a record variable: it is an object that has built-in methods to handle any task involving its data fields. A major benefit of encapsulation is that it allows us to hide even more information inside various compartments of the program. Just as using global variables in a subroutine without declaring them as parameters violates the principle of information hiding and must be avoided whenever possible, so too any attempt to manipulate an object's fields without using its methods violates the same principle and must be avoided.

The key to preserving the integrity of your object variables is to make sure that your object type definition includes *all* the methods that the object will need to manipulate the data in its fields. If one or more methods are left out of your object type definition, then you will have no choice but to manipulate object fields directly, which you do not want to do.

Obviously, which methods an object will require depends on the purpose of the object. Our student object variable needs methods to initialize its fields, to load them with data, to report that data to the screen, and to print out a letter when appropriate. A stack object variable would also need an **Init** method, and methods to do pushes and pops.

Because you can create descendant object types and add methods that are not in their ancestor types, you can even do this with precompiled libraries of objects, as we will see in the next section.

INHERITANCE

In this section, we will discuss how to create and use descendant object types that are derived from already-existing object types. Just as human children inherit characteristics from their parents—hair color, height, and so forth—Pascal objects inherit fields and methods from their parent objects, as well as from all their other ancestor objects up the line.

The first thing we want to do is put the object and method declarations from Listing 21.2 into a unit. Listing 21.3 shows how to do this.

Once you have keyed in Listing 21.3, save it as *MY_OBJS.PAS*. Go into Turbo Pascal's Compile menu and set the Destination option to "Disk." Then, compile the unit and copy the compiled .TPU file to your Turbo Pascal program directory (probably C:\TP). Finally, go back into the Compile menu and set the Destination option back to "Memory."

You can see in Listing 21.3 that, from the standpoint of creating a unit, there is nothing unusual about setting up a unit with object types. The object type definition itself goes in the INTERFACE section of the unit, while the details of the methods go in the IMPLEMENTATION section, just as you would expect.

The trick comes in Listing 21.4, a program that uses the object type and method definitions in the unit. In this program, we create a **GradStudentRec** object type which is a descendant of the **StudentRec** object type. To do this, we simply include the identifier **StudentRec** in parentheses after the word **OBJECT** in the object type definition.

Notice that we declared three methods in the **GradStudentRec** object type: **Init**, **FillRecord**, and **SendHonorsLetter**. Because these methods have the same names as methods in their ancestor type, they *override* the methods from the ancestor type. If we create a variable of type **GradStudentRec** and send it a message to initialize itself, it will use its own **Init** routine; likewise for the other methods.

The **DisplayNameAndGPA** method did not have to be changed, so we did not have to declare it in **GradStudentRec** at all. Because it is part of the **StudentRec** object type, it is inherited by the **GradStudentRec** object type.

```
UNIT my_objs;   { Listing21.3 }

  { Demonstrates how to move object types into a unit for
    re-use in other programs. }

INTERFACE

USES CRT, MyUtils;

CONST
  formfeed = #12;

TYPE
  string15 = STRING[15];
  studentrec = OBJECT
                 fname,
                 lname : string15;
                 GPA           : REAL;
                 PROCEDURE init;
                 PROCEDURE fillrecord;
                 PROCEDURE SendHonorsLetter;
                 PROCEDURE DisplayNameAndGPA;
                 END;


IMPLEMENTATION

PROCEDURE studentrec.init;
  BEGIN
  fname     := space;
  lname     := space;
  GPA       := 0.00
  END;

PROCEDURE studentrec.FillRecord;
  BEGIN
  CLRSCR;
  WRITE(' Enter the student''s first name: ');
  READLN(fname);
  WRITE(' Enter the student''s last name: ');
  READLN(lname);
  WRITE(' Enter the student''s current GPA: ');
  READLN(GPA);
  END;

PROCEDURE studentrec.SendHonorsLetter;
  VAR
    letterfile: TEXT;
    counter   : INTEGER;
  BEGIN
    ASSIGN(letterfile, 'prn');
    REWRITE(letterfile);
    FOR counter := 1 TO 10 DO WRITELN(letterfile);
    WRITELN(letterfile, 'Dear Mr./Ms. ', lname, ':');
    WRITELN(letterfile);
    WRITELN(letterfile, 'Your grade point average is over 3.5. This');
    WRITELN(letterfile, 'means that you will graduate cum laude from');
    WRITELN(letterfile, 'this institution. Congratulations.');
    WRITELN(letterfile);
    WRITELN(letterfile, 'Sincerely,');
    WRITELN(letterfile);
    WRITELN(letterfile, 'V. Wormer');
```

Listing 21.3: A unit with studentrec object declarations.

```
     WRITELN(letterfile, 'Dean of Students');
     WRITELN(letterfile, formfeed);
     close(letterfile)
  END;

PROCEDURE studentrec.DisplayNameAndGPA;
  BEGIN
  CLRSCR;
  WRITELN(' The student''s name is: ', fname, space, lname, '.');
  WRITELN(' The student''s GPA is:  ', GPA:0:2, '.');
  IF GPA > 3.5  THEN SendHonorsLetter;
  END;


END.
```

Listing 21.3: A unit with studentrec object declarations. (cont.)

Another trick demonstrated by Listing 21.4 is that in an object type's methods, you can make explicit calls to the methods of ancestor types by using the dot notation with the name of the ancestor type. In the **GradStudentRec.Init** method, for example, there is no need to repeat the code that gets the student name and GPA, because this code is part of the ancestor type **StudentRec**. Instead, we simply include an explicit call to **StudentRec**'s **Init** routine *inside* the **GradStudentRec**'s **Init** routine. When this line of code is reached, **StudentRec.init** executes just like any other subroutine. The rest of the **GradStudentRec.init** routine then gets the information that is unique to the **GradStudentRec** type. The same trick is used in the **GradStudentRec.fillrecord** method.

In summary, to override a method from an ancestor object type, you simply declare a new method in the descendant object type with *the same name* as the method in the ancestor type. To add a new method or field, as we did with the **PhDCandidate** field in the **GradStudentRec** type, simply add it to the descendant type declaration.

Note one very important point: only *methods* can be overridden, *not* data fields. The data fields of an ancestor type are an ineradicable part of all its descendant types, and they cannot be changed. If you have some descendant types that will need a certain field and others that will not need it, you should simply leave that field out of the ancestor type.

Once you have keyed in Listing 21.4, compile and run it. You will see that, as advertised, the **GradStudentRec** methods collect the information and process it as needed—that is, with one exception.

```
PROGRAM Listing21_4;

   ( Shows how the creation of descendant object types saves
     considerable programming work. Principal features shown:

       INHERITANCE, whereby an object type automatically includes
                    fields and methods from its ancestor types; and

       OVERRIDING, whereby an object type can (but does not have to)
                   replace methods from ancestor types with more ap-
                   propriate methods for itself. )

USES CRT, MyUtils, my_objs;

TYPE
   gradstudentrec = OBJECT (studentrec)
                    PhDcandidate : BOOLEAN;
                    PROCEDURE init;
                    PROCEDURE FillRecord;
                    PROCEDURE SendHonorsLetter;
                    END;

PROCEDURE gradstudentrec.init;
   BEGIN
   CLRSCR;
   studentrec.init;
   PhDcandidate := FALSE;
   WRITELN(' The PhDcandidate field has been initialized to false.');
   pause
   END;

PROCEDURE gradstudentrec.fillrecord;
   VAR candidate : CHAR;
   BEGIN
   studentrec.fillrecord;
   WRITE(' Is the student a Ph.D. candidate (Y/N)? ');
   READLN(candidate);
   IF UPCASE(candidate) = 'Y'
      THEN PhDcandidate := TRUE
      ELSE PhDcandidate := FALSE
   END;

PROCEDURE gradstudentrec.SendHonorsLetter;
   VAR
     letterfile: TEXT;
     counter   : INTEGER;
   BEGIN
     ASSIGN(letterfile, 'prn');
     REWRITE(letterfile);
     FOR counter := 1 TO 10 DO WRITELN(letterfile);
     WRITELN(letterfile, 'Dear Mr./Ms. ', lname, ':');
     WRITELN(letterfile);
     WRITELN(letterfile, 'Your grade point average is over 3.5. This');
     WRITELN(letterfile, 'means that you will receive your Ph.D. "with');
     WRITELN(letterfile, 'distinction" from this institution.');
     WRITELN(letterfile, 'Congratulations.');
     WRITELN(letterfile);
     WRITELN(letterfile, 'Sincerely,');
     WRITELN(letterfile);
     WRITELN(letterfile, 'V. Wormer');
     WRITELN(letterfile, 'Dean of Students');
     WRITELN(letterfile, formfeed);
     CLOSE(letterfile)
   END;
```

Listing 21.4: Creating and using a descendant object type.

```
VAR
  gradstudent : gradstudentrec;

BEGIN
  gradstudent.init;
  gradstudent.fillrecord;
  gradstudent.displaynameandGPA;
  pause
END.
```

Listing 21.4: Creating and using a descendant object type. (cont.)

VIRTUAL METHODS
AND POLYMORPHISM

The exception is the **GradStudentRec.SendHonorsLetter** method, which does not seem to execute at all. Instead, we get the letter from the ancestor **StudentRec** object type! Something is clearly going wrong.

The problem is that the **DisplayNameAndGPA** method, which calls the **SendHonorsLetter** method, is *inherited* from the ancestor object type. When the program is compiled, the **DisplayNameAndGPA** method is given the memory address of the **SendHonorsLetter** method that it should use. Because the copy of **DisplayNameAndGPA** we are using is part of the **StudentRec** object type, it naturally uses the SendHonorsLetter method that is *also* part of the **StudentRec** object type. Because everything is determined at compile time, this is called an example of *early binding:* the method call is *bound* to a certain copy of the **SendHonorsLetter** method when the program is compiled, and this cannot be changed later on when the program is run. Methods that are bound at compile time are called *static methods* because they cannot be changed after compilation.

The obvious solution to the problem is to put a new method declaration for **DisplayNameAndGPA** into the **GradStudentRec** object type. Then, when the program is compiled, this method is part of the **Grad-StudentRec** type, so it is bound to the appropriate copy of the **Send-HonorsLetter** method. This solution is demonstrated in Listing 21.5.

This approach will work: if you run the program in Listing 21.5, you will see that the correct copy of the **SendHonorsLetter** method is being used.

```
PROGRAM Listing21_5;

    { Shows a static-method solution to the problem of the inherited
      "DisplayNameAndGPA" method calling the ancestor object type's
      "SendHonorsLetter" routine instead of the current object type's
      "SendHonorsLetter" routine. This approach requires more code
      than the virtual method solution in Listings 21.6 and 21.7. }

USES CRT, MyUtils, my_objs;

TYPE
    gradstudentrec = OBJECT (studentrec)
                        PhDcandidate : BOOLEAN;
                        PROCEDURE init;
                        PROCEDURE FillRecord;
                        PROCEDURE SendHonorsLetter;
                        PROCEDURE DisplayNameAndGPA;
                        END;

PROCEDURE gradstudentrec.init;
  BEGIN
  CLRSCR;
  studentrec.init;
  PhDcandidate := FALSE;
  WRITELN(' The PhDcandidate field has been initialized to false.');
  pause
  END;

PROCEDURE gradstudentrec.fillrecord;
  VAR candidate : CHAR;
  BEGIN
  studentrec.fillrecord;
  WRITE(' Is the student a Ph.D. candidate (Y/N)? ');
  READLN(candidate);
  IF UPCASE(candidate) = 'Y'
     THEN PhDcandidate := TRUE
     ELSE PhDcandidate := FALSE
  END;

PROCEDURE gradstudentrec.SendHonorsLetter;
  VAR
    letterfile: TEXT;
    counter   : INTEGER;
  BEGIN
    ASSIGN(letterfile, 'prn');
    REWRITE(letterfile);
    FOR counter := 1 TO 10 DO WRITELN(letterfile);
    WRITELN(letterfile, 'Dear Mr./Ms. ', lname, ':');
    WRITELN(letterfile);
    WRITELN(letterfile, 'Your grade point average is over 3.5. This');
    WRITELN(letterfile, 'means that you will receive your Ph.D. "with');
    WRITELN(letterfile, 'distinction" from this institution.');
    WRITELN(letterfile, 'Congratulations.');
    WRITELN(letterfile);
    WRITELN(letterfile, 'Sincerely,');
    WRITELN(letterfile);
    WRITELN(letterfile, 'V. Wormer');
    WRITELN(letterfile, 'Dean of Students');
    WRITELN(letterfile, formfeed);
    CLOSE(letterfile)
  END;
```

Listing 21.5: Static-method solution to a problem in Listing 21.4.

```
PROCEDURE gradstudentrec.DisplayNameAndGPA;
  BEGIN
  CLRSCR;
  WRITELN(' The student''s name is: ', fname, space, lname, '.');
  WRITELN(' The student''s GPA is:  ', GPA:0:2, '.');
  IF GPA > 3.5 THEN SendHonorsLetter;
  END;

VAR
  gradstudent : gradstudentrec;

BEGIN
  gradstudent.init;
  gradstudent.fillrecord;
  gradstudent.displaynameandGPA;
  pause
END.
```

Listing 21.5: Static-method solution to a problem in Listing 21.4. (cont.)

Notice, however, that apart from the fact that it is in the **GradStudentRec** object declaration, there is *no difference* between the **DisplayNameAndGPA** routine in Listing 21.5 and the corresponding routine in the ancestor **Student-Rec** type. This means we are writing the same code all over again.

One of the advantages of object-oriented programming was *supposed* to be that it reduces the amount of code we have to write. If we have to keep rewriting the same methods in each descendant object type just to make sure that they are bound to the appropriate copies of other methods, then it would seem that we should sue somebody for false advertising: interesting as it is, object-oriented programming would not be making good on its promises.

However, there is a better solution than repeating the same method code in each descendant type (or suing somebody): using *virtual methods,* which are not bound at compile time. Declaring a method as *virtual* tells Turbo Pascal that it is unknown at compile time *which* copy of the method will need to be used, and that this decision should be put off until the program is actually run—an approach called *late binding.* This powerful approach also enables an object and its methods to be *polymorphic*—i.e., to respond to the same messages in different ways. Polymorphism is one of the most useful features of objects. When an object gets a message to **DisplayNameAndGPA**, it first checks to see which sort of object it is, and therefore, which version of **SendHonorsLetter** to call.

To declare a method as a virtual method, we add the Turbo Pascal reserved word *virtual* at the end of the method header in the object type definition. Listing 21.6 shows how we can change the MY_OBJS unit so that it causes **SendHonorsLetter** to become a virtual method.

Notice that there are two key differences between Listing 21.6 and Listing 21.3. First, of course, we have added the word *virtual* after the **SendHonorsLetter** method in the object type definition. Second—and this is vitally important—we have a new name for the **Init** routine: instead of being called a procedure, it is now called a *Constructor*.

Let's review the situation to see why this is so important. When the program is compiled, any calls to static (nonvirtual) methods are given the memory addresses where those methods can be found—an instance of early binding. With virtual methods, however, it is not known at compile time *which* virtual method will be needed by a particular method call: the method call is *not* given the memory address of a virtual method because it is not known which address (i.e., the address of which method) will be needed. This means that when the program is compiled, these method calls *do not know where to find* the virtual methods that they are supposed to call. When the program finally is run, we need a way to tell these method calls where to find the methods that they need.

This task is performed by the **Constructor** routine. When the program is run, an object variable's **Constructor** routine must be called before any calls are made to the object's virtual methods. The **Constructor** routine sets up a *virtual method table (VMT)* that tells the program where to find the object variable's virtual methods. Note that if you fail to put in a call to the **Constructor** routine before calling a virtual method, your program will crash.

The good news is that all this work is done simply by including the word **constructor**. As long as you call a routine designated as an object's constructor, the VMT will be set up automatically. This means that, even though the **studentrec.init** routine in Listing 21.6 does some other work as well, you could have a **Constructor** routine that did nothing except set up the VMT, as in

```
CONSTRUCTOR AnotherInitMethod;

    BEGIN

    END;
```

```
UNIT my_objs2;   { Listing21.6 }

   { Changes the unit in Listing 21.3 to make SendHonorsLetter
     a virtual method instead of a static method. Principal
     features illustrated:

         VIRTUAL METHODS, whereby a program can choose at run-time
                    which method should be executed, and
         A CONSTRUCTOR routine, which is absolutely required in any
                    object type that uses virtual methods. An object
                    variable's constructor MUST be called to set up
                    the VMT before any calls are made to the object's
                    other methods. }


INTERFACE

USES CRT, MyUtils;

CONST
  formfeed = #12;

TYPE
  string15 = STRING[15];
  studentrec = OBJECT
               fname,
               lname : string15;
               GPA         : REAL;
               CONSTRUCTOR init;
               PROCEDURE fillrecord;
               PROCEDURE SendHonorsLetter; VIRTUAL;
               PROCEDURE DisplayNameAndGPA;
               END;


IMPLEMENTATION

CONSTRUCTOR studentrec.init;
  BEGIN
  fname      := space;
  lname      := space;
  GPA        := 0.00
  END;

PROCEDURE studentrec.FillRecord;
  BEGIN
  CLRSCR;
  WRITE(' Enter the student''s first name: ');
  READLN(fname);
  WRITE(' Enter the student''s last name: ');
  READLN(lname);
  WRITE(' Enter the student''s current GPA: ');
  READLN(GPA);
  END;

PROCEDURE studentrec.SendHonorsLetter;
  var
    letterfile: text;
    counter   : integer;
  BEGIN
    assign(letterfile, 'prn');
    rewrite(letterfile);
    for counter := 1 to 10 do WRITELN(letterfile);
    WRITELN(letterfile, 'Dear Mr./Ms. ', lname, ':');
```

Listing 21.6: Changing the MY_OBJS unit to use virtual methods.

```
      WRITELN(letterfile);
      WRITELN(letterfile, 'Your grade point average is over 3.5. This');
      WRITELN(letterfile, 'means that you will graduate cum laude from');
      WRITELN(letterfile, 'this institution. Congratulations.');
      WRITELN(letterfile);
      WRITELN(letterfile, 'Sincerely,');
      WRITELN(letterfile);
      WRITELN(letterfile, 'V. Wormer');
      WRITELN(letterfile, 'Dean of Students');
      WRITELN(letterfile, formfeed);
      close(letterfile)
   END;

PROCEDURE studentrec.DisplayNameAndGPA;
   BEGIN
   clrscr;
   WRITELN(' The student''s name is: ', fname, space, lname, '.');
   WRITELN(' The student''s GPA is:  ', GPA:0:2, '.');
   IF GPA > 3.5 THEN SendHonorsLetter;
   END;


END.
```

Listing 21.6: Changing the MY_OBJS unit to use virtual methods. (cont.)

A call to this routine will set up the VMT and make it possible for the object variable to use virtual methods, even though it does not do anything else. It's simply the word *constructor* that is important in setting up the VMT.

It is so important that it must be repeated: *every* object variable that uses virtual methods *must* have a **Constructor** method and the program *must* call that method before attempting to use any of the object variable's virtual methods. Failure to abide by this rule can result in disaster.

Now, let's recode the program from Listing 21.5 and make the **Send-HonorsLetter** method a virtual method. First, save Listing 21.6 as MY_OBJS2 and compile it to disk. Copy the MY-OBJS2.TPU file to your Turbo Pascal program directory (probably C:\TP). Then, key in the program in Listing 21.7. Do not forget to change the compilation destination back to disk, and be sure that you name MY-OBJS2, not MY_OBJS, in the USES clause of Listing 21.7.

In Listing 21.7, we declare the **Init** method as a **constructor** method and make **SendHonorsLetter** into a virtual method. Now, because **Send-HonorsLetter** is virtual (in both the **studentrec** and **gradstudentrec** object types), its memory address is not bound to the method call in **DisplayNameAndGPA** when the program is compiled. The decision on which version of **SendHonorsLetter** to use is put off until the program

```
PROGRAM Listing21_7;

  ( Changes the program in Listing 21.5 by using virtual methods
    to eliminate the redundant code in the program. Principal
    features demonstrated:

        VIRTUAL METHODS, whereby a program can choose at run-time
                        which method should be executed, and
        A CONSTRUCTOR routine, which is absolutely required in any
                        object type that uses virtual methods. An object
                        variable's constructor MUST be called to set up
                        the VMT before any calls are made to the object's
                        other methods. )


USES CRT, MyUtils, my_objs2;

TYPE
  gradstudentrec = OBJECT (studentrec)
                      PhDcandidate : BOOLEAN;
                      CONSTRUCTOR init;
                      PROCEDURE FillRecord;
                      PROCEDURE SendHonorsLetter; VIRTUAL;
                      END;

CONSTRUCTOR gradstudentrec.init;
  BEGIN
  CLRSCR;
  studentrec.init;
  PhDcandidate := FALSE;
  WRITELN(' The PhDcandidate field has been initialized to false.');
  pause
  END;

PROCEDURE gradstudentrec.fillrecord;
  VAR candidate : CHAR;
  BEGIN
  studentrec.fillrecord;
  WRITE(' Is the student a Ph.D. candidate (Y/N)? ');
  READLN(candidate);
  IF UPCASE(candidate) = 'Y'
     THEN PhDcandidate := TRUE
     ELSE PhDcandidate := FALSE
  END;

PROCEDURE gradstudentrec.SendHonorsLetter;
  VAR
     letterfile: TEXT;
     counter   : INTEGER;
  BEGIN
  ASSIGN(letterfile, 'prn');
  REWRITE(letterfile);
  FOR counter := 1 TO 10 DO WRITELN(letterfile);
  WRITELN(letterfile, 'Dear Mr./Ms. ', lname, ':');
  WRITELN(letterfile);
  WRITELN(letterfile, 'Your grade point average is over 3.5. This');
  WRITELN(letterfile, 'means that you will receive your Ph.D. "with');
  WRITELN(letterfile, 'distinction" from this institution.');
  WRITELN(letterfile, 'Congratulations.');
  WRITELN(letterfile);
  WRITELN(letterfile, 'Sincerely,');
```

Listing 21.7: A virtual-method solution to the problem in Listing 21.4.

```
     WRITELN(letterfile);
     WRITELN(letterfile, 'V. Wormer');
     WRITELN(letterfile, 'Dean of Students');
     WRITELN(letterfile, formfeed);
     CLOSE(letterfile)
   END;

VAR
   gradstudent : gradstudentrec;

BEGIN
   gradstudent.init;
   gradstudent.fillrecord;
   gradstudent.displaynameandGPA;
   pause
END.
```

Listing 21.7: A virtual-method solution to the problem in Listing 21.4. (cont.)

is run. When a call is actually made to **SendHonorsLetter** during a program run, the program first checks to see what type of object is making the method call. It then calls the *correct* **SendHonorsLetter** method for that object type. In the case of Listing 21.7, **SendHonorsLetter** is being called by a **gradstudentrec**-type object, so it gets the version of **SendHonorsLetter** from the **gradstudentrec** object declaration.

By using virtual methods, we can avoid repeating code in descendant object types. Object-oriented programming has made good on its promise to reduce the amount of code we must write.

AN OBJECT-ORIENTED STACK

As one more illustration, let's look at an object-oriented version of a stack. As you may recall, a stack is a list in which all additions and deletions are made at one end of the list. In Chapter 17, we implemented stacks as both arrays and linked lists by using standard structured programming techniques. Here, we will create an array-based stack (Listing 21.8) with object-oriented techniques: the corresponding listing in Chapter 17 is Listing 17.1.

We first create a generic ("abstract") object type that can serve as an ancestor type for both stacks and queues: we call this abstract type *list*. This type contains the data fields and methods that will be common to all the list object types that we plan to create. Having created this ancestor type, all we need to add when we declare the stack object type are methods to push items onto the stack and to pop items off of the stack.

Note that the methods for pushing and popping have to take only a single parameter: the character that is being pushed or popped. It is not necessary to include the stack object as a parameter because, as discussed earlier, the push and pop routines are *part of* the stack object, not external to it. When a call is made to an object's push or pop methods, it automatically knows that it is supposed to do a push or pop on its own **listitem** data field.

As in Listing 17.1, we also include routines to prompt the user for input and then display the results on the computer screen. These routines *are* external to the stack object and, therefore, the object is passed to them as a parameter.

The rest of the stack operations go pretty much as expected. We first tell the stack object **charlist** to initialize itself. Then, we call the **PushItems-OnStack** and **PopItemsOffStack** routines to get input and display it. These routines, in turn, instruct the stack object to push items onto its **listitem** data field and pop them off.

DYNAMIC OBJECT
VARIABLES AND POINTERS

Although the procedures are a little more complicated, objects can be used with pointers just like any other variables:

```
TYPE

    studentrecptr = ^studentrec;

    studentrec = OBJECT

                { object fields and methods }

                END;
```

```
PROGRAM Listing21_8;

    ( Demonstrates an object-oriented implementation of a stack.
      As in Chapter 17, the program prompts the user to enter
      enough characters to fill up the stack, then pops them off
      the stack in reverse order. Note the key difference between
      this stack and the one in Listing 17.1: while the stack in
      Listing 17.1 was a passive array structure on which some
      procedures operate, this stack is an active data structure
      that includes methods so that it can perform the same stack
      operations on itself. Instead of calling a procedure to do
      something to the stack, as in 17.1, we send a message to the
      stack instructing it to do something on its own. )

USES CRT, MyUtils;

CONST
  Max = 5;

TYPE
    ( GENERIC LIST OBJECT TYPE )
    ( The list type is an abstract object type. This means that
      we never intend to create any variables of the list type
      itself. The list type is created solely as an ancestor type
      for other list object types, such as stacks and queues. We
      will actually create variables of these descendant types.
      Here, we demonstrate a stack object which is a descendant
      of the abstract list type. )
    list = OBJECT
            listitem  : array[1..Max] OF CHAR;
            count     : 0..Max;
            PROCEDURE init;
            FUNCTION full    : BOOLEAN;
            FUNCTION empty   : BOOLEAN;
            END;

    ( STACK OBJECT TYPE )
    stack = OBJECT (list)
             ( Because the top of the stack will always be
               the same as the "count" field inherited from
               the list object type, there is no need for a
               separate stacktop field. )
             PROCEDURE push(item : CHAR);
             PROCEDURE pop(VAR item : CHAR);
             END;

( -------------------------------------------------------------- )
(                 METHODS FOR THE LIST OBJECT TYPE                )
( -------------------------------------------------------------- )
PROCEDURE list.init;
  VAR
    counter : INTEGER;
  BEGIN
    CLRSCR;
    FOR counter := 1 TO max DO
        listitem[counter] := space;
    count := 0
  END;

FUNCTION list.full : BOOLEAN;
  BEGIN
```

Listing 21.8: An object-oriented version of a stack.

```
      IF count = max
         THEN full := TRUE
         ELSE full := FALSE
   END;

FUNCTION list.empty : BOOLEAN;
   BEGIN
   Empty := (count = 0)
   END;



{ --------------------------------------------------------------- }
{                 METHODS FOR THE STACK OBJECT TYPE               }
{ --------------------------------------------------------------- }
PROCEDURE stack.push(item : CHAR);
   BEGIN
     IF full    ( test FOR full stack )
     THEN BEGIN
          WRITELN(' Sorry, full stack!');
          exit
          END
     ELSE BEGIN
          count := count + 1;
          listitem[count] := item
          END
   END;

PROCEDURE stack.pop(VAR item : CHAR);
   BEGIN
     IF empty
     THEN BEGIN
          WRITELN(' Sorry, stack is empty!');
          exit
          END
     ELSE BEGIN
          item := listitem[count];
          listitem[count] := space;
          count := count - 1
          END
   END;

{ --------------------------------------------------------------- }
{                 VARIABLE DECLARATION SECTION                    }
{ --------------------------------------------------------------- }
VAR
   charlist : stack;




{ --------------------------------------------------------------- }
{  NON-OBJECT PROCEDURES TO DISPLAY RESULTS ON THE PC'S SCREEN    }
{ --------------------------------------------------------------- }
PROCEDURE PushItemsOnStack(VAR charlist : stack);
   VAR
     newitem : CHAR;
     counter : INTEGER;
   BEGIN
     FOR counter := 1 TO max DO
       BEGIN
       WRITE(' Enter a character to push onto the stack: ');
       READLN(newitem);
```

Listing 21.8: An object-oriented version of a stack. (cont.)

```
            charlist.push(newitem);
            WRITELN
            END
        END;

    PROCEDURE PopItemsOffStack(VAR charlist: stack);
        VAR
            counter : INTEGER;
            item    : CHAR;
        BEGIN
            CLRSCR;
            WRITELN(' The stack items are popped off in reverse order');
            WRITELN(' because a stack is a last-in-first-out list.');
            WRITELN;
            WRITE(' Items popped from the stack: ');
            FOR counter := 1 TO max DO
                BEGIN
                delay(700);
                charlist.pop(item);
                WRITE(item, space)
                END
        END;

    { ------------------------------------------------------------- }
    {                    MAIN BODY OF THE PROGRAM                    }
    { ------------------------------------------------------------- }
    BEGIN
        charlist.init;
        PushItemsOnStack(charlist);
        PopItemsOffStack(charlist);
        pause
    END.
```

Listing 21.8: An object-oriented version of a stack. (cont.)

```
VAR

        student : studentrecptr;

BEGIN

        New(student);

        { ... other program statements }

END.
```

With objects, Turbo Pascal extends the **New** procedure so that you can create a dynamic object variable and initialize it in a single step. You can still do things the traditional way, as in

```
New(student);

student.init;
```

but you can also include the initialization method in the call to the **New** procedure, as in

```
New(student, init);
```

In Turbo Pascal 6, you can also use **New** as a function as well as a procedure. If *ThisPtr* is a pointer variable of the same type as *ThatPtr*, you can create a dynamic variable, initialize it, and assign it to *Thisptr* as follows:

```
ThisPtr := New(ThatPtr, Init);
```

Turbo Pascal also extends the **Dispose** procedure to do extra work in handling object variables. Because objects are more complicated than other data types, you can now include a shutdown routine called a **Destructor** in your object type definition to handle any special cleanup chores that are needed. The **Dispose** procedure can now call this **destructor** method at the same time as it deallocates a dynamic object variable. If your **destructor** method is called **Done**, then it would be written as:

```
Dispose(student, done)
```

SUMMARY

Object-oriented programming provides an immensely powerful tool to reduce the amount of work required in complex programming projects. An object is a *smart* data structure that encapsulates in itself all the subroutines (called "methods") that it needs to operate. Any object type also can have descendants that inherit all of its data fields and methods. The methods of an ancestor type can be overridden when different methods are needed for the descendant type, and virtual methods allow the postponement of decisions about which methods to use until the program is run.

Turbo Pascal extends the capabilities of the **New** and **Dispose** procedures for use with dynamic object variables, allowing initialization and shutdown to be handled in the same program commands as allocation and deallocation of a dynamic object.

REVIEW EXERCISES

1. Explain the idea of an object. What does it mean to say that an object is an "intelligent" data structure?

2. Explain how object-oriented programming is similar to traditional structured programming, as well as how it differs.

3. Suppose that you wanted to create an object-oriented version of a queue. How would you determine what methods were needed, and what methods those would be?

4. Explain how an object inherits methods from ancestor objects, and how those inherited methods can be used. Give at least two examples.

5. What is wrong with the following code fragment? Explain your answer.

```
rock = OBJECT
        composition : string15;
        weight      : INTEGER;
        PROCEDURE Init;
        PROCEDURE GetData;
        PROCEDURE DisplayData;
        END;
moonrock = OBJECT
        composition : string80;
        PROCEDURE Init;
        PROCEDURE GetData;
        PROCEDURE DisplayData;
        END;
```

6. What is wrong with the following code fragment? Explain your answer.

```
rock = OBJECT
  composition : string15;
  weight      : INTEGER;
  PROCEDURE Init;
  PROCEDURE GetData; VIRTUAL;
  PROCEDURE DisplayData;
  END;
```

7. Explain the difference between static and virtual methods, as well as the difference between early and late binding.

8. What is a VMT and why is it important?

9. What is wrong with the following code fragment? Explain your answer.

```
rock = OBJECT
  composition : string15;
  weight      : INTEGER;
  CONSTRUCTOR Init;
  PROCEDURE GetData;
  PROCEDURE DisplayData;
  END;
```

10. Try your hand at writing a program that uses an object-oriented version of a queue.

C H A P T E R

Introducing Turbo Vision

It follows that these bouts of college days with intractable assignments, witless classmates, and professorial ogres are not mere shadow boxing. They are the means of finding yourself and thereby finding your niche in the scheme of things. They are the means of acquiring that art of thinking without which our world is becoming an increasingly insoluble puzzle.

—Brand Blanshard, *The Uses of a Liberal Education*

WHAT IS TURBO VISION?

Turbo Vision is the remarkable new library of object types included with Turbo Pascal 6. By using Turbo Vision, you can incorporate pull-down menus, dialog boxes, mouse support, and a host of other sophisticated features into your applications—all without having to write the code yourself! It's all prepackaged in the Turbo Vision units.

Once you learn to use Turbo Vision, your own programs can have the same professional and easy-to-use screen interface as Turbo Pascal itself. However, learning Turbo Vision can be very difficult. Turbo Vision is essentially a specialized I/O (input-output) programming language built on top of Turbo Pascal. This means that the normal Pascal I/O commands you have learned up to now, such as WRITELN, often cannot be used in Turbo Vision programs.

In their place, you will learn completely new ways to display text and get user input through menus, dialog boxes, and windows. Some of these new methods are quite intricate—so much so that even the Turbo Vision manual and example programs, which were written by the people at Borland who *created* Turbo Vision, *still* contain a few errors.

Consequently, learning Turbo Vision will require tremendous effort and determination on your part—but such effort will produce an equally tremendous benefit at the end. In this chapter, we will be able to introduce only some of the most basic features of Turbo Vision, but they will be enough to get you started. To acquire a fuller understanding of Turbo Vision, you should consult your Turbo Pascal Turbo Vision manual.

Turbo Vision programming requires a solid grasp of both (1) object-oriented programming concepts and (2) operations with pointers and dynamic allocation. If you feel at all insecure about either of these topics, you should review Chapters 11 and 21 before going ahead with this chapter.

STRUCTURE OF TURBO VISION

Turbo Vision is a library of object types that can handle most tasks involved in getting input from the user and displaying output on the screen. Aspects of your program that do not involve I/O tasks can be handled the same way as before: for example, sorting an array or searching through a linked list. Turbo Vision makes changes primarily in the way your program interacts with the user.

The biggest conceptual change in Turbo Vision is that it causes your programs to be *event-driven*. In our previous program examples, we set up menus and prompts that allowed the user to make choices in the program. Our programs were prepared to accept certain kinds of input at certain times, and would not accept such input at any other times. This meant, for instance, that the user could not merely press the Escape key at any time to back out of a program task. Instead, he or she had to wait for an appropriate on-screen prompt.

Turbo Vision, however, allows programs to accept and use input in a more flexible way, called "event-driven." An event can be a keypress, a mouse click, a request for context-sensitive help, or a message from one part of a program to another. The advantage of this approach is that it does not limit the user to a specific set of menu choices: a Turbo Vision program is ready to perform a wide variety of tasks depending on the event that it detects, and its object types use a special method, **HandleEvent**, to do this.

TURBO VISION AND TURBO PASCAL FOR WINDOWS

By the time this book is in print, Borland will have announced Turbo Pascal for Windows, which provides full support for object-oriented programming with the Microsoft Windows graphic user interface. Because Turbo Vision and Microsoft Windows both provide standardized menus, mouse support, and screen displays, you may wonder if Turbo Vision is merely a transitional product on the way to Microsoft Windows. Will it be obsolete as soon as you take it out of the box?

The answer is that Turbo Pascal 6 (with Turbo Vision) and Turbo Pascal for Windows stand side-by-side as powerful solutions to different problems. For applications that demand a graphic interface such as that provided by Microsoft Windows, Turbo Pascal for Windows is an ideal choice. On the other hand, the majority of applications do not require a graphic interface but can benefit from event-driven programming and standardized screen displays—as provided by Turbo Vision.

Moreover, if and when you *do* need to program for Microsoft Windows, Turbo Vision will have prepared you for all the basic ideas and operations that you will have to perform.

BASIC TURBO VISION OBJECT TYPES

Turbo Vision is a hierarchy of object types, all of which are descended from a single ancestor object type. Turbo Vision object types divide neatly into two categories: those that are *views* and those that are not views.

A view is anything in the program that can be displayed on the screen. Views are descended from the **TView** object type and include menus, dialog boxes, windows, scroll bars, and text elements. Because Turbo Vision operates in character mode instead of in graphics mode, its views are all rectangular and can draw or redraw themselves very quickly on the screen. Because Turbo Vision views are objects, they have built-in methods that enable them to handle any tasks that come their way.

It is important to remember that in a Turbo Vision program, *only* views are allowed to display anything on the screen. If you try to display text with a WRITELN statement, for example, you will obliterate part of the Turbo Vision screen display, perhaps overwriting a dialog box or part of a window.

Like many Turbo Vision object types, the **TView** object type is very complex, but you can learn its basic features in a fairly short time. Any view must be able to initialize itself, draw itself on the screen, change size or position on the screen if needed, and shut itself down when its work is finished. Turbo Vision view types are shown in Figure 22.1. Ancestor objects are toward the left of the figure, and descendants are connected with their ancestors by horizontal lines.

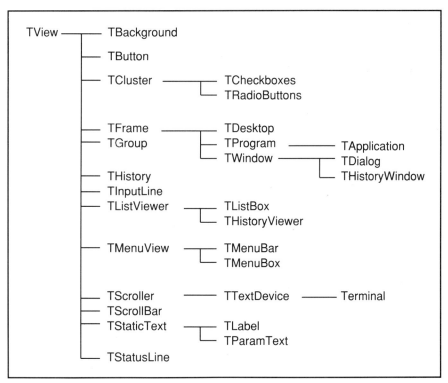

Figure 22.1: Turbo Vision View Types.

Turbo Vision object types that are not views are the **TCollection, T-Stream, TResourceFile, TStringList,** and **TStrListMaker** types: these perform a variety of tasks in the background to support view objects.

CREATING PULL-DOWN MENUS

The best way to learn Turbo Vision is to jump right in and examine a Turbo Vision program. Listing 22.1 shows how to set up the Turbo Vision desktop, create a status line at the bottom of the screen, and create a menu bar with pull-down menus at the top of the screen.

The first thing we do in the program is to name the Turbo Vision units we need in the USES clause: in this case, we need object types from the Objects, Drivers, Views, Menus, and App units. We then declare a constant to serve as an intermediary between a menu option to open a window and the actual method in the window object that opens the window.

The only object type that we use in this program is **TMyApp**, which is a descendant of the **TApplication** object type. It has two methods, both of them virtual methods: first, a method to set up a menu bar, and second, a method to set up a status line.

Before we go into the details of setting up the menu bar and status line, however, let's take a quick look at the end of the listing. The main body of the program has three lines in it: **MyApp.Init, MyApp.Run,** and **MyApp.Done**. These are all methods that our variable *MyApp*, which is of the **TMyApp** object type, inherited from its ancestor **TApplication**. The point is that the ancestor object type's methods do a tremendous amount of behind-the-scenes work in setting up the Turbo Vision program—work that you as the programmer almost never have to worry about.

Now let's go back to look at **TMyApp.InitMenuBar**, which sets up the menu bar and pull-down menus for our Turbo Vision program. The first thing to ask is: what does a menu bar look like on the screen? Well, it's a rectangle one line high and 80 columns wide. To represent our menu bar on the screen, we declare a variable of type *TRect*, a view that comes from the Objects unit. A *TRect* type variable is specified by giving the screen coordinates of its upper-left corner (denoted by *a*) and its lower-right corner (denoted by *b*).

```
PROGRAM Listing22_1;

   { Demonstrates how to set up menus and a status line in
     a Turbo Vision program. Note, however, that none of the
     menu options is implemented yet. The only thing you can
     do at this stage is to exit from the program with Alt-X. }

USES OBJECTS, DRIVERS, VIEWS, MENUS, APP;

CONST
  cmNewWindow = 101;

TYPE
  TMyApp = OBJECT (TApplication)
    PROCEDURE InitMenuBar; VIRTUAL;
    PROCEDURE InitStatusLine; VIRTUAL;
    END;

{ ------------------------------- }
{ METHODS FOR TMYAPP OBJECT TYPE  }
{ ------------------------------- }
PROCEDURE TMyApp.InitMenuBar;
  VAR
    r: TRect;
  BEGIN
    GetExtent(r);
    r.b.y := r.a.y + 1;
    MenuBar := New(PMenuBar, Init(r, NewMenu(
      NewSubMenu('~F~ile', hcNoContext, NewMenu(
        NewItem('~N~ew', 'F4', kbF4, cmNewWindow, hcNoContext,
        NewLine(
        NewItem('E~x~it', 'Alt-X', kbAltX, cmQuit, hcNoContext,
        NIL)))),
      NewSubMenu('~W~indow', hcNoContext, NewMenu(
        NewItem('~N~ext', 'F6', kbF6, cmNext, hcNoContext,
        NewItem('~Z~oom', 'F5', kbF5, cmZoom, hcNoContext,
        NIL))),
      NIL))
    )));
  END;

PROCEDURE TMyApp.InitStatusLine;
  VAR
    r: TRect;
  BEGIN
    GetExtent(r);
    r.a.y := r.b.y - 1;
    StatusLine := New(PStatusLine, Init(r,
      NewStatusDef(0, $FFFF,
        NewStatusKey('', kbF10, cmMenu,
        NewStatusKey('~Alt-X~ Exit', kbAltX, cmQuit,
        NewStatusKey('~F4~ New', kbF4, cmNewWindow,
        NewStatusKey('~Alt-F3~ Close', kbAltF3, cmClose,
        NIL)))),
      NIL)
    ));
  END;

{ ------------------------------- }
{ GLOBAL VARIABLE DECLARATIONS    }
{ ------------------------------- }
```

Listing 22.1: Creating menu bar, status line, and pull-down menus.

```
VAR
  MyApp: TMyApp;

{ ----------------------------------------------------------- }
{                    MAIN BODY OF PROGRAM                      }
{ ----------------------------------------------------------- }
BEGIN
  MyApp.Init;
  MyApp.Run;
  MyApp.Done;
END.
```

Listing 22.1: Creating menu bar, status line, and pull-down menus. (cont.)

When we call the **TView.GetExtent** method, it sets the **TRect** object to include all of the current view: here, the whole Turbo Vision screen. To reduce its height to a single line at the top of the screen, we then reset its *b.y* coordinate (the height of the lower-right corner) so that it is just one line below the *a.y* coordinate (the upper-left corner). This gives us a rectangle that is one line high, at the top of the screen, and extends from the left to the right edge of the screen.

So far, however, it's just a rectangle—not a menu bar. To turn it into a menu bar, we call the **MenuBar** method, and this is one of the places where Turbo Vision starts to get complicated.

One of the innovations in Turbo Pascal 6 is that it allows you to use the **New** procedure as a function—something that is unheard of in traditional Pascal programming. Remember also that Turbo Pascal allows you to initialize dynamic object variables in the same **New** command that creates them, as in **New(p,init(p))**.

Here, we use **New** as a function to create a dynamic menu bar object with **New(PMenuBar** (where **PMenuBar** is a predefined pointer type in Turbo Vision) and use **Init(r,NewMenu(** to put the menu bar in the *TRect* variable we have created.

The **NewMenu** part of the call to **Init** is actually what sets up the pull-down menus attached to the menu bar. For each pull-down menu, we call the **NewSubMenu** method. The **NewSubMenu** method takes four parameters: the name of the menu, a constant that indicates the on-screen help (if any) available for this menu, a pointer to the first item in the menu, and a pointer to the next pull-down menu in the menu bar. Notice that **NewSubMenu, NewMenu**, and **NewItem** are all functions that return pointers to various menu objects.

In each call to **NewSubMenu** and **NewItem**, the name of the submenu or menu item is a string in single quotes. To highlight a letter in the string, you enclose it in tilde marks, e.g., as in '~F~ile' for the File submenu. In each call to **NewItem**, you also use one of Turbo Vision's predefined key constants, such as **kbF4**, to specify that key as a speed key for the menu choice. The command constants, such as **cmNewWindow**, generally, are not predefined in Turbo Vision and must be defined in your program. The **HcNoContext** in this example shows that we are not making on-screen help information available for these menu choices.

At the end of the method to define a menu bar, we have a bewildering sequence of parentheses and **NIL**s: this is because we have nested menus and menu items several levels deep. There is no way to avoid this, but it is one place where Turbo Pascal 6's pair-matching feature (see Chapter 4) can be very handy.

Creating the status line is similar to creating the menu bar. We first define a *TRect* variable and then put the status line into it. Using **PStatusLine**, a predefined Turbo Vision pointer to a status line object, we call **New** as a function to create a dynamic status line variable. The first two parameters, **0**, **$FFFF** define help contexts and can be ignored in this example.

Each call to **NewStatusKey** displays a string (which can be an empty string) in the status line and binds a certain key or key combination to a certain command. In this case, **cmQuit** is a predefined Turbo Vision command; we must define the others, as we will do in the listings that follow this one. As before, we end up with a messy but unavoidable sequence of parentheses and **NIL**s.

Until now, we have simply been defining the **TMyApp** object type. It inherits both fields and methods from its ancestor type **TApplication**, and we have added two new methods to set up a menu bar and a status line. We now declare *MyApp*, a variable of this object type, and call its methods in the main body of the program. The result is shown in Figure 22.2.

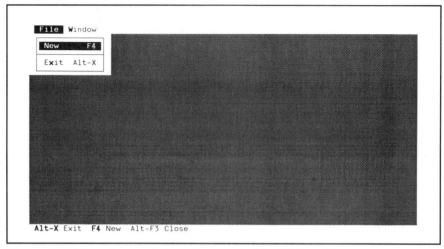

Figure 22.2: Menu bar and status bar created by Listing 22.1.

CREATING SCREEN WINDOWS

Now we will look at three main problems: first, how to bind specific commands to items in pull-down menus; second, how to create and open screen windows; and third, how to display text in those screen windows. These operations are illustrated in Listing 22.2. Because of the tremendous amount of detail, we will look only at the most important points in this listing, as we did with Listing 22.1.

The first thing you will notice is that we have added two new methods to our **TMyApp** object type: a **HandleEvent** method to get input from the user, and a **NewWindow** method to set up and initialize windows. We also declare a window object type as a descendant of **TWindow**, a predefined Turbo Vision type, and set up a pointer type to point to dynamic window variables.

Here's where you may need to do a quick mental reset. A window is just a frame: it can *contain* something, but it does not come with an interior as standard equipment. If we want something to be in the window, we

```
PROGRAM Listing22_2;

  { Demonstrates how to set up commands, open screen windows,
    and display text in the screen windows. }

USES OBJECTS, DRIVERS, VIEWS, MENUS, APP;

CONST
  WinCount: INTEGER =    0;
  cmNewWindow       = 101;

TYPE
  TMyApp = OBJECT (TApplication)
    PROCEDURE HandleEvent(VAR Event: TEvent); virtual;
    PROCEDURE InitMenuBar; virtual;
    PROCEDURE InitStatusLine; virtual;
    PROCEDURE NewWindow;
    END;

  PDemoWindow = ^TDemoWindow;
  TDemoWindow = OBJECT (TWindow)
    CONSTRUCTOR Init(Bounds: TRect; WinTitle: STRING;
                              WindowNo: WORD);
    END;

  PInterior = ^TInterior;
  TInterior = OBJECT (TView)
    CONSTRUCTOR Init(VAR Bounds: TRect);
    PROCEDURE Draw; virtual;
    END;

{ ------------------------------- }
{ METHODS FOR TINTERIOR           }
{ ------------------------------- }
CONSTRUCTOR TInterior.Init(VAR Bounds: TRect);
  BEGIN
  TView.Init(Bounds);
  GrowMode := gfGrowHiX + gfGrowHiY;
  Options := Options or ofFramed;
  END;

PROCEDURE TInterior.Draw;
  CONST
    Greeting: STRING = 'Hello, new programmer!';
  BEGIN
  TView.Draw;
  WriteStr(4, 2, Greeting,$01);
  END;


{ ------------------------------- }
{ METHODS FOR TDEMOWINDOW         }
{ ------------------------------- }
CONSTRUCTOR TDemoWindow.Init(Bounds: TRect; WinTitle: STRING;
                                   WindowNo: WORD);
  VAR
    S: STRING[3];
    Interior: PInterior;
  BEGIN
  Str(WindowNo, S);
  TWindow.Init(Bounds, WinTitle + ' ' + S, wnNoNumber);
  GetClipRect(Bounds);
```

Listing 22.2: Setting up screen windows.

```
    Bounds.Grow(-1,-1);
    Interior := New(PInterior, Init(Bounds));
    Insert(Interior);
    END;


{ ------------------------------- }
{ METHODS FOR TMYAPP             }
{ ------------------------------- }
PROCEDURE TMyApp.HandleEvent(VAR Event: TEvent);
  BEGIN
  TApplication.HandleEvent(Event);
  if Event.What = evCommand then
     BEGIN
     CASE Event.Command OF
         cmNewWindow: NewWindow;
         ELSE
         Exit;
         END;
     ClearEvent(Event);
     END
  END;

PROCEDURE TMyApp.InitMenuBar;
  VAR
    r: TRect;
  BEGIN
    GetExtent(r);
    r.b.y := r.a.y + 1;
    MenuBar := New(PMenuBar, Init(r, NewMenu(
      NewSubMenu('~F~ile', hcNoContext, NewMenu(
        NewItem('~N~ew', 'F4', kbF4, cmNewWindow, hcNoContext,
        NewLine(
        NewItem('E~x~it', 'Alt-X', kbAltX, cmQuit, hcNoContext,
        NIL)))),
      NewSubMenu('~W~indow', hcNoContext, NewMenu(
        NewItem('~N~ext', 'F6', kbF6, cmNext, hcNoContext,
        NewItem('~Z~oom', 'F5', kbF5, cmZoom, hcNoContext,
        NIL)))),
      NIL))
    )));
  END;

PROCEDURE TMyApp.InitStatusLine;
  VAR

    r: TRect;
  BEGIN
    GetExtent(r);
    r.a.y := r.b.y - 1;
    StatusLine := New(PStatusLine, Init(r,
      NewStatusDef(0, $FFFF,
        NewStatusKey('', kbF10, cmMenu,
        NewStatusKey('~Alt-X~ Exit', kbAltX, cmQuit,
        NewStatusKey('~F4~ New', kbF4, cmNewWindow,
        NewStatusKey('~Alt-F3~ Close', kbAltF3, cmClose,
        NIL)))),
      NIL)
    ));
  END;

PROCEDURE TMyApp.NewWindow;
  VAR
```

Listing 22.2: Setting up screen windows. (cont.)

```
       Window : PDemoWindow;
       r      : TRect;
    BEGIN
    INC(WinCount);
    r.Assign(0, 0, 32, 7);
    RANDOMIZE;
    r.Move(RANDOM(47), RANDOM(16));
    Window := New(PDemoWindow, Init(r, 'Greeting Window', WinCount));
    DeskTop^.Insert(Window);
    END;


    ( -------------------------------- )
    ( GLOBAL VARIABLE DECLARATIONS      )
    ( -------------------------------- )
    VAR
      MyApp: TMyApp;

    ( ------------------------------------------------------------ )
    (                 MAIN BODY OF THE PROGRAM                      )
    ( ------------------------------------------------------------ )
    BEGIN
      MyApp.Init;
      MyApp.Run;
      MyApp.Done;
    END.
```

Listing 22.2: Setting up screen windows. (cont.)

have to define it ourselves. To that end, we define a **TInterior** object type that can draw itself inside of a window object. We also create a pointer type for this type.

TInterior's constructor method calls the **init** method of its ancestor, **TView**. Using predefined Turbo Vision constants, it also sets up the interior so it can grow, shrink, or move along with the window in which it finds itself.

TInterior's **Draw** method first calls **TView.Draw** to clear the interior of the window, then uses the Turbo Vision **WriteStr** method to display a greeting in the window.

The **TDemoWindow init** method sets up a pointer to connect the window (i.e., the frame) with the interior of the window. It then inserts the interior into the frame.

TMyApp.HandleEvent sets up a CASE statement so that it tells the application object which method to execute if it receives a certain command constant: here, only one command constant is defined and it activates the **NewWindow** method.

The **TMyApp.NewWindow** method itself sets up a pointer to the new (dynamic) window object. It then calls the **Assign** method of the **TRect** object to set up a rectangle of a certain size—the size of the window we want. After initializing Turbo Pascal's random number generator, it selects a random location on the screen for the window's upper-left corner, creates a new window with a call to **New**, and displays the window on the screen with a call to the Turbo Vision **Desktop** object's **Insert** method.

The result of all this is shown in Figure 22.3.

ADDING SCROLL BARS TO WINDOWS

Another thing we can do with screen window objects is to add scroll bars that allow us to move around in the window by using a mouse. Listing 22.3 illustrates how to modify the program in Listing 22.2 so that the on-screen windows have scroll bars. In addition, it displays a text file (Listing 22.3 itself) in the window so that you have enough text to scroll around in.

A key change that we made in this listing was to change the ancestry of our **TInterior** object type. Previously, it was a descendant of the **TView**

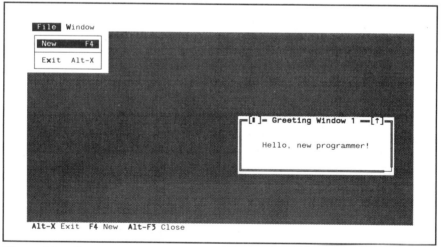

Figure 22.3: Creating screen windows in Turbo Vision.

```
PROGRAM Listing22_3;

   { Demonstrates how to add scroll bars to a screen window and
     display a text file in the window. }

USES OBJECTS, DRIVERS, VIEWS, MENUS, APP;

CONST
  SourceFile        = 'list22_3.pas';
  MaxLines          = 200;
  WinCount: INTEGER =   0;
  cmNewWindow       = 101;

( ------------------------------- )
( GLOBAL VARIABLE DECLARATIONS    )
( ------------------------------- )
VAR
  LineCount: INTEGER;
  Lines: ARRAY[0..MaxLines - 1] OF PString;


( ------------------------------- )
( OBJECT TYPE DECLARATIONS        )
( ------------------------------- )
TYPE
  TMyApp = OBJECT   (TApplication)
    PROCEDURE HandleEvent(VAR Event: TEvent); VIRTUAL;
    PROCEDURE InitMenuBar; VIRTUAL;
    PROCEDURE InitStatusLine; VIRTUAL;
    PROCEDURE NewWindow;
  END;

  PInterior = ^TInterior;
  TInterior = OBJECT (TScroller)
    CONSTRUCTOR Init(VAR Bounds: TRect; AHScrollBar,
                                   AVScrollBar: PScrollBar);
    PROCEDURE Draw; VIRTUAL;
    END;

  PDemoWindow = ^TDemoWindow;
  TDemoWindow = OBJECT (TWindow)
    CONSTRUCTOR Init(Bounds: TRect; WinTitle: STRING;
                                WindowNo: Word);
    PROCEDURE MakeInterior(Bounds: TRect);
    END;


( ------------------------------------------------------------ )
( MISCELLANEOUS GLOBAL PROCEDURES NOT TIED TO OBJECT TYPES }
( ------------------------------------------------------------ )
PROCEDURE ReadFile;
  VAR
  FileToRead: Text;
  LineString: STRING;
BEGIN
  LineCount := 0;
  Assign(FileToRead, SourceFile);
  {$I-}
  Reset(FileToRead);
  {$I+}
  IF IOResult <> 0
    THEN BEGIN
         Writeln(SourceFile, ' not found.');
```

Listing 22.3: Adding scroll bars to a Turbo Vision window object.

```
                    Halt(1);
                END;
        WHILE NOT EOF(FileToRead) AND (LineCount < MaxLines) DO
                BEGIN
                    READLN(FileToRead, LineString);
                    Lines[LineCount] := NewStr(LineString);
                    INC(LineCount);
                END;
            Close(FileToRead);
    END;  { of ReadFile procedure }


PROCEDURE DoneFile;
    VAR
        counter: INTEGER;
    BEGIN
        FOR counter := 0 TO LineCount - 1 DO
            IF Lines[counter] <> NIL
            THEN DisposeStr(Lines[counter]);
    END;


{ ------------------------------- }
{ METHODS FOR TINTERIOR OBJECT TYPE }
{ ------------------------------- }
CONSTRUCTOR TInterior.Init(VAR Bounds: TRect; AHScrollBar,
                              AVScrollBar: PScrollBar);
    BEGIN
    TScroller.Init(Bounds, AHScrollBar, AVScrollBar);
    GrowMode := gfGrowHiX + gfGrowHiY;
    Options := Options or ofFramed;
    SetLimit(100, LineCount);
    END;

PROCEDURE TInterior.Draw;
    VAR
        Color: Byte;
        I, Y: INTEGER;
        b: TDrawBuffer;
    BEGIN
        Color := GetColor(1);
        for Y := 0 to Size.Y - 1 do
            BEGIN
            MoveChar(b, ' ', Color, Size.X);
            i := Delta.Y + Y;
            IF (I < LineCount) and (Lines[I] <> nil) THEN
            MoveStr(b, Copy(Lines[I]^, Delta.X + 1, Size.X), Color);
            WriteLine(0, Y, Size.X, 1, b);
            END
    END;


{ ------------------------------- }
{ METHODS FOR TDEMOWINDOW OBJECT TYPE }
{ ------------------------------- }
CONSTRUCTOR TDemoWindow.Init(Bounds: TRect; WinTitle: STRING;
                                 WindowNo: Word);
    VAR
        NumString: STRING[3];
    BEGIN
    Str(WindowNo, NumString);
```

Listing 22.3: Adding scroll bars to a Turbo Vision window object. (cont.)

```
    TWindow.Init(Bounds, WinTitle + ' ' + NumString, wnNoNumber);
    MakeInterior(Bounds);
    END;

PROCEDURE TDemoWindow.MakeInterior(Bounds: TRect);
  VAR
    HScrollBar, VScrollBar: PScrollBar;
    Interior: PInterior;
    r: TRect;
  BEGIN
    VScrollBar := StandardScrollBar(sbVertical + sbHandleKeyboard);
    HScrollBar := StandardScrollBar(sbHorizontal + sbHandleKeyboard);
    GetExtent(Bounds);
    Bounds.Grow(-1,-1);
    Interior := New(PInterior, Init(Bounds, HScrollBar, VScrollBar));
    Insert(Interior);
    END;


    ( ------------------------------ )
    ( METHODS FOR TMYAPP OBJECT TYPE  )
    ( ------------------------------ )
PROCEDURE TMyApp.HandleEvent(VAR Event: TEvent);
  BEGIN
    TApplication.HandleEvent(Event);
    IF Event.What = evCommand THEN
        BEGIN
        CASE Event.Command OF
            cmNewWindow: NewWindow;
            ELSE Exit;
            END;
        ClearEvent(Event);
        END;
    END;

PROCEDURE TMyApp.InitMenuBar;
  VAR
    r: TRect;
  BEGIN
    GetExtent(r);
    r.b.Y := r.a.Y + 1;
    MenuBar := New(PMenuBar, Init(r, NewMenu(
      NewSubMenu('~F~ile', hcNoContext, NewMenu(
        NewItem('~N~ew', 'F4', kbF4, cmNewWindow, hcNoContext,
        NewLine(
        NewItem('E~x~it', 'Alt-X', kbAltX, cmQuit, hcNoContext,
        nil)))),
      NewSubMenu('~W~indow', hcNoContext, NewMenu(
        NewItem('~N~ext', 'F6', kbF6, cmNext, hcNoContext,
        NewItem('~Z~oom', 'F5', kbF5, cmZoom, hcNoContext,
        nil)))),
      nil))
    )));
    END;

PROCEDURE TMyApp.InitStatusLine;
  VAR
    r: TRect;
  BEGIN
    GetExtent(r);
    r.a.Y := r.b.Y - 1;
```

Listing 22.3: Adding scroll bars to a Turbo Vision window object. (cont.)

```
      StatusLine := New(PStatusLine, Init(r,
        NewStatusDef(0, $FFFF,
          NewStatusKey('', kbF10, cmMenu,
          NewStatusKey('~Alt-X~ Exit', kbAltX, cmQuit,
          NewStatusKey('~F4~ New', kbF4, cmNewWindow,
          NewStatusKey('~Alt-F3~ Close', kbAltF3, cmClose,
          nil)))),
        nil)
      ));
    END;


  PROCEDURE TMyApp.NewWindow;
    VAR
      Window: PDemoWindow;
      r: TRect;
    BEGIN
    Inc(WinCount);
    r.Assign(0, 0, 24, 7);
    RANDOMIZE;
    r.Move(RANDOM(55), RANDOM(16));
    Window := New(PDemoWindow, Init(r, 'Window', WinCount));
    DeskTop^.Insert(Window);
    END;



  { -------------------------------- }
  { MORE GLOBAL VARIABLE DECLARATIONS }
  { -------------------------------- }
  VAR
    MyApp: TMyApp;

  { ----------------------------------------------------------- }
  {                      MAIN BODY OF PROGRAM                    }
  { ----------------------------------------------------------- }
  BEGIN
    ReadFile;
    MyApp.Init;
    MyApp.Run;
    MyApp.Done;
    DoneFile;
  END.
```

Listing 22.3: Adding scroll bars to a Turbo Vision window object. (cont.)

type. Now, however, it is descended from the **TScroller** type so that we can move around in it by using the scroll bars.

The **ReadFile** and **Done** procedures are not tied to any object type. They open a text file, load it into a window's interior, and shut it down when the window closes. They manage the trick of loading the file into the interior object by creating an array of pointers to text strings; each string holds one line of the file.

The scroll bars themselves are additional dynamic objects that we create in the **TDemoWindow.MakeInterior** method, using predefined Turbo Vision scroll bar object types. The result is shown in Figure 22.4.

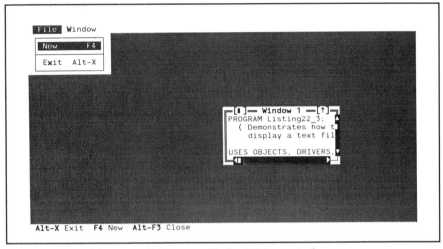

Figure 22.4: Adding scroll bars to a Turbo Vision window.

CREATING DIALOG BOXES

Creating a dialog box involves just as much intricate work as the other things we have done in Turbo Vision, but it proceeds in much the same way. This is illustrated in Listing 22.4.

First, we create a dialog box object type that is descended from the predefined **TDialog** object type, along with a pointer to that type. We add an additional item to the File menu and another command constant to the CASE statement in the **HandleEvent** method.

In the dialog box itself, we create rectangles to hold the title of the dialog box. We also use predefined Turbo Vision types to create checkboxes, pushbuttons, and radio buttons in the same way that we created menu items in earlier listings.

When we have finished setting up the dialog box, we insert it into the Turbo Vision **desktop** with a call to the **Desktop** object type's **ExecView** method. At this stage, of course, the program is not set up to do any actual sorting in response to the user's actions with the dialog box. The result is shown in Figure 22.5.

```
PROGRAM Listing22_4;

  { Demonstrates how to set up a dialog box with pushbuttons,
    checkboxes, and radio buttons. }

USES OBJECTS, DRIVERS, VIEWS, MENUS, APP, DIALOGS;

CONST
  WinCount: Integer =   0;
  cmNewWindow      = 101;
  cmSortDialog     = 102;

TYPE
  TMyApp = OBJECT (TApplication)
    PROCEDURE HandleEvent(VAR Event: TEvent); VIRTUAL;
    PROCEDURE InitMenuBar; VIRTUAL;
    PROCEDURE InitStatusLine; VIRTUAL;
    PROCEDURE SortDialog;
    PROCEDURE NewWindow;
    END;

  PDemoWindow = ^TDemoWindow;
  TDemoWindow = OBJECT (TWindow)
    CONSTRUCTOR Init(Bounds: TRect; WinTitle: STRING; WindowNo: WORD);
    END;

  PDemoDialog = ^TDemoDialog;
  TDemoDialog = OBJECT (TDialog)
                END;

  PInterior = ^TInterior;
  TInterior = OBJECT (TView)
                CONSTRUCTOR Init(VAR Bounds: TRect);
                PROCEDURE Draw; VIRTUAL;
                END;

{ TInterior }
CONSTRUCTOR TInterior.Init(VAR Bounds: TRect);
  BEGIN
  TView.Init(Bounds);
  GrowMode := gfGrowHiX + gfGrowHiY;
  Options := Options or ofFramed;
  END;

PROCEDURE TInterior.Draw;
  CONST Greeting: STRING = 'Hello, new programmer!';
  BEGIN
  TView.Draw;
  WriteStr(4, 2, Greeting,$01);
  END;

{ TDemoWindow }
CONSTRUCTOR TDemoWindow.Init(Bounds: TRect;
                             WinTitle: STRING; WindowNo: WORD);
  VAR
    S: STRING[3];
    Interior: PInterior;
  BEGIN
  Str(WindowNo, S);
  TWindow.Init(Bounds, WinTitle + ' ' + S, wnNoNumber);
  GetClipRect(Bounds);
  Bounds.Grow(-1,-1);
```

Listing 22.4: Creating a dialog box.

```
    Interior := New(PInterior, Init(Bounds));
    Insert(Interior);
    END;

{ TMyApp }
PROCEDURE TMyApp.HandleEvent(VAR Event: TEvent);
  BEGIN
    TApplication.HandleEvent(Event);
    if Event.What = evCommand then
    BEGIN
      CASE Event.Command OF
          cmNewWindow: NewWindow;
          cmSortDialog : SortDialog
          ELSE
          Exit;
          END;
    ClearEvent(Event);
    END;
  END;

PROCEDURE TMyApp.InitMenuBar;
  VAR
    r: TRect;
  BEGIN
    GetExtent(r);
    r.B.Y := r.A.Y + 1;
    MenuBar := New(PMenuBar, Init(r, NewMenu(
      NewSubMenu('~F~ile', hcNoContext, NewMenu(
        NewItem('~S~ort', 'F3', kbF3, cmSortDialog, hcNoContext,
        NewItem('~N~ew', 'F4', kbF4, cmNewWindow, hcNoContext,
        NewLine(
        NewItem('E~x~it', 'Alt-X', kbAltX, cmQuit, hcNoContext,
        nil)))),
      NewSubMenu('~W~indow', hcNoContext, NewMenu(
        NewItem('~N~ext', 'F6', kbF6, cmNext, hcNoContext,
        NewItem('~Z~oom', 'F5', kbF5, cmZoom, hcNoContext,
        nil))),
      nil))
    )));
  END;

PROCEDURE TMyApp.InitStatusLine;
  VAR
    r: TRect;
  BEGIN
    GetExtent(r);
    r.A.Y := r.B.Y - 1;
    StatusLine := New(PStatusLine, Init(r,
      NewStatusDef(0, $FFFF,
        NewStatusKey('', kbF10, cmMenu,
        NewStatusKey('~Alt-X~ Exit', kbAltX, cmQuit,
        NewStatusKey('~F4~ New', kbF4, cmNewWindow,
        NewStatusKey('~Alt-F3~ Close', kbAltF3, cmClose,
        nil)))),
      nil)
    ));
  END;

PROCEDURE TMyApp.SortDialog;
  VAR
    SDView: PView;
    Dialog: PDemoDialog;
```

Listing 22.4: Creating a dialog box. (cont.)

```
      r: TRect;
      C: WORD;
    BEGIN
    r.Assign(20, 6, 60, 19);
    Dialog := New(PDemoDialog, Init(r, 'Sorting Algorithms'));

    WITH Dialog^ DO
      BEGIN
      { create checkboxes }
      r.Assign(2, 3, 16, 6);
      SDView := New(PCheckBoxes, Init(r,
        NewSItem('~S~creen',
        NewSItem('~F~ile',
        NewSItem('~P~rinter',
        nil)))
      ));
      Insert(SDView);

      { create label for checkboxes }
      r.Assign(2, 2, 10, 3);
      Insert(New(PLabel, Init(r, 'Sort To', SDView)));

      { create radio buttons }
      r.Assign(18, 3, 38, 6);
      SDView := New(PRadioButtons, Init(r,
        NewSItem('~Q~uicksort',
        NewSItem('~I~nsertion Sort',
        NewSItem('~R~adix Sort',
        nil)))
      ));
      Insert(SDView);

      { create label for radio buttons }
      r.Assign(21, 2, 33, 3);
      Insert(New(PLabel, Init(r, 'Algorithm', SDView)));

      { create pushbuttons }
      r.Assign(15, 10, 25, 12);
      Insert(New(PButton, Init(r, '~O~k', cmOK, bfDefault)));
      r.Assign(28, 10, 38, 12);
      Insert(New(PButton, Init(r, 'Cancel', cmCancel, bfNormal)));
      END; { of "with Dialog^ do" statement }

    C := DeskTop^.ExecView(Dialog);
    Dispose(Dialog, Done);
    END;

  PROCEDURE TMyApp.NewWindow;
    VAR
      Window  : PDemoWindow;
      r       : TRect;
    BEGIN
    Inc(WinCount);
    r.Assign(0, 0, 32, 7);
    RANDOMIZE;
    r.Move(RANDOM(47), RANDOM(16));
    Window := New(PDemoWindow, Init(r, 'Greeting Window', WinCount));
    DeskTop^.Insert(Window);
    END;
```

Listing 22.4: Creating a dialog box. (cont.)

```
VAR
  MyApp: TMyApp;

BEGIN
  MyApp.Init;
  MyApp.Run;
  MyApp.Done;
END.
```

Listing 22.4: Creating a dialog box. (cont.)

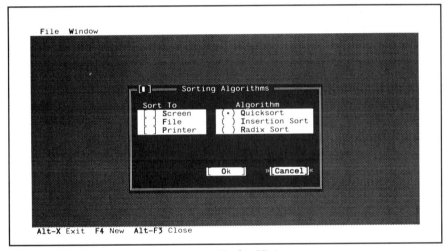

Figure 22.5: Creating a dialog box in Turbo Vision.

SUMMARY

Turbo Vision is a tremendously powerful, but tremendously complicated, library of object types for use in Turbo Pascal programs. It allows you to add pull-down menus, dialog boxes, mouse support, and many other features to your programs. In this book, we have given only a brief taste of the true power of Turbo Vision. For more complete information, you should consult your Turbo Pascal Turbo Vision manual.

REVIEW EXERCISES

1. Explain what an object library is and how an object library can be used in your own programs.

2. Explain the main tasks performed by Turbo Vision as they have been explained and demonstrated in this chapter.

3. Explain the difference between event-driven programming and the traditional Pascal programming.

4. List the main Turbo Vision object types that have been discussed in this chapter and give a brief explanation of each.

5. (Challenging) Add a new menu option to the File menu that allows the user to select a text file from a directory, open it, and load it into the interior of a Turbo Vision window.

6. (Challenging) Add a new pushbutton to the dialog box in Listing 22.4.

7. (Challenging) Delete a checkbox and a radio button from the dialog box in Listing 22.4.

8. (Very challenging) Modify the Turbo Tunemaker program developed in Chapter 20 so that it takes advantage of the facilities provided by Turbo Vision.

A P P E N D I X

Turbo Pascal
Reserved Words

Turbo Pascal Reserved Words

AND	GOTO	RECORD
ASM[*]	IF	REPEAT
ARRAY	IMPLEMENTATION[*]	SET
BEGIN	IN	SHL[*]
CASE	INLINE[*]	SHR[*]
CONST	INTERFACE[*]	STRING[*]
CONSTRUCTOR[*]	LABEL	THEN
DESTRUCTOR[*]	MOD	TO
DIV	NIL	TYPE
DO	NOT	UNIT[*]
DOWNTO	OBJECT[*]	UNTIL
ELSE	OF	USES[*]
END	OR	VAR
FILE	PACKED	WHILE
FOR	PROCEDURE	WITH
FUNCTION	PROGRAM	XOR[*]

*Not in ISO Standard Pascal

A P P E N D I X

The Ten Most Common
Programming Mistakes

Appendix B: The Ten Most Common Programming Mistakes

1. Unterminated statement (BEGIN, CASE, etc.); too many (or too few) ENDs. Often results from overly complex code.

2. Unterminated comment bracket.

3. Failure to declare global variables as parameters when they are used by a subroutine.

4. Failure to declare global variables as VAR parameters when they need to be *changed* by a subroutine.

5. Loop control variable in a WHILE or REPEAT loop never changes its value inside the loop, resulting in an endless loop. Usually results from either (a) the omission of a statement that changes the value of the variable, or (b) the mis-positioning of the statement so that it is outside of the loop.

6. Confusing the declaration of a data type with the creation of a variable of that type.

7. Failure to initialize variables when needed. This can result in bizarre program behavior that has no obvious connection to the un-initialized variables that are causing the problem.

8. Too much detail at the global level of the program, e.g., (a) declaring too many variables and subroutines as global when they could be local, or (b) having too many lines of code in the main body of the program.

9. Conflict between identifiers, including "unknown identifier" error: usually results from confusion over scope of identifiers.

10. Failure to analyze problems carefully before starting to write code. Usually results in programs that compile but produce incorrect results when they are run.

APPENDIX

Solutions to
Selected Exercises

Appendix C: Solutions to Selected Exercises

This appendix contains solutions to the even-numbered review exercises, except for diagrams and programming projects.

CHAPTER 1

2. Three ways to open Turbo Pascal's drop-down menus are the following:

   (a) Hold down the Alt key and press the highlighted letter in the menu.

   (b) Press the F10 function key, use the arrow keys to highlight the name of the menu you want, and press Enter.

   (c) With a mouse, click on the name of the menu you want.

4. (a) Open the File menu and select *Save*. (b) Press the F2 key.

6. When a program is compiled, it is translated from source code (words that can be understood by a human being) into object code, which can be understood by a computer. A Turbo Pascal program can be compiled by (a) selecting *Compile* from the Compile menu or (b) pressing Alt-F9.

8. Turbo Pascal units are separately compiled files that have two important uses: first, to hold often-used routines so that they are easily available to different programs; and second, to allow the development of Turbo Pascal programs larger than 64K in size.

10. In Listings 1.1 and 1.2, WRITELN displays a text string on the computer screen and then moves the cursor down one line. WRITELN differs from WRITE in that WRITE does not move the cursor down one line.

12. False. Semicolons are used in Pascal to separate statements from each other. You should end any statement with a semicolon (whether or not it is on a line by itself) if it is immediately followed by another statement.

14. (a) Press the F1 key. (b) Open the pull-down Help menu. (c) Position the cursor on a Pascal word with which you want

help and press Ctrl-F1.

CHAPTER 2

2. A computer stores and processes information as sequences of zeros and ones, called *bits*. Sequences of bits (such as eight bits, which is also called a *byte*) can be used to represent information, in much the same way as Morse Code uses sequences of short and long signals to represent letters of the alphabet.

4. (b)

6. A high-level programming language consists of words that can be understood by human programmers. When the program is compiled, the words are translated into object code that can be understood by the computer.

8. Structured programs are easier to understand, debug, and modify than unstructured programs. Unstructured programs are easier to write, and for small programming projects, using unstructured programming may save time.

10. You start at the bottom of the program listing, in the main body of the program. This part shows the overall structure of the program. Work your way line-by-line through the main body of the program. At each line, look in the code above for the details of the subroutines used in that line.

12. Top-down program development means that you first design a program "framework" that includes all the main subroutines, but without developing any of the details of those subroutines. In the second step, bottom-up program development, you code and test each subroutine separately before plugging it into the framework of the main program.

14. Program comments can be used (a) to explain the overall purpose of a program or individual lines in a program; (b) to "comment out" sections of program code while they are still under development and testing; and (c) to insert compiler directives into a program.

CHAPTER 3

2. An identifier must begin with a letter or an underscore. It can contain letters, digits, and underscores, but it cannot contain spaces or special characters such as *, +, or $. Identifiers can be as long as you like, but only the first 63 characters are significant to Turbo Pascal.

4. The eight main parts of a Pascal program are as follows:

   (a) the program declaration line, which gives the name of the program and, in standard Pascal, the names of any file variables used by the program;

   (b) the USES clause, which names any units that are used by the program (not in ISO Standard Pascal);

   (c) the CONST section, which declares any global constants used by the program;

   (d) the LABEL section, which declares any global line identifiers used by GOTO statements in the program;

   (e) the TYPE section, which declares any global user-defined data types used by the program;

   (f) the VAR section, which declares any global variables used by the program;

   (g) the procedures and functions section, which declares any global subroutines used by the program;

   (h) the main body of the program, which actually carries out the actions defined in other parts of the program.

6. No. **MyNumber** is the name of an integer data type, not the name of an integer variable. You can assign values only to variables, not to data types.

8. The main numeric types in Pascal are *integer,* which in Turbo Pascal has a range from −32,768 to +32,767, and *real,* which in Turbo Pascal has a range from 2.9×10^{-39} to 1.7×10^{38}. There are also "fancy" integer and real types for special purposes.

12. An array is like a rack of slots that can hold items of a certain type. Arrays can be used to keep lists of related data items (such as student records) or tables of reference information (such as tax rates).

14. Procedures and functions are named blocks of code that perform sequences of actions and return values. A procedure is similar to a complete sentence, while a function is similar to a word.

CHAPTER 4

2. The pull-down menu choices are as follows:

(a) File/New

(b) Search/Replace

(c) System/Clear Desktop

(d) Debug/Watches/Add Watch. A watch allows you to view how the value of a variable changes during a program run.

(e) Options/Editor

(f) Compile/Destination to change destination to disk; then Compile/Compile

(g) Window/Cascade

(h) Run/Step (Generally, though, you would use the F7 or F8 speed key instead.)

(i) Run/Go to Cursor

(j) Mark the block of text, then use Edit/Copy.

(k) File/Print

(l) Window/Next, Window/Previous, or Window/List

(m) Help/Contents

4. The parts of a dialog box are as follows:

(a) Close button: used to close the dialog box.

(b) Input box: used to type in a text string.

(c) Check boxes: used to select multiple options.

(d) Radio buttons: used to select single options.

(e) Pushbuttons: used to carry out operations.

6. Highlight the directory you want and select it by pressing Enter or double-clicking with the mouse. Then highlight and select the file you want in that directory.

8. The active window has various devices in the frame, such as scroll bars and a zoom button. Also, the frame itself is highlighted and thickened.

10. You can select a block of text by:

(a) Pressing Ctrl-K-B to mark the beginning of the block and Ctrl-K-K to mark the end;

(b) Positioning the cursor at the beginning of the block, holding down the shift key, and pressing the down arrow until you reach the end of the block; or

(c) Holding down the left mouse button and dragging the mouse cursor from the beginning to the end of the block. You then copy the text block to the Turbo Pascal "clipboard" by pressing Ctrl-Ins or by selecting Copy from the Edit menu. You can paste the block to another location by moving the text cursor to the new location and (a) pressing Ctrl-K-C or (b) choosing Paste from the Edit menu.

12. You create a bookmark by positioning the text cursor where you want the bookmark to be, then pressing Ctrl-K-n, where n is a digit from 0 to 9. You jump back to a bookmark by pressing Ctrl-Q-n, where n is the number of the bookmark. You can have up to 10 bookmarks in a Turbo Pascal program file.

14. Open the File menu and select *Save As*, then key in the new name of the file.

CHAPTER 5

2. An ordinal data type has members that are in a specific order, as well as being discrete and not continuous.

(a) Predefined ordinal data types in Pascal are integers, characters, and truth values (Boolean values).

(b) The **SUCC()** function, which returns the next ordinal value after the one used with **SUCC()**, and the **PRED()** function, which returns the previous ordinal value.

4. The integer data types in Turbo Pascal are as follows:

(a) Shortint, –128 to +127; eight bits

(b) Integer, –32,768 to + 32,767; 16 bits

(c) Longint, –2,147,483,648 to +2,147,483,647; 32 bits

(d) Byte, 0 to 255; eight bits

(e) Word, 0 to 65,535; 16 bits

You should not use "fancy" integer types unless it is really necessary.

6. A compiler directive is a special kind of program comment that gives Turbo Pascal special instructions on how to compile the program. The directives to turn 80x87 code generation and emulation on are {$N+} and {$E+}; to turn them off, {$N-} and {$E-}. The odd thing about compiler directives is that, unlike other program comments, they are not ignored by Turbo Pascal.

8. Expressions inside of parentheses are evaluated first. Then, expressions with operators of higher precedence are evaluated. Finally, if parentheses and precedence rules do not completely determine how the expression should be evaluated, it is evaluated from left to right.

10. Because there are only 256 different ordered sequences of eight zeros and ones ($256 = 2^8$).

12. Languages = (Pascal, BASIC, Modula2, C, Jovial, Ada, Snobol)

14. The statements are wrong because:

(a) **PRED()** is a function and cannot be on a program line by itself.

(b) **DEC** is a procedure and cannot be embedded in a program statement.

(c) First, **INC** is a procedure and cannot be embedded in a program statement. Second, **INC(Sun)** is not a text string and cannot be used with a WRITELN statement.

CHAPTER 6

2. Looping statements, such as FOR statements, and branching statements, such as IF..THEN..ELSE statements. A FOR statement causes a (simple or compound) statement to repeat for a predetermined number of times. An IF..THEN..ELSE statement causes the program to branch in one of two directions based on the truth value of the expression in the IF clause.

4. Assertive statements are not officially considered statements in Pascal; instead, they are called *Boolean expressions*. The reason is that Pascal programs are action-oriented, not assertion-oriented: official Pascal statements are all commands.

6. The statements are the following:

    (a) simple

    (b) simple (does only one program action)

    (c) two simple statements

    (d) compound (one statement does two actions)

    (e) simple

    (f) simple

8. A statement-oriented programming language executes one statement at a time, which means that usually a statement can be spread over two or more lines if needed. A line-oriented language executes one line at a time, and does not allow statements to be spread over more than one line.

10. An I/O statement moves data and instructions to and from the computer's processor and input/output devices, such as from the keyboard to the processor and from the processor to the screen. Examples of I/O statements are WRITELN, which sends a text string to an output device (a disk file, printer, or the

screen); READLN, which reads data from the keyboard or a disk file into one or more variables; WRITE, which works the same as WRITELN but does not add an end-of-line marker at the end of the text string; and READ, which works like READLN but does not move the file pointer or screen cursor down a line.

12. The answers are the following:

(a) True: 6 > 4 {stop here}

(b) True: (6 > 4) AND (5 > 3) {stop here}

(c) True: (6 > 4) OR {stop here}

(d) True: (6 > 7) OR (5 > 3) {stop here}

(e) True: (6 > 7) OR (5 > 3) XOR False {stop here}

(f) True: ((6 > 7) AND (5 > 3)) XOR (17 div 3 = 5) {stop here}

14. You should use a FOR statement when a loop must repeat a predetermined number of times. FOR can be used either with TO, which counts upward, or DOWNTO, which counts downward. There is nothing wrong with the code fragment: a FOR loop counter need not be an integer—it can be any ordinal data type.

CHAPTER 7

2. **QuitNum** is a variable; only constants or lists of constants can be used as the selector values in a CASE statement.

4. A FOR statement repeats for a predetermined number of times and requires a counter variable. A WHILE statement repeats only as long as a certain condition is true, and is used when the number of loops needed is not known in advance. If the loop condition is never true, a WHILE loop will never execute.

6. Three potential pitfalls are the following:

(a) A WHILE loop might never execute at all even when it should. If you want the loop to execute at least once, make sure that the loop condition is set to True before the program gets to the loop. Better still, use a REPEAT loop.

(b) A WHILE loop might never terminate, resulting in an endless loop. You should make sure that the loop condition is adjusted *inside* the loop each time the loop executes.

(c) A WHILE loop might not include everything it is supposed to include. You should remember that only the *first* statement after the WHILE clause is repeated; if multiple actions must be in the loop, use BEGIN..END to make a compound statement.

8. You should use WHILE loops when (a) you do not know in advance how many times the loop should execute, and (b) there are conditions under which the loop should never execute at all. You should not use WHILE loops when (c) you know in advance how many times the loop should execute, or (d) you want to make sure that the loop executes at least once.

10. The error is that a REPEAT loop will repeat all the statements between the REPEAT and UNTIL clauses, so using BEGIN..END to combine the loop statements into a single compound statement (as you *should* in a WHILE loop) is a waste of effort. The program will compile.

12. The error is that the GOTO statement attempts to jump out of the current code block (the DoingSomething subroutine). In Turbo Pascal, GOTO allows you to jump only *within* the current code block.

14. When range checking is on, Turbo Pascal checks during compilation to see if your program tries to assign out-of-range values to variables, such as trying to put something in the 11th slot of a 10-slot array. When stack checking is on, Turbo Pascal checks for *stack overflow*— i.e., whether your program's subroutine calls need more stack space in your computer's memory than is currently available.

CHAPTER 8

2. An abstract data type specifies what a data structure needs to do, but does not refer to how that data structure is created or to any specific features of any programming language. A fixed-length list

is an abstract data type which, in Pascal, can be implemented in an array—but it is *not* the same thing as an array.

4. The *MyList* variable and the **MyList** parameter are only *compatible,* not identical, data types. Variables passed to subroutines must be of a data type *identical* to that of the parameters. This code will not compile.

6. To initialize an array means to put *blank* values into its slots in preparation for using the array to hold actual values. This is important when you need to determine if a slot is occupied yet or not. The *blank* value should be one that will never be used for an *actual* value in the array—e.g., –10 for an array that will hold only positive numbers, or a space character for an array that will hold only letters.

8. The most important advantage of arrays over individual variables is that they can keep a unified list of related items; this list can then be searched, sorted, and traversed. The main disadvantage is that arrays must be large enough to hold all the items that might possibly be used, so arrays often will use more memory than is actually needed to hold the items.

12. The explanations are as follows:

    (a) A set is an un-ordered collection of items, all of which are of the same data type.

    (b) Two sets are compatible when they contain elements of the same data type.

    (c) An item is a member of a set if it is of a compatible data type and is assigned to that set variable.

    (d) Sets in Turbo Pascal cannot contain more than 256 members, and the ordinality of any item in a set cannot be larger than 255.

CHAPTER 9

2. Information hiding means that the internal details of a subroutine should be hidden from the rest of the program, so that a

change in those internal details should have no effect on anything outside the subroutine.

4. *Name* is a local variable inside the **GetNames** routine and is not accessible from the main body of the program. The program will not compile. To correct the problem, you could make **Name** a global variable and pass it to the **GetNames** routine as a VAR parameter.

6. The **String15** data type is used before it is declared. The code will not compile. To correct the problem, move the line declaring **String15** so that it comes before the student record declaration.

8. Information that must be in a procedure declaration header: name of procedure, names and data types of parameters, and whether or not parameters are VAR parameters. Information that must be in a function declaration header: the same as for a procedure, but must *also* include the data type of the function.

10. Some major blunders are the following:

    (a) Failure to use VAR when needed;

    (b) Failure to declare all outside variables as parameters if they are used by the subroutine;

    (c) Parameters in the wrong order.

12. True: you can change the internal details of a properly designed subroutine without having to change anything outside of the subroutine.

14. The *Name* variable is not declared as a VAR parameter.

CHAPTER 10

2. Similar: both help compartmentalize a program and hide their internal details. Different: units are compiled separately from the main program.

4. In the program code, you:

    (a) name the unit in a USES clause,

(b) name the include file in an *include file* compiler directive, as in {$I myfile.inc }.

6. False: you should not need to know *anything* about the implementation section of a unit in order to use its subroutines; the details are (and should be) hidden.

8. The initialization section comes at the end of the Implementation section. It is used to initialize variables used by the unit. However, units do not require an initialization section to compile properly.

10. The five routines are the following:

(a) CLRSCR: clears the computer screen (or the current screen window).

(b) Keypressed: determines if a key has been pressed.

(c) Readkey: reads a keypress from the keyboard buffer.

(d) GotoXY: moves the cursor to a specified screen position in the current screen window.

(e) ClrEOL: clears the current screen line including and to the right of the cursor position.

12. Standard Turbo Pascal units are the following:

(a) System unit: provides many standard Turbo Pascal procedures and functions.

(b) DOS unit: provides routines to access DOS and BIOS services, as well as to interact directly with the PC's hardware.

(c) Graph unit: provides routines for graphics programming.

(d) CRT unit: provides many screen-handling routines.

(e) Overlay unit: provides support for developing very large programs that will not fit into standard PC memory.

(f) Printer unit: contains predefined support for working with a printer.

(g) Turbo Vision units: provide object types and subroutines for object-oriented programming with Turbo Vision.

14. False: subroutines that are declared only in the Implementation section of the unit are private to the unit and cannot be called by any programs using the unit. Such subroutines are accessible only to the subroutines inside the unit.

CHAPTER 11

2. Static variables can be accessed very quickly; this applies especially to arrays. However, static variables cannot be added or changed after the program is compiled; arrays also tend to waste memory because they must be designed to hold as much data as will ever possibly be used by the program.

4. False: a pointer can be either a static or a dynamic variable. In fact, to create a linked list, there must be at least *one* static pointer declared in the program code; this is to give the linked list an "anchor point," a known memory location from which to start.

6. The code tries to assign an integer to **RecPtr^**. However, **RecPtr** is the *data type*, not a variable of that type, so it cannot be dereferenced and you cannot assign any values to it. Also, the line that defines the **RecPtr** type should end with a semicolon.

10. The heap is an area of memory where Pascal stores dynamic variables. The stack is an area of memory where Pascal stores local variables in subroutines and the return addresses for those subroutines. Also, the stack is normally set to a size of 16K, while the heap normally takes up all DOS memory not already used by the program, the operating system, and memory-resident software.

12. Yes. A pointer variable takes up 4 bytes. If the items in a list are smaller than this, then the pointers in the list would require more memory than the items in the list. Depending on the size of an array used to implement the list as a static list, this could mean that a linked list with a certain number of items would take up more memory than an array-based list containing the same number of items. This problem increases with more complex

linked data structures: in a doubly linked list, each item has two pointers, one to the next item and one to the previous item. In this case, pointers will take up 8 bytes (64 bits) per item.

14. The heap memory allocated to the variable is freed up for use by other dynamic variables, and the pointer becomes undefined. This effectively destroys the dynamic variable that has been disposed.

CHAPTER 12

2. File variables:

(a) a file variable is a variable that is associated with a disk file or device in the PC.

(b) File variables insulate the programmer (and the Pascal language) from details of how particular computers and operating systems handle files and devices.

(c) First, you declare the file variable in the VAR section. A text file variable is of type TEXT, while a typed file variable is declared as a FILE OF <type>, where <type> is the data type of the elements in the file. You then associate the variable with a disk file or device by using the ASSIGN procedure and open the file with RESET, REWRITE, or APPEND.

4. Keep all file-handling routines together in a separate section of the program code. Also, use text files instead of typed files whenever possible, because text files are more portable.

6. They perform the following tasks:

(a) Associates a file variable with a disk file or device.

(b) Opens a file for reading.

(c) Creates a new file for writing; if called with a file that already contains data, wipes out all the old data.

(d) Opens a text file for writing, so that new data can be added at the end of the file.

(e) Closes a file variable and writes any remaining file data to the disk file or device.

10. **EOF(MyFile)** returns a value of True if the end of the file **My-File** has been reached. **EOLN(MyFile)** returns a value of True if the end of the current line in a text file has been reached. Both are used with WHILE loops to keep repeating an operation until the end of the file or line is reached.

14. Yes. Sometimes, you are moving through a file and need to move the file pointer back to the beginning of the file. Reset will accomplish this.

CHAPTER 13

2. False: typed files are not always smaller. Typed files are larger than text files when there is wide variation in the size of the individual items in the file, such as text strings.

4. The most important difference is that before noncharacter data can be written to a text file, it must be translated into text characters; when it is read back from a text file, it must be translated back into its appropriate data type. This means that it takes more time to handle noncharacter data with text files than with typed files.

6. The main advantage of text files is that they are simple and highly portable. The main disadvantage is that they slow down file handling operations in your program.

8. Some factors to consider are the following:

   (a) Speed: typed files may be faster than text files.

   (b) Ease of programming: in some situations, it is easier to write the code for text files, while in other situations, it is easier with typed files.

   (c) Portability: if the program might be moved to another Pascal compiler, then text files are better because they are more portable than typed files.

14. Untyped files actually represent a very fast way of reading from and writing to text and typed files without any regard for their content.

CHAPTER 14

2. Compile-time bugs are errors in the syntax of your program code that prevent your program from compiling properly. Runtime bugs are problems that occur when you try to run the program, such as not being able to find a needed file. Logical bugs are errors in the way you analyzed the problem your program is trying to solve. Logical bugs are the most dangerous because they are hardest to detect and can make your program produce incorrect results.

4. By reducing the size of the code segments with which you must deal at any one time, structured programming reduces the complexity of the problems you must analyze. This makes errors less likely in the first place and makes it easier to find and correct them when they do occur.

8. Debug code consists of program statements that show how the values of variables change during the course of a program run.

10. To step through a program, you press the F8 key to move one line at a time. To trace through a program, press the F7 key. The difference is that if a subroutine is called, F8 will simply execute the subroutine in a single step, while F7 will trace into the subroutine, executing it one line at a time.

12. You open the Evaluate/Modify dialog box from the Debug menu. You can enter a variable name and see the current value of the variable. You can also change the value to a new value: this allows you to try out different variable values in the middle of a program run to see the result.

14. The problems are the following:

    (a) The *Continue* variable is never initialized. It should be assigned an initial value of 'Y'.

    (b) There are too many ENDs. Eliminate the second END from the bottom of the code fragment.

CHAPTER 15

2. Programming in graphics mode is far more flexible than in text mode, but it is also much more complex. Because the resolution of monitors and video adapters can vary considerably, graphics items must be positioned using relative rather than absolute screen coordinates. This is a fairly complicated business.

4. **InitGraph** initializes the PC's graphics hardware and puts the screen in graphics mode. **Initgraph** takes three parameters: the graphics driver for the video card, the graphics mode, and the location on-disk of the graphics driver files. Ordinarily, you should set the graphics driver to *detect*, which allows **Initgraph** to detect whatever graphics hardware is installed.

8. Items must be positioned using relative coordinates. You first call the **GetMaxX** and **GetMaxY** functions in the Graph unit to get the maximum x and y coordinates of the current graphics screen. Then, you use various arithmetic tricks to position items, e.g., in the middle of the screen where x = **MaxX** div 2 and y = **MaxY** div 2.

CHAPTER 16

2. Registers provide for on-chip storage of data and instructions so that they can be accessed more quickly by the processor. Each register can hold 16 bits (two bytes) of data and has its own job to perform.

4. An interrupt (whether a software or hardware interrupt) tells the computer's processor to stop what it is doing and perform some other task, after which it goes back to what it was doing when the interrupt occurred.

6. You indicate a hex number in a program by prefacing it with a dollar sign, as in **$10**. Hex numbers are used because they are a convenient shorthand for binary numbers, which correspond to the computer's on/off switches. Each hex number can stand for four binary digits.

10. Interrupt hex 21 (**$21**) is used to call DOS functions. First, you load the function number into the AH register, then call interrupt **$21** to carry out the function.

12. In order to run an external program with the **Exec** procedure, enough computer memory must be free to load and run the program. However, a Turbo Pascal program (from which you would call the external program with **Exec**) normally reserves all unused DOS memory for the heap—leaving no free memory in which to run an external program. The solution is to reduce the amount of heap memory by using the **$M** compiler directive.

14. You first call the **Swapvectors** procedure to save a copy of your interrupt vector table. Then call **Exec**, including the name and directory path of DOS's command interpreter and (if appropriate) the name of the external program to be run. On the line after calling **Exec,** you should call **Swapvectors** again (as a safety measure) to restore your original copy of the interrupt vector table.

CHAPTER 17

2. A queue is a list in which all deletions are made from one end (the front) and all additions are made at the other end (the rear); for this reason, queues are also referred to as First-In-First-Out (FIFO) lists.

6. A circular array is one with special routines that "circle back" to the start of the array when attempting to add a new item at the end of the array. If the array is full, then no new item is added. If deleted items have left open space at the beginning of the array, new items are added there.

8. The mod operator returns the remainder from integer division. It is used to set up a circular array for an array-based queue because any deletions will be made toward the beginning of the array, thereby opening up space for new queue items.

10. The principal difference between the array-based and the linked versions is that the array-based version must include code to check for a full-array condition.

CHAPTER 18

2. An algorithm should run with *maximum* speed while using a *minimum* amount of memory. These aspects of algorithmic efficiency are often in conflict because things you can do to increase speed (e.g., storing data in an array) also increase the memory needs of your program, while things that decrease memory requirements (e.g., storing data in a linked list) slow down the program.

4. You should concentrate your efforts on routines that (a) are called many times during a program run, and (b) on routines that require the user to wait while something is happening. The reason for (a) is that the more times a routine is called, the greater will be its impact on the overall speed and efficiency of your program. The reason for (b) is that users become impatient when they have to wait too long for a routine to run.

6. A sentinel node is inserted at the end of a list (or file) to make sure that a searched-for value will be found. This allows you to make the search algorithm slightly more efficient.

8. In **Insertion Sort,** you create a sorted sublist of the list you are sorting. One at a time, you add items from the unsorted part of the list onto the sorted sublist, making sure that each item goes into its correct position in the sorted sublist. When the process is done, the list is completely sorted.

CHAPTER 19

2. The tones will last:

  (a) one second

  (b) one second

  (c) a fifth of a second

  (d) 10.5 seconds

  (e) one thousandth of a second

CHAPTER 21

2. Object-oriented programming is similar to structured programming in that it divides the program into sealed compartments, thereby making it easier to understand, modify, and debug the program. It differs from structured programming in that it creates "intelligent data structures" that handle most tasks themselves, instead of having passive data structures that are operated on by independent subroutines.

4. When you declare an object type, you declare its ancestor type (if any) in parentheses after the name of the new type. All fields and methods in the ancestor type are inherited in the new (descendant) object type. To call one of these methods in an object variable, you simply use a dot notation similar to that for accessing the fields of a record: if the object variable is **MyObject** and the method is **Init**, you would write **MyObject.init**.

6. It contains a virtual method but no CONSTRUCTOR routine to set up the Virtual Method Table for an object variable of this type.

8. Program statements that call virtual methods are not given the memory addresses of those methods when the program is compiled. Therefore, a Virtual Method Table must be set up for each object that uses virtual methods so that the object can find the memory addresses of the methods it needs to use.

CHAPTER 22

2. Turbo Vision is a library of object types that can handle most tasks involved in getting input from the user and displaying output on the screen. It allows programs to accept and use input in a flexible, event-driven way. An event can be a keypress, a mouse click, a request for context-sensitive help, or a message from one part of a program to another.

4. A Turbo Vision *View* (**TView**) is anything that can be displayed on the screen. Descendants of the **TView** object type include

window frames, dialog boxes, radio buttons, checkboxes, and the Turbo Vision Desktop itself. **TMenuBar** allows you to set up a menu bar from which pull-down menus can be opened, while **TStatusLine** allows you to create a status line that displays important keys and information about the program. **TScroller** allows you to put scroll bars on the frame of a file window. There are many other Turbo Vision object types.

INDEX

Selections from The SYBEX Library

LANGUAGES

The ABC's of GW-BASIC
William R. Orvis
320pp. Ref. 663-4

Featuring two parts: Part I is an easy-to-follow tutorial for beginners, while Part II is a complete, concise reference guide to GW-BASIC commands and functions. Covers everything from the basics of programming in the GW-BASIC environment, to debugging a major program. Includes special treatment of graphics and sound.

BASIC Programs for Scientists and Engineers
Alan R. Miller
318pp. Ref. 073-3

The algorithms presented in this book are programmed in standard BASIC code which should be usable with almost any implementation of BASIC. Includes statistical calculations, matrix algebra, curve fitting, integration, and more.

Encyclopedia C
Robert A. Radcliffe
1333pp. Ref. 655-3

This is the complete reference for standard ANSI/ISO programmers using any Microsoft C compiler with DOS. It blends comprehensive treatment of C syntax, functions, utilities, and services with practical examples and proven techniques for optimizing productivity and performance in C programming.

FORTRAN Programs for Scientists and Engineers (Second Edition)
Alan R. Miller
280pp. Ref. 571-9

In this collection of widely used scientific algorithms—for statistics, vector and matrix operations, curve fitting, and more—the author stresses effective use of little-known and powerful features of FORTRAN.

Introduction to Pascal: Including Turbo Pascal (Second Edition)
Rodnay Zaks
464pp. Ref. 533-6

This best-selling tutorial builds complete mastery of Pascal—from basic structured programming concepts, to advanced I/O, data structures, file operations, sets, pointers and lists, and more. Both ISO Standard and Turbo Pascal.

Mastering C
Craig Bolon
437pp. Ref. 326-0

This in-depth guide stresses planning, testing, efficiency and portability in C applications. Topics include data types, storage classes, arrays, pointers, data structures, control statements, I/O and the C function library.

Mastering QuickBASIC
Rita Belserene
450pp. Ref. 589-1

Readers build professional programs with this extensive language tutorial. Fundamental commands are mixed with the author's tips and tricks so that users can create their own applications. Program templates are included for video displays, computer games, and working with databases and printers. For Version 4.5.

Mastering Turbo C (Second Edition)
Stan Kelly-Bootle
609pp. Ref. 595-6

With a foreword by Borland International President Philippe Kahn, this new edition has been expanded to include full details on Version 2.0. Learn theory and practical programming, with tutorials on data types, real numbers and characters, controlling program flow, file I/O, and producing color charts and graphs. Through Version 2.

Systems Programming in Microsoft C
Michael J. Young
604pp. Ref. 570-0
This sourcebook of advanced C programming techniques is for anyone who wants to make the most of their C compiler or Microsoft QuickC. It includes a comprehensive, annotated library of systems functions, ready to compile and call.

Systems Programming in Microsoft C (Second Edition)
Michael J. Young
600pp; Ref. 1026-6
This book offers detailed information on advanced programming techniques for Microsoft C, as well as a comprehensive library of ready-to-use functions. It covers both the Microsoft C optimizing C compiler through version 6.0, and Microsoft QuickC (versions 1.0 and later). With complete code for converting a Microsoft Cprogram into a memory-resident utility.

Turbo Pascal Toolbox (Second Edition)
Frank Dutton
425pp. Ref. 602-2
This collection of tested, efficient Turbo Pascal building blocks gives a boost to intermediate-level programmers, while teaching effective programming by example. Topics include accessing DOS, menus, bit maps, screen handling, and much more.

ASSEMBLY LANGUAGES

Programming the 6809
Rodnay Zaks
William Labiak
362pp. Ref. 078-4
A step-by-step course in assembly-language programming for 6809-based home computers. Covers hardware organization, the instruction set, addressing, I/O, data structures, program development and complete sample applications.

Programming the 68000
Steve Williams
539pp. Ref. 133-0
This tutorial introduction to assembly-language programming covers the complete 68000 architecture and instruction set, as well as advanced topics such as interrupts, I/O programming, and interfacing with high-level languages.

Programming the 8086/8088
James W. Coffron
311pp. Ref. 120-9
A concise introduction to assembly-language programming for 8086/8088-based systems, including the IBM PC. Topics include architecture, memory organization, the complete instruction set, interrupts, I/O, and IBM PC BIOS routines.

Programming the 80386
John H. Crawford
Patrick P. Gelsinger
775pp. Ref. 381-3
A detailed tour of the 80386 for assembly-language programmers. Topics include registers, data types and instruction classes, memory management, protection models, multitasking, interrupts, the numerics coprocessor, and more.

Programming the Z80 (Third Edition)
Rodnay Zaks
624pp. Ref. 069-5
A self-teaching guide to assembly-language programming for the wide range of Z80-based microcomputers. Includes the Z80 architecture and instruction set, addressing, I/O techniques and devices, data structures and sample programs.

Z80 Applications
James W. Coffron
295pp. Ref. 094-6
A handbook for assembly-language programmers on the principles of Z80 hardware operations. Topics include using ROM, static and dynamic RAM, I/O, interrupts, serial communication and several specific LSI peripheral devices.

APPLICATION DEVELOPMENT

The ABC's of ToolBook for Windows
Kenyon Brown
300pp. Ref. 795-9

Gain the skill and confidence you need to create sophisticated applications for Windows. This hands-on introduction teaches you how to build custom graphical applications, without the need for traditional computer language. Learn to use the Script Recorder to create scripts and add animation to presentation applications.

The Elements of Friendly Software Design
Paul Heckel
319pp. Ref. 768-1

Here's what you *didn't* learn in engineering school! This entertaining, practical text shows how the same communication techniques used by artists and filmmakers can make software more appealing to users. Topics include visual thinking; design principles to follow—and mistakes to avoid; and examples of excellence.

Up & Running with ToolBook for Windows
Michael Tischer
138pp. Ref. 816-5

In just 20 time-coded steps (each taking no more than 15 minutes to an hour), you can begin designing your own Windows applications. Learn to add visual interest with lines, colors, and patterns; create a customized database form; navigate the user interface; draw and paint with Tool-Book, and more.

COMMUNICATIONS

Mastering Serial Communications
Peter W. Gofton
289pp. Ref. 180-2

The software side of communications, with details on the IBM PC's serial programming, the XMODEM and Kermit protocols, non-ASCII data transfer, interrupt-level programming, and more. Sample programs in C, assembly language and BASIC.

Mastering UNIX Serial Communications
Peter W. Gofton
307pp. Ref. 708-8

The complete guide to serial communications under UNIX. Part I introduces essential concepts and techniques, while Part II explores UNIX ports, drivers, and utilities, including MAIL, UUCP, and others. Part III is for C programmers, with six in-depth chapters on communications programming under UNIX.

Understanding PROCOMM PLUS 2.0 (Second Edition)
Bob Campbell
393pp; Ref. 861-0

This in-depth tutorial on communications with PROCOMM PLUS is now updated and expanded for version 2.0. It's still the best guide to PROCOMM PLUS, showing how to choose and install hardware; concect with on-line services and other computers; send and receive files; create and use MetaKeys and scripts; and more.

AMAZING DISK OFFER!

If you do not want to key in the example programs in this book, they are available on disk.

In addition to all program listings from this book, the disk includes other Turbo Pascal programs with completely commented source code. These include *Turbo Resume*, which enables you to create a Turbo Vision "executable resume." Disk space permitting, other games and utilities will be added as they are developed.

To order, send a check or money order payable to Scott D. Palmer for $25.00 plus $2.50 shipping/handling for North American orders and $5.00 shipping/handling for overseas orders. Virginia residents must add 4.5 percent to the total as sales tax. (For fastest service, enclose a crisp new $100 bill or a blank check made out to the author. No junk bonds, please.) Send your order to:

Scott D. Palmer
RGMS Computer Systems
310 Maple Avenue West
Vienna, VA 22180

Don't forget to:

- Include your name and address
- Specify if you want a 5.25-inch or a 3.5-inch disk

The author is also available as a consultant to provide on-site training or to help solve specific problems.

FREE CATALOG!

SYBEX ®

Mail us this form today, and we'll send you a full-color catalog of Sybex books.

Name _____

Street _____

City/State/Zip _____

Phone _____

Please supply the name of the Sybex book purchased.

_____

How would you rate it?

_____ Excellent   _____ Very Good   _____ Average   _____ Poor

Why did you select this particular book?

_____ Recommended to me by a friend

_____ Recommended to me by store personnel

_____ Saw an advertisement in _____

_____ Author's reputation

_____ Saw in Sybex catalog

_____ Required textbook

_____ Sybex reputation

_____ Read book review in _____

_____ In-store display

_____ Other _____

Where did you buy it?

_____ Bookstore

_____ Computer Store or Software Store

_____ Catalog (name: _____)

_____ Direct from Sybex

_____ Other: _____

Did you buy this book with your personal funds?

_____ Yes   _____ No

About how many computer books do you buy each year?

_____ 1-3   _____ 3-5   _____ 5-7   _____ 7-9   _____ 10+

About how many Sybex books do you own?

_____ 1-3   _____ 3-5   _____ 5-7   _____ 7-9   _____ 10+

Please indicate your level of experience with the software covered in this book:

_____ Beginner   _____ Intermediate   _____ Advanced

Which types of software packages do you use regularly?

_____ Accounting	_____ Databases	_____ Networks
_____ Amiga	_____ Desktop Publishing	_____ Operating Systems
_____ Apple/Mac	_____ File Utilities	_____ Spreadsheets
_____ CAD	_____ Money Management	_____ Word Processing
_____ Communications	_____ Languages	_____ Other _____
		(please specify)

Which of the following best describes your job title?

_____ Administrative/Secretarial	_____ President/CEO
_____ Director	_____ Manager/Supervisor
_____ Engineer/Technician	_____ Other _____
	(please specify)

Comments on the weaknesses/strengths of this book: _____

_____

_____

_____

_____

PLEASE FOLD, SEAL, AND MAIL TO SYBEX

- - - - - - - - - - - - - - - - - - - -

SYBEX, INC.
Department M
2021 CHALLENGER DR.
ALAMEDA, CALIFORNIA USA
94501

SYBEX ®

SEAL

PREDEFINED UNITS IN
TURBO PASCAL

SYSTEM UNIT: Contains standard Turbo Pascal procedures and functions.

DOS UNIT: Contains procedures, functions, constants, and data types for doing low-level programming with MS-DOS, the PC BIOS, and the PC's processor registers.

CRT UNIT: Contains procedures, functions, constants, and data types for screen-handling operations, such as clearing the screen or moving the cursor to a desired location.

GRAPH UNIT: Contains procedures, functions, constants, and data types for graphics programming on a wide variety of PC monitors and video adapters.

OVERLAY UNIT: Contains procedures, functions, constants, and data types for creating programs too large to fit into standard DOS memory; these programs swap parts of themselves out to disk or to expanded (EMS) memory.

TURBO VISION UNITS: Contain predefined object types for object-oriented programming with Turbo Vision. Predefined object types include pull-down menus, dialog boxes, and mouse support.